DEMOCRACY

DEMOCRACY

A CASE STUDY

David A. Moss

The Belknap Press of Harvard University Press
CAMBRIDGE, MASSACHUSETTS
LONDON, ENGLAND
2017

Library of Congress Cataloging-in-Publication Data
Names: Moss, David A., 1964– author.
Title: Democracy : a case study / David A. Moss.
Description: Cambridge, Massachusetts : The Belknap Press of Harvard
University Press, 2017. | Includes bibliographical references and index.
Identifiers: LCCN 2016020796 | ISBN 9780674971455 (alk. paper)
Subjects: LCSH: Democracy—United States—History—Case studies. |
Social conflict—Political aspects—United States—Case studies. |
United States—Politics and government—Case studies.
Classification: LCC E183 .M876 2017 | DDC 320.473—dc23
LC record available at https://lccn.loc.gov/2016020796

Book design by Dean Bornstein

For my parents

CONTENTS

DEMOCRACY

Introduction: *E Pluribus Unum*

ON JULY 4, 1776, after formally adopting the Declaration of Independence, the Continental Congress appointed a committee of three to design an official seal for the fledgling United States of America. The appointees were John Adams, Thomas Jefferson, and Benjamin Franklin, each of whom had served on the earlier Committee of Five tasked with drafting the Declaration. Their goal now was to produce an emblem reflecting the spirit and character of the new nation. A little over six weeks later, on August 20, the three men reported back with a recommendation; they offered a seal with the Goddesses of Justice and Liberty on one side and Moses parting the Red Sea on the other. Although their design was not adopted, the seal that Congress finally did approve in 1782, a bald eagle with thirteen arrows and an olive branch in its talons, included three Latin words that Adams, Jefferson, and Franklin had recommended as a motto for their seal: *E Pluribus Unum*.

It was a curious phrase, with deep resonance for American democracy. Often translated as "out of many, one," the three Latin words effectively served as the national motto until 1956, when Congress finally threw its weight behind "In God We Trust." The older Latin expression continued to grace the Great Seal of the United States, however, and arguably remains the most concise statement ever put forth on the essence of democratic governance in America.

The phrase itself, "E Pluribus Unum," has long been shrouded in mystery. Commonly thought to have hailed from ancient Rome (uttered by the likes of Virgil, Cicero, or Horace), it is apparently of much humbler origin, most likely proposed by Benjamin Franklin, who had seen it displayed on the cover of *Gentleman's Magazine,* a popular British periodical. Dating back to 1731, *Gentleman's Magazine* had helped break new ground in the publishing world, providing a broad assortment of literary pieces in each issue and relying mainly on reprinted fragments and extracts in its early years. This was apparently the first time the word "magazine," meaning storehouse or repository, had ever been used in reference to a publication, evidently to suggest a repository of diverse literary works. Reinforcing the notion of a unified collection of independent pieces, *"E Pluribus Unum"* appeared on the magazine's cover beside a sketch of a hand grasping a bouquet of flowers. The message was clear: out of many flowers, one bouquet, and out of many literary works, one magazine. For Franklin, it was but a small leap to his preferred use of the Latin expression: out of many states and peoples, one nation.[1]

Gentleman's Magazine, it appears, borrowed the motto from another publication, the short-lived *Gentleman's Journal* from the early 1690s.[2] But here, in the words of one scholar, "the trail ends."[3] It is possible that *Gentleman's Journal* adapted the phrase from Horace. If so, Franklin likely knew nothing about this. He recommended the expression in 1776 not because of any classical lineage—as one historian put it, the eminently practical "Franklin would not . . . have had any scruples" about adopting the nation's motto from a popular magazine—but rather because the words spoke to him.[4]

Bringing together thirteen disparate colonies to fight for their common independence from Britain was the central challenge of the time. Beyond that, forming one out of many would become the central challenge of America from that moment forward. Franklin, characteristically, was far ahead of his time. He recognized from the republic's first breath that the unique promise of America lay in harnessing difference toward a common purpose through self-governance; and in just three words, taken from the eighteenth-century equivalent of *Reader's Digest,* he found the means to express that aspiration: *E Pluribus Unum*—out of many, one.

Like *Gentleman's Magazine,* this book brings together seemingly disparate parts—nineteen case studies highlighting key episodes in the history of American democracy. Together these cases form the basis of a course at Harvard University open to both undergraduates and MBA students. Although the cases traverse broad expanses of American history, they do not provide the sort of comprehensive coverage typical of a textbook. Instead, they focus on pivotal decisions facing lawmakers and private citizens alike, and offer the historical background necessary to inform those decisions. Very much in the spirit of the Harvard course, therefore, this book encourages critical thinking on the essence of the nation's democracy, both past and present.

One of the most notable features of a case-method course is that students are asked—even actively pushed—to draw their own conclusions. Case studies are not supposed to editorialize, and the cases that make up this book largely follow that rule, inviting readers to form their own judgments and interpretations. It is not uncommon, however, for a case-method teacher to suggest a few broad themes at the beginning of a course, and much the same seems appropriate here, in the Introduction. Franklin's three-word motto, with its dual emphasis on difference and unity, provides a particularly fitting place to begin.

American Democracy and the Power of Productive Tension

As the cases presented here will reveal, democracy in America has always been a contact sport. Words like "cooperation" and "consensus" may sound appealing and even comforting, but American democracy has survived and thrived from one generation to the next on the basis not principally of harmony but of conflict—sometimes intense conflict—mediated, generally, by shared ideals.

Indeed, democratic decision making in the United States has nearly always been rooted in disagreement and tension, including plenty of bare-knuckle politics. The nation has witnessed sharp partisan, ideological, and often sectional conflict in everything from the battle over ratification of the Constitution in 1787–1788 to the repeated fights over a national bank (in the 1790s, 1830s, and 1910s) to the bitter struggles over health care and gun laws today. Intense political conflict has always been with us and is, in fact, profoundly American.

The critical question is what makes this conflict either constructive or destructive. Indeed, this is the central question of this book. Political conflict is not a disease, as some pundits contend, but instead an essential feature of American democracy. In most periods across the nation's history, it has served as a powerful source of strength. But not always. And this, in a nutshell, is what we need to figure out. Why has fierce political conflict proved highly constructive at many historical moments and severely destructive at others, and which type of conflict—constructive or destructive—characterizes the nation's democracy today?

We'll return to this question shortly. First, though, it is worth taking a closer look at the idea of democracy itself.

If you ask family members or friends what democracy is, they are likely to begin by saying that it is a system of government in which people cast votes for representatives and in which laws are determined by majorities. It is also possible that some of them will distinguish *representative* democracy (also known as republican government) from the type of *direct* democracy practiced in a New England town meeting or in ancient Greece. If you give them a bit more time and you're having the discussion in the United States, they will likely tell you about the three branches of government as set out in the Constitution, about the checks and balances between these branches, and possibly about the importance of individual liberty and the various protections written into the Bill of Rights. Occasionally someone may warn that not all of these things are quite as straightforward as they seem—that majorities don't always get their way, for example—and this is where the conversation will start to get interesting.

James Madison suggested back in the mid-1780s, when he was contemplating the creation of a new constitution for the young nation, that the "majority who rule" in a representative democracy are ideally "the safest Guardians both of public Good and of private rights." Yet he also recognized that representative democracy inevitably confronts two foundational problems. The first is that elected representatives may end up deferring to powerful special interests rather than to their constituents, and in this way majority rule may be subverted as special interests gain control of the policymaking process at the expense of the "public Good." By the twentieth century, this sort of special interest influence was sometimes referred to as "capture," indicating that special interests could be so powerful as to effectively capture public officials for their own benefit. The second foundational problem, which Madison regarded as even more dangerous than the first, is that majorities, when they do exercise power in a democracy, are liable to oppress or tyrannize minorities, violating those minorities' "private rights." A dominant religious group, for instance, might use its power in the political system to persecute smaller religious groups. When this happens, legitimate majority rule is not subverted or captured by special interests but instead perverted by the passions of the majority itself.[5]

The core challenge of democracy, as Madison saw it, was to empower the people to select their lawmakers while somehow avoiding these twin evils, special interest capture of government on the one hand and tyranny of the majority on the other. Particularly fearful of the latter, he came to see conflict—continuous political struggle across a multitude of widely dispersed factions—as the key to preventing tyrannical majorities from forming. His formula was far from foolproof, allowing numerous majoritarian abuses over the course of the nation's history, including the most horrific of all, slavery, which Madison himself participated in. The more difficult question is not whether it was foolproof—nothing in human affairs ever is—but instead whether it was better or worse than the alternatives.

We'll have a chance to examine Madison's conception of a healthy republic in detail in Case 1. For now, however, it is enough to highlight three core elements of his understanding of democratic governance: first, that democracy is inherently fragile, likely to be subverted by special interests or perverted by majority passions unless the proper checks and balances are in place; second, that the necessary checks and balances extend far beyond the *formal* structures of government, such as the three branches that Madison would play a large role in designing at the Constitutional Convention in 1787; and finally, that political conflict—at every level of society—is central to a vibrant democracy.

Successfully building and sustaining a democracy, in other words, is about much more than simply ensuring broad suffrage and majority rule, although both are vital. Nor is it enough to provide a compelling blueprint, like the one crafted at the Constitutional Convention in Philadelphia, which specifies formal governing structures and the rules of the game, although this too has proved to be an essential feature of American democracy. Equally necessary, it seems, is a vibrant spirit of political engagement among the people themselves that yields productive conflict in the marketplace of ideas, presumably along the lines Madison envisioned.

If so, this brings us back to the question of what separates *constructive* political conflict from *destructive* political conflict in a democracy. Unfortunately, there exists no perfect theory or framework that we can rely on in answering this question. We can draw lessons from historical examples, however, on both the positive and the negative sides. The Civil War—by far the most violent episode in the nation's history—provides a natural starting point.

Needless to say, the lead-up to the Civil War represents a powerful example of destructive conflict in American politics. Although there was plenty of political tension in the late 1850s and the start of the 1860s, very little of it was in any way constructive. But why, exactly?

In February 1861—not long after Lincoln had been elected president and Southern states had begun to secede from the Union, but before Lincoln had taken the oath of office—the editor of the *Atlantic Monthly,* James Russell Lowell, suggested that political tensions had turned destructive in the United States because Americans had come to take effective self-governance for granted. He claimed that the Southern secessionists, in particular, had given up on the idea of national democracy altogether:

> they now question the right of the majority to govern, except on their terms, and threaten violence in the hope of extorting from the fears of the Free States. . . . Their quarrel is not with the Republican Party, but with the theory of Democracy.[6]

Most secessionists continued to believe in the application of democratic procedures at the state level (at least for white men), but apparently not at the federal level. When Lincoln won the election in November 1860, many Southerners—perhaps a majority—were unswayed by the fact that he had secured more votes, both popular and electoral, than any other candidate. In their eyes, he was illegitimate because he opposed the expansion of slavery.

So perhaps conflict in American politics turned destructive when common faith in the democracy itself broke down and could no longer hold Americans together. Fortunately, the rupture that occurred in the early 1860s was very much the exception, not the rule, across the nation's history. In nearly every other period, conflict was a given, but a shared belief in democratic self-governance helped channel that conflict in constructive directions—or, at the very least, helped prevent partisan conflict from degenerating into violence.

As readers make their way through the cases that follow, they will see this dynamic of productive tension play out again and again, in a host of different contexts. In some cases they will observe controversial policies gaining acceptance through appeals to democratic process or principles. Several years after the Panic of 1837, for example, budget hawks in New York State proposed a constitutional provision that would severely limit lawmakers from authorizing public borrowing, but with a democratic escape hatch allowing state debt to be issued so long as voters approved it in a statewide referendum. At roughly the same time, education reformers were calling for a significant expansion of government spending to fund "free" schools, arguing that public education was essential not only for building a more capable workforce but also—and perhaps most importantly—for ensuring a more informed and responsible electorate. On both ends of the political spectrum, therefore, political actors tied controversial proposals to core democratic values.

Significantly, as we will see in Cases 6 and 7, New York lawmakers of the 1840s considered both of these proposals nearly simultaneously—fiscal retrenchment on the one hand, and fiscal expansion to support public education on the other. This sort of dissonance was not uncommon in American politics. Instead of meeting in the middle or splitting the difference, two competing factions or parties frequently both secured what they most wanted. It was a distinctive form of compromise, with the classic American example being the so-called Great Compromise, proposed by the illustrious Connecticut delegation at the Constitutional Convention in 1787. As the convention debated how Congress should be structured, delegates from large states insisted that representation ought to be proportional to population, whereas those from small states favored equal representation by state, irrespective of population. Instead of meeting in the middle (for example, by adopting a proportional model weighted somewhat toward small states), delegates from both sides agreed to a two-part solution: proportional representation in the House and equal representation in the Senate. Each side, in other words, achieved its preferred option, but had to tolerate the other side also getting what it wanted. Such horse-trading could be explicit, as it was in the Great Compromise, or it could be implicit or even coincidental, as in New York in the 1840s. Either way, it was indicative of the productive tension that so often characterized American politics.

From a policy perspective, vigorous political conflict—especially when rooted in shared democratic ideals—thus had the potential to surface good ideas from all sides, generating a best-of-both dynamic where lawmakers might pick the best from Column A *and* the best from Column B. The author F. Scott Fitzgerald famously wrote that the "test of a first-rate intelligence is the ability to hold two opposed ideas in the mind at the same time, and still retain the ability to function."[7] By this standard, the institutions of American policymaking must be judged to have been rather ingenious, at least across much of the nation's history. Conflicting ideas, interests, and policies, not ideological consistency, have long been the stock and trade of American politics.

But the logic of what I call productive political tension also runs deeper, beyond policymaking to the very foundation of democratic governance itself. Productive tension between competing factions serves not only as a vital source of diverse policy ideas, but also as a critical check on democratic excess, as Madison observed on the eve of the Constitutional Convention. Indeed, the paramount role of productive tension in American politics is apparent throughout the nation's history and, consequently, in all of the case studies that compose this volume. The words "productive tension" appear nowhere in the Constitution, of course, nor is there any certain recipe or formula for creating and sustaining it. But it is no less important, as a result. It is, in short, one of the intangibles of American democracy, which breathes life into the republic in the most mysterious of ways, animating an otherwise static set of structures and rules as powerfully—and as subtly—as the oxygen carried in our bloodstreams.

An Organism, Not a Machine

All too often, in civics and government classes from grade school to high school and beyond, American democracy is characterized as a machine built to specification. Students learn, appropriately, about the intricate checks and balances across the three branches of government, about the strict division of powers between the states and the federal government, and about the explicit limitations placed on lawmakers to protect the rights of individuals against improper infringement by government. All are essential elements of the American political system, and all flow directly from the Constitution. And yet, with so much emphasis on constitutional design and mechanics, students are often left with the impression that a successful democracy is virtually automatic, given the right blueprint.

Such is not the case, of course. If it were, then exporting American democracy to other countries would simply be a matter of exporting the Constitution itself, just as a manufacturer might export the plans for a piece of machinery to be built and operated abroad. But as Americans have learned time and again through hard experience, exporting a democratic system of governance is exceedingly difficult to do. A working democracy requires much more than a successful blueprint.

A closely related observation has to do with the way democracy is modeled in the social sciences. One very influential strain of thought, drawn mainly from economics, focuses on equilibrium conditions in democratic decision making. The basic idea is that given people's preferences, societies can potentially fashion governing arrangements that are self-sustaining in equilibrium. One of the nation's leading theorists of political institutions, Barry Weingast, has argued that "democratic stability depends on a self-enforcing equilibrium: It must be in the interests of political officials to respect democracy's limits on their behavior."[8]

As an example from American history, Weingast highlights the Missouri Compromise of 1820, which attempted to ensure a political balance of power between the slave states of the South and the free states of the North, in part by drawing a line at the 36°30′ parallel and permanently banning slavery in territories north of the line. Weingast concludes that "over the long run, balance provided the basis for sectional cooperation. Because it meant that radical measures could not succeed, balance induced moderates in each section to cooperate with one another."[9]

Although the equilibrium model has a certain appeal, it nonetheless feels strangely at odds with the relentless storm and stress of American history. Indeed, the closer one gets to the historical record, the more it seems that democracy is never in equilibrium: lawmakers are forever testing the limits of their power; interests are constantly looking for ways to tilt policymaking to their advantage; and reformers of all stripes are endlessly seeking to change the underlying rules of the game in line with their biases and aspirations.

Following the Missouri Compromise, the United States held together for another forty years, yet sectional divisions and slavery itself continued to roil the nation. In 1828, Northerners infuriated Southerners by passing the so-called Tariff of Abominations, leading ultimately to the Nullification Crisis of 1832. Nat Turner's slave rebellion of 1831, meanwhile, sent shockwaves through the South, and a surge of Northern abolitionist petitions during the 1830s so unnerved certain—especially Southern—members of Congress that they passed a "gag rule" in 1836 barring such petitions from consideration, despite the First Amendment guarantee of "the right . . . to petition the

Government for a redress of grievances." The nation was further riven by the Mexican War of 1846–1848 and the bitter fights that ensued over whether territories acquired in the war should be slave or free. In the end, the Missouri Compromise was overturned not once but twice—first by Congress in the fiercely controversial Kansas-Nebraska Act of 1854, which gave rise to the Republican Party, and next by the Supreme Court in the infamous *Dred Scott* decision of 1857.

In fact, the Missouri Compromise that Weingast characterized as a "self-enforcing equilibrium" was prophetically described by Thomas Jefferson in 1820 as the "knell of the Union." In Jefferson's view, the Missouri Compromise was not self-sustaining at all, but instead self-delusional and ultimately self-destructive: "A geographical line, coinciding with a marked principle, moral and political, once conceived and held up to the angry passions of men, will never be obliterated," he wrote, "and every new irritation will mark it deeper and deeper."[10]

As this example suggests, equilibrium analysis—drawn from economics and, before that, from physics—may not be the best framework for understanding democracy. A better approach, perhaps, can be derived from the field of biology, which offers a strikingly different take on the notion of equilibrium. As one well-known biology textbook bluntly explains, "a cell that has reached metabolic equilibrium is dead! The fact that metabolism as a whole is never at equilibrium is one of the defining features of life."[11]

The very same might be said of democracy. A healthy democracy, like a healthy organism, is constantly fighting *against* the forces of equilibrium—the forces of entropy—which drive fragmentation, breakdown, and decay. It's an imperfect analogy, to be sure. All analogies are. But the comparison to a living organism reveals some fundamental truths about democracy—about its complexity and its animating spirit—and is far more apt than the mechanistic conception of democracy so pervasive in civics classrooms and, to a large extent, in the public mind.

A little more than a quarter century after James Russell Lowell characterized the breakdown of the Union in 1861 as a breakdown of faith in the democracy, he famously declared that "after our Constitution got fairly into working order it really seemed as if we had invented a machine that would go of itself, and this begot a faith in our luck which even the civil war itself but momentarily disturbed."[12] Of course, Lowell knew as well as anyone that democracy is not "a machine that would go of itself"—that for it to survive and thrive, human agency is critically required. Woodrow Wilson had much the same thing in mind when he declared that "government is not a machine, but a living thing. It falls, not under the theory of the universe, but under the theory of organic life. It is accountable to Darwin, not to Newton. It is modified by its environment, necessitated by its tasks, shaped to its functions by the sheer pressure of life."[13]

Although a working democracy may appear simple, particularly in civics class, it in fact comprises an enormously complex array of human institutions, both formal and informal, all of which interact and need constantly to change and adapt to fight off threats of various kinds. The formal institutions, ranging from the three branches of government to the Bill of Rights, are all relatively fixed in the short run, but can be modified in various ways over the medium term and can be more profoundly changed through constitutional amendments over the long term. Informal institutions, meanwhile, ranging from civil society to social reform movements to the press, are equally vital to the health of the overall system and can change rapidly or barely at all, depending on conditions.

In these ways and many others, democracy is indeed more like a living, breathing organism than a machine built to specification. And like an organism, it can't stand still. It needs to actively work against corrosive forces, both moral and institutional, or succumb to them. We will see this, for example, in the battle to replace the Articles of Confederation with the Constitution in the late 1780s (Cases 1 and 2), and in an effort in New York State in the late 1830s to clean up a corrupt banking system intimately tied to the state's politics (Case 4). We will see it in the rise of independent administrative agencies in the late nineteenth century and the drive for the direct election of U.S. senators in the early twentieth (Cases 12 and 13). We will see it in battles to expand the franchise (Cases 5, 16, and 17), in the fight for public education (Case 7), and in the adoption of the secret ballot (Case 10) and the initiative and referendum (Case 13). We will see it in the growth and transformation of political parties (Cases 2, 4, and 10, among others), in the development of the abolitionist movement (Case 8), and in the rise of muckraking journalism (Cases 12 and 13). And we will see it in countless softer, but no less significant, changes in outlook and understanding across the nation's history—including, especially, changed perceptions of African Americans, Native Americans, Catholics, women, and gays and lesbians—often with dramatic political and legal consequences.

American democracy has always been a relentless struggle, both to expand its promise and to protect itself against forces of decay and corruption. It is a remarkable process, to say the least, but *not* an automatic one. It requires constant vigilance. As we have seen, this struggle—at its best—implies productive tension in the nation's politics: tension, in the form of competing ideas, interests, and institutions, made productive, ultimately, by a deep faith in—and a shared commitment to—the nation's system of democratic self-governance. This is what gives life to American democracy and has sustained it through countless trials.

E Pluribus Unum

Today we are frequently told by pundits of various kinds that American democracy is broken—that it is riven by partisanship, corrupted by wealth, and racked by distrust. These are hardly new concerns. In fact, charges of democratic dysfunction are almost as old as the republic itself. In virtually every generation, critics have warned that the democracy was not working as well as it once had and that this or that reform was urgently needed to prevent collapse. Sometimes these critics may have been right. Most often, probably not. But even when the democracy was not at death's door, such political hypochondria probably served a useful purpose in focusing attention on the health of the political system and stimulating public discussion about possible ailments and remedies. The same may be true today.

One of the most familiar claims of this sort in recent years is that the nation is being ripped apart by forces of division, including ideological extremism, populist anger, and especially hyperpartisanship. Some observers blame partisans on both the right and the left for the problem; others blame just the right or the left. There is no question, however, that the gap between the two sides has increased. In particular, partisan polarization in Congress—as measured by the political scientists Nolan McCarty, Keith Poole, and Howard Rosenthal—has reached record levels, higher now in both the House and the Senate that at any time since at least 1879.[14]

Clearly, as anyone who has even glanced at a newspaper recently can attest, there is no shortage of tension in American politics. But that, by itself, shouldn't set off alarm bells. After all, it is the presence of tension and conflict in democratic politics that ensures the best ideas win out, that guards against tyranny of the majority, and that helps mitigate capture by special interest groups. The critical question is not whether there is tension in our politics, partisan or otherwise, but rather whether it is constructive or destructive. And that depends, as I have tried to suggest, on the interplay of a broad range of democratic institutions and, perhaps most fundamentally, on whether our common faith in the democracy itself is strong enough to hold us together, to make one out of many, however intense our differences and disagreements.

If political conflict in America has indeed taken a turn for the worse and become less constructive (or possibly even destructive) in recent years or decades, it could be—as Lowell observed under far more extreme circumstances in February 1861—that we have come to take the democracy itself for granted. Perhaps we have become so distracted by our disagreements over big versus small government, over whose tax rates should be higher or lower, over the best and worst ways to deliver health care, and so forth, that we have lost track of what most powerfully binds us together.

We will return to these issues in the Conclusion, focusing especially on whether America's culture of democracy has in fact atrophied in recent decades and, if it has, why this might be the case and what might be done about it. My hope is that readers will reach the end of this book with many conclusions of their own, having worked through the individual case studies that make up this volume. To get the most out of the various cases, readers should think carefully about the decision point that is summarized at the start and end of each one—not only keeping the core decision in mind while reading the case, but also taking time to actively grapple with it after finishing the chapter. A quick summary of what happened in the aftermath of each case is presented in the Appendix, but readers should try to avoid peeking until after they have wrestled with all of the relevant issues in the case themselves. One of the premises of this book (and of the course on which it is based) is that readers who put themselves in the shoes of case protagonists and struggle with the decisions that the protagonists struggled with will experience history in a far more dynamic way, and will derive insights that they might not otherwise have seen.

One of those insights, on which I place particular weight, goes back to the three Latin words that Benjamin Franklin apparently plucked from the cover of *Gentleman's Magazine* in 1776 as a motto for the new nation: *E Pluribus Unum*. Out of many flowers, one bouquet; out of many literary works, one magazine; and out of many states and peoples, one nation. Franklin's elegant repurposing of the Latin phrase should remind us that our differences as Americans are in fact a profound source of strength, not weakness, but only so long as we find enough in common to see ourselves as one nation.

Faith in the democracy and in the essential principles of self-government has long been what most united Americans—what most bound them together. Yet sustaining and nourishing that faith, particularly in the face of unending crises, scandals, and transgressions, has always been part of the grand struggle of democracy. Legend has it that as Franklin was exiting the Constitutional Convention in September 1787, a woman asked him if the delegates had created a republic or a monarchy, and he responded, "A republic, madam, if you can keep it."[15] Perhaps the struggle to sustain our faith in self-governance—and in each other—is part of what he had in mind. It is to that struggle, and the broader story of American democracy, that we now turn.

NOTES

1. The story of the adoption of *E Pluribus Unum* as America's first national motto is drawn principally from Monroe E. Deutsch, "E Pluribus Unum," *Classical Journal* 18, no. 7 (Apr. 1923): 387–407. See also W. C. Harris, *E Pluribus Unum: Nineteenth-Century American Literature and the Constitutional Paradox* (Iowa City: University of Iowa Press, 2005), esp. 196–200; Gaillard Hunt, *The History of the Seal of the United States* (Washington: GPO, 1909), esp. 7–17; George Henry Preble, *Origin and History of the American Flag* (Philadelphia: Nicholas L. Brown, 1917), 2:694–697. On the etymology of the word "magazine," see "magazine, n." at *OED Online*.

2. Deutsch noted that whereas *Gentleman's Journal* used the phrase *"E Pluribus Unum"* to mean "one selected from many" (the *Journal* explained in 1692 that its use of the phrase "implies that tho' only one of the many Pieces in it were acceptable, it might gratify every reader"), *Gentleman's Magazine* used the phrase to mean "one composed of many" (the *Magazine* included a poem in 1734 that explained, "To your motto most

true, for our monthly inspection, You mix various rich sweets in one fragrant collection"). See Deutsch, "E Pluribus Unum," 392.

3. Harris, *E Pluribus Unum,* 197.

4. Deutsch, "E Pluribus Unum," 403.

5. James Madison, "Vices of the Political System of the United States" (Apr. 1787), §11.

6. James Russell Lowell, "E Pluribus Unum," *Atlantic Monthly,* Feb. 1861, 235–236, 240.

7. F. Scott Fitzgerald, "The Crack-Up," reprinted in *The Crack-Up,* ed. Edmund Wilson (New York: New Directions, 1945), 69.

8. Barry Weingast, "The Political Foundations of Democracy and the Rule of Law," *American Political Science Review* 91, no. 2 (June 1997): 245 (abstract).

9. Ibid., 259.

10. Thomas Jefferson, letter to John Holmes, 22 Apr. 1820, Library of Congress, available at http://www.loc.gov/exhibits/jefferson/159.html.

11. Jane B. Reece et al., *Campbell Biology,* 9th ed. (Boston: Pearson Benjamin Cummings, 2011), 148.

12. James Russell Lowell, *Political Essays* (Boston: Houghton, Mifflin, and Co., 1888), 312. These lines are included in the essay "The Place of the Independent in Politics," 295–326, which was based on an address to the Reform Club of New York on 13 Apr. 1888. See also Michael Kammen, *A Machine That Would Go of Itself: The Constitution in American Culture* (New York: Alfred A. Knopf, 1986).

13. Woodrow Wilson, *The New Freedom: A Call for the Emancipation of the Generous Energies of a People* (New York: Doubleday, Page, 1913), 47. Wilson described the book as "the result of the editorial literary skill of Mr. William Bayard Hale, who has put together here in their right sequences the more suggestive portions of my campaign speeches [from 1912]" (vii).

14. See Nolan McCarty, Keith T. Poole, and Howard Rosenthal, *Polarized America: The Dance of Ideology and Unequal Riches* (Cambridge, MA: MIT Press, 2006). Updated data (through 2014) available at http://voteview.com/political_polarization_2014.htm.

15. Quoted in Richard Labunski, *James Madison and the Struggle for the Bill of Rights* (New York: Oxford University Press, 2006), 13.

James Madison, the "Federal Negative," and the Making of the U.S. Constitution (1787)

ON JUNE 8, 1787, at the Constitutional Convention in Philadelphia, delegates from across the United States began discussing a curious proposal to expand federal power over the states. James Madison of Virginia had suggested that the new constitution include a "federal negative," which would give Congress the authority to veto any law passed by a state legislature. He viewed this as a critical safeguard against unchecked power at the state level. In late May, Madison's Virginia delegation had presented a plan for the constitution that included a watered-down version of the federal negative. Now, in June, Charles Pinckney of South Carolina revived the original version, calling it "the corner stone of an efficient national Gov^t [Government]."[1]

Not everyone agreed with Pinckney's assessment, however. Opponents charged that Madison's federal negative would allow Congress to "enslave the states" and let "large States crush the small ones."[2] Indeed, the question of how much power—and what types of power—to vest in the federal government went to the very heart of the debate that unfolded in Philadelphia that summer.

The Constitutional Convention of 1787 capped a tumultuous period in American history. In 1783, after eight years of war, Britain formally recognized its former colonies as the independent United States of America. Within just a few years, however, the triumphant Americans found themselves facing calamities on many fronts, ranging from federal insolvency and widespread economic recession to an armed rebellion in western Massachusetts. Said

---

Reprinted with permission from Harvard Business School Publishing. "James Madison, the 'Federal Negative,' and the Making of the U.S. Constitution." HBS Case 716-053. This case was prepared by David A. Moss and Marc Campasano, and draws significantly in parts on a previous case by Moss: "Constructing a Nation: The United States and Their Constitution, 1763–1792" (HBS Case 795-063, 1994).

George Washington, the hero of the Revolutionary War, "I am really morti-fied beyond expression that in the moment of our Acknowledged Indepen-dence we should, by our conduct, verify the predictions of our transatlantic foe, & render ourselves ridiculous & contemptible in the eyes of all Europe."[3]

Sharing Washington's frustration and embarrassment, James Madison came to believe that the economic and social turmoil plaguing America in the mid-1780s could be traced to defects in the Articles of Confederation, which had been adopted as the nation's governing document in 1781. After extensive research on past republics and confederacies, Madison concluded that the theory of state sovereignty underlying the Articles was deeply flawed: lodging nearly all power in the states was a recipe for disaster. What was needed, Madison argued, was an entirely new constitution that would create a strong but limited central government with well-defined powers, including the power to veto state laws. Whether Madison could persuade his fellow delegates at the Constitutional Convention was far from clear, but there could be little doubt how much was at stake as the new nation struggled to find its footing in Philadelphia.

Toward a New Nation

The United States began as thirteen British colonies located along the eastern seaboard of North America. The region possessed an abundance of natural resources—especially land—and the typical colonist lived well by world stan-dards. One prominent historian maintained that as of 1774 the colonists' living standards were "probably the highest achieved for the great bulk of the population in any country up to that time."[4] Between 1650 and 1750, the population of the North American colonies increased from 50,000 to nearly 1.2 million, even as the Native American population fell sharply, particu-larly as a result of disease. By 1770 the colonial population had nearly doubled again, reaching over 2 million. More than three-quarters of the colonial population worked in agriculture, and about two-thirds of white male farmers owned their own land. Blacks, nearly all of whom were slaves, comprised about one-fifth of the colonial population as of 1770.[5] Although slavery was legal in all of the colonies, most slaves worked in the South, typically cultivating rice and tobacco for export. Cotton was not yet an important crop.

Although disputes occasionally arose between the colonies and the mother country, before the 1760s they were few and far between. The British government controlled trade and foreign policy but otherwise left the colonists a great deal of authority over their own affairs. Although in principle most colonies were run by governors appointed by the British crown, in practice the colonies' elected assemblies enjoyed considerable power and discretion. Apart from a few import duties that were set in Britain, these assemblies decided local tax policy themselves.[6] The colonists were legally required to trade within the British Empire in most cases but still benefited from guaranteed markets for their agricultural products, access to English manufactured goods, and the protection of the British military.

This mutually beneficial relationship began to deteriorate only as the British felt new financial pressures in the 1760s. After concluding a very long but ultimately successful war against French and Native American forces on North American soil in 1763, the British government determined that the colonists were vastly undertaxed. Compared to citizens of the British Isles, the American colonists paid next to nothing in taxes. British officials, who faced a dramatically enlarged national debt after the French and Indian War, believed that the Americans should begin to share the costs of their own defense.[7]

In 1764, therefore, the British Parliament passed the Sugar Act, which placed new regulations on the colonial sugar trade and imposed heavy taxes on a number of popular colonial imports, including wine and silk. Although some New Englanders attempted to fight the edict by refusing to buy British goods, their nonimportation campaign failed to achieve widespread acceptance. The colonists' response was far more dramatic the following year when the British passed the Stamp Act, which levied taxes on nearly all types of colonial documents, from newspapers to licenses. Incensed colonists reacted violently, burning effigies of British officials and physically threatening tax collectors. In most places the colonists' tactics effectively blocked implementation of the Stamp Act. The nonimportation campaign also took on new life during the crisis and began exacting a heavy toll on British exporters.

In the emerging rebellion, the colonists coalesced around the principle of "no taxation without representation." The British Parliament had seized the power to tax from the monarchy in the Glorious Revolution of 1688, and this right was often celebrated as a foundation of British freedom and parliamentary democracy. The colonists viewed the new taxes in North America as a violation of these same ideals because they had no elected representatives in Parliament. The British government strenuously disagreed, claiming that the colonies *did* have a voice in Parliament through the principle of "virtual representation." This idea, championed by Chancellor of the Exchequer George Grenville, suggested that each member of Parliament represented the entire empire, not only those who voted him into office.[8]

Although Parliament bowed to political pressures at home and repealed the Stamp Act, the conflict was by no means over. British military commanders in North America began redeploying troops from the interior to the coastal cities in response to the colonists' increasingly organized resistance. Meanwhile, in 1767 Parliament passed the Townshend Acts, which levied a variety of new taxes on colonial imports, riling the colonists once again. By 1770 tempers were so short in Boston that nervous British troops fired on an unruly group of demonstrators, killing five of them. The "Boston Massacre" only further inflamed the colonists' feelings of injustice and mistrust.

After yet another tactical retreat in 1770, involving the repeal of most of the Townshend duties, Parliament passed the Tea Act in 1773. The Tea Act offered special advantages to British traders who re-exported tea to the colonies. Its primary purpose was to eliminate smuggled Dutch tea from the American market and thus bolster Britain's troubled East India Company. As a by-product it also severely undercut New England merchants who had enjoyed a lucrative trade in smuggled tea, and it effectively reimposed an existing tax on tea imports, which the smuggling operations had circumvented. Convinced that these new British rules further infringed on their independence, the colonists again resorted to violence. They threatened incoming ships carrying tea, and one night in December they dramatically dumped 105,000 pounds of British tea cargo into Boston Harbor. Outraged at the "Boston Tea Party," the royal government immediately shut down Boston's port and attempted to place Massachusetts under military rule. Declared King George III, "The die is now cast. The Colonies must either submit or triumph."[9]

As the king suspected, dissent was now spreading rapidly and threatening to become a full-scale rebellion. In September 1774, representatives from twelve colonies (all except Georgia) met in Philadelphia for a "Continental

Congress," which quickly revived and intensified the nonimportation campaign. Massachusetts citizens began establishing their own governmental institutions the very same year. The growing resentment between the Americans and the British came to a head on April 19, 1775, when the first shots of the American Revolution were fired just outside of Boston, on the Lexington town green. To their astonishment, British military leaders soon discovered that the American rebels—though highly unconventional and undisciplined by traditional standards—constituted a formidable challenge.

Managing the War Effort

By the time the American colonists formally declared their independence from Britain on July 4, 1776, the philosophical question about what form of government was best had become a pressing practical one. British administrative structures began crumbling in the early 1770s as the rebellion took hold, leaving the colonists little choice but to erect new governmental institutions. Revolutionary leaders in most states established ad hoc legislative bodies in order to raise taxes and form militias. Through the pivotal year of 1776 seven states adopted formal constitutions, and most of the others soon followed. By embracing these new legal frameworks, "Americans had discovered a way to legalize revolution."[10] Significantly, all of the state constitutions were grounded on the principle of popular sovereignty and, in most cases, extended suffrage to all white males who owned at least a small amount of property.[11]

Although most governmental authority and responsibility remained firmly lodged at the state level, the Continental Congress played an important role in coordinating the war effort against Britain—for example, by creating the Continental Army and appointing George Washington of Virginia as its commander in chief. Over the course of the war, the army never reached the full strength that many national leaders envisaged. The American people largely distrusted centralized military power, especially given their experience under British rule. Reflecting this anxiety (and adding to the challenge of managing the war effort), the Americans fielded at least fourteen distinct force structures during the war: "the thirteen state militias and the Continental Army."[12]

Financing the war effort proved equally challenging, especially because it was unclear whether the Continental Congress had the legal authority or the popular support necessary to levy taxes. Perhaps as a consequence, Congress initially financed the war at least in part through extensive issues of paper money. The bills, known as "Continentals," were ostensibly backed by future tax revenues rather than gold or silver. From 1775 until 1780, when the printing stopped, Congress had issued well over $200 million in paper currency, triggering severe depreciation and bringing the phrase "not worth a Continental" into common parlance.[13] The scientist and statesman Benjamin Franklin, however, argued that the inflation was not such a bad thing: "The general Effect of the Depreciation among the Inhabitants of the States, has been this, that it has operated as a *gradual Tax* upon them. . . . Thus it has proved a Tax on Money, a kind of Property very difficult to be taxed in any other Mode; and it has fallen more equally than many other Taxes, as those People paid most who being richest had most Money passing thro' their Hands."[14]

Although issues of paper money covered a large portion of federal spending until 1780, the Continental Congress also financed the war through borrowing—particularly from France, Spain, and Holland, but also from domestic creditors. Because investors were naturally wary about loaning large sums to a new government, interest rates rose as wartime borrowing accelerated.[15]

Like Congress, most states initially tried to avoid levying taxes, relying instead on paper money to finance the war effort. As inflation rose, however, many states finally began imposing higher taxes. In some cases wartime taxes exceeded those collected under British rule, provoking citizens to protest, evade payment, and even sometimes riot. Ultimately even these higher taxes proved insufficient, forcing states to rely on extensive borrowing and, in some cases, continued use of the printing press to finance the war.[16]

Forging a Confederation

As early as 1775 a number of political leaders, including Benjamin Franklin, had suggested that the authority of the Continental Congress should be grounded in a written constitution. Lawmakers began working on such a document in June 1776, based on the general understanding that the states would be left to manage their internal affairs while Congress would handle foreign affairs. Several significant points of contention emerged during the drafting process, however, including whether more populous states would have more votes in Congress and whether slave populations would be counted when calculating each state's share of wartime expenses.

As the summer of 1776 came to a close, the drafting process was largely put aside—in part because several core issues remained contentious, but also because the military situation was becoming increasingly dire. British forces seized control of New York City in September, and the city became a stronghold for colonists loyal to Britain. General Washington fled with his troops to Pennsylvania, but over the winter captured Trenton and Princeton in New Jersey. In October 1777 the British took Philadelphia, the nation's capital, but this victory proved costly to the British in both money and lives as a result of their generals' poor coordination and George Washington's clever maneuvering. Although Washington's army faced starvation conditions at Valley Forge in Pennsylvania that winter, the Americans' strategic position had already begun to improve in October 1777, when the American general Horatio Gates succeeded in halting a British army descending from Canada in the Battle of Saratoga.[17]

That same month, members of the Continental Congress resumed work on a governing document. Worsening inflation as well as the potential for an alliance with France renewed the desire for a formal accord to undergird and clarify Congress's authority. Lawmakers ultimately resolved their differences by agreeing that each state would have one vote in the unicameral Congress, war expenses would be distributed based on the value of each state's land and improvements, and Congress would not manage state boundaries or western lands. Representatives finally completed drafting the document, called the Articles of Confederation, in mid-November 1777.[18]

As the war gradually turned in the Americans' favor, individual states began ratifying the Articles. Virginia moved first, approving the document near the close of 1777, and Maryland completed the process as the last state to ratify in early 1781. Just seven months later, the British commander Lord Cornwallis found himself surrounded by American forces and their newfound French allies, and he surrendered to General Washington at Yorktown, Virginia, on October 19, 1781.[19] Although the war was not yet officially over, it was now rapidly winding down, and the victorious Americans increasingly turned their attention to matters of domestic governance.

The Articles of Confederation, which announced that each state "retains its sovereignty" (Art. 2) and that together the states would form "a firm league of friendship with each other" (Art. 3), vested limited authority in a national Congress without creating either a chief executive or a judiciary. Specifically, the Articles conferred upon Congress the authority to borrow as well as the exclusive power to declare war, to enter into treaties and alliances, to settle disputes between the states, to regulate weights and measures, and to oversee a national postal system. Nowhere, however, did the Articles grant the national government superiority relative to the states or the means to compel them to follow its laws.

Although the Articles placed relatively few restrictions on the states, there was a clear attempt to prevent states from discriminating against each other's citizens. The people of each state, the document declared, "shall be entitled to all privileges and immunities of free citizens in the several States; and . . . shall have free ingress and regress to and from any other State, and shall enjoy therein all the privileges of trade and commerce, subject to the same duties, impositions, and restrictions as the inhabitants thereof."[20] Significantly, the Articles also left virtually all control over both foreign and interstate commerce with the states, rather than with Congress.

While permitting the various states to collect taxes and impose tariffs, and requiring the federal government to honor its war debts, the Articles did not grant Congress the power to levy taxes. Instead the Articles asserted: "All charges of war, and all other expenses that shall be incurred for the common defense or general welfare, and allowed by the United States in Congress assembled, shall be defrayed out of a common treasury, which shall be supplied by the several States in proportion to the value of all land within each State."[21]

Finally, in terms of representation, the Articles granted each state delegation one vote in Congress and mandated that the members of each delegation (who could not hold office for more than three years out of six) "shall be annually appointed in such manner as the legislature of each State shall direct."[22] On important bills, nine votes out of thirteen would be necessary for passage, and unanimous consent of the states would be required in order to amend the Articles themselves.[23]

A "Critical Period"

Although 1781 was a glorious year for the young United States, with the victory at Yorktown and the ratification of the Articles of Confederation, the struggle to establish a viable nation had only just begun. Indeed, the new nation faced enormous challenges after the war came to a close. One of Harvard's student commencement speakers in 1787, John Quincy Adams, declared that during this "critical period," Americans found themselves "groaning under the intolerable burden of . . . accumulated evils."[24] Similarly, John Jay of New York had warned in a letter to George Washington the previous year, "Our affairs seem to lead to some crisis, some revolution—something that I cannot foresee or conjecture. I am uneasy and apprehensive; more so than during the war. . . . The case is now altered; we are going and doing wrong."[25] Anxiety was in the air during this "critical period," and with good reason.

Congress's Limited Power

One of the first major problems to become apparent, even before the war officially ended, was the appallingly weak financial position of the new federal government. Congress had accumulated $27 million in debt during the war.[26] Yet under the Articles it was unable to impose national taxes or force the states to provide funds. In 1781 Congress collected only $422,000 of $5 million requested from the states, with no contribution at all from Georgia, North or South Carolina, or Delaware.[27] Two years later, after persistent attempts to put Congress's fiscal house in order, Superintendent of Finance Robert Morris asked to be "dismissed" from his position, writing in frustration, "It can no longer be a doubt to Congress *that our public credit is gone*."[28]

Congress could not pay its expenses, or its debts, without reliable income. Soldiers expecting payment for their wartime service were particularly alarmed, and several officers in Newburgh, New York, even threatened mutiny until George Washington himself intervened, delivering a moving speech to his officer corps in defense of the republic. Although a frightened Congress temporarily calmed the waters by enacting an expansive military pension in 1783, Pennsylvania soldiers who were tired of waiting for compensation literally ran Congress out of Philadelphia later that same year. Lacking funds well into the decade, Congress repeatedly defaulted on its debt obligations, both foreign and domestic.[29] At the urging of anxious creditors, Congress began transferring some of its debt burden into the more capable hands of the states. Several states had already been contributing to cover a portion of the debt since 1780, and many state leaders viewed the assumption of the debt as an expression of the "right to take care of [their] subjects."[30] By the middle of the decade, Pennsylvania, Maryland, and New York alone had assumed $9 million of the national debt. Because states had the authority to tax their citizens, most were more successful at managing this debt than Congress had been. Congress did resume some interest payments in 1784 but paid creditors in new certificates rather than specie (that is, gold or silver). These certificates—essentially a replacement of new debt for old—were naturally unpopular with recipients and quickly depreciated in value.[31]

Congress's weakness under the Articles was also evident in its inability to enforce the terms of the Treaty of Paris, the peace agreement between Britain and the United States that officially brought the war to a close in September 1783. With Congress lacking any real coercive power, the states defied important provisions of the treaty designed to protect loyalists from abuse and ensure payment of private debts to British creditors. Furious about these blatant violations, the British retaliated by keeping troops garrisoned in frontier forts on American soil, also in clear contravention of the treaty.[32]

Beyond treaty violations, the states frequently flouted the Articles of Confederation—for example, by enacting laws that discriminated against out-of-state merchants. As a case in point, New York laid heavy duties on New Jersey and Connecticut merchants who shipped their products to New York City, provoking retaliatory sanctions from the affected states. In fact, numerous states had begun imposing tariffs on their neighbors, dramatically impeding interstate commerce.[33]

Beggar-thy-neighbor policies at the state level also sharply limited American effectiveness in negotiations over international trade. Because Congress lacked the power to impose tariffs and thus to retaliate against trade protection, it lacked the necessary bargaining power to negotiate a reasonable trade treaty with a foreign power. In fact, the British government simply refused to negotiate with Congress at all, recognizing early on that Congress was virtually powerless and that the various states could easily be played against one another. The result was that British goods poured into the states while American exports to Britain remained severely depressed by prewar standards. American commercial interests actively looked for alternative markets, particularly in Continental Europe, but they faced the same obstacles again and again. As John Adams, the American liaison to Great Britain (and John Quincy Adams's father), struggled to respond to Britain's aggressive posture, he fretted that a sound commercial standing for the United States would "never be secured until Congress shall be made supreme in foreign commerce."[34]

Immediately after the war, several "nationalist" politicians who worried about the consequences of an enfeebled Congress had suggested enhanced powers for the national government. In his role as finance superintendent, for example, Robert Morris of Pennsylvania proposed several amendments to the Articles that would have authorized national taxes, and James Madison of Virginia supported an amendment to grant Congress the power "to employ the force of the United States as well by sea as by land" to ensure compliance with national laws.[35] Such proposals, however, consistently failed to win the unanimous consent of the states that was required to amend the Articles (Rhode Island, sometimes referred to as "Rogue Island," was a frequent dissenter), and the nationalists' energy soon faded after 1783, at least temporarily.[36]

Other critics of Congress, meanwhile, harbored even more radical ideas for restoring order. In the middle of the military pension dispute, Colonel Lewis Nicola wrote to George Washington about the officers' grievances. Most famously, he suggested that an American monarchy be erected with Washington as king. Washington responded that if Nicola had "any regard for your Country, concern for yourself or posterity—or respect for me, to banish these thoughts from your Mind & never communicate, as from yourself, or any one else, a sentiment of the like nature."[37]

Recession and Rebellion

Amid such political turmoil—and perhaps in part because of it—the American economy soon took a turn for the worse. Historians continue to debate the extent of the economic downturn in the mid-1780s, but nearly all agree that it was a difficult period and some believe that the downturn may have been extremely sharp. The most pessimistic estimates suggest that per capita GNP fell by more than half. If so, then the economic collapse in the mid-1780s was even worse than that experienced between 1929 and 1933 (the worst phase of the Great Depression). According to two scholars of the period, "While the extent of the reduction in gross national product remains uncertain, it is clear that per capita product fell and that it fell enough to affect all levels of society."[38]

One consequence of the downturn is that many individual debtors found it difficult to make good on their obligations. Their woes were only compounded by the fact that the federal government, as well as a number of states, had fallen behind on servicing their own debts, leaving many former soldiers who had accepted bonds and certificates as payment for their wartime service in a tough financial squeeze. Many of these former soldiers had no choice but to sell their government certificates to speculators at deep discounts. In Massachusetts, for example, a farmer who had served in the Revolutionary War complained in a local newspaper that neither vendors nor workers would accept the government notes at par. "The necessities of my family," he lamented, "obligated me to alienate [the notes] at one quarter part of their original value."[39] Adding to the burden, many state governments raised taxes to pay off war debts, pushing numerous taxpayers with heavy financial commitments of their own to the breaking point.[40]

With countless farmers petitioning for debt relief, several state legislatures responded around 1786 by issuing substantial amounts of paper money, thereby allowing debtors to repay their debts in inflated currency. Rhode Island took the policy to its logical extreme, inducing rapid inflation and imposing penalties on creditors who refused to accept payment in the sharply depreciated paper money. Within a year, Rhode Island's paper dollar was worth only sixteen cents in gold. Although other states exercised more restraint, creditors across the country claimed that their property was being confiscated as a result of the inflationary policies.[41] In Virginia, James Madison warned that paper money "affects the Rights of property as much as taking away equal value in land."[42]

In contrast to Rhode Island, neighboring Massachusetts remained committed to both fiscal and monetary conservatism. The state legislature raised taxes to repay its debts and resolutely avoided a policy of inflation. The resulting pressure on small farmers was enormous, and many lost their property in court-ordered foreclosures. One former Revolutionary officer, Daniel Shays, was so angry about the plight of farmers in the state that starting in the summer of 1786 he helped to lead a growing rebellion in western Massachusetts, its ranks eventually surging to over 2,000 men. One goal of the rebels was to prevent the courts—through either force or intimidation—from seizing the delinquent farmers' property. Although rumors circulated that the rebels intended to unseat the state government, nothing of the sort ever happened and the uprising was ultimately put down in early 1787. There is little doubt, however, that the newly elected legislature in Massachusetts heard Shays' message, for they quickly passed a variety of relief measures, including a moratorium on debts.[43]

In the minds of many Americans, the crisis in Massachusetts epitomized all that was wrong with the new confederation. Economic elites who had never been very comfortable with the idea of broad-based democracy wondered whether they were headed for a future of class warfare and even mob rule. George Washington saw the whole episode as a terrible embarrassment: "To be more exposed in the eyes of the world & more contemptible than we already are, is hardly possible," he lamented.[44] Particularly after the nation's extraordinary triumph over the British, what could explain its shocking fall from grace in the eyes of so many Americans, including the hero of the Revolution himself?

Madison's Diagnosis

This question of what had gone wrong captivated James Madison, a Virginia statesman who had been active in both national and state politics throughout the revolutionary and postwar eras. Born in 1751 into an affluent slaveholding family,* Madison has been described as possessing "a keen and inquiring mind coupled with a voracious intellectual appetite."[45] He attended the College of New Jersey, which later became Princeton University, and went on to study with its president, John Witherspoon.

Although physically diminutive and reserved in personality, Madison had a penchant for politics and political battles. Frustrated upon returning from New Jersey in the early 1770s that his own Virginia Anglican Church was a

---

* Although Madison would later speak out against slavery, he never freed his own slaves. Significantly, he also wrote a precursor to the infamous Three-Fifths Compromise as a proposed amendment to the Articles of Confederation, though the provision was not adopted.

source of intolerance against other denominations, he furiously denounced its "diabolical, hell-conceived principle of persecution."[46] Not long afterward, as the rebellion against Britain took hold, Madison began to assist county and state governments, and at the age of 25 helped to write Virginia's state constitution. Elected to the Continental Congress in 1780, Madison had borne witness to its various deficiencies, and he was disappointed when his nationalist projects failed to take hold. After rejoining the Virginia legislature in 1784, he and his allies successfully defeated proposals both to declare Christianity the state religion and to expand issuances of paper money. Nevertheless, the mere existence of these movements likely contributed to his growing unease about the direction of American politics.[47]

In March 1784 Madison asked his friend Thomas Jefferson, then in Paris on a diplomatic mission, to send him whatever books "may throw light on the general Constitution & droit public [public law] of the several confederacies which have existed."[48] Madison reasoned that by understanding why past confederations had succeeded or failed, he could better identify what ailed the American confederation. By January 1786 he had received two trunks of books in English, French, and Latin at Montpelier, his family's plantation estate.[49] Sitting in his library, Madison began working through the books, conducting a thorough historical review spanning thousands of years. The lessons he gleaned would shape his thinking on the young American republic as well as his arguments at the Constitutional Convention in Philadelphia the following year.

History as a Guide

The books on Madison's reading list included, among others, recent French works in the Enlightenment *philosophe* tradition and numerous classical Greek texts.[50] The confederations he surveyed ranged from the Amphyctionic and Achaean confederacies of ancient Greece to the Belgic confederacy in the Netherlands (also known as the United Netherlands), which was still in place in the 1780s.

Madison took careful notes on each confederation's structure and operations, specifically commenting on the deficiencies he perceived in each. He noted that several confederation governments had been unable to control their members, even in policy areas where they held explicit authority. For example, he pointed out that Athens and Sparta had waged their many wars against each other while co-members of the Amphyctionic confederacy, despite the federal authority's prerogative to mediate such conflicts.[51] In the Belgic confederacy, the central authority had to consult fifty-two cities—and sometimes procure their unanimous consent—when negotiating any treaty, which resulted in long delays and easy manipulation by foreign powers. With each member city able to hold up the whole, the confederacy proved exceedingly slow in enacting policies. Madison believed that such a "weak constitution must necessarily terminate in dissolution for want of proper powers."[52]

"Vices of the Political System of the United States"

Having completed his historical investigation of confederations from around the world, Madison began preparing a critique of the new confederation in America. The resulting 1787 document, entitled "Vices of the Political System of the United States," identified a range of national failings and attributed them to deficiencies "radically and permanently inherent in . . . the present System."[53]

He began by highlighting the states' persistent violations of the Articles of Confederation, such as their breaches of international treaties and their regular refusal to honor Congress's requests for funds. Although Madison criticized the states for these actions, he mainly faulted the Articles for denying the national government the capacity to enforce its policies. The authors of the Articles, he wrote, had trusted too much "that the justice, the good faith, the honor, [and] the sound policy" of the state legislatures would obviate the need for such enforcement power at the federal level. "A sanction is essential to the idea of law, as coercion is to that of Government," he explained, and without either he believed the existing system had little to recommend it.[54]

Even the state legislatures' constitutional actions, Madison lamented, had often undercut the national interest. He complained that the states had regularly failed to pursue "concert in matters where public interest require[d] it," particularly in setting uniform commercial policies. Instead, they had passed laws to limit interstate trade or to support debtors at the expense of out-of-state creditors, which pit states and citizens against each other in a manner Madison called "destructive of the general harmony."[55]

In the final section of "Vices," Madison went beyond merely listing the country's problems and proposed an explanation as to why there had been so much "injustice" in the states' laws.[56] In doing so, he rejected the traditional assumption—perhaps most strongly associated with Montesquieu and his studies of the ancient Greek republics—that republican government worked best on a small scale.[57] Madison began by observing that all communities contained various factions such as economic classes, religious groups, and political parties. If a single faction, or a small concert of factions, won control of a legislature, "what [was] to restrain them from unjust violations of the rights and interests of the minority, or of individuals?" Madison suggested that small republics, with less competition among political groups, were more vulnerable to this problem of tyranny of the majority. In large republics, by contrast, "the Society becomes broken into a greater variety of interests, of pursuits, of passions, which check each other, whilst those who may feel a common sentiment have less opportunity of communication and concert." With diverse factions tempering each other's influence, he suggested, a larger republic's legislature would enact sounder and fairer policies.

Implicit throughout "Vices" was Madison's longing for constitutional reforms that would strengthen the national government and expand its influence over the states. He clearly articulated his desire to grant Congress powers of "sanction" and "coercion." But his frustrations about the states' failure to work together implied that the federal government required not only greater enforcement power, but also a broader span of authority. Notably, he wished to see an "enlargement of the sphere" of democratic policy-making to weaken the influence of faction, implying a shift in power from the state to the national level.[58] Such changes would be impossible under the current system, however, because the states' "sovereignty, freedom, and independence" were enshrined in the Articles of Confederation.[59] Madison thus intimated that only fundamental changes to the nation's constitution—or perhaps a completely new one—would be sufficient to correct the republic's flaws.

Vision for a New Constitution

By the time he completed "Vices," Madison had begun describing potential constitutional reforms in his correspondence with other national leaders.[60]

Together these proposals comprised a program that would "lead to such a systematic change" in American governance, he wrote, that it would replace, rather than merely alter, the Articles of Confederation.[61]

Madison's proposed system would be built on "a due supremacy of the national authority" and would leave the states with enough power to be "subordinately useful." To that end, he sought to grant the national government "positive and compleat authority in all cases which require uniformity," such as the setting of trade regulations and customs rates. This federal supremacy would extend to new judicial and executive branches of the national government, each superior to the analogous state institutions. To further bolster the national government's authority, Madison proposed a "right of coercion" against delinquent states that would enable the federal government to carry out its laws "by force."[62]

As a further check on the states, Madison proposed that Congress hold a veto over state laws "in *all cases whatsoever.*"[63] He explained his reasoning in a letter to Jefferson:

> The effects of this provision would be not only to guard the national rights and interests against invasion, but also to restrain the States from thwarting and molesting each other, and even from oppressing the minority within themselves by paper money and other unrighteous measures which favor the interest of the majority.[64]

Madison believed that this veto, which scholars call the "federal negative," was essential to Congress's supremacy under his model.[65] "Without this defensive power," he warned, "every positive power that can be given on paper will be evaded & defeated."[66]

In addition to suggesting new powers for Congress, Madison also recommended modifications to its structure and mechanisms of representation. His proposal would split the existing unitary Congress into two houses: one elected by the people or state legislatures and another "to consist of a more select number, holding their appointments for a longer term."[67] Within those houses, Madison desired a "change [to] be made in the principle of representation" to foster greater equality between the states. Although each state was nominally equal in Congress under the Articles' one-state-one-vote system, the larger states had always enjoyed more clout in national affairs due to their legislatures' greater "weight and influence." Madison hoped to see these inequalities reduced "under a system which would operate . . . without the intervention of the State legislatures."[68]

The Constitutional Convention of 1787

An emerging national "consensus" for constitutional reform would soon give Madison the chance to present his ideas on a national stage.[69] In 1785, as the individual states struggled against Britain's trade laws, support had grown for an amendment to the Articles of Confederation that would grant Congress new powers over international trade. At Madison's recommendation, a convention met the following September in Annapolis to discuss such an amendment, but only five states sent representatives who arrived in time to participate.[70] Although the conference remained brief because of sparse attendance, the conferees suggested that another meeting be held the next year to discuss a wider array of constitutional issues. Congress sat on this recommendation for months. Some observers say that it was ultimately propelled to action only by fears of general unrest stemming from Shays' Rebellion. Whatever the cause, Congress in February 1787 formally called for a new convention in Philadelphia "for the sole and express purpose of revising the Articles of Confederation."[71]

Madison was one of fifty-five delegates who attended the convention that began on May 25. George Washington presided over the convention, and every state except Rhode Island sent a delegation. Seated in a central location from which he could easily hear all members and take detailed notes, Madison was a leading contributor to the discussions.[72] Throughout the debates he shared the theories he had derived from his extensive study of republics and confederacies, and peppered the debate with arguments he had rehearsed in "Vices of the Political System." Georgia delegate William Pierce described Madison as "blend[ing] together the profound politician, with the Scholar . . . the best informed Man of any point in debate."[73]

Madison's outsized influence over the convention was further enhanced by his Virginia delegation, which presented a preliminary outline for the new constitution, inspired heavily by Madison's own recommendations. The "Virginia Plan," as it became known, dominated early discussions at the convention.

The Structure of the New Government under the Virginia Plan

The Virginia Plan included Madison's proposal for a bicameral Congress, specifying that the American people would elect representatives to the lower house, who in turn would select members of the upper house from candidates nominated by the state legislatures. State representation in Congress would be "proportioned to the Quotas of contribution [taxes], or to the number of free inhabitants."[74] The delegates quickly agreed to the bicameral structure, but remained at odds over how to select the members of each house.[75]

Some delegates worried about giving the people too much power. According to Elbridge Gerry of Massachusetts, the United States already suffered from an "excess of democracy." The people of his home state, he asserted, had been "misled into the most baneful measures and opinions" by "pretended patriots," and these episodes had convinced him of the dangers of too much democracy. Agreeing that the people were unqualified to choose their congressmen, South Carolina's Charles Pinckney proposed that the selection of the lower house be left to the state legislatures instead.[76]

Supporters of a popularly elected house, meanwhile, were quick to invoke democratic ideals in its defense. It was only just, Virginia's George Mason argued, that "every class of the people" be represented in the government. Madison, responding to Pinckney's proposal, spoke at length on his theory of faction and the virtues of a large republic. He repeated the criticisms of faction-prone state legislatures that he had developed in "Vices." Keeping state politics out of the lower house of Congress, he maintained, would "enlarge the sphere," ensuring a greater variety of interests.[77] Ultimately Madison and his allies prevailed on this issue: Pinckney's proposal was rejected, and control over selecting the lower house was placed in the people's hands.

The Senate (as the conferees called the upper house) would be built on less democratic principles. Many delegates envisioned the Senate as the more careful and deliberative house, containing "the most distinguished characters, distinguished for their rank in life and their weight of property."[78] Madison predicted that the Senate, given its makeup, would stand as a vital bulwark against tyranny of the majority, even as American society evolved and (in his estimation) the proportion of poor laborers increased over time:

In framing a system which we wish to last for ages, we sh^d not lose sight of the changes which ages will produce. An increase in population will of necessity increase the proportion of those who will labour under all the hardships of life, & secretly sigh for a more equal distribution of the blessings. These may in time outnumber those who are placed above the feelings of indigence. According to the equal laws of suffrage, the power will slide into the hands of the former. No agrarian attempts have yet been made in this Country, but symptoms, of a leveling spirit . . . have sufficiently appeared . . . to give notice of the future danger. How is this danger to be guarded agst on republican principles? How is the danger in all cases of interested coalitions to oppress the minority to be guarded agst? Among other means by the establishment of a body in the Gov^t sufficiently respectable for its wisdom & virtue, to aid on such emergences, the preponderance of justice by throwing its weight into the scale.[79]

Although the delegates largely agreed on the desired character of the Senate, there was considerable debate over how members of the upper house should be selected. Mirroring Pinckney's earlier idea for the lower house, John Dickenson of Delaware suggested that the state legislatures should select their senators, asserting, "The preservation of the States in a certain agency is indispensable."[80] He hoped that the Senate, selected in this way, would be a body through which the states could exert an additional check on federal power. Madison opposed Dickenson's suggestion because he preferred a small Senate composed of just a few elite leaders. Under Dickenson's proposal, the smallest states would each have at least one senator and, because Madison and his Virginia colleagues favored proportional representation, larger states would require proportionally larger numbers of senators, as in the lower house. The Virginia Plan had ingeniously avoided this problem by granting election of the Senate to the lower house. In this way, *votes* for senators would be proportionally distributed among the states, while the final number of senators selected could remain small. Although Madison attempted to rally support for his model by reminding listeners of the state legislatures' role in the paper money crises, the delegates ultimately endorsed Dickenson's method of selection instead.[81]

Beyond the bicameral legislature, the Virginia Plan also included a new national executive branch with "a general authority to execute the National laws." When James Wilson of Pennsylvania moved that the executive be vested in one person, rather than a small council, there was "a considerable pause" in the discussion. Americans had been ruled by one man before, the king of England, and there was concern that Wilson's proposal might prove to be "the fœtus of monarchy."[82] Wilson countered that a council would involve "nothing but uncontrouled, continued, & violent animosities," whereas a unitary executive would be steadier and more decisive. Wilson also reassured the convention that the executive's powers would be sufficiently limited that he could never rule like a king; instead, he would more closely resemble the governors to whom Americans had already entrusted their state operations.[83] In the end, the assembly agreed with Wilson that a single executive would be best, in part because nearly all assumed that George Washington, whom they admired and trusted, would become the first president.

Elbridge Gerry of Massachusetts next recommended granting the executive veto power over laws passed by Congress. The Virginia Plan would have conferred this power to a "Council of Revision" made up of the executive and members of the judicial branch, but Gerry wished to separate the judiciary from the laws it would be asked to rule upon. Delegates had already expressed anxiety about the creation of a single executive, and the prospect of empowering it still further immediately provoked opposition. As a matter of democratic principle, critics resisted "enabling any one man to stop the will of the whole."[84] They also feared that veto power would, in practice, give the executive nearly absolute control over the entire government.[85] This issue, like so many others, was ultimately settled through compromise: the executive would have veto power, but two-thirds votes in both houses of Congress could override it.

National Supremacy?

As the delegates gradually worked out the structure of the new federal government, they also had to decide on its role vis-à-vis the states. One of the first general principles voted on was "that a *national* Government ought to be established consisting of a *supreme* Legislative, Executive & Judiciary." Gouverneur Morris of Pennsylvania "explained the distinction between a *federal* and *national, supreme* government; the former being a mere compact resting on the good faith of the parties; the latter having a complete and *compulsive* operation. He contended that in all Communities there must be one supreme power, and one only." Perhaps not surprisingly, some delegates wondered if the notion of national supremacy over the states went too far. Pinckney even questioned whether this new dynamic was intended to "abolish the State Governments altogether," though Edmund Randolph, the leading presenter of the Virginia Plan, assured him that it was not.[86] After relatively brief deliberation on the issue, the convention voted to endorse the supremacy provision.

A closely related issue was how to draw a dividing line between the powers of Congress and those of the states. The Virginia Plan proposed that Congress have "Legislative power in all cases to which the State Legislatures were individually incompetent." Some delegates, however, worried this language was excessively vague. To combat concerns that the convention was "running into an extreme in taking away the powers of the States,"[87] many delegates believed that Congress's authority should be limited by specifically enumerating its powers. Madison largely agreed with them, but he made it clear that in any future discussions of such powers "he would shrink from nothing which should be found essential to such a form of Government as would provide for the safety, liberty, and happiness of the community."[88] With the understanding that specifics might be discussed at a later date, the convention voted at the end of May in favor of the Virginia Plan's language on Congress, empowering it to act where the states "were individually incompetent."[89]

The Federal Negative

Madison's proposal for a congressional veto over state laws—his federal negative—finally took center stage at the convention on June 8. Whereas his original proposal would have applied in "all cases whatsoever," Madison's Virginia colleagues had included a narrower version in the Virginia Plan that limited Congress's veto only to state laws that "contraven[ed] in the opinion of the National Legislature the articles of Union." The convention had assented to this more limited federal negative early on and without argument. On June 8, however, Pinckney suggested extending the veto to "all laws which [Congress] should judge to be improper," in line with Madison's original conception. Pinckney doubted that the Virginia Plan's more limited approach would be sufficient to keep the states in line and that "a universality of the power was indispensably necessary to render it effectual." He judged the absolute approach that he was proposing to be "the corner stone of an efficient national Gov^t," without which Congress would prove unable to enforce its policies.[90]

Madison seconded Pinckney's motion. He warned that a limited federal negative, intended to nullify only unconstitutional state laws, was liable to become "a fresh source of contention" between the states and the federal government, as they battled over the question of constitutionality. Perhaps most troubling, while such disagreements might necessitate that Congress impose its decisions by force, Madison questioned whether such federal coercion would be feasible:

> Could the national resources, if exerted to the utmost, enforce a national decree against Massachusetts, abetted, perhaps, by several of her neighbours? It would not be possible. A small proportion of the community, in a compact situation, acting on the defensive, and at one of its extremities, might at any time bid defiance to the national authority.[91]

Fortunately, Madison predicted, an absolute federal negative would eliminate such potentially violent disagreements. "The negative would render the use of force unnecessary," he declared. "The States could of themselves pass no operative act, any more than one branch of a legislature, where there are two branches, can proceed without the other. But in order to give the negative this efficacy, it must extend to all cases."[92]

Wilson joined Pinckney and Madison in supporting the absolute federal negative, stressing that excessive state independence threatened national unity. He reviewed the history of American attitudes toward federalism, noting that an early confidence that the United States would "bury all local interests & distinctions" had gradually dissolved under the "jealousy & ambition" of the state governments. "Leave the whole at the mercy of each part," he asked, "and will not the general interest be continually sacrificed to local interests?"[93]

Opponents of the absolute negative expressed horror at the thought of so explicitly sacrificing the states' control over their own affairs. Although Gerry of Massachusetts saw the usefulness of vetoing paper money laws, he feared that an absolute negative would allow Congress to "enslave the states."[94] Delegates also argued that empowering the national government in this way would *enable* interstate abuses rather than curtail them. Gerry suggested that the negative might dissuade new states from joining the Union, and Delaware's Gunning Bedford worried that the more populous states, which would have greater influence in Congress, might use the negative to impose their will on smaller states. He offered his own state as an illustration of the point: under proportional representation, Pennsylvania and Virginia would together control one-third of Congress, while Delaware would control just one-nineteenth. "Will not these large States crush the small ones [with the negative]," he asked, "whenever they stand in the way of their ambitious or interested views?"[95]

With both sides having made their case, the proposal was finally put to a vote at the end of the day's session on June 8, 1787. Whether Madison's notion of an absolute federal veto over state laws would live or die was now up to the fifty-five delegates who together comprised the Constitutional Convention in Philadelphia.

NOTES

1. James Madison, *Notes of Debates in the Federal Convention of 1787* (Athens: Ohio University Press, 1984), 88 (8 June 1787). Although Madison himself does not appear to have used the phrase "federal negative," he commonly used the word "negative" in describing the proposal. In a letter to Thomas Jefferson on 19 March 1787, for example, he wrote that it was necessary "to arm the federal head with a negative *in all cases whatsoever* on the local Legislatures." Numerous historians have subsequently referred to Madison's proposal as the "federal negative." See esp. Alison L. LaCroix, "The Authority for Federalism: Madison's Negative and the Origins of Federal Ideology," *Law and History Review* 28, no. 2 (May 2010): 462, 462n29.

2. Madison, *Notes of Debates,* 89, 91.

3. George Washington, "To David Humphreys, 22 October 1786," in *The Papers of George Washington Digital Edition,* http://rotunda.upress.virginia.edu/founders/GEWN.html.

4. Alice Hanson Jones, "Wealth Estimates for the American Middle Colonies, 1774," *Economic Development and Cultural Change* 18, no. 4, pt. 2 (1970): 130.

5. John J. McCusker, "Population, by Race and by Colony or Locality: 1610–1780," in *Historical Statistics of the United States, Earliest Times to the Present: Millennial Edition,* ed. Susan B. Carter, Scott Sigmund Gartner, Michael R. Haines, Alan L. Olmstead, Richard Sutch, and Gavin Wright (New York: Cambridge University Press, 2006), series Eg1, Eg41; Russell Thornton, "Population History of Native North Americans," in *A Population History of North America,* ed. Michael R. Haines and Richard H. Steckel (New York: Cambridge University Press, 2000), esp. 9–24 (see also table A.1, p. 694);

Allan Kulikoff, *From British Peasants to Colonial American Farmers* (Chapel Hill: University of North Carolina Press, 2000), esp. 3, 291. With regard to the Native American population, Thornton emphasizes that estimates vary widely. According to one set of estimates (presented in Haines and Steckel, *Population History*, table A.1), the Native American population north of the Rio Grande fell from 1.15 million in 1650 to 780,000 in 1750. Although disease (especially smallpox) played a large role in the decline of the Native American population, Thornton stresses that other factors associated with contact with the colonists, including violent conflict, also played a significant role (see Thornton, "Population History," 21–23).

6. Edmund S. Morgan, *The Birth of the Republic, 1763–89* (Chicago: University of Chicago Press, 1977), 8–9.

7. The so-called French and Indian War was part of a larger global conflict known as the Seven Years' War. The total cost of this war to Britain was more than double its annual gross national product in 1760. See Nancy F. Koehn, *The Power of Commerce: Economy and Governance in the First British Empire* (Ithaca, NY: Cornell University Press, 1994), 5.

8. Morgan, *Birth of the Republic*, 16–19. See also Bernard Bailyn, *The Ideological Origins of the American Revolution* (Cambridge, MA: Harvard University Press, 1967), 160–175.

9. Quoted in Merrill Jensen, *The Founding of a Nation* (Indianapolis: Hackett, 1986), 572.

10. Samuel Eliot Morison, Henry Steele Commager, and William E. Leuchtenburg, *The Growth of the American Republic*, 2 vols. (New York: Oxford University Press, 1969), 1:209.

11. Several of the new constitutions were only slightly revised versions of existing colonial charters. See Donald S. Lutz, "State Constitution-Making, through 1781," in *A Companion to the American Revolution*, ed. Jack P. Greene and J. R. Pole (Malden, MA: Blackwell, 2000), 270–271, 277–279. Most states also created bicameral legislatures. See Gordon S. Wood, *The Creation of the American Republic, 1776–1787* (Chapel Hill: University of North Carolina, 1998), 197–256; Lutz, "State Constitution-Making," esp. 274.

12. Holly A. Mayer, "The Continental Army," in Greene and Pole, *American Revolution*, 309; Merrill Jensen, *The New Nation* (New York: Knopf, 1950), 30 (quotation).

13. Robert A. Becker, "Currency, Taxation, and Finance, 1775–1787," in Greene and Pole, *American Revolution*, 388–389. The extent of the inflation apparently occasioned some alarm in Congress. Benjamin Franklin wrote (most likely in 1780): "The excessive Quantities which Necessity oblig'd the Americans to issue, for continuing the War, occasion'd a Depreciation of Value. . . . To put an End to this Evil, which destroy'd all Certainty in Commerce, the Congress first resolved to diminish the Quantity gradually by Taxes. . . . By these Taxes 15 Millions of Dollars, of the 200 Millions extant, are to be brought in monthly and burnt. . . . Thirty Millions have already been so destroy'd" (Benjamin Franklin, "Of the Paper Money of America" [1780?], *The Papers of Benjamin Franklin*, vol. 34, http://franklinpapers.org/franklin/framedVolumes.jsp?vol=34&page=228b).

14. Franklin, "Of the Paper Money of America."

15. E. James Ferguson, *The Power of the Purse* (Chapel Hill: University of North Carolina Press, 1961), 35–44.

16. Becker, "Currency, Taxation, and Finance," 391–392.

17. Jack N. Rakove, "The Articles of Confederation, 1775–1783," in Greene and Pole, *American Revolution,* 281–283; Don Higginbotham, "The War for Independence, to Saratoga," in Greene and Pole, *American Revolution,* 287–296.

18. Rakove, "The Articles of Confederation," 283–284.

19. Ibid., 285; Don Higginbotham, "The War for Independence, after Saratoga," in Greene and Pole, *American Revolution,* 298–302.

20. Art. 4, §1.

21. Art. 8.

22. Art. 5, §1.

23. Art. 5, §4, §2; Art. 9, §6; Art. 13.

24. Quoted in Gordon S. Wood, *The Creation of the American Republic, 1776–1787* (New York: W. W. Norton, 1969), 393.

25. John Jay to George Washington, 27 June 1786, in *The Correspondence and Public Papers of John Jay,* vol. 3, *1782–1793* (New York: G. P. Putnam's Sons, 1891), 204.

26. Becker, "Currency, Taxation, and Finance," 394. In 1782 Congress consolidated all of its various forms of debt (paper money, military certificates, and so forth), arriving at the $27 million figure.

27. John Fiske, *The Critical Period of American History* (Cambridge: Riverside Press, 1898), 109.

28. Robert Morris, "Letter to the President of Congress," in *The Revolutionary Diplomatic Correspondence of the United States,* ed. Francis Wharton (Washington, DC: GPO, 1889), 6:309–311. Significantly, the role "superintendent of finance" was not an executive-branch position—none existed under the Articles.

29. Fiske, *Critical Period,* 109–118; Becker, "Currency, Taxation, and Finance," 395.

30. Stephen Higginson, quoted in Ferguson, *The Power of the Purse,* 222.

31. Becker, "Currency, Taxation, and Finance," 395–396.

32. Higginbotham, "War for Independence, after Saratoga" 305; Fiske, *Critical Period,* 135, 137.

33. Fiske, *Critical Period,* 148–152.

34. Ibid., 142–148, quotation at 146.

35. Ibid., 108–109; and James Madison, "Proposed Amendment of Articles of Confederation" (12 Mar. 1781), in *The Papers of James Madison Digital Edition,* ed. J. C. A. Stagg, http://rotunda.upress.virginia.edu/founders/JSMN.html.

36. Mark D. Kaplanoff, "Confederation: Movement for a Stronger Union," in Greene and Pole, *American Revolution,* 460–463.

37. Robert F. Haggard, "The Nicola Affair: Lewis Nicola, George Washington, and American Military Discontent during the Revolutionary War," *Proceedings of the American Philosophical Society* 146, no. 2 (June 2002): 156–158. Washington's letter to Nicola was dated May 22, 1782.

38. John J. McCusker and Russell R. Menard, *The Economy of British North America, 1607–1789* (Chapel Hill: University of North Carolina Press, 1985), 373–376. For a less severe assessment of the postwar economic downturn, see Gordon S. Wood, *The Creation of the American Republic* (Chapel Hill: University of North Carolina Press, 1969), 394–395.

39. Quoted in William G. Anderson, *The Price of Liberty: The Public Debt of the American Revolution* (Charlottesville: University Press of Virginia, 1983), 33.

40. Woody Holton, "Did Democracy Cause the Recession That Led to the Constitution?," *Journal of American History* 92, no. 2 (Sept. 2005): 445.

41. Fiske, *Critical Period,* 190; Holton, "Did Democracy Cause the Recession?," esp. 444–463.

42. Quoted in James W. Ely Jr., *The Guardian of Every Other Right: A Constitutional History of Property Rights* (New York: Oxford University Press, 1992), 37.

43. See, e.g., Richard D. Brown and Jack Tager, *Massachusetts: A Concise History* (Amherst: University of Massachusetts Press, 2000), 100–106; Anderson, *Price of Liberty,* 32–35.

44. George Washington, "To Henry Lee, Jr., 31 October 1786," in *Papers of George Washington.*

45. "People and Ideas: James Madison," http://www.pbs.org/godinamerica/people /james-madison.html.

46. Quoted in Irving Brant, "Madison: On the Separation of Church and State," *William and Mary Quarterly* 8, no. 1 (Jan. 1951): 5.

47. *James Madison, a Biography in His Own Words,* ed. Merrill D. Peterson (New York: Newsweek, 1974), 14–41, 90; Ketcham, *James Madison* (New York: MacMillan, 1971), 172.

48. James Madison, "To Thomas Jefferson, 16 March 1784," in Stagg, *Papers of James Madison.*

49. James Madison, "Notes on Ancient and Modern Confederacies" (April–June? 1786), in Stagg, *Papers of James Madison,* editorial note.

50. Ketcham, *James Madison,* 183.

51. Madison, "Notes on Ancient and Modern Confederacies."

52. James Madison (with Alexander Hamilton), "The Federalist No. 20," in *The Federalist,* ed. Jacob E. Cooke (Middletown: Wesleyan University Press, 1961), 127.

53. James Madison, "Vices of the Political System of the United States," in Stagg, *Papers of James Madison,* §1.

54. Ibid., §7.

55. Ibid., §5, §4.

56. Ibid., §11.

57. Charles F. Hobson, "The Negative on State Laws: James Madison, the Constitution, and the Crisis of Republican Government," *William and Mary Quarterly* 36, no. 2 (Apr. 1979): 225; George Klosko, *History of Political Theory: An Introduction,* vol. 2, *Modern,* 2nd ed. (Oxford: Oxford University Press, 2013), 249–251. See also Jacob T. Levy, "Beyond Publius: Montesquieu, Liberal Republicanism, and the Small-Republic Thesis," *History of Political Thought* 27, no. 1 (2006): 50–90.

58. Madison, "Vices," §7, §11.

59. Art. 2.

60. Madison completed "Vices" in April 1787. In March he wrote to Thomas Jefferson describing several of the proposals discussed here. See Madison, "To Thomas Jefferson, 19 March 1787," in Stagg, *Papers of James Madison*.

61. Madison, "To Edmund Randolph, 8 April 1787," in Stagg, *Papers of James Madison*.

62. Madison, "To George Washington, 16 April 1787," in Stagg, *Papers of James Madison*.

63. Madison, "To Thomas Jefferson, 19 March 1787." Emphasis in original.

64. Ibid.

65. In his letters Madison compared the federal negative to the powers of the king of Great Britain. During the colonial era, the Privy Council, made up of the king and his councilors, could review colonial court decisions and legislative acts and approve or reject them. Reviews of court decisions required an appeal from a colonist about a specific case, but legislative acts could be examined and negated at the Council's whim. Madison based the federal negative on this second power. (LaCroix, "The Authority for Federalism," 464–466, 472.)

66. Madison, "To George Washington, 16 April 1787."

67. Madison, "To Edmund Randolph, 8 April 1787."

68. Madison, "To George Washington, 16 April 1787."

69. Kaplanoff, "Confederation," 468.

70. Madison may have prepared his "Notes on Ancient and Modern Confederacies" for consultation at this convention (see editor's commentary to that essay in Stagg, *Papers of James Madison*).

71. Kaplanoff, "Confederation," 467–468.

72. Ketcham, *James Madison*, 195–196.

73. Quoted in Kevin R. C. Gutzman, *James Madison and the Making of America* (New York: St. Martin's Press, 2012), 49.

74. The Virginia Plan appears in Madison, *Notes of Debates*, 30–33 (29 May). Because Delaware's delegates had been instructed not to agree "to any change of the rule of suffrage" (37–38), discussion of proportional representation of the states was postponed to a later period beyond the scope of this case. Mark D. Kaplanoff, "The Federal Convention and the Constitution," in Greene and Pole, *American Revolution*, 472, clarifies that "quotas of contributions" meant taxes.

75. Madison, *Notes of Debates*, 38 (31 May).

76. Ibid., 39 (31 May), 73 (6 June).

77. Ibid., 40 (31 May), 77 (6 June).

78. John Dickenson, in ibid., 82 (7 June).

79. Madison, *Notes of Debates*, 194–195 (26 June).

80. John Dickenson, in ibid., 84 (7 June).

81. Madison, *Notes of Debates*, 83, 86–87 (7 June).

82. Edmund Randolph (VA), in ibid., 45–46 (1 June).

83. Madison, *Notes of Debates*, 59 (4 June).

84. Roger Sherman, quoted in ibid., 62 (June 4). Sherman would be the author of the "Great Compromise," through which the Virginia Plan, with its proportional state

representation scheme for Congress, was combined with the competing New Jersey Plan, which gave each state equal representation. The resulting plan called for one proportional chamber and one with equal numbers of delegates for each state.

85. Madison, *Notes of Debates,* 62–65 (4 June).
86. Ibid., 34–35, 34 (30 May).
87. Pierce Butler, quoted in ibid., 44 (31 May).
88. Madison, *Notes of Debates,* 44 (31 May).
89. Ibid., 43 (31 May).
90. Ibid., 44 (31 May), 88 (8 June).
91. Ibid., 88–89 (8 June).
92. Ibid., 89 (8 June).
93. Ibid., 90–91 (8 June).
94. Ibid., 89–90 (8 June).
95. Ibid., 89–92 (8 June), quotation at 91.

·{ 2 }·

Battle over a Bank: Defining the Limits of Federal Power under a New Constitution (1791)

IN THE DARK, early morning hours of February 23, 1791, the candles were lit at 79 Third Street in Philadelphia. Inside, Treasury Secretary Alexander Hamilton and his wife, Elizabeth, were hurriedly finishing a report that President George Washington was expecting to receive in just a few hours.[1] The report was a defense of Hamilton's recent proposal for a national bank, which he hoped would bolster the American economy and assist the federal government in managing its finances. Congress had approved the plan, but some of the president's advisers warned that the federal government lacked the authority to establish a bank because the Constitution did not grant it the power to charter corporations. Washington, "greatly perplexed" by the constitutional issue, had requested a rebuttal from Hamilton.[2] After many hours of work on the document, "which occupied him the greatest part of the night," Hamilton finally delivered it to the president after the sun rose that morning.[3]

In his rebuttal, Hamilton argued that Congress had "implied powers," not specifically listed in the Constitution, which lawmakers could use when necessary to achieve legitimate goals. As a sovereign entity, he maintained, the federal government inherently possessed certain fundamental capabilities, including the power to charter corporations. He also interpreted the Constitution's "necessary and proper" clause, which authorized Congress to "make all Laws which shall be necessary and proper for carrying into Execution" its specified powers, as a license to act in this case. Because the proposed bank would assist Congress in executing its fiscal responsibilities,

---

Hamilton believed that incorporating the bank fell well within Congress's constitutional authority.

As President Washington considered all of the arguments, he knew that his decision to sign or veto the bank bill would extend far beyond the issue of the bank itself. If he approved, his assent would potentially encourage the broad exercise of implied powers in the future. A veto, on the other hand, would send the message that Congress had no authority beyond the powers explicitly listed in the Constitution. Either way, President Washington would be lending his considerable weight and prestige to one side of this seminal constitutional debate, and he was well aware that much was riding on his decision.

Toward a New Constitution: The Debate over Federal Power, and Its Limits

The United States' first national constitution, the Articles of Confederation, had quickly proved inadequate after its ratification in 1781. Although the intention had been to create an extremely weak federal government, with most powers (including the power to tax) reserved for the states, many of the nation's leading figures had concluded by 1786 that the experiment was failing. Trade was collapsing, the economic outlook was bleak, the federal government was in default, and a rebellion over debt collection had broken out in western Massachusetts. Stunned by the turn of events since leading the nation to victory over the British just a few years before, George Washington declared that he was "mortified beyond expression" in witnessing "the clouds which have spread over the brightest morn that ever dawned upon any Country."[4] By 1787 there was a growing belief among many of the nation's political leaders that only revision or even total replacement of the Articles of Confederation could save the republic. From May through September of that year, fifty-five delegates representing twelve of the thirteen states (all but Rhode Island) convened in Philadelphia to draft a new constitution.[5]

The delegates' first major task was to design a structure for the new government. On May 29 the Virginia delegation presented a proposal that would divide federal power among three branches—an executive, a judiciary, and a bicameral legislature where each state would be represented in proportion to its population. Although the "Virginia Plan" became the basis for much of the discussion at the convention, it was not without competition. In mid-June, New Jersey's William Paterson offered a plan that included the same three branches but retained the Articles' unicameral Congress in which each state had one vote. The two different models for Congress provoked vigorous debate, as populous states tended to support proportional representation while smaller ones feared being "destroyed" or "enslaved" unless they were guaranteed an equal voice in Congress.[6] The disagreement lasted until July when the delegates finally embraced Roger Sherman's "Great Compromise," which included the Virginia Plan's bicameral legislature and proportional representation in the lower house, but granted each state equal representation in the upper house.*

The convention's next major task was to decide what this new legislature would do. The Virginia Plan recommended that Congress be authorized "to legislate in all cases to which the separate States are incompetent," but several delegates thought this formulation was too general, preferring instead that the new constitution identify specific congressional powers. A full list finally emerged on August 6, when the convention's Committee of Detail distributed a written draft of the Constitution for discussion. Ultimately, the Constitution would grant Congress a broad range of powers, including the power to "lay and collect Taxes, Duties, Imposts and Excises, to pay the Debts and provide for the common Defence and general Welfare of the United States," to "borrow money on the credit of the United States," to "regulate Commerce with foreign Nations, and among the several States," and to "coin Money, regulate the Value thereof . . . and fix the Standard of Weights and

---

* An important later compromise concerned how to account for slaves when determining the size of each state's delegation in the lower house of Congress. Southern delegates wanted to count slaves, at least in part, but some northerners accused these delegates of hypocrisy. "Upon what principle is it that the slaves shall be computed in the representation," Gouverneur Morris of New Jersey asked. "Are they men? Then make them Citizens and let them vote. Are they property? Then why is no other property included?" The convention ultimately decided to count three-fifths of a state's slave population for purposes of both congressional representation and taxation by state, which became known as the Three-Fifths Compromise. See James Madison, *Notes of Debates in the Federal Convention of 1787* (Athens: Ohio University Press, 1984), 411 (8 Aug. 1787). See also Donald L. Robinson, *Slavery in the Structure of American Politics, 1765–1820* (New York: Harcourt Brace Jovanovich, 1971), chap. 5.

Measures." Congress would also gain authority over naturalization and bankruptcy, and it would be empowered to establish a postal system, safeguard intellectual property rights, set up a system of federal courts, administer a national capital, call forth militia to enforce federal laws and combat insurrection or invasion, organize the nation's armed forces, and declare war. Finally, Congress would have the authority to "make all Laws which shall be necessary and proper for carrying into Execution the foregoing Powers, and all other Powers vested by this Constitution in the Government of the United States, or in any Department or Officer thereof."[7]

To complement the list of congressional powers, some delegates also hoped to include an explicit list of limitations on federal authority. Several of their proposed restrictions took the form of declarations of what the government could *not* do, while others were phrased as obligations to citizens. The convention voted to bar both the federal government and the states from passing bills of attainder (laws that declared specific individuals guilty of crimes without trial) and ex post facto laws (which retroactively made past actions illegal and punishable). The federal government was also prohibited from suspending the right of habeas corpus (the right of a prisoner to appear before a court), except in cases of rebellion or foreign invasion, and trial by jury was guaranteed for all criminal cases. Although the final document that the convention produced offered no general statement of freedom of religion, it did prohibit religious qualifications for government offices.[8]

Delegates who favored a more extensive list of limitations were disappointed. When Charles Pinckney of South Carolina and Elbridge Gerry of Massachusetts recommended a clause ensuring "liberty of the Press," Connecticut's Roger Sherman replied that such language was "unnecessary," arguing that "the power of Congress does not extend to the Press," and a majority of delegates voted against the language. Suggestions for limitations on standing armies, the right to a jury trial in civil cases, and a prohibition against forced quartering of soldiers were also successfully resisted.[9]

As the convention drew to a close, however, some delegates continued to insist that the limitations on federal power did not go far enough. In their view, the proposed Constitution would create a federal government that was too strong. On September 8, for example, Edmund Randolph of Virginia highlighted a number of features to which he objected, including the vague "necessary and proper" clause, the extent of Congress's enumerated powers, and "the want of a more definite boundary between the General & State Legislatures—and between the General and State Judiciaries." Discouraged, he announced that "he verily believed [the Constitution] would end in Tyranny" and called for a second convention to consider amendments.[10]

Randolph's fellow Virginian George Mason objected in equally blunt terms, having earlier declared that "he would sooner chop off his right hand than put it to the Constitution as it now stands." With little time remaining at the convention, he suggested that "he wished the plan had been prefaced with a Bill of Rights" to protect against government overreach.[11] Mason was well acquainted with the idea of a bill of rights. In 1776 he had been the principal author of Virginia's Declaration of Rights, which had included freedoms of the press and of religion, a ban on cruel and unusual punishments, and other protections for Virginia's citizens. In the intervening years, similar statements modeled after the Virginia Declaration had been approved in other states as well.[12] Mason's suggestion that the convention adopt a national bill of rights was not nearly as successful, however. Roger Sherman swiftly deflected the proposal, arguing that the rights granted in the state constitutions were sufficient to protect the people, and Sherman's position prevailed once again.[13]

Yet Randolph and Mason's fears of government tyranny were hardly assuaged. When the time came to sign the document on September 17, 1787, they and Elbridge Gerry were the only delegates present (of those still attending) who refused to add their names.[14] Other delegates, led by the elderly and esteemed Benjamin Franklin, beseeched them to lend their signatures to make the convention's verdict unanimous, but the three abstainers held fast. Randolph declared that he "was dictated by his conscience" and warned that presenting the Constitution to the states without opportunity for amendment beforehand would "produce . . . anarchy & civil convulsions."[15]

Of the thirty-nine delegates who signed the Constitution, few, if any, were completely satisfied with the result. Most signed despite lingering concerns and objections, believing that rejecting the document would be a far worse option. "Considering the present plan as the best that was to be attained," said Gouverneur Morris, no doubt summarizing the sentiments of many, "[I] should take it with all its faults."[16] After the convention adjourned, the document was sent to the states for ratification, sparking intense debate from one end of the country to the other.

The Fight over Ratification

Although the Articles of Confederation required unanimity among the states for any amendment to its provisions, the framers of the Constitution decided that the Articles could be replaced altogether if nine of the thirteen states ratified the new document. Even after the bar had been lowered in this way, however, winning the approval of nine states was far from certain. A powerful "Anti-Federalist" opposition was determined to prevent ratification. Anti-Federalists waged their campaign in the press and in convention halls across the nation, warning that the Constitution would create an undemocratic and oppressive government. An early manifesto by Mason expressed the core of their critique: "There is no Declaration of Rights, and . . . the Declarations of Rights in the separate States are no security."[17] In their literature and speeches at the ratifying conventions, Anti-Federalists listed the fundamental protections they believed the Constitution lacked, such as freedom of the press and prohibitions on standing armies during peacetime.[18] "The liberties of America were not secured by the system," asserted Elbridge Gerry in Massachusetts, defending his refusal to sign the Constitution, "[and] it was my duty to oppose it."[19]

Among proponents of the Constitution, known as Federalists, one of the first to argue against the proposed bill of rights was James Wilson of Pennsylvania. Wilson asserted that because Congress would be limited to the powers specified in the Constitution, it would be unable to infringe on the people's rights. In fact, he suggested that an additional declaration of rights might "imply that some degree of power was given" to Congress that had never been intended.[20] Alexander Hamilton developed Wilson's arguments in essay 84 of *The Federalist* (which would later become known as *The Federalist Papers*), a collected series of essays Hamilton authored with James Madison and John Jay in support of the Constitution. "The Constitution is itself, in every rational sense, and to every useful purpose, A BILL OF RIGHTS," he wrote. The fact that the Constitution proclaimed itself an instrument of "We, the people," Hamilton insisted, signified that the people retained their natural rights without having to declare them. Hamilton also repeated

Wilson's assertion that specifying further rights was unnecessary and potentially dangerous. "Why declare that things shall not be done which there is no power to do?" he asked.[21]

Although Hamilton was unequivocal in his argument in *Federalist* 84, an earlier *Federalist* essay—by one of Hamilton's colleagues—had suggested a somewhat different perspective. In *Federalist* 44, James Madison wrote at length on the "necessary and proper" clause, explaining that such language was a practical necessity, the only viable alternative to detailing a "complete digest of laws . . . accommodated . . . to all the possible changes which futurity may produce." The clause, Madison argued, granted Congress all the powers it needed to fulfill its obligations, whatever those powers might be. "No axiom is more clearly established in law, or in reason," he wrote, "than that wherever the end is required, the means are authorized; wherever a general power to do a thing is given, every particular power necessary for doing it is included."[22]

Despite strong Anti-Federalist efforts, the Federalists repeatedly triumphed at the ratifying conventions, and on June 21, 1788, New Hampshire became the ninth state to ratify. This ensured that the Constitution would enter into force and become the foundation of a new government. On the day New Hampshire breathed life into the Constitution, however, Virginia, New York, North Carolina, and Rhode Island had still yet to ratify, and they would not fall under the new government's purview unless they did. The absence of Virginia and New York, large and economically influential states that together contained nearly a third of the country's population, would seriously undermine the legitimacy of the Union if they failed to approve the document. Furthermore, if Virginia rejected the Constitution, then its favorite son, George Washington, would be ineligible for the presidency. Washington was the clear favorite to become the nation's first chief executive, and a government devoid of his leadership would find it almost impossible to achieve legitimacy in the eyes of countless Americans.[23] Ratification by only nine states, in other words, would not be sufficient after all.

Virginia Debates Ratification

The Virginia ratifying convention had begun on June 2, 1788. Although 170 delegates attended, Anti-Federalist leader Patrick Henry alone spoke for nearly a fourth of the total time.[24] In his lengthy speeches, Henry warned that "Congress will have an unlimited, unbounded command over the soul of this Commonwealth [of Virginia]" under the new Constitution. He believed that the Constitutional Convention had gone too far by replacing the Articles of Confederation instead of simply revising them. "A general peace, and [a] universal tranquility prevailed in this country" under the Articles, he asserted, and it was now threatened by a "consolidated" national government.[25] One of Henry's vocal allies at the Virginia convention, George Mason, reiterated his pleas for a bill of rights.[26]

Virginia Federalists, led by Madison and—quite surprisingly—Governor Edmund Randolph, defended the Constitution against Henry's attacks. Randolph stood by his decision not to sign the document, but explained, "When I withheld my subscription, I had not even a glimpse of the genius of America, relative to the principles of the new Constitution."[27] He argued that although the document was far from perfect, refusing to ratify it was not worth the threat to national unity that Virginia's rejection would pose.[28] Madison buttressed Randolph's case and directly addressed Henry's arguments. He challenged the assertion that the Constitution somehow empowered Congress to oppress the states and the people, and all but mocked Henry's contention that the nation had been tranquil under the Articles. "If this be their happy situation," Madison asked, "why has every State acknowledged the contrary?" Echoing a blistering critique of the Articles he had prepared in advance of the Constitutional Convention, Madison attacked the lack of a "general controuling power" under the old system, and explained his theory that "the loss of liberty very often resulted from factions and divisions . . . [and] local considerations," rather than excessive power in the center.[29]

Madison and Randolph carried the day, and on June 25 the Virginia convention narrowly agreed to ratify the Constitution. At the same time, however, the Virginians approved forty amendments that they thought should be incorporated into the Constitution, including provisions asserting freedom of religion, speech, and the press, protections against unreasonable search and seizure, a right to bear arms, and several modifications of federal rules and procedures. Massachusetts, South Carolina, and New Hampshire had similarly recommended amendments as part of their ratification processes. After New York did the same, becoming the eleventh state to ratify in late

July, the fate of the Constitution was far more certain, but approximately 200 amendments, containing perhaps seventy-five different recommendations, were now part of the public debate alongside the Constitution itself.[30]

Madison and the Bill of Rights

The states' proposed amendments reflected a widespread sentiment that the Constitution, while necessary and acceptable, needed improvement. Having failed to prevent ratification, the Anti-Federalists now championed amending the Constitution, especially with a bill of rights, and planned and petitioned (unsuccessfully) for a second constitutional convention to achieve that end.[31] No state voiced its dissatisfaction with the Constitution more loudly than North Carolina, which rejected the document in the summer of 1788 due largely to its lack of a bill of rights. Many leaders believed that the right amendments might draw North Carolina back into the fold.[32]

Even Madison, the principal intellectual force behind much of the Constitution, supported amending it with a bill of rights. Madison outlined his nuanced opinion on the matter in an October 1788 letter to Thomas Jefferson. He first asserted that a bill of rights was technically unnecessary because such rights were already implied, and that enumerating them might suggest that Americans lacked other rights that were not specified. He was also certain that the powers of the federal government were already significantly constrained and that bills of rights were nothing but "parchment barriers" whose "inefficacy" had been demonstrated in the past "on those occasions when [their] controul [was] most needed." Yet Madison also wrote that his "own opinion has always been in favor of a bill of rights." While he doubted that a list of this sort would be sufficient to contain "overbearing majorities," he believed it could provide a basis from which to criticize such abuses of power. If rights were declared, he reasoned, they would "become incorporated with the national sentiment" and discourage factions from infringing on others' rights. Furthermore, if the federal government ever became too strong, "a bill of rights will be a good ground for an appeal to the sense of the community."[33]

In March 1789 Madison departed Montpelier, his slave plantation in Virginia, to join the national legislature in New York City as a member of the newly created U.S. House of Representatives. He soon announced that he would present a federal bill of rights for the chamber's consideration. The proposal Madison prepared derived many of its amendments from the states' recommendations.[34] It opened with a new preamble for the Constitution, which declared that "all power is originally vested in, and consequently derived from, the people." The rights that followed included freedom of religion, speech, assembly, petition, and the press, as well as "the right of the people to keep and bear arms." While these protections were aimed mainly at safeguarding the people against federal power, Madison specified that the states too would be prohibited from infringing on freedom of religion, speech, and the press, as well as on the right to trial by jury for criminal cases. The proposed amendments also contained protections against forced quartering of soldiers during peacetime, "cruel and unusual punishment," and "unreasonable searches and seizures."[35]

Madison's proposal went beyond merely listing basic rights. It also clarified the nature of rights and of government powers enumerated in the Constitution. So as not to insinuate that unlisted rights were not protected, Madison wrote that the "exceptions here or elsewhere in the Constitution, made in favor of particular rights, shall not be so construed as to diminish the just importance of other rights retained by the people, or as to enlarge the powers delegated by the Constitution." He declared further that the "powers not delegated by this Constitution, nor prohibited by it to the states, are reserved to the States respectively." His proposal also incorporated several additional constitutional revisions suggested by the state conventions. These included enlarging the House of Representatives, which proponents believed would make its members more responsive to their constituents, and barring any law that changed the compensation of members of Congress from becoming operational "before the next ensuing election of Representatives."[36]

When Madison presented his work to the House on June 8, 1789, several lawmakers showed little interest in discussing it. There were plenty of other important tasks for the young government to attend to—such as setting up courts and executive offices and passing revenue laws—which they believed were more urgent than producing a bill of rights. Opponents also contended that the Constitution had not yet been tested and that it was unwise to modify it until its weaknesses had been determined. "The Constitution may be compared to a ship that has never yet put to sea," said Georgia's

James Jackson, ". . . she is now laying in the dock—we have had no tryal as yet; we do not know how she may steer."[37] Even after Madison guided his colleagues through his proposed amendments, one by one in a speech lasting hours, many congressmen remained unconvinced. The House voted to delay further discussion of the bill until July 21, and when that day arrived Madison was exasperated to find many in the House still unwilling to discuss his amendments in any detail. Although Madison "begged" his fellow congressmen to at least "indulge him," they instead forwarded the bill to a select committee for revision, and included Madison on the committee.[38]

The House finally took up the edited proposals in the middle of August.[39] One significant debate concerned the final provision, which reserved to the states all powers "not delegated by this Constitution, nor prohibited by it to the states." Thomas Tucker of South Carolina and Elbridge Gerry wanted the amendment to read, "The powers not *expressly* delegated by this Constitution," so as to clearly bar congressional assumption of unwritten powers. Madison forcefully opposed this recommendation, however, declaring that "it was impossible to confine a government to the exercise of express powers . . . there must necessarily be admitted powers by implication, unless the constitution descended to recount every minutiae."[40] The House rejected Tucker and Gerry's proposals, and in the end—even over stalwart opposition to the very idea of amending the Constitution—approved some form of each of Madison's amendments except for the new preamble, which it removed.[41]

The Senate received the amendments on August 25, but details of its deliberations remain largely unknown because early Senate discussions were not reported. The Senate made primarily cosmetic changes to the House bill, rewording several clauses and consolidating the House's seventeen amendments into twelve. One significant modification dropped Madison's proposal to extend rights to speech, conscience (religious conviction), and trial by jury to the states. That is, these protections, like the others, would only constrain the federal government, not the states. Members of the House and Senate soon met to reconcile their versions into a consolidated Bill of Rights, and approved the final language in late September 1789. President Washington, who had taken office in April, then sent the twelve proposed amendments to the states. Each amendment would have to be ratified by three-quarters of the states in order to be added to the Constitution.[42]

Madison and Hamilton

During the first year of the new government, Madison did not limit his attention to the Bill of Rights. In fact, he established himself as one of the most influential figures in national politics, even though he sat in the popularly elected House of Representatives rather than in the more elite Senate or in the executive branch. When Congress turned to the important task of raising revenues, Madison took a leading role and shepherded successful legislation relating to tariff and trade policy. He even acted as an unofficial adviser to the president, counseling him on both how to behave and how to govern—to such an extent that some historians have suggested Madison nearly filled the role of "prime minister" in the early Washington administration.[43]

One of Madison's most important contributions in 1789 was the creation of the office of Secretary of the Treasury. Since 1784, national financial policy had been managed by a three-member Treasury Board, but Madison believed that a single head of the Treasury Department would be more likely to produce "well-digested plans."[44] Sympathetic to Madison's argument, but fearful of centralizing too much power in the executive branch, Congress created the department with a single secretary, but mandated that he prepare reports for Congress, not the president, though the president could remove him from office. To fill this influential position, Madison recommended his longtime friend and collaborator on the *Federalist Papers,* Alexander Hamilton, whom President Washington appointed in September.[45]

Hamilton was a committed nationalist who had long believed in the federal government's potential to bolster the nation's economy. As a New York delegate to the Constitutional Convention, he had proposed a plan that would have granted the national government superiority over the states to a far greater degree than was ultimately established under the Constitution.[46] In Hamilton's opinion, "American liberty and happiness had much more to fear from the encroachments of the great states, than from those of the general government." As the first secretary of the Treasury, he would inevitably set precedents for future secretaries, and, as he himself put it, he aspired "to trace out his own path, and to adjust for himself the import and bearings of the delicate and important provisions in the Constitution and in the laws."[47]

The Report on Public Credit

One of Hamilton's most important responsibilities as treasury secretary was managing the national debt, which in 1789 exceeded $50 million.[48] Congress had amassed this substantial debt during the rebellion against Britain and the early postwar years, and had fallen behind on servicing its debt in large measure because it lacked the power to tax under the Articles of Confederation. The new Constitution, which granted Congress the power to tax, required that "All Debts contracted and Engagements entered into, before the Adoption of this Constitution, shall be as valid against the United States under this Constitution, as under the Confederation."[49] As the nation's creditors began petitioning for payment, Congress directed Hamilton to draft a report on how the government could best meet its obligations.[50]

Hamilton replied promptly, submitting his "Report on Public Credit" in January 1790. The report began by emphasizing the importance of good credit: "States, like individuals, who observe their engagements, are respected and trusted." Toward this end, Hamilton recommended funding the entire national debt, even though many parts of it were currently in arrears and some government bonds were trading in the market for as little as 25 cents on the dollar. In many cases the original holders of the debt—such as former soldiers who had been paid for their wartime service in bonds—had since sold out to speculators, often at significant discounts, once the government had failed to pay interest on these bonds under the Articles. Hamilton now proposed that the federal government pay the current holders of the debt, rather than the original owners (i.e., the speculators, rather than the former soldiers). To do otherwise, he reasoned, would have been "a breach of contract; a violation of the rights of a fair purchaser," and plainly unconstitutional.[51]

Hamilton also boldly recommended that the federal government assume all of the states' war debts, which in 1790 amounted to about $26 million. Such an arrangement, he contended, would better serve creditors because the national government would be better at raising revenue. Hamilton believed that if the states were left to raise the funds themselves, "collision and confusion" among the states' "interfering regulations" would depress the nation's economy, the revenue extracted from it, and creditors' receipts. Federal assumption, he reasoned, would also ensure that creditors had a stake in the success of the entire nation and its revenue stream, rather than in individual states that might have different interests and "give place to mutual jealousy and opposition." Hamilton believed, moreover, that the national government had an obligation to treat the nation's creditors equally. Particularly because the states themselves had assumed responsibility for much of the national debt during the 1780s, when the federal government was unable to pay, he suggested it would be "most equitable, that there should be the same measure of retribution for all." Furthermore, he appealed to American patriotism by arguing that the war against Britain had been a collective struggle, and that there was no "good reason why the expenses for the particular defense of a part, in a common war, should not be a common charge."[52]

Debate over the Debt

Although Madison agreed on the need to fully fund the debt, he strongly objected to the rest of Hamilton's plan. To begin with, the idea of paying speculators who, in his view, had traded on the federal government's weakness under the Articles of Confederation (buying up distressed government bonds from financially desperate veterans for a fraction of their par value) struck Madison as "radically immoral and consequently impolitic." Instead, he sought to divide payment between the two main classes of claimants, reimbursing the current holders of the debt (i.e., the so-called speculators) at the highest market rate and delivering the remainder to the original holders, many of whom had been forced to sell their claims under immense financial pressure. Madison also opposed Hamilton's proposal to assume the states' debts at their 1790 values. Doing so, Madison claimed, would be an "injustice" to the states that had already paid off much of their debts.[53] "A simple unqualified assumption of the existing debts would bear peculiarly hard on Virginia," he noted. "If such an assumption were to take place she would pay towards the discharge of the debts, in the proportion of 1/5 and receive back to her Creditor Citizens 1/7 or 1/8, whilst Massts. [Massachusetts] would pay not more than 1/7 or 1/8 and receive back not less than 1/5." Madison again offered a counterproposal, suggesting that the federal government assume the states' debts at the levels pertaining at the end of the war in 1783, which would cost the federal government more but would, in Madison's eyes, be "more just & satisfactory."[54] For his part, Hamilton expressed outrage at Madison's fierce opposition to his plan, calling it "a perfidious desertion of the principles which [Madison] was solemnly pledged to defend."[55]

Debate over the debt program divided Congress into Hamilton and Madison blocs, and in the words of one observer "seemed to unchain all those fierce passions which a high respect for the government and for those who administered it, had in a great measure restrained."[56] Although Madison's proposal to discriminate between current and original debt holders never gained much traction, his opposition to Hamilton's plan for assumption of state debts attracted many adherents, who insisted that the proposal to fully fund the debt be voted on separately from the proposal to assume state debts. Hamilton and his supporters, however, demanded that the two be voted on together. The controversy had a sectional dimension to it: Perhaps in part because many people believed the northern states had retired less of their war debt than their southern counterparts, and that much of the debt was owed to northern creditors, northern congressmen tended to side with Hamilton and southern ones with Madison. As threats of secession began to circulate among New Englanders weary of southern resistance, the debate over Hamilton's proposals on the public debt seemed to threaten the very survival of the Union.[57]

The contentious debate lasted until July 1790, when Hamilton, Madison, and Secretary of State Thomas Jefferson finally arrived at a deal over dinner in New York City. Madison and Jefferson, both of Virginia, agreed to persuade southern congressmen to support Hamilton's plan, but in exchange the national capital would be removed from New York City—temporarily to Philadelphia (which helped ensure a few critical votes from the Pennsylvania delegation) and then permanently to a spot on the Potomac River on the northern edge of Virginia. With this compromise, along with some monetary compensation for the less indebted states, including Virginia, Congress passed most of the core elements of Hamilton's plan in August 1790.[58]

By this time all thirteen states were officially members of the Union. Congress's proposed Bill of Rights had convinced North Carolina to ratify the Constitution in November 1789, and Rhode Island had followed suit the following May. By the middle of 1790, nine of the thirteen states—one shy of the three-quarters necessary for adoption—had ratified most of the twelve amendments that made up the proposed Bill of Rights. Not all of these states, however, had approved the two amendments (the first two on Congress's list of twelve) that dealt with the allocation of representation in the House and congressional salaries.[59] As the nation waited for one more state to approve the other ten amendments, a new battle broke out over the meaning of the Constitution's existing text.

Imagining a National Bank: Power, Principle, and the Constitution

Although Secretary Hamilton had scored a significant victory with the passage of his debt plan, he regarded it as only one part of a broader financial program. In December 1790 he presented a new report to Congress, this time recommending the establishment of a national bank. The proposal attracted a great deal of attention as there were then only three banks operating in the United States—the Bank of North America in Philadelphia, the Bank of New York in Manhattan, and the Bank of Massachusetts in Boston—whose combined authorized capital was less than $3.5 million.[60] The national bank Hamilton was proposing would have authorized capital of up to $10 million, giving it, in his words, "a scale which will entitle it to the confidence, and be likely to render it equal to the exigencies, of the public."[61]

Hamilton opened his *Report on a National Bank* by highlighting three major benefits he believed a large, federally chartered bank would confer upon the nation. First, he noted the "active and productive quality" of specie (gold and silver) when deposited in a bank, where it could undergird a disproportionate volume of new loans. "The money which a merchant keeps in his chest, waiting for a favourable opportunity to employ it, produces nothing till that opportunity arrives," Hamilton wrote. "But if . . . he either deposits it in a bank, or invests it in the stock of a bank," this helps build "a fund upon which himself and others can borrow to a much larger amount." In this way, "banks become nurseries of national wealth." Second, he believed that the bank could aid the government in times of emergency by providing loans as needed. Third, he suggested that the bank could facilitate tax collection, both by providing loans to taxpayers who needed funds to cover their obligations to the government and by providing a "circulating medium" (banknotes backed by specie) in which those obligations could be paid.

"Whatever enhances the quantity of circulating money," he wrote, "adds to the ease with which every industrious member of society may acquire that portion of it, of which he stands in need; and enables him the better to pay his taxes, as well as to supply his other wants."[62]

In the December report, Hamilton also rebutted a number of popular objections to banking, such as fears of usury and unsound speculation. His last and most detailed rebuttal was to the claim that banks "tend to banish gold and silver out of the country" and replace them with unbacked paper money—a fear that Hamilton acknowledged was rooted in memories of financial and monetary turmoil during and after the war.[63] He made it clear that the national bank's notes would be backed by specie and that there was a vital difference "between a paper currency, issued by the mere authority of government, and one issued by a bank, payable in coin." Paper notes issued by the new national bank, he insisted, would promote productive economic activity by unlocking "passive" wealth, greatly facilitate both private and public transactions, and ultimately bolster the nation's standing in the international economy.[64]

The Senate passed a bill on January 20, 1791, to create the bank Hamilton was proposing, but the legislation was briefly slowed down in the House, where James Madison, with support from Secretary of State Jefferson, was leading a group of southern congressmen in resisting the bill. Many southern farmers harbored strong suspicions of the banking sector, and their representatives in Congress argued that a government-backed bank would hoard the nation's specie, provoke inflation by printing paper money, and give undue advantage to northern commercial interests.[65] One opponent in the House announced "that he would no more be seen entering a bank than a house of ill fame."[66] Many southerners also feared that the proposal to establish the bank in Philadelphia would ensure a strong northern orientation within the Treasury, and potentially someday reverse the recent agreement to move the nation's capital southward.[67]

Constitutional Objections

Madison himself objected to the bank principally on constitutional grounds, insisting that the Constitution granted Congress no power to charter a national bank or any other corporation. In fact, Madison had been wrestling with the issue of national incorporation for many years. In 1781 he had cast "an acquiescing, rather than affirmative vote" in the Continental Congress to charter the national Bank of North America,* which he believed was not authorized under the Articles of Confederation but nonetheless economically necessary.[68] At the Constitutional Convention in 1787, he had proposed that Congress be empowered "to grant charters of incorporation where the interest of the U.S. might require & the legislative provisions of individual States may be incompetent," but a majority of his fellow delegates had voted down the idea.[69] Now that Hamilton was attempting what the convention had rejected, Madison declared that the Constitution "is a grant of particular powers only, leaving the general mass in other hands." He could find no power granted in the Constitution that would allow Congress to charter the bank, irrespective of Congress's powers to tax, borrow, and provide for the general welfare. Even the "necessary and proper" clause, Madison now maintained, was "merely declaratory of what would have resulted by unavoidable implication, as the appropriate, and, as it were, technical means of executing those powers." Under any wider interpretation of that clause, he suggested, the "essential characteristic of the Government, as composed of limited and enumerated powers, would be destroyed."[70]

Despite Madison's objections, the bank bill passed the House of Representatives on February 8, 1791, and reached President Washington a week later. The president appeared to have concerns about the proposed legislation, and Madison later recalled that Washington had "held several free conversations with me on the Subject, in which he listened favorably as I thought to my views of it, but certainly without committing himself in any manner whatever." Washington subsequently asked Madison to write a statement for him on the issue in case he ultimately decided to veto the bill.[71]

Thomas Jefferson and his fellow cabinet member Edmund Randolph, now the U.S. attorney general, also opposed the bill and conveyed their views in writing directly to the president. Central to both of their arguments was a strong belief that the federal government was one of limited, enumerated

---

* The Bank of North America shifted to become a state bank, rather than a national bank, when the State of Pennsylvania rechartered it in 1787. See F. Cyril James, "The Bank of North America and the Financial History of Philadelphia," *Pennsylvania Magazine of History and Biography* 64, no. 1 (Jan. 1940): 67–68.

powers. Both mentioned the provision in the proposed Bill of Rights, only slightly revised from Madison's original wording, that "all powers not delegated to the United States, by the Constitution, nor prohibited by it to the States, are reserved to the States or to the people."[72] Although the Bill of Rights had not yet been ratified by the requisite number of states, Jefferson considered the principle behind this provision to be "the foundation of the Constitution" and warned: "To take a single step beyond the boundaries thus specially drawn around the powers of Congress, is to take possession of a boundless field of power, no longer susceptible of any definition."[73] Randolph interpreted Congress's approval of the amendment in 1789 as tantamount to an official declaration that the national legislature "claim[ed] no powers which are not delegated to it."[74]

Having asserted the primacy of the Constitution's written text, both Jefferson and Randolph set out to prove that none of the enumerated powers allowed for a national bank. Both men focused on Congress's powers to tax, borrow, and regulate commerce as being potentially related to the bank, but ultimately rejected the notion that any of the three provided the requisite authority. The Constitution allowed Congress to levy taxes and pay debts, Jefferson wrote, but "no debt is paid by this bill, nor any tax laid."[75] Randolph acknowledged that the provision of banknotes might make taxes *easier* to pay, but insisted that finding "the mode of procuring the money [rested] on the resources of the debtors" and was not the government's responsibility.[76] Acknowledging similarly that Congress had the power to borrow, Jefferson noted that the bill "neither borrows money nor ensures the borrowing of it," because the bank would not be obligated to lend to the government. Nor did he believe that the power to *establish* a bank—"a subject of commerce," in Jefferson's parlance—could conceivably be derived from Congress's authority to *regulate* commerce. "To make a thing which may be bought and sold," he wrote, "is not to prescribe regulations for buying and selling."[77]

Both Jefferson and Randolph also grappled with the possibility that the power to incorporate a bank could potentially be based on one of the Constitution's other, more open-ended provisions. Jefferson first examined the clause authorizing Congress to "lay taxes for *the purpose of* providing for the general welfare," and considered whether "providing for the general welfare" might encompass the creation of a bank. His answer, in a word, was no. Members of Congress were "not *to do anything they please* to provide for the general welfare," Jefferson declared, "but only to *lay taxes* for that purpose. To consider the latter phrase, not as describing the purpose of the first, but as giving a distinct and independent power to do any act they please, which might be for the good of the Union, would render all the preceding and subsequent enumerations of power completely useless."[*] He next turned to the "necessary and proper" clause, suggesting that it should only enable Congress to do what was strictly needed to operationalize the enumerated powers, not to do anything "merely 'convenient' for effecting" them. "If such a latitude of construction be allowed to this phrase as to give any non-enumerated power," he wrote, "it will go to everyone, for there is not one which ingenuity may not torture into a *convenience* in some instance *or other,* to *some one* of so long a list of enumerated powers."[78]

Hamilton's Defense of the Bank

Washington sent the opinions of Jefferson and Randolph to Hamilton and asked for his response. On February 22 the secretary of the Treasury worked through the night penning a defense of his proposal that directly answered the Virginians' criticisms.[79] He showed little deference to their arguments, suggesting from the start that "principles of construction like those espoused by the Secretary of State and Attorney General, would be fatal to the just and indispensable authority of the United States." While acknowledging the obvious—that the Constitution did not specifically authorize Congress to charter a bank—he offered a detailed and closely reasoned argument for the constitutionality of the bill. First, he referenced the

> general principle . . . inherent in the very definition of government . . . that every power, vested in a government, is in its nature sovereign, and includes by force of the term, a right to employ all the means requisite, and fairly applicable, to the attainment of the ends of such power and which are not precluded by restrictions and exceptions specified in the constitution, or not immoral, or not contrary to the essential ends of political society.[80]

---

[*] The relevant clause from the Constitution (Art. I, §8) reads as follows: "The Congress shall have Power To lay and collect Taxes, Duties, Imposts and Excises, to pay the Debts and provide for the common Defence and general Welfare of the United States; but all Duties, Imposts and Excises shall be uniform throughout the United States."

Hamilton argued that sovereign authorities inherently possessed all powers germane to their spheres of responsibility, limited in these spheres only by what their constitutions specifically prohibited, adding that "it is unquestionably incident to sovereign power to erect corporations." The power to charter the bank, in Hamilton's mind, was so basic and essential to government that it could be safely assumed to exist.[81]

Although Hamilton believed that this reasoning alone should be sufficient, he laid siege to Jefferson and Randolph's central argument that the power to charter a corporation had to be enumerated in the Constitution to be valid. Their belief that the bill assumed a significant new congressional power, he argued, was fundamentally misguided. Incorporating a bank, Hamilton explained, was not "some great independent substantive thing" like trade or tax collection, but merely a tool to help achieve those goals—a "mean to an end," not an end in itself. Such measures, he maintained, were protected by the "necessary and proper" clause. He excoriated Jefferson for suggesting a dangerously restrictive interpretation of the word "necessary," which he believed would unduly constrain Congress. Admitting that "no government has a right to do merely what it pleases," Hamilton nonetheless offered a far more liberal interpretation of what "necessary and proper" implied: "The relation between the measure and the end; between the nature of the mean employed toward the execution of a power, and the object of that power must be the criterion of constitutionality, not the more or less of necessity or utility." He warned, moreover, that "adherence to the letter of [the Constitution's enumerated] powers would at once arrest the motion of government."[82]

Armed with this interpretation of the "necessary and proper" clause, Hamilton demonstrated the connections he perceived between the bank and the powers expressly listed in the Constitution. He observed, for example, that through the issuance of paper banknotes, a national bank would assist Congress in implementing its taxing power "by increasing the quantity of circulating medium" and "by creating a convenient species of medium in which [taxes] are to be paid." Observing further that "[m]oney is the very hinge on which commerce turns," Hamilton suggested that nationally recognized banknotes would facilitate interstate commerce, another field in which Congress had explicit constitutional authority. Hamilton also highlighted the bank's potential role as a lender to the government itself, which he believed was consistent with Congress's power to borrow and to defend the nation, particularly because such loans could prove vital in times of national emergency.[83]

President Washington received Hamilton's memorandum on the morning of February 23, 1791. Having consulted his closest advisers on the constitutionality of the bank, he had obtained sharply conflicting advice. The decision to sign or veto the bank bill was now solely in his hands. Given his extraordinary stature as the hero of the Revolution and the nation's first president, the path he chose promised to set a powerful precedent. One observer reported that on February 25, as Congress awaited Washington's judgment, "there was general uneasiness . . . the President stood on the brink of a precipice" and the "glorious reputation he has so deservedly established" hung in the balance.[84] As Washington weighed the arguments on each side, he understood what was at stake and knew that his decision, whichever direction he chose, would become a defining feature of his presidency.

NOTES

1. David Jack Cowen, *The Origins and Economic Impact of the First Bank of the United States, 1791–1797* (New York: Garland, 2000), 7.

2. James Madison quoted in ibid., 20.

3. Report cover letter quoted in ibid., 7.

4. George Washington, "To Henry Lee, Jr., 31 October 1786," in *The Papers of George Washington Digital Edition,* http://rotunda.upress.virginia.edu/founders/GEWN .html.

5. Although 55 delegates attended at the start of the Constitutional Convention, only 41 were in attendance on the last day, 17 Sept. 1787.

6. David Brearly (NJ) and Luther Martin (MD) in James Madison, *Notes of Debates in the Federal Convention of 1787* (Athens: Ohio University Press, 1984), 94, 203.

7. Madison, *Notes,* 31, 43–44, 389–390. The powers of Congress are listed in the U.S. Constitution, Art. I, §8.

8. Many of these rights were summarized in a proposal by Charles Pinckney on 20 Aug. 1787. See Madison, *Notes,* 485–487; Robert Allen Rutland, *The Birth of the Bill of Rights, 1776–1791* (Boston: Northeastern University Press, 1991), 114–115.

9. Madison, *Notes,* 640, See also 486, 630, 639.

10. Ibid., 614–615.

11. Ibid., 566, 630. See also Rutland, *Bill of Rights,* 115–116; Richard Labunski, *James Madison and the Struggle for the Bill of Rights* (New York: Oxford University Press, 2006), 8–11.

12. Rutland, *Bill of Rights,* chaps. 3 and 4, esp. pp. 38–39. The Virginia Declaration incorporated language dating back to the 1689 English Bill of Rights, which limited the power of the monarchy, forbade "excessive bail" and "cruel and unusual punishment," protected Englishmen's right to petition the king, and allowed Protestants to keep weapons for self-defense (see ibid., 8–9). "An Act Declaring the Rights and Liberties of the Subject and Settling the Succession of the Crown," at the Avalon Project, Yale Law School. http://avalon.law.yale.edu/17th_century /england.asp.

13. Madison, *Notes,* 630.

14. Although three of the 41 delegates in attendance on 17 Sept. 1787 refused to sign the proposed constitution, one delegate signed in absentia, bringing the total number of signers to 39.

15. Ibid., 657.

16. Ibid., 656.

17. Rutland, *Bill of Rights,* 124. Quotation from George Mason, "Objections to This Constitution of Government," online at Chapin Library of Rare Books, Williams College, http://chapin.williams.edu//collect/masonobj.html. Also quoted in Rutland, 120.

18. See Mason, "Objections to this Constitution," and Rutland, *Bill of Rights,* chap. 7.

19. Quoted in Rutland, *Bill of Rights,* 123.

20. Quoted in ibid., 133.

21. *Federalist* 84.

22. *Federalist* 44. See also Cowen, *Origins and Economic Impact,* 18.

23. Labunski, *James Madison,* 60, 28.

24. Ibid., 68, 73–74.

25. Quotations in ibid., 61, 77.

26. Ibid., 104–105.

27. Quoted in ibid., 78.

28. Ibid., 78.

29. Quotations in ibid., 90, 91.

30. Ibid., 114, 199.

31. Rutland, *Bill of Rights,* 188–189; Labunski, *James Madison,* 190.

32. Rutland, *Bill of Rights,* 185–187; Labunski, *James Madison,* 202.

33. Madison, "To Thomas Jefferson" (17 Oct. 1788), in *The Papers of James Madison Digital Edition,* http://rotunda.upress.virginia.edu/founders/JSMN.html.

34. Labunski, *James Madison,* 184, 187, 199.

35. "James Madison's Proposed Amendments," included in ibid., append. 1, 265–268.

36. Ibid.

37. Labunski, *James Madison,* 192–196, quotation at 195.

38. Ibid., 197–216, quotation at 213.

39. Ibid., 217; see append. 2, 269–271, for the full committee bill.

40. Quoted in ibid., 230.

41. Ibid., 218, 231–232. In a contentious change, the House also converted the amendments from modifications of the Constitution's original text into new articles to be appended to it.

42. Ibid., 235–240.

43. John C. Miller, *The Federalist Era, 1789–1801* (New York: Harper, 1960), 15; Labunski, *James Madison,* 187.

44. Quoted in Miller, *The Federalist Era,* 26.

45. Ibid., 26, 36.

46. See Madison, *Notes,* 138–139. Under Hamilton's plan, state governors would have been appointed by the national government, and these governors would have had the authority to veto any laws passed by their legislatures.

47. Quotations in Miller, *The Federalist Era,* 33, 34.

48. Miller, *The Federalist Era,* 38.

49. Art. VI. See also Miller, *The Federalist Era,* 37.

50. Miller, *The Federalist Era,* 39.

51. Alexander Hamilton, "Report on Public Credit," in the *Annals of Congress,* House of Representatives, vol. 1, 1st Congress, 3rd Sess., pp. 2042, 2046, 2049. Online at http://memory.loc.gov/ammem/amlaw/lwac.html.

52. Ibid., 2050, 2051, 2052, 2053.

53. Miller, *The Federalist Era,* 42, 45–47, quotations at 42, 47. See also Madison's letter to Edmund Pendleton (4 Mar. 1790) in *Papers of James Madison.*

54. Madison, letter to Pendleton.

55. Miller, *The Federalist Era,* 41–42, quotation at 41.

56. John Marshall's biography of Washington quoted in ibid., 47.

57. Ibid., 41–48. See also Benjamin Ulysses Ratchford, *American State Debts* (Durham, NC: Duke University Press, 1941), esp. 56–68.

58. Miller, *The Federalist Era,* 48–49.

59. Rutland, *Bill of Rights,* 216–217. Virginia, Massachusetts, Georgia, and Connecticut were the four states that hadn't ratified the Bill of Rights by the end of 1790.

60. Bray Hammond, "Long and Short Term Credit in Early American Banking," *Quarterly Journal of Economics* 49, no. 1 (1934): 86; Robert E. Wright, "Origins of Commercial Banking in the United States, 1781–1830," at https://eh.net/encyclopedia/origins-of-commercial-banking-in-the-united-states-1781-1830, table 1. A fourth state bank, the Bank of Maryland, was chartered in 1790 with authorized capital of $300,000; it opened for business early the next year. See Alfred Cookman Bryan, *History of State Banking in Maryland* (Baltimore: Johns Hopkins Press, 1899), 19–20.

61. Alexander Hamilton, *The Report of the Secretary of the Treasury on the Subject of a National Bank* (New York: S. Whiting and Co., 1811), 36, 3. Online at http://fraser.stlouisfed.org/docs/bankunitedstates/bankoftheunitedstates_hamilton_1790.pdf.

62. Ibid., 5, 7, 8–9.

63. Ibid., 15; for Hamilton's discussion of the Articles period, see 19, 20.

64. Ibid., 22, 21.

65. Cowen, *Origins and Economic Impact,* 16–17.

66. Miller, *The Federalist Era,* 56. The language is Miller's and is not a direct quote from the (unspecified) congressman.

67. Cowen, *Origins and Economic Impact,* 17–18.

68. Quoted in Miller, *The Federalist Era,* 57. During debates over Hamilton's bank proposal, Madison said that the Bank of North America was "the child of necessity. It could never be justified by the regular powers of the articles of Confederation." *Annals of Congress,* House of Representatives, vol. 1, 1st Congress, 3rd Sess., p. 1947, online at http://memory.loc.gov/ammem/amlaw/lwac.html.

69. Madison, *Notes,* 638–639.

70. *Annals of Congress,* pp. 1945, 1946–1947, 1947.

71. Cowen, *Origins and Economic Impact,* 19–20.

72. Thomas Jefferson, "Jefferson's Opinion on the Constitutionality of a National Bank," at the Avalon Project, Yale Law School, http://avalon.law.yale.edu/18th_century /bank-tj.asp. Note than in referencing what Congress had originally proposed as the Twelfth Amendment, but which was later ratified by the states as the Tenth, Jefferson used wording (quoted here) that differs slightly from the wording of the actual amendment.

73. Ibid.

74. Randolph's opinion is reprinted in Walter Dellinger and H. Jefferson Powell, "The Constitutionality of the Bank Bill: The Attorney General's First Constitutional Law Opinions," *Duke Law Journal* 44, no. 110 (1994): 121–130, quotation at 123.

75. "Jefferson's Opinion."

76. Randolph in Dellinger and Powell, "Constitutionality of the Bank Bill," 126.

77. "Jefferson's Opinion."

78. Ibid.

79. Cowen, *Origins and Economic Impact,* 20–21.

80. Alexander Hamilton, "Hamilton's Opinion as to the Constitutionality of the Bank of the United States," at the Avalon Project, Yale Law School, http://avalon.law.yale .edu/18th_century/bank-ah.asp.

81. Ibid.

82. Ibid.

83. Ibid.

84. John Rutledge, Jr. quoted in Cowen, *Origins and Economic Impact,* 22.

Democracy, Sovereignty, and the Struggle over Cherokee Removal (1836)

THE CHEROKEE COUNCIL HOUSE at New Echota, Georgia, was burning. On December 24, 1835, as Major Benjamin Currey spoke to a committee from the tribe about a potential treaty with the United States, an ember from the hearth fire had floated to the ceiling and set the roof ablaze. Vigilant Cherokee jumped into action, attacking the flames with blankets and buckets of water. The fire was soon extinguished, and Currey resumed his speech. Although the meeting continued without further interruption, at least one Cherokee in attendance who opposed the treaty later acknowledged that he saw the fire as a sign of disapproval from the heavens.[1]

The number of Cherokee assembled at New Echota—possibly as many as several hundred—was but a small fraction of the full tribe. Although the federal government and the State of Georgia had for years been pushing the Cherokee to turn all of their territory over to white settlers and move west, most Cherokee wanted to keep their ancestral homeland. In October 1835 the Cherokee General Council had named a committee of leaders to work out a mutually agreeable solution with the federal government in Washington. However, U.S. Indian Commissioner John Schermerhorn had called a meeting at New Echota with a separate committee of Cherokee who he believed would be more willing to "remove" the entire tribe to the West. This was the committee listening to Major Currey speak on December 24. Five days later, on December 29, its members agreed to the Treaty of New Echota, ceding all of the Cherokee's eastern territory in exchange for $4.5 million, land in the West, and other sundry benefits.

Reprinted with permission from Harvard Business School Publishing. "Democracy, Sovereignty, and the Struggle over Cherokee Removal," HBS Case 716-051. This case was prepared by Marc Campasano, Dean Grodzins, and David A. Moss. Copyright ©2016 by the President and Fellows of Harvard College: all rights reserved.

U.S. President Andrew Jackson, who had battled Native American tribes during much of his former military career, was eager to oust the Cherokee from the eastern states. However, several members of the Senate criticized the Treaty of New Echota as a "phantom treaty," claiming that it was signed by an illegitimate council without the consent of the Cherokee people.[2] Approving the treaty, they insisted, would be a grave wrong against the Cherokee Nation and its official government, which the United States had long recognized.

On May 18, 1836, the U.S. Senate finally put the Treaty of New Echota to a vote. If ratified, the treaty would bind all Cherokee to the decisions of the committee at New Echota, and the Cherokee Nation would have to leave its native land.

The Meeting of Different Worlds

When European explorers arrived in North America, they claimed control of territory inhabited by millions of indigenous people (the exact number is unknown) whom Europeans called "Indians."* These Native Americans called themselves by many names. They were divided into hundreds of tribes that spoke different languages and lived diverse ways of life and that had long and complex histories of alliances and rivalries with each other. Among them were the Cherokee.[3]

The earliest recorded contact between Europeans and Cherokee occurred in 1540, when the Spanish conquistador Hernando de Soto reached the Cherokee village of Guasili in what is now North Carolina. At the time, the Cherokee clans were centered in roughly 40,000 square miles of the southern Appalachian Mountains, where their ancestors had migrated, most likely from the Great Lakes region many centuries before. Although the Cherokee had only limited dealings with Europeans before 1700, these interactions had nonetheless significantly affected them. Cherokee obtained their first guns, horses, and alcohol from Europeans, and possibly even the practice of referring to themselves as "Cherokee," a term that

---

* In this case study, indigenous American peoples will be referred to sometimes as "American Indians" or "Indians," the terms used in the era under discussion and used by many indigenous peoples today, and sometimes as "Native Americans," the more common modern term.

may originally have been what a neighboring tribe called them. Also, like other native populations, they contracted a host of diseases to which they had never before been exposed. The most devastating was smallpox. A series of epidemics beginning at least as early as 1697 had sharply reduced the Cherokee population, roughly estimated at 22,000 in 1650, to about 10,000–12,000 by 1720. A subsequent smallpox outbreak in the late 1730s again proved devastating, and the Cherokee population recovered only slowly thereafter. Still, the Cherokee may have been able, for a time, to expand their territory, as nearby tribes were also weakened by European conquest and disease. Cherokee lands eventually recognized by Britain and the United States covered some 125,000 square miles across what is today Kentucky, West Virginia, Virginia, North and South Carolina, Tennessee, Georgia, and Alabama.[4]

British migrants began arriving in North America in large numbers in the seventeenth century. They came expecting to take possession of land on which indigenous peoples lived, but at the same time they asserted that they would not behave like their hated international rivals, the Spanish, who had already conquered the Indians of Central and South America. Stories of the conquistadors' atrocities and cruelties were widely publicized in Britain. The British declared that they would do better, taking territory only by treaty, achieved through fair negotiation, while converting willing American Indians to Christianity and "civilizing" them. The Massachusetts Bay Colony, founded in 1630, placed on its first official seal the image of a Native American quoting, from the New Testament, the plea of the Macedonians to St. Paul: "Come over and help us" (Acts 16:9). The struggle over territory, however, was not mainly resolved through goodwill or negotiation, in Massachusetts or elsewhere. In 1675–1676, relations between settlers and Native Americans in southern New England degenerated into a brutal and exceedingly bloody conflict, known as King Philip's War, which killed thousands, destroyed whole communities, and, in the end, sharply diminished Native American presence in the region.[5]

Farther south—and far beyond the reach of King Philip's War—British merchants began visiting Cherokee villages in the late seventeenth century, marking the beginning of the Cherokee's closest relationship with a colonial power. The British and the Cherokee were signing military and commercial treaties with each other by 1684 and together fought against the Tuscarora, another southeastern Native American tribe, in the early 1710s.[6] They solidified their partnership in 1730, when seven Cherokee visited London to negotiate a treaty called the Articles of Friendship and Commerce.[7] The Articles, drawn up by the British, declared that "the great nation of Cherokees [are] now the children of the Great King of Great Britain [George II]," and that "as the King has given his land on both sides of the great mountains to his own children the English, so he now gives to the Cherokee Indians the privilege of living where they please." The Cherokee would promise to trade and ally only with England in exchange for weapons and supplies. The Cherokee delegates assented to these terms on September 9, 1730, in a response notable for its extreme deference to the British monarchy: "We came hither naked and poor, as the worm out of the earth, but you have everything; and we that have nothing must love you, and can never break the chain of friendship that is between us."[8]

Although the two nations entered the French and Indian War of 1754–1763 as allies, the Anglo-Cherokee "chain of friendship" fell apart over the course of the war. Trouble began in 1756, when a group of Virginia settlers killed twenty-four Cherokee warriors and delivered their scalps to the colonial governor, seeking a bounty for "enemy" scalps. The Cherokee retaliated with their own atrocities, and the violence escalated into a conflict called the "Cherokee War" by the British. Despite a significant victory in which the Cherokee seized a British fort on the Tennessee River, a British assault on their homeland later in 1760 severely weakened the tribe. The two sides signed peace treaties the next year.[9]

Victory in the French and Indian War left Britain as the dominant power in North America, and its people were eager to settle the frontier—regardless of whether or not Britain had already legally recognized the land as Indian territory. Many Native American tribes had long struggled with colonists' settlement on their lands. Unlike the Cherokee, most tribes had fought against the British in the war to avenge such intrusions. Hoping to calm these tensions, King George III issued the Proclamation of 1763, which forbade all English settlement west of the Appalachian Mountains. Colonists widely ignored the Proclamation, however, and continued to settle lands belonging to the Cherokee and other tribes. At the same time, the official Cherokee territory shrunk as a series of treaties ceded more and more of their land to the colonies. The Cherokee had signed their first treaty transferring land to the British in 1721. By the end of 1777 they had ceded more than 68,000 square miles in nine treaties.[10]

The conflict between the settlers and the Cherokee escalated when the colonists declared their independence from Britain in 1776. Most Cherokee (and other Native Americans) sided with the Crown in the war, preferring a government that respected treaties over its rebellious subjects, who often did not. To weaken the Cherokee threat, American troops attacked and destroyed Cherokee villages. The invasion was brutal, and some American soldiers scalped and tortured their enemies—horrors that Cherokee themselves had sometimes been known to practice in battle. The attack crippled the tribe, which ceded over 8,000 square miles to the Americans in peace deals the next spring.[11] Irrespective of these deals, many Cherokee continued fighting for years afterward, and one group called the Chickamaugans kept up attacks on U.S. communities until well after the Revolution had ended. Another smallpox epidemic in 1783 is estimated to have killed 2,500 more Cherokee and further weakened the reeling tribe.[12]

Cherokee Policy of the Early United States

The United States finally signed a comprehensive peace treaty with the Cherokee on November 28, 1785. The Treaty of Hopewell declared "all the Cherokees to be under the protection of the United States of America, and of no other sovereign whatsoever." It delineated the borders of the Cherokee Nation and prohibited American settlement within those borders. The treaty also stated that Congress would "have the sole and exclusive right of regulating trade with the Indians, and managing their affairs in such manner as they think proper," and it allowed the Cherokee to send a deputy to Congress whenever they wished to communicate with the U.S. government. Finally, the treaty declared, "The hatchet shall be forever buried, and the peace given by the United States, and friendship re-established between the said states on the one part, and all the Cherokees on the other, shall be universal."[13]

As with the Proclamation of 1763, the Treaty of Hopewell proved ineffective in curbing white settlement on Cherokee lands. Thousands continued migrating into the territory, joining those who had traveled there before Hopewell. Under the existing national charter of the United States, the Articles of Confederation, the federal government lacked the authority to stop these incursions. The situation changed only after the ratification of the U.S. Constitution in 1788.

A Newly Empowered Federal Government

In addition to broadly expanding federal authority, the Constitution contained a number of provisions pertaining to Native Americans in U.S. territory. It declared that "Indians not taxed" were not to be counted toward apportionment of the House of Representatives or direct federal taxes, indicating that they were not to be regarded as citizens (Art. I, §2). It further declared that Congress had the authority "to regulate commerce with foreign Nations, and among the several States, and with the Indian tribes" (Art. I, §8); that all existing treaties (the large majority of which were with Native American tribes) were to be held as valid by the new federal government; and that all treaties made under the authority of the federal government were to be the "supreme Law of the Land . . . any Thing in the Constitution or Laws of any State to the Contrary notwithstanding" (Art. VI).[14] As a result of these provisions, relations with the Native Americans were now seen as exclusively a federal matter; the Cherokee, like other tribes, would negotiate treaties only with the federal government, never with states. The Constitution specified, moreover, that the power to "make Treaties" rested with the Executive, meaning Native Americans from this point forward would have to deal with the president or his representatives, and that all treaties had to be ratified by a two-thirds vote of the U.S. Senate (Art. II, §2).

In 1789, shortly after ratification of the Constitution and the inauguration of the first president, George Washington, the Cherokee sent a delegation to the national capital to complain about the ongoing treaty violations. They caught the sympathetic ear of Secretary of War Henry Knox, who had responsibility for Indian relations. On July 7 he wrote to President Washington, insisting that the settlers showed "direct and manifest contempt of the authority of the United States," which if unmet would lead "Indian tribes [to] have no faith in such imbecile promises."[15] In response, the federal government reiterated the illegality of settlement on Cherokee lands in a proclamation, but settlers ignored this as well. These continuing intrusions led to the Treaty of Holston (July 1791), in which the Cherokee handed over large tracts of land in the Carolinas in exchange for an annual $1,000 payment and a new prohibition on trespassing. An amendment in February 1792 raised the annual payment to $1,500.[16]

The Treaty of Holston also promised that the United States would "furnish gratuitously the said [Cherokee] nation with useful implements of husbandry," in order "that the Cherokee nation may be led to a greater degree of civilization, and to become herdsmen and cultivators, instead of remaining in a state of hunters." This strategy of "civilization," conceived by Secretary Knox, formed the core of the federal government's early Indian policy.[17] The agreement authorized up to four federal officials, who would become known as "Indian agents," to live among the Cherokee and oversee this effort. The first such agent, Benjamin Hawkins, established his headquarters in Tellico, Tennessee, along with a trading post (called a "factory") where the Cherokee could obtain U.S. goods. Knox hoped these arrangements would familiarize the tribes with a more commercial lifestyle and, ideally, ease their assimilation into the United States.[18]

Meanwhile the federal government negotiated an end to its conflict with the Chickamaugans, the Cherokee holdouts who had never abandoned warring against the States. In the early 1790s they were still attacking settlers near the frontier. In September 1794 the United States invaded Chickamaugan territory in northwest Georgia and destroyed their towns, finally breaking the resistance. "I want peace," Chickamaugan leader Bloody Fellow pleaded that October, "that we may . . . sleep in our houses, and rise in peace on both sides."[19] Chickamaugan leaders signed a peace treaty the next month at Tellico. Hoping for continued tranquility, the governor of the Southwest Territory, William Blount, proudly declared, "Peace with the Indians exists now not only in name or upon paper in form of treaty but in fact, and he who shall violate it shall deserve the severest punishment of the laws and execrations of his fellow citizens."[20]

Tellico was also the site of yet another treaty that transferred land from the Cherokee. After Tennessee became a state in 1796, many of its citizens settled in the eastern Powell Valley, which belonged to the Cherokee. The settlers were frequent targets of Cherokee attacks and of federal officers attempting to enforce the Treaty of Holston. Many Tennesseans were upset that the government was exercising, in their eyes, "partial conduct in favour of a Savage tribe," and state leaders reported that some settlers were fleeing to Spanish-held territory to escape both the violence and the law. At the urging of Tennessee's congressmen, including a young senator named Andrew Jackson, the administration of President John Adams negotiated with the Cherokee and signed the First Treaty of Tellico on October 2, 1798.[21] The treaty ceded the lands in question to the United States, in exchange for $5,000 and an increase of $1,000 to the preexisting annual payment, to be paid in merchandise.[22]

Adams's successor, Thomas Jefferson, was eager to continue the country's expansion as well as the "civilization" of the American Indians. The two processes were linked in his mind: he believed that as the Native Americans ceded their hunting grounds to the States, they would have to abandon their culture for the whites' way of life.[23] Jefferson made his first major deal concerning Native American lands with the State of Georgia rather than with a particular tribe. In 1802 many Georgians were outraged after the state legislature sold approximately 80,000 square miles of western land to wealthy speculators in a deal that enriched a number of political elites and their allies. In an attempt to wash away the scandal, the state transferred all of the contested land to the federal government (the land would later become Alabama and Mississippi). In exchange, the federal government paid for all of the speculators' holdings and promised eventually to clear for settlement all of the land in Georgia that belonged to the Cherokee and Creek tribes. The contested land was transferred to the federal government and the speculators were paid, but President Jefferson did not immediately act on his promise to acquire Cherokee and Creek territory. The Pact of 1802 remained on the books, however, and Georgia's leaders would cite it years later in their efforts to oust the Cherokee.[24]

Disagreement within the Cherokee Tribe

In the meantime, President Jefferson continued to deal with the issue of Native American lands through traditional treaty acquisitions. Between 1804 and 1806, a federal Indian agent named Return Jonathan Meigs secured four agreements with the Cherokee, netting land in Georgia, Tennessee, Kentucky, and Alabama.[25] These agreements, however, served to exacerbate internecine conflicts within the tribe. Although by this point there existed a national tribal council with supposed authority over all of the Cherokee, the tribe was unofficially divided into two subgroups: the southern "Lower Towns" and the northern "Upper Towns." Meigs had negotiated his treaties primarily with Lower Towns leaders and had often enticed them with what he called "silent considerations" of money and goods. After Lower Towns chiefs ceded much of the Cherokee land, Upper Towns leaders demanded that future treaties be worked out with the consent of the entire Cherokee Nation. The conflict came to a head in August 1807, after word leaked that Meigs had bribed Doublehead, a Chickamaugan leader who had once participated in the fighting against the United States.[26] To punish Doublehead, another leading Cherokee known as "The Ridge" (an English translation of one of his Cherokee names, "The Man Who Walks On Mountain's Top") gathered a group to confront Doublehead at his favorite tavern. The Ridge's men brutally killed Doublehead, ostensibly in accordance with tribal law.[27]

After the Doublehead killing, several Lower Towns leaders orchestrated the very first Cherokee "removal" operation. Beginning to doubt the viability of federal "civilization" policy, Meigs had come to believe that westward relocation—or "removal"—was the only means by which the Cherokee could "preserve their national existence."[28] Lower Towns chiefs nearly negotiated a formal removal treaty with the federal administration in Washington, but Upper Towns chiefs in the National Council sent a delegation to block it. Still, in 1808 President Jefferson offered an exchange of western lands for eastern ones to any Cherokee willing to leave their homelands. The Cherokee Council rejected this offer, but 1,023 Lower Towns Cherokee—led by Doublehead's brother-in-law—voluntarily migrated west to Arkansas. Two years later, in 1810, the Council revoked the migrants' citizenship in the Cherokee Nation, accusing them of "treason against the motherland."[29]

Cherokee Culture and Government

The defeat of the Cherokee during the American Revolution seems to have convinced most members of the tribe that conflict with America would lead only to the loss of more lives and land. In 1811, therefore, they gave a cool reception to the charismatic Shawnee warrior Tecumseh, who was traveling south from his native Ohio territory in search of allies. Tecumseh believed that if all western tribes formed a united military front against the United States, they could prevent it from taking any more of their land and could preserve their traditional ways of life. He had been able to bring together warriors from most of the tribes of the Great Lakes region under his leadership and found friends among a faction of Creeks, the Cherokee's neighbors, who became known as "Red Sticks" after they adopted Tecumseh's symbol (a bundle of red sticks) as their own. Cherokee leaders, however, thought Tecumseh's plan would lead their nation to disaster. In the summer of 1813, The Ridge confronted a large meeting of Cherokee who wanted to join with Tecumseh, telling them bluntly that to do so "would lead us to war with the United States, and we should suffer." Some listeners were so angered by The Ridge's words that they attacked him, but he was mostly able to fend off the assault until friends came to his aid and helped him escape. Tecumseh was killed later that year, fighting alongside the British against the United States in the War of 1812, and support for his ideas among the Cherokee seems to have died with him.[30]

Instead of pursuing warfare, the Cherokee opted to try to save their nation by transforming their system of governance and way of life, a process already long under way. At the time of European contact, Cherokee had been organized into scores of autonomous towns, each with its own chief, but governed in most matters by local councils in which all adults, male and female, participated. Particularly after the disasters suffered during the Revolution, however, the Cherokee began to centralize their administration. They gradually invested authority in a national council of chiefs and warriors (all men), headed by a principal chief. By the 1790s the council had established the first national police force, later known as the Light Horse Guard, tasked initially with suppressing horse stealing and eventually with enforcing the council's decisions. By 1808 the most important council decisions began to be written down as a national legal code, in the formal English of legislation (*"Whereas . . . , Be it resolved by the Council . . ."*). By 1821 the Cherokee had established their own system of district courts and marshals.[31]

Meanwhile, in October 1820 the Council restructured itself into a bicameral General Council, with the National Committee as the upper house and the National Council as the lower house. Eight districts would each send four delegates to the National Council for two-year terms, and the National Council would select the thirteen members of the National Committee. A principal chief and second chief would hold executive power. In 1822 the General Council established a National Superior Court of four judges to oversee the judicial system. In the early years of this new government, Pathkiller served as principal chief, John Ross as committee president, and The Ridge as speaker of the National Council.[32]

The changes in Cherokee governance accompanied deeper changes in Cherokee society, ones that started before Knox established a federal "factory" in Cherokee territory and that persisted after it closed in 1811.[33] Before European contact, the Cherokee had lived by hunting deer and bear (seen as the work of men) and growing fields of maize and other crops (seen as the work of women). In the eighteenth century the Cherokee economy came to be based largely on trading deerskins (used in luxury European clothing) and other goods with the British in return for consumer goods. In 1745 a Cherokee chief complained, "My people cannot live independent of the English. . . . The clothes we wear we cannot make ourselves. They are made for us. We use their ammunition with which to kill deer. We cannot make our guns. Every necessary of life we must have from the white people."[34] By 1800, overhunting and habitat loss had depleted the deerskin trade, producing an economic crisis. In response the Cherokee increasingly turned to making a living as their white neighbors did, through trade, herding, and commercial agriculture. In wealthier and more acculturated households, Cherokee women began to live as housewives, although in poorer and more traditional households, planting and tending crops remained women's work. Meanwhile, Cherokee–white intermarriages became increasingly common. The children of such unions, even if fully acculturated to white ways, were regarded as "half-breeds" by most whites and subjected to various legal disabilities. The Cherokee, by contrast, accepted them as full tribal members—especially, in their matrilineal society, if their mother was Cherokee. Cherokee therefore respected both The Ridge and John Ross as tribal leaders, not caring that the former was "full-blooded" and eloquent in Cherokee, while the latter was mostly of white ancestry and felt more comfortable speaking English than Cherokee, or that both men lived in the style of prosperous white southern planters (both owned slaves).[35]

Another major shift in Cherokee life was the spread of literacy. In 1799 the Cherokee allowed Moravian missionaries to establish a school among them; later they would allow in other missionaries, most notably from the influential American Board of Commissioners of Foreign Missions (ABCFM), an organization dominated by Congregationalists and Presbyterians. Most Cherokee leaders sent their children to be educated in mission schools, although few showed any interest in converting from traditional Cherokee beliefs to Christianity. Among those who did express interest were The

Ridge's son John Ridge and his cousin Gallegina ("Buck") Watie, who furthered their education at an academy in Connecticut, popularly known as the "Heathen School." The school had been established by the ABCFM to train "natives" from around the world to spread the Gospel in their homelands. Watie identified with the cause so strongly that he adopted the name of a prominent ABCFM patron, the New Jersey philanthropist (and former president of the Continental Congress) Elias Boudinot.[36]

The spread of literacy made its greatest advance, however, owing to the efforts of a silversmith named (by his white father) George Guess, but more widely known by his Cherokee name, Sequoyah. Himself illiterate, he is generally believed to have started by 1809, if not earlier, to devise a system of written symbols to represent the sounds of the Cherokee language. Working entirely alone, by 1821 he had developed an 86-character syllabary (later reduced to 85). Many Cherokee speakers found they could learn it in just a few days. The system spread rapidly, possibly in part as an act of resistance against a separate plan by missionaries to make Cherokee a written language. By the 1830s, observers reported that half or more of all Cherokee households had a member who could read and write using Sequoyah's syllabary, while one in six households contained a member literate in English.[37] In 1828 Boudinot established the first Native American–run newspaper with the authorization of the Cherokee Council and the backing of the ABCFM. The paper was called the *Cherokee Phoenix* (its motto, "I Will Arise"), and Boudinot had special fonts designed for Sequoyah's symbols so he could print columns in both English and Cherokee. The *Phoenix* found readers across the United States and served as a platform for publicizing the tribe's cause and achievements.[38]

The Cherokee found many sympathizers among American whites, especially northern and evangelical Protestant supporters of the ABCFM, who saw the Cherokee as the successful fulfillment of all the old missionary promises, and validation of the early goal to "civilize the Indian." Yet in at least one critical respect, "civilization" for the Cherokee meant something very different from what it meant for its original white advocates. Whereas the latter had envisioned that "civilized" Indians would eventually assimilate fully into white society, the Cherokee did not seek to assimilate because even the most acculturated of them had come to believe that whites would never accept them as equals. Such had been the bitter lesson learned by

John Ridge and Elias Boudinot at the "Heathen School" in Connecticut. Each, during his time there, had won the heart of a young woman from a prominent local family (in Ridge's case the daughter of the school steward, and in Boudinot's the daughter of a leading school patron), and married her. Yet the marriages, both in 1824, provoked consternation in the women's families and a huge public outcry. Many white Americans professed shock and disgust that respectable white ladies had been allowed to wed "savages." The controversy grew so fierce that the ABCFM eventually decided to close the school. This painful episode provoked a backlash against missionary activity in Cherokee lands and helped convince Ridge and Boudinot that the Cherokee could retain their dignity only under the aegis of their own sovereign government.[39]

General Jackson

The U.S. wars against both British and Native American foes in the 1810s would have lasting consequences for the Cherokee. A pivotal figure in the events of this era, both on the battlefield and in the political arena, was Andrew Jackson. Born on the Carolina frontier in 1767, Jackson as a child had witnessed Native American attacks on his community, including one that reportedly killed a member of his family.[40] In 1788 he moved to Nashville, Tennessee, where settlers are said to have lived in fear of Cherokee raids. Jackson distinguished himself as a dogged enemy of the local tribes and, in the words of one nineteenth-century historian, "had great ambition for encounters with the savages."[41] He served in a militia that fought the Chickamaugans in the early 1790s, and later joined the U.S. House of Representatives in 1796 as Tennessee's first delegate. Jackson was elected to the U.S. Senate in 1797, but disliked the job and resigned the next year. He returned to the Tennessee militia, where he reached the rank of major general in 1802.[42]

The Creek War

The perennial clashes between Tennessee settlers and Native Americans continued, and attacks by the Creek tribe in particular roused Jackson's anger. When the Red Stick faction attacked Fort Mims in Alabama in August 1813, killing hundreds, Jackson led his militia into Alabama to avenge their deaths.[43] At the urging of The Ridge, who feared war with the United States, the Cherokee allied with Jackson in this "Creek War." The Red Stick leader William Weatherford had promised to punish members of other tribes who did not fight for his cause, but Jackson assured his allies, "If one hair of your head is hurt or of your family or of any who are friendly to the whites, I will sacrifice a hundred lives to pay for it."[44] Jackson and his Native American allies smashed the Red Sticks by the spring of 1814. In this campaign, The Ridge served as major of the 800-member Cherokee regiment (whose ranks included John Ross), and he got to know Jackson. After the war he was always called "Major Ridge." Meanwhile, in August 1814 the Creeks agreed to the Treaty of Fort Jackson, in which they ceded approximately 36,000 square miles of land in Alabama and Georgia.[45]

The treaty still required ratification by the U.S. Senate before it could become official, but international political developments complicated matters. When Andrew Jackson was fighting the Creeks, the United States was simultaneously engaged in the War of 1812 against Britain. In fact, Britain had been arming Native American tribes, including in Florida, to the great consternation of U.S. settlers. Immediately after the Creek War, Jackson was promoted to major general of the U.S. Army and placed in charge of the southern military district. He led a campaign into Florida, and in January 1815 he defended New Orleans from British invasion in a victory that earned him national admiration. Unbeknownst to Jackson, however, the United States and Britain had already signed the Treaty of Ghent on December 24, 1814, formally ending the war. The treaty included an article requiring the United States to end its wars against Native Americans and to return to the tribes all land it had acquired since 1811. This clause threatened the Creek concessions in the Treaty of Fort Jackson.[46]

Despite this tension between the two treaties, Jackson's status as a national hero persuaded the Senate to ratify the Fort Jackson agreement on February 16, 1815, and to do so unanimously. President James Madison's acting secretary of war, Alexander J. Dallas, encouraged Jackson to "cooperate with all means in your power to conciliate the Indians, upon the principles of our agreement with Great Britain," but Jackson largely ignored the Treaty of Ghent in construing his settlement with the Creeks. With the war over, Jackson returned to Tennessee to oversee the surveying of boundaries agreed upon in the Treaty of Fort Jackson.[47]

Jackson and the Cherokee

The Treaty of Fort Jackson ended up posing a significant problem for the Cherokee, even though they had assisted Jackson in the Creek War. In particular, they believed that some of the land the Creeks had ceded actually belonged to them. Creek chiefs insisted that the disputed lands had been "only loaned to the Cherokees, and that the said lands were always considered the property of the Creek Nation."[48] Major Ridge led a Cherokee delegation to Washington to settle the issue. On March 22, 1816, the Madison administration awarded them a new treaty that granted them the contested lands, plus $25,500 for damages done by Jackson's militia in the Creek War, in exchange for some Cherokee lands in South Carolina.[49]

Jackson found the treaty revision troubling, asserting that it could inflame tensions on the frontier and, in turn, bring about "the destruction of the whole cherokee nation, and of course . . . a [civil] war." In other words, he believed that southern whites would defy the government if he attempted to enforce the treaty provisions.[50] Jackson also made it clear, in letters to his superiors in Washington, that he thought treaty negotiations were an "absurd" and atavistic relic of an earlier era, when American Indian tribes were powerful and independent nations. Because this was no longer true, he suggested, the treaties were no longer relevant and Congress should simply enact laws to remove Indians from their land. Besides, he asserted, only "designing half-breeds and renegade white men" who lived among the Indians protested removal. In his view, "real" Indians did not oppose removal, because, as "natives of the forest," they wished to escape from what they viewed as the corrupting influence of whites.[51]

Despite such attitudes, Jackson was duty-bound, as a U.S. Army general, to enforce the new treaty—or at least to work out a new one more to his liking. In September 1816 Jackson and his treaty commissioners met leaders of the Cherokee and Chickasaw (another tribe that contested the Fort Jackson boundaries) at the Chickasaw Council House in Mississippi to press for a new agreement. In a speech on September 12, Jackson's commissioners pushed the cause of "civilization," saying that the Cherokee and Chickasaw "must cultivate the Earth like your white Brethren & your women like their white sisters must learn to spin & weave." The commissioners insisted that the lands the United States desired were "of no value to you . . . [and] will only be a fruitful source of Bloodshed & strife."[52] Finally—after some "presents" had been offered—the Cherokee and Chickasaw chiefs agreed to land cession treaties on September 14 and 20, respectively. A meeting with the Cherokee National Council at Turkey Town, Alabama, beginning on September 28 finalized the treaty with the Cherokee, over the opposition of several leaders and only after further bribes had been granted. A year later, leading Cherokee chiefs alleged that the treaty had been ratified only by representatives of a few towns and not the entire nation, but the federal government never investigated the matter.[53]

As the negotiations progressed, some Cherokee leaders hinted that they might be willing to abandon their lands entirely and "remove" themselves west. The Monroe administration, seeking to acquire Cherokee lands along the Tennessee River, was willing to offer U.S. property along the Arkansas River in exchange. In June 1817 President Monroe sent Jackson to the government's Cherokee Agency in Tennessee to negotiate with both the eastern Cherokee and the Arkansas Cherokee, those who had taken up President Jefferson's offer to move west years before.[54] In his presentation to the Cherokee Council and its new National Committee of thirteen leading men, Jackson argued that the Cherokee who had discussed removal with Jefferson in 1808 had accepted an exchange of lands between the West and the East on behalf of the whole tribe. The Arkansas Cherokee had acted on this first and moved before any land was officially transferred, and now the time had come to finalize the exchange. "Go where game is plentiful & corn is plenty," he encouraged the easterners, and enticed them with promises of supplies and a trading factory. Anyone who did not go, Jackson promised, would become a U.S. citizen and be assimilated into the "civilized life."[55]

This offer divided the leaders of the two Cherokee populations. Although barred from the meeting with Jackson, the Arkansans agreed with his telling of events, and were willing to trade the ancestral territory for official ownership of their land in the West. The easterners saw things quite differently. They claimed that the tribe had made no such agreement with Jefferson, and that those who had gone west had had no official sanction from the Cherokee Nation. Even Cherokee delegates who had been at the meeting with Jefferson could not agree on exactly what had happened there. The easterners presented two of those delegates to support their story, but the principal chief of the tribe, named Tochelar, had also been present and agreed with

Jackson's account. Incensed at the thought of removal, the easterners ousted Tochelar from their council and on July 4 declared, "We wish to remain on our land, and hold it fast."[56]

The statement enraged Jackson, who told the chiefs that they were reneging on a promise to the United States. "Look around you and recollect what happened to . . . the Creeks," he warned.[57] On July 6 his commissioners delivered the chiefs a draft treaty, which included a "private article" offering eastern and Arkansan chiefs thousands of dollars each for their approval. On July 8, a number of chiefs—though not the Council, or even a majority of the chiefs present—consented, signing over a thousand square miles in Georgia, Alabama, and Tennessee for equivalent territory in the West. The Senate approved the treaty on December 11, 1817, and the first party to migrate west under the treaty, numbering about 700, departed in February 1818. (Among them was Sequoyah. His syllabary first grew popular when migrants and their families realized they could use it to write letters to one another.)[58]

Most of the eastern Cherokee opposed removal and disagreed with those who had moved west. In late 1818 the new Cherokee National Committee president John Ross led a delegation to Washington with the aim of revising the 1817 treaty. Although the Cherokee ceded an even greater amount of land—nearly 6,000 square miles—to the United States in the resulting Treaty of 1819, their negotiators agreed to this with the understanding that their boundaries would never be further diminished. They believed that on the basis of this new treaty, the more than 12,000 square miles of their homeland they still held, which Principal Chief Pathkiller called the "last little," would always remain in Cherokee hands. Confident that they had finalized their borders, the Council rescinded citizenship in the Cherokee Nation to any member who moved to a reservation outside the traditional homeland.[59]

Georgia Demands Cherokee Lands

In the 1820s about two-thirds of all Cherokee lived in Georgia, and the General Council met at New Town, Georgia. The existence of a separate government within Georgia's borders, as well as a large Cherokee population, disturbed state leaders, representing (in their eyes) an unnecessary constraint on white settlement and a clear violation of Georgia's sovereignty. After the

Treaty of 1819, state lawmakers had complained that the state received no lands in the deal, despite the Pact of 1802, which seemed to promise that all the Cherokee lands in Georgia would someday be cleared.[60] Now that the Cherokee were re-forming, centralizing, and strengthening their government, the state stepped up its effort to collect on Jefferson's promise.

President Monroe responded to Georgia's complaints in March 1823, announcing that the Cherokee "in their present temper . . . can only be removed by force . . . and there is no obligation on the United States to remove the Indians by force."[61] With the president showing no interest in a conflict, Congress appropriated money for peaceful removal, and Secretary of War John Calhoun sent commissioners to the October 1823 General Council meeting to urge emigration. In a Supreme Court decision that year, *Johnson v. M'Intosh,* Chief Justice John Marshall ruled that the states owned their Native American territories by a "right of discovery" transferred from the British Crown. The Native Americans themselves only had a "right of occupancy," not complete ownership of their lands.[62] Calhoun's commissioners invoked this argument at the General Council meeting. Offering another exchange of western lands for eastern lands, they claimed that previous treaties had acknowledged only the Cherokee's right to live on the land, not ownership of it. When the Council turned down their offer, the commissioners attempted to bribe its leaders with $12,000. The commissioners secured the representation of a Creek named William McIntosh to make the offer, but Pathkiller, Ross, and Major Ridge roundly rejected McIntosh's overtures and sent him fleeing from New Town.[63]

With officials from Georgia and the federal government continuing to harangue the Cherokee Council over emigration, Ross, Major Ridge, and others journeyed to Washington in January 1824 to discuss the issue with Secretary Calhoun and President Monroe. They told the president that they would not cede any more territory and urged him to disavow the Pact of 1802: "An exchange of territory twice as large . . . or all the money now in the coffers of your treasury, would be no inducement for the Nation to exchange or sell their country." In his annual message of March 1824, Monroe reiterated that the United States had no responsibility or obligation to remove the Cherokee by force.[64]

Monroe's inaction aggravated Georgia's leaders, and John Forsyth, the state's only U.S. House representative, put forward a resolution calling for the United States to force the Cherokee out of Georgia. John Ross traveled to Washington to confront Forsyth personally and on April 15, 1824, brought a petition against the resolution to Congress. In his testimony, Committee President Ross insisted that the Cherokee were more "civilized" than other tribes, and would remain peaceful, seeking only to "enjoy the blessings of civilization and Christianity, on the soil of their rightful inheritance." Ross's plea proved successful, with enough northern congressmen voting against Forsyth's resolution to block its passage.[65]

The Question of Sovereignty

Over the next few years the government of Georgia eased its pursuit of the Cherokee lands, and the Cherokee continued to develop their governance institutions. The General Council announced in 1825 the creation of a capital called New Echota, near New Town, to house the government. Under the guidance of Committee President Ross, the Cherokee elected delegates to a constitutional convention, which on July 4, 1827, published a national constitution. It was modeled on the U.S. Constitution, as was evident from its preamble: "We, the Representatives of the People of the Cherokee Nation . . . in order to establish justice, ensure tranquility, promote our common welfare, and secure to ourselves and our posterity the blessings of liberty . . . do ordain and establish this Constitution." The Cherokee constitution affirmed the Nation's existing borders, indicating that no more land would be ceded, and defined its governmental structures, declaring that "the sovereignty & jurisdiction of this Government shall extend over the country within the boundaries . . . described." The next February, the government began publishing the *Cherokee Phoenix.*[66]

Just months before the birth of the *Phoenix,* however, the Georgia legislature approved a resolution (on December 26, 1827) challenging Cherokee sovereignty: "That the policy which has been pursued by the United States toward the Cherokee Indians has not been in good faith toward Georgia. . . . That all the lands, appropriated and unappropriated, which lie within the conventional limits of Georgia belong to her absolutely . . . and that Georgia has the right to extend her authority and her laws over . . . all descriptions of people, be they white, red, or black, who may reside within her limits."[67] Although passage of the resolution had no immediate consequences, many Cherokee were understandably alarmed. Elias Boudinot later wrote in protest, "How is it possible that [the Cherokee] will establish for themselves good laws, when an attempt is made to crush their first feeble effort toward it?"[68]

Georgia took no further legal action until December 20, 1828, when John Forsyth, now governor, approved a law asserting that all Cherokee laws were null and that beginning in June 1830 the Cherokee lands would be subject to state law and annexed to nearby counties. The law, while not unexpected, further offended the Cherokee and threatened their sovereignty. In January 1829 John Ross, now principal chief, carried a petition to Washington signed by 3,095 Cherokee protesting Georgia's new law. Ross found the capital crowded with people eager to meet the same man he had come to see, President-elect Andrew Jackson. Chief Ross never met with Jackson, and by the time he departed Washington in April his only response from the administration was a letter from the new secretary of war, John Eaton, urging removal.[69]

The Lure of Gold and "War in Georgia"

The threat to the Cherokee grew more serious in mid-1829 after a gold vein was discovered running through their territory. "Within a few days it seemed as if the world must have heard of it, for men came from every state," recalled one fortune seeker. At its height the gold rush would draw more than 10,000 people to the area. The mania tempted some Cherokee to sell their land, which in turn led the General Council to declare unanimously in October that any who did so were outlaws and that it was permissible for any Cherokee to kill them if spotted within the Nation. The Georgia legislature countered with laws of its own, forbidding the Cherokee from digging for gold on their own land and banning the Council from preventing land sales.[70]

Driven by the lure of gold, the new arrivals harassed the Cherokee living in the territory. There were frequent raids against Cherokee communities, and many settlers took up residence in abandoned Cherokee homesteads. Despite complaints from the Cherokee, the Jackson administration did nothing to combat these illegal incursions. The Cherokee began fighting back in February 1830, when Major Ridge led a Council-approved force to oust settlers from Cherokee homes near the Alabama border and to burn down buildings so they could not return. Violence between whites and Cherokee soon escalated, and the national press spoke of "War in Georgia." The Cherokee's retaliation and subsequent fights with settlers fed many whites' perceptions that the Cherokee were belligerent savages. Elias Boudinot wrote in the *Cherokee Phoenix* that this was "a circumstance which we have for a long time dreaded. . . . It has been the desire of our enemies that the Cherokees may be urged to some desperate act. . . . We would say, *forbear, forbear*—revenge not, but leave vengeance 'to whom vengeance belongest.' "[71]

The Indian Removal Act

In his first message to Congress, in December 1829, President Jackson acknowledged Georgia's ongoing conflict with the Cherokee and urged congressional action. In particular, he asked Congress to allot "an ample district west of the Mississippi, and without the limits of any State or Territory now formed, to be guaranteed to the Indian tribes as long as they shall occupy it. . . . This emigration should be voluntary, for it would be as cruel as unjust to compel the aborigines to abandon the graves of their fathers and seek a home in a distant land. But they should be distinctly informed that if they remain within the limits of the States they must be subject to their laws."[72] With anti-Cherokee sentiment rising, particularly in Georgia, the Senate Indian Affairs Committee reported a bill in line with Jackson's recommendation on February 22, 1830. The bill would authorize the president to offer western lands in exchange for Native American holdings in the states and territories. The president would be empowered to provide aid to any Native Americans who emigrated, and would be bound to protect the émigrés in their new lands.[73]

When Senate debate over the removal bill began in April, opinions divided largely along regional lines, with support coming from the South and opposition from the North. Although the bill would apply to five different tribes, discussion focused on the Cherokee. The tribe's most vigorous defender in the Senate was Theodore Frelinghuysen of New Jersey, who had once served as president of the ABCFM. In a six-hour speech stretched over three days, Frelinghuysen insisted on equal justice for the Cherokee irrespective of race, the sovereignty of the Cherokee Nation, and the Cherokee's inherent right to their lands. The bill would only authorize the president to negotiate an exchange of lands, but Frelinghuysen and other opponents believed that Jackson would negotiate aggressively and with threats of force, effectively seizing Cherokee lands.[74] "God, in his providence, planted these tribes on this western continent, for aught that we know, before Great Britain herself had a political existence," he argued. "Where is the decree or ordinance, that has stripped of their rights these early and first lords of the soil? . . . [N]o argument can shake the political maxim—that where the Indian always *has been,* he enjoys an absolute right still *to be,* in the free exercise of his own modes of thought, government and conduct." Comparing the United States to a "horseleech" that sought more land than it needed, he declared that Georgia's 1828 law was illegitimate and that removal was profoundly unjust.[75]

John Forsyth, who was now a U.S. senator from Georgia, responded in a speech that likewise spanned three days. He suggested that Frelinghuysen was a hypocrite because the northern states had seized Native American lands long ago and were now criticizing southern states for doing the same. "The Indians in New York, New England, Virginia, &c. &c. are to be left to the tender mercies of those states, while the arm of the General Government is to be extended to protect the Choctaws, Chickasaws, Creeks, and especially the Cherokees, from the anticipated oppressions of Mississippi, Alabama, and Georgia." Forsyth reviewed the history of Native American treaties with the United States, the British colonies, and the individual states, and concluded that Georgia had been well within its rights in passing the 1828 law. He concluded by accusing Senator Frelinghuysen of "prejudiced examination, and unjust condemnation of our cause," and of wanting the federal government to violate "the personal rights of its people" and "to make war upon a State."[76]

The Senate approved the federal removal bill on April 26, and the House began its debate on May 13. The House discussion was similarly heated, with speeches invoking themes of Cherokee sovereignty, the validity of prior treaties, and states' rights. In a long speech on the first day, New York's Henry Storrs lamented that the removal bill showed little respect for Cherokee sovereignty, which previous treaties had assumed to exist. "If the question [of Cherokee sovereignty] before us is not settled at this day, there is nothing settled in the Government. Every thing is to be kept floating. We shall never know what our institutions are, nor will others know when or whether to trust us at all." Supporters, by contrast, argued that the bill would benefit Native Americans. "It is a measure of life and death," argued Georgia's Wilson Lumpkin. If the Native Americans did not move west, he warned, "they will

every day be brought into closer contact and conflict with the white population, and this circumstance will diminish the spirit of benevolence and phi-
lanthropy towards them which now exists."[77]

In a 103–97 vote, the House passed the removal bill on May 26, 1830, and
President Jackson signed it into law two days later.[78] Following passage,
Georgia and the federal government pressured the Cherokee to abandon
their lands. Georgia's 1828 law had declared that the state would extend its
authority over the Cherokee in June 1830, and Governor George Gilmer sent
the Georgia Guard into the Cherokee Nation beginning that month. Mindful
that many Americans were sympathetic to the Cherokee, the Guard did not
begin full-scale enforcement of state law but apparently did harass Cherokee
with arrests over trivial, invented, or provoked offenses. At the same time,
President Jackson pressed for the Cherokee to give up their land by treaty.
Of the five tribes with lands eligible for exchange under the new federal
law, the Cherokee were the only tribe that refused to meet with Jackson. In
retaliation, the president changed the way the federal government paid its
annuity to the Cherokee. Traditionally the government had paid the annuity to Cherokee leaders, but Jackson now required that individual Cherokee collect their share from the Indian agent. Because most Cherokee would
likely not travel a long distance to obtain the small sum due to them, this
had the effect of reducing federal payments to the tribe.[79]

The Cherokee Go to Court

With state and federal governments turning up the heat, the Cherokee General Council sought to fight back in court.

Cherokee Nation v. Georgia

Chief Ross hired the former U.S. Attorney General William Wirt to guide
the Cherokee's legal efforts, which initially relied on the case of a Cherokee
named Corn Tassel to get to the U.S. Supreme Court. Tassel had been accused of murdering another Cherokee, and the tribe had arrested him and
planned a trial. However, state officials in Georgia intervened, seizing Tassel,
trying him in state court, and sentencing him to hang. Wirt argued that the
state had violated tribal sovereignty. The Georgia Superior Court ruled for
the state, and on December 12, 1830, Wirt appealed to the U.S. Supreme Court

to halt the execution. Chief Justice John Marshall proved responsive and ordered the governor of Georgia to appear before the court. Instead, the governor summoned a special session of the Georgia legislature, which instructed the sheriff detaining Tassel to move forward with the execution. Tassel was hanged on December 24. Three days later, Wirt and his co-counsel, John Sergeant, a congressman from Pennsylvania, filed a new case before the Supreme Court, claiming that the Cherokee qualified as a foreign nation. Georgia sent no counsel to rebut them, because it refused to acknowledge that the Supreme Court had jurisdiction over what it called an internal state matter.[80]

Chief Justice Marshall handed down a decision in *Cherokee Nation v. Georgia* on March 5, 1831. Although sympathetic to the Cherokee, Marshall's opinion held that the U.S. Supreme Court was not the proper venue for the case. The U.S. Constitution stated that federal judicial power pertained to cases "between a State, or the Citizens thereof, and foreign States, Citizens, or Subjects."[81] Marshall maintained that the Cherokee Nation was not a foreign state, but rather a "domestic dependent nation" within the United States:

> In general, nations not owing a common allegiance are foreign to each other. . . . But the relation of the Indians to the United States is marked by peculiar and cardinal distinctions which exist nowhere else. The Indian territory is admitted to compose a part of the United States. In all our maps, geographical treatises, histories, and laws, it is so considered. In all our intercourse with foreign nations, in our commercial regulations, in any attempt at intercourse between Indians and foreign nations, they are considered as within the jurisdictional limits of the United States, subject to many of those restraints which are imposed upon our own citizens. . . .
>
> Though the Indians are acknowledged to have an unquestionable, and, heretofore, unquestioned right to the lands they occupy, until that right shall be extinguished by a voluntary cession to our government; yet it may well be doubted whether those tribes which reside within the acknowledged boundaries of the United States can, with strict accuracy, be denominated foreign nations. They may, more correctly, perhaps, be denominated domestic dependent nations. They occupy a territory to which we assert a title independent of their will, which must take effect in point of possession when their right of possession ceases. Meanwhile they are in a state of pupilage. Their relation to the United States resembles that of a ward to his guardian.[82]

Because Georgia's seizure of Tassel had not violated the rights of a foreign nation, Marshall ruled, the Supreme Court had no authority to reverse the state court's decision.

Settler incursions and abuses in Cherokee territory increased after the decision. Civilians and guardsmen alike engaged in violence against the Cherokee, and Governor Gilmer and President Jackson did little to stop them. In a meeting with Cherokee leaders after the decision, Jackson swore that he was "the friend of the Cherokees" but asserted, "You can live on your lands in Georgia if you choose, but I cannot interfere with the laws of that state to protect you."[83]

Worcester v. Georgia

The Cherokee had another chance to challenge Georgia before the U.S. Supreme Court the following year. In December 1830 the Georgia legislature had passed a bill directing settlers on Cherokee land to obtain a permit that required an oath of loyalty to the state. Supporters of the law intended to target evangelical Protestant missionaries, sent by the American Board of Missions, who had settled among the Cherokee and, according to Senator Lumpkin, spread defiant "religious fanaticism" throughout the tribe.[84] The Georgia Guard selectively enforced the law and in March 1831 arrested several missionaries who had not taken the oath. The state judge who heard the case, Augustin Clayton, ruled that the missionaries' work with the Indians made them in effect federal agents and so exempt from arrest. Apparently, Judge Clayton did not want to give these missionaries standing to challenge the constitutionality of the Georgia law. However, the Jackson administration soon denied that they were federal agents, and the Guard arrested them again, along with more missionaries. After a retrial in September, most of the accused took the oath and subsequently fled Georgia. Two of the original defendants, Elizur Butler and Samuel Worcester (a founder, with Boudinot, of the *Cherokee Phoenix*), refused and were sentenced to jail. Wirt brought their case to the U.S. Supreme Court, arguing that Georgia had violated U.S.-Cherokee treaties with the 1830 law. In this case, unlike *Cherokee Nation v. Georgia,* the Court's jurisdiction was unquestioned, because the plaintiff was a U.S. citizen alleging wrongdoing by a U.S. state.[85]

Once again, Wirt and Sergeant argued the Cherokee case; once again, Georgia refused to send anyone in response. The Marshall Court ruled on

March 3, 1832, in *Worcester v. Georgia,* that Georgia's law was unconstitutional. The law, Marshall wrote, violated the Cherokee's right to self-government, which treaties with the U.S. and Britain had always recognized. The Cherokee Nation existed within Georgia's borders, but was not subject to Georgia law:

> The very fact of repeated treaties with them recognizes [Cherokee self-government]; and the settled doctrine of the law of nations is, that a weaker power does not surrender its independence—its right to self-government, by associating with a stronger, and taking its protection. A weak state, in order to provide for its safety, may place itself under the protection of one more powerful, without stripping itself of the right of government, and ceasing to be a state. . . . The Cherokee nation, then, is a distinct community occupying its own territory, with boundaries accurately described, in which the laws of Georgia can have no force, and which the citizens of Georgia have no right to enter, but with the assent of the Cherokees themselves, or in conformity with treaties, and with the acts of Congress. The whole intercourse between the United States and this nation, is, by our constitution and laws, vested in the government of the United States.[86]

In *Cherokee Nation v. Georgia,* the Court had ruled that the Cherokee did not constitute a foreign nation. Now it made clear the Cherokee were a sovereign nation, though dependent on and not foreign to the United States, and that the states were bound to observe U.S. treaties delineating tribal borders.

The decision was initially greeted with jubilation among the Cherokee. John Ross reported "great rejoicings throughout the nation," and Elias Boudinot believed that the "question is forever settled as to who is right and who is wrong."[87] It soon became clear, however, that the ruling was not a panacea for the Cherokee. Wilson Lumpkin, now governor, refused to release Worcester and Butler from prison, and President Jackson made it known that he had no intention of enforcing the decision. The ruling, he said, was "stillborn," and his allies in Washington continued to pressure the Cherokee to accept a removal treaty.[88]

At first, some Cherokee held out hope that President Jackson would be defeated for reelection in 1832. Among Jackson's opponents were prominent supporters of the Cherokee, including both of the attorneys who represented them at the Supreme Court: Sergeant was running on the National Republican ticket as the vice presidential running mate of Jackson's political archenemy, Henry Clay, and Wirt was running as the presidential nominee of a large third party, the Anti-Masons. In the fall elections, however, Jackson won over 54 percent of the popular vote, as opposed to 37 percent for the Clay-Sergeant ticket and 8 percent for Wirt. In Georgia, Jackson was so popular that his opponents did not even mount campaigns, and he won 100 percent of the vote.[89]

Contemplating Removal

As a growing number of Cherokee came to see the *Worcester* decision as an empty victory, they began to conceive of removal as a necessary evil. In a meeting with Jackson soon after the decision, Committee President John Ridge, son of Major Ridge, became "convinced that the only alternative to save his people from moral and physical death was to make the best terms they could with the government, and remove out of the limits of the States," according to a close Jackson ally.[90] Elias Boudinot and Major Ridge began seriously considering removal at about the same time, and some Cherokee started migrating west in the spring of 1832 in anticipation of full removal. In May, Boudinot printed a story in the *Phoenix* reporting that Committee President Ridge had attempted to negotiate a land sale with Jackson. Although Ridge himself denied this, the article angered Principal Chief Ross, who feared it would be read as suggesting his government was considering removal. Ridge and Boudinot broached the topic in July, when the General Council gathered at Red Clay, Tennessee, a new center of Cherokee government beyond the reach of the Georgia Guard. Perhaps because most Cherokee leaders continued to oppose removal, Ridge and Boudinot were careful not to endorse it explicitly, but they did encourage the Council to consider negotiations.[91]

Chief Ross emerged as the foremost opponent of removal at the July 1832 meeting. In his opening address, he hinted that he would reject any negotiations without full tribal consent, declaring that a "man who will forsake his country in time of adversity and will cooperate with those who oppress his own kindred is no more than a traitor and should be viewed and shunned as such."[92] Leadership changes made at the meeting further strengthened Ross's hand. Boudinot resigned as editor of the *Phoenix,* complaining that Ross was attempting to block all dissent within its pages. Ross's brother-in-law, Elijah Hicks, became the new editor of the *Phoenix,* and proved receptive to

Ross's guidance. When, for example, President Jackson's Indian Affairs commissioner, Elisha Chester, came to the Red Clay meeting to offer a removal treaty, Hicks honored Ross's request not to print any of Chester's testimony in the *Phoenix*. At the same meeting, the General Council agreed to postpone the elections constitutionally mandated for that year, thereby ensuring that Ross would retain power. Although the Council ostensibly did this to avoid the prospect of changing leaders in the midst of a crisis, some dissenters believed the measure was instead intended simply to shield Ross from challengers.[93]

At its October 1832 meeting, the General Council decided Ross should go to Washington to confront the Jackson administration. Ross met with Jackson twice in February 1833, and the exchanges were heated. Jackson made two offers for the Cherokee lands: $2.5 million for assisted removal, or $3 million if the Cherokee left without any government help. Ross refused, replying, "If you have so much money at your disposal, buy off the Georgia settlers and end this dispute." Finally, Jackson offered a grim prediction of the Cherokee's fate if they did not leave their ancestral land. Georgia would not back down, he promised, and eventually there would be war. The U.S. government would not help the Cherokee, for fear of sectional discord, and the tribe's people would either be killed or brought under Georgia law.[94]

A Growing Divide

When Ross returned to the Cherokee Nation that spring, divisions over removal ran deep. Cherokee leaders had split into a pro-removal "Treaty Party" and an anti-removal "National Party," and isolated acts of violence had broken out between the two factions. At a meeting in May 1833, Committee President Ridge expressed his disapproval of Ross's decision to dismiss Jackson's offer, and others in the Treaty Party composed a letter to the General Council warning that continued resistance to removal would "not result in the restoration of those rights" the tribe had lost. Ross persuaded the authors of this letter, including Major Ridge and Boudinot, to postpone publication until the October Council meeting, hoping that the situation would improve in the meantime. It did not. That summer, white settlers who had been granted title to Cherokee land by the state began seizing land and homes, and more and more Cherokee opted to head west.[95]

The extent to which removal divided the Cherokee—and even individual families—became apparent in the months that followed. In October 1833 the General Council again sent Ross to meet with President Jackson. In January, Ross's younger brother Andrew and his relative Thomas Jefferson Pack secretly traveled to Washington as well. Pack and the younger Ross were emissaries of William Hicks, a former principal chief whom John Ross had ousted in the election of 1828. Hicks had formed a shadow government of pro-removal Cherokee and hoped that Pack and Andrew Ross could negotiate a treaty with Jackson. Jackson, however, knew that they lacked authority and that neither the Cherokee governing bodies nor the U.S. Senate would approve any treaty they signed. He thus dismissed Pack and Ross, requesting that they return with leaders of greater stature within the Cherokee Nation.[96]

Andrew Ross returned to Washington in May, this time with Major Ridge and Elias Boudinot at his side. Although both soon lost confidence in his negotiating skills and abandoned him, the discussions continued (despite Jackson's earlier position) and Andrew Ross's delegation hammered out a removal treaty with the administration in June. The treaty would award the Cherokee an annual payment of $25,000 for twenty-four years. Funds were also allocated to Andrew Ross himself. However, John Ross denounced the treaty, insisting that Andrew's men had "no authority whatever from the nation to do what they have done," and the U.S. Senate rejected it.[97]

Chief Ross's own mission to Washington, meanwhile, once again yielded no progress. In discussions with Secretary of War Lewis Cass, Ross offered a partial cession in exchange for protection of the Cherokee lands that would remain, and, failing that, requested that the Cherokee be allowed to apply for citizenship if they relinquished all of their lands. Cass refused both offers, claiming that only full removal would be satisfactory. Even when Ross presented President Jackson with an anti-removal petition signed by 13,000 Cherokee (out of 16,000 tribal members still living on their traditional lands), the president dismissed it as a fake.[98]

By 1834 the rupture within the tribe was becoming ever more dangerous. Andrew Ross faced death threats, and the Ridges confronted calls for their assassination at an August meeting at Red Clay. That same month a Treaty Party leader named John Walker Jr. was shot and killed, raising tensions and provoking Georgia settlers to form a "Citizens Committee" to defend against the "constant danger of assassination and other lawless violence."[99] The conflict finally split the Cherokee government in two when John Ridge, his father, Boudinot, and other Treaty Party leaders walked out of the October 1834 Council meeting to form a separate council. From John Ridge's home at Running Waters, this alternative council sent a message to the U.S. Congress announcing that they had "turned their eyes to the country west of the Mississippi" and were prepared to leave for good.[100]

Both councils sent delegations to Washington that winter. Aware that the Treaty Party was negotiating as well, Chief Ross made his first offer to Jackson for removal: $20 million for all of the lands, plus extra money for past treaty violations. When Jackson dismissed this price as "preposterous," Ross suggested he would take any price the Senate proposed. Jackson approved, and a week later the Senate Committee on Indian Affairs offered $5 million. Having expected a much larger sum, Ross rejected the deal and left Washington.[101] Arriving at his home in Georgia late one evening, he found strangers living there: the state of Georgia had confiscated all of his property and awarded it to a white family in a lottery. Ross had little choice but to rent a room, and he left the next morning to find his family and set up a new home in Tennessee. In the meantime, Committee President Ridge had been negotiating with Reverend John F. Schermerhorn, Jackson's new treaty commissioner. Schermerhorn proposed paying $4.5 million, plus extensive western lands, for the Cherokee homeland. Ridge believed this to be "very liberal in its terms," and a provisional treaty along these lines was signed on March 14, 1835.[102]

Many—and likely most—Cherokee still opposed removal, and in May the General Council voiced its disapproval of the Treaty Party's negotiations and invested John Ross with "full power to adjust the Nation's difficulties in whatever way he might think most beneficial."[103] Ross encouraged his supporters to attend a July meeting at Running Waters that the Treaty Party was holding with Schermerhorn, with the aim of scuttling the negotiations. Approximately 2,600 Cherokee answered Ross's call, and those assembled rejected a key provision concerning annuity payments in a 2,225 to 114 vote. Foiled by the National Party, Schermerhorn waited until the October Council meeting to make his next move.[104]

The Treaty of New Echota

Chief Ross did not permit Schermerhorn to address the Council at Red Clay in October 1835 until the very end of the meeting. At that point, Schermerhorn spelled out the specific terms of the treaty he offered: $3.4 million plus more than 21,000 square miles of land in the West (mostly land already guaranteed to the western Cherokee). The Council rejected this offer, even after Schermerhorn raised his price to $5 million. Finally, Ross claimed that Schermerhorn's offer was illegitimate anyway, since he had no formal commission document from Secretary of War Cass. With this in mind, the Council voted to send a committee to negotiate a new treaty with the U.S. government. The committee would include John Ross, Elijah Hicks, John Ridge, and Elias Boudinot, among others.[105]

Commissioner Schermerhorn, meanwhile, called for negotiations at New Echota, the abandoned Cherokee capital in Georgia. As two historians have explained, "Schermerhorn wanted a treaty, and he knew that "the Cherokees most likely to show up [there] would be those nearby who were hurting the most," owing in part to Georgian policies.[106] While Ross led the Council-approved committee in Washington, Ridge and Boudinot, who had resigned their positions on the committee, met with Schermerhorn and his team (which included Major Benjamin Currey) at New Echota on December 21, declaring their delegation to be the true negotiating body for the tribe. Estimates vary widely, but perhaps up to several hundred Cherokee, women and children included, attended the meeting, many enticed by a promise of free blankets. Major Ridge and Andrew Ross were also present. In the agreement worked out there, the United States promised $4.5 million, plus western lands, removal assistance, support for Cherokee education, and the possibility of a Cherokee delegate to the U.S. House of Representatives, if Congress approved. The Cherokee would have to leave their lands within two years.[107]

"We Are Few, and They Are Many"

On December 24, Major Ridge, speaking in Cherokee, offered the following comments on the treaty:

> I am one of the native sons of these wild woods. I have hunted the deer and turkey here, more than fifty years. I have fought your battles, have defended

your truth and honesty, and fair trading. I have always been the friend of honest white men. . . . I know the Indians have an older title than theirs. We obtained the land from the living God above. They got their title from the British. Yet they are strong and we are weak. We are few, and they are many. We cannot remain here in safety and comfort. . . . There is but one path to safety, one road to future existence as a Nation. That path is open before you. Make a treaty of cession. Give up these lands and go over beyond the great Father of Waters [Mississippi River].[108]

Major Ridge's plea moved many of the older chiefs to tears, and they vowed to support the treaty. The Ridge-Boudinot committee approved the deal on December 28, 1835, and the next day, at Boudinot's house, committee members signed the Treaty of New Echota. They were well aware of how unpopular the treaty would be with the tribe, and of the Cherokee law declaring cession of territory a capital crime.[109] Major Ridge, who had helped kill Doublehead for ceding territory contrary to tribal law, announced after making his mark on the document, "I have signed my death warrant."[110] Boudinot also thought he was risking his life by signing, but asked, "What is a man worth who is not willing to die for his people?"[111]

When Chief Ross, then in Washington, learned what had happened, he immediately sought to persuade the Jackson administration that the negotiations at New Echota were illegitimate. Presenting Secretary of War Cass with a petition signed by almost 14,000 Cherokee against the treaty (hastily assembled by Assistant Chief George Lowrey), Ross hoped that federal lawmakers would reject the treaty, as they had in the case of his brother's treaty the year before. Unmoved by Ross's pleas, Jackson backed the New Echota treaty and pressed for its ratification in the U.S. Senate, where it had substantial support. Elbert Herring, commissioner of Indian Affairs, wrote to Ross: "You are laboring under extreme misapprehension in believing that you have been recognized . . . as the duly constituted representatives of the Cherokee Nation."[112]

The Senate Votes

The U.S. Senate began debating the Treaty of New Echota on March 7, 1836, and the next day Chief Ross delivered a long memorial against its ratification. "This instrument purports to be a contract with the Cherokee people," he declared, "when in fact it has been agreed upon, in direct violation of their will, wishes, and interests, by a few unauthorized individuals of the Nation. . . ." After reviewing the sequence of events that had led to the document, he argued that it was "a fraudulent treaty, false upon its face," and begged senators not to "drive us from the land of our nativity and from the tombs of our Fathers and of our Mothers."[113]

Discussion within the Senate chamber remained confidential, but Ross clearly had supporters at the Capitol. Lawmakers who had opposed the 1830 removal law condemned the treaty as unjust. Senator Daniel Webster of Massachusetts called it "a great wrong."[114] Henry Clay, senator from Kentucky, announced, "I tremble that God is just and that His justice cannot sleep forever," quoting (in part) what Thomas Jefferson had once said regarding slavery. There were even opponents among those directly involved in the removal process. Major William M. Davis, who operated inside the borders of the Cherokee Nation enrolling Cherokee for removal, had written to Secretary Cass that the "treaty is no treaty at all . . . it would be instantly rejected by 9/10 of [the Cherokees] and I believe 19/20 of them."[115]

The final Senate vote on the treaty came on May 18, 1836. At the last moment Senator Clay attempted to introduce an amendment that would have nullified the whole treaty, but this was rejected. Southern and western senators largely supported the treaty, despite the considerable passion of its opponents. One southern senator, Thomas Hart Benton of Missouri, later explained that he hoped it would transform "Indian soil to slave soil."[116] Nonetheless, Chief Ross believed the treaty would fail, based on his discussions with numerous senators.[117] With the vote commencing in the Senate chamber, the result would be known soon enough.

NOTES

1. Brian Hicks, *Toward the Setting Sun: John Ross, the Cherokees, and the Trail of Tears* (New York: Atlantic Monthly Press, 2011), 279; Samuel Carter III, *Cherokee Sunset: A Nation Betrayed* (Garden City, NY: Doubleday, 1976), 189; A. J. Langguth, *Driven West: Andrew Jackson and the Trail of Tears to the Civil War* (New York: Simon and Schuster, 2010), 232; Gary E. Moulton, *John Ross: Cherokee Chief* (Athens: University of Georgia Press, 1978), 72.
2. Quotation from Tennessee's Hugh Lawson White in Carter, *Cherokee Sunset,* 197.

3. For estimates of North American population at the time of the early European explorers, see Charles C. Mann, *1491: New Revelations of the Americas before Columbus* (New York: Knopf, 2005), 132–133.

4. Carter, *Cherokee Sunset*, 8; Grace Steele Woodward, *The Cherokees* (Norman: University of Oklahoma Press, 1963), 18–19, 21–22; Alvin M. Josephy Jr., *500 Nations: An Illustrated History of North American Indians* (New York: Knopf, 1994), 232; Russell Thornton, *The Cherokees: A Population History* (Lincoln: University of Nebraska Press, 1990), 11–12, 15–18, 21–23, 28–30, 42.

5. Jill Lepore, *The Name of War: King Philip's War and the Origin of American Identity* (New York: Knopf, 1998), xiv–xvi, xi–xiii, 183–184; Colin G. Calloway, "Introduction: Surviving the Dark Ages," in *After King Philip's War: Presence and Persistence in Indian New England,* ed. Colin G. Calloway (Hanover: University Press of New England, 1997), 1–4; Eric B. Schultz and Michael J. Tougias, *King Philip's War: The History and Legacy of America's Forgotten Conflict* (Woodstock, VT: Countryman Press, 1999), 1–5.

6. Theda Perdue and Michael D. Green, *The Cherokee Nation and the Trail of Tears* (New York: Penguin, 2007), 15–16; Robert V. Remini, *Andrew Jackson and His Indian Wars* (New York: Penguin Group, 2001), 10.

7. Carter, *Cherokee Sunset*, 7.

8. The treaty and response are available via the British History Online website at http://www.british-history.ac.uk/cal-state-papers/colonial/america-west-indies/vol37/pp291-298. Robert J. Conley, *The Cherokee Nation: A History* (Albuquerque: University of New Mexico Press, 2005), 34–35, argues that the Cherokee delegates probably did not compose this response themselves.

9. Conley, *Cherokee Nation*, 45–53. For detailed accounts of Anglo–Cherokee relations during the French and Indian War, see John Oliphant, *Peace and War on the Anglo-Cherokee Frontier 1756–63* (Baton Rouge: Louisiana State University Press, 2001); Tyler Boulware, *Deconstructing the Cherokee Nation: Town, Region, and Nation among Eighteenth-Century Cherokees* (Gainesville: University Press of Florida, 2011), chaps. 5–6; and Woodward, *The Cherokees*, 69–79.

10. Perdue and Green, *Cherokee Nation*, 17–18; Thornton, *The Cherokees*, 40–41.

11. Carter, *Cherokee Sunset*, 10; Woodward, *The Cherokees*, 41, 96–98; Thornton, *The Cherokees*, 41. For a detailed account of the Cherokee during the Revolution, see Boulware, *Deconstructing the Cherokee Nation*, chap. 8.

12. Perdue and Green, *Cherokee Nation*, 19; Woodward, *Cherokees*, 97–101; Carter, *Cherokee Sunset*, 10.

13. The treaty is reprinted in Charles J. Kappler, ed., *Indian Affairs: Laws and Treaties,* vol. 2 (Washington: GPO, 1904), 8–11, available at http://digital.library.okstate.edu/kappler/vol2/treaties/che0008.htm.

14. Charles F. Wilkinson, "Indian Tribes and the American Constitution," in *Indians in American History,* ed. Frederick E. Hoxie (Wheeling, IL: Harlan Davidson, 1988), 119.

15. Carter, *Cherokee Sunset*, 12–13, quotation at 13. Knox's letter is available via the National Archives at http://founders.archives.gov/documents/Washington/05-03-02

-0067. The Cherokee complaint, dated May 19, is at http://founders.archives.gov /documents/Washington/05-02-02-0237.

16. Carter, *Cherokee Sunset*, 12–13. The treaty and amendment are reprinted in Kappler, *Indian Affairs*, 2:29–33, available at http://digital.library.okstate.edu/kappler/vol2 /treaties/che0029.htm.

17. Perdue and Green, *Cherokee Nation*, 23–29.

18. Carter, *Cherokee Sunset*, 13, 21; Perdue and Green, *Cherokee Nation*, 30.

19. Quoted in Woodward, *Cherokees*, 116. See also John R. Finger, *Tennessee Frontiers: Three Regions in Transition* (Bloomington: University of Indiana Press, 2001), 146–147.

20. Carter, *Cherokee Sunset*, 13–14; Woodward, *Cherokees*, 115–117, quotation at 116. See Remini, *Andrew Jackson*, 32–35, for a more detailed account of the Chickamauga conflict.

21. Remini, *Andrew Jackson*, 43–44, quotation from a letter to Jackson from Tennessee governor John Sevier on 44.

22. The treaty is reprinted in Kappler, *Indian Affairs*, 2:51–55, available at http://digital .library.okstate.edu/kappler/Vol2/treaties/che0051.htm.

23. Perdue and Green, *Cherokee Nation*, 31.

24. Carter, *Cherokee Sunset*, 27–28; Langguth, *Driven West*, 28–29; George R. Lamplugh, "Yazoo Land Fraud," available at http://www.georgiaencyclopedia.org/articles /history-archaeology/yazoo-land-fraud.

25. Perdue and Green, *Cherokee Nation*, 31; Carter, *Cherokee Sunset*, 29; Woodward, *Cherokees*, 128–129.

26. Perdue and Green, *Cherokee Nation*, 37.

27. For a detailed account of this confrontation, see Hicks, *Toward the Setting Sun*, 18–25.

28. Perdue and Green, *Cherokee Nation*, 37–38, quotation at 38.

29. Ibid., 38–39; Carter, *Cherokee Sunset*, 29; Hicks, *Toward the Setting Sun*, 33–36; Remini, *Andrew Jackson*, 115. Quotation in Perdue and Green, *Cherokee Nation*, 39.

30. Hicks, *Toward the Setting Sun*, 53–60; Josephy, *500 Nations*, 308–317.

31. Perdue and Green, *Cherokee Nation*, 10, 16, 36; John Demos, "The Tried and the True: Native American Women Confronting Colonization," in *No Small Change: A History of Women in the United States*, ed. Nancy Cott (New York: Oxford University Press, 2000), 36; Hicks, *Toward the Setting Sun*, 32; *Laws of the Cherokee Nation* (Tahlequah, Cherokee Nation, 1852).

32. Carter, *Cherokee Sunset*, 54–55.

33. Perdue and Green, *Cherokee Nation*, 29–30.

34. Quoted in John Demos, *The Heathen School: A Story of Hope and Betrayal in the Age of the Early Republic* (New York: Knopf, 2014), 213–214. See also Demos, "Tried and the True," 36–38.

35. Perdue and Green, *Cherokee Nation*, 35–36; Josephy, *500 Nations*, 322; Hicks, *Toward the Setting Sun*, 116, 28–31; Demos, *The Heathen School*, 200–203.

36. Perdue and Green, *Cherokee Nation*, 32–34; Demos, *The Heathen School*, 146–148.

37. Jill Lepore, *A is for American: Letters and Other Characters in the Newly United States* (New York: Knopf, 2002), 65–67, 74–75; Barry O'Connell, "Literacy and Colonization: The Case of the Cherokees," in *An Extensive Republic: Print, Culture, and Society in the New Nation; A History of the Book in America*, vol. 2, ed. Robert A. Gross and Mary Kelley (Chapel Hill: University of North Carolina Press, 2010), 510–515.

38. Lepore, *A is for American*, 81–84; Perdue and Green, *Cherokee Nation*, 75–76.

39. Demos, *The Heathen School*, 149–154, 175–195, 219–221.

40. Remini, *Andrew Jackson*, 14. This anecdote originates from Jackson's childhood neighbor, Susan Alexander. Alexander reported that the family member killed was Jackson's oldest brother, but this could not have been accurate. Both of Jackson's older brothers died during the Revolutionary War.

41. Albigence W. Putnam, *History of Middle Tennessee* (Nashville, 1859), 317–318, quoted in Remini, *Andrew Jackson*, 27.

42. Remini, *Andrew Jackson*, 34–47.

43. Ibid., 55–61; Carter, *Cherokee Sunset*, 2.

44. Remini, *Andrew Jackson*, 62; Carter, *Cherokee Sunset*, 33–34. Quotation in Remini from a letter to Cherokee Principal Chief Pathkiller (23 Oct. 1813).

45. Remini, *Andrew Jackson*, 62–92; Hicks, *Toward the Setting Sun*, 61–63, 71–72; Langguth, *Driven West*, 35. Fort Jackson was an old French fort, rebuilt in 1814 and named after Jackson himself (Remini, *Andrew Jackson*, 81). The treaty is reprinted in Kappler, *Indian Affairs*, 2:107–110, available at http://digital.library.okstate.edu/kappler/Vol2/treaties/cre0107.htm.

46. Remini, *Andrew Jackson*, 86, 94–95.

47. Ibid., 95–98, quotation from a letter of 15 June 1815.

48. Statement from Creek leaders of 22 Jan. 1816, quoted in ibid., 102.

49. Hicks, *Toward the Setting Sun*, 84–87; Carter, *Cherokee Sunset*, 35–36. The treaty is reprinted in Kappler, *Indian Affairs*, 2:125–126, available at http://digital.library.okstate.edu/kappler/Vol2/treaties/che0125.htm.

50. Quoted in Remini, *Andrew Jackson*, 105.

51. Perdue and Green, *Cherokee Nation*, 50; Remini, *Andrew Jackson*, 105.

52. Quoted in Remini, *Andrew Jackson*, 110–111.

53. Ibid., 111–114. The treaties are reprinted in Kappler, *Indian Affairs*, 2:133–137, available at http://digital.library.okstate.edu/kappler/Vol2/treaties/che0133.htm and . . . /chi0135.htm. A third tribe, the Choctaws, also settled Treaty of Fort Jackson objections in a separate meeting.

54. Remini, *Andrew Jackson*, 114–115, 120–121; Hicks, *Toward the Setting Sun*, 95.

55. Quoted in Remini, *Andrew Jackson*, 122–123.

56. Ibid., 124–125, quotation at 125.

57. Ibid., 126.

58. Ibid., 127–129; Hicks, *Toward the Setting Sun*, 98; Thornton, *The Cherokees*, 55; Carter, *Cherokee Sunset*, 38. The treaty is reprinted in Kappler, *Indian Affairs*, 2:140–144, available

at http://digital.library.okstate.edu/kappler/Vol2/treaties/che0140.htm; Lepore, *A Is for American*, 86, 89.

59. Carter, *Cherokee Sunset*, 40; Hicks, *Toward the Setting Sun*, 101–105; Thornton, *The Cherokees*, 55. The treaty is reprinted in Kappler, *Indian Affairs*, 2:177–181, available at http://digital.library.okstate.edu/kappler/Vol2/treaties/che0177.htm; Langguth, *Driven West*, 36. Hicks estimates the Cherokee had "about eight million acres" left, or 12,500 square miles (*Toward the Setting Sun*, 105), whereas Carter offers a higher estimate of "approximately ten million acres," or 15,625 square miles (*Cherokee Sunset*, 40).

60. Carter, *Cherokee Sunset*, 40, 55; Perdue and Green, *Cherokee Nation*, 55.

61. Quoted in Perdue and Green, *Cherokee Nation*, 56.

62. Langguth, *Driven West*, 39. The case is available online at http://supreme.justia.com /cases/federal/us/21/543/case.html.

63. Carter, *Cherokee Sunset*, 56–57; Hicks, *Toward the Setting Sun*, 122–128.

64. Carter, *Cherokee Sunset*, 57–58, quotation at 58; Hicks, *Toward the Setting Sun*, 132–138.

65. Hicks, *Toward the Setting Sun*, 138–140, quotation at 140.

66. Carter, *Cherokee Sunset*, 64, 68–70, 70–71, 74–75. The constitution appears in *Laws of the Cherokee Nation*, 118–130.

67. Quoted in Carter, *Cherokee Sunset*, 71, 73.

68. *Cherokee Phoenix* (6 Mar. 1828), quoted in ibid., 76.

69. Carter, *Cherokee Sunset*, 83, 83–84; Hicks, *Toward the Setting Sun*, 166–167.

70. Carter, *Cherokee Sunset*, 88, 89–90.

71. Hicks, *Toward the Setting Sun*, 178–180; Carter, *Cherokee Sunset*, 91–96. Quotation from the *Phoenix* (10 Feb. 1830).

72. The speech is available via the American Presidency Project of the University of California, Santa Barbara, at http://www.presidency.ucsb.edu/ws/index.php?pid=29471.

73. The bill reported by the Senate Indian Affairs Committee on 22 Feb. 1830 (S. 102, 21st Cong, 1st Sess.) is available online at https://memory.loc.gov/cgi-bin/ampage ?collId=llsb&fileName=011/llsb011.db&recNum=223. See also Senate Committee on Indian Affairs, Report of 22 Feb. 1830, available at https://memory.loc.gov/cgi-bin /ampage?collId=llrd&fileName=009/llrd009.db&recNum=551.

74. Ronald M. Satz, *American Indian Policy in the Jacksonian Era* (Norman: University of Oklahoma Press, 2002), 21–23; Carter, *Cherokee Sunset*, 96; Hicks, *Toward the Setting Sun*, 181–182; Langguth, *Driven West*, 148.

75. *Register of Debates in Congress*, vol. 6, 311, online at http://memory.loc.gov/ammem /amlaw/lwrd.html.

76. Ibid., 325, 339.

77. Ibid., 1010, 1016.

78. Ibid., 1135. The final text of the law is available at http://www.civics-online.org /library/formatted/texts/indian_act.html.

79. Carter, *Cherokee Sunset*, 102, 101; Hicks, *Toward the Setting Sun*, 186, 187.

80. Hicks, *Toward the Setting Sun*, 187–192; Perdue and Green, *Cherokee Nation*, 81, 79.

81. Art. III, §2.

82. 30 U.S. 1 (1831), pp. 11–12. Opinion available online at laws.findlaw.com/us/30/1.html.

83. Quoted in Carter, *Cherokee Sunset*, 117.

84. Ibid., 106.

85. Perdue and Green, *Cherokee Nation*, 84–85; Hicks, *Toward the Setting Sun*, 198–199; Tim Alan Garrison, *The Legal Ideology of Removal: The Southern Judiciary and the Sovereignty of Native American Nations* (Athens: University of Georgia Press, 2002), 171–172. One of the missionaries was released because, as a U.S. postmaster, he was a federal employee; the Jackson administration fired him, allowing him to be rearrested.

86. 31 U.S. 515 (1832), p. 560. Opinion available online at laws.findlaw.com/us/31/515.html.

87. Quotations from Hicks, *Toward the Setting Sun*, 214–215, and Carter, *Cherokee Sunset*, 131.

88. Carter, *Cherokee Sunset*, 132; Hicks, *Toward the Setting Sun*, 214. Rumors abounded that Jackson said, "John Marshall has made his decision, now let him enforce it." However, this quotation appears to have been invented by the editor Horace Greeley, reporting on the president's inaction after the decision. Langguth writes, "Jackson may not have put it so tersely, but Greeley's version reflected his sentiments" (Langguth, *Driven West*, 190). See also Hicks, *Toward the Setting Sun*, 214.

89. Perdue and Green, *Cherokee Nation*, 86; Presidential general election, all states, 1832 summary (2003), available at *CQ Voting and Elections Collection*, http://library.cqpress.com/elections/AVg1832-1us1.

90. Amos Kendall quoted in Carter, *Cherokee Sunset*, 135.

91. Hicks, *Toward the Setting Sun*, 218–223.

92. Carter, *Cherokee Sunset*, 136–137, quotation at 137.

93. Hicks, *Toward the Setting Sun*, 222–224; Carter, *Cherokee Sunset*, 137–141.

94. Hicks, *Toward the Setting Sun*, 227–231, quotation at 230.

95. Ibid., 231–237, quotation at 234; Carter, *Cherokee Sunset*, 149–150.

96. Hicks, *Toward the Setting Sun*, 240–241; Carter, *Cherokee Sunset*, 151–152.

97. Hicks, *Toward the Setting Sun*, 242–244; Carter, *Cherokee Sunset*, 152–153; Langguth, *Driven West*, 214–215, quotation at 215.

98. Carter, *Cherokee Sunset*, 153; Hicks, *Toward the Setting Sun*, 244.

99. Hicks, *Toward the Setting Sun*, 246–248. Quotation in Carter, *Cherokee Sunset*, 164.

100. Carter, *Cherokee Sunset*, 164–165; Hicks, *Toward the Setting Sun*, 250.

101. Remini, *Andrew Jackson*, 263–265. Remini provides the most detailed account of this negotiation, but says that it occurred in February 1834. However, several other authors are clear that it took place in 1835 (Carter, *Cherokee Sunset*, 169; Hicks, *Toward the Setting Sun*, 252; Langguth, *Driven West*, 219; Woodward, *Cherokees*, 179). Remini's footnotes and chronology suggest that he may have made a typographical error.

102. Perdue and Green, *Cherokee Nation*, 105; Carter, *Cherokee Sunset*, 168–170, quotation at 169. See also Hicks, *Toward the Setting Sun*, 252–253, 255.

103. Hicks, *Toward the Setting Sun*, 256; Carter, *Cherokee Sunset*, 173; Woodward, *Cherokees*, 182.

104. Hicks, *Toward the Setting Sun*, 257–261; Woodward, *Cherokees*, 182–183.

105. Langguth, *Driven West*, 229; Carter, *Cherokee Sunset*, 184–185; Woodward, *Cherokees*, 186–187. On Nov. 7, 1835, after the Council meeting had ended, the Georgia Guard arrested Ross and accused him of interfering with a census of the Cherokee. He was released on Nov. 16, thanks to the assistance of President Ridge. See Hicks, *Toward the Setting Sun*, 269–276, for a detailed account.

106. Perdue and Green, *Cherokee Nation*, 110.

107. Carter, *Cherokee Sunset*, 189; Hicks, *Toward the Setting Sun*, 277–279; Langguth, *Driven West*, 232–234; Woodward, *Cherokees*, 190.

108. Quoted in Hicks, *Toward the Setting Sun*, 280 and Carter, *Cherokee Sunset*, 189.

109. The following resolution was approved by the Cherokee Council in October 1829: "*Whereas,* a law has been in existence for many years, but not committed to writing, that if any citizen or citizens of this Nation shall treat and dispose of any lands belonging to this Nation without special permission from the national authorities, he or they, shall suffer death, therefore, *Resolved by the Committee and Council in General Council* . . . That any person or persons who shall, contrary to the will and consent of the Legislative Council of this Nation, in General Council convened, enter into a treaty with any Commissioner or Commissioners of the U. States or any officers instructed for the purpose, and agree to sell or dispose of any part or portion of the National lands defined in the Constitution of this Nation, he or they so offending upon conviction before any of the Circuit Judges or the Supreme Court, *shall suffer death* . . . [and] any person or persons who shall violate the provisions of this act and shall refuse by resistance to appear at the place designated for trial, or abscond, are hereby declared to be outlaws, and any person or persons citizens of this Nation may kill him or them so offending in any manner most convenient." *Laws of the Cherokee Nation*, 136–137.

110. Langguth, *Driven West*, 234–235; Carter, *Cherokee Sunset*, 190; Hicks, *Toward the Setting Sun*, 282. The treaty is reprinted in Kappler, *Indian Affairs*, 2:439–449, available at http://digital.library.okstate.edu/kappler/Vol2/treaties/che0439.htm.

111. Quoted in Demos, *The Heathen School*, 247.

112. Hicks, *Toward the Setting Sun*, 284–286, quotation at 286.

113. Reprinted in Gary Moulton, ed., *The Papers of John Ross* (Norman: University of Oklahoma Press, 1985), 1:394–413.

114. Quotation in Carter, *Cherokee Sunset*, 196.

115. Quoted in Robert A. Rutland, "Political Background of the Cherokee Treaty of New Echota," *Chronicles of Oklahoma* 27, no. 4 (Dec. 1949): 405. Originally in C. C. Royce, *The Cherokee Nation of Indians* (1883).

116. Quoted in Rutland, "Political Background," 406. Originally in Benton's book *Thirty Years' View, 1820–1850*, published in 1854–1856.

117. Carter, *Cherokee Sunset*, 197.

·{ 4 }·

Banking and Politics in Antebellum
New York (1838)

IN MID-APRIL 1838, when a bill to overhaul the New York banking system was presented to Governor William L. Marcy, banks throughout the state were still refusing to redeem their banknotes in specie (gold and silver coins). This was a problem because privately issued banknotes—not government-printed dollar bills—circulated as the most common form of money at the time, and the main reason banknotes were accepted as money is that people believed they could be converted to specie on demand.

The weakness of several state banks, combined with a nationwide financial panic, had led to the abandonment of specie convertibility in 1837 and had only intensified New Yorkers' perennial calls for banking reform. Amid the financial calamity, a Whig-controlled Assembly was elected, deposing the long-standing majority of Democratic-Republicans, known since the mid-1830s simply as Democrats.* The new Whig lawmakers responded to the

* The Democratic-Republican Party was born from the political philosophy of Thomas Jefferson and James Madison in the early 1790s. Although Madison had been a Federalist during the debate over ratification of the Constitution in 1787–1788 (meaning that he favored ratification), the Democratic-Republican Party opposed the Federalist Party of Alexander Hamilton, also established in the early 1790s. By the end of the period covered in this case (and particularly after 1832), the Democratic-Republican Party had evolved into the Democratic Party and its members were commonly referred to as Democrats. The Whig Party, dating from about 1834, was founded by former Federalists and Democratic-Republicans who opposed President Andrew Jackson and the Democratic Party.

crisis and the cries of a frustrated public with the radical bill that now sat on Governor Marcy's desk. The bill offered a "free banking" solution that, if enacted, would mark a major departure from the chartering regime that had long dominated New York banking.[1]

Under the chartering system, banks were required to obtain specific approval from the legislature before they could open. By 1838 many New Yorkers had come to view this as an inefficient and crooked process that delivered banking monopolies to the powerful and rewarded politicians with kickbacks. This popular belief was supported by widespread corruption allegations, the occasional fraud trials, and the connection of the chartering system with the Democratic-Republican bloc known as the Albany Regency. In addition to the allegations of impropriety, the Albany Regency, which controlled New York politics through most of the 1820s and 1830s, had not always been responsive to New Yorkers' repeated demands for more banking capital, and over time both the chartering process and the political machine had fallen out of public favor.[2]

The free banking bill put forth by the newly ascendant Whigs in 1838 sought to remove the "monopolistic" aspects of the state banking system by circumventing the chartering mechanism altogether, essentially allowing anyone with sufficient capital to open a bank, even without specific approval from the legislature. The bill also contained a novel limitation on banknotes, mandating that every note issued be fully backed by high-grade bonds or mortgages. Supporters believed that their plan would allow banks to sprout up wherever they were needed, guarantee the convertibility of banknotes at all times, and protect the economy against inflation.[3]

Skeptics, including Governor Marcy, a member of the crumbling Albany Regency, had reservations about displacing the chartering mechanism. Marcy's Democrats had long relied on their capacity to grant special bank charters as a bulwark of party strength and discipline. In addition, from a policy standpoint, the governor had previously stated his belief that note-issuing entities should be required to obtain government charters, and he had expressed apprehension about chartering any new banks during the financial chaos of the late 1830s.[4] A rush of new banks was likely to be unleashed if the free banking bill became law, though how many new banks and how much new banking capital would be created was unknown. The decision facing Governor Marcy was not easy: he could quell public ire by signing this unproven set of proposals into law, or he could veto the legislation and seek a less extreme response to the crisis.

The Chartering Process

During the late eighteenth century, numerous organizations—including banks—sought corporate charters from state legislatures because the corporate form offered a number of advantages over the type of partnership that was then typical of most American firms. Agreements made by any member of a partnership were binding on the firm, which meant that a dissenting party could cause trouble for his partners. A corporation could eliminate this problem by designating a management team to conduct business on its behalf. Unlike partnerships, moreover, corporations could survive the death of a founding member, had the ability to sue and be sued like an individual, and often (but not always) afforded limited liability to shareholders.[5]

States assumed the power to issue corporate charters after the Revolution, and at the outset more than 95 percent of charters were granted to companies that promised to develop vital infrastructure—both physical and financial. At that time corporate charters were official acts of legislation that were drawn up, debated, and voted upon by members of the state legislature. The process of chartering a corporation was thus akin to enacting a law. By the end of the eighteenth century, state legislatures had granted corporate charters to at least 29 banks, 32 water supply companies, 33 insurance companies, 66 canal companies, 69 toll-bridge companies, and 72 turnpike companies.[6]

Although no manufacturing companies obtained corporate charters in New York State over the first seven years of the nineteenth century, twenty-four secured charters from 1808 to 1810.[7] The process proved highly political. In the words of one historian, "Lawmakers enjoyed complete discretion over the process, often wielding their authority with all the subtlety of a sledgehammer. Special favors, connections, and payoffs frequently made the difference in a rough-and-tumble political system where successful appeals were more the exception than the rule."[8]

In 1811, New York passed "the world's first general incorporation law for manufacturing companies."[9] The "Act Relative to Incorporations for

Manufacturing Purposes" applied to firms in the glass, metal, paint, and textile industries with capitalizations up to $100,000.[10] It enabled entrepreneurs in the relevant manufacturing sectors to bypass the legislature, guaranteeing applicants permission to incorporate so long as they met the minimal standards specified in the law.

In banking and other sectors, however, those seeking a corporate charter in early nineteenth-century New York still had to secure a special act of the legislature to get one. The typical bank charter limited "total amounts of debts, over and above the moneys actually deposited in the vaults of the bank" to three times the paid-in capital, fixed the bank's capital stock at a given sum, designated the location where the bank could operate, laid out the bank's governing structure, prohibited the bank from trading in any type of goods or stocks, and held the bank legally accountable for the paper money, or banknotes, that it issued.[11]

The banknotes emitted by individual banks were essentially "non-interest-bearing IOUs, and these notes constituted the bulk of the circulating media" in the antebellum United States. Banknotes thus served as a convenient form of money, which was relied upon for making transactions. The farther a note traveled from its point of issue, the greater the effort required to redeem it. As a result, banknotes typically traded at discounts related to their distance from the issuing bank. In addition, because a banknote was only as secure as the bank that issued it, discounts also reflected the issuing bank's perceived risk of failure. Throughout the antebellum era, newspapers published the going discount rates on the banknotes that traded in their regions. New York's earliest charters mandated that banks redeem their notes on demand either in specie or in another bank's notes. After 1816 banknotes had to be redeemed in specie alone if so demanded by the note holder.[12]

The Politics of Bank Chartering in Early New York State

The chartering process was always subject to extensive political maneuvering whereby "lawmakers were able to favor their friends and allies in the way they distributed (or refused to distribute) charters."[13] This system of patronage was so common that "early banks . . . were popularly identified by their founders' political affiliations."[14]

Federalists vs. Democratic-Republicans

In 1784 the young lawyer and Revolutionary War hero Alexander Hamilton drafted articles of association for the Bank of New York. Hamilton's bank was only the "third organized bank in the United States," after Philadelphia's Bank of North America, which had been chartered by the Continental Congress in December 1781, and Boston's Bank of Massachusetts, which was granted a state charter in February 1784.[15]

Despite repeated appeals for a charter, the Bank of New York operated without official state sanction for seven years. The bank was finally granted a charter in 1791, marking the first time that New York State lawmakers had chartered a homegrown bank.[16] Shortly before the Bank of New York was granted its charter, the federal government established the Bank of the United States, also the brainchild of Alexander Hamilton, who now served as Treasury secretary. In 1792 a branch of the Bank of the United States opened on Wall Street, not far from the Bank of New York. For the next seven years, these would be the only two banks in New York City.[17]

The Bank of Albany became the state's second homegrown bank to receive a charter, in 1792, and the next year a charter was granted to a bank in Hudson, New York. The second New York City bank to earn a state charter was the Bank of the Manhattan Company, an institution established by Democratic-Republican Aaron Burr, whose political and personal differences with the Federalist Alexander Hamilton were well known. Burr had tried several times in the 1790s to charter a Democratic-Republican-controlled bank, but the Federalist-dominated legislature repeatedly denied his requests. So in 1799 Burr turned his attention to obtaining a charter for a completely different type of company.[18]

New York City had suffered a particularly frightening outbreak of yellow fever in 1798, and the source of the scourge was believed to be the city's "unwholesome water."[19] Burr, then a member of the state legislature, drafted a bill to charter a company that could deliver clean water to the city. Hopeful that this proposed company could rid New York City of the recurrent deadly outbreaks, the state legislature approved Burr's plan with bipartisan support.[20] But the bill did not simply establish a waterworks; rather, it established a company with a $2 million capitalization that could invest any "surplus capital" over and above its water delivery expenses "in the purchase of public stocks or in any other moneyed transactions." Although the Manhattan Company had laid "twenty miles of wooden pipe" and provided clean water to some 1,400 homes by 1802, the company's water supply duties quickly became a secondary concern. Within "the first year of its existence $1,000,000 was employed in banking," and thus was born the Bank of the Manhattan Company.[21]

Federalists, and Hamilton in particular, were indignant, not only because they felt Burr had exploited public sentiment to further his own personal and political interests, but also because the Bank of New York now had to contend with a powerful Democratic-Republican-controlled rival. The Manhattan Company's $2 million capitalization was twice that of the Bank of New York, and unlike its older competitor, its "charter was perpetual" and lacked the typical restrictions of a bank charter.[22]

Burr's use of the Manhattan Company charter to create a large new bank drew the ire of many citizens. Said Jabez Hammond, himself a Democratic-Republican and New Yorker, "It is probable that in 1799 many [Democratic-Republicans] voted the Federal ticket in consequence of their dissatisfaction with the manner in which the law granting banking powers to the Manhattan Company had been smuggled through the legislature and for the reason that Colonel Burr, who was confessedly the contriver and the agent who effected that extraordinary measure, was then a candidate."[23]

But in spite of the anti–Manhattan Company sentiments of 1799, Democratic-Republicans regained favor and won control of the New York legislature from Federalists in 1803, mirroring a trend that was occurring throughout much of the nation.[24] That year, state lawmakers heard a charter request for a second bank in Albany. This request came from a group of Democratic-Republicans who claimed that the Bank of Albany was a Federalist-dominated institution that was "oppressive" to Democratic-Republican businessmen.[25] With their Jeffersonian roots, Democratic-Republicans were typically more averse to banking than were Federalists. However, certain pro-bank Democratic-Republicans believed that "banks, *in the proper hands* . . . could be great levelers, tremendous aids to respectable, trustworthy yeomen, mechanics, and traders in need of a little working capital."[26] Of course, "the proper hands" referred to those of fellow party members. And thus, with a little help from a backroom deal that allowed some lawmakers to "subscribe for a certain number of [the bank's] shares," the legislature granted the charter, thereby incorporating the Democratic-Republican-controlled New York State Bank in Albany in 1803.[27]

The Bank of America

By January 1810, New York State had chartered nine banks with a combined capitalization of $6,215,000. Over the next four years, fourteen additional banks would be chartered, and total banking capitalization would nearly quadruple to $22,215,000. This rapid increase was sparked largely by Congress's decision to allow the charter of the Bank of the United States to expire in March 1811. In 1812, in an effort to fill the sizable banking void, New York shareholders of the now-defunct national bank applied for a state charter. They sought to reincorporate the New York City branch of the Bank of the United States as the state-chartered Bank of America.[28]

The largely Federalist sponsors of the Bank of America sought a capitalization of $6,000,000, which would make the institution the biggest state bank in the nation and give an edge to New York City in its "financial and commercial rivalry" with Philadelphia.[29] Democratic-Republicans, including Governor Daniel D. Tompkins, were wary of such a large Federalist presence, and New York's existing banks vigorously opposed a rival institution whose capitalization would be three times as large as that of its nearest competitor.[30]

To help build support for the Bank of America, supporters offered concessions, including a payment of $600,000 to the state, "of which $400,000 was for the use and encouragement of common schools, $100,000 for roads and navigation, and $100,000 for the encouragement of literature."[31] It was also stipulated that the bank would lend the state $2,000,000, "at any time it might require it."[32] By the time the state assembly approved the charter in late March 1812, allegations of bribery and other unethical behavior had surfaced. Before the senate could vote on the matter, an incensed Governor Tompkins prorogued* the legislature until May 21, "practically the maximum period for which he had authority."[33] This marked the first and only time that the power of prorogation had been exercised in New York State

---

* "Proroguing" means officially suspending or concluding a legislative session, but without dissolving the legislative body itself. New York governors would lose the power of prorogation when the state amended its constitution in 1821.

since the height of the American Revolution.[34] Although Tompkins had used this authority in an effort to draw attention to the accusations of corruption surrounding the Bank of America's chartering, it appears that his tactic only intensified the legislature's ill feelings toward him. When the legislative session resumed eight weeks later, the charter quickly passed.[35]

The Restraining Acts and the Politics of Scarcity

Up until the Restraining Acts of 1804 and 1818, banks were not required to obtain charters; charters were often sought, however, because they "relieved . . . shareholders of personal liability" and "conferred [upon banks] monopoly privileges and an honorific legal status." With passage of the Restraining Act of 1804, it became "illegal for any person 'unauthorized by law' to become a proprietor of a bank or member of a banking company."[36] In 1818 lawmakers amended the Restraining Act, making it illegal for individuals to engage in the practice of banking on their own, even apart from a larger organization.[37] Through these laws the legislature made banking services the exclusive purview of state-sanctioned banks, further enhancing the value of a bank charter.

The desirability of a state charter gave the legislature great leverage, which lawmakers often used to demand concessions from banks. Typically lawmakers required banks to pledge a certain amount of money or allot a given amount of stock to the state or its agencies.[38] The City Bank of New York's charter of 1812, for example, mandated a payment of $120,000 toward "the common school fund of New York."[39] Other charters simply exacted an un-earmarked fee—or "bonus"—from banks, such as that of the Fulton Bank in 1824, which mandated that the bank pay the state $133,000 for its charter.[40]

But the power wielded by the legislators in the chartering process was not always used to serve a public purpose. In 1805 the Merchants' Bank applied for a charter. The resulting partisan debate was so heated that lawmakers "came to actual fisticuffs within the senatorial precincts."[41] Although the charter eventually passed by three votes, two senators were later alleged to have "accepted stock in the bank with the understanding that it was to be taken off their hands at twenty-five per cent. advance."[42]

The way in which shares in new banks were allocated presented another avenue for politicians to divert resources toward their associates and themselves. "Beginning in 1811," writes one financial historian, "every incorporation act appointed administrators charged with distributing shares in the new bank."[43] Because almost every new bank faced excess demand for its shares at the initial price, it was left to the administrators to decide who should receive shares and how many they should receive. Lawmakers typically appointed allies as commissioners, who in turn distributed stock among themselves and other party stalwarts. This practice ensured that party loyalists were rewarded and control of the banks remained in party hands. After the Seventh Ward Bank received its charter in 1833, for example, only 40 of 3,710 shares were distributed to the public; the rest were given to the commissioners' friends and various state officials.[44] Even with repeated calls to modify the distribution process, it was not ultimately reformed until 1837.[45]

Credit, Currency, and Crises

Despite widespread dissatisfaction with the chartering system, New Yorkers, eager for access to loanable funds, continuously beseeched the state legislature to charter new banks. Prior to the 1800s, most loans in America were made among family and friends.[46] But by the turn of the nineteenth century, the United States had emerged as an important developing country with a burgeoning economy, and its residents craved the regular credit and financial services that banks could supply.[47]

A bank's balance sheet typically included specie (gold and silver coins), various securities, and especially a portfolio of loans on the asset side, and banknotes and deposits (as well as bank capital) on the liability side. Banks were sometimes thought to create credit out of thin air, because most of the funds that stood behind banknotes and deposits were used to make loans, rather than kept in a vault. In fact, all bank liabilities were backed by assets. What was peculiar about banks is that a large portion of their liabilities (especially banknotes and deposits) could be liquidated on demand, whereas most of the assets (particularly the loans) could not. Bankers counted on the expectation that not all note holders and depositors would demand specie at the same time; for if they did, even the sturdiest bank would likely fail.

Most of the time, deposits were patiently held and banknotes circulated as currency in the economy, without being immediately returned for payment in specie. Yet if a bank was perceived (rightly or wrongly) to be nearing insolvency, note holders and depositors would often feel compelled to seek immediate liquidation of their claims on the bank. If they waited too long and the bank ran out of specie (and other liquid reserves), the bank would then be unable to make good on its commitments to them—at least not immediately.[48] When banks experienced such "runs," they were often forced to call in loans, which placed immense pressure on borrowers and could even lead to serious "interruptions of investment and production."[49] Such runs could also become contagious, potentially producing more generalized banking panics.

When bankers saw a run or a panic beginning to take hold, one potential response was the suspension of specie convertibility.[50] By refusing to redeem notes or deposits in specie, the banks could temporarily contain the crisis, though at the expense of "obstructing normal payments and consumption." Although suspensions proved to be a valuable protective tool for banks, they were notably unpopular among note holders and depositors and typically sanctioned by the government only during times of widespread financial emergency.[51]

For all of these reasons, banking in early nineteenth-century New York had not only great economic salience but great political significance as well.

The Albany Regency

Around 1819 the Democratic-Republican Party in New York was reorganized and whipped into a powerful bloc under the deft leadership of state legislator Martin Van Buren.[52] The resulting "party machine" was "perhaps the most efficient . . . in American history."[53] This "superbly drilled" political apparatus would come to be known as the Albany Regency and would dominate New York politics over the next two decades.[54] Van Buren and his Regency cohorts "devised a symbiosis between business and party in which both prospered."[55] Eventually this "symbiosis" would lead to the Regency's downfall, as many New Yorkers would grow to distrust the Democratic-Republican machine—in large measure because of its intimate and allegedly corrupt relationship with the business of banking.[56]

Commonly referred to as the "Little Magician" or the "Red Fox," Van Buren was a consummate politician.[57] According to one historian, "Mr Van Buren's tact was extraordinary; he had superlative skill in political manipulation and the advancement of his own interest without friction or apparent effort."[58] Van Buren's political acumen would eventually lead him to the pinnacle of American politics. He served as state senator, attorney general of New York, U.S. senator, and governor of New York, a position he quickly vacated to join Andrew Jackson's cabinet in 1829. He then served as vice president during Jackson's second term and eventually succeeded Jackson as president of the United States in 1837.[59]

By the time Van Buren first won election to the New York Senate in 1812, the Federalist Party was sufficiently weakened that many of the most important debates were taking place between rival factions of the Democratic-Republican Party.[60] It was in this atmosphere of intraparty strife that the Albany Regency began to take shape under the leadership of Van Buren.

Van Buren's chief rival during this period was DeWitt Clinton, whose uncle, George Clinton, had served as governor of New York during the Revolutionary War. DeWitt Clinton, like Van Buren, was a Democratic-Republican, but Clinton represented a traditional style of politics in which supporters showed more loyalty to individual leaders than to the party itself. Instead of granting appointments and nominations to party men alone, Clinton distributed the spoils of office to his friends, both Democratic-Republican and Federalist.[61]

For Van Buren and his group of Bucktails, as they were known, Clinton's personal style of politics was anathema. In the words of one historian, "The Bucktails asserted that a party organized about an individual or patrician family was unacceptable as it was not republican. Personal parties were not parties at all, but factions, aristocratic remnants from the deferential days of colonial politics. . . . The proper form of political organization in a democratic state, the Bucktails argued, was not a personal faction but a political party."[62]

Credited with having "developed the modern concept of a political party," Van Buren reimagined the party as a vital expression of majoritarian politics, and he actively used this new conception to "discredit both Clinton and his style of politics." Parties, the Bucktails believed, "should be democratic associations, run by the majority of the membership. It was a simple assertion, but it immediately put them in a position of strength. The ideal was virtually unassailable; to undermine the Bucktail position, critics would have to denounce republicanism itself."[63]

At the same time, Van Buren developed his political party as a highly disciplined and effective operation—more akin to a business corporation than a traditional political organization.[64] From an organizational standpoint, Clinton was simply outclassed:

> Although DeWitt Clinton was a charismatic visionary who could rally popular support for specific projects, such as the Erie Canal, he was unable to organize supporters into a unified political party. Where Clinton fell short, Martin Van Buren excelled. Van Buren's gift was his ability to transform a loose coalition of sometimes cooperative but often bickering factions into a powerful, focused, and reasonably stable political machine.[65]

Already by 1821 the Bucktails had largely taken control of the legislature; and although Clinton had been reelected as governor, "he was surrounded by Bucktails who controlled the Council of Appointment and swept the state's appointive offices of Clinton supporters, replacing them with Bucktail men. . . . By 1823 the Regency was a well-entrenched, well-organized, smoothly operating political machine—the pride of its supporters, the envy of its rivals, and the prototypical machine for the next century."[66]

For Van Buren, the reality of a disciplined political machine was in no way inconsistent with the majoritarian politics that he believed a modern political party should represent. On the contrary, the main purpose of party discipline, in his view, was to ensure that minority factions always accepted the verdict of the majority in intraparty decision making. This was the essence of the so-called caucus doctrine: "In its mature form, the caucus doctrine required minority factions in party conclaves to submit to the will of the greater number: party discussion in private was to be followed by party unity in public."[67] As a Bucktail newspaper put it, "brethren of the same principle [meet] together—the minority yield to the majority—and the result is announced as the will of the whole." In fact, party newspapers and other publications operated under the same principle. Wrote one party loyalist, "The proprietor of a party journal is entitled to all the profits and emoluments arising out of his establishment; and so far as pecuniary matters extend, none ought to control him. But . . . [t]o the political opinions and views of his party, he should ever be subservient. It is upon this principle that a party newspaper is commenced."[68]

Van Buren and his allies powerfully demonstrated their commitment to the caucus principle in 1817 when the party nominated Clinton for governor.

Many Bucktails advocated ignoring the caucus decision and bolting; their New York City allies, the Tammanyites, did just that. But Van Buren firmly believed in the caucus doctrine. . . . Under his leadership, the Bucktails supported the caucus decision. As Van Buren explained, "If we could be found capable of opposing [the caucus's] decision for no other reason than because we found ourselves in a minority, our bad faith would reduce us from our present elevated position as the main body . . . of the [Democratic-Republican] party of the State, to that of a faction."[69]

Two years later, when Clinton's faction refused to abide by a majority decision of the party, now led by the Bucktails, the latter used this transgression to "virtually excommunicate" the Clintonians from the party.[70] As Jabez Hammond later observed, the Clintonians' decision to violate the caucus principle "was the cause of [their] prostration and ruin."[71]

While highly partisan, the Albany Regency was not an ideological organization, nor did it push a particular policy agenda. "There were virtually no substantive planks in regency platforms. . . . Their basic campaign appeal was aimed at those who already identified with them, and it was simple enough: now is the time for all good men to come to the aid of their party."[72]

Central to sustaining party loyalty was the spoils system, and it was a member of the Regency—William Marcy—who first coined the phrase "to the victors belong the spoils."[73] Officials loyal to the Regency had the power to fill vast numbers of state and local offices. By placing party loyalists in these positions, the Regency was able to reward supporters, punish dissenters (by removing disloyal men from office), and extend its influence to "the remotest areas in the State."[74] As one member of the Regency explained to another in 1827, "On the subject of these appointments you know well my mind. Give them to good and true and useful friends who will enjoy the emolument if there is any, and who will use the influence to our benefit, if any influence is [conferred] by the office. This is the long and short of the rule by which to act."[75]

Even beyond their ability to allocate government positions, members of the Regency were also able to distribute significant financial resources to loyalists, particularly as a result of their authority to charter banks, so long as they retained power in Albany. Precisely because bank charters were limited in number, they could be exceedingly valuable, which in turn gave lawmakers the ability to greatly reward friends and punish enemies. The system also potentially favored party members in the allocation of credit: "As dispensers of credit, banks favored those to whom they loaned, and, if controlled by a political party, a bank could insure that party supporters were disproportionately advantaged with share ownership and, perhaps, access to credit."[76]

While leaders of the Regency clearly used their control over bank chartering to enrich loyalists and strengthen the party, they did not typically exploit the process to enrich themselves. "If they were selfish," one observer noted at the time, "they were sensible. They seldom committed an indiscretion, and personally they were above reproach." Even their fiercest enemies acknowledged that "no accusation of [direct] pecuniary impropriety was ever made."[77] One historian of New York banking has explained their behavior this way: "Although the party's leaders did not line their own pockets, they made it possible for others to line theirs. . . . Regency leaders understood that bending the system to their personal benefit would quickly alienate voters. But the party leadership realized that political machinery was fueled with money and jobs, and they distributed both to their friends and supporters."[78]

With so much at stake and so many favors being dispensed, "charges of corruption swirled around nearly every bank charter introduced between 1813 and 1821"[79]—that is, even before the Bucktails fully solidified their control of the machinery of government. But the charges of corruption continued, and in some cases even intensified, after the Regency's ascendance. Although the top leadership of the party machine generally avoided diverting funds into their own personal coffers, rank-and-file lawmakers were more likely to engage in such behavior. A revision to the state constitution in 1821 required a two-thirds majority of both houses of the legislature to pass a bank charter, ostensibly to make it more difficult for prospective bankers to buy the requisite number of votes. According to contemporary observer Jabez Hammond, however, the new two-thirds requirement only served to "increase the evil [of the chartering process], by rendering necessary a more extended system of corruption."[80] When the Chemical Bank of New York sought and received a charter three years later, allegations of impropriety were widespread. Describing an investigation of the matter, Hammond depicted the chartering process and the legislature itself as rife with corruption:

> The evidence given before the committee afforded a most disgusting picture of the depravity of the members of the legislature. . . . The attempt to corrupt, and in fact, corruption itself, was not confined to any one party. It extended to individuals of all parties, and it is not improbable that the interest of members in these applications for moneyed incorporations had an effect on the political action of some of them.[81]

Despite repeated calls for reform after the Chemical Bank episode, Regency members "used all of their efforts to prevent the passage of any long-term banking legislation that might undermine the Regency's banking alliance."[82] One economic historian has even described the Regency's relationship with the banks as one of "systematic corruption"—that is, "the idea that political actors manipulated the economic system to create economic rents that politicians could use to secure control of the government."[83]

While the Bucktails clearly played to win, and largely controlled New York politics for nearly two decades, they showed little interest in actually destroying their political opponents. They saw partisan competition as one of the foundations of a healthy and vibrant democracy.[84] To be sure, Van Buren and his compatriots "thought that the party that obtained a majority of the votes of the state should rule completely," but only "until such time as the minority party managed to convert itself into the majority party." In the view of one leading historian of the Regency, the Bucktails' approach to power "was not vindictive but democratic."[85]

Banking Reform under the Regency

When Van Buren assumed the governorship of New York in 1829, he quickly made banking reform a top priority. Since early 1825 four banks had failed, and the average discount on banknotes had climbed from 0.33 percent to 9.57 percent.* In reaction, the state legislature had ceased granting bank

---

* Although 9.57 percent was the average banknote discount in 1829, the median discount was only 0.5 percent and the vast majority of notes still traded at less than 1 percent discount.

charters after 1825. Adding to the disarray, over three-quarters of the state's banks held charters that were due to expire by 1833.[86]

Legislators were divided on how best to respond to the bank failures and the impending spate of charter renewal requests. Some believed that a dramatic change was needed; others felt that it was too risky to shift to an entirely new banking regime at such a crucial moment. In 1827 lawmakers had attempted to reinvigorate the chartering process by enacting a statute that would apply double liability to all stockholders of newly chartered banks, believing this would reaffirm faith in the stability of New York's banking system. "Double liability" meant that shareholders could not only lose their stock, but also be held personally "liable for an equal sum, provided the debts due and owing at the time of dissolution, are of such magnitude as to require it."[87] Some of the legislation's detractors claimed that double liability would actually increase the likelihood of bank failures by deterring honest and reliable individuals from banking and thus leave the industry to those of "lower character"—a belief that was only strengthened by the fact that two of the banks that failed in 1825 had double liability clauses in their charters.[88] As banks continued to fail in 1827 and 1829, the chartering standoff persisted and the new double liability rule remained in abeyance.[89]

The Birth of the Safety Fund

With so many banks seeking charter renewals and the state legislature currently refusing recharter requests, Governor Van Buren believed that a complete overhaul of New York's banking system was necessary and called on Joshua Forman to draw up a plan for doing so.[90] Forman had been "one of the most influential promoters of the Erie Canal," and had learned a great deal about banking through his involvement in the financing of that project.[91]

Like Van Buren, Forman was wary of the 1827 double liability law, believing the legislation would leave banking to "swindlers," increase the rate of bank failures, and cause the public to lose faith in banknotes.[92] Forman's keen observation that one bank's failure could lead to a lack of confidence in all banks' notes showed an "understanding that banks constitute a system, being peculiarly sensitive to one another's operations, and not a mere aggregate of free agents."[93] With these observations in mind, Forman sought to lay a more solid foundation for the state banking system, but one that did not place excessive restraints on credit extension and liquidity, as the public continued its demands for ever more banking capital. In Van Buren's words, Forman's goal was to refit the state's banking system with a "more efficient safeguard."[94]

The first of two major provisions in Forman's plan was an insurance fund, which Forman claimed was adapted from a system used by Cantonese merchants.[95] This provision called on all state banks to "contribute a small percentage of their capital to a common fund."[96] This fund, which Forman suggested need only be $500,000 to $1,000,000, would serve as an insurance pool that could be drawn on to repay creditors (specifically, note holders and depositors) of failed banks. He insisted that this form of mandatory bank insurance would strengthen the public's confidence in banknotes, thereby reducing or eliminating the problem of contagious bank runs.[97] Forman's second major provision called for a supervisory body to oversee banking within the insurance fund system. He recommended that a board of commissioners "be appointed by the banks, as he thought the State should interfere as little as possible."[98] These commissioners would inspect the state's banks and enforce compliance with regulations.[99]

The Assembly Committee on Banking Corporations offered a bill drawn "almost entirely" from Forman's proposal. Their bill mandated that all state banks, upon their chartering or rechartering, participate in a common insurance fund. Member banks would contribute 0.5 percent of their stock of capital into the fund on a yearly basis until an amount equal to 3 percent of their capital stock had been paid in. If the fund subsequently dipped below this target sum (as a result of payouts to cover the obligations of failed banks), additional contributions by member banks would be required. No newly chartered bank would be allowed to begin operations until its capital had been paid in by investors and verified by state banking commissioners. If a bank failed, the fund would fully compensate all of that bank's note holders and all of its depositors who had not already been reimbursed after the bank's assets had been liquidated.[100]

The bill also laid out how Forman's proposed banking commission would function. The body would be composed of three commissioners, who would oversee the fund as well as its member banks. Barred from owning bank stock themselves, the commissioners would "inspect each bank at least once in every four months," and would inspect a bank on demand if three or more other banks requested the commission to do so.[101]

The insurance fund bill sparked strong protest upon its arrival on the floor of the assembly. The speaker of the assembly questioned how such a small fund (at the beginning of 1829, 3 percent of bank capital in New York would have amounted to about $850,000) "could possibly guarantee note issues that were authorized to reach nearly $75 million."[102] Another state representative warned that the insurance fund would lead to overconfidence in bank solvency and thereby reduce the "public scrutiny and watchfulness which now serve to restrain or detect mal-conduct . . . and that bankruptcy and loss would ensue."[103] Others disliked the notion that the fund system essentially made "stockholders of one bank . . . responsible for all the rest."[104] Adherents of *laissez-faire* denounced the proposed insurance fund network as a burdensome and unnecessary intrusion into the business of banking, even going so far as to liken the planned banking oversight commission to a group of "inquisitors."[105] The large metropolitan banks of New York City and Albany, meanwhile, balked at the tax structure underpinning the fund. Because the insurance fund was intended primarily to back note issues, the metropolitan banks felt it unjust that a tax be levied on bank capital, as city banks tended to have lower note-to-capital ratios than did their rural counterparts.[106]

Opponents were unable to stop the legislation, however. After favorable votes in both the assembly and the senate, the Safety Fund bill was signed into law on April 2, 1829, by Governor Enos T. Throop, who had taken office after Van Buren left to become secretary of state under President Andrew Jackson.[107] The legislation was certainly novel: the bank insurance fund was arguably the first of its kind anywhere in the world, and the regulatory commission is said to have been "the first special supervisory authority established over banking in the States."[108]

The New York City Banks and Jackson's War

Despite their initial opposition, New York City banks eventually grew to accept the fund. In one sense they had no choice, because banks that wished to recharter had to join the fund or go out of business. In 1831 eight New York City banks were rechartered into the Safety Fund network. The legislature also eased the transition somewhat by removing an "unlimited [bank] director liability" clause from the Safety Fund law and by repealing a "local tax on bank capital, which the New York City banks had found particularly objectionable."[109]

In Washington, D.C., meanwhile, President Andrew Jackson was laying the groundwork for his "war" on the Second Bank of the United States, a federally chartered bank that served both as the nation's chief fiscal agent and as a quasi-central bank. Jackson told Congress in his first annual message in 1829 that "both the constitutionality and the expediency of the law creating the [Second Bank] were well questioned by a large portion of our fellow-citizens, and it must be admitted by all that it has failed in the great end of establishing a uniform and sound currency."[110] Convinced that the Second Bank was both illegitimate and ineffective, not to mention unpopular, Jackson set out to destroy it. He is said to have tapped into "Wall Street's jealousy of Chestnut Street [the street in Philadelphia where the Second Bank was located], the business man's dislike of the federal Bank's restraint upon bank credit, the politician's resentment at the Bank's interference with states' rights, popular identification of the Bank with the aristocracy of business, and . . . agrarian antipathy" toward banking in general and the Second Bank in particular.[111]

Van Buren's role in the attack on the Second Bank has long been debated. Knowing how heavily Jackson relied on the advice of his inner circle—his "Kitchen Cabinet"—some historians have argued that it was Van Buren who instigated the bank war. Among Jackson's close friends and advisers, Van Buren "was probably the most influential . . . and highest in esteem." The historian Bray Hammond has famously argued that Van Buren's principal aim was "to end Philadelphia's rivalry of New York as financial center" and that it was Van Buren who urged Jackson to challenge the Second Bank.[112] Other historians have disagreed, however, arguing that Van Buren would have been foolish to go after Philadelphia, because he would need Pennsylvania to win the presidency, and that back in New York, Regency members were hardly enthusiastic about the bank war, following only "haltingly and often halfheartedly."[113]

Whatever Van Buren's role in the bank war, the Safety Fund that he had helped to create emerged as a strong "potential weapon against the Second Bank of the United States."[114] Even an adviser to Nicholas Biddle, the

Second Bank's president, acknowledged that a successful Safety Fund would render New York banks "sufficiently safe to be entrusted with the collection and disbursement of the public monies."[115] Indeed, New York City bankers believed that they stood to benefit if the charter of the Second Bank of the United States was allowed to lapse (without renewal, it would expire in 1836), because they expected the federal government would call upon them to act as the nation's fiscal agents, with their banks as depositories for federal funds.[116]

By 1836 the Second Bank of the United States was in serious trouble. Facing the imminent expiration of its federal charter—nearly four years after President Jackson had famously vetoed a bill to recharter it—the Second Bank converted itself into a private state-chartered institution in February 1836.[117] The erstwhile national bank sputtered as a purely private entity, suspending payments multiple times and ultimately failing and being forced to liquidate its assets in 1841.[118]

Safety, Security, and Scandal

Following passage of the Safety Fund law in 1829, the New York State legislature heard a spate of new charter requests. By the close of the year, the network of insured banks had already grown to twenty-six members, eleven of which were new banks with the remaining fifteen being recharters. Fifty-three more would be chartered through 1836.[119] During this time not a single member bank failed. Impressed with the ingenuity and apparent security of New York's Safety Fund network, Vermont in 1831 adopted its own bank insurance fund system, modeled largely on that of its neighbor.[120]

But for all of the fund's apparent success, there was still much public dissatisfaction with the condition of banking in New York State. The perennial calls for greater capital availability continued, especially from the state's western counties. And although the Safety Fund had restructured much of the banking system, it had retained the chartering process. In fact, some critics believed that the Safety Fund system was expressly constructed to allow corrupt lawmakers even greater control over banking.[121] In an 1831 address, William Seward, who would be elected governor of New York (as a Whig) in 1838, gave voice to the growing frustration with the Regency and its ties to banking:

We are constrained to believe that the political organization which controls this state is combined with a moneyed aristocracy, existing in the city of Albany, which owns the Mechanics' and Farmers' bank. We find the officers and large stockholders of that institution, and their immediate connections, the most prominent leaders in the dominant party, and influencing every executive and legislative measure. We find them embarking with the highest officers in the state, in speculations where the power of government, or the influence of its officers, can be brought to aid their projects of aggrandizement. We find them owning banks in the interior, and establishing associations with those institutions in every part of the state. . . . Their identity of interest with the canal commissioners, with the canal board, with the comptroller, and with a majority of the bank commissioners, enables them to exercise a more dangerous influence over all the moneyed institutions in the state. . . . This identity of interests causes a combination of political influence, which bids defiance to all legislative control.[122]

New Demands for Radical Reform

In addition to the mounting distrust of the Albany Regency and the bank chartering system in the 1830s, the period was marked by rising antimonopoly sentiments and wariness over the increasing reliance on paper money, instead of specie, as the nation's principal form of currency. In combination these fears produced a generalized sense of anxiety about banking and spurred calls for further reform.[123]

Nowhere was the spirit of banking distrust more prevalent than in the Locofoco movement of the middle-to-late 1830s. The Equal Rights Party, whose members would come to be known popularly as "Locofocos," was a Democratic Party offshoot that sought to do away with banking corporations completely.* Although the Locofoco movement was popular among

---

* At a Democratic Party meeting at Tammany Hall, New York City, on October 29, 1835, the Equal Rights wing of the party "tussled" with the party regulars, seizing control of the chair and the platform of the meeting hall. In response to the "mutiny," the party regulars retreated to the building's basement and shut off the gas to the lamps, thus leaving the Equal Rights members in the dark. Undeterred, the Equal Rights group "produced candles and loco focos, as the recently invented friction matches were popularly called." From then on, in reference to their candlelit meeting, the Equal Rights Party was known as the Locofocos. For more on the Locofocos, see Bray Hammond, *Banks and Politics in America,* 493–499 (quotations on 494).

city-dwelling laborers and industrial workers, the party's roots were in Jeffersonian agrarianism. They espoused Thomas Jefferson's belief "that banks were privileged, aristocratic monopolies," and their message resonated strongly with a public that had grown increasingly suspicious of the political machine in Albany and its tight links to banking.[124]

Much to the chagrin of the true Locofocos, their momentum and message were often usurped and reframed to fit the anti-charter, "free banking" movement. Indeed, free banking advocates frequently echoed the Locofocos' calls to end the "monopolistic" practice of chartering; however, the goal of the free banking proponents was to institute a charter-free system of bank incorporation, not to eliminate banks altogether as the Locofocos desired.[125]

Supporters of free banking sought to replace what they viewed as a corrupt Albany-dominated banking system with one that promoted competition. They believed that if bank creation could be freed from the bonds of politics—and essentially anyone with sufficient capital was permitted to open a bank—financial power would be more democratically distributed and banking capital would increase statewide to a level that could finally meet public demand. Some advocates of free banking believed that their proposed system could be integrated with the Safety Fund, by retaining the mandatory insurance provision but discarding the charter requirement. Others, however, wished to start fresh.[126]

The call to end chartering had strong public support, and in March 1837 members of the state senate recommended a bill that would install a free banking structure supported by unlimited liability for shareholders. A modified version of the bill earned majorities in both houses but could not produce "the requisite two-thirds majorities necessary for enactment."[127]

A very different sort of idea for amending the banking system had been proposed several years earlier by the Safety Fund commissioners themselves. In 1833 the commissioners suggested, "The legitimate use of banks is not for the purpose of loaning capital, but for the purpose of furnishing a currency. . . . If loans of capital are required, it is better for the community as well as the borrower, that they should be made of individuals or corporations not having the power of issuing currency."[128] The commissioners were thus recommending separation of the lending and note-issuing functions of banks into two separate sets of institutions. According to their proposal, the lending institutions would be funded by long-term deposits, while the note-issuing institutions would "be backed only with short-term loans and preferably trade credits." The commissioners considered it somewhat illogical and dangerous for highly liquid banknotes, which were redeemable at any time, to be backed by illiquid assets (such as small business loans). A rather similar proposal had been suggested by Joshua Forman during the drafting of the Safety Fund system four years earlier. In both instances, however, the state legislature paid little heed.[129]

The Panic of 1837

A financial panic in 1837 led to a nationwide suspension of specie payments, sparking public indignation and adding significant momentum to the nation's various banking reform movements. After several years of rapid economic expansion, "speculative fever," and liberal credit extension during the early to mid-1830s, two federal government policies of 1836 were thought to have drained banks of their specie reserves, forcing them to call in their loans and cut back on their note-discounting operations.[130] On top of this, a rapid drop in the Bank of England's own specie reserves prompted it to raise its discount rate in June and again in August 1836.[131] A breakdown in "credit arrangements between major American and British banking houses" ensued.[132]

The tightening of credit markets in England led to a drop in demand for American goods, a draw on American specie, and a sharp decline in the prices of American exports. Cotton—"the most important single crop in the country, [and] the primary source of foreign exchange"—was especially hard hit, with prices dropping by more than 50 percent in New Orleans from February to March 1837.[133] But even at drastically reduced prices, cotton traders found it difficult to find buyers. By early March the rapid price drop, combined with the cessation of credit extension from England, had forced many merchants, trading houses, and banks associated with the cotton industry into default. A wave of business failures spread throughout the country and a general panic took hold. The loss of faith in the nation's financial system resulted in runs on banks and individual hoarding of gold and silver, which only exacerbated the problems of insufficient specie reserves.[134]

By early May 1837 the growing financial distress had led four New York banks to suspend payments. Three of the troubled banks, all in Buffalo, were members of the Safety Fund. The fourth bank was the Dry Dock Bank of New York City, which was not a Safety Fund participant. On May 10, in response to the financial turmoil, New York City banks suspended all payments in specie. Banks throughout the nation soon followed suit. Within a week of the suspension, New York State lawmakers made the discontinuance of specie payments legal for one year.[135] New York's banks would use almost the entire twelve months granted to them, not feeling confident enough to resume payments in specie until late April 1838.[136]

The state insurance fund was quick to compensate the creditors of the broken banks; in fact, the commissioners bypassed the original Safety Fund rules (with special legislative permission) and reimbursed note holders even before the liquidation of the insolvent banks' assets had been completed.[137] The state comptroller notified the public that bills issued by the Buffalo banks "would be received in payment of canal tolls and all other debts to the State; a measure which gave general credit to the bills in actual circulation." With such assistance, the Buffalo banks were able to regain their financial footing, allowing them eventually to repay their debts to the Safety Fund at 7 percent interest.[138] Ultimately only one New York bank closed permanently during the panic: the Lockport Bank, a Safety Fund bank whose charter had been revoked by the legislature in May 1837.[139] Although the Safety Fund was never seriously depleted during the crisis, it had originally been promoted as a means to *prevent* bank runs and specie suspensions; and thus in the wake of the panic, many New Yorkers considered it a failure. As the depression and suspension of specie payments stretched into 1838, calls for an overhaul of the banking system grew louder.[140]

Another Free Banking Bill

In 1837, amid all the financial turbulence, the Albany Regency was deposed from power in the state assembly. Although Martin Van Buren was then president of the United States and Regency member William L. Marcy still retained the governorship of New York, "opposition to the Regency had been building for many years," due in large part to the powerful Democratic bloc's intimate connection with the bank chartering process.[141] The newly installed Whig majority in the assembly revived the free banking proposal that had been debated during the previous session, while also adding several unique provisions that had not been included in the earlier bill.[142]

The 1838 free banking bill, if enacted, would allow any prospective bank with at least $100,000 of capital to start up with no special act of the legislature required.[143] Remarkably, to get around the state's constitutional provision requiring two-thirds majorities for passing legislation establishing (or renewing) corporations, the free banking bill defined the new banks as "associations" rather than "corporations."[144] Except for this clever rhetorical maneuver, the free banking bill closely resembled a general incorporation statute, like the one New York lawmakers had enacted for manufacturing corporations back in 1811.

Aside from divorcing bank formation from the chartering process, Whig lawmakers, who were clearly affected by the ongoing financial panic, also sought to protect note holders from loss and thus inserted a novel note-security requirement into the bill. This provision mandated that every note issued by a free bank be fully backed by "high-grade bonds" or "low-risk mortgages."[145] These securities were to be deposited with the state comptroller. Should a free bank be unable to redeem its notes in specie when demanded, the state comptroller would be authorized to sell the bank's deposited securities and use the proceeds to repay the bank's note holders.[146] By requiring a one-to-one ratio between banknotes and deposited securities, the bill's backers hoped finally to have found a solution that would prevent inflation (by discouraging the overissue of banknotes) and guarantee banknote convertibility under all circumstances.[147]

With the bill having passed both houses of the legislature by mid-April 1838,* Governor Marcy had to decide what to do. A member of the Albany Regency, the governor was now countered by a Whig-led Assembly that was hostile to Democrats and their long-standing association with chartered banking. Marcy, in official messages in 1837 and 1838, "expresse[d] fear of

---

* According to Bray Hammond ("Free Banks and Corporations," 196), the bill "was adopted by a two-thirds majority of the legislators voting, but not by a two-thirds majority of those elected," as required by the constitutional provision, adopted in New York State in 1821, regarding the establishment or renewal of corporations.

the injurious consequences which would result from granting to individuals the unrestrained license to issue paper," and "insisted . . . that no new charters be granted as long as the economic climate remained so unsettled."[148]

Although the notion of free banking had existed in New York for many years (a bill advancing an early form of free banking was first officially proposed in the New York legislature in 1825), free banking as government policy was unproven in the United States.[149] And the one-to-one note-to-security provision written into the free banking bill was equally untested. Opponents of the bill argued that the chartering system and the insurance fund were sufficient to ensure the stability of banking in the state, and they worried about the flood of new bank incorporations that could ensue if the free banking bill became law. Proponents, meanwhile, maintained that chartering was an inefficient system that would always be subject to the corrupt machinations of bankers and politicians. Governor Marcy listened to the impassioned arguments on both sides as he weighed whether or not to veto the free banking bill.

NOTES

1. David A. Moss and Sarah Brennan, "Managing Money Risk in Antebellum New York," *Studies in American Political Development* 15 (Fall 2001): 152–155.

2. Ibid., 143–155.

3. John Jay Knox, *A History of Banking in the United States* (New York: Bradford Rhodes, 1903), 413–416; Moss and Brennan, "Managing Money Risk," 152–155; Bray Hammond, *Banks and Politics in America from the Revolution to the Civil War* (Princeton, NJ: Princeton University Press, 1957), 595.

4. Moss and Brennan, "Managing Money Risk," 154.

5. David A. Moss, *When All Else Fails: Government as the Ultimate Risk Manager* (Cambridge, MA: Harvard University Press, 2002), 56–57.

6. Joseph S. Davis, "Charters for American Business Corporations in the 18th Century," *Publications of the American Statistical Association* (Dec. 1916): 428; Bray Hammond, "Free Banks and Corporations," *Journal of Political Economy* 44, no. 2 (Apr. 1936): 185; E. Merrick Dodd, "The Evolution of Limited Liability in American Industry: Massachusetts," *Harvard Law Review* (Sep. 1948): 1354.

7. Naomi R. Lamoreaux, "Business Incorporations, by Industry: 1800–1930 [Five states]," table Ch330–379, in *Historical Statistics of the United States, Earliest Times to the*

Present: Millennial Edition, ed. Susan B. Carter, Scott Sigmund Gartner, Michael R. Haines, Alan L. Olmstead, Richard Sutch, and Gavin Wright (New York: Cambridge University Press, 2006), series Ch354.

8. Moss, *When All Else Fails,* 56.

9. Ibid.

10. W. C. Kessler, "A Statistical Study of the New York General Incorporation Act of 1811," *Journal of Political Economy* (Dec. 1940): 877.

11. John Cleaveland, *The Banking System of the State of New York: With Notes and References to Adjudged Cases; Including also an Account of the New York Clearing House* (New York: John S. Voorhies, 1857), xiv–xvi.

12. Naomi R. Lamoreaux, *Insider Lending: Banks, Personal Connections, and Economic Development in Industrial New England* (New York: Cambridge University Press, 1994), 3; "Report on Currency; by a Committee of the New-York Convention of the Friends of Domestic Industry," *American Quarterly Review (1827–1837)* 11, no. 21 (Mar. 1832): 252; Moss and Brennan, "Managing Money Risk," 144.

13. Moss and Brennan, "Managing Money Risk," 143.

14. Howard Bodenhorn, "Bank Chartering and Political Corruption in Antebellum New York: Free Banking as Reform," in *Corruption and Reform: Lessons from America's Economic History,* ed. Edward L. Glaeser and Claudia Goldin (Chicago: University of Chicago Press, 2006), 234.

15. Ron Chernow, *Alexander Hamilton* (New York: Penguin, 2004), 200–201; Knox, *History of Banking,* 393, quotation at 393; J. Van Fenstermaker, *The Development of American Commercial Banking: 1782–1837* (Kent, OH: Kent State University, 1965), 139, 169; Richard P. McCormick, "Ambiguous Authority: The Ordinances of the Confederation Congress, 1781–1789," *American Journal of Legal History* 41, no. 4 (Oct. 1997): 435–436.

16. Henry W. Domett, *A History of the Bank of New York: 1784–1884: Compiled from Official Records and Other Sources at the Request of the Directors* (New York: G. P. Putnam's Sons, 1884), 32–36. New York had previously awarded a charter to the Philadelphia-based Bank of North America in 1782, but this charter was essentially voided when the Bank of New York was chartered in 1791 (Knox, *History of Banking,* 393–394). See also L. Carroll Root, "New York Bank Currency: Safety Fund vs. Bond Security," in *Sound Currency 1895: A Compendium of Accurate and Timely Information on Currency Questions Intended for Writers, Speakers and Students* (New York: Reform Club Sound Currency Committee, 1895), 286.

17. Chernow, *Alexander Hamilton,* 349–354; Van Fenstermaker, *American Commercial Banking,* 159; Chauncey M. Depew, *1795–1895: One Hundred Years of American Commerce* (New York: D. O. Haynes and Co., 1895), 67–68; B. Hammond, *Banks and Politics in America,* 149.

18. Van Fenstermaker, *American Commercial Banking,* 159; Knox, *History of Banking,* 395.

19. Knox, *History of Banking,* 395.

20. B. Hammond, *Banks and Politics in America*, 152.

21. Knox, *History of Banking*, 395.

22. Ibid., 396; B. Hammond, *Banks and Politics in America*, 152, 154–157; Van Fenstermaker, *American Commercial Banking*, 159.

23. Quoted in B. Hammond, *Banks and Politics in America*, 157.

24. Knox, *History of Banking*, 396; H. James Henderson, "Quantitative Approaches to Party Formation in the United States Congress: A Comment," *William and Mary Quarterly*, 3rd ser., vol. 30, no. 2 (Apr. 1973): 315.

25. Knox, *History of Banking*, 396.

26. Robert E. Wright, "Banking and Politics in New York, 1784–1829" (PhD diss., SUNY Buffalo, 1996), 231, emphasis in original.

27. Knox, *History of Banking*, 396; Van Fenstermaker, *American Commercial Banking*, 159.

28. Root, "New York Bank Currency," 287; James O. Wettereau, "The Branches of the First Bank of the United States," *Journal of Economic History* 2, suppl.: *The Tasks of Economic History* (Dec. 1942): 98; B. Hammond, *Banks and Politics in America*, 162. Today's Bank of America, originally a California-based company, is not a corporate descendant of the Bank of America that received its charter in New York State in 1812. See, e.g., Steven H. Jaffe and Jessica Lautin, *Capital of Capital: Money, Banking, and Power in New York City, 1784–2012* (New York: Columbia University Press, 2014), 25, 50, 65n14.

29. B. Hammond, *Banks and Politics in America*, 162.

30. Van Fenstermaker, *American Commercial Banking*, 159–160; B. Hammond, *Banks and Politics in America*, 162.

31. B. Hammond, *Banks and Politics in America*, 162.

32. Knox, *History of Banking*, 397.

33. B. Hammond, *Banks and Politics in America*, 162–163.

34. The last time the power had been used was under New York State's first governor, George Clinton, who twice prorogued the legislature before its very first session in 1777. See Charles Z. Lincoln, *The Constitutional History of New York from the Beginning of the Colonial Period to the Year 1905, Showing the Origin, Development, and Judicial Construction of the Constitution*, vol. 1 (Rochester, NY: Lawyers Co-Operative Pub. Co., 1906), 451; George Clinton, *Public Papers of George Clinton, First Governor of New York, 1777–1795, 1801–1804*, vol. 1, ed. Hugh Hastings et al. (New York: Wynkoop Hallenbeck Crawford Co., 1900), 184.

35. Jabez Hammond, *History of Political Parties in the State of New York: From the Ratification of the Federal Constitution to December, 1840*, vol. 1 (Cooperstown, NY: H. and E. Phinney, 1846), 309; B. Hammond, "Free Banks and Corporations," 188; Van Fenstermaker, *American Commercial Banking*, 160.

36. Bray Hammond, "Free Banks and Corporations," 185, 187.

37. Knox, *History of Banking*, 398–399.

38. Van Fenstermaker, *American Commercial Banking*, 15–20; William J. Shultz and M. R. Caine, *Financial Development of the United States* (New York: Prentice-Hall, 1937), 126; Moss and Brennan, "Managing Money Risk," 144.

39. Van Fenstermaker, *American Commercial Banking*, 16, 160; B. Hammond, *Banks and Politics in America*, 162. Similarly, up until the War of 1812, most New York bank charters "contained provisions authorizing the colleges of the State (Hamilton, Union, and Columbia) to subscribe for portions of the stock, and in many charters the State itself was authorized to be a subscriber" (Root, "New York Bank Currency," 286).

40. Moss and Brennan, "Managing Money Risk," 143; Van Fenstermaker, *American Commercial Banking*, 19, 161.

41. Quoted in Knox, *History of Banking*, 397; Van Fenstermaker, *American Commercial Banking*, 159.

42. Knox, *History of Banking*, 397.

43. Bodenhorn, "Bank Chartering," 242.

44. Ibid.; J. Hammond, *History of Political Parties*, 447; Ronald Seavoy, *The Origins of the American Business Corporation, 1784–1855* (Westport, CT: Greenwood Press, 1980), 123.

45. Bodenhorn, "Bank Chartering," 242.

46. Moss and Brennan, "Managing Money Risk," 152; Robert E. Wright, *Hamilton Unbound: Finance and the Creation of the American Republic* (Westport, CT: Greenwood Press, 2002), 153.

47. Moss and Brennan, "Managing Money Risk," 152, 158; B. Hammond, "Free Banks and Corporations," 191; Wright, *Hamilton Unbound*, 102, 130–134.

48. Douglas W. Diamond and Philip H. Dybvig, "Bank Runs, Deposit Insurance, and Liquidity," *Journal of Political Economy* 91, no. 3 (June 1983): 401.

49. George Selgin, "In Defense of Bank Suspension," *Journal of Financial Services Research* 7, no. 4 (Dec. 1993): 357.

50. Charles W. Calomiris, *U.S. Bank Deregulation in Historical Perspective* (New York: Cambridge University Press, 2000), 97–99.

51. Selgin, "In Defense of Bank Suspension," 360, 357.

52. Benson J. Lossing, *The Empire State: A Compendious History of the Commonwealth of New York* (Hartford, CT: American Pub. Co., 1888), 445–446; Moss and Brennan, "Managing Money Risk," 152.

53. B. Hammond, *Banks and Politics in America*, 351.

54. Frank Otto Gatell, "Sober Second Thoughts on Van Buren, the Albany Regency, and the Wall Street Conspiracy," *Journal of American History* 53, no. 1 (June 1966): 20; John J. Lalor, *Cyclopaedia of Political Science, Political Economy, and of the Political History of the United States, by the Best American and European Writers*, vol. 1 (Chicago: Melbert B. Cary and Co., 1883), 45–46.

55. B. Hammond, *Banks and Politics in America*, 351.

56. Moss and Brennan, "Managing Money Risk," 154–155.

57. Robert V. Remini, *Daniel Webster: The Man and His Time* (New York: W. W. Norton, 1997), 142.

58. B. Hammond, *Banks and Politics in America*, 332.

59. Lossing, *The Empire State*, 445–446.

60. Donald B. Cole, *Martin Van Buren and the American Political System* (Princeton, NJ: Princeton University Press, 1984), 33; Edward Countryman, "The Empire State and the Albany Regency," in *The Empire State: A History of New York,* ed. Milton M. Klein (Ithaca, NY: Cornell University Press, 2001), 297.

61. Michael Wallace, "Changing Concepts of Party in the United States: New York, 1815–1828," *American Historical Review* 74, no. 2 (Dec. 1968): 456.

62. Ibid., 458.

63. Ibid., 453, 457.

64. Ibid., 458.

65. Bodenhorn, "Bank Chartering," 236.

66. Ibid., 237. See also Robert Remini, "The Albany Regency," *New York History* 39, no. 4 (Oct. 1958): 353.

67. Wallace, "Changing Concepts of Party," 461.

68. Ibid., quotations at 461, 464.

69. Ibid., 462.

70. Ibid., 463.

71. Quoted in ibid.

72. Ibid., 470.

73. Quoted in ibid., 478.

74. Remini, "The Albany Regency," 343–344, quotation at 344.

75. Quoted in ibid., 345.

76. Bodenhorn, "Bank Chartering," 238, 234–235.

77. Quotations in Remini, "The Albany Regency," 346.

78. Bodenhorn, "Bank Chartering," 241.

79. Ibid., 237.

80. J. Hammond, *History of Political Parties,* 337.

81. Ibid., 178. Originally found in B. Hammond, "Free Banks and Corporations," 190.

82. Seavoy, *American Business Corporation,* 106.

83. John Joseph Wallis, "The Concept of Systematic Corruption in American Political and Economic History," NBER Working Paper 10952 (abstract), available at http://www.nber.org/papers/w10952.

84. Wallace, "Changing Concepts of Party," 476–466, 489–490. Van Buren himself observed, "In a Government like ours founded upon freedom in thought and action . . . occasional differences are not only to be expected, but to be desired. They rouse the sluggish to exertion, give increased energy to the most active intellect, excite a salutary vigilance over our public functionaries, and prevent that apathy which has proved the ruin of Republics" (quoted in ibid., 489).

85. Ibid., 478.

86. Knox, *History of Banking,* 400; Moss and Brennan, "Managing Money Risk," 148.

87. *Briggs v. Penniman,* 8 Cowen (N.Y. Com. Law) 387, 392 (1826).

88. Knox, *History of Banking,* 400; Moss and Brennan, "Managing Money Risk," 147; Van Fenstermaker, *American Commercial Banking,* 160.

89. Moss and Brennan, "Managing Money Risk," 146–150.

90. Seavoy, *American Business Corporation,* 118.

91. B. Hammond, *Banks and Politics in America,* 557; Moss and Brennan, "Managing Money Risk," 148.

92. Knox, *History of Banking,* 400; Moss and Brennan, "Managing Money Risk," 148.

93. B. Hammond, *Banks and Politics in America,* 558–559.

94. Quoted in Moss and Brennan, "Managing Money Risk," 149, 152.

95. Joshua Forman noted that the Hong merchants of Canton were given exclusive government licenses that allowed them to trade with foreigners. And although each merchant within the licensed trading group acted individually, they were all held collectively liable for debts incurred by any failed member. Forman, adapting this idea to the banking system, stated that New York banks "enjoy[ed] in common the exclusive right of making a paper currency for the people of the State, and by the same rule should in common be answerable for that paper." For more, see Root, "New York Bank Currency," 288.

96. Moss and Brennan, "Managing Money Risk," 149.

97. Knox, *History of Banking,* 401; Moss and Brennan, "Managing Money Risk," 148–150.

98. Knox, *History of Banking,* 401.

99. Moss and Brennan, "Managing Money Risk," 149.

100. Knox, *History of Banking,* 403–405; Shultz and Caine, *Financial Development of the United States,* 204.

101. B. Hammond, *Banks and Politics in America,* 559; Knox, *History of Banking,* 404.

102. Moss and Brennan, "Managing Money Risk," 150; Root, "New York Bank Currency," 287.

103. Quotation in Moss and Brennan, "Managing Money Risk," 150.

104. Quoted at ibid.

105. B. Hammond, *Banks and Politics in America,* 559.

106. Ibid., 558; Moss and Brennan, "Managing Money Risk," 150.

107. Knox, *History of Banking,* 403–404; Moss and Brennan, "Managing Money Risk," 150.

108. B. Hammond, *Banks and Politics in America,* 559.

109. Moss and Brennan, "Managing Money Risk," 150–151.

110. Bray Hammond, "Jackson, Biddle, and the United States Bank," *Journal of Economic History* 7, no. 1 (May 1947): 5.

111. B. Hammond, *Banks and Politics in America,* 329.

112. Ibid., 331, 365–366.

113. Gatell, "Sober Second Thoughts," 36–39.

114. Moss and Brennan, "Managing Money Risk," 151.

115. Quoted in ibid.

116. B. Hammond, *Banks and Politics in America,* 392; Moss and Brennan, "Managing Money Risk," 151; Knox, *History of Banking,* 68–75.

117. B. Hammond, "Jackson, Biddle," 11–12. For more on the political war over rechartering the Second Bank of the United States and for a discussion of Jackson's famous veto message, see Edwin J. Perkins, "Lost Opportunities for Compromise in the

Bank War: A Reassessment of Jackson's Veto Message," *Business History Review* 61, no. 4 (Winter 1987): 531–550.

118. B. Hammond, "Jackson, Biddle," 15.

119. Moss and Brennan, "Managing Money Risk," 150; Van Fenstermaker, *American Commercial Banking,* 161–164.

120. Moss and Brennan, "Managing Money Risk," 151; Shultz and Caine, *Financial Development of the United States,* 204.

121. Robert E. Chaddock, *The Safety Fund Banking System in New York: 1829–1866* (Washington: GPO, 1910), 375, 377; Moss and Brennan, "Managing Money Risk," 152.

122. William H. Seward, "Address of the Minority of the Members of the Legislature of 1831," in *The Works of William H. Seward,* vol. 3, ed. George E. Baker (New York, 1853), 341. The editor notes that among "the names signed to this address, we find those of Trumbull Cary, Philo C. Fuller, William H. Maynard, Albert H. Tracy, Millard Fillmore, and John C. Spencer. While Mr. Seward was a member of the legislature, and ever since that period, the task of preparing the annual legislative address of the political party to which he is attached, has frequently been assigned to him" (338).

123. Carl Degler, "The Locofocos: Urban 'Agrarians,'" *Journal of Economic History* 16, no. 3 (Sept. 1956): 322–326; Moss and Brennan, "Managing Money Risk," 152.

124. B. Hammond, *Banks and Politics in America,* 493–495; Moss and Brennan, "Managing Money Risk," 152–155.

125. B. Hammond, *Banks and Politics in America,* 576–584.

126. Moss and Brennan, "Managing Money Risk," 152–155. During the early debates over the 1838 free banking bill in the state assembly, an amendment was proposed "that would have incorporated free banks into the safety fund." This amendment was rejected. Ibid., 154n127.

127. Moss and Brennan, "Managing Money Risk," 154; Chaddock, *Safety Fund Banking System,* 375–376.

128. Quoted in Moss and Brennan, "Managing Money Risk," 151.

129. Ibid., 151–152; Knox, *History of Banking,* 402.

130. Harry N. Scheiber, "The Pet Banks in Jacksonian Politics and Finance, 1833–1841," *Journal of Economic History* 23, no. 2 (June 1963): 202–214; Van Fenstermaker, *American Commercial Banking,* 62–63; B. Hammond, "Free Banks and Corporations," 191; B. Hammond, *Banks and Politics in America,* 454–457, 582; Shultz and Caine, *Financial Development of the United States,* 221–226. The traditional account of how the government played a role in sparking the Panic of 1837, which remains contested among economic historians, goes as follows: In July 1836, President Andrew Jackson issued the Specie Circular, which required all western land to be purchased from the government in gold, silver, or Virginia land scrip. The result was a drop in land sales and an increase in the redemption of banknotes for specie, draining banks of their reserves and forcing them to cut back on lending and note discounting. Just prior to Jackson's issuance of the Circular, Congress had passed a law to redistribute the federal budget surplus, in the form of specie, to the individual states based on their

congressional representation. Because much of the country's revenue came from the sale of frontier lands, a disproportionate share of federal deposits was held in the less populated West. Prior to the Specie Circular, most frontier land had been purchased in loaned bank money and not in silver or gold, and thus, when the redistribution bill passed, western banks "scrambled to accumulate specie" for shipment to the more populous East. On the ongoing debate about the role of federal policy in sparking the panic, see, e.g., Peter L. Rousseau, "Jacksonian Monetary Policy, Specie Flows, and the Panic of 1837," *Journal of Economic History* 62, no. 2 (Jun. 2002): 457–488.

131. Van Fenstermaker, *American Commercial Banking,* 63.
132. Scheiber, "Pet Banks," 208.
133. Peter Temin, "The Causes of Cotton-Price Fluctuations in the 1830's," *Review of Economics and Statistics* 49, no. 4 (Nov. 1967): 463; Van Fenstermaker, *American Commercial Banking,* 63; B. Hammond, *Banks and Politics in America,* 459–461.
134. Shultz and Caine, *Financial Development of the United States,* 224–225; Van Fenstermaker, *American Commercial Banking,* 62–64; B. Hammond, *Banks and Politics in America,* 457–467.
135. Moss and Brennan, "Managing Money Risk," 154; B. Hammond, *Banks and Politics in America,* 560; Shultz and Caine, *Financial Development of the United States,* 225; Knox, *History of Banking,* 408.
136. Shultz and Caine, *Financial Development of the United States,* 226.
137. B. Hammond, *Banks and Politics in America,* 560.
138. Root, "New York Bank Currency," 292.
139. Paulette Peca, *Lockport* (London: Arcadia, 2003), 55; Van Fenstermaker, *American Commercial Banking,* 161; Moss and Brennan, "Managing Money Risk," 154. The Lockport Bank's charter was repealed "for fraudulent accounting practices" (Peca, *Lockport,* 55).
140. Moss and Brennan, "Managing Money Risk," 154–155.
141. Ibid.
142. B. Hammond, *Banks and Politics in America,* 582–583; Moss and Brennan, "Managing Money Risk," 155.
143. Root, "New York Bank Currency," 300.
144. B. Hammond, "Free Banks and Corporations," 194.
145. B. Hammond, *Banks and Politics in America,* 595–596; Moss and Brennan, "Managing Money Risk," 155. More specifically, according to the bill, the free banks' notes would be printed by the state comptroller, and in order to receive them, the banks would be required to deposit "with the comptroller an equivalent value (1) of federal bonds, New York State bonds, or bonds of other states approved by the comptroller, or (2) of mortgages on improved real estate with a fifty per cent or better equity." However, many further restrictions were placed on the types of mortgages allowable, and thus it would appear that bonds were to compose the vast majority of banknotes' backing. See Shultz and Caine, *Financial Development of the United States,* 229.

146. Knox, *History of Banking*, 415–416; Moss and Brennan, "Managing Money Risk," 156.

147. B. Hammond, *Banks and Politics in America*, 595; Knox, *History of Banking*, 416.

148. Knox, *History of Banking*, 414; Moss and Brennan, "Managing Money Risk," 154–155.

149. Wright, "Banking and Politics," 572. A free banking law, modeled on a New York bill, had been passed in Michigan in 1837, but it was soon suspended and ultimately repealed. See Kevin Dowd, "US Banking in the 'Free Banking' Period," in *The Experience of Free Banking*, ed. Kevin Dowd (New York: Routledge, 1992), 211.

·{ 5 }·

Property, Suffrage, and the "Right of Revolution" in Rhode Island (1842)

"RHODE ISLAND IS THE THEATRE of a great and angry controversy," wrote an observer in nearby Boston in 1842. "It is a collision not of men, but of *principles*."[1] He did not exaggerate. In a still-young nation that had recently undergone a seismic shift into greater democratic rights for the Jacksonian "common man," Rhode Island continued to be governed by a charter issued in the seventeenth century by King Charles II. The small New England state now seemed an anachronism, the last holdout of a colonial past dominated by a landed aristocracy. The "collision . . . of *principles*" to which the Boston observer referred, moreover, was nothing less than a contest between two rival state governments—one claiming the right of law (the charter government), the other claiming the right of popular sovereignty (the rebel government).

The leader of the rebel government seemed an unlikely rallying figure for the landless masses. Thomas W. Dorr, putative governor of Rhode Island, was an Exeter- and Harvard-educated lawyer, the firstborn son of a wealthy merchant, and "was considered, like Jefferson, a traitor to his class."[2] As a member of the Rhode Island General Assembly, Dorr had fought fiercely but in vain to relax his state's voting qualifications, which were the most restrictive in the country. Only adult white males with real estate worth $134 or more, and their firstborn sons, could be registered as "freemen," and only freemen could vote. As the state's industrialized and urban populations swelled, the fraction of its adult men who qualified as freemen had shrunk from more than half to roughly a third over the course of Dorr's lifetime.[3]

Finding little support within the system, Dorr resolved to circumvent it. In 1840 he joined the Rhode Island Suffrage Association, a political organization committed to suffrage reform, which in 1841 carried out an extralegal constitutional convention. The draft constitution that emerged ultimately won approval from a majority of adult white males in the state, "freeman" status notwithstanding. Declaring the "People's Constitution" duly ratified, the Suffrage Association, reinvented as the "Suffrage Party," held elections and inaugurated a new government in May 1842, meeting in an unfinished foundry building in Providence. Dorr assumed the governorship, knowing that doing so would incur charges of treason.[4]

As the charter government began arresting officers in the rebel government, Dorr left for Washington to seek the support of President John Tyler. Although many in Congress supported Dorr, the president rebuffed him, while privately urging the charter government to find a compromise with the rebels. On his way home, Dorr found a sympathetic audience among the Tammany Hall Democrats of New York, who pledged their own military support should it become necessary.[5]

Dorr returned to Providence to find his government cornered by the charter government, which had issued a warrant for his arrest. The collision of principles had yielded an impasse, and a collision of men seemed imminent. Although the reforms that Dorr had been fighting for were in jeopardy, they were not definitively out of reach. The spring of 1842 seemed the last best opportunity for Dorr and his compatriots to secure their objectives. But how could they do it?

The Radical Origins of Rhode Island

Although by the 1840s Rhode Island seemed, by comparison to its neighbors, a political laggard, it began as a radically progressive experiment. Its founding father, Roger Williams, was banished from the Massachusetts Bay Company in 1635 for sedition and heresy, after steadfastly refusing to recant his views that a government should not use its power to enforce religious doctrine, and—still more dangerously—that colonial governments chartered on stolen Indian lands possessed no legitimate authority.[6] Rather than return to England, Williams fled into the New England wilderness in January 1636.

True to his beliefs, Williams founded the town of Providence on a tract of land he acquired from the Narragansett tribe.[7] For all the piety of its name, the settlement's government was explicitly secular—as well as radically democratic, at first eschewing all magistrates and favoring purely collective decision making among heads of households. Yet the separatist strand uniting these settlers soon led to divisions among themselves, and the settlement fractured into several towns, which remained effectively autonomous political units until King Charles II issued a charter to the "Governor and Company of the English Colony of Rhode Island and Providence Plantations" in 1663.[8] Fittingly for a colony that had become a refuge for religious outcasts of all types, the charter included a unique provision that "no person within the said colony . . . shall be any wise molested, punished, disquieted, or called in question, for any differences in opinion in matters of religion, [who] do not actually disturb the civil peace."[9]

The charter was a remarkable document in another respect as well: it explicitly adopted a republican form of government, complete with fixed apportionment of representatives to the legislative body, or General Assembly, based on the size of the various towns. Representatives were to be elected by a majority vote of the freemen, and the General Assembly could decide who should be admitted as new freemen, although in 1666 the Assembly delegated this power to the towns. Compared to its New England neighbors, Rhode Island's 1663 charter was extraordinarily lax with respect to suffrage—in fact, it did not specify any qualifications at all. In New Hampshire, by contrast, a voter needed to own land worth twenty pounds sterling, while in Massachusetts, as of 1631, a voter needed to be a "church member in full communion," a "householder," at least 24 years old, and have a yearly income of at least ten shillings.[10]

New Restrictions on Suffrage

As the admission of new freemen from the towns accelerated in the early eighteenth century, however, lawmakers in Rhode Island began to think suffrage ought to be more tightly controlled. In 1724 the General Assembly adopted a landholding qualification. To attain the status of "freeman," a person now had to own an estate worth one hundred pounds, or pay forty shillings rent, or be the firstborn son of a freeman. At the time, because Rhode Island remained overwhelmingly agricultural, such landholding qualifications excluded relatively few adult males.[11]

A more profound change occurred in 1742, when the General Assembly revised the meaning of "freeman" from its original sense—that is, a lifelong status denoting full membership in the corporate body—to a temporary and rescindable label signifying a certain level of property ownership.[12] Under this new rule, a large number of privileges depended on an individual's economic position. Non-freemen lacked not only the right to vote but also many other rights, such as the right to file suit in court, even though they could still be required to pay taxes and serve in the militia.[13] This legal innovation invited abuse, however, as landowners found they could split their land into so-called "fagot freeholds" in advance of an election, and give out temporary deeds to men who otherwise would not be able to vote. After the election concluded, the title would transfer back to the original owner, but in the process the owner would have multiplied votes for his preferred candidate. In time, Rhode Island's elections grew so notoriously corrupt that one observer from Connecticut deemed the state a "licentious Republic."[14]

"A Downright Democracy"

True to its radical roots and in keeping with its mercantile interests, Rhode Island was among the first of the thirteen colonies to agitate for separation from Britain. In 1774 it became the first colony to select delegates for a Continental Congress. On May 4, 1776, it also became the first to declare its separation from the British crown, when the newly elected General Assembly passed a resolution to replace all of the charter's references to the king, from whom the government's authority supposedly derived, with "The Governor and Company of the English Colony of Rhode Island and Providence Plantations."[15]

Rhode Island also played a crucial role in the War for Independence, providing the colonists with their first naval force. Like the other colonies, Rhode Island amassed a significant debt in the process—more than $700,000. In neighboring Massachusetts, where eastern merchant elites dominated the legislature, the debt and tax burden shifted in part to the cash-poor farmers of the western lands, helping to prompt Shays' Rebellion in 1786.[16] Landed rural interests controlled the General Assembly in Rhode Island, however, and pursued a very different strategy by printing paper money to pay back the bonds held by wealthy individuals and towns, effectively at a deep discount.[17] This policy generated considerable inflation, but the General Assembly passed a law forcing Rhode Islanders to accept the local paper money at face value, under penalty of losing their freeman status.[18]

During the "critical period" of the mid-1780s, such policies struck many Americans as deeply irresponsible. James Madison decried Rhode Island's "wickedness and folly" and George Washington considered its policies "scandalous."[19] Others deemed the state a "moral sewer" and "a downright democracy"[20]—terms of contempt encapsulating the fear, articulated again in the debates over the federal constitution, that Rhode Island exemplified the perils Americans could expect from popular politics.[21]

Rhode Islanders were evidently as skeptical of the proposed federal constitution as their would-be confederates were of them. Citing concerns that the Constitution did not sufficiently protect individual liberties, the General Assembly rejected thirteen resolutions favoring ratification between 1787 and 1789. In January 1790, well after the Constitution had been ratified by the other states, Alexander Hamilton proposed that the new federal government assume the states' war debts. When Rhode Island again refused to join the Union in March, Congress's patience was exhausted. The Senate passed a resolution in May to prohibit commerce between Rhode Island and the other states, and to force Rhode Island to repay $27,000 in specie.[22] As the U.S. House of Representatives debated the resolution, Rhode Island finally ratified the Constitution on May 29, 1790, becoming the last of the thirteen original states to do so.[23]

Constitution Making in the New Republics

Although Rhode Islanders had been quickest to declare their separation from Britain, they had done so without writing a constitution, relying instead on their existing charter. In the years between 1776 and 1780, eleven of the other twelve states undertook this exercise, many with guidance and instruction from the Continental Congress, which exhorted the states to ground their governments on "the authority of the people." Connecticut also declined to write a constitution, but it did take the added step of calling a special legislative session to affirm that the existing charter embodied the people's will and their consent.[24]

Among the many ways these various constitutions differed were in their extension of suffrage. Although New Hampshire passed a resolution in 1775 extending the vote to all taxpaying males, and Pennsylvania's 1776 constitution contained a similar provision, four of the northern states passed constitutions specifying property requirements of varying sizes. The southern states, which had more extensive territories and economies reliant on large plantations, tended to adopt constitutions with landholding requirements defined in terms of acreage.

Rhode Island's landholding qualifications were thus not unusual, and in practice they did not prove especially restrictive. During the Revolutionary period, three-quarters of the adult men in Rhode Island qualified as freemen, and even in the urban center of Providence, more than half could vote in 1790. Nor did the composition of the electorate prevent the state from undertaking meaningful reforms, including an emancipation act in 1784 to gradually end slavery, and another to restructure the General Assembly into a bicameral legislature in 1796. Yet enthusiasm for an entirely new governing document seemed muted. One notable exception was George R. Burrill, a Providence lawyer, who delivered an oration on July 4, 1797, urging the Rhode Islanders to replace their charter with a more equal constitution.[25] He warned, however, that the members of the General Assembly would never make the necessary changes themselves. "To petition this legislature for equal representation," he wrote, "is to require the majority to surrender their power—a requisition which it is not in human nature to grant."[26]

Transformation and Intransigence

The economic and demographic transformations that ensued over subsequent decades only compounded the problem Burrill attributed to human nature. Following Eli Whitney's invention of the mechanical cotton gin in 1793, cotton production in the South exploded, and Rhode Island experienced the rise of cotton by way of manufacturing. The Revolutionary War had delayed somewhat the widespread adoption of cotton mill machinery in America, but Rhode Island proved to be the site of its earliest surge. Pawtucket was home to the first cotton-spinning mill in the country, founded in 1790,[27] and within a year the state was producing nearly 6,000 yards of cotton cloth. The War of 1812 provided the new industry with a major boost, as the American textile industry became a serious transatlantic competitor.[28] Within three years the number of mills in Rhode Island jumped from thirty-eight to ninety-nine, and Rhode Island contained more than three-fifths of the mills in southern New England. By 1816 the area within a thirty-mile radius of Providence accounted for about a fourth of all domestic consumption of raw cotton.[29]

At the same time, the expansion of manufacturing spurred urbanization, emptying country towns of their young people and attracting foreign labor. By 1832 the mills employed over 8,500—a large portion of whom were children. During this period the original apportionment set by King Charles II in the seventeenth century became increasingly problematic. Providence, for example, had surpassed Newport as Rhode Island's largest city by 1800, but it still had only four seats to Newport's six. By 1824, Providence County—which included nine surrounding towns—was home to three-fifths of the state population, but sent only twenty-two representatives out of seventy-two total in the General Assembly.[30]

Until the 1820s serious efforts at reform were as infrequent as they were unsuccessful. For example, when Democratic-Republicans introduced a bill to the General Assembly in 1811 to relax suffrage restrictions, mostly out of concern for electoral abuses such as "fagot freeholds" perpetuated largely by Federalists, the Federalist majority in the House immediately blocked the bill. Not long afterward, with the people of neighboring Connecticut at last agitating to replace their colonial charter with a new constitution, the ensuing debates garnered considerable attention in Rhode Island. In October 1817 the state's House of Representatives appointed a committee to draft a call for Rhode Island's first constitutional convention. As soon as the committee produced a draft, however, the House postponed consideration, and the issue again faded from view.[31]

Only in 1820, as Massachusetts undertook its own constitutional convention, did the Providence press return to the issue. By 1821 interest was sufficiently large that another convention bill passed both chambers of the General Assembly, at which point the issue went before the freemen. Partisan disputes hijacked the issue, however, and in October the freemen nixed the proposed convention by a margin of two to one.[32] Strikingly, amid the fierce but short-lived debates, suffrage reform was hardly mentioned.

Thomas W. Dorr: An Unlikely Rebel

That very winter, 15-year-old Thomas Wilson Dorr was a sophomore at Harvard College in Cambridge, Massachusetts, and had recently alienated himself from the majority of the student body.

Like most of his classmates, Thomas was the son of a prosperous New England family. His father, Sullivan Dorr, was a Boston native and the first-born son of an immigrant Irish Protestant merchant, Ebenezer Dorr. Just a child during the Revolution, Sullivan entered the fur trade as a young man in the Pacific Northwest before migrating to China, where he spent five years amassing a small fortune trading Chinese goods through a firm his brothers owned in Boston. In 1803 he returned to the United States, settled in Providence with his new wife, Lydia, continued his success as a merchant, and raised seven children, the eldest of whom was Thomas.[33]

Thomas Dorr may have had the pedigree to match any of his classmates, but he did not quite fit in. The class of 1823 was a notoriously rowdy one—over half of the students would eventually be expelled over repeated spats with the administration, which one historian later described as a "rebellion."[34] In one episode, a student named Russell Sturgis had organized an illicit alcohol-fueled feast at a local tavern the night before exams—in protest over the administration's recent decision to stop paying for the entire student body, composed of mostly teenage boys, to do just that.[35] Sturgis was enormously popular. The administration suspended him, and Thomas Dorr took their side.[36] In so doing, he became a faculty favorite and garnered membership in a "black list" among his classmates.[37] The grudge proved durable. Celebrating the two-year anniversary of the "black list," a group of students stole the bathtub from Dorr's suite in Stoughton Hall and set it on fire in Harvard Yard, an event commemorated in student-spun verses as "the splendid conflagration of Dorr."[38]

At about the time Dorr was graduating second in his half-expelled class of 1823, the General Assembly in his hometown of Providence was entertaining, for the third time in three years, a motion to call a constitutional convention.[39] Now 17 years old, Dorr moved to New York City to study law, where he remained until 1825. By then the constitutional convention of 1824 had come and gone—the delegates, selected by the freemen, had declined to propose any changes to suffrage, and the popular vote had struck down the proposed constitution by a margin of nearly two to one. By the time Dorr began practicing law in Providence in 1827, the state was home to over 12,000 white men of voting age who were legally barred from casting ballots.[40] Dorr, firstborn son of a freeman, was not one of them.

The young lawyer, however, proved as restless as his father had been at his age, and shortly after his twenty-third birthday, in November 1828, Thomas Dorr left his law practice in Providence and embarked on a "journey thro' the Western & Southern states."[41] Thus Dorr was absent for the next serious push for suffrage reform, which occurred in 1829 when a series of petitions, or "memorials," arrived at the Rhode Island House of Representatives. Hundreds of citizens, including hundreds of freemen, had committed their signatures to the cause of expanded suffrage without a property requirement. In response, the House dutifully formed a committee, to be chaired by Benjamin Hazard of Newport.[42]

Hazard's Report

Hazard had gone on record five years prior saying he was in favor of constitutional reform that entailed more equitable representation.[43] Yet in the opening lines of his report on the petition for white male suffrage, he dismissed it entirely, writing that he found "nothing in those memorials, either of facts or reasoning, which requires the attention of the House," except perhaps the "little sense of propriety" with which they were drafted.[44] The unabashed hostility of Hazard's report suffused more than twenty dense pages of discourse on constitutionalism, immigration, and the decline of American republicanism.

Hazard had no patience for the tone the citizens of his state had used in requesting the right to vote, which, Hazard reasoned, was like the right to property: "Every man has a right, honestly, to acquire property; but his right to possess and enjoy property accrues and commences only with the acquirement." So, too, every man was entitled to vote only after acquiring its qualifications. The oft-touted principle of "majority rule" or "popular sovereignty," moreover, lent the suffragists no logical support. "What is it that any man means, when he says, that *a majority of the people ought to govern?*" asked Hazard:

> In this State, the number of the people is ninety-seven thousand: In South Carolina, it is four hundred and ninety thousand. Is it meant that a majority of these in either instance, is to exercise the sovereign power; or to elect those who shall govern in their stead? No man, however visionary, entertains such an idea. Every one in the outset, excludes all but free males of twenty-one

years of age and upwards; and most men exclude all but free *white* males of lawful age.[45]

It seemed obvious, therefore, that the principle of majority rule was consistent with restrictive suffrage. The report went on to impugn the petitioners for the alleged hypocrisy of their argument for adult male suffrage. If the basis was "public utility," it was not at all evident why suffrage should stop there. "As if," Hazard wrote sarcastically, "all living things in the human shape; (except females, and those who lack a single day or more of the precise age of twenty-one-years,) are worthy agents" to elect representatives. The hypocrisy, he continued, was even more flagrant in the petitioners' tacit acceptance of more onerous property requirements for officers than electors—as was typical of many states at the time. If the argument for expanded suffrage was one of principle, wrote Hazard, "we cannot perceive the consistency of prohibiting those who have the right to vote, from voting for one another."[46]

Because suffrage had to be regulated in some way, it seemed only reasonable to Hazard and the committee to maintain the status quo. The alternative—opening up the affairs of the state to the landless, and especially to immigrants—would only invite disaster, for such persons "cannot feel the same strong interest [in the state] as native citizens." Hazard could thus divine "no better general rule" than that "which requires that most probable evidence of permanent interest and attachment."[47] The property requirement was to stay in force, and Hazard's report ensured that there would be no more petitions requesting its abolition.

The Suffrage Movement Intensifies

The immigrants whom Hazard so disdained had indeed been flowing steadily into Rhode Island, thanks to the state's early industrialization. Of particular concern to many were Catholics, hailing mostly from Ireland, who grew more and more numerous starting in the late 1820s, supplying virtually all of the labor for the Boston-to-Providence railroads in the early 1830s, and settling into towns where they gravitated toward manufacturing and various unskilled and semiskilled jobs.[48] Surely these were among the people Hazard had in mind when he wrote that "a great majority" of immigrants had arrived "in as degraded a condition, as men can be brought to, by abject servitude, poverty, ignorance, and vice."[49]

Hazard and his home town of Newport, meanwhile, continued to enjoy a plum deal. In the royal charter of 1663, Newport had been apportioned six representatives—more than any other town. Thanks to the rise in industry and the attendant influx of labor, however, Providence had twice Newport's population by 1824. By 1834 Providence contained 17 percent of the state's population and supplied two-thirds of its taxes, but elected only 5 percent of its representatives.[50] Such were the circumstances that compelled Seth Luther—carpenter, firebrand, and Providence native—to declare in 1833 that "all men are created equal, except in Rhode-Island."[51]

In the early 1820s, Luther had served time in debtors' prison and had been thrown out of his Baptist congregation for a vague charge of "disorderly walking," but in the 1830s he rose to prominence as an eloquent spokesman and organizer of the artisans and laborers of Providence County. He also urged all non-freemen to refuse service in the militia until they gained the right to vote.[52] After Hazard's rebuke of the petitions for wider suffrage in 1829, Luther's rhetoric grew more incendiary. "If it was the right of British subjects not to be taxed without their consent before the Revolution," he asked in his 1833 address, "and the General Assembly now tax twelve thousand citizens of this state directly or indirectly without their consent, what has that body of men gained by the Revolution but a change of masters?"[53]

Luther was not alone in thinking the time for orderly protest was over. William Tillinghast, a Providence barber and fellow suffragist, complained the same year that the suffragists "might as well petition Engine Company No. 2" in place of the farmer-dominated General Assembly. "Both would throw a vast quantity of cold water and in a very short time; the Engine Company to extinguish fire, and the General Assembly to extinguish the flame of liberty." Working-class reformers such as Tillinghast and Luther had good reason to be pessimistic, especially in light of the persistent intransigence from, in the words of one historian, "a state legislature dominated by farmers and urban elites."[54] Yet they were just about to find an ally among the ranks of the latter class—for Thomas Dorr, after six years of traveling and occasionally practicing law in New York City and Providence, had decided it was time to join the political fray in his home state.

Representative Dorr and the Constitutional Party

Dorr's personal motivations for entering politics would later become the subject of partisan controversy. His detractors alleged in 1840 that he joined the radical cause of suffrage reform after failure as a lawyer.[55] His professional trajectory notwithstanding, Dorr's political interests and values were already apparent by the early 1830s. In a letter he penned in 1832 to the prominent British reformer William Bridges Adams, he conveyed his keen interest in—and support for—the pending Reform Bill, which broadened English suffrage. He also praised Adams's recent pamphlet on the subject, with only one caveat: it was too prone to radical interpretations. "Now I complain that the poor man may be led to think, by your book, that he has a present right to a portion of the great heritage, and may help himself without waiting for the slow process of legislation," Dorr wrote. "True, you tell him to be careful lest he make his condition worse by attempting to do himself justice; but his reply will be, concede my right, and I will take the risk of the consequences."[56]

Dorr made a bold and rapid entrance into Rhode Island politics in 1834, when he won a seat in the state House of Representatives from the fourth ward of Providence. Originally a member of the Whig party, his early causes included expanding public education and abolishing debtors' prisons. Suffrage reform soon became his top priority, however, and in the spring of 1834 he joined the newly formed Constitutional Party, which aimed to call a constitutional convention that would likely weaken the General Assembly and establish a bill of rights.[57] The Constitutional Party was less radical in its specific aims than the earlier movement led by Seth Luther, but in its 1834 "Address to the People of Rhode Island," it too argued for the end of property requirements for voting, and drew an analogy—identical to Luther's one year prior—between the Rhode Island taxpayers and the British subjects before the American Revolution.[58]

When the bill to form a constitutional convention came before the Rhode Island House of Representatives, Dorr found himself fending off another volley of attacks from Benjamin Hazard, still resolute as ever in his opposition to broader suffrage.[59] Hazard quickly made the debate personal, speculating that the reformers' behavior, traitorous to their class, must be "mortifying for the relations of these young gentlemen."[60] Dorr responded that Hazard was espousing "old fashioned prejudices," and that whatever scandal his politics may have roused among his family attested only to the Constitutional Party's integrity "in postponing private interests to what they deemed the welfare of the state."[61]

Ultimately the House agreed to a constitutional convention in the fall of 1834, but rejected Dorr's motion to relax suffrage requirements for the selection of delegates. The convention, partly for this reason, "was doomed to failure"; the delegates failed to reach a quorum, adjourned after a few days, and allowed the convention to expire the following June—when only Dorr and one other Constitutionalist showed up.[62]

The Constitutional Party collapsed two years later, after Dorr waged a controversial and unsuccessful bid for a seat in the U.S. Congress in 1837.[63] By Dorr's own account, "after a three year struggle against every discouragement," his cause "was totally overthrown and annihilated."[64] Frustrated and disheartened, Dorr noted in personal correspondence that the disfranchised men of his state "seemed quite willing to have [Tyranny's] foot set upon their necks. Such being the case, they deserve their fate."[65] For the next several years Dorr avoided the issue of suffrage reform.

The Rhode Island Suffrage Association

With the demise of the Constitutional Party, suffrage reform faded temporarily from public view.[66] On the national stage, the Panic of 1837 had plunged the nation into a recession, earning President Martin Van Buren the moniker "Martin Van Ruin."[67] The Whigs mounted a spirited campaign to defeat him in 1840, nominating William Henry Harrison and John Tyler for the presidential ticket.

Back in Rhode Island, the General Assembly passed an act in early 1840 making it a crime for any man to refuse service in the state militia. Since the 1830s the disfranchised men of Rhode Island had occasionally abstained from militia duty, or made a mockery of it, as a form of political protest.[68] The so-called Assembly Act therefore struck many of these men as a political attack and became the catalyst for a new activist organization in Providence, which called itself the Rhode Island Suffrage Association. At first little more than a gathering of tradesmen in the vein of Seth Luther, the Suffrage Association soon gained momentum in the politically charged climate of 1840. Its aims were radical from the start. The preamble of the organization's

constitution, written in March 1840, called the state government "a despotism, and totally unworthy the name of republican, and having no just claim
to the confidence and respect of any American citizen."[69]

As the elections of 1840 drew closer, a mysterious pamphlet began circulating in Rhode Island, fanning the flames of the rising suffrage movement.
The pamphlet, titled "Address to the Citizens of Rhode Island, Who Are Denied the Right of Suffrage," had no listed author and was attributed only to
the "Social Reform Society of New York."[70] Neither Whigs nor Democrats
were keen to take credit for the pamphlet, which quoted extensively from
the Declaration of Independence before encouraging the disfranchised men
of Rhode Island to "[let] your will be known by the sovereign act of framing
a Constitution to supersede the Charter of a King." Worse, the short pamphlet
concluded with a how-to guide to peacefully overthrow the government—
beginning with open primaries to select delegates, continuing with a convention, popular ratification of the draft constitution, and election of officers. The plan concluded at the steps of the U.S. Congress, which the
pamphlet promised would inherit "the responsibility . . . of deciding"
which delegation to acknowledge as legitimate.[71]

By September even Thomas Dorr, now chairman of the state Democratic
committee, could hardly avoid the topic of suffrage reform. Looking forward
to an uphill battle in the federal elections, Dorr confessed in a letter to a
prominent Democrat in Washington that the "democratic phalanx" would
not be enough to overcome the Whig majority. Expanding suffrage, however, could reverse the balance: "16000 out of 24000 white males over 21 years
in this state are deprived of the right of suffrage. . . . Our friends in the
country are now reaping the fruits of disfranchising their natural allies
the mechanic & working men, to say nothing of their own young sons. . . .
Two thirds of the mechanics and workingmen are democrats; and if they
were possessed of the rights of freemen, with a vote by ballot, we should
carry the state even against the combined powers of the banks and
manufacturers."[72]

Sure enough, after the Democrats suffered a crushing defeat in both the
state and the federal elections of 1840, Dorr was not alone in looking to the
rising suffrage movement with newfound interest. The Democrat-friendly
Republican Herald acknowledged that the thousands of disfranchised men
in Rhode Island might well have turned the balance of the elections—or at

least made defeat by the "whole people and not a select few merely" a less bitter pill to swallow.[73]

The Rhode Island Suffrage Association, meanwhile, was keeping busy. In December it acquired its own newspaper, the Providence-based *New Age*. That same month the association submitted its final petition—a token gesture to the legal political process—to request a constitutional convention to reform suffrage qualifications.[74] In February the General Assembly tabled the petition without comment, but it responded to a "similar memorial" from the town of Smithfield, requesting a convention to address "the extreme inequality of the present representation." Without calling for a statewide vote, the General Assembly authorized a convention for November. The resolution made no mention of suffrage, nor of relaxing the voting qualifications for the election of delegates.[75] The Suffrage Association dismissed the motion entirely, writing that "the whole affair will result precisely as did the last attempt of the kind. These contradictions only show the necessity of the people's taking the matter into their own hands."[76]

Even as it espoused more dramatic action, the suffrage movement was spreading. Suffrage organizations were already springing up in other Rhode Island towns in late 1840, and by the spring of 1841 nearly every town in the state had its own suffrage association.[77] In late February and March, the Rhode Island Suffrage Association held public debates on questions as provocative as "Is it expedient for the non-freeholders to form associations for the purpose of military discipline?"[78] The association also began to employ new forms of political agitation, including "parades, spectacles, processions and collations." On April 17, 1841, as many as 3,000 people participated in a procession through the streets of Providence, waving banners bearing pro-suffrage slogans—including "Peaceably if we can, forcibly if we must."[79]

The occasionally ominous overtones of the movement did not prevent some of Rhode Island's prominent politicians from declaring their support. Two leading Democrats in the state House of Representatives, Dutee J. Pearce of Newport and Samuel Y. Atwell of Glocester, both delivered addresses at the April 17 festivities. Thomas Dorr, however, declined an invitation to speak at the next rally, to be held in Newport in May. He missed a big one. Although not as large as the rally in April, the procession in Newport contained a number of men carrying swords and guns, and concluded by adopting a set of bold resolutions.[80] The resolutions denounced the state's charter, dismissed the upcoming convention in November, and "empowered a committee to initiate plans for a People's Convention."[81]

"Whatever they want the people must do for themselves"

Sensing, perhaps, the rising discontent among the disfranchised of the state, the General Assembly made a small concession. The apportionment of delegates to the November convention would better reflect population. The *New Age* dismissed this as a "feint."[82] In May 1841, Representative Atwell submitted a resolution to admit all taxpayers to vote in the choice of delegates. The resolution won only three votes.[83]

Observing these events from fifty miles away at Harvard College, Henry Crawford Dorr wrote a letter to his eldest brother conveying his views. While supportive of suffrage "as well as other radical reforms," he confessed his fear "that they will be managed & directed by a few narrow minded politicians who will render them subservient to the purposes of their own political elevation." Henry was especially keen that the suffrage movement remain a truly popular one. Mindful, perhaps, of Thomas's crushing failure in the mid-1830s, he concluded his thoughts with a warning: "On former occasions a few enlightened persons have endeavored to bring about a change in existing institutions in favour of the people, and as friends of the people, they forgot that whatever they want the people must do for themselves."[84]

The Suffrage Association evidently shared a similar sentiment. That same week it published an address formally announcing its more radical approach. "The friends of reform must depend on their own active energies," read the address. When all other forces in the state were allied against them, the people would need to invoke their *"numerical force"* and "resume their original powers, and assert their original rights." Enacting a constitution would be their "legitimate" way to "[consign] an unequal government to the grave."[85] At the next rally, in July, the association formed a committee to set the process for a people's convention in motion, and later that month the committee called for the election of delegates on August 28, 1841.[86]

Rival Conventions, Rival Constitutions

The turnout for the association's August elections was disappointing to a movement premised on the principle of popular sovereignty. Only 7,512 citizens submitted votes for the uncontested seats. Roughly 2,500 of these were freeholders and the rest disenfranchised adult white men, meaning that well under half of each group participated. Nevertheless, every town in Rhode Island, with the exception of three primarily agricultural country towns in the south, sent delegates to the People's Convention. Three days later the freemen voted on delegates to the charter government's "Landholders' Convention," as it was officially known. This delegation skewed conservative, with a few notable exceptions such as Samuel Atwell. Another five reformers from Providence won seats in both conventions—including Thomas Dorr.[87]

The People's Convention had the critical advantage of speed. Deliberately scheduled ahead of the Landholders' Convention in November, the People's Convention also progressed rapidly—on October 4–9 they drafted a nearly complete constitution. The draft extended suffrage to all adult white males who had resided in the state for one year, although it limited the right to vote on matters relating to taxation to men who paid taxes on property worth $150. The disputes among the delegates were few but significant—and the most heated of all centered on the question of black suffrage, of which Dorr was a leading advocate. Although few delegates opposed black suffrage on principle, the more moderate delegates warned that such a radical extension would alienate the more conservative freemen voters, making ratification less likely. Caution ultimately won the day, although the draft included a provision allowing the new legislature, when formed, to immediately revisit the question of black suffrage and grant it with a simple majority vote. Still, a few lingering points of dispute prompted the convention to adjourn and reconvene the following month.[88] Throughout the entire process in October, the convention encountered no resistance from the existing government—despite being "so loudly denounced" for its "monstrous tyranny."[89]

When the Landholders' Convention met in November, Dorr worked strenuously to convince the delegates to adopt the same suffrage extension that the People's Convention had in its constitution.[90] His motion failed 8 votes to 61, as the delegates rehearsed an argument similar to the one that defeated his earlier push for black suffrage at the People's Convention. Atwell was more pragmatic but equally unsuccessful in his pleas, cautioning the convention not to force the people to choose between "blind submission or open rebellion." In a testament to the ambivalence of the official convention, after only a few days it adjourned until February, without producing anything resembling a complete constitution.[91]

The People's Convention made quick work when it resumed on November 15, and by November 18 it had finished the draft constitution. Dorr prepared an 8,000-word address for the occasion, declaring that the people had a right to compose their own constitution and that ratification would not require a majority of the freemen's votes to be legitimate. The statewide vote on the People's Constitution began on December 27, 1841. Voting took place at town meetings staffed by clerks and moderators appointed by the convention, and every ballot included the voter's name and a statement attesting to his qualifications.[92]

The charter government greeted the news with a mixture of indifference and hostility. As the date for releasing the results approached, Samuel Atwell submitted a resolution in the General Assembly to suspend the Landholders' Convention and disband the charter government in May, but the proposal was easily dismissed. The results of the vote on the People's Constitution arrived at the General Assembly on January 14. The Assembly debated what to do until January 22, when it defeated Atwell's motion to review the results. In the same session, it passed resolutions rejecting the People's Convention and declaring that the Assembly would not disband.[93]

Even as the government declared the results irrelevant, supporters of the People's Constitution celebrated them as a spectacular success. A total of 13,944 votes were cast in favor of the constitution, a figure that represented— by anybody's count—a majority of the adult white males in the state. Moreover, the committee reported that 4,960 freemen had voted in favor of the People's Constitution, which meant a majority of legal voters also endorsed the document. There were reasons to doubt the numbers—especially given the large number of proxy votes, as well as hundreds of votes cast in Newport that turned out to be fraudulent—but the General Assembly refused to investigate a process they considered illegitimate. The leaders of the suffrage movement, meanwhile, satisfied that ratification had been achieved, declared the People's Constitution to be the fundamental law of the state.[94]

The leaders of the charter government were hardly oblivious to the mounting pressure. That month they made another surprising concession— passing a resolution that allowed all taxpayers to vote for the constitution that the Landholders' Convention would produce. This convention reconvened in February 1842 with a newfound sense of urgency, and within two weeks completed a draft constitution, to be voted on in late March.[95] In the meantime, citizens of Providence requested that the state Supreme Court weigh in on the legality of the People's Constitution. In a succinct proclamation, the three justices concluded that "the convention which formed the 'People's Constitution' assembled without law; that in forming it they proceeded without law . . . and however strong an expression of public opinion they may present, that said constitution . . . is of no binding force whatever . . . and that any attempt to carry it into effect by force will be treason against this State, if not against the United States."[96]

The opinion demanded a response from the movement's leaders, and again Thomas Dorr assumed the role of spokesman. In a pamphlet co-signed by Atwell, Pearce, and six other prominent Rhode Island lawyers, Dorr restated the movement's claim to legitimacy on the basis of popular sovereignty. What had begun decades prior as a request for a modest extension of suffrage had transformed into a statewide public debate about the very nature of written constitutions and the so-called "right of revolution."[97]

As the debate raged in the press, the charter government submitted the proposed Landholders' Constitution to the same population that had, just three months prior, ratified the People's Constitution. In certain key respects, the two constitutions were oddly similar. The Landholders' Constitution adopted nearly identical suffrage qualifications for native Rhode Islanders, although it retained the property requirement for naturalized citizens with fewer than three years' residence. Both constitutions failed to apportion legislative seats fairly on the basis of population, although the imbalance in the Landholders' Constitution was more severe.[98] Critics of the Landholders' Constitution also claimed that it replicated the flaws of the royal charter, including an "indistinct separation of powers" and a lack of any enumerated individual rights.[99] Ultimately the Landholders' Constitution failed by a margin of 676 votes, out of 16,702 cast.[100]

"Forcibly if We Must"

The fight over the rival constitutions precipitated a profound change in the state's politics. The Rhode Island Suffrage Association, having achieved its paramount goal, transformed into the "Suffrage Party," and its members deemed Dorr their "Political *Mentor*."[101] Their conservative opponents, meanwhile, coalesced into the "Law and Order Party," a grouping "virtually coextensive with the Charter Government." The Suffrage Party set immediately to nominating candidates for the new government, while the Law and Order Party intensified their efforts to stop them.[102]

As the crisis grew increasingly grave, Samuel Atwell continued to present the General Assembly with opportunities for a peaceful way out. On March 30 he submitted a resolution to resubmit the People's Constitution to the public in an official, legally sanctioned vote. He found only two representatives willing to support the measure.[103] The next day the General Assembly passed "An Act in Relation to Offenses against the Sovereign Power of the State," which declared null and void any unauthorized meetings or elections to select state officers, and declared anyone involved in such activities guilty of a criminal offense and subject to fines or imprisonment. Clerks and moderators were subject to six months, anyone listed as a candidate would serve a year, and anyone assuming office, finally, would be guilty of treason and subject to life in prison.[104] Such laws were not unprecedented—Virginia, for example, carried a death sentence for the latter offense—but in Rhode Island the act was immediately derided as the "Algerine Law," a reference to a "contemporary tyrant," the Dey of Algiers.[105]

Whatever the General Assembly hoped to achieve with the Algerine Law, its effect was to further radicalize the Suffrage Party, as its more "respectable" elements distanced themselves from the cause. Eight of the nine lawyers who had joined in the bold statement of sovereign rights in the ideological debates of March withdrew from the party. Even Atwell distanced himself. The one exception was Thomas Dorr. After every nominee for major office withdrew his candidacy, Dorr, an active member of the nominating committee, scrambled to fill the ticket. In an unsent letter dated April 2, Dorr had written that he did not want to run for any office.[106] Yet in the days to follow, looking at an incomplete slate of nominees and the April 18 elections fast approaching, he found himself short on options.

At this point Sullivan and Lydia Dorr caught wind of certain rumors circulating about their son, and they wrote him a letter, full of anguish, on April 8:

We hear with great pain that you are about publishing a prox [ticket] at the head of which you are named for Governor of this state which is a violation of the lawful authority of the State. It grieves us to the heart to know that a son of ours . . . should be a participant in acts calculated to bring the state into destruction, around passions which you cannot allay and which God forbid produce civil strife attended with bloodshed and murder. We beseech you. We pray you to pause before you pass the Rubicon and become engulfed in political criminal degradation, where our feeble prayers will not avail to save you from disgrace and ruin.

The letter was signed, "Your affectionate parents and best friends."[107]

Meanwhile the governor of the charter government, the aptly named Samuel Ward King, was sending letters of his own. Not content to rely on the deterrent effect of the Algerine Law, on April 4 he wrote two letters to President John Tyler, entreating him for military support. The first letter was a formal request that the executive branch uphold the Constitution's guaranty clause and defend the legally constituted state government of Rhode Island. The second was a personal letter suggesting that the mere display of force would be enough to settle the commotion. To deliver the letters, he sent a delegation of three of the leading Law and Order men—all lawyers—to explain the situation to Tyler.[108]

Days later Dorr and the Suffrage Party sent their own delegate, a Providence-based manufacturer of root beer by the name of John Brown, to meet with the president of the United States. Tyler received Brown on April 10 and offered him vague assurances that he would not send federal troops to Rhode Island, which Brown accepted. The next day, as Brown was returning to Rhode Island and Tyler was writing his response to Governor King's letters, the Suffrage Party published its list of candidates for office. At the top of the ticket, recorded as candidate for governor, was the name Thomas Wilson Dorr.[109]

Governor Dorr

When President Tyler's response to Governor King arrived, it satisfied no one. "His Accidency," as the successor to the short-lived President Harrison was often called, had far too much on his plate to embroil himself in the domestic affairs of a state.[110] Fortunately, as he saw it, his hands were tied, for he could not legally intervene with military force unless the conflict in Rhode Island became an armed insurrection. This response, conciliatory as it was, only intensified the conflict in Rhode Island. The letter simultaneously gave the Law and Order supporters something to flaunt and the Suffrage Party supporters reason to redouble their nonviolent activities. This left the charter government in a difficult spot. It was public knowledge that the elections for a rival government were less than a week away. Yet the only way to enforce the Algerine Law against some 180 Suffrage Party members, with thousands behind them in support, would be to call out the militia. But with the men of the state so evenly divided, calling them to arms could easily end in disaster.[111]

Dorr, meanwhile, sent out a series of letters to friendly Democratic senators from other states, seeking their support in the event of federal intervention. In a letter to New Hampshire senator Levi Woodbury, he pleaded, "Will the friends of American Democracy in the two Houses of Congress permit such a proceeding to take place in violation of the rights & expressed opinions of the Sovereign people of a State . . . without one word of remonstrance?"[112] He sent out similar letters to Pennsylvania senator James Buchanan and Ohio senator William Allen.[113]

On April 18 the elections for the People's Government proceeded as planned, without any interruption from the charter government. Voter turnout, dampened by the Algerine Law, was only 6,400. That very day Senator Allen introduced a resolution in Washington, D.C., demanding that President Tyler explain to Congress why he had interfered—or threatened to interfere—in the affairs of Rhode Island.[114]

Yet when the charter government held its elections two days later, the turnout suggested it still enjoyed significant support. Governor King won reelection with 4,864 votes—a majority of all freemen in the state—and defeated the suffragist challenger, who won only 2,211. Before the end of the month Governor King took additional steps to head off any violent conflict, calling a special session of the General Assembly to form a new Board of Councilors to advise him during the ongoing "state of emergency." The General Assembly also repealed the section of the "riot act" that required one hour's notice before using military force on civilians.[115]

The "People's Government" Convenes

Thousands of onlookers joined the curious festivities surrounding the formation of a rebel government in Providence on May 3, 1842. An escort of armed militiamen accompanied Dorr through the streets of Providence, and before dispersing they passed a resolution pledging their allegiance to Dorr as their commander in chief. They had not brought him to the state House—which at the moment was unoccupied.[116] Instead, they met in an unfinished foundry building nearby. Onlookers scrambled onto the exposed rafters to watch Dorr and nearly eighty other officers and members of the assembly, elected under the People's Constitution, openly commit treason by taking their oaths of office. Notably, one of the earliest acts of the new rebel government was to repeal the Algerine Law.[117]

First, however, Governor Dorr delivered his inaugural address. "The sovereignty of the people has been vindicated," he announced, before launching into another soaring exegesis of the principle of popular sovereignty. "The idea that government is in any proper sense the source of power in this country," he argued, "is of foreign origin, and at war with the letter and spirit of our institutions." The "war" of which Dorr spoke was purely rhetorical, however, and in his speech he denied revolutionary aims. The Assembly had threatened military action, said Dorr, and the people were "consequently put on the defensive." Yet he reassured his audience, "There is reason to believe that [President Tyler's letter] to Governor King . . . was written under a mistake of the facts, occasioned by the misrepresentation of the character, motives, and objects of the constitutionalists of this State."[118]

Still, Dorr wanted the state House.[119] Reflecting later on the events of May 3 and 4, he wrote, "The period for decided action had now arrived. If the government were such, it was entitled to sit in the usual places of legislation." The rebel House of Representatives, however, "preferred to *request* the surrender" of the state House, and on the second day of its first session, the rebel legislature passed "an act *requiring* all persons to deliver to the proper custody the possession of any public property in their hands," the enforcement of which act would be left to the executive magistrate—that is, Governor Dorr.[120]

Renewed Appeals to Washington

In the first week of May 1842, President Tyler was presented with an oddity no American president had ever encountered. Two sets of resolutions announcing the formation of the Rhode Island state government, sent by two different governors on the same day—and somehow, both bearing the official state seal—arrived within days of each other.[121] The resolutions from the charter government came attached to a small delegation.[122] The People's Government sent their own delegation days later. Before these delegates could leave the state, however, they needed to make bail—for on May 4 one government of Rhode Island began arresting the other.

Daniel Brown of Newport was the first to be arrested under the Algerine Law, and he was released the same day on $5,000 bail. The next day the authorities did the same to Dutee Pearce, Dorr's longtime ally and a member of the delegation heading to Washington. A warrant was also issued for Dorr's arrest. On May 6 a second member of the delegation, Burrington Anthony, was arrested and arraigned, but he too was released on bail. Frightened members of the People's Assembly began to resign, and at a rally in Providence the crowd requested that Governor Dorr himself represent their interests to the president in Washington.[123]

President Tyler, meanwhile, received the charter government delegation and contemplated his reply. In the letter he wrote the next day, he informed Governor King that his "opinions as to the duties of this Government to protect the State of Rhode Island against domestic violence remain unchanged," but that certain new information had led him "to believe that the lawless assemblages . . . have already dispersed."[124] Although he could not have known it, he was right in one critical respect: Governor Dorr had left the state, departing under cover of darkness only hours after Pearce and Anthony.[125]

Upon learning of Dorr's disappearance, the *Providence Journal* accused him of cowardice, and days later an editorial in the same journal gleefully reported, "The revolution is in a state of suspended animation."[126] At this point President Tyler, having already sent the charter government delegation on its way, wrote a confidential letter to Governor King, urging "conciliation." He said he had been "advised" that if "the General Assembly would authorize you to announce a general amnesty and pardon for the past, without making any exception, upon the condition of a return to allegiance, and follow it up by a call for a new convention upon somewhat liberal principles, that all difficulty would at once cease." Reminding the governor that a "government never loses anything by mildness and forbearance to its own citizens," President Tyler urged him to "try the experiment" of amnesty and compromise, "and if it fail, then your justification in using force becomes complete."[127]

Governor Dorr met with the president the next day. Whatever the content of their discussions, Dorr left thoroughly unimpressed. "The President," he wrote two days later, "is apparently a very good natured weak man, unequal to his situation, and having his mind made up for him by others." Dorr reported that the president and his secretary of state, Daniel Webster, rejected outright the idea that the people could cast off a government to establish their own—and were therefore "both Tories of the rankest sort."[128]

His meeting with members of Congress, however, seemed more promising. "The Democrats in Congress and some of the Whigs are with us," he wrote in one letter on his way home.[129] "We have the moral & intellectual weight of Congress on our side," he wrote in another, "and perhaps the numerical weight, after a full and fair discussion."[130] The one reservation he detected came from "some of the Southern members"—they were "with the People of Rhode Island, but not with all People in asserting a principle, which might be construed to take in the southern blacks and to aid the abolitionists."[131] Nonetheless, he remained optimistic, pinning his hopes on "the aid & strength of the People of the States, to whom, I am happy to say, we shall not look in vain."[132]

The Tammany Hall Democrats

Governor Dorr had good reason to suspect that New York, his onetime professional home, would greet his cause with sympathy. After all, the powerful Tammany Hall Democrats of New York had already tried to convince the U.S. House of Representatives to impeach President Tyler for his "armed interference, or threatened coercive measures, against the people of Rhode Island, in their struggle to cast off the authority claimed over them under King Charles Second's charter."[133] After departing Washington on May 11, Dorr made a four-day stop in New York City. There he was surely not disappointed—for the Tammany Hall Democrats received "Governor T. W. Dorr, of Rhode Island" with all the pomp they could muster, treating him to a performance at the Bowery Theatre and a reception at Tammany Hall, where he delivered an address to great applause. Even on his way out of the city to catch a steamboat, he enjoyed an escort of hundreds of citizens, complete with firemen and a brass band.[134]

His visit contained more than mere festivities, however. On May 13 he attended a semi-secret meeting held in his hotel, organized by Daniel Webster and attended by the charter government's delegation, but Dorr resisted Webster's overtures for compromise.[135] He took greater interest in a letter he received that same day from two officers in the New York State militia, informing him that "several military companies of this city and vicinity" had "tendered their services . . . to form a military escort to accompany you to Providence."[136] Dorr graciously declined, but confessed that "the time may not be far distant, when I may be obliged to call upon you for your services."[137]

Return to Providence

When Governor Dorr arrived in Stonington, Connecticut, by steamboat on May 15, he was greeted by a small delegation from Providence and soon joined by a chartered train containing 200 supporters, many of whom were armed.[138] Back in Rhode Island, the suffragist Aaron White Jr. penned Dorr a letter to warn him of the delicate—and dangerous—situation he was about to reenter:

> I wish to advise that all our proceedings be purely defensive—and that we avoid all conflict as long as possible and if possible let the conflict first come some distance from Providence. The preparations of our adversaries are all made for Providence. You may depend that Col. Blackhead [the commanding federal officer at nearby Fort Adams] with all his troops will be in Providence within a few hours after an outbreak. We should incur great danger of defeat & if defeated many would leave us & few come to our aid in season. Every day is now adding to efficiency while we delay. You have returned & can see to the organization of our men & also restrain all rash proceedings, which timid men in times of danger are very apt to adopt.[139]

When Dorr's train arrived in Providence, he was welcomed by a crowd of thousands. A procession of 1,200 men—300 of whom were armed, and 75 mounted on horseback—led him to the home of Burrington Anthony, which was to become Dorr's headquarters.[140] Before the procession dispersed, Dorr delivered a fiery speech—the content of which later eyewitness accounts would dispute.[141] Most, however, agreed that Governor Dorr at one point addressed the rumor that he had asked his friends in neighboring states for 500 men. He denied this—but announced it was true that he had been promised 5,000.[142] At the climax of his speech he drew a sword that he had been given in New York, and declared that he would not shy from using it.[143]

With that, he and the leading officers of the People's Government retreated into the Anthony house, and spent the evening of May 16, 1842, deciding what to do.

NOTES

1. *Facts Involved in the Rhode Island Controversy with Some Views upon the Rights of Both Parties* (Boston: B. B. Mussey, 1842), 3.
2. Chilton Williamson, *American Suffrage: From Property to Democracy, 1760–1860* (Princeton, NJ: Princeton University Press, 1960), 247.
3. William G. McLoughlin, *Rhode Island: A Bicentennial History* (New York: W.W. Norton, 1978), 128.
4. McLoughlin, *Rhode Island,* 132; Arthur May Mowry, *The Dorr War: The Constitutional Struggle in Rhode Island* (Providence, RI: Preston and Rounds, 1901), 111, 135; Marvin E. Gettleman, *The Dorr Rebellion: A Study in American Radicalism, 1833–1849* (New York: Random House, 1973), 90–91.
5. Gettleman, *The Dorr Rebellion,* 109, 111; Mowry, *The Dorr War,* 169–173.
6. Sydney V. James, *Colonial Rhode Island: A History* (New York: Charles Scribner's Sons, 1975), 16; Donald A. Grinde Jr. and Bruce E. Johansen, *Exemplar of Liberty: Native America and the Evolution of Democracy,* chap. 5, at http://www.ratical.org/many_worlds /6Nations/EoL/chp5.html.
7. James, *Colonial Rhode Island,* 7.
8. Sydney V. James, *The Colonial Metamorphoses in Rhode Island: A Study of Institutions in Change* (Hanover, CT: University Press of New England, 2000), 16, 17–20; "The Charter Granted by King Charles II," reprinted in Mowry, *The Dorr War,* 307.
9. Quoted in Mowry, *The Dorr War,* 309.
10. Ibid., 311–312; *Facts Involved,* 10; Francis Newton Thorpe, *A Constitutional History of the American People, 1776–1850,* vol. 1 (New York: Harper and Brothers, 1898), 192–193 (quotation at 192–193).
11. Albert Edward McKinley, *The Suffrage Franchise in the Thirteen English Colonies in America* (Philadelphia: University of Pennsylvania Press, 1905), 453–454; Mowry, *The Dorr War,* 19–20; *Facts Involved,* 11.
12. Mowry, *The Dorr War,* 20.
13. Williamson, *American Suffrage,* 246. Thomas Dorr himself discussed the history of militia duty for non-freemen, in "Address to the people of Rhode Island, from the convention assembled at Providence on the 22nd day of February, and again on the 12th day of March, 1834, to promote the establishment of a State constitution," in *Rhode Island—Interference of the Executive in the Affairs of, June 7, 1844,* Report No. 546, for the U.S. House of Representatives, 28th Congress, 1st Sess., 355 (hereafter Burke's Report).
14. Williamson, *American Suffrage,* 54.
15. McLoughlin, *Rhode Island,* 92, 94; "The May 4, 1776, Act of Renunciation," at *State of Rhode Island Secretary of State,* http://sos.ri.gov/divisions/Civics-And-Education /ri-history/archives-treasures/renunciation/.

16. McLoughlin, *Rhode Island,* 93–94; Samuel Greene Arnold, *History of the State of Rhode Island and Providence Plantations,* vol. 2 (Providence, RI: Preston and Rounds, 1894), 500; David P. Szatmary, *Shays's Rebellion: The Making of an Agrarian Insurrection* (Amherst: University of Massachusetts Press, 1980), 25–34.

17. Arnold, *History,* 2:505.

18. John Fiske, *The Critical Period of American History* (Boston: Houghton, Mifflin and Co., 1898), 109; Arnold, *History,* 2:521.

19. McLoughlin, *Rhode Island,* 103–104.

20. Joseph M. Parent, *Uniting States: Voluntary Union in World Politics* (Oxford: Oxford University Press, 2011), 55.

21. Madison Debates, 18 July 1787, at The Avalon Project, Lillian Goldman Law Library, Yale Law School, http://avalon.law.yale.edu/18th_century/debates_718.asp.

22. McLoughlin, *Rhode Island,* 103; Arnold, *History,* 2:561.

23. D. Jonathan White, "The 'Wayward Sisters' and Constitutional Interpretation," *Humanitas* 26, nos. 1–2 (2013): 64–68; Arnold, *History,* 2:541.

24. Willi Paul Adams, *The First American Constitutions* (Chapel Hill: University of North Carolina Press, 1980), 63, 66–67.

25. McLoughlin, *Rhode Island,* 128, 106; Williamson, *American Suffrage,* 244–245; Mowry, *The Dorr War,* 22; George R. Burrill, "Extracts from the oration of George R. Burrill, delivered in Providence in 1797, in favor of a republican constitution," in Burke's Report, 271–274.

26. Mowry, *The Dorr War,* 27–28; Burke's Report, 271–272.

27. Josiah B. Bowditch, "Industrial Development," chap. 4 of *State of Rhode Island and Providence Plantations at the End of the Century: A History,* vol. 3, ed. Edward Field (Boston: Mason, 1902), 342; John K. Towles, "Factory Legislation of Rhode Island," *American Economic Association Quarterly,* 3rd ser., vol. 9, no. 3 (Oct. 1908): 2.

28. Bowditch, "Industrial Development," 343; Clive Day, "The Early Development of the American Cotton Manufacture," *Quarterly Journal of Economics* 39, no. 3 (May 1925): 463.

29. Bowditch, "Industrial Development," 347, 351; Peter J. Coleman, *The Transformation of Rhode Island, 1760–1860* (Providence, RI: Brown University Press, 1963), 86–87; Howard Kemble Stokes, "Public and Private Finance," in Field, *State of Rhode Island,* 3:287.

30. Coleman, *Transformation,* 228; Bowditch, "Industrial Development," 354; Lynne Withey, *Urban Growth in Colonial Rhode Island: Newport and Providence in the Eighteenth Century* (Albany: SUNY Press, 1984), 115; Jacob Frieze, *A Concise History of the Efforts to Obtain an Extension of Suffrage in Rhode Island, from the year 1811 to 1842* (Providence, RI: Benjamin F. Moore, Printer, 1842), 15–16.

31. Williamson, *American Suffrage,* 178; Mowry, *The Dorr War,* 28–29; Frieze, *Concise History,* 14.

32. Mowry, *The Dorr War,* 29–30; Burke's Report, 151.

33. *Biographical Cyclopedia of Representative Men of Rhode Island* (Providence, RI: National Biographical Pub. Co., 1881), 198, 328, available at Rhode Island Historical Society, Manuscripts Division.

34. Gettleman, *The Dorr Rebellion,* 14; for the 1821 "rebellion," see Dean Grodzins and Leon Jackson, "Colleges and Print Culture," in *An Extensive Republic: Print, Culture, and Society in the New Nation, 1790–1840,* ed. Robert A. Gross and Mary Kelley (Chapel Hill: University of North Carolina Press, 2010), 331.

35. Megan Marshall, *The Peabody Sisters: Three Women Who Ignited American Romanticism* (Boston: Houghton Mifflin, 2005), 110.

36. Evelyn Savidge Sterne, *Ballots and Bibles: Ethnic Politics in the Catholic Church in Providence* (Ithaca, NY: Cornell University Press, 2003), 17. Sterne concludes that Dorr "cast his lot with the administration." Nonetheless, a close family friend, Jason Whitman, expressed his condolences in a letter to Dorr. "I was very sorry to hear that your classmate Sturges [*sic*] was suspended," Whitman wrote, adding, "I hope however it will do him good." "Jason Whitman to Thomas Wilson Dorr," 24 June 1821, electronic transcription at http://library.providence.edu:8080/xtf/view?docId=tei/L0002 .xml.

37. Sterne, *Ballots and Bibles,* 17.

38. "Black List Convention," 2nd ed., 27 Aug. 1823, Harvard College Library, quoted in Gettleman, *The Dorr Rebellion,* 14.

39. Introduction to "Draft letter from Thomas Wilson Dorr to Chief Justice John Savage, May 16, 1831," Dorr Letters Project, electronic transcription at http://library.prov idence.edu:8080/xtf/view?docId=tei/L0003.xml; Mowry, *The Dorr War,* 30. The General Assembly put the question to a referendum in 1821 and in April 1822.

40. "Draft letter from Thomas Wilson Dorr to Chief Justice John Savage, May 16, 1831"; *Manufacturers and Farmers Journal,* 4 Nov. 1824, cited in Mowry, *The Dorr War,* 32–33; Petitions Not Granted, May 1829, in Outsize Petitions, box 1, quoted in Coleman, *Transformation,* 268.

41. "Draft letter from Thomas Wilson Dorr to Chief Justice John Savage, May 16, 1831."

42. Mowry, *The Dorr War,* 35–36.

43. Ibid., 31.

44. Rhode Island House of Representatives, Report of the Committee on the Subject of an Extension of Suffrage. Author: B. Hazard, June 1829, 1, at http://digitalcommons .providence.edu/cgi/viewcontent.cgi?article=1015&context=dorr_pamphlets (hereafter Hazard's Report).

45. Ibid., 6 (emphasis in the original).

46. Ibid., 20, 22.

47. Ibid., 9, 8.

48. Sterne, *Ballots and Bibles,* 14; Austin Dowling, "The Diocese of Providence," in *History of the Catholic Church in the New England States,* ed. William Byrne (Boston: Hurd and Everts, 1899), 356, 359; Coleman, *Transformation,* 229; Christopher Malone, *Between Freedom and Bondage: Race, Party, and Voting Rights in the Antebellum North* (New York: Routledge, 2008), 114; for a discussion of the Rhode Islanders' perception of Irish immigration into the state, see Gabriel J. Loiacono, "Poverty and Citizenship in Rhode Island, 1780–1870" (PhD diss., Brandeis University, Waltham, Massachusetts, 2008), 217.

49. Hazard's Report, 11.

50. "The Charter Granted by King Charles II," in Mowry, *The Dorr War,* 311; Frieze, *Concise History,* 18; Sterne, *Ballots and Bibles,* 14.

51. Seth Luther and Stephen Randall Weeden, "An Address on the Right of Free Suffrage," quoted in Alexander Keyssar, *The Right to Vote: The Contested History of Democracy in the United States* (New York: Basic Books, 2000), 57.

52. Sterne, *Ballots and Bibles,* 15–16.

53. Luther and Weeden, "Right of Free Suffrage," quoted in Sterne, *Ballots and Bibles,* 16.

54. Sterne, *Ballots and Bibles,* 16–17.

55. A Citizen of Massachusetts [George Ticknor Curtis], *The Merits of Thomas W. Dorr and George Bancroft as they are Politically Connected* (Boston: John H. Eastburn, 1844), 5.

56. "Thomas Dorr to William B. Adams," 28 May 1832, electronic transcription at http://library.providence.edu:8080/xtf/view?docId=tei/L0004.xml.

57. Gettleman, *The Dorr Rebellion,* 17; McLoughlin, *Rhode Island,* 129; Williamson, *American Suffrage,* 249.

58. For a comparison between the two movements, see Gettleman, *The Dorr Rebellion,* 24; for the full text of the 1834 Address, see Burke's Report, 151–176.

59. Gettleman, *The Dorr Rebellion,* 26.

60. Ibid., quoting from Debates in the General Assembly, June 1834, reported in *Manufacturers and Farmers Journal* (Providence), 1 Sept. 1834.

61. Ibid., 27, quoting from General Assembly debates reported in *Manufacturers and Farmers Journal* (Providence), 1, 3, and 8 Sept. 1834.

62. Mowry, *The Dorr War,* 41; Gettleman, *The Dorr Rebellion,* 28.

63. Gettleman, *The Dorr Rebellion,* 29.

64. "Thomas Wilson Dorr to Amos Kendall," 24 Sept. 1840, electronic transcription at http://library.providence.edu:8080/xtf/view?docId=tei/L0008.xml.

65. "Dorr's remarks on reverse of Philip B. Stinness to Dorr, November 18, 1837," available at Brown University, quoted in Gettleman, *The Dorr Rebellion,* 29.

66. Gettleman, *The Dorr Rebellion,* 30–31.

67. Michael A. Genovese, "Martin Van Buren," in *Encyclopedia of the American Presidency* (New York: Infobase, 2010), 503–504.

68. Frances H. (Whipple) McDougall, *Might and Right by a Rhode Islander* (Providence, RI: A. H. Stillwell, 1844), 70; see also John Russell Bartlett, "Index to the Acts & Resolves of Rhode Island 1758–1850 Part 2 (H-O)" (1856), *Library Archive,* paper 13, p. 235, at http://helindigitalcommons.org/lawarchive/13; Sterne, *Ballots and Bibles,* 15.

69. McDougall, *Might and Right,* 73.

70. See Gettleman, *The Dorr Rebellion,* 31, note 3; Mowry, *The Dorr War,* 48, also expresses some doubt as to the origins of the pamphlet.

71. "Address to the Citizens of Rhode Island, Who Are Denied the Right of Suffrage," Periodical No. 3, Social Reform Society of New York, 1840, 6, 8.

72. Thomas Dorr to Amos Kendall, 24 Sept. 1840. John Hay Library, Rider Collection, Dorr Correspondence (box 3, folder 9).

73. *Republican Herald,* 14 Nov. 1840, quoted in Mowry, *The Dorr War,* 53.

74. Mowry, *The Dorr War,* 53–54; *New Age,* 18 Dec. 1840, quoted in Mowry, *The Dorr War,* 56; "Petition of Elisha Dillingham and Others," in Burke's Report, 402–403.

75. Gettleman, *The Dorr Rebellion,* 37–38; Mowry, *The Dorr War,* 58–59.

76. Mowry, *The Dorr War,* 60.

77. "Historical sketch of the adoption of the People's Constitution, and their action in reference to the Landholders' Constitution, and also to the existing Constitution," in Burke's Report, 16; Mowry, *The Dorr War,* 50.

78. *New Age,* 26 Feb., 5 Mar., and 12 Mar. 1841, quoted in Mowry, *The Dorr War,* 61–62.

79. Gettleman, *The Dorr Rebellion,* 39.

80. Ibid.; letter from Jesse Calder to Thomas Dorr, 3 May 1841, cited in ibid., 39–40; Mowry, *The Dorr War,* 65–66; "Proceedings of the mass convention held at Newport, R.I., May 5, 1841," in Burke's Report, 256–259, 404–407.

81. Gettleman, *The Dorr Rebellion,* 41.

82. *New Age,* 14 May 1841, quoted in ibid., 42.

83. Gettleman, *The Dorr Rebellion,* 42; Mowry, *The Dorr War,* 68–69; see also "Address of Governor Dorr to the People of Rhode Island, August 1843," in Burke's Report, 733.

84. Henry C. Dorr to Thomas Dorr, 17 June 1841, electronic transcription at http://library.providence.edu:8080/xtf/view?docId=tei/L0009.xml.

85. "Address of the State suffrage committee, setting forth the principles of the suffrage movement," in Burke's Report, 267.

86. Mowry, *The Dorr War,* 70–71, citing *New Age,* 23 July 1841, *Newport Mercury,* 24 July 1841, and Burke's Report, 269–271, 410–412.

87. Mowry, *The Dorr War,* 95; ibid., citing *New Age,* 3 Sept. 1841; Gettleman, *The Dorr Rebellion,* 44; [Edward Field], "The Dorr War and Its Results, in Field, *State of Rhode Island,* 339; see also the account of Convention proceedings in *Providence Journal,* 2–15 Nov. 1841, cited in Gettleman, *The Dorr Rebellion,* 44.

88. *New Age,* 15 Oct. 1841, cited in Mowry, *The Dorr War,* 96; People's Constitution, Art. II, §4 (reprinted in Mowry, *The Dorr War,* 326); Gettleman, *The Dorr Rebellion,* 47; Mowry, *The Dorr War,* 46–47, 98–99; People's Constitution, Art. XIV, §22 (reprinted in Mowry, *The Dorr War,* 346); Gettleman, *The Dorr Rebellion,* 45–46.

89. *The Providence Journal,* quoted in Mowry, *The Dorr War,* 96.

90. Gettleman, *The Dorr Rebellion,* 49, citing *Providence Journal,* 2–13 Nov. 1842.

91. Ibid., 49–50, citing *Providence Journal,* 13 Nov. 1842.

92. Mowry, *The Dorr War,* 96, 107–108; "Speech of Thomas W. Dorr, on the Right of the People of Rhode Island to Form a Constitution: Delivered in the People's Convention on the 18th day of November, 1841," in Burke's Report, 851–864.

93. Mowry, *The Dorr War,* 121–123, citing *Rhode Island House Journals,* 14 and 18 Jan. 1842, Burke's Report, 443, and *Rhode Island Acts and Resolves,* Jan. 1842, 45.

94. Burke's Report, 438–439, 353, 436–437; Mowry, *The Dorr War,* 115, 111–112, 115–116; Gettleman, *The Dorr Rebellion,* 58.

95. Gettleman, *The Dorr Rebellion,* 59 (citing Act of the General Assembly, Jan. 1842, in Burke's Report, 646), 60–61.

96. Mowry, *The Dorr War,* 128–129.

97. Ibid., 129–130; Gettleman, *The Dorr Rebellion,* 64–68.

98. Mowry, *The Dorr War,* 351 (quoting The Landholders' Constitution, Art. II), 326 (quoting The People's Constitution, Art. II), 104–105.

99. Gettleman, *The Dorr Rebellion,* 61–63.

100. Burke's Report, 119; Mowry, *The Dorr War,* 124, citing *Rhode Island House Journals,* 30 Mar. 1842, *New Age,* 2 Apr. 1842, *Providence Express,* 31 Mar. 1842, and *Rhode Island Manual, 1696–7,* 128.

101. Letter from Suffrage Party men in North Scituate, Alexander Allen, Harley Luther, Simon Mathewson to Dorr, 22 Feb. 1842, quoted in Gettleman, *The Dorr Rebellion,* 81–82.

102. Gettleman, *The Dorr Rebellion,* 82, 82–84.

103. Mowry, *The Dorr War,* 131–132, citing *Rhode Island House Journals,* 30 Mar. 1842 and 1 Apr. 1842.

104. Mowry, *The Dorr War,* 133, citing *Rhode Island House Journals,* 1 Apr. 1842, *Rhode Island Acts and Resolves,* Mar. 1842, 16–18, and Burke's Report, 133–135.

105. Mowry, *The Dorr War,* 134 (citing *Providence Express,* 5 Apr. 1842), 134 and 89 (citing John Pitman, *A Reply to the Letter of the Hon. Marcus Morton, Late Governor of Massachusetts, on the Rhode-Island Question* [Providence: Knowles and Vose, 1842], 20).

106. Gettleman, *The Dorr Rebellion,* 92; letter from Dorr to "Gentlemen of the State [Suffrage Party] Nominating Committee," 2 Apr. 1842 (draft), Dorr MSS, quoted in ibid., 84.

107. Letter from Sullivan and Lydia Dorr to Thomas Dorr, 8 Apr. 1842, electronic transcription at http://library.providence.edu:8080/xtf/view?docId=tei/L0012.xml.

108. Mowry, *The Dorr War,* 141–142; "Two letters of Governor King to the President," in Burke's Report, 656–657; Gettleman, *The Dorr Rebellion,* 94.

109. Gettleman, *The Dorr Rebellion,* 95; Mowry, *The Dorr War,* 135, citing *Providence Journal,* 11 Apr. 1842.

110. Gettleman, *The Dorr Rebellion,* 95, citing the Boston *Bay State Democrat,* 13 May 1842.

111. Gettleman, *The Dorr Rebellion,* 97; Mowry, *The Dorr War,* 144, 139–140.

112. "Thomas Wilson Dorr to Levi Woodbury, April 13, 1841," electronic transcription at http://library.providence.edu:8080/xtf/view?docId=tei/L0013.xml. Note that there is an error in the transcription of the passage quoted in the text; we follow the version in the original letter, an image of which can be found at http://library.providence.edu:8080/xtf/data/tei/bookreader/letter13/#page/1/mode/1up.

113. Erik Chaput, introduction to "Levi Woodbury to Thomas Wilson Dorr, April 15, 1841," electronic transcription at http://library.providence.edu:8080/xtf/view?docId=tei/L0014.xml.

114. Gettleman, *The Dorr Rebellion,* 86, 87, 100.

115. Mowry, *The Dorr War,* 136, 147, 148.

116. Gettleman, *The Dorr Rebellion,* 101–102; Mowry, *The Dorr War,* 151–152.

117. Gettleman, *The Dorr Rebellion,* 102 (citing *New Age,* 7 May 1842, and Frieze, *Concise History,* 70–71); Mowry, *The Dorr War,* 151–155; testimony of Jeremiah Briggs, in "Report of Treason Trial of Dorr," in Burke's Report, 874; "Proceedings and Journals of the People's Legislature," in Burke's Report, 462–466.

118. "Organization of the Government under the People's Constitution, and Message of Governor Dorr," in Burke's Report, 720, 726, 730.

119. Mowry, *The Dorr War,* 155; Burke's Report, 738.

120. "Governor Dorr's address to the People of Rhode Island, August, 1843," in Burke's Report, 738.

121. The *Providence Journal,* 6 May 1842, quoted in Mowry, *The Dorr War,* 158. For Governor King's letter, see Burke's Report, 672–673; for Governor Dorr's letter, see Burke's Report, 675. Dorr's letter is undated, but Mowry, *The Dorr War,* 158, states that the letters were "transmitted" the same day.

122. "Letter of Governor King to the President, transmitting resolutions of the General Assembly, declaring the State of Rhode Island in a state of insurrection, and calling for the military interference of the United States," in Burke's Report, 672–673; "The President's letter to Governor King, in reply to his letter of May 4, 1842," in Burke's Report, 674.

123. Mowry, *The Dorr War,* 160–163 (citing *Providence Journal,* 5–7 and 9–14 May 1842, inclusive, and *Providence Express,* 9–14 May 1842, inclusive); Gettleman, *The Dorr Rebellion,* 108 (citing Providence *Evening Chronicle,* 7 May 1842); see also "Governor Dorr's Address to the People of Rhode Island, August, 1843," in Burke's Report, 750.

124. "The President's letter to Governor King, in reply to his letter of May 4, 1842," in Burke's Report, 674.

125. McDougall, *Might and Right,* 239; "Dutee Pearce's Testimony in the Trial of Thomas Dorr," in Burke's Report, 876.

126. *Providence Journal,* 9 and 17 May 1842, quoted in Mowry, *The Dorr War,* 161, 163.

127. "Confidential Letter of the President [Tyler] to Governor King, May 9, 1842," Burke's Report, 676.

128. "Thomas Dorr to Aaron White, Jr.," 12 May 1842, electronic transcription at http://library.providence.edu:8080/xtf/view?docId=tei/L0017.xml.

129. "Thomas Dorr to Walter S. Burges," 12 May 1842, electronic transcription at http://library.providence.edu:8080/xtf/view?docId=tei/L0018.xml.

130. "Thomas Dorr to Aaron White, Jr.," 12 May 1842.

131. "Thomas Dorr to Walter S. Burges," 12 May 1842.

132. "Thomas Dorr to Aaron White, Jr.," 12 May 1842.

133. *New York Evening Post,* 16 Apr. 1842, quoted in Mowry, *The Dorr War,* 168.

134. "Thomas Dorr to Walter S. Burges," 12 May 1842. Dorr writes that he departed Washington on Wednesday morning (i.e., 11 May); Mowry, *The Dorr War,* 169, citing *New York New Era,* quoted by the *New York Evening Post,* 16 May 1842, *New York American,* 18 May 1842, and *New York Evening Post,* 13 May 1842.

135. Gettleman, *The Dorr Rebellion*, 111–112, citing McDougall, *Might and Right*, 258–259, Daniel Webster to John Whipple, 9 May 1842, Webster Papers, New Hampshire Historical Society, W. Channing Gibbs to Webster, 12 May 1842, Webster Papers, New Hampshire Historical Society, Dorr to Walter S. Burges, 12 May 1842, Dorr MSS, and *Providence Journal*, 26 May 1842.

136. "Alex Ming Jr. and Alexander Craston to Thomas Dorr," 13 May 1842, electronic transcription at http://library.providence.edu:8080/xtf/view?docId=tei/L0020 .xml. Note that this source erroneously transcribes "Crasto" as "Craston."

137. Mowry, *The Dorr War*, 173.

138. Ibid., 175, citing *Providence Journal*, 16 May 1842.

139. "Aaron White Jr. to Thomas Dorr, May 15, 1842," electronic transcription at http://library.providence.edu:8080/xtf/view?docId=tei/L0021.xml.

140. Mowry, *The Dorr War*, 175 (citing *Providence Express*, 17 May 1842), 175–176 (citing *Providence Journal*, 17 May 1842).

141. See "Trial of Dorr," in Burke's Report, 878–879; Mowry, *The Dorr War*, 176.

142. Mowry, *The Dorr War*, 176 (citing Joseph S. Pitman, *Report on the Trial of Thomas Wilson Dorr for Treason against the State of Rhode Island* [Boston: Tappan and Dennet, 1844], 26–27; testimony of Wm. P. Blodget).

143. Mowry, *The Dorr War*, 176; Burke's Report, 876–878.

·{ 6 }·

Debt and Democracy: The New York Constitutional Convention of 1846

ON SEPTEMBER 23, 1846, the convention to revise the constitution of New York State prepared to vote on a proposal that its principal proponent, Michael Hoffman, conceded would be "a serious change in the form of our government."[1] The proposal would place tight restrictions on the state's ability to borrow money.

Delegates had been meeting since June in the newly built Albany statehouse, writing constitutional amendments to submit to the voters in November. The delegates had wrangled over weighty problems, such as whether to make the judiciary elective, how to restructure the system of representation, and whether to give "colored male citizens" the vote. They had even received a petition, the first of its kind, asking them to give women the vote, but had tabled it without discussion.[2] Yet everyone knew that the main reason the convention had been called, and the most explosive issue it would consider, was how to deal with the public debt.

New York State debt had grown from under $8 million in 1837 to nearly $27 million in 1842.[3] The new debt had been incurred mostly to build canals during a major economic depression, precipitated by consecutive financial panics in 1837 and 1839. By the end of 1841, many feared that New York was teetering on the brink of default. Hoffman himself, in the state legislature, had written a bill "for paying the debt and preserving the credit of the state."[4] The bill, which became law in March 1842, levied a statewide property tax, devoted the proceeds to debt repayment, and abruptly suspended the canal-building program. Known as the "Stop and Tax" policy, Hoff-man's law provoked furious debate, with opponents intent on reversing it altogether.

Anti-debt reformers had been agitating for an amendment to the state constitution since the 1830s. It took various forms over the years, but by 1846 the version presented to the convention placed a cap on state debt of $1 million, which could be exceeded for only two reasons. Lawmakers would be able to borrow above the cap to meet an extraordinary emergency, such as repelling an invasion or putting down an insurrection. Alternatively, they could exceed the cap if they (1) authorized the additional debt for a specific, clearly identified purpose, (2) enacted an associated tax sufficient to pay off the additional debt within eighteen years, and (3) obtained approval of the debt and the tax from a majority of voters in a statewide referendum.

Critics had long denounced the idea of a debt-restriction amendment as unnecessary, unworkable, and subversive of republican government. They also objected that it would reverse three decades of state policy regarding "public improvements" and debt, dating back to 1817, when New York undertook to build the celebrated Erie Canal. Yet popular support for the idea had steadily grown as a tool to limit legislative irresponsibility and corruption. Debt reformers, led by Hoffman and his friend Arphaxed Loomis, had been instrumental in calling the constitutional convention, and now at last, on September 23, after days of fierce debate, the convention was about to vote on their big idea. If the convention approved it, it would almost certainly become part of the new constitution, because all amendments that the convention proposed would be submitted together (as a single package) to the voters, who were unlikely to reject the entire constitutional revision. The delegates thus had to decide: Should the fundamental law of the state restrict public debt, and if so, was the proposal before them the right way to do it?

The Struggle over Building and Financing Canals

By 1817 the New York State legislature had been debating for nearly a decade whether to construct a canal from Lake Erie to the Hudson River. Canal supporters envisioned it as a great avenue of commerce, but opponents insisted the project would fail, pointing out that western New York (and, for that matter, the entire Great Lakes region) as yet contained few towns and relatively little commercial activity. Critics also questioned whether the proposed canal was technically feasible. The longest existing American canal, the Middlesex Canal in Massachusetts, ran 27 miles with 20 locks to deal with a rise in elevation of 170 feet. This one would run over 360 miles and was projected to require over 60 locks to address a rise in elevation of 565 feet.[5]

Principally, however, critics objected to the high cost of the canal, projected at over $6 million. This amount was apparently beyond the ability of private corporations to raise on their own. Two private entities had already tried to build major canals in western New York and failed for lack of sufficient capital.[6] Meanwhile, the federal government had refused to help, which meant New York State would have to pay for the project alone, at a time when its annual "General Fund" revenues totaled less than $1.5 million. The largest portion of these revenues (about a third) came from a general property tax, but representatives in the legislature from New York City and towns along the lower Hudson River blocked any attempt to fund the Erie Canal with property taxes, on the grounds that the project would not raise their property values. The only way to build the canal, in short, would be for the state to take on substantial debt—a prospect that alarmed many. "Depend upon it," one anti-canal legislator declared, "if we vote for the canal . . . we mortgage the state forever."[7]

Despite such concerns, canal proponents, led by Governor DeWitt Clinton, persuaded the legislature to authorize the project. Work began on July 4, 1817, and was completed in October 1825. The state financed the work in part by dedicating two existing taxes to canal building, one tax on the auction of imports in New York City and the other on the production of salt near Syracuse, but mostly by taking out loans in the form of state-issued 5 percent "stock" (hereafter referred to simply as "bonds").* In the end, the state borrowed nearly $7.9 million to build the canal.[8]

Clinton and his allies remained confident that canal tolls would generate more than enough revenue to fund the debt, and they turned out to be right.

---

* These "stocks" were like bonds in that they paid fixed interest at regular intervals and, after a certain number of years, could be redeemed for the principal. They were traded on the "stock market," with "par value" equaling the face value listed on the instrument itself. The rate at which the "stock" traded below par (its "discount"), or above par, was often regarded as a measure of state credit.

In 1825–1826, the Erie Canal's first year of full operation, it produced over $687,000 in tolls, and the sum increased each year thereafter.[9] The tolls more than paid for canal upkeep and interest on the debt. In fact, the surplus was sufficiently large that when the existing general property tax expired in 1826 (it had been imposed to pay off debts incurred by the state during the War of 1812), the legislature saw no need to replace it with a new one.[10] Looking back on this era many decades later, one historian remarked that the people of New York began "to think that taxes need never again be imposed, for the waterways were looked upon as a veritable treasure-house for supplying funds."[11]

The economic benefits of the canal turned out to be greater than even Clinton himself had hoped. Before the canal opened, the cost to haul a ton of goods from Buffalo to Albany had been $100. After the canal opened, it was $10.[12] As costs plummeted, trade increased dramatically. In the 1845 season, "total traffic arriving at the Hudson . . . included nearly 2,000,000 bushels of wheat, 2,500,000 barrels of flour, 20,000,000 pounds of butter, and nearly 30,000,000 pounds of cheese," as well as "237,000,000 feet of boards and 70,000 tons of staves." The business generated by the canal drew a tide of migrants, swelling villages along the canal route into cities. Between 1820 and 1850, the population of Syracuse grew from 1,814 to 22,271; Rochester grew from 1,502 to 36,403; and Buffalo, from 2,095 to 42,261. Some observers have attributed the rapid growth between 1820 and 1850, not only of western New York but also of the entire Great Lakes region, in significant part to the canal. And although the leaders of New York City had generally opposed the canal (Clinton, a former New York mayor, was a conspicuous exception), it turned out that the city benefited greatly from the booming business the canal brought down the Hudson, becoming the principal commercial gateway between the American interior and the Atlantic.[13]

The success of the canal made Clinton a political hero to many, hailed both before and after his death in 1828 as the "great projector." Business and political leaders across New York began petitioning the state to build canals through their towns and villages. As early as 1825, the legislature authorized the surveying of seventeen more canals.[14] Direct opposition to state-sponsored canal building had by this point disappeared from mainstream political discourse, yet there remained strong disagreements over how canals should be financed.[15] Because canals were now by far the largest expense of state government, as well as its principal source of revenue, these disagreements would play a considerable role in shaping New York politics over the coming decades.

Two major national political parties emerged in these years, the Democrats and the Whigs. Democrats dominated state politics from 1829 to 1837, controlling the governorship and large majorities in the legislature. The state Democratic Party was in turn dominated by a powerful political machine, popularly known as the "Albany Regency," founded and led by Martin Van Buren, who became U.S. senator from New York (1821–1828), governor of New York (1829), U.S. secretary of state (1829–1831), vice president of the United States (1833–1837), and U.S. president (1837–1841). Although Van Buren had been DeWitt Clinton's chief political rival, and he and his followers had been critics of the Erie Canal proposal, Van Buren Democrats ultimately became canal promoters. Largely under their administration, New York built five "lateral" canals, feeding into the Erie Canal—a total of 165 new miles of inland waterway.[16]

Although New York Democrats appeared united through the 1830s, they disagreed internally about both public works and debt. These disagreements would harden in the 1840s and divide the party into factions. One group, generally referred to as "Conservatives," were principally interested in maintaining party unity and discipline and were open to using debt to finance canal building. Their support for debt financing, however, was restrained by their desire to maintain unity with the "Radicals," who shared Thomas Jefferson's view that public debt was a tax on posterity and a tool of political corruption, and who wanted canals to be built on a pay-as-you-go basis, if at all.[17]

The Radical position was forcefully stated in 1827 by Silas Wright Jr. when he chaired the Committee on Canals in the state Senate. His committee had received a petition asking the state to support construction of a major new waterway that would connect the Erie Canal to the Allegheny River, to facilitate trade with Pennsylvania. Wright rejected the proposal in a widely noticed report.

Wright argued that the existing canal debt should be paid off before the state used any canal revenue to finance new projects. "That the state has borrowed money for the construction of canals is true,—that it can again do it, the committee do not doubt," he observed; "but that *it has paid* the money so borrowed, is not true." He considered the amount of revenue produced by the canals to be "highly exaggerated in the public opinion" and predicted that canal revenues in the coming years would not significantly increase. Wright expressed concern that the state had nonetheless undertaken to build more canals, thereby increasing the state debt to a level where it could not be paid with canal revenue (plus the auction and salt duties, which continued). He therefore recommended that a canal should be built only when it clearly would "reimburse the treasury for the expense of making it." The proposed canal to Pennsylvania did not meet this standard, in his view. To build unprofitable canals, Wright insisted, would only "hasten the period when direct taxation must be resorted to."[18]

New York Whigs, most of whose leaders had been Clinton supporters, identified themselves as the true heirs of the "great projector." Whigs gained power in New York after the Panic of 1837 turned voters against the incumbent Democrats. In the state elections that fall, Whigs won a large majority in the New York State Assembly, the lower house of the legislature. In 1838, William H. Seward, today remembered as Abraham Lincoln's secretary of state, won election as the first Whig governor of New York, and he was re-elected two years later. When Whigs also secured a majority in the state Senate in 1839, this gave them full control of state canal policy for the first time.

The Whig view of canals and debt was expressed in a famous 1838 report prepared by Samuel B. Ruggles, a businessman, philanthropist, and lawmaker who chaired the Ways and Means Committee in the state Assembly. Ruggles severely criticized Wright's 1827 report and offered a powerful affirmative case for canal building. He likely agreed with many other Whigs that even if a canal were "profitless," in the narrow sense of revenues not exceeding expenses, it still might be worth building for the sake of economic development. Here, however, he focused on the more obvious point that Wright's pessimistic predictions about Erie Canal revenue had been wrong. Revenue had in fact almost doubled between 1826 and 1835, even as canal tolls had been cut by nearly a third.[19]

More broadly, Ruggles attacked the Radical view that "internal improvement is but another name for eternal taxation." Ruggles found this belief "strange," considering that since 1817, when work on the Erie Canal began, state revenues had increased more than threefold (despite elimination of the property tax), while the "productive property" of the state had more than quadrupled in value. He expressed frustration with what he regarded as the Radicals' irrational obstructionism, which he alleged had forced the state to pursue canal building in an "irregular and disconnected" way, "yielding only to occasional impulses, and proceeding without much plan or method." If New York could only build a "great and harmonious system of intercommunication," he suggested, this would yield extraordinary benefits, "in augmenting the aggregate riches of our State;—in covering its surface with opulent cities; . . .—in securing its political supremacy;—and in enlarging, in all respects, its prosperity, power, and glory."[20]

To realize this vision, Ruggles argued, New York need not levy new taxes, because more and bigger canals would produce more revenue. He calculated that if the state expanded its spending on public improvements to $4 million a year over the following ten years, financed entirely with 5 percent bonds, net annual canal revenue would rise from $800,000 in 1838 to $3 million in 1849. He produced tables demonstrating that under these circumstances, the entire $40 million debt, interest and principal, would be fully repaid by 1865. As soon as his report was published, in 1838, New York Whigs celebrated it, and they turned its ideas into a central plank of the platform on which they ran and won elections over the next several years.[21]

The Politics of Public Debt

When the New York legislature decided in 1827 not to authorize a new statewide property tax, few expected that surplus canal tolls would, in and of themselves, be sufficient to cover government expenses. Instead, annual revenue shortfalls would be offset by drawing down the state General Fund, which was at this time flush with tax revenue, proceeds from the sale of public lands, and bank stock. Once canal revenues had paid off the original Erie Canal debt, so the thinking went, the General Fund could then be further augmented by restoring to it the salt and auction taxes, which had been diverted to canal building. From the beginning, however, some Radical Democrats objected that this approach would inevitably deplete the General Fund. Among them were the two comptrollers who held office through the 1830s, Silas Wright and Azariah Flagg, who in their annual reports repeatedly urged the legislature to replenish the General Fund with a small statewide property tax. Yet legislators showed no desire to impose new taxes; a bill proposed in 1832 to levy a property tax of one-tenth of a cent on the dollar received only 5 votes in the state senate. Just as Wright and Flagg predicted, without new taxes the General Fund was ultimately depleted—by 1835, in fact. Although the auction tax was restored to the fund that year, as the salt tax would be later, deficits proved unavoidable.[22]

The Expansion of Public Works

In 1836, meanwhile, the state legislature approved the most ambitious canal project to date: enlargement of the Erie. The canal had been built forty feet wide and four feet deep, with single locks. By the mid-1830s, however, with the number of boats continuing to rise, and relentless economic pressure to increase their size, most observers predicted that desired canal traffic would soon exceed capacity, forcing trade away to other channels (up the new Canadian ship canal around Niagara Falls, for example). In 1835, therefore, the legislature authorized the Canal Board to devise an enlargement plan. The board, whose "guiding spirit" was William Bouck, a Conservative Democrat, came back in 1836 with a proposal to increase the dimensions of the Erie to seventy feet wide by seven feet deep, with double locks throughout, for an estimated cost of about $12.5 million.[23] Also in 1836, legislators approved two ambitious new lateral canals. The Genesee Valley Canal would run 100 miles from the Erie Canal at Rochester south to the Allegheny River—essentially the same route Silas Wright had rejected as unprofitable in his 1827 report—and would cost an estimated $1.9 million to build. The second canal would connect the Erie Canal at Rome to the Black River in the north, and so to the eastern part of Lake Ontario; it would run only 35 miles, but as the route snaked through the Allegheny foothills, it would require more than a hundred locks, which brought the estimated building cost to just over $1 million.[24]

The legislature, under pressure from Radical Democrats, had authorized no loans to pay for these projects, which meant that spending on a pay-as-you-go basis had been slow—about $600,000 by 1838. That year, however, the Assembly, for the first time under Whig control, with Ruggles as its dominant figure, allied with Conservative Democratic governor William Marcy and Conservatives in the state Senate to approve a bill authorizing the Canal Board to borrow $4 million and to begin securing construction contracts to expand the Erie Canal as quickly as possible. In January 1839 William Seward took office as the first Whig governor. In his first annual message, he recommended that the legislature act in the spirit of Ruggles's report and accelerate public works spending, not only on the Erie expansion but also on the lateral canals, based on an additional $4 million of new debt per year.[25]

Rising Costs, Recession, and Reaction

Shortly thereafter the Canal Board made an alarming announcement. It had discovered that the price of the various projects now under contract would be much higher than originally estimated. The Black River Canal would cost not $1 million but $2.1 million; the Genesee River Canal not $1.9 million but $5 million; the Erie enlargement not $12 million but $24 million—more than New York had spent on all other canal projects combined. (And the revised figures all proved too low in the end.) These disparities were so great that many concluded the engineers who made the original estimates "were either grossly and culpably ignorant or negligent or . . . were corrupt."[26] At the same time, the deepening economic crisis following the Panic of 1837 depressed canal revenues, so that Ruggles's projections, on which the Whig program rested, proved overly optimistic. He had calculated a revenue surplus in 1840 of $2 million, for example, but there turned out to be no surplus at all.[27]

These developments alarmed Democrats, who, with Radicals taking the lead, in 1839 began to attack the Whigs' "Forty Million Dollar Debt." Democrats pronounced Whig policy wrong in principle, because each generation, in their view, should leave future generations debt free. Democrats also denounced Whig public works policy as fostering corruption. Above all, they insisted that expanding public works through debt financing would soon bankrupt the state. They therefore urged that the Erie project be radically scaled back and the Genesee and Black River projects be abandoned altogether. That these arguments began to resonate with voters could be seen in the 1840 elections. Seward only barely won reelection, and although the Whigs retained control of the state legislature, their majority in the Assembly narrowed. Moreover, two leading critics of Whig policy— Michael Hoffman and his younger, more introspective colleague Arphaxed Loomis—won Assembly seats. Both were Radical Democrats and former

U.S. congressmen from upstate Herkimer County. Loomis immediately introduced resolutions calling for a constitutional limit on debt, which nearly passed the Assembly.[28]

Despite growing public unease, Whigs refused to alter their canal policy, except to concede that canal building should be pursued with a new emphasis on "moderation and economy." They claimed that their opponents exaggerated the size of the state debt, reminded everyone that the original "deceptive" cost estimates for the canal projects had been made by Democrats, and insisted above all that these projects were far too important for the long-term economic growth of the state to be scaled back or abandoned. More broadly, they attacked the Democratic concept that each generation should operate independently of the next, because this idea seemed to reject one of the most "benevolent" and patriotic human impulses, to leave a great legacy for posterity.[29] Furthermore, as Governor Seward pointed out in his annual message in January 1840, state spending on public works helped ease the negative effects of the economic depression:

> During the severe pressure we have experienced, the industry of the citizen has been stimulated, and the wages of labor, the prices of the products of the earth, and the value of property have been sustained by expenditures in the prosecution of this system. The sudden arrest of such expenditures, and the discharge of probably ten thousand laborers, now employed upon the public works, at a time when the circulation of money in other departments of business is so embarrassed as almost to have ceased, would extend throughout the whole community, and with fearful aggravation, the losses and sufferings that as yet have been in a great measure confined to the mercantile class.[30]

Default and Repudiation outside of New York State

Despite Whig efforts to blunt public concern about the state debt, events outside New York gave Democratic alarm bells growing resonance. During the 1830s other states had been inspired to emulate the success of the Erie Canal with their own ambitious public works projects. To finance them, many had not levied new taxes but like New York had floated bonds, initially at 5 or 6 percent interest, which were sold in large measure to British investors. State officials had expected the new public works to yield extraordinary returns. Most were disappointed, however, when the American economy contracted sharply after the Panics of 1837 and 1839. In fact, many state governments now found themselves struggling to meet millions of dollars in obligations. They were forced to float bonds at ever higher interest rates, and they in turn forced state-chartered banks to give them loans, which only weakened the banks. Many states increased property taxes, but found that because property values were falling with the shrinking economy, even higher tax rates failed to generate the revenues they needed.[31]

In the spring of 1841, two states defaulted on their debts by missing payments: Michigan, which had borrowed $5 million to build, simultaneously, a canal and three railroads (parallel to one another) from Lake Erie to Lake Michigan; and Indiana, which had borrowed over $10 million to construct a "lattice-work" of interconnecting "canals, roads, and railroads." More state defaults, also associated with significant spending on canals and railroads, soon followed: in October 1841, Maryland (with $14 million of debt); the same month, Illinois ($10 million); and in August 1842, Pennsylvania ($40 million). In the South, meanwhile, numerous state governments defaulted after having invested millions in banks that collapsed in the panics: Mississippi (May 1841), Arkansas (October 1841), the Florida Territory (February 1842), and Louisiana (January 1843).[32]

In response to this fiscal disaster, Mississippi and the Territory of Florida repudiated their debts completely, while Michigan, Arkansas, and Louisiana repudiated a portion of their debts. Other defaulting states missed payments, but ultimately paid in full over time. The arguments for repudiation varied. Michigan refused to pay certain bondholders because it had not actually received money for the bonds they held: American banks had bought the Michigan bonds on credit, used them as security for loans from English and Dutch banks, but collapsed before paying the state what it was owed. Elsewhere, government officials pointed out (often correctly) that a large portion of their debts had been contracted without legislative consent, or in direct violation of legislative intent or even state law. Some advocates of repudiation, meanwhile, declared that American taxpayers should not be forced to bail out greedy European investors. The governor of Mississippi, merging this argument with rank anti-Semitism, singled out for denunciation a major British bondholder who was a member of the Jewish Rothschild family. "The blood of Judas and Shylock flows in his veins," the governor declared, "and he unites the qualities of both his countrymen."[33]

For their part, foreign investors were understandably alarmed. One British correspondent, writing for an American publication, suggested that opinion was growing "among the more reflecting, that the original cause of danger is to be found in the too democratic nature of the institutions of your country, which, by throwing all elections in the hands of the multitude, and by making those elections recur perpetually, cause those institutions to be attacked by demagogues, addressing themselves to the passions of the ignorant who form the numerical majority."[34]

Mounting Financial Troubles in New York

Although the doctrine of "repudiation" (i.e., refusing to pay debts) found almost no support in New York, by late 1841 many observers did fear the state might be unable to avoid missing payments and thus headed for default. One obvious sign of trouble was the falling value of New York bonds. Its 5 percent bonds, which in 1833 had sold above par, were now selling at nearly 20 cents below par, and its 6 percent bonds also sold at steep discounts.[35] Unwilling to contract long-term debt at "ruinous" interest, the state began taking out short-term loans, due in six months to a year. Moreover, the state was nearly a million dollars in arrears to its canal contractors, who began taking out loans themselves to cover their labor costs.[36]

In January 1842, Governor Seward confessed in his annual message that "the prosecution of the public works is embarrassed." He insisted, however, that the problem did not lie in state fiscal policy. New York actually had ample resources to pay its debts, for example from the millions in revenue that would certainly flow once the Erie Canal improvement was complete. Instead, he argued, "our [bonds] . . . are depressed by some general cause affecting all American governmental securities." The defaults and repudiation of some states had damaged the credit of all, especially in England, where the differences between state governments in the United States was not well understood. True, the various public improvement projects had been undertaken on the assumption that interest rates would be 5 percent, and they were now around 7, but "it would certainly be the worst of all economy to discontinue enterprises so important for a reason so inadequate."[37]

Despite Seward's assurances, public concern about Whig debt policy won the Democrats increasing support. In the 1841 elections, voters gave Democrats control again of both houses of the state legislature, and in January 1842 Michael Hoffman, who had been reelected to the Assembly, took over as chair of the Ways and Means Committee. Shortly afterward, he gave a speech condemning Seward's policies:

> You may follow in the course of other states and other institutions—offer seven, seven and a half—go to eight—continue the process until, like Indiana, Illinois, and Michigan, your stocks are sold at forty or fifty cents on the dollar. But sooner or later the hour is approaching when you must stop in this profligate course. . . . Lives there any thing so base on earth, that to work itself out of difficulty, would bring this state where Indiana and Illinois are? . . . where Michigan is? where deficit has put Maryland, an Atlantic state? . . . If we will only stand by our credit—cease our expenditures—pay as we go—we shall overcome this storm. . . . But if, seeking popularity for an hour . . . we go on [spending] . . . the credit of the state in peril, and itself on the verge of bankruptcy . . . the ashes of the dead on which we stand would be dishonored. The damned would mock us and drive us from their society. No language of reprobation can express the deep indignation that men must feel when they see their country urged—urged—urged to the fatal verge of ruin.[38]

"Stop and Tax"

Soon after Hoffman spoke, the Democratic legislature brought back as comptroller Azariah Flagg, who had been out of office during the years of Whig control. Flagg promptly produced a report pronouncing the fiscal situation of the state dire, with pressing obligations that could not currently be met. He recommended, as he had throughout the 1830s, reimposition of a general property tax.[39] On March 7, Hoffman issued his own report, which found that Flagg had, if anything, understated the gravity of the fiscal situation. Hoffman calculated the overall state debt as $25.5 million, higher than previously estimated. Even worse, when he took into account all *"present, available, and prospective"* means, he still found a deficiency of over $5 million "to meet existing present demand upon the treasury, pressing demands on the Canal Fund in 1842, and demands to be matured in 1845."[40] In an appendix to the report, Hoffman published a letter he had received from the presidents of the four largest Wall Street banks, including the widely esteemed former

Treasury secretary Albert Gallatin, declaring that unless New York reversed its fiscal course, any further extension of credit to the state would be "highly inexpedient and improper."[41]

Hoffman concluded that there was only one "safe policy" open to the state: expenditures on public works "must cease" and "a tax of one mill on the dollar . . . of the assessed value of all taxable property, should be imposed."[42] For its first two years, the new revenue would go to pay off debts to the General Fund, and thereafter to pay off the canal debt. These recommendations were embodied in his "Stop and Tax" bill, which he promptly introduced.

Voting on the bill proved highly partisan. A Whig member of the Assembly tried unsuccessfully to amend it to allow appropriations for the unfinished canals and to strike out the tax provision. As a contemporary observer noted, these "amendments were supported by *all* the whigs, and opposed by *all* the democrats." Similar amendments were proposed by Whigs in the state Senate "and were rejected there by a similar party vote." Tensions between Conservative and Radical Democrats became apparent, however, when a Conservative senator from a canal district tried and failed to amend the act to allow some work on the canals to proceed. In the end, the two wings of the party united for the final vote, but some Conservatives evidently worried that stopping the works altogether and indefinitely would be going too far.[43]

The bill next went to the governor for approval. In a special memorandum, Seward remarked that the proposed legislation ran "contrary to the policy which I have on all proper occasions recommended" and that he dissented entirely from the view of "the fiscal administration" (meaning Comptroller Flagg) that the legislation was "absolutely and urgently necessary." Yet he also observed that "the Executive could not, consistently with the spirit of the [state] Constitution, attempt to control the deliberate action of the Legislature in regard to such measures under such circumstances," and he therefore reluctantly signed the Stop and Tax bill, which became law on March 29, 1842.[44]

Just a few months later, however, Governor Seward sent a special message to the legislature urging it to reconsider the "radically wrong" legislation. He lamented that for the first time in a quarter century, no progress could be reported on the "system of internal improvements," and that this "high career of prosperous and well-directed enterprise has been brought to a sudden and humiliating close." He argued that if the policy were to continue in force, the "present generation . . . must abandon all hopes of seeing the system resumed, and it will only remain for them to pay the whole cost of the works, in a great degree useless, because left unfinished, and hastening rapidly to dilapidation and ruin." The Stop and Tax policy would not, in Seward's view, even meet its stated objective of decreasing indebtedness. New York was now "liable to contractors for heavy damages which might have been avoided by prosecuting the works, while by discontinuing the necessary enlargement of the Erie canal, the increase in revenues hitherto so constant, and so confidently relied upon for the reimbursement of the debts, is checked, and must ultimately cease."[45]

The Democratic legislature declined to act on Seward's recommendation, and Hoffman, in a speech to the Assembly, answered him at length. Hoffman pointed out that the governor had not even mentioned the main problem that Stop and Tax had been implemented to address. "Yes," he exclaimed, "like the strolling players in a country village, who gave notice that they would perform Hamlet, at the same time stating that the part of Hamlet would be entirely omitted . . . the Governor had sent in a message here on finance, without a word in it of the amount of the state debt, of the arrearages—of the appropriations necessary to carry on and finish works begun—not a syllable as to the many millions it would take to execute '*the system*,' which had found favor with him." This omission made the governor's message not only "worthless, but so far as it can have any effect, positively mischievous."[46]

Hoffman denied that the Stop and Tax law had, in actual fact, stopped the works. The works had "suspended themselves" because "the contractors, pushed to the wall, could go no further." The stoppage "could not have been prevented, law or no law. . . . The want of funds had arrested the public works; and it is not in your power now, nor in the power of the Executive, to do what you will do in the statute book. You can't command money.—It can only be had by prudence, economy, by some effort towards paying as well as borrowing."[47]

As for Seward's overall recommendation to repeal Stop and Tax, Hoffman branded it as nothing less than "perfidy." Under this policy, he explained,

> the public officers have gone to the widow, the trustee of the property of minors and orphans, the capitalist and the hard working man—to everybody that had funds—have borrowed their money and have pledged this tax and the guaranty of this law as security. . . . Whatever hardships have existed (and the bill has operated severely in some quarters)—still, we have been saved from the general wreck. And now that we have got the advantage of it, shall we in treachery . . . repeal the act? . . . It is to say to the public creditors, after you have got their money and delivered over the securities, "give them up." It is the language of the highwayman—except that the person who undertakes to say it, does not evince the courage of the highwayman, in exposing himself to be shot.[48]

Barnburners and Hunkers

The bond market appeared to react quickly and positively to the Stop and Tax law. By the end of April 1842, New York 5 percent bonds, which just before the law took effect had been trading at 76 cents on the dollar, increased to 84, while 6 percent bonds rose from 80 to 88.5. A month later, 7 percent bonds were selling at par; before the end of the year, 6 percents had reached par, and by August 1843 even 5 percents were at par.[49] Moreover, the public seemed to support Stop and Tax. In the 1842 state elections, the Democrats united around the policy, declaring that it had saved the state, while Whigs denounced it as "ruinous." Whigs claimed Stop and Tax had benefited only "stock-gamblers" and not the ordinary people of New York, decried the waste of money on projects that now languished unfinished and unusable, and charged that the real purpose of the new property tax was not to rescue state finances, which did not need rescuing, but to "make Internal Improvement unpopular."[50] Apparently unconvinced by Whig arguments, voters gave Democrats a decisive victory at election time, allowing them to retain control of the legislature and electing the Democratic gubernatorial candidate, William Bouck, by a wide margin.[51]

At the same time, pressure to restart the state's public works remained strong. It came first from contractors, many of whom had political connections. In 1842, shortly after the Stop and Tax policy went into effect, a canal commissioner complained of being "daily beset by a hungary [*sic*] & starving throng of contractors upon our public works, begging for money or State stocks, or even a promise of money."[52] Contractors were not alone. Towns along the unfinished Black River and Genesee Valley Canals, for example, complained bitterly about the policy, dwelling especially on the financial distress of people who had sunk their savings into new homes along the projected routes. In 1846 a Whig described the situation along an abandoned section of the Genesee Valley Canal:

> The . . . desolation along its borders [presents] . . . a mournful appearance that beggars description; you will there find mounds of earth and excavation grown over with grass, locks partly finished, piles and acres of stone, decaying timbers and plank prepared for finishing the work; you will find farms cut in two, the roads everywhere obstructed and in places rendered almost impassable; . . . you will see the deserted shantees [*sic*] of the workmen, the forsaken homes of the injured victims of a cruel disappointment, and you will see those who continue to reside there brooding over their hard fate.[53]

The issue that no doubt resonated most strongly with the new governor, Bouck, was the future of the Erie Canal enlargement. The legislature had originally approved this project because so many observers predicted that demand for canal transport would soon exceed existing capacity. Although canal traffic had slowed during the economic downturn, it began to increase again as the economy recovered, and by the mid-1840s, with recovery in full swing, it would approach levels predicted by Samuel Ruggles in 1838. Yet when the Stop and Tax Act passed, only a fraction of the enlargement had been completed.[54]

Hoffman and other Radicals argued that the plan for Erie Canal enlargement had been the product of heady dreams during the boom years of the mid-1830s and that enlargement was not needed. Realistic projections of increased canal traffic, they insisted, could be met by modest improvements, such as installing faster-operating lock gates. Governor Bouck disagreed. In 1836 he had led the Canal Commission in approving the 70-by-7 enlargement plan, and he still believed in it. Bouck had been persuaded to suspend canal building only as a "temporary necessity." In his first message to the legislature, therefore, in January 1843, Bouck cautiously suggested that the works be restarted, "of course . . . with strict reference to the financial condition of the state." Hoffman was not in the legislature that year, but he privately fumed to his friend Flagg that Bouck had betrayed the Democratic platform: "To change sides on coming into power is such an open profligacy . . . as has never been exhibited on this side of the Atlantic!"[55]

The Democratic disagreements between Conservatives and Radicals over spending and public works, already apparent in 1842, reached a new level of intensity starting in 1843. The Radicals began referring to the Conservatives as "Hunkers," presumably because they cared less about principles than about getting "a large 'hunk' of the spoils of office."[56] Radicals were in effect alleging that the Conservatives wanted to keep building canals as a resource for political patronage and favors, a function the public works had in fact long served. As a leading historian of the Erie Canal has noted, every "shift in political power in the state brought new engineers, collectors, weigh masters, boat inspectors, superintendents, and lock tenders to the entire line of the canal. . . . Working under the direction of the engineers were the contractors, whose political loyalties were also weighed on a partisan scale. . . . After every election the press took note of the displacement of the incumbents and printed the list of the new appointees."[57] Conservatives, meanwhile, began calling the Radicals "Barnburners," after an old story of a farmer who foolishly "burned down his barn to rid it of the rats—the implication being that the Barnburners were willing to destroy the public works . . . to stop the abuses connected with them."[58]

Hoffman and the Barnburners grew convinced that "an association had been formed, with Governor Bouck at its head . . . the object of which was to change the policy established by the act of 1842."[59] Democrats managed to pull together for the legislative elections that year, which they again won, but the unity did not last long. In January 1844, Bouck once again suggested in his annual message that the works be restarted, and this became the principal issue considered by the legislature that year.[60]

As the Whigs were now in the minority, the debate was mainly between the Barnburners, led by Hoffman, who had returned to the Assembly and once again chaired the Ways and Means Committee, and the Hunkers, led in the legislature by the young chair of the Canal Committee, Horatio Seymour (who would become governor during the Civil War and the Democratic presidential nominee in 1868). The differences between the two sides appeared large, with Barnburners charging Hunkers with repudiating Stop and Tax, and Hunkers charging Barnburners with hostility to the canals and adherence to "abstract theories." Yet in fact, as one contemporary remarked, the real difference was the "true construction of the act of 1842":

> Mr. Hoffman contended that, according the spirit of that act, nothing ought to be expended [on canals] other than for necessary repairs until the entire debt should be paid. Mr. Seymour, on the contrary, though he explicitly took ground in favor of the law of 1842, and urged that all its guarantees and pledges should be rigidly observed, contended that any surplus, beyond the amount pledged, should be applied to the *extension* and preservation of the public works.[61]

Seymour won this argument. In 1844, Hunkers united with the minority Whigs to enact a bill that restarted work on the Erie, Genesee, and Black River Canals.[62]

Although these new projects were to proceed more slowly than under the Whigs, the renewed spending on public works would inevitably put off the day when the state's debts could be extinguished. This development only reinforced Hoffman's view that a more complete—constitutional—solution to the problem of public debt was required. As he had written to his friend Flagg in the summer of 1842, "If we are to have further loans and additional debts, I go for a convention and a new constitution. Monopoly may hiss and locality may yell, but a convention of the people must be called to sit in judgment of the past and command the future."[63]

A New Constitution?

The idea of using the state constitution to limit debt had originated with Hoffman's friend Arphaxed Loomis. One commentator speculated that because Loomis was nearly deaf, he was "isolated from the ordinary commerce of thought," which forced him into independent study and reflection that led him to original ideas. In 1835 Loomis had proposed a resolution to the Herkimer County Democratic Party convention calling for the state constitution to be amended so that if the government went into debt to build a public project, and the project did not generate enough revenue to pay the annual interest, the state must levy taxes to pay the difference. The delegates liked the proposal, which they added to their platform. Two years later,

Loomis resubmitted the proposal to the convention, with the significant addition that any new tax had to be approved by a public referendum as well. Again, the Herkimer convention approved his plan.[64]

Other than some Radical newspapers, however, few people outside Herkimer paid attention to Loomis's idea until 1840, when he and Hoffman were elected to the state Assembly. There, in February 1841, Loomis proposed, with Hoffman's support, what came to be called "The People's Resolutions." The key passage demanded that

> the constitution of the state be so amended, that every law authorizing the borrowing of money . . . shall specify the object for which the money shall be appropriated; and that every such law shall embrace no more than one such object, which shall be singly and specifically stated; and that no such law shall take effect until it shall be distinctly submitted to the people at the next general election, and be approved by a majority of the votes cast. . . . This provision shall not extend or apply to any law to raise money for the purpose of suppressing insurrection, repelling a hostile invasion, or defending the state in war.[65]

Although Whigs held a narrow majority in the Assembly that year, the resolutions failed on a tie vote. Some Whigs apparently were absent or abstained, while some Hunkers, ominously for Democratic unity, voted against it. In 1842, with Democrats in the majority, Loomis tried again, but once more Whig and Hunker votes united against him, and his resolution lost outright, 49–53.[66]

Loomis insisted that his proposal was "eminently democratic—perfectly in harmony with the spirit of our government and institutions," but many disagreed. One critic noted that only constitutional provisions, not laws, should be enacted by referendum. If laws were enacted by referendum, "the power and glory of the constitution" would be transformed "into a perfect image of ordinary laws." This would be "precisely tantamount to having no constitution at all. Its power will be destroyed, and the majority will wield the power of sovereignty without limitation or control and the government will be nothing more or less than a majority despotism."[67] The only proper way, argued another critic, to correct the errors and restrain the abuses of legislation, was "not by constitutional fetters, but by elevating the representative standard, and holding the servant to a strict and fearful accountability."[68]

Supporters of Loomis's idea, however, thought that punishing legislators after the fact for excessive spending was like locking the barn door after the horse had bolted.[69] They argued that the referendum would act as a check on legislative "log rolling" and the power of lobbyists. On a deeper level, they argued that the system of representative government had shown itself flawed, because it gave legislators every incentive to "become advocates of partial interests, instead of the representatives of the people." Loomis's allies also rejected the idea that representative democracy was the cornerstone of American government. The real cornerstone, they insisted, was popular sovereignty. As one Barnburner newspaper asserted, the legislature "is a mere labor-saving machine, an invention to save time and trouble; but the power of which is with the people, and whose machinery, is under their control."[70]

Although the People's Resolutions were defeated, Barnburners refused to let the anti-debt amendment die. Neither Hoffman nor Loomis sat in the Assembly in 1843, but they were doubtless behind a memorial to the Assembly from Herkimer County Democrats, again asking for an amendment forbidding the legislature to contract debts without the express consent of the voters. The petition was referred to a select committee, which was unable to unite on a recommendation. The majority report favored the proposed amendment, on the grounds that recent state history had shown the need for stronger safeguards against excessive spending. The minority report, written by a Whig from a canal district, replied that the real issue was not the state debt—which had been necessary to achieve the state's internal improvements—but instead whether the government would substitute the "anarchy and confusion" of direct democracy for the "order and efficiency which prevails under a representative or republican form of government." Besides, the minority argued, a referendum rule, had it been in effect in 1839–1841, would not have changed history. The "measures adopted, by which the state has become heavily indebted, whether wise or unwise, were the *measures* of the people themselves, enacted through their representatives. The judgment of the representative was a true index to that of the people. The voice of one was the voice of the other."[71]

Because, in the end, the state legislature took no action on the "Herkimer Memorial," Barnburners launched a campaign for a constitutional convention. Hoffman led the agitation, becoming president of the new State Association for Constitutional Reform.[72] From the Barnburner perspective, a constitutional convention had two advantages. First, it would take the process of writing and approving an anti-debt amendment out of the hands of the legislature, whose powers the amendment would limit. Second, because a convention could consider all aspects of the constitution, it could enact other useful and popular reforms that would help the anti-debt cause.

Of particular interest to the Barnburners, beyond the anti-debt amendment itself, was the judicial system. The state at this time had three distinct court systems, with overlapping jurisdictions, a structure left over from colonial times that was now widely viewed as confusing, burdensome, and inefficient. Hoffman thought that only a new court system, one truly responsive to and respected by the people, would have the authority to interpret the anti-debt provisions of a new constitution strictly, should some future legislature try to circumvent them. He therefore favored replacing the existing system of judges appointed for life with a system of judges elected for fixed terms.[73]

Hoffman laid out this broader reform program in a letter read to a pro-convention mass meeting in New York City in August 1843.[74] A new constitution, he declared, must not only "retrench expenditure," "make the revenues equal, in a short and reasonable period, to the payment of the whole of the public debt," and "limit the legislative power over debt and expenditure," but should also "provide Courts of law and equity . . . to be held by Judges to be elected by the people for a reasonable term of years." Further, these "Courts of the people must have the power to decide on constitutional questions, and thus maintain in practice the limits set by the constitution on delegated power."[75] Hoffman and the Barnburners also favored a number of other constitutional provisions, including "individual liability" for bankers.[76]

Whigs decided to support the convention movement—in part because they wanted to enact reforms of their own, including a new legislative districting system and black suffrage, and in part because they wanted to sow dissension between the two Democratic factions, the Barnburners and the Hunkers. The former strongly supported the proposed convention, the latter staunchly opposed it. The leading Hunker newspaper, for example, worried that the convention movement arose from a "spirit of demogoguism [sic]—a desire to overturn and remodel, for the sake of overturning—a desire of political and personal capital, from the belief that popularity will follow in the wake of a forward advocacy of sweeping changes through a convention," which, according to the newspaper, was not needed or even widely sought by the public.[77]

Hunkers also insisted that a constitutional convention would itself be unconstitutional. They pointed out that the original state constitution, from 1777, contained no provision for amendment, so when pressure arose to reform the document, the only recourse had been for the legislature to "recommend" that the people elect delegates to a constitutional convention, which had met in 1821. That convention had created a regular amendment process: a proposed amendment would have to be approved by a majority of elected members of the legislature and, the following year, by a two-thirds majority, and finally by a majority of voters in a statewide referendum. The 1821 delegates had made clear that they thought this procedure dispensed with the need for *"all future conventions."*[78]

Advocates of a new convention countered that the changes they wanted were necessary and could not be achieved by the regular amendment process and, more importantly, that the people had always retained the "right of *revolution"*—to change their government however they saw fit.[79] Hoffman considered the lack of a convention option in the 1821 constitution as another of its flaws to be reformed. One of his demands for a new constitution was that it require a new convention be called at least once every twenty years.[80]

In 1844, with the support of Governor Bouck, Hunkers in the legislature tried to forestall the convention movement by proposing a series of constitutional amendments to be approved by the 1821 procedure. Among them were amendments that incorporated the Stop and Tax law into the constitution, required a popular referendum to increase the debt, and made modest changes to the court system. Although the Barnburners still agitated for a convention, there were strong reasons not to split the party. A presidential election was taking place in 1844, and New York was the largest swing state. The amendments therefore passed with majorities in the legislature, while Hunkers agreed, in the face of Barnburner pressure, not to renominate Bouck for governor. Instead the state party convention gave the nod to Silas Wright, by now an elder statesman, who despite his Radical history had done little to offend Hunkers because he had been out of the state for a decade serving as a U.S. senator.[81]

By remaining united, New York Democrats won the fall elections. They retained control of the legislature; Wright became governor; and the

Democratic presidential nominee, James K. Polk of Tennessee, carried the state and the election. When Polk became president, he rewarded Hoffman, a personal friend, by appointing him to the lucrative post of Naval Officer for the Port of New York. Hoffman continued, however, to agitate for a convention.[82]

The new governor, Wright, tried in his first annual message to unify the party around the Stop and Tax and anti-debt amendments approved by the legislature in 1844, which now, in 1845, had to be approved again by a two-thirds majority. He failed. The Barnburners still wanted a convention and found allies in the Whigs, who disagreed with Barnburners on debt but wanted a convention for their own reasons. The Whigs and Barnburners therefore joined forces to defeat the anti-debt amendments and approve a bill (introduced by a Barnburner after consulting with Hoffman and Loomis, and bitterly opposed by Hunkers) calling for a constitutional convention, to open the following summer. In November, the voters approved the proposal by a margin of 213,257 to 33,860. Elections for delegates to the convention took place in the spring of 1846, and both Hoffman and Loomis were chosen, along with 125 others.[83]

Debate at the Constitutional Convention in Albany

The delegates assembled in Albany on June 1, 1846, and met continuously, six days a week, for the next four months. Hoffman and Loomis quickly established themselves as dominant figures; one Whig even referred to them as the "Ajax Telamon" and "Ulysses" of the convention.[84] Loomis joined the committee considering amendments for judicial reform, while Hoffman became chair of the committee considering amendments related to "Canals, internal improvements, public revenues and property, public debt, and the powers and duties of the Legislature in reference thereto."[85]

On July 30 Hoffman's committee proposed two amendments. The first, a variation on the 1842 Stop and Tax law, would deal with existing debt; and the second, an elaboration on the People's Resolutions, would deal with future debt. On August 1, meanwhile, the judiciary committee presented its report, recommending an amendment to restructure the courts along the lines Barnburners favored, with an elected judiciary.[86]

The convention considered the judiciary report first and on September 10 adopted an amendment that largely followed its recommendations. The very next day, delegates took up Hoffman's first amendment on existing debt—the Stop and Tax amendment. Hoffman himself opened the debate with a speech that lasted almost the entire day, in which he reviewed the financial situation of the state in elaborate detail. Hoffman aimed to prove that if the public works did not stay stopped, the state would never relieve itself from crushing debt. He argued, moreover, that the Erie enlargement and the Genesee and Black River Canals were all poor investments. He predicted that Erie Canal revenue would soon start falling, owing to increased competition from other waterways and from railroads. As for the Genesee and Black River Canals, he thought they would never generate enough tolls to turn a profit for the state.[87]

With respect to state revenues, Hoffman argued for repeal of the auction and salt taxes. He also rejected the long-standing state policy of using canal tolls for general revenues. The state should hold rights of way, he argued, "in trust for the million—to promote travel, transportation, and commerce." If the state "makes advances and incurs a reasonable risk in making a road or canal, the State from the tolls should fully indemnify itself for those expenses and that risk." To use the tolls for general revenue, however, makes "the government a real highwayman—odious, and an oppressor." Such an "abuse" would in the end fail even to produce revenue: "Trade, travel, and transportation will be driven from us, and our industry must languish. . . ." Hoffman concluded that ever higher general taxes would be needed unless New York firmly rejected "our debtor system for internal improvements," which had falsely "promised exemption from taxes and with it the endowment of schools and charities," but which had "already made us feel these taxes, and will leave us long to their mercy."[88]

Debate over Hoffman's first amendment lasted until September 22, often running late into the night. Whigs and Hunkers denounced Hoffman's plan as too extreme and proposed substitute after substitute that authorized the public works to be restarted. Eventually Hoffman and Loomis realized they had to compromise, and so they reluctantly agreed to a substitute amendment, which basically put into the constitution, not the 1842 act, but instead the 1844 act (which had allowed further canal building, but on a restricted basis).

With this long struggle out of the way, debate immediately began on Hoffman's second proposed amendment. Regarding the contracting of state debt, it read as follows:

> The State may, to meet casual deficits or failures in revenues, or for expenses not provided for, contract debts, but such debts, direct or contingent, singly or in the aggregate, shall not, at any time, exceed one million of dollars. . . .
>
> In addition to the above limited power to contract debts, the State may contract debts to repel invasion, suppress insurrection, or defend the State in war. . . .
>
> Except the debts specified [above], no debt or liability shall be hereafter contracted by or on behalf of this State, unless such debt shall be authorized by a law for some single work or object to be distinctly specified therein, and such law shall impose and provide for the collection of a direct annual tax, to pay, and sufficient to pay the interest on such debt as it falls due, and also to pay and discharge the principal of such debt within eighteen years from the time of the contracting thereof. No such law shall take effect until it shall, at a general election, have been submitted to the people and have received a majority of all the votes cast for and against it at such election. . . .
>
> The money arising from any loan or stock creating debt or liability shall be applied to the work or object specified in the act authorizing such debt or liability, or for the repayment of such debt or liability, and for no other purpose whatever.[89]

The arguments for and against the amendment largely followed the lines that had been laid down over the previous five years. The most controversial aspect of the amendment remained the referendum provision. Supporters believed that it would serve as a check on legislative corruption and "log rolling," while opponents saw it as "going back to the old form of personal government as practised by the Athenians and Romans."[90] According to one opponent, Alvah Worden of Ontario County, the amendment falsely implied that "the experiment of a republican, representative, responsible form of government, after a trial of more than 70 years, had proved a failure." He also argued that the referendum provision would actually encourage the government to be fiscally reckless: "While members of the legislature acted upon their individual responsibility, they would be cautious in their acts; but relieve them from that responsibility by giving to the people the approval of all laws to create debt, and this conservative feature of our representative government is gone, and log-rolling would be open and bold in the halls of legislation, invited by this very provision."[91]

An interesting twist in the debate came when some Barnburners objected that the debt amendment was too lenient. It already allowed for a million dollars of debt, and it already made an exception in cases of war and insurrection. Why not, asked Lorenzo Shepard of New York City, just ban all other debts outright? The escape hatch of a referendum would still leave the government "at liberty to run wild as heretofore in pursuit of . . . visionary schemes." Loomis himself replied in defense of his idea that "the legislature and the people might with perfect propriety dispose of the immediate subject before them . . . but they never had the right to legislate for the future, to enthrall and bind down those who came after them," and "in the future there might be some occasion for creating a debt."[92]

After two days of discussion, the delegates at last faced a choice. Should they accept the debt-restriction amendment, accept it with modifications, or simply reject it altogether?

NOTES

1. S. Croswell and R. Sutton, *Debates and Proceedings in the New-York State Convention for the Revision of the Constitution* (Albany, NY: Argus Press, 1846), 723.

2. William G. Bishop and William H. Attree, *Report of the Debates and Proceedings of the Convention for the Revision of the Constitution of the State of New York* (Albany: Evening Atlas, 1846), 284; Jacob Katz and Lori D. Ginzberg Cohen, "1846 Petition for Women's Suffrage, New York State Constitutional Convention," *Signs* 22, no. 2 (Winter 1997): 427–439.

3. Don C. Sowers, *The Financial History of New York State, from 1789 to 1912* (New York: Columbia University, 1914), 336.

4. Laws of New York, 65th sess., chap. 114.

5. Ronald E. Shaw, *Erie Water West: A History of the Erie Canal, 1792–1854* (Lexington: University of Kentucky Press, 1966), 57, 69, 87–88; Daniel Walker Howe, *What Hath God Wrought: The Transformation of America, 1815–1848* (New York: Oxford University Press, 2007), 117; Christopher Roberts, *The Middlesex Canal, 1793–1860* (Cambridge: Harvard University Press, 1938), 191–192. In fact, the Erie Canal would turn out to need eighty-three locks, plus eighteen aqueducts, to address changes in elevation of

675 feet. Note that although Buffalo was 565 feet above the level of Albany, the total of changes in elevation was greater, including falls as well as rises on the route.

6. On $6 million projection, see Shaw, *Erie Water West*, 26. For the histories of the Western Inland Lock Navigation Company and the Northern Inland Lock Navigation Company, both chartered in 1792 and both of which went bankrupt, see ibid., 15–21. "Their failures," concludes Shaw, ". . . gave clear indication that such a work [as the Erie Canal] in that day was beyond the resources of private enterprise alone" (21).

7. Sowers, *Financial History*, 61–62, 324–325; Shaw, *Erie Water West*, 66–68, 73.

8. Shaw, *Erie Water West*, 84, 181; Sowers, *Financial History*, 62–63, 138–139; L. Ray Gunn, *The Decline of Authority: Public Policy and Political Development in New York, 1800–1860* (Ithaca, NY: Cornell University Press, 1988), 115–116.

9. Shaw, *Erie Water West*, 49–50, 299.

10. New York levied a general property tax from 1799 to 1803 and again from 1815 to 1826, to pay specific debts. In each case, the rate was one-tenth of a cent for each dollar of personal and real property; the valuation was made by the taxpayer, attested to in a sworn statement. See Sowers, *Financial History*, 114–116, 324.

11. Noble E. Whitford, *History of the Canal System of New York* (1906), quoted in Herbert D. A. Donovan, *The Barnburners: A Study of the Internal Movements in the Political History of New York State and of the Resulting Changes in Political Affiliation, 1830–1852* (New York: NYU Press, 1925), 15.

12. Edwin P. North, "Erie Canal and Transportation," *North American Review* 179 (Jan. 1900): 123. The figures are in the money of the times. See Shaw, *Erie Water West*, 72.

13. Shaw, *Erie Water West*, 297, 263, quotations at 297; Howe, *What Hath God Wrought*, 216–217.

14. Jabez Delano Hammond, *Life and Times of Silas Wright, Late Governor of New York* (Syracuse, NY: Hall and Dickson, 1848), 84. On "great projector," see e.g. Janet D. Larkin, "'Mr. Merritt's Hobby': New York State in the Building of Canada's First Welland Canal," *New York History* 86, no. 2 (Spring 2005): 188–189.

15. Gerrit Smith, a millionaire advocate of radical causes, most notably absolute racial equality and John Brown's 1859 attempt to start a slave insurrection in Virginia, was also among the very few people to call for New York to give up canal building altogether, on the grounds that it was beyond the proper scope of a republican government. See Shaw, *Erie Water West*, 308.

16. *Documents of the Assembly of the State of New-York* (1842) [hereafter cited as *Documents of the Assembly*], no. 61, pp. 11–13. The full volume is available at https://books.google.com/books?id=E1gbAQAAIAAJ&pg=RA1-PA1#v=onepage&q&f=false. On Van Buren, see Ted Widmer, *Martin Van Buren* (New York: Henry Holt, 2005).

17. Donovan, *Barnburners*, 15–16, 19–21.

18. Hammond, *Silas Wright*, 86–88, emphasis in original; Samuel B. Ruggles, *Report upon the Finances and Internal Improvements of the State of New-York* (New York: John S. Taylor, 1838), 12–13.

19. Shaw, *Erie Water West*, 318–319; Ruggles, *Report*, 12–15.

20. Ruggles, *Report*, 22–23, 8, 63.

21. Ibid., append.; Shaw, *Erie Water West*, 311.

22. Ruggles, *Report*, 17–18; Hammond, *Silas Wright*, 120–121; Donovan, *Barnburners*, 15–16; Gunn, *Decline of Authority*, 159–161; Sowers, *Financial History*, 254, 133, 138–139.

23. "Address of the Whig Members of the Legislature," *New-York Daily Tribune*, 28 Apr. 1841; Shaw, *Erie Water West*, 306–307, 320; William H. Seward, Annual Message (1840), in *State of New York: Messages from the Governors*, vol. 3, ed. Charles Z. Lincoln (Albany, NY: J. B. Lyon, 1909), 787–789.

24. Seward, Annual Message (1840), 789; Hammond, *Silas Wright*, 408.

25. Shaw, *Erie Water West*, 307–308, 315; *Laws of the State of New York, of a General Nature; Passed, from 1828, to 1841, Inclusive* (Rochester, NY: Thomas H. Hyatt, 1841), 91. Seward, Annual Message (1839), in Lincoln, *Messages from the Governors*, 3:735.

26. Seward, Annual Message (1840), 790; Hammond, *Silas Wright*, 408–409.

27. Shaw, *Erie Water West*, 318.

28. Shaw, *Erie Water West*, 322–323; George W. Smith, "Arphaxed Loomis: His Career and Public Services," *Papers Read before the Herkimer County Historical Society* 2 (1912): 109–127; James A. Henretta, "The Strange Birth of Liberal America: Michael Hoffman and the New York Constitution of 1846," *New York History* 77, no. 2 (Apr. 1996): 151–176; Gunn, *Decline of Authority*, 154; Hammond, *Silas Wright*, 287–288.

29. "Address of the Whig Members"; Seward, Annual Message (1841), in Lincoln, *Messages from the Governors*, 3:892, 814–816, 801–803.

30. Seward, Annual Message (1840), 795.

31. Alasdair Roberts, *America's First Great Depression: Economic Crisis and the Political Disorder after the Panic of 1837* (Ithaca, NY: Cornell University Press, 2012), 25–48.

32. Ibid., 53–65, quotations at 55.

33. Ibid., 58–59, 60–63, 64–65, quotation at 62. On state defaults and repudiation, see also John Wallis, "Constitutions, Corporations, and Corruption," *Journal of Economic History* 65 (2005): esp. 216–217.

34. Quoted in Gunn, *Decline of Authority*, 147.

35. Gunn, *Decline of Authority*, 146–147.

36. Hammond, *Silas Wright*, 268; Shaw, *Erie Water West*, 336; Gunn, *Decline of Authority*, 146.

37. Seward, Annual Message (1842), in Lincoln, *Messages from the Governors*, 3:966–968.

38. Quoted in Hammond, *Silas Wright*, 270–271.

39. *Documents of the Assembly*, no. 61, p. 5.

40. *Documents of the Assembly*, no. 88, pp. 12–13, 32, 26.

41. Albert Gallatin et al. to Hoffman, 28 Feb. 1842, in ibid., 52–59, quotation at 53.

42. *Documents of the Assembly*, no. 88, pp. 36–37.

43. Hammond, *Silas Wright*, 314, 283–284, quotations at 314.

44. Lincoln, *Messages from the Governors*, 3:1008–1009. Seward's understanding of the limits of his veto power grew from his concern, which he shared with most Whigs, about the abuse of executive power generally; Whigs had signaled how important

this issue was to them when they named their party after the Whigs of England, who had opposed the abuse of royal power. On this point, see Michael F. Holt, *The Rise and Fall of the American Whig Party: Jacksonian Politics and the Onset of the Civil War* (New York: Oxford University Press, 1999), 27–30. Seward had explained his view of the proper use of the governor's veto in a special message to the legislature in January 1842: "The general responsibilities of making laws rest with the legislature, while on the executive are devolved only the duties of recommending measures and of rejecting for sufficient causes bills originated and perfected by the representatives of the people. Although the executive might reluctantly feel himself obliged to interpose objections in a case where a proposed law should have hastily and inconsiderately passed the legislature, or should contravene the letter or spirit of the constitution, or infringe individual rights or impair the necessary efficiency of the executive administration, or invade the constitutional or appropriate powers of any department of the government or threaten any pervading or lasting injury to the public welfare, or should tend to produce inequality or injustice or deeply compromise any recognized principles of republican institutions, yet the person administering the government could not interpose objections to less important bills upon the mere ground of a difference of opinion concerning their expediency." Seward, Memorandum to the Senate (1842), in Lincoln, *Messages from the Governors*, 3:973–974.

45. Seward, Special Message (1842), in Lincoln, *Messages from the Governors*, 3:1045, 1041, 1042–1043, 1044.

46. Michael Hoffman, *Finances, Faith & Credit of the State: Mr. Hoffman's Speech . . . on the Governor's Message* (Albany, NY: Argus Press, 1842), 3, 5, emphasis in original.

47. Ibid., 7, 8.

48. Ibid., 10–11.

49. Gunn, *Decline of Authority*, 166.

50. "The Everlasting Water Wheel and the Man at the Pump," *New-York Daily Tribune*, 28 Sept. 1842, "ruinous" at 4; "An Eye to Windward," *New-York Daily Tribune*, 15 Nov. 1842, "stock gambler" at 2; "The Stop and Tax Policy," *New-York Daily Tribune*, 29 Oct. 1842, "make Internal Improvement unpopular" at 2.

51. Donovan, *Barnburners*, 34.

52. Shaw, *Erie Water West*, 338.

53. Speech of William G. Angell, in Croswell and Sutton, *Debates*, 666.

54. Shaw, *Erie Water West*, 352, 362–363; 337–339.

55. Hammond, *Silas Wright*, 278–279n; Donovan, *Barnburners*, 24, 35, 37.

56. Donovan, *Barnburners*, 33.

57. Shaw, *Erie Water West*, 253.

58. Donovan, *Barnburners*, 32.

59. Hammond, *Silas Wright*, 386–387.

60. Donovan, *Barnburners*, 44–48.

61. Hammond, *Silas Wright*, 419, emphasis in original.

62. Shaw, *Erie Water West*, 345; Donovan, *Barnburners*, 50.

63. Donovan, *Barnburners,* 44.

64. Smith, "Arphaxed Loomis," 120, 116; Donovan, *Barnburners,* 23; Hammond, *Silas Wright,* 287.

65. Hammond, *Silas Wright,* 286–287.

66. Donovan, *Barnburners,* 23; Gunn, *Decline of Authority,* 154.

67. Gunn, *Decline of Authority,* 155, 157.

68. Smith, "Arphaxed Loomis," 110.

69. Ibid.

70. Quoted in Gunn, *Decline of Authority,* 155, 157–158.

71. Quoted in ibid., 173–174, emphasis in original. The author of the minority report was Wells Brooks of Erie County.

72. Ibid., 174–175.

73. Ibid., 63–64, 193; Henretta, "Strange Birth," 170–171; "General Intelligence," *New York Evangelist,* 17 Aug. 1843 (section titled "Convention for Altering the Constitution").

74. Gunn, *Decline of Authority,* 175–177.

75. "General Intelligence."

76. Gunn, *Decline of Authority,* 177.

77. Ibid., 177–179 (quotation at 177).

78. Ibid., 179; Hammond, *Silas Wright,* 422–423, emphasis in original.

79. Gunn, *Decline of Authority,* 177–179; Hammond, *Silas Wright,* 423–424.

80. "General Intelligence."

81. Gunn, *Decline of Authority,* 179–180; Shaw, *Erie Water West,* 345–348; Donovan, *Barnburners,* 57–59.

82. Shaw, *Erie Water West,* 346–347; Donovan, *Barnburners,* 59–64.

83. Gunn, *Decline of Authority,* 180–181; Hammond, *Silas Wright,* 542; Croswell and Sutton, *Debates,* vii–viii; Bishop and Attree, *Report,* 4–6.

84. Bishop and Attree, *Report,* 843.

85. Croswell and Sutton, *Debates,* 64.

86. Bishop and Attree, *Report,* 461–463, 481–482.

87. Michael Hoffman, *Speech of Michael Hoffman on the State Finances, in Convention Friday, September 11, 1846* (Albany, NY: Argus Press, 1846). Hoffman's presentation can also be found in Croswell and Sutton, *Debates,* 647–652, 917–938.

88. Hoffman, *Speech of Michael Hoffman,* 5–6, 5, 23. The relevant passages can also be found in Croswell and Sutton, *Debates,* 921, 920, 938.

89. Bishop and Attree, *Report,* 462.

90. Ibid., 947.

91. Croswell and Sutton, *Debates,* 724, 725; Bishop and Attree, *Report,* 945, 947.

92. Bishop and Attree, *Report,* 944, 949, 944–945.

The Struggle over Public Education
in Early America (1851)

ON MARCH 26, 1849, the New York State legislature passed "An Act Establishing Free Schools throughout the State." The act mandated that "common schools in the several school districts . . . shall be free to all persons residing in the district over five and under twenty-one years of age."[1] At a time when the well-to-do had near-exclusive access to higher education through secondary schools and colleges, common schools were created to offer basic, primary education to the state's rich and poor alike. Prior to 1849, however, many common schools in New York were less accessible than their name implied, often relying on tuition payments from parents, known as "rate-bills," to cover costs unmet by limited state and county resources. The "Free School Law" would abolish these rate-bills and, for the first time in New York, require school districts to levy taxes to cover the difference. The 1849 act also specified that these provisions would become law only if approved in a statewide referendum that November.

Although the Free School Law was ultimately approved by a large majority of the state's voters, opposition remained fierce even after the law went into effect. Detractors complained especially about the burden of new taxes and the injustice of having to support other people's children. Some critics also charged that the law was unconstitutional because—by requiring a referendum—the legislature had delegated its exclusive lawmaking authority to the people. Opponents in the legislature secured a new bill in 1850 proposing to repeal the Free School Law altogether, and again submitted the

---

question to voters in November.[2] The electorate supported the law for a second time—in this case by rejecting the repeal proposal—but the margin of victory was now considerably narrower.

Still not satisfied, two state lawmakers put forward a bill in early 1851 that would eliminate the key funding provision of the 1849 law and reinstate tuition payments. Echoing the Free School Law, the new bill was entitled "An Act to Establish Free Schools throughout the State." Unlike the earlier statute, however, the new bill would mandate that any expenses not covered by available state and local funds "shall be raised by rate-bill, to be made out by the [district] trustees against those sending [children] to school."[3] After having approved the Free School Law in 1849 and seen the electorate endorse it twice in two years, the state legislature once again faced the decision of who should pay for primary education across the state and, ultimately, how public their schools should be.

Schooling in Colonial America

Approaches to education in the American colonies varied significantly by geographic region. The New England, middle, and southern colonies each adopted educational systems that reflected the unique character of their settlements.

The earliest form of public education emerged in New England, starting with the Massachusetts Bay Colony. In 1642 the provincial legislature, the Massachusetts General Court, called for all children to be educated and made "profitable to the Commonwealth."[4] Authorities could fine parents and masters who failed to ensure that their children "read and understand the principles of religion and the capital laws" of their predominantly Puritan settlement.[5] Five years later, the general court made towns principally responsible for education.[6] The 1647 law compelled towns with over fifty families to employ a schoolmaster, whose foremost duties were to teach children to read the Bible and write. The Puritan members of the general court acted on a religious imperative: "Knowledge of the Scriptures" would guard young minds from the clutches of "that old deluder, Satan."[7] Despite the religious motivations behind the law, town schools were public in the sense that they were controlled by civil officials, on both local and provincial levels. Towns that lacked such schools could incur fines—paid to neighboring town schools. Although many towns levied taxes to fulfill the 1647 mandate, the early schools were not always free to residents. Some towns also chose to meet expenses by imposing tuition charges known as rate-bills on parents who sent their children to school.[8]

Most New England colonies followed the Massachusetts example with town schools of their own.[9] In 1693, thirteen years after separating from Massachusetts, New Hampshire went one step further by making taxation for the support of town schools mandatory, rather than optional. The New Hampshire provincial legislature ordered towns to raise taxes for schoolhouses and teacher salaries "by an equal rate and assessment upon the inhabitants," becoming the first to establish free, public schools in America.[10]

Although town schools grew quickly in popularity, private education still flourished in New England. So-called Dame schools preceded town schools, and they remained the most common form of private education. Female teachers ran these modest schools in their own homes, where they taught the alphabet and basic reading skills for small fees. They also served the important function of educating children who could not attend town schools. Many town schoolmasters excluded students who did not know the alphabet and permitted girls to attend only after regular hours, if at all. In such cases, families often sent their children to Dame schools.[11]

In the middle colonies of Pennsylvania, Delaware, New Jersey, and New York, education was seldom legally regulated. Colonial governments sometimes oversaw teacher licensing, but beyond this they generally left education to parents, private schoolmasters, or churches. Many children had their first reading lessons at home, but parents intermittently sent them to church schools or private, in-home teachers.[12] With so many unregulated, private facilities, the schooling provided could be disjointed and inconsistent. According to one historian, this was particularly true in urban New York and other "coastal towns," where "parents bought schooling as a commodity in an open market. Schoolmasters competing for students offered subjects ranging from the alphabet to astronomy, for children of all ages, at all times of the day. Schooling arrangements were haphazard and temporary; people in all ranks of society gained their education in a patchwork, rather than a pattern, of teachers and experiences."[13]

The most stable source of schooling in the middle colonies came from churches and religious organizations, which took the lead in providing rudimentary education. As compared to Puritan-dominated New England, the middle colonies were home to a more diverse array of ethnicities and religious denominations, all competing to impart their traditions and beliefs on local children. Parochial institutions of various types also played an important role in educating the poor, whose options were limited in the educational market of the middle colonies. When impoverished children went to school at all, they attended charity schools supported by local churches. Although these schools often charged tuition, they offered a limited number of stipends to those in need. In some circumstances, charity schools also accepted girls from families too poor to provide basic schooling.[14]

Education in the southern colonies (Maryland, Virginia, North Carolina, South Carolina, and Georgia) often conformed to the vast class divides surrounding the region's agricultural economy. At the top of the class hierarchy, wealthy landowners typically supplied their children with private tutors and often sent them to England for higher education. In contrast, the white servant and laboring classes—comprising the vast majority of the southern labor force until the African slave trade expanded dramatically in the eighteenth century—frequently relied on home schooling and the apprenticeship system to teach their children a trade, though not necessarily reading or writing. Already by 1646, a Virginia apprenticeship law "empowered local authorities to round up and send to public workhouses boys and girls who, whether by parental neglect or absence, were not being instructed 'in some good and lawful calling.'" It was not until 1701 that the Virginia government began to require masters to teach their apprentices literacy skills. Charity schools of various kinds also educated poor white youth to read and write, although their reach is thought to have been limited, partly due to the region's "scattered and sparse population." Unlike the religiously diverse charity schools of the middle colonies, moreover, southern charity schools were mainly associated with the Church of England, as the southern colonies remained committed to the religious and social values of Britain.[15]

Across all regions, access to education was restricted by race and sex. Although some religious groups sought to provide schooling for black freemen and slaves, governmental efforts to educate blacks during the pre-Revolutionary period were far less common. In the South, legal prohibitions on educating slaves would become more extensive in the early nineteenth century, but even in the colonial era it was sometimes illegal and more often discouraged to teach slaves to read or write.[16] With respect to white children, churches and governments as well as schoolmasters and parents nearly always prioritized the educational pursuits of boys prior to the Revolution. Fortunate girls learned basic reading and writing in preparation for marriage and motherhood. Yet even for daughters of the well-to-do, lessons in reading and writing were often limited in scope to make time for other activities; dancing, embroidery, and good manners were thought by many—though by no means all—to be every bit as important.[17]

The Massachusetts Experiment
Educational Reform in the Early National Period, 1780–1837

Building on its colonial legacy, Massachusetts boasted the most developed and widely accessible town school system of any state during the American Revolution. Soon after the colonists declared independence in 1776, John Adams, Samuel Adams, and James Bowdoin wrote education into the founding document of the Commonwealth of Massachusetts. Ratified on June 15, 1780, the Massachusetts State Constitution affirmed the value of public education for all members of society:

> Wisdom, and knowledge, as well as virtue, diffused generally among the body of the people, [are] necessary for the preservation of their rights and liberties; as these depend on spreading the opportunities and advantages of education . . . it shall be the duty of legislatures and magistrates . . . to cherish the interests of literature and the sciences, and all seminaries of them; especially the university at Cambridge, public schools, and grammar-schools in the towns.[18]

After the thirteen colonies won their war for independence, Massachusetts legislators returned to the issue of education, as directed by the state constitution. In 1789 they enacted a law quite similar to the 1647 colonial legislation, requiring towns with over fifty families to employ a schoolmaster to teach at least six months of reading, writing, arithmetic, and "decent behavior" each year; towns with more than one hundred families were obligated to offer year-round instruction.[19] However, the 1789 legislation included two significant additions to the system established in 1647: first, it required locally appointed supervisors to inspect schools once every six months, en-force regular attendance, and ensure the "proficiency" of students; and second, it gave towns the right to divide themselves into school districts, which would oversee school expenditures.

When the legislature sanctioned the district system in 1789, it affirmed the prevailing public opinion that education should remain a local enterprise. As one citizen put it, local residents were considered "the properest judges of what schools are most suitable" for their communities.[20] Indeed, most communities prized their long-established town schools and resisted state interference. In 1800 the state legislature determined that towns should have the option of collecting tax revenue for schools and dispersing it among their districts, ensuring local control over spending. One consequence of local con-trol during this early period was that the quality and duration of instruction across common schools, as town schools came to be known, varied consid-erably.[21] As a result, schools in poorer districts—limited in their funding and resources—often appeared neglected relative to their richer counterparts.

These poorer schools found a fierce advocate in James G. Carter, a Har-vard graduate and Whig who took it upon himself to shape public opinion and make the quality of all schools a legislative priority. In the *Boston Patriot,* he wrote of the deteriorating caliber of teachers and the need for official school administration. Largely due to his efforts, the state expanded its role in education, and in 1826 a new law mandated that towns appoint special committees to oversee schools, choose textbooks, and evaluate all publicly employed teachers.[22]

The renewed interest in common schools also led to concerns about funding and access. Carter and other advocates argued that broad-based ed-ucation could prevent societal decay by teaching even the poorest children to become proper, moral, and responsible citizens. However, poor families often failed to send their children to school in districts that required parents to pay rate-bills. Residents in poorer districts began to demand quality edu-cation and schoolhouses, even for families who could not afford these charges. And increasingly, reformers advocated a scheme of universal taxation and free schools to support the ever-growing educational needs of Massachusetts communities. Their free school movement culminated on March 10, 1827, when Governor Levi Lincoln approved "An Act to Provide for the Instruction of Youth," which required towns to support their common schools entirely through taxation.[23] Tuition payments and rate-bills were rendered obsolete for Massachusetts families sending their children to public schools.

The school law of 1827 included one other critical feature: section 7 required that town committees "shall never direct any school books to be purchased or used . . . which are calculated to favor any particular religious sect or tenet."[24] Over the course of the early nineteenth century, the Congregationalist Church, which descended from the Puritan churches of the Massachusetts Bay Colony, split into orthodox Calvinist and liberal Unitarian branches. Section 7 of the 1827 law was almost certainly informed by this controversy and may have even represented a limited attempt to keep the sectarian dispute out of the schools.[25]

After spurring the legislation of 1826 and 1827, Carter continued to press for reform. A decade later, as chairman of the Committee on Education for the Massachusetts House of Representatives, he led the campaign to create the Massachusetts State Board of Education, which would report to the state legislature on the performance of public schools and recommend improvements.[26] Once the bill was enacted in April 1837, another Whig lawmaker, Horace Mann, was selected to head the new board.[27] According to some historians, Mann would go on to lead an "educational renaissance" in Massachusetts.[28]

The Educational Vision of Horace Mann

Horace Mann left his post as president of the Massachusetts Senate to become the first secretary of the State Board of Education on June 29, 1837. A member of the Whig Party, he believed that free, universal education was the key to greater political and social stability. He viewed free schooling as "the great equalizer of the conditions of men,—the balance wheel of the social machinery," and the most dependable path toward national prosperity.[29] According to Mann, the state had a duty to provide poor and neglected children with the skills and discipline necessary to become productive members of society. He argued that government-supported schools reduced crime by teaching common political, moral, and cultural values. This, in turn, would foster higher living standards for all. "An educated people is always a more industrious and productive people. . . . Intelligence is a primary ingredient in the wealth of nations," he once declared.[30] Above all else, Mann asserted that universal education was a necessary ingredient for a healthy democracy: "It may be an easy thing to make a republic; but it is a very laborious thing to make republicans; and woe to the republic that rests upon no better foundations than ignorance, selfishness, and passion!"[31] He went on to claim that for the democratic process to succeed in the United States, the government must educate and instill values in its citizens, lest voters abuse their liberties.[32]

Although Mann developed a lengthy reform agenda, translating his vision into reality would not be easy. As one historian observed, "Probably the most important single thing about the position [of Secretary of the Board of Education], at least in retrospect, is that it had no power . . . [and] in the absence of power Mann was forced to rely upon his wit." The 1819 valedictorian of Brown University, Mann had worked as a tutor, had created a successful law practice, and was elected to the Massachusetts House and Senate before becoming secretary of the Board of Education. There he served for over a decade, until he was elected to the U.S. House of Representatives as an antislavery Whig in 1848. As secretary, Mann especially promoted three broad principles of education: universal access, increased control at the state level, and religious neutrality.[33]

UNIVERSAL ACCESS Mann famously claimed that the "well-being of a community is to be estimated not so much by its possessing a few men of great knowledge, as by having many men of competent knowledge."[34] To achieve this objective, Mann sought to ensure free schooling for "every child."[35] The 1827 abolition of parents' tuition payments was an important first step, but Mann still sought to curb absenteeism in order to fully achieve his goal. According to his *First Annual Report of the Secretary of the Board of Education,* which appeared in early 1838, an alarming one-third of the students who "depend[ed] wholly upon the Common Schools" were permanently absent from the winter school session, and many more were absent in the summer.[36] Reformers feared that these children would fail to learn basic lessons in everything from literacy to morality and discipline.

During an Independence Day address in 1842, Mann argued that the democratic principles on which the United States was founded necessitated universal education. "In these schools," he announced, "the first great principle of a republican government,—that of native, inborn equality, should have been practically inculcated, by their being open to all, good enough for all, and attended by all."[37] Common school advocates insisted that education was the best way to prepare children for the civic duties of adulthood—those of a parent, voter, witness, or juror—and to make society prosper. Mann stressed that through universal education,

> the children of a republic [must] be fitted for society as well as for themselves. As each citizen is to participate in the power of governing others, it is an essential preliminary that he should be imbued with a feeling for the wants, and a sense of the rights, of those whom he is to govern; because the power of governing others, if guided by no higher motive than our own gratification, is the distinctive attribute of oppression.[38]

There were many obstacles to universal education, however. Children played important roles in family economies, including as farmhands and as wage laborers in factories. Although many families felt sure they could not afford to lose the extra help or income, Mann was unsympathetic: "How can any man . . . use the services of a child in his household, his shop, his office, or his mill . . . to enlarge his own gains, or to pamper his own luxurious habits, by taking the bread of intellectual and moral life from the children around him?"[39] Still, to many citizens, the idea of making school attendance compulsory not only posed a significant economic challenge, but was also deeply at odds with core American values of liberty and freedom. Sensitive to these objections, Mann initially favored a gradual "process of enlightenment" to change public sentiment on the matter and encourage families to send their children to school, rather than force attendance.[40] Later in his tenure as secretary, however, he decided that the slow pace of change came at too great a cost, and began to push for compulsory schooling.

INCREASED STATE CONTROL A second core principle of Mann's educational vision related to the need for state-level regulation, which he hoped would ensure uniformly high standards across diverse local schools. In particular, the Board of Education, working under Mann's direction, actively collected data on school attendance and efficacy. This was a first step toward broader state oversight, allowing the board to monitor local schools and suggest necessary reforms.

The Board of Education also borrowed specific practices from the Prussian educational model, in which the state government assumed central authority for education throughout the country. In Prussia, aspiring teachers could not instruct students until they themselves had studied the "Art of Teaching" at state-specified schools.[41] Seeking to emulate Prussia in this regard, the board encouraged statewide standards for the education of teachers. They followed the lead of James G. Carter, whose dearest cause was to ensure the competency of common school teachers, and pushed Massachusetts to establish "normal schools" for teacher training. For Mann, perhaps the single most effective feature of the centralized Prussian system—apart from teacher training—was compulsory schooling, although he struggled over the use of compulsion in a democratic context.[42]

To ensure that students and teachers had access to quality resources, Mann also lobbied for the adoption of standardized schoolbooks. In visiting Massachusetts schools, he had found that books written for adults were in common use but that many of these were unsuitable for children. Mann worked to solve this problem, and by 1842 the Board of Education had published "The School Library," which included a collection of educational books recommended specifically for children.[43]

Although Mann's reforms involved a significant increase in state control over primary education, local school boards continued to exercise considerable discretion over their schools.[44] According to Mann, this local element ensured that *"upon the people,* will still rest the great and inspiring duty of prescribing to the next generation what their fortunes shall be, by determining in what manner they shall be educated."[45]

RELIGIOUS NEUTRALITY Prior to 1833, the Massachusetts constitution required towns to support "publick worship of GOD and . . . maintenance of publick protestant teachers of piety, religion and morality, in all cases where such provision shall not be made voluntarily." Most citizens were taxed at the local level to fund the established Congregationalist church in their parish. Although in principle a taxpayer could direct his taxes "to the support of the publick teacher or teachers of his own religious sect or denomination," in practice many so-called dissenters had no choice but to support the local Congregationalist church. Massachusetts finally disestablished religion in 1833 (the last state to do so), amending its constitution to abolish "the churches established by law in this government."[46] Even after 1833, however, religious differences remained pronounced, and the feud between two main offshoots of the original Congregationalist Church—the orthodox Congregationalists and the liberal Unitarians—had only intensified.

In the face of such religious divisions, Mann argued that common schools must serve all children, whether they were of Congregationalist, Unitarian, Catholic, or any other Christian faith. While touring Europe, he came to admire the "spirit of toleration" in Dutch common schools, which educated Holland's religiously diverse citizens by "elevat[ing] the ideals of children without introducing issues of religious controversy."[47] Looking to the Dutch model of nonsectarianism, Mann advocated religiously neutral instruction. He argued that such an education would instill students with "immeasurable virtue" and prepare them for the responsibilities of democratic citizenship.[48]

While he believed that the virtues taught in common schools must be broadly Christian in nature, Mann also felt strongly about section 7 of the 1827 law, which barred the use of sectarian books in public schools. When the Board sanctioned "The School Library," it cautioned those who might recommend books for the collection: "Being intended for the whole community, no work of a sectarian or denominational character in religion . . . will be admitted."[49] Although Mann characterized the King James Bible as the most important text for common schools and the ultimate guide to morality, he stressed that teachers and students should read the Scriptures "without note or comment."[50]

Opposition to Mann's Reforms

In trying to advance their educational reform agenda, Mann and the Massachusetts State Board of Education faced considerable resistance. In fact, as secretary, Mann spent much of his time answering critics in public speeches and popular publications.

RELIGIOUS OPPOSITION Mann's harshest critics opposed his work on religious grounds. Many detractors—especially orthodox Congregationalists—saw the Board of Education as irreligious, and they feared that Mann himself was effectively trying to secularize schools.[51]

By his own admission, Mann was not unbiased when it came to the sectarian divide in Massachusetts. He identified as Unitarian, after becoming alienated from the orthodox Congregationalist church of his youth. When Mann was fourteen, his older brother Stephen drowned swimming in a pond while skipping church on Sunday. At the funeral service, the local minister told parishioners that Stephen was destined for hell because he had died "unconverted."[52] Mann later recalled this as the moment when he began to reject Calvinism.[53] Although Mann endeavored to keep his personal distaste for orthodox Congregationalism separate from his actions as secretary, one historian has argued that "he appears sincerely not to have recognized the extent to which his own belief in human goodness and the centrality of morality to religion constituted an alternative faith—essentially that preached Sunday by Sunday in Unitarian churches—which could not fail to conflict with traditional Christian beliefs, whether of Protestants or of Roman Catholics."[54]

In early March 1838, the first in a series of challenges to Mann's version of nonsectarianism arrived in the form of a letter from Congregationalist Frederick A. Packard. As the editor of publications for the American Sunday School Union, Packard wrote asking Mann to include one of the Union's volumes, *Abbott's Child at Home,* in the Massachusetts School Library. After reading the book, Mann replied that its sectarian character would offend Unitarians. He criticized passages focusing on damnation and hellfire, and complained, "There is scarcely anything in the book which presents the character of God in an amiable or lovely aspect."[55]

Packard continued to correspond with Mann, trying to convince him that the Union books were not sectarian, but rather conveyed core Christian beliefs. Indeed, the American Sunday School Union was nondenominational, serving Congregationalists, Presbyterians, Baptists, Methodists, and other evangelical Protestant sects—all of whom were able to agree on the Union school library.[56] Packard asserted that Mann had grossly misinterpreted the 1827 law, turning it into a "monstrous" piece of legislation with the power to remove religion from Massachusetts schools.[57] Instead, he argued, people in local districts should choose the character of their texts.[58] Over the course of Mann's career, Packard—writing under a pseudonym—continued to denounce the board and its secretary, urging Massachusetts residents to "put down this new-fangled philosophy of education."[59]

Mann vehemently denied charges that he was trying to take religion out of the schools. Indeed, although he was a Unitarian, not an evangelical revivalist, the common school movement that he helped to lead has been characterized as "one of a variety of social and moral reform movements inspired by the 'Second Great Awakening,' a religious revival of evangelical Protestantism that swept the northern United States in the late 1820s and 1830s."[60] Far from removing religion, Mann saw himself as removing doctrine, while allowing the true essence of religion to speak through Bible readings in the classroom. Furthermore, if a majority in any town could decide what books would be taught, children of religious minorities might be forced from common schools. Books controversial to any particular sect, he argued, could be used in Massachusetts churches, Sunday schools, or homes, but their sectarian doctrines had no place in common schools.[61]

LOCALIST SKEPTICISM Many critics also claimed Mann was trying to exert too much state control over education—a domain widely seen as the special responsibility of parents and local communities. Opponents of centralization, known as localists and frequently associated with the Democratic Party, preferred that towns and districts control education, particularly at the primary school level. One of Mann's most vocal critics on the issue was Marcus Morton, who was elected as the state's first Democratic governor in November 1839. Morton agreed with Mann on the importance of common schools, but fiercely opposed state control and even proposed a bill in 1840 that would have eliminated both the Board of Education and the normal schools, although the bill ultimately failed in the legislature. Mann and the board faced a similar bill the following year; and although a Whig, John Davis, had by this time replaced Morton as governor, Mann still could not count on his support. Davis steered clear of educational reform because he regarded it as politically unpopular.[62] Still, despite formidable localist opposition, Mann and his political disciples continued on their course, further strengthening the state's authority over education.

SCHOOLMASTER RESISTANCE A group of thirty-one Boston schoolmasters formed yet another point of resistance to Mann's educational vision. They especially objected to his call for state management of teacher qualifications, but also criticized his pedagogical methods, including his emphasis on conversational instruction and his distaste for the use of corporal punishment. Of all his detractors, the schoolmasters probably caused Mann the most personal pain, as he felt a certain kinship with them through his dedication to education, and he claimed to have read their criticisms "with grief and astonishment."[63]

Progress toward Mann's Goals

Despite significant opposition, by the end of his tenure on the Massachusetts State Board of Education, Mann had achieved much of what he had set out to do. New state and local investments in schools had expanded access to education. In numerous communities, old schoolhouses were repaired and new ones built. Although primary education in Massachusetts had yet to become compulsory, by 1848 another month had been added to the academic term. Mann and other reformers founded three normal schools for teacher training with both state and private funds. These schools began the work of standardizing and advancing teaching practices. Respect for the occupation grew, the ranks of professional teachers swelled, and the average teacher's salary increased by more than 50 percent during Mann's eleven-year term. Mann also achieved considerable success in implementing his interpretation of nonsectarian education. Reading of the King James Bible, without comment, became standard, and sectarian (especially orthodox) texts were generally not permitted in the district school libraries of Massachusetts.[64] Perhaps most importantly, Mann succeeded in making public education a higher priority in Massachusetts, reversing widespread indifference over the quality and accessibility of common schools. Indeed, as a result of his work, Mann became known as the "Father of the Common School Movement."[65]

The Battle over Education in New York State

Just as Horace Mann was leaving his post at the Massachusetts Board of Education to serve in Congress in 1848, lawmakers in New York State were gearing up for a battle over free schooling. The question taking shape in Albany and across the state was whether primary education should be fully financed out of taxes, without any tuition charges—an issue that lawmakers in Massachusetts had settled more than twenty years before, in 1827. The context in New York was quite different, however. Whereas the legacy of local schools supported by town governments spanned centuries in

Massachusetts, the experience with public schools was far more limited in New York. By the late 1840s, moreover, New York had seen a much larger inflow of immigrants as compared to Massachusetts and arguably faced greater religious and ethnic divisions. Although officials in New York were well aware of what reformers had accomplished in neighboring Massachusetts, they also recognized that they confronted a very different climate and that new solutions would be required.

Background

Over the first half of the nineteenth century, New York State experienced extraordinary growth and development, leaping ahead of virtually all competing states. As one historian has written:

> By whatever measurement of growth—population, wealth, agricultural production, manufacturing output, transportation facilities, or commerce— the state had earned the renown increasingly accorded it at home and abroad. By the 1830s, New York had already outdistanced its rivals Massachusetts and Pennsylvania in the quest for economic supremacy of the nation. . . . Rapid population growth, urbanization, improved communications, the expansion and integration of the market, and the growth of manufacturing fundamentally altered traditional patterns of social and economic behavior in the state and laid the foundation for a modern social order.[66]

The Panic of 1837 and the recession that followed temporarily slowed the state's progress and diminished its confidence. The downturn also triggered a sharp political reaction against continued public investment in large-scale infrastructure, such as the Erie Canal, which had been completed in 1825. Yet, despite the panic and its aftermath, there was no denying that New York was an economic powerhouse with strength in virtually every sector, from finance to manufacturing to commerce. While New York was hardly the only state to have experienced rapid growth and industrialization during this period, it definitely seemed to live up to its moniker as the "Empire State."

As the state's economy was galloping forward, its educational system was also developing, though perhaps not quite as rapidly. At the start of the nineteenth century, school offerings still depended to a significant extent on local churches, philanthropic societies, and private schoolmasters. The state's existing array of schools had been built on the fading colonial notion that, as one scholar put it, "a certain type of education was necessary for each class in society."[67] Particularly during and after the Revolutionary War, however, New Yorkers began to undergo an ideological shift that proved more favorable to broad-based education, and soon the common school movement was born.

After a preliminary attempt in the final years of the eighteenth century, the New York State legislature established a permanent common school fund on April 2, 1805. Seven years later, the legislature passed "An Act for the Establishment of Common Schools," which created the nation's first office of state superintendent for the administration of schools. New York's superintendent of common schools was charged with distributing proceeds from the common school fund to local communities. The 1812 law also required towns, in order to receive aid, to match state funds with local tax revenue and to distribute the money among districts based on the number of children of primary school age. The new legislation targeted rural districts and explicitly exempted New York City, where common school funds were channeled entirely to schools established by charities, churches, and philanthropic organizations.[68]

Under the 1812 arrangement (which was further revised by the legislature in 1814), each rural district was responsible for constructing and maintaining its own common schoolhouse, open to local children. State aid was to be used only for teacher salaries. However, state funds often came up short, and local authorities required parents of schoolchildren to pay rate-bills in order to meet expenses and compensate schoolmasters. The rate-bills were "frequently quite burdensome" on poor and middle-class families.[69] While there was typically an exemption for families unable to pay, the social stigma of publicly declaring impoverishment likely prevented many from taking advantage of it, and the common schools suffered from extensive absenteeism.[70] The problem continued for decades. In an 1831 report to the legislature, Superintendent Azariah Flagg declared: "Intelligence has been regarded as the vital principle of a free government; and every parent, guardian or master who neglects or refuses to give the children under his charge the advantages of a Common School education . . . is [effectively] an offender against the State."[71]

Charity Schools, Catholic Schools, and Common Schools in New York City

By the time the state legislature enacted the 1812 common school law, New York City already had an extensive network of privately run charity schools. Thus, legislators addressed the growing metropolis in a separate 1813 law, giving charity schools access to taxpayer dollars through the common school fund. These schools—run by churches or philanthropic institutions—became nearly synonymous with "common" schools, as they taught nonsectarian curricula and were open to children, rich and poor, of all religious backgrounds. In fact, until the 1840s, privately run charity schools received the bulk of public funds in New York City.[72]

THE PUBLIC SCHOOL SOCIETY The foremost charity school in New York City was the Public School Society. Privately founded as the Free School Society in 1805 by the city's Protestant elite, the Society's original purpose was to establish—through donations and government aid—a free school for poor boys neglected by church charity schools. As the school became known for its thrift and commitment to providing a nonsectarian but "virtuous education," the state gave the Society public funds to expand; and in 1808 the legislature sanctioned the Free School Society's education of all poor children, including those who already belonged to religious associations.[73]

The Society's founders rejected the aristocratic orientation that had formerly viewed the poor as inferior citizens. In an 1809 address, DeWitt Clinton, president of the Free School Society and mayor of New York City, implored the public to see that "the fundamental error of Europe has been, to confine the light of knowledge to the wealthy and the great, while the humble and depressed have been . . . excluded from its participation." He claimed that the whole of New York would benefit from the education of the poor, which would prevent impoverished youth from becoming a burden on society and instead turn them into good citizens. America's democratic principles rested on education, Clinton continued, because "ignorance is the cause as well as the effect of bad governments."[74]

Although the 1813 state law gave church schools access to the common school fund if they committed to nonsectarian education, in 1825 the Common Council of New York City passed a local law that restricted religious organizations' access to these funds. The following year the state legislature gave the Free School Society a new charter, renaming it the Public School Society. It authorized the Society to educate children of all classes and religions, and placed it in charge of nine-tenths of all common school fund resources earmarked for New York City.[75] The state also put the Public School Society in charge of the Female Association and the African Free School, organizations long dedicated to the education of girls and black children in New York.[76]

In 1832, to further increase enrollment and encourage students to attend common schools, the Public School Society adopted a resolution abolishing rate-bills, effectively making education free to all students attending schools under the Society's purview in New York City.[77] While this represented a major advance for education reformers, not everyone approved of the Society's handling of the city's schools, and criticism would soon reach a deafening pitch.

CATHOLIC IMMIGRANTS AND THE CLASH OVER COMMON SCHOOLS Beginning in the 1820s, increasing waves of immigrants entered the United States, including those fleeing famine and political strife in Europe. They saw opportunity in the ever-increasing demand for laborers in America, especially in the industrializing Northeast. In part because of the large inflow of immigrants, New York State's population more than doubled between 1820 and 1850, and New York City's population more than quadrupled over the same period. Nearly half of the two million immigrants arriving in the United States between 1840 and 1851 were Irish, and it is estimated that up to 90 percent of these Irish immigrants were Catholic. Many landed and remained in New York City.[78] Germans were the second-largest immigrant group. Most settled in the Midwest, but many German Catholics remained in New York City. In a city historically dominated by Protestants, the enormous influx of Catholic immigrants proved unsettling to many existing residents and communities, especially as it created a powerful new force in New York politics.

For many Catholic immigrant families, the education of their children was not only part of the new beginning they sought in America, but also a means of preserving the faith of old. They did not find New York City's common schools hospitable to their religious beliefs, however. With the city's

TABLE 7.1

Immigration into the United States (1821–1850)

Years	Total	From Ireland (% of total)	From Germany* (% of total)	From All Other Countries (% of total)
1821–1825	40,503	31.9	3.4	64.6
1826–1830	102,936	36.7	5.2	58.1
1831–1835	252,494	28.6	18.1	53.3
1836–1840	346,631	39.0	30.8	30.2
1841–1845	430,336	43.5	24.4	32.1
1846–1850	1,222,939	46.1	25.7	28.3

Source: Adapted from Robert Barde, Susan B. Carter, and Richard Sutch, "Immigrants, by Continent of Last Residence: 1820–1997," table Ad90–97, and Barde, Carter, and Sutch, "Immigrants, by Country of Last Residence—Europe: 1820–1997," table Ad106–120, both in *Historical Statistics of the United States, Earliest Times to the Present: Millennial Edition,* ed. Susan B. Carter, Scott Sigmund Gartner, Michael R. Haines, Alan L. Olmstead, Richard Sutch, and Gavin Wright (New York: Cambridge University Press, 2006).

* German states, prior to national unification in 1871.

Catholic charity schools filled beyond capacity, the diocese could not afford to keep up with the waves of immigrant children, and the law of 1825 barred them from drawing on the common school fund. Led by Bishop John Dubois, Catholics challenged the Public School Society's claim to nonsectarianism, charging that the Society's textbooks, while uncontroversial to Protestants, were patently anti-Catholic. In 1834 Dubois sent a petition to the Board of Trustees of the Public School Society, requesting state funds for a new common school with a Roman Catholic teacher, but the petition was denied.[79]

Concerns over educating the electorate had steadily increased after 1821, when property requirements for suffrage in New York were eliminated and the franchise was extended to virtually all white males. Indeed, as wave upon wave of Catholic immigrants settled into New York City, the issue of education increasingly attracted the attention of nativists, including Samuel Morse, an artist and inventor who helped to develop the electric telegraph and Morse code. In Catholic schools, Morse and fellow nativists warned, future voters were being brainwashed to act as political servants of the pope. *"Popery is the natural enemy of general education,"* Morse wrote. "If the [Catholic Church] is establishing schools, it is to make them *prisons* of the youthful intellect of the country."[80]

Dubois's successor, Bishop John Hughes, confronted such attacks head-on and quickly became a leading voice of Irish and German Catholics in city politics. Hughes, himself an Irish immigrant, boldly declared in response to nativist sentiment:

> I was born under the scourge of Protestant persecution, of which my fathers, in common with our Catholic countrymen, had been the victim for ages. Hence, I know the *value* of that civil and religious liberty which our happy government secures to all; and I regard, with feelings of abhorrence, those who would sacrilegiously attempt . . . to deprive any citizen of those inestimable blessings.[81]

Known as "dagger John" for his combative personality, Hughes challenged the dominance of the Public School Society in City Hall debates and appearances before the state legislature. He was convinced that common schools were part of an institutionalized effort to turn Catholic children into Protestants, and he actively discouraged families from enrolling their children. To give his flock an alternative, he established eight free Catholic schools with diocese funds, in addition to several tuition-based schools, which together enrolled approximately 5,000 students by 1840.[82] Still, as one historian has noted, these schools provided for only "one-fourth to one-third of the Catholic children of school age in New York at that time."[83]

To keep up with the influx of Catholic immigrant children, in 1840 Hughes appealed to the Common Council for school funds. He questioned how Catholic parents could in good conscience send their children to common schools—to which they paid their fair share of taxes—while the Public School Society continued to use textbooks with anti-Catholic and anti-immigrant passages. One such textbook, *The New York Reader,* painted the pope as an evil tyrant.[84] Another, *An Irish Heart,* warned that Irish immigrants, "in many cases drunken and depraved," were entering the United States on such a scale that they would turn the country into "the common sewer of Ireland."[85] Hughes was not satisfied when the Society volunteered to cover such lines with ink, or glue offending pages together. Nor did he accept the King James Bible—used for readings in common schools without comment—which he considered to be a Protestant version of the Scriptures. In fact, the very notion of reading the Bible without the guidance of clerical authority profoundly offended his Catholic sensibilities.[86]

William H. Seward, New York's first Whig governor, came to the defense of Catholics in 1841, recommending "the establishment of schools in which they may be instructed by teachers speaking the same language with themselves and professing the same faith."[87] Disheartened over low rates of school attendance within immigrant communities, he suggested that he would rather see Irish-American children go to publicly supported Catholic schools than no schools at all. Nativists accused him of being "in league with the pope" and "sapping the foundations of liberty," but Seward, an Episcopalian, denied any particular affinity for Catholicism.[88]

When the Common Council denied the Catholic appeal for public funds, Seward and Hughes took the case before the state legislature. Although Catholics never succeeded in gaining access to the common school fund, they did help to secure passage of the Maclay Bill in 1842, which stripped the Public School Society of its control over state funds. In time the Society was gradually absorbed by the city's ward school system, ending the private provision of public education in New York. As one scholar observed, "For the first time in its history, New York City would have a school system that was directly controlled by the people and entirely financed from the public treasury. Almost inadvertently, the people of New York had a public school system."[89]

The city's common schools, now officially public, did not lose their Protestant character, however. As one historian noted, "the majority of New Yorkers were Protestant and in all but a few of the city's wards, the public schools remained largely Protestant in tone and curriculum."[90] The new Board of Education elected in 1842 was "dominated by opponents of the Catholics," and the new superintendent of education was a well-known nativist. "Daily Bible reading was official school policy," a leading historian explained: "The Catholics protested the use of the Protestant Bible, but, in 1844, the Board of Education ruled that Bible reading without note or comment did not constitute sectarianism."[91]

Deeply frustrated, Bishop Hughes and New York City Catholics resolved to expand their system of parochial free schools, even without public funding.[92] William Seward, meanwhile, appears to have paid a political price for his advocacy on behalf of Catholic schools. Catholic support never materialized in numbers able to offset nativist disapproval within his own Whig

Party, and he was replaced by another Whig candidate for governor in the 1842 election, who in turn lost to the Democratic candidate that fall.

Common and Free?

Despite ongoing religious tensions, Protestant education reformers widely considered the public school system of New York City a success, with one major exception: Common schools still had a reputation as pauper schools. Although these schools had been free in the city since 1832 (as a result of public financing), leading reformers believed that affluent citizens needed not only to put their taxes toward common schools, but also to send their own children to study there alongside the poor.

Rural districts, outside of the major cities, had a different problem: many still operated under rate-bills, limiting access to adequate schooling among poor children. The state had yet to ensure that all common schools, rural and urban alike, were fully financed through taxation. For the schools in New York State to reach their full potential as public institutions, reformers argued, the entire system had to be both *common* across classes and *free* of tuition.

At the intersection of these issues, few reformers were as vocal as John Orville Taylor, a professor at the University of the City of New York and one of the nation's foremost experts on popular education.[93] Taylor aimed to convince New Yorkers statewide that rate-bills should be abolished and that common schools should be seen as a place for all children, not just one class or the other. Speaking at the New York Public Library in 1842, he argued that class differences had to be put aside in the spirit of democratic equality. The wealthy who had children should see the common school, "not as inferior; not as the school for poor men's children; but as the light and the air are common. And what is common to all should be the best of all." He also fiercely criticized state legislators who, in their "semi-barbarism," showed more concern for state-funded "courts, jails, prisons, and the gallows" than for education, which "is the cheap defense of nations . . . it is cheaper to educate the infant mind, than to support the aged criminal."[94]

THE CONSTITUTIONAL CONVENTION OF 1846 In 1846, New York State held its third constitutional convention. Although the main issues on the agenda were fiscal and judicial reform, some education reformers also saw the convention as an opportunity to bypass the legislature and write a require-ment for fully tax-financed schools (so-called free schools) directly into the state constitution.[95] Indeed, on October 1, delegates at the convention voted 57 to 53 to submit the following provision for ratification as the ninth article of the state constitution: "The Legislature shall provide for the free educa-tion and instruction of every child of the State in the common schools, now established, or which shall hereafter be established therein."[96] To this they added, by a vote of 82 to 26, that the legislature should "provide for raising the necessary taxes in each school district, to carry into effect the provisions contained in the preceding section."[97] Following the adoption of this article, the delegates took a recess for dinner. When they returned, they mysteriously reversed their original vote, choosing to "strike out all that portion relating to the establishment of free schools."[98] To the dismay of free school advocates, their initial victory had swiftly turned to defeat.

PASSAGE OF THE 1849 ACT The next major effort to eliminate rate-bills did not materialize until 1849. On March 26 of that year, the Whig-dominated New York State legislature passed "An Act Establishing Free Schools throughout the State," mandating that "common schools in the several school districts . . . shall be free to all persons residing in the district over five and under twenty-one years of age."[99] (By this point, "all persons" included both males and females, as there were almost as many girls as boys in school in New York State; the enrollment rate of blacks, however, was sharply lower than that of whites.)[100] The Free School Law, as it became known, required that common schools be tuition-free and financed through a combination of state funds and local taxes necessary to cover schooling in each district for at least four months out of the year.[101] Yet the full enactment of the leg-islation was left conditional on a referendum. Still unsure about how resi-dents would respond to an increased tax burden, legislators decided that the Free School Law would go into effect only if approved by a majority of the voters in November. Predicting a victory for free school advocates, the edi-tors of the *New-York Daily Tribune* saw a chance for New York to finally catch up to its rival Massachusetts, making "our school houses . . . open to all, rich and poor alike," and allowing the "Empire State, being foremost in all the attributes of commercial greatness, [to also] be behind no other state in her support of the great cause of Education."[102] As the *Tribune* predicted, on

November 6, 1849, the citizens of New York State voted overwhelmingly in favor of the Free School Law, 249,872 to 91,951.[103]

1850 ACT TO REPEAL THE FREE SCHOOL LAW When the Free School Law went into effect, many districts, especially in rural areas, found "operation of the new law burdensome and oppressive." In a majority of counties, officials had already settled their budgets and "no provision had been made for the additional town tax required by the law." Numerous wealthy landowners, moreover, used their influence to oppose "the support of the schools beyond the minimum term of four months required," and some schools that had operated eight months out of the year under the former system, now felt pressure to operate only half that time.[104] Given these and other problems that emerged after enactment, petitions complaining about the Free School Law flooded the state legislature. The House proposed a new general tax of $800,000 to address the law's operational difficulties, but the proposal died in the Senate.[105] The flood of complaints prompted legislators, on April 10, 1850, to call for another November referendum, this time proposing the repeal of the Free School Law of 1849. Once again, the final decision would be left to the voters.

The Free School Debates of 1850

The repeal legislation spawned some of the fiercest debates over education in New York's history, as supporters and opponents of the Free School Law vied to sway popular opinion before the November 1850 referendum. Although virtually everyone agreed that the law was imperfect, most supporters urged that it be strengthened through amendments, whereas opponents favored outright repeal.

Free school advocates were quick to highlight the "emphatic vote of the people, at the last election, in favor of the act establishing *Free Schools* throughout the State," and insisted that "no defect" in the law could "justify the abandonment of that principle, or the total repeal of the law."[106] Some supporters conceded that the old system of rate-bills should be brought back, at least for a few years, given the extent of opposition to the law.[107] For the most part, however, free school supporters argued that repeal would be both bad policy (for all of the reasons reformers like Mann and Taylor had enumerated) and a clear violation of the popular will.

Opponents of free schooling, meanwhile, clearly took pleasure in the fact that, as they put it, even "the friends of this law themselves admit that, unamended, it is a bill of abominations."[108] Their strongest arguments, however, revolved around the issues of taxation and coercion. For many city dwellers, the new law would not mark much of a change because numerous cities, from Brooklyn to Buffalo, had already abolished rate-bills on their own, substituting taxpayer financing for tuition.[109] For most rural New Yorkers, however, the Free School Law meant higher taxes, and this sparked staunch resistance. One group of rural opponents of the law declared, "If the life of Free Schools depends upon the *taking of one man's property* for the purpose of *educating another man's children,* when that other person is abundantly able, and bound by reason and humanity, to educate his own children, [then the free schools] *ought not to exist by such support.*"[110] Similarly, a petition from central New York, circulated in 1849, had warned that the Free School Law would create "strifes, jealousies, divisions and animosities in every district" by allowing people to "put their hands into their neighbors' pockets" to obtain support for common schools.[111]

The battle only intensified as the date of the referendum grew near. It was said, for example, that some employers who opposed higher taxes threatened to fire any worker who voted against repeal. The editors of the *Tribune* responded by advising workers facing such threats to hold their ground when voting, being "faithful to your children and your children's children, even though you should have to go hungry a few days because of it."[112]

Although the debate over taxes loomed especially large in 1850, it was by no means the only front in the war over free public schooling. Catholic leaders, in particular, opposed the Free School Law as an assault on freedom of religion. Although Superintendent McKeen surmised that those favoring parochial schools did not "amount to more than from three to five per centum of [New York City] voters and tax payers," they were a vocal minority.[113] James McMaster, editor of the *New York Freeman,* a prominent Catholic publication in New York City, lauded the state legislature for its push to repeal the law:

HURRAH FOR REPEAL!—The Free School law, voted blindly at the general election last fall, has been submitted anew by the Legislature to the popular vote. Many thanks to the Legislature for the opportunity thus offered us for making our step backward from the downward course of State monopoly, State despotism, and State socialism into which recent legislative movements have been hurrying us.[114]

Horace Greeley of the *New-York Tribune* countered that the public vote for free schools was just the opposite of despotism: "What was the State? Who constitute the commonwealth? The people were the State, and we, the people, could do by our majorities what might be deemed essential for the public good."[115]

A Constitutional Challenge

Although supporters like Greeley took comfort in the fact that the electorate had decisively endorsed the Free School Law in late 1849, New York officials faced difficulty enforcing the statute almost from the moment it went into effect. In some cases, rural New Yorkers refused to cooperate with their school district trustees, who were responsible under the law for levying taxes on local inhabitants. Disgruntled residents in some counties took their complaints to court, as they attempted to recover property confiscated under tax warrants.

One such suit, filed by Henry D. Barto in July 1850, directly challenged the constitutionality of the Free School Law. In pursuit of damages amounting to $50 for a wagon confiscated by school district trustees, Barto's attorney alleged that the tax levied by the trustees "was illegal because the said free school law was . . . and is void, and all acts done by virtue thereof are void and of none effect." He argued that the Free School Law "was not constitutionally passed by the legislature of the State of New York, but the same became a law, if at all, only by virtue of a vote of the people . . . at the annual election in November, 1849, and at a time when no legislative body known and recognized by the constitution was in session."[116] The case thus hinged on whether it was constitutional for a legislature to delegate its power to enact a statute to the electorate, in the form of an up or down referendum, as had occurred with the Free School Law. On October 11, 1850, after taking additional time to consider "the questions of law arising" from the case, Justice William Shankland of the state's Supreme Court, Tompkins County Circuit, ruled in favor of the plaintiff, Henry Barto.

TABLE 7.2

Impact of Urban Counties on the Vote for Repeal
of the Free School Law, November 1850

Position	Total Vote	Vote of 6 Urban Counties*	Vote of 52 Rural Counties**
For repeal	184,308	16,240	168,068
Against repeal	209,346	78,889	130,457

Source: Data adapted from the "official returns to the Secretary of State's office" as reported by Silas M. Burroughs and Benjamin G. Ferris, "Report No. 42, in Assembly, February 6, 1851," in *Free Schools: A Documentary History of the Free School Movement in New York State,* ed. Thomas E. Finegan (Albany: University of the State of New York, 1921), 462–463.

* Urban counties, according to the 1851 report by Assemblymen Silas Burroughs and Benjamin Ferris (referenced in the text below), refer to the "counties in each of which large cities are located." The relevant urban counties were: New-York (city and county), Kings, Albany, Dutchess, Erie, and Rensselaer. Burroughs and Ferris maintained that the large cities that were part of these counties already had "special [free] school laws for their government [at the municipal level], which would not in any degree be affected by" acceptance or repeal of the Free School Law at the state level.

** Vote excluding the six urban counties.

Not surprisingly, the school district trustees appealed Justice Shankland's decision. Yet as the November referendum approached, the issue remained unsettled: "the validity and constitutionality of the act were, in some influential quarters, seriously questioned, upon the ground of its conditional submission to the people."[117] If Shankland's ruling were upheld, the Free School Law would cease to exist, with or without repeal.

Decision

On November 5, 1850, New York voters rejected repeal of the Free School Law by a vote of 209,346 to 184,308. The statute had now twice been put to the people, and twice they had supported it. Yet advocates and detractors alike concluded that the law could not stand as it was, given its many acknowledged imperfections as well as fierce rural opposition.

Three months later, therefore, members of the New York Assembly's Committee on Colleges, Academies, and Common Schools proposed two different bills to replace the Free School Law. Both would levy taxes to raise $800,000 per year, to be divided among the districts along with the common school fund. Both also sought to eliminate a key source of rural discontent—mandatory district property taxes, which the Free School Law had triggered in lieu of rate-bills. But the two proposals would achieve this result in sharply different ways. The first bill, introduced by the majority of the committee, suggested a poll tax to replace district property taxes. Concerns immediately arose, however, that a poll tax would not exempt the poor, as it could be charged to "persons having no taxable property." Assemblymen Silas Burroughs and Benjamin Ferris, both from rural districts, introduced a second option that would reinstitute the rate-bill (which in principle had exempted the poor) and also extend the length of the required school term to seven months, rather than four.[118] Opposing an untried poll tax, Burroughs (a Democrat) and Ferris (a Whig) beseeched their fellow legislators to return to the old rate-bill system by voting for their "Act to Provide for the Support of the Common Schools."

Although their bill would no longer guarantee that all necessary school expenses would be covered by taxes (some tuition charges, or rate-bills, might be required), Burroughs and Ferris justified this, at least in part, by warning that free schooling would be seen by many as low-quality schooling, and would inevitably become compulsory, as it had in Prussia. "Compulsion in this country, on this subject," they wrote, "is entirely out of the question. Our citizens cannot be compelled to receive these benefits for their children without adopting a despotic principle entirely at war with our free institutions."[119]

After a protracted debate, legislative opinion began shifting toward the second bill, which mandated that any "balance required to be raised in any school district for the payment of teachers' wages, beyond the amount apportioned to such district . . . and other public moneys belonging to the district . . . shall be raised by rate-bill, to be made out . . . against those sending [children] to school."[120] As the Assembly vote approached, the bill's framers looked to make it more palatable to free school advocates by renaming it "An Act to Establish Free Schools throughout the State," arguing that common schools under their bill would be "nominally free," despite the provision for rate-bills.[121] With this last rhetorical flourish, the fate of common schools in New York State was, once again, in the hands of the full legislature.

NOTES

1. "An Act Establishing Free Schools throughout the State" (Albany, NY: Weed, Parsons and Co., 1849), 1.

2. See "An Act Submitting the Question of the Repeal of the Act Establishing Free Schools" (Albany: Weed, Parsons and Co., 1850).

3. "An Act to Establish Free Schools throughout the State. Passed April 12, 1851," in *Statutes of the State of New York, of a Public and General Character, Passed from 1829 to 1851, Both Inclusive,* ed. Samuel Blatchford (Auburn, NY: Derby and Miller, 1852), 849. See also S. S. Randall, *History of the Common School System of the State of New York, from Its Origin in 1795 to the Present Time* (New York: Ivison, Blakeman, Taylor, and Co., 1871), 284–285.

4. Nathaniel B. Shurtleff, ed., *Records of the Governor and Company of the Massachusetts Bay in New England,* vol. 2 (Boston: Press of William White, 1853), 6 (enacted by the General Court on 14 June 1642). Shurtleff printed the records in their original form. Original reads: "proffitable to the common wealth" and has been modified to contemporary English for this case.

5. Shurtleff, *Records,* 6. Original reads: "read & understand the principles of religion & the capitall lawes of this country" and has been modified to contemporary English for this case.

6. See, e.g., George H. Martin, *The Evolution of the Massachusetts Public School System* (New York: D. Appleton and Co., 1915), 14–16, 83–86.

7. Shurtleff, *Records,* 203 (enacted by the General Court on 11 Nov. 1647). Original reads "knowledge of ye Scriptures" and "y^t ould deluder, Satan" and has been modified to contemporary English for this case.

8. Paul Monroe, *Founding of the American Public School System: A History of Education in the United States, from the Early Settlements to the Close of the Civil War Period,* vol. 1 (New York: Macmillan, 1940), 114; Shurtleff, *Records,* 203; Ellwood P. Cubberley, *Public Education in the United States: A Study and Interpretation of American Educational History* (Cambridge, MA: Riverside Press, 1934), 198.

9. Monroe, *Founding,* 123–127.

10. "An Act for the Maintenance and Supply of the Ministry within this Province," in *Acts and laws of His Majesty's Province of New-Hampshire* (Portsmouth, NH: Daniel Fowle, 1761), 58.

11. Monroe, *Founding,* 127, 128; David Tyack and Elisabeth Hansot, *Learning Together: A History of Coeducation in American Public Schools* (New York: Russell Sage Foundation, 1992), 16–21.

12. New York and Pennsylvania both had basic legal requirements for teacher qualifications and licensing. See Monroe, *Founding,* 84, 89, 95; Carl F. Kaestle, *The Evolution of an Urban School System: New York City, 1750–1850* (Cambridge, MA: Harvard University Press, 1973), 3–5.

13. Kaestle, "Common Schools before the 'Common School Revival': New York Schooling in the 1790s," *History of Education Quarterly* 12, no. 4 (1972): 465.

14. Monroe, *Founding*, 103–104, 89, 95; Kaestle, *Urban School System*, 3.

15. Monroe, *Founding*, 32–35, 42–43, 53–68; Marcus W. Jernegan, "Compulsory Education in the Southern Colonies," *The School Review* 27, no. 6 (Jun. 1919), 405–425; Wayne J. Urban and Jennings L. Wagoner Jr., *American Education: A History*, 4th ed. (New York: Routledge, 2009), 23–29, quotations at 29 and 24.

16. R. Freeman Butts, *Public Education in the United States: From Revolution to Reform* (New York: Holt, Rinehart and Winston, 1978), 60–62; A. Leon Higginbotham, Jr., *In the Matter of Color: Race and the American Legal Process, the Colonial Period* (New York: Oxford University Press, 1980), 198–201, 259; Clarence J. McGivens, "Colonial Statutes Restricting Negro Education," in *Studies in the History of American Education*, ed. Claude Eggertsen (Ann Arbor: University of Michigan School of Education, 1947), 37–38; Charles L. Glenn, *African-American / Afro-Canadian Schooling: From the Colonial Period to the Present* (New York: Palgrave Macmillan, 2011), chap. 2.

17. See, e.g., Tyack and Hansot, *Learning Together*, 16–21; Cynthia A. Kierner, *Beyond the Household: Women's Place in the Early South, 1700–1835* (Ithaca, NY: Cornell University Press, 1998), 59; Sarah E. Fatherly, " 'The Sweet Recourse of Reason': Elite Women's Education in Colonial Philadelphia," *Pennsylvania Magazine of History and Biography* 128, no. 3 (July 2004): 229–256.

18. *The Constitution, or Frame of Government, for the Commonwealth of Massachusetts* (Worcester, MA: Isaiah Thomas, 1787), 80 (chap. 5, §2, in the Massachusetts Constitution of 1780).

19. "An Act to Provide for the Instruction of Youth, and for the Promotion of Good Education," chap. 19 (May Session 1789), in *Acts and Resolves of Massachusetts, 1788–1789* (Boston: Wright and Potter), 416.

20. As quoted in Oscar Handlin and Mary Handlin, eds., *The Popular Sources of Political Authority: Documents on the Massachusetts Constitution of 1780* (Cambridge, MA: Harvard University Press, 1966), 29; spelling has been slightly modified to contemporary English.

21. "An Act in Addition to an Act Entitled, 'An Act to Provide for the Instruction of Youth, and for the Promotion of Good Education'" (28 Feb. 1800), in *The Laws of the Commonwealth of Massachusetts from November 28, 1780 to February 28, 1807*, vol. 2 (Boston: J. T. Buckingham, 1807), 906–908; Martin, *Massachusetts Public School System*, 93–99.

22. *Biographical Sketch of James G. Carter, with His Outline of a Plan of an Institution for the Education of Teachers* (Hartford, CT: F. C. Brownell, [1858]), 16–24; "An Act Further to Provide for the Instruction of Youth" (approved by the governor on 4 Mar. 1826), in *Laws of the Commonwealth of Massachusetts Passed by the General Court* (Boston: True and Greene, 1826), 299.

23. "An Act to Provide for the Instruction of Youth" (approved by the governor on 10 Mar. 1827), http://books.google.com/books?id=6Xl9ye3JkxsC&pg.

24. Ibid., 10.

25. See, e.g., David Robinson, *The Unitarians and the Universalists* (Westport, CT: Greenwood Press, 1985), 3–5; Conrad Wright, *The Unitarian Controversy: Essays on American*

Unitarian History (Boston: Skinner House Books, 1994), 30–31; R. Laurence Moore, "Bible Reading and Nonsectarian Schooling: The Failure of Religious Instruction in Nineteenth-Century Public Education," *Journal of American History* 86, no. 4 (2000): 1588.

26. Lawrence A. Cremin, *American Education: The National Experience, 1783–1876* (New York: Harper and Row, 1980), 135.

27. When the time came to choose a leader for the Board, Carter was passed over despite his many contributions. A political scandal in the town of Lancaster—where he had mismanaged government-provided land and finances intended for a normal school—severely damaged his reputation. See James G. Carter, *Letter to the Rev. Nathaniel Thayer, D.D.* (Boston: J. E. Hinckley and Co, 1833); and also Nathaniel Thayer, *Records of the Church in the Case of Deacon James G. Carter and Reply* (Lancaster, MA: Carter, Andrews, and Co., 1832).

28. "The Centennial of the Birth of Horace Mann," *The Outlook* 53, no. 19 (9 May 1896): 844; Martin, *Massachusetts Public School System*, 154–155; Cremin, *American Education*, 137.

29. Horace Mann, "Report for 1848" ("Twelfth Annual Report of the Secretary of the Board of Education of Massachusetts,"), in *Life and Works of Horace Mann*, 5 vols., ed. Mary Mann (Boston: Lee and Shepard, 1891), 4:251–252.

30. Mann, "Report for 1846" ("Tenth Annual Report of the Secretary of the Board of Education of Massachusetts"), in *Life and Works*, 4:114.

31. Mann, "Twelfth Annual Report," 4:271.

32. Mann, "An Oration Delivered to the Authorities of the City of Boston July 4, 1842," in *Life and Works*, 4:346.

33. Cremin, *American Education*, 136, 137, quotation at 136.

34. Horace Mann, "Lecture VI: On District-School Libraries," in *Life and Works*, 2:315.

35. Horace Mann, "Report for 1839" ("Third Annual Report of the Secretary of the Board of Education of Massachusetts"), in *Life and Works*, 3:10.

36. Horace Mann, "Report for 1837" ("First Annual Report of the Secretary of the Board of Education of Massachusetts"), in *Life and Works*, 2:399–401.

37. Mann, "An Oration . . . July 4, 1842," 4:363.

38. Mann, "Report of 1845" ("Ninth Annual Report of the Secretary of the Board of Education of Massachusetts"), in *Life and Works*, 4:4.

39. Mann, "Report of 1847" ("Eleventh Annual Report of the Secretary of the Board of Education of Massachusetts"), in *Life and Works*, 4:207.

40. Martin, *The Evolution of the Massachusetts Public School System*, 212.

41. John Orville Taylor, "J. Orville Taylor's Lecture on Common Schools and Education," *New York Herald*, 3 Mar. 1842.

42. Monroe, *Founding*, 249; Henry J. Perkinson, *Two Hundred Years of American Educational Thought* (Lanham, MD: University Press of America, 1987), 77–78.

43. Horace Mann, ed., *The Common School Journal*, vol. 4 (Boston: William B. Fowle and N. Capen, 1842), 106–107.

44. Butts, *Public Education,* 84–85.

45. Mann, "Lecture I: Means and Objects of a Common-School Education," in *Life and Works,* 2:41, emphasis in original.

46. *The Constitution, or Frame of Government,* 7–9 (Art. III of the "Declaration of Rights" in the Massachusetts Constitution of 1780); John D. Cushing, "Notes on Disestablishment in Massachusetts, 1780–1833," *William and Mary Quarterly* 26, no. 2 (Apr. 1969): 172–173, 190.

47. Charles Leslie Glenn, *The Myth of the Common School* (Oakland, CA: Institute for Contemporary Studies Press, 2002), 110.

48. Mann, "Lecture II: Special Preparation a Prerequisite to Teaching," in *Life and Works,* 2:109.

49. Mann, ed., *Common School Journal,* 4:106.

50. Burke Aaron Hinsdale, *Horace Mann and the Common School Revival in the United States* (New York: Charles Scribner's Sons, 1898), 225.

51. Glenn, *Myth of the Common School,* 154. See also Cubberley, *Public Education,* 233–235.

52. Letter from a personal friend to Mary Mann, as quoted in Mary Mann, "Life of Horace Mann," in *Life and Works,* 1:16.

53. Letter from Horace Mann to a friend, as quoted in Mary Mann, "Life of Horace Mann," 1:15.

54. Charles Glenn Jr., "Mann, Horace," in *The Praeger Handbook of Religion and Education in the United States,* ed. James C. Carper and Thomas C. Hunt (Westport, CT: Praeger, 2009), 295.

55. As quoted in Raymond B. Culver, *Horace Mann and Religion in Massachusetts Public Schools* (New York: Arno Press / New York Times, 1969), 59.

56. Isaac Collins and John S. Powell, *A List of Some of the Benevolent Institutions of the City of Philadelphia* (Philadelphia: Henry B. Ashmead Book and Job Printer, 1859), 33.

57. Quoted in Culver, *Horace Mann and Religion,* 77.

58. Ibid., 56.

59. As quoted in ibid., 94.

60. Diane Ravitch, "American Traditions of Education," in *A Primer on America's Schools,* ed. Terry M. Moe (Stanford, CA: Hoover Institution Press, 2001), 9. See also Daniel Walker Howe, "Protestantism, Voluntarism, and Personal Identity in Antebellum America," in *New Directions in American Religious History,* ed. Harry S. Stout and D. G. Hart (New York: Oxford University Press, 1997), 224–225.

61. Mann wrote in his journal, "I would rather no District Library should ever be formed, than to have them, if they must be composed of such books" (as quoted in Culver, *Horace Mann and Religion,* 57).

62. Maris Vinovskis, "Horace Mann on the Economic Productivity of Education," *New England Quarterly* 43, no. 4 (Dec. 1970): 559–560.

63. Mann, *Reply to the "Remarks" of Thirty-One Boston Schoolmasters on the Seventh Annual Report of the Secretary of the Massachusetts Board of Education* (Boston: William B. Fowle and Nahum Capen, 1844), 3.

64. Monroe, *Founding*, 248–249; Robert Laurence Moore, *Selling God: American Religion in the Marketplace of Culture* (New York: Oxford University Press, 1994), 62.

65. Dionne Danns and Christopher M. Span, "History of Schooling," in *21st Century Education: A Reference Handbook*, vol. 2, ed. Thomas L. Good (Thousand Oaks, CA: Sage, 2008), 267.

66. L. Ray Gunn, *The Decline of Authority: Public Economic Policy and Political Development in New York State, 1800–1860* (Ithaca, NY: Cornell University Press, 1988), 23.

67. Monroe, *Founding*, 185.

68. Benjamin Justice, *The War That Wasn't: Religious Conflict and Compromise in the Common Schools of New York State, 1865–1900* (Albany: SUNY Press, 2005), 31.

69. Charles Z. Lincoln, *The Constitutional History of New York*, 5 vols. (Rochester: Lawyers Co-operative Pub. Co., 1906), 3:526–527. See also Randall, *Common School System*, 19–21; William A. Fischel, *Making the Grade* (Chicago: University of Chicago Press, 2009), 59.

70. Lincoln, *Constitutional History of New York*, 3:526–527.

71. As quoted in Randall, *Common School System*, 70.

72. William Oland Bourne, *History of the Public School Society of the City of New York* (New York: William Wood and Co., 1870), 48; Cremin, *American Education*, 164; Diane Ravitch, *The Great School Wars: A History of the New York City Public Schools* (Baltimore: Johns Hopkins University Press, 2000), 79–81.

73. Bourne, *Public School Society*, 3–12, quotation at 3. See also Ravitch, *The Great School Wars*, 11. Ravitch makes clear that the 1808 extension applied to "all poor boys."

74. Bourne, *Public School Society*, 15.

75. Cremin, *American Education*, 166; Bourne, *Public School Society*, 429.

76. The African Free School was the first nonsectarian free school in New York City, founded in 1787 by the Manumission Society to give black children the benefits of education and the "right understanding of their future privileges, and relative duties, when they should become free men and citizens." Society members—including Alexander Hamilton, George Clinton, and John Jay—believed that education was the way to right the evils of slavery. Its members acknowledged that even "those [white men] who are most sincere and zealous in reprobating slavery" struggled with prejudice because of false associations between skin color and poor character. They argued that the institution of slavery unjustly imparted such associations; the hope was that educational institutions would impart new, positive associations. However, when the African Free School was transferred from the Manumission Society to the Public School Society in 1826, these same prejudices were used to justify and reaffirm segregated schools for blacks. The Female Association founded a free school for girls in New York City in 1802, and later partnered with the Public School Society to ensure that girls were educated alongside boys and not just taught outside of regular school hours. See Charles C. Andrews, *The History of the New-York African Free Schools* (New York: Mahlon Day, 1830), 7; and Edward Augustus Fitzpatrick, *The Educational Views and Influence of DeWitt Clinton* (New York: Teachers College, Columbia University, 1911), 121–122.

77. Bourne, *Public School Society,* 626.

78. Jay P. Dolan, *The Irish Americans: A History* (New York: Bloomsbury Press, 2010), 75; Ravitch, *The Great School Wars,* 27.

79. Jay P. Dolan, *The Immigrant Church: New York's Irish and German Catholics, 1815–1865* (Baltimore: Johns Hopkins University Press, 1975), 100; Bourne, *Public School Society,* 161–162.

80. Samuel F. B. Morse, *Foreign Conspiracy against the Liberties of the United States* (New York: Leavitt, Lord and Co., 1835), 103, emphasis in original.

81. John Hughes, in *A Discussion of the Question: Is the Roman Catholic Religion . . . Inimical to Civil and Religious Liberty?* (Philadelphia: Carey, Lea, and Blanchard, 1836), 20, emphasis in original.

82. Richard Shaw, *Dagger John: The Unquiet Life and Times of Archbishop John Hughes of New York* (New York: Paulist Press, 1977); Timothy Walch, "Hughes, John," in *The Praeger Handbook of Religion and Education in the United States,* vol. 1, ed. James C. Carper and Thomas C. Hunt (Westport: Praeger, 2009), 244. See also Dolan, *The Immigrant Church,* 106.

83. Walch, "Hughes, John," 244.

84. Baron George Littleton, "A Dialogue between Fernando Cortes and William Penn," in *New York Reader,* no. 3 (New York: Samuel Wood and Sons, 1815), 200–205.

85. John Hughes, speech from "Meeting in the Basement of St. James' Church, July 27, 1840," in *The Complete Works of the Most Rev. John Hughes,* vol. 1, ed. Laurence Kehoe (New York: American News Co., 1864), pt. 3 *(Lectures, Letters and Speeches of Archbishop Hughes),* 7.

86. Bourne, *Public School Society,* 456.

87. As quoted in Vincent Peter Lannie, "William Seward and Common School Education," *History of Education Quarterly* 4, no. 3 (Sept. 1964): 185.

88. Frederick W. Seward, *Autobiography of William H. Seward from 1831 to 1834 with a Memoir of His Life and Selections from His Letters from 1831–1846* (New York: Derby and Miller, 1877), 462. See also Lannie, "William Seward," 188.

89. Ravitch, *The Great School Wars,* 76.

90. Walch, "Hughes, John," 245.

91. Ravitch, *The Great School Wars,* 80.

92. Ibid.

93. Paul D. Travers, "John Orville Taylor: A Forgotten Educator," *History of Education Quarterly* 9, no. 1 (Spring 1969): 58.

94. "J. Orville Taylor's Lecture."

95. Randall, *Common School System,* 236.

96. As quoted in ibid., 230.

97. As quoted in Lincoln, *Constitutional History of New York,* 2:205.

98. As quoted in Randall, *Common School System,* 230.

99. "An Act Establishing Free Schools," 1.

100. Based on data from the U.S. Census of 1850, the number of children in New York State reported by their families as attending school, as a share of school-age children

(ages 5–19), was 69.2 percent for white males, 63.3 percent for white females, 39.3 percent for free black males, and 32.8 percent for free black females; at the national level, the proportion for free black males was 18.4 percent and for free black females 16.0 percent. *Statistical View of the United States . . . Being a Compendium of the Seventh Census* (Washington, DC: Beverley Tucker, Senate Printer, 1854), tables 30 (p. 52), 33 (p. 56), 57 (p. 70), 147 (p. 144). Tyack and Hansot (*Learning Together,* 51–52) report similar attendance rates for white children in the Middle Atlantic states as of 1850 (66.1 percent for white males and 59.6 percent for white females), but somewhat lower national rates for free black children (13.6 percent for males and 10.8 percent for females); they do not report free black attendance rates for the Middle Atlantic states. The economic historian Claudia Goldin finds national school enrollment rates of 59.0 percent for white males and 53.3 percent for white females, but just 2.0 percent for nonwhite males and 1.8 percent for nonwhite females, where the nonwhite population here includes both black slaves (accounting for the vast majority of the black population) and free blacks. See "School Enrollment Rates, by Sex and Race: 1850–1994," in *Historical Statistics of the United States, Earliest Times to the Present: Millennial Edition,* ed. Susan B. Carter et al. (New York: Cambridge University Press, 2006), tables Bc438–Bc446.

101. "An Act Establishing Free Schools," 1–3.
102. "Our State Legislature," *New-York Daily Tribune,* 14 Apr. 1849, 1.
103. Lincoln, *Constitutional History of New York,* 3:529.
104. Randall, *Common School System,* 255, 255–256.
105. Samuel Sidwell Randall, ed., *District School Journal of the State of New York,* vol. 11 (Albany, NY: C. Van Benthuysen and Co., 1851), 7.
106. Randall, *Common School System,* 264, emphasis in original.
107. Ibid., 260.
108. As quoted in ibid., 275.
109. Charles E. Fitch, *The Public School: History of Common School Education in New York from 1633 to 1904* (Albany, NY: J. B. Lyon, 1905), 36.
110. As quoted in Randall, *Common School System,* 275, emphasis in original.
111. As quoted in Carl F. Kaestle, *Pillars of the Republic: Commons Schools and American Society, 1780–1860* (New York: Hill and Wang, 1983), 150.
112. "The Free School System—A General Appeal," *New-York Daily Tribune,* 18 Oct. 1850, 3.
113. Joseph McKeen, "Annual Report of the County Superintendent of Common Schools of the City and County of New York," *New-York Daily Tribune,* 6 Jan. 1851, 7
114. As quoted in Randall, *Common School System,* 273, emphasis in original.
115. As quoted in ibid., 266–267.
116. *In Court of Appeals: Henry D. Barto, Respondent, against David W. Himrod & Eber Lovell, Appellants* (Ithaca, NY: Andrus, Gauntlet, and Co., 1852), 6–7.
117. Randall, *Common School System,* 256.
118. Silas M. Burroughs and Benjamin G. Ferris, "Report No. 42, in Assembly, February 6, 1851," in *Free Schools: A Documentary History of the Free School Movement in New York*

State, ed. Thomas E. Finegan (Albany: University of the State of New York, 1921), 468, 470.

119. Ibid., 463–464.
120. Ibid., 470.
121. Ibid., 468. See also Randall, *Common School System,* 284.

·{ 8 }·

A Nation Divided: The United States
and the Challenge of Secession (1861)

*Let the consequences be what they may—whether the Potomac is crimsoned in
human gore, and Pennsylvania Avenue is paved ten fathoms in depth with
mangled bodies, or whether the last vestige of liberty is swept from the face of
the American continent, the South will never submit to such humiliation and
degradation as the inauguration of Abraham Lincoln.*[1]

THIS CHILLING LANGUAGE APPEARED in the *Atlanta Confederacy* newspaper
shortly after the election of Abraham Lincoln, the nation's first Republican
president. Northern political leaders had formed the Republican Party only
a few years before, in large measure to combat the spread of slavery in America. Southerners had long been wary of Northern hostility toward their "peculiar institution," and Lincoln's 1860 victory proved to be the last straw in
this sectional rivalry that had deeply influenced American culture and politics since the nation's earliest days.

By the time of Lincoln's inauguration five months later, in March 1861,
seven Southern states had announced their decision to secede from the
Union, making it clear that they preferred disunion to the rule of a Republican president elected almost entirely on the strength of Northern support.
Lincoln rejected secession as unlawful, declaring that "no State upon its own
mere motion can lawfully get out of the Union," and he pledged that his government would continue to exercise its authority, as best it could, in the rebellious states.[2]

A crisis in South Carolina, the first state to secede, tested Lincoln's mettle in the opening days of his presidency. Federal troops still held Fort Sumter in Charleston harbor, but their supplies were running low. Lincoln would either have to evacuate the fort or risk war by sending provisions. Throughout the month of March, he consulted his advisers about Sumter as public pressure mounted for decisive action. At the end of the month, with most of his Cabinet members in agreement, Lincoln prepared a mission to resupply the fort. Aware that the move would be risky, however, he withheld final orders for putting the plan into action. The possibility of a peaceful evacuation still appealed to him, particularly if his government could hold its ground elsewhere. With Sumter's provisions dwindling as Lincoln pondered his options, voices in the press and Lincoln's own Republican Party increasingly demanded a solution. The new president understood the weight of the choice he faced: nothing less than the survival of the Union was at stake.

The Struggle for Political Dominance

The division of the United States into a slave South and a free North had its roots in the regional economies of the original colonies. The large plantations that dominated the Southern economy relied on African slaves to harvest cash crops like tobacco and, especially after 1793, cotton.* Slavery was far less prevalent in the more diversified economies of New York, New Jersey, and Pennsylvania, and was even less common in many parts of New England.[3] Accordingly, the vast majority of slaves lived in the South, which by the middle of the Revolutionary War in 1780 held over 90 percent of the nation's almost 578,000 black residents.[4] As Southern slavery expanded, many Northerners embraced moral and religious objections to the institution. By the early 1800s, all of the states from New Jersey and Pennsylvania northward had taken action to emancipate their resident slaves, either immediately or over time.[5]

The South held a minority of the nation's white population, but exercised outsized influence at the federal level due to two important constitutional

---

* Eli Whitney's invention of the cotton gin in 1793 contributed to a dramatic increase in the production of cotton.

TABLE 8.1

Population of the United States, North and South, 1790–1860

Year	Total U.S.	Original Northern States[a]			Original Southern States[b]			Northern Territories and Later Northern States, plus Western Territories and States[c]			Southern Territories and Later Southern States[d]		
		Total	% Black	% Blacks Enslaved	Total	% Black	% Blacks Enslaved	Total	% Black	% Blacks Enslaved	Total	% Black	% Blacks Enslaved
1790	3,929,625	1,881,856	3.6	60.0	1,853,060	36.4	95.2	85,341	0.3	0	109,368	14.9	97.1
1800	5,308,483	2,481,111	3.3	44.0	2,286,494	37.6	93.0	205,471	0.6	11.3	335,407	17.5	97.9
1810	7,239,881	3,268,780	3.1	26.7	2,674,891	40.4	91.0	490,219	0.9	10.2	805,991	23.7	94.0
1820	9,638,453	4,123,935	2.7	16.4	3,061,063	41.6	90.8	1,028,700	0.8	12.9	1,424,755	26.7	95.4
1830	12,860,702	5,261,729	2.4	2.2	3,611,022	41.9	89.9	1,750,670	1.0	4.7	2,237,281	30.2	95.6
1840	17,063,353	6,469,134	2.2	0.5	3,870,822	40.6	89.1	3,259,788	0.9	1.2	3,463,609	32.7	96.0
1850	23,191,876	8,312,731	1.8	0.2	4,591,645	39.7	89.2	5,214,489	0.9	<0.1	5,073,011	32.0	97.4
1860	31,443,321	10,279,170	1.5	<0.1	5,224,279	38.2	89.1	8,848,778	0.8	<0.1	7,091,094	31.3	98.0

a. Massachusetts (including Maine, which was part of Massachusetts until 1820), New Hampshire, Rhode Island, Connecticut, New York, New Jersey, and Pennsylvania. All of these states either had abolished slavery or had begun a process of gradual emancipation laws by 1790, except for New York and New Jersey. New York enacted a gradual emancipation law in 1799, and New Jersey enacted a gradual emancipation law in 1804.

b. Virginia (including West Virginia, which was part of Virginia until 1861), Delaware, Maryland, North Carolina, South Carolina, Georgia, and the District of Columbia (which was part of Maryland and Virginia until 1801; Virginia took its part back in 1846).

c. Vermont (which became a state in 1791), Ohio (1803), Indiana (1816), Illinois (1818), Michigan (1837), Iowa (1846), Wisconsin (1848), California (1850), Minnesota (1858), and Oregon (1859). Also included are organized territories in 1860: Kansas (which became a state in 1861), Nevada (1864), Colorado (1876), Dakota (which became two states, South and North Dakota, 1889), Washington (1889), Utah (1896), and New Mexico (1912). Slaves were held in a number of northern and western territories which either abolished slavery or began a process of gradual emancipation on becoming states.

d. Kentucky (which became a state in 1792), Tennessee (1796), Louisiana (1812), Mississippi (1817), Alabama (1819), Missouri (1821), Arkansas (1836), Florida (1845), and Texas (1845).

Source: Adapted from Michael R. Haines, "State Populations" (table group Aa2244–6550), and Susan B. Carter, "Black Population, by State and Slave/Free Status: 1790–1860" ("Table Bb1–98), in Historical Statistics of the United States, Earliest Times to the Present: Millennial Edition, ed. Susan B. Carter, Scott Sigmund Gartner, Michael R. Haines, Alan L. Olmstead, Richard Sutch, and Gavin Wright (New York: Cambridge University Press, 2006).

TABLE 8.2

Population in 1790: Total, Free, and Three-Fifths Rule, by Region

	Total	North	South	North %	South %
Total population (1790)	3,929,000	1,967,000	1,962,000	50.1	49.9
Free population (1790)	3,231,000	1,927,000	1,304,000	59.6	40.4
Three-fifths rule (1790)	3,651,000	1,951,000	1,700,000	53.4	46.6

Source: Adapted from Donald L. Robinson, *Slavery in the Structure of American Politics, 1765–1820* (New York: Harcourt Brace Jovanovich, 1971), 180.

Note: Populations rounded to nearest thousand.

provisions. First, although slaves could not vote, three-fifths of their population was counted when calculating the size of each state's delegation in the House of Representatives (and thus its number of electoral votes for president). This arrangement—the so-called Three-Fifths Compromise—had itself resulted from contentious debates between Northern and Southern delegates at the Constitutional Convention in 1787. Second, the Constitution guaranteed each state two U.S. senators regardless of its population. This meant that although the Northern states' populations had grown faster than those of the Southern states, their representation in the Senate never increased as a result.[6]

Against this constitutional backdrop, politicians nationwide understood that the status of slavery in the territories—which were potential future states—could determine the balance of power between slave and free states in Congress. In 1787 the Confederation Congress voted to prohibit slavery in territories northwest of the Ohio River, ensuring that states formed from those lands would be free. This did not trouble most Southerners at the time because they expected that northwestern farmers would emerge as political allies against northeastern mercantile elites. Nearly two decades later, in 1803, many New Englanders opposed the enormous "Louisiana Purchase" of western territory for fear of incubating future slave states. Southerners also grew wary as settlers populated the Purchase, but for exactly the opposite reason. Because slavery had failed to gain political traction in the Northwest, even outside the lands governed by the 1787 ordinance, Southerners increasingly feared that the new territories could become free states, tipping the federal balance of power. Congress handled this delicate issue by regularly admitting new states to the Union in pairs, one free and one slave, to preserve a rough balance in the Senate.[7]

Even beyond slavery itself, debates in Congress regularly divided along North–South lines, reflecting sharply differing interests across the two regions. The pro-business Federalist Party controlled the government in the 1790s, instituting policies that benefited Northern commerce such as a national bank and a close trade relationship with Great Britain. When the Southern-based Democratic-Republican Party* took control in 1801, beginning more than two decades of essentially single-party rule, its leaders let the bank expire and also embargoed trade with Britain. These policies infuriated Northern commercial communities and their Federalist representatives, who argued that the South's constitutional advantages unfairly kept the Democratic-Republicans in power. Northern resentment peaked after the United States went to war with Britain in 1812. Some angry New Englanders called for repeal of the Three-Fifths clause in the Constitution and even threatened to "cut the connection" with the rest of the nation altogether.[8]

The Missouri Crisis

The early power struggle between North and South came to a head after the government of Missouri, a territory that was part of the Louisiana Purchase, petitioned for statehood in late 1818. The following February, Representative James Tallmadge of New York proposed that Congress ban the introduction of new slaves into Missouri and eventually emancipate all slaves born there. Southern congressmen attacked the proposal as "a prohibition of the emigration of the Southern people to the State of Missouri." Antislavery Northerners defended it just as passionately.[9] After Georgia's Thomas W. Cobb warned that the proposal's supporters were "kindling a fire . . . which could be extinguished only in blood," Tallmadge responded that "if blood is necessary to extinguish any fire which I have assisted to kindle . . . I shall not forbear to contribute my mite."[10]

Northerners who supported the Tallmadge proposal offered both moral and political rationales. Opposition to slavery was growing in the

---

* Contemporaries typically called this party simply "Republican," but historians often use the terms "Democratic-Republican" or "Jeffersonian Republican" to distinguish it from the modern Republican Party formed in the 1850s.

North as the region's emancipation laws gradually diminished the practice, and by 1820 Northerners would own less than 2 percent of the nation's slaves.[11] Arthur Livermore of New Hampshire, one of Tallmadge's allies in the House, reflected this trend by calling slavery "the foulest reproach of nations" and "a sin which sits heavy on the souls of every one of us."[12] Humanitarian concern for the plight of black slaves was far from the only motivation, however. Fearful of the political consequences of a new slave state, Tallmadge argued that to expand slavery further beyond the states that the Three-Fifths Compromise had been designed for "would be unjust in its operations, unequal in its results, and a violation of [the compromise's] original intention."[13]

As Northern opposition to slavery was hardening, many white Southerners were becoming even more fervent supporters of the institution. Southern orators had traditionally treated slavery as a "necessary evil" that they hoped would someday fade away. After the cotton industry boomed in the 1810s, however, more of them spoke of the practice as a "positive good" that kept slaves "well clothed, well fed, and treated with kindness and humanity."[14] Some Southern congressmen voiced this opinion in opposition to the Tallmadge amendment. Others, still in the "necessary evil" camp, argued that spreading slavery over the United States would, as the esteemed Virginian, and slaveholder, Thomas Jefferson put it, "dilute the evil everywhere, and facilitate the means of getting finally rid of it."[15]

Although Tallmadge's proposal passed the House, the Senate rejected it in 1819 and the Missouri question spilled into 1820. In the meantime, the debate had become increasingly acrimonious both within and outside of Congress. One New York paper warned that allowing Missouri to become a slave state would be "the death-warrant of the political standing and influence of the free states," and many Northern congressmen who voted against the amendment faced the ire of disgruntled constituents when they returned home from Washington.[16] Meanwhile, pro-slavery Missourians promised "'to kill, or drive out of the country' any man who should open his mouth against slavery," and some Southern congressmen threatened to break the Union itself.[17] Despite the ferocity on both sides, Congress finally reached a compromise in March 1820. Missouri would join the Union without restrictions on slavery at the same time as Maine, a new northeastern free state that had previously been part of Massachusetts. Furthermore, slavery would be prohibited in all other Louisiana Purchase lands above the latitude of 36°30', Missouri's southern border.

Reactions to the Missouri Compromise were mixed. Although many leading political figures regarded it as a Southern victory, Tallmadge himself reported "great Joy" at the compromise.[18] Perhaps the most ominous response came from Thomas Jefferson, who wrote, "I considered it at once as the knell of the Union. It is hushed indeed for the moment. But this is a reprieve only, not a final sentence. A geographical line, coinciding with a marked principle, moral and political, once conceived and held up to the angry passions of men, will never be obliterated; and every new irritation will mark it deeper and deeper."[19]

Southern Opposition to the Tariff

By the early 1820s, although the Democratic-Republican Party controlled the federal government more thoroughly than ever, many Southern leaders felt increasingly under siege and regularly attacked policies that they claimed favored the North. Having become more national in scope, the Democratic-Republican Party now included many members who no longer embraced the party's founding ideals of states' rights and small government. Jefferson, who had helped to found the party, observed in 1822 that the apparent "amalgamation" of all interests under the Democratic-Republican umbrella was "of name only, not of principle."[20] Indeed, when Democratic-Republicans in Washington allowed the enactment of protective tariffs, the funding of major infrastructure projects, and even the reinstatement of a national bank in 1816, these essentially Federalist policies delighted northeastern businessmen but irked proponents of the Democratic-Republicans' original platform.[21] Some Southerners particularly feared that a more active federal government would threaten slavery. "If Congress can make canals," warned one North Carolina senator, "they can with more propriety emancipate."[22]

No policy issue in the 1820s riled Southern interests more than rising tariff rates. Although Southerners had supported prior tariff increases, especially following the War of 1812, by the early 1820s they increasingly saw the tariff as a means to "sacrifice the South to the North."[23] While the tariff benefited Northern industry by raising the cost of competing manufactured imports, Southerners claimed that it hit agriculture hard, inflating nonagricultural prices and deflating agricultural exports.[24] Despite Southern opposition, Congress passed a new tariff in 1824 and another in 1828 that opponents called the Tariff of Abominations. One South Carolinian warned that the government had "pressed this most iniquitous Tariff against the South with I believe the express hope of driving us into Rebellion."[25]

Many Southerners also charged that the way Congress had been exercising tariff policy was unconstitutional. Since 1816 Congress had primarily imposed tariffs as a means of bolstering American industry, which was mainly concentrated in the North.[26] Southerners, however, pointed out that the Constitution authorized Congress to use its taxing power only "to pay the Debts and provide for the common Defence and general Welfare of the United States."[27] They interpreted this to mean that Congress could enact tariffs only in order to raise revenue, and never principally to promote domestic industry through trade protection.[28]

John Calhoun of South Carolina, who served as vice president under President John Quincy Adams in the late 1820s, believed that the states possessed a special means to resist the tariff. Formerly a pro-tariff nationalist, Calhoun had grown convinced that Southerners had become "serfs" to Northern manufacturers, and he opposed tariff hikes otherwise supported by the Adams administration.[29] Calhoun posited that every state had the authority to "nullify"—and thus not to abide by—any federal law it judged unconstitutional.[30] As Calhoun characterized it, this extraordinary nullification power was essential to defend individual and state rights against the "unrestrained will of a majority," which he believed had the capacity to abuse federal power.[31]

Calhoun's theory of nullification was put to the test in 1832, when the government of South Carolina asserted that it had nullified the Tariff of Abominations and threatened secession if the federal government tried to enforce it. The president at the time was Andrew Jackson of Tennessee, the head of a new Democratic Party formed in opposition to the nationalist policies of John Quincy Adams. Calhoun had joined Jackson, a fellow slaveholder, as vice president with hopes that he would end the protective tariff, but by 1832 Jackson had sorely disappointed Calhoun and only slightly modified the tariff. After South Carolina's announcement, Jackson attacked nullification as "incompatible with the existence of the Union, contradicted expressly by the letter of the Constitution, unauthorized by its spirit, inconsistent with every principle on which It was founded, and destructive of the great object for which it was formed." Accordingly, he requested legislation from Congress that would allow him to enforce tariff collection, despite the resistance from South Carolina.[32]

Many observers warned that the nullification debate threatened the nation's very survival. While Calhoun, who left the Jackson administration for the Senate, asserted that nullification prevented the need for state secession, the president claimed it was a "mask which concealed the hideous features of disunion." Another major national political figure and slave owner, Kentucky senator Henry Clay, warned that unless the debate was resolved, "civil war shall be lighted up in the bosom of our own happy land."[33] To avoid such a calamity, Clay pushed through Congress compromise legislation that included both a lower tariff *and* Jackson's requested enforcement bill. The standoff ended in March 1833 when South Carolina's legislature accepted the lower tariff (but, ever rebellious, symbolically asserted that it had nullified the enforcement act). Although tariff debates would never again reach the intensity that characterized the Nullification Crisis, they would continue to be an important source of sectional division over the ensuing decades.[34]

The "Subterranean Fire" of Slavery and Abolition

The 1833 compromise succeeded in allaying immediate fears of sectional conflict, but as one Northern antislavery activist warned, settlements like this one concealed a "subterranean fire" of regional struggle, "fed by slavery."[35] Although Congress rarely discussed the topic of slavery in the 1830s, Northern antislavery activists grew more outspoken in this period. The Second Great Awakening, a national religious revival that peaked around these years, filled many Northerners with the belief that they must "abolish" the national "sin" of slavery. Leaders of the abolitionist movement, dedicated to the peaceful but "immediate" emancipation of Southern slaves and to civil equality for blacks and whites, included the antislavery evangelist Theodore Dwight Weld, the journalist William Lloyd Garrison (who founded the *Liberator* newspaper, in Boston, to "lift the standard of emancipation in the eyes of the nation"), the best-selling writer Lydia Maria Child, and, later on, the escaped slave, author, and orator Frederick Douglass.[36] By 1840 more than 200,000 Americans (many, if not mostly, nonvoting women) had joined abolitionist societies. This was a small portion of the total population (about 17 million), but more than enough to unsettle slaveholders.[37]

Southerners feared the abolitionist movement not only as a threat to slavery but also as a potential incitement to violence against slaveholders. Particularly after Virginia slave Nat Turner led a failed but bloody revolt in 1831, many Southerners feared new rebellions. Political leaders like Calhoun who sought a united South pointed to the Northern abolition movement as evidence of irreconcilable sectional differences and warned that abolitionists had control "of the pulpit, of the schools, and to a considerable extent, of the press" in the North. Critics of abolitionism in North and South alike characterized the movement as a form of aggression against the South that, if unabated, would cause "the destruction and disunion of our happy government."[38]

President Martin Van Buren, a New York Democrat, noted confidently in 1837 that the growing popular clamor over slavery had "signally failed [to] reach the stability of our institutions."[39] Some Northern congressmen—most of them members of the new Whig Party—would have liked to debate slavery and emancipation, but their Southern colleagues were unwilling to broach the topic at all. After receiving over 300 abolitionist petitions with more than 40,000 signatures, House Democrats had passed a "gag rule" in 1836 banning discussion of such petitions. The Senate observed the same prohibition, and over the next several years Congress effectively ignored the pleas of abolitionists as it focused on other issues, such as the tariff and relief for victims of a recent economic downturn.[40] By the early 1840s, the geographic divide in Congress appeared less pronounced as loyalty to party seemed to eclipse regional disagreements on most issues, though there continued to be sectional alignment on the tariff.[41] Congress's official silence on the abolitionists' petitions lasted until 1844, when a coalition of Whigs and Northern Democrats finally overturned the gag rule.[42]

The Territory Debate Revisited

The battle over slavery in the territories returned with a vengeance in the mid-1840s and exploded dormant divisions within both parties. The country went to war with Mexico in 1845, stemming from a dispute over Mexico's border with Texas, a slave state newly annexed to the United States. Democratic president James K. Polk of Tennessee, a slaveholder and a believer in the expansionist doctrine of "manifest destiny," had his eye on acquiring more southwestern land as part of an eventual peace deal. The thought of more Southern territory horrified many Northerners who already considered the annexation of Texas "monstrous beyond all expression."[43] Polk's desire for even more land led many to conclude that his true motivation for taking the country to war was "to Strengthen the 'Slave Power.'"[44]

In August 1846 Representative David Wilmot, a Pennsylvania Democrat, proposed an amendment to a war appropriation bill, stipulating that "neither slavery nor involuntary servitude shall ever exist in any part of the territory" acquired from Mexico. Wilmot did not show any particular concern for the plight of slaves when defending his amendment, but instead expressed his desire to "preserve to free white labor a fair country, a rich inheritance, where the sons of toil, of my own race and color can live without the disgrace which association with negro slavery brings upon free labor."[45] Debate over the Wilmot Proviso provoked hostility between Northern and Southern leaders that degenerated into attacks on each other's character and culture. Northern supporters derided "the frantic struggles of an infatuated slave power," which threatened disunion whenever slavery seemed imperiled, while their opponents accused Northerners of seeking "mastery" over the Southern states.[46]

Political Divisions

The territory question became still more urgent after the war ended in February 1848 and the United States gained more than 1.2 million square miles of land between the Rio Grande and the Pacific Ocean.[47] Battles erupted within both major political parties over the morality of slavery, constitutional limits on its containment, and the rights of settlers in the territories. Observers noted that Democrats were becoming "denationalized" into sectional blocs: Northern Wilmot supporters believed that Congress had the constitutional authority to limit slavery in the territories, whereas Southern followers of the "Calhoun Doctrine" contended that only state governments, never Congress or the territorial governments, could enact such restrictions.[48] Both views conflicted with the opinion of President Polk, also a Democrat, that the territories should adhere to the Missouri Compromise line, as well as with Michigan Democratic senator Lewis Cass's "popular sov-

ereignty" proposal to grant "the people of any territory . . . the right to regulate [slavery] themselves."[49] At the same time, Northern Whigs increasingly
split between "Conscience Whigs," who supported the Wilmot Proviso, and
"Cotton Whigs," who were more amicable to the South.

Perhaps not surprisingly, 1849 proved to be an unproductive year in Washington. The 1848 elections had split the federal government, awarding the
presidency to the Whig Zachary Taylor (a Louisiana slave owner renowned
for his victories in the Mexican War), leaving the Senate in the hands of
Democrats, and producing a House where a new Free-Soil Party (which opposed slavery in the territories) held enough seats to narrowly deny either
major party a majority. While divisions over the territories remained sharp,
other slavery-related issues also stoked sectional passions. Momentum was
growing behind an effort to ban the slave trade—or even to emancipate the
slaves—within the borders of Washington, D.C., and several Northern states
passed "personal liberty laws" to protect runaway slaves (despite the Constitution's mandate that "No person held to service or labor in one state,
under the laws thereof, escaping into another, shall, in consequence of any
law or regulation therein, be discharged from such service or labor; but shall
be delivered up, on claim of the party to whom such service or labor may be
due"). These developments infuriated Southerners, and even produced
open talk of secession.[50] Observing the growing bitterness, John Calhoun
wrote in April 1849 that "the alienation between the two sections has . . .
gone too far to save the union."[51]

The quandary of the western territories, meanwhile, grew ever more
tangled. Although California saw its population grow rapidly after the discovery of gold there in 1848, it had not yet been formally organized as a territory. With so many settlers already there, President Taylor sought to
circumvent the long-running debate over the territories by immediately
turning California and the bordering region of New Mexico into states. This
possibility angered Southerners, because they expected that these new states
would ban slavery before slaveholders could establish a presence there. Com-
plicating matters still further, the government of Texas claimed that its
border with New Mexico extended much farther west than Taylor recognized. Taylor's plan to grant the disputed land not just to another state, but
to one that would ban slavery, infuriated Texans, even provoking threats of
military action from some Texan leaders.[52]

The Compromise of 1850

With tensions potentially spiraling out of control, in January 1850 Henry Clay (now a Whig) offered a plan to resolve all of these issues at once. Echoing Lewis Cass, Clay proposed that Congress organize New Mexico as a territory without imposing "restriction or condition on the subject of slavery," a position that rejected the Wilmot Proviso but left open the possibility that either popular sovereignty or the Calhoun Doctrine would rule in the territories.[53] (The new Territory of Utah would be granted the same option.) California, however, would become a state and would almost certainly ban slavery. Texas would not get its extreme border under the plan, but the federal government would assume some of the state's public debt in return. To settle the question of Washington, D.C., Clay proposed abolishing the slave trade in the district but forbidding complete abolition there until Maryland and the district consented. The plan also included a stricter fugitive slave law. In a historic speech on February 5, Clay insisted that only such mutual concessions from the North and South could quiet the "uproar, confusion and menace to the existence of the Union."[54]

While many moderates favored Clay's compromise, critics on both sides sharply attacked it. Free-Soil senator Salmon P. Chase of Ohio derided the plan as "sentiment for the North [but] substance for the South," while Calhoun, in one of his last speeches, asserted that the South had "already surrendered so much that she [had] little left to surrender."[55] At the same time, President Taylor continued to demand the immediate incorporation of all of the new lands as states. These disagreements broke party allegiances as Wilmot Democrats and Conscience Whigs supported Taylor, moderate Democrats and Cotton and Southern Whigs backed Clay, and Southern radicals rejected both plans.[56]

In the end, a different president and a different senator succeeded in driving the compromise through Congress. President Taylor unexpectedly died of an illness that July and was replaced by his vice president, Millard Fillmore of New York, who "announced he would accept any compromise passed by Congress." Clay, feeling unwell himself, temporarily departed Washington a month later and Illinois Democrat Stephen Douglas took up his cause in the Senate. To win passage, Douglas introduced the plan's various components as separate bills. Each individual piece won the approval of one region's congressmen, plus a few moderates, sufficient to overcome opposition from the other region.[57] Contemporaries noted that the factions had not truly come to an agreement. "The question of slavery in the territories has been avoided," commented Senator Chase. "It has not been settled."[58]

The divisive sectional battles of the late 1840s demolished the party unity that had reigned earlier in the decade. Partisan loyalty declined sharply, and the parties ultimately proved able to keep their members in line in only about half of the votes in Congress. One historian characterized this tellingly as "the apparent disappearance of the parties."[59]

Two Cultures and Two Economies

Although tensions in Washington calmed markedly after 1850 as a result of the compromise, Northern citizens came out in force against the new Fugitive Slave Act. Many Northerners resisted enforcing it, and several states passed further personal liberty laws to undercut its enforcement. Northern citizens confounded Southerners and federal law enforcement by helping fugitive slaves escape their captors and by maintaining the "Underground Railroad," a network of sympathizers who provided shelter to at least 50,000 runaway slaves as they fled to Canada.[60] Enraged Southern leaders attacked these violations of the Fugitive Slave Act and warned that such disregard for the law would crush the Union into "a vast pile of ruin and desolation."[61]

The publication of Harriet Beecher Stowe's *Uncle Tom's Cabin* in 1852 further radicalized both sides of the slavery debate. This extraordinarily popular novel (and its countless stage dramatizations), about the martyrdom of an old slave man sold to a violent drunkard and of a young runaway slave mother, reached millions of American readers and is said to have turned many solidly against slavery and the Fugitive Slave Act. In the meantime, Southern leaders attacked "dangerous and dirty little volumes" by antislavery authors such as Stowe.[62] Apologists insisted that slavery maintained whites' equality by preventing economic stratification among them and that it provided slaves with better lives than they would have had in Africa. Claiming that *Uncle Tom's Cabin* ignored these "peculiar advantages," Southern critics denounced the novel as a "pathetic tale" and "willful slander."[63]

"Stupendous Wrongs"

As the nation debated Stowe's fictional account, more than three million African-Americans lived the reality of slavery in the 1850s.[64] Slaves were used in several industries, but most worked on plantations harvesting cotton, tobacco, and other crops. Legally slaves were "chattel," or property, and as such had few legal rights, if any. Most slave states banned slaves from formally marrying, owning property, or even learning to read and write. Owners were allowed to buy and sell them as they wished, often breaking up families. Scholars estimate that on average approximately 50,000 slaves were sold between Americans each year from 1820 to 1860. Furthermore, owners could abuse, rape, or kill their slaves with few or no repercussions. Certainly some slaveholders treated their slaves better, either out of a sense of paternalism or as a strategy for maximizing economic output, but even the slaves of these masters had to endure the curtailment of individual rights and security inherent in the practice of slavery.[65] As Frederick Douglass lamented,

> The physical cruelties are indeed sufficiently harassing and revolting; but they are but as a few grains of sand on the sea shore, or a few drops of water in the great ocean, compared with the stupendous wrongs which it inflicts upon the mental, moral and religious nature of its hapless victims. . . . The first work of slavery is to mar and deface those characteristics of its victims which distinguish *men* from *things,* and *persons* from *property.* Its first aim is to destroy all sense of high moral and religious responsibility. It reduces man to a mere machine. It cuts him off from his maker, it hides from him the laws of God, and leaves him to grope his way from time to eternity in the dark, under the arbitrary and despotic control of a frail, depraved and sinful fellow-man.[66]

Of course, some slaves resisted this degradation. Slaves had protested their status, peacefully and violently, since the early days of colonial America. Some stole from their masters, disobeyed them, or destroyed their property. Others fought them, in rare instances murdered them, and tens of thousands ran off, most for short periods, but sometimes permanently, with a few thousand a year fleeing the slave states altogether. Some of this resistance was seen as mere disobedience; one slave-owning woman from North Carolina reported in 1850 that "I have not a single servant at my command."[67] Other forms of resistance, up to and including violent insurrection, were more explosive. From 1856, a particularly tumultuous year, there are accounts of failed escape plans that involved hundreds of slaves, plots to blow up bridges, and violent confrontations that left both white and black combatants dead. Slaveholders constantly feared insurrections and regularly arrested slaves for plotting them, although how many of these conspiracies were real and how many were figments of slaveholders' imaginations is unknown. Slaves who did participate in organized resistance risked horrific punishments, and might be beaten, whipped, hanged, burned, or otherwise abused or executed, whether by law enforcement, by their owners, or by mobs. Whites who assisted slaves in acts of rebellion could likewise receive corporal or capital punishments for their involvement.[68]

Diverging Regional Economies

The continued polarization of Northern and Southern attitudes toward slavery paralleled the regions' divergent courses of economic development. By the 1850s, the Industrial Revolution was transforming Northern manufacturing and society. As factory labor replaced artisan labor, Northern firms shipped increasingly mass-produced textiles and machinery across the nation via canals, most of them state-built, and freshly laid railroad tracks— approximately 22,000 miles of tracks in the North alone by 1861. With thriving commercial, financial, industrial, and agricultural sectors, Northern capitalists accumulated vast fortunes and employed a growing urban labor class. Such prosperity attracted over 2.8 million immigrants to the United States in the 1850s, the majority of whom settled in the North.[69]

Although the Southern economy also boomed during this decade, its growth was rooted in increasing production of its traditional cash crops, especially cotton, rather than an embrace of manufacturing. By 1860 the South was responsible for less than a tenth of the nation's manufacturing and had not developed its railroad network nearly as extensively as the North. Nor did the South have much that was comparable to the financial or commercial engines of the North. In fact, a significant volume of its agricultural profits flowed to Northern investors, and by 1860 its people would be more than $200 million in debt to Northern creditors. The South was far from impoverished in the 1850s, but its slave economy was very different—and arguably far less dynamic—than the "free-labor" economy of the North.[70]

TABLE 8.3

North versus South: Economic Comparison in 1860

	North	South
Bank deposits ($m)	189	47
Gold specie ($m)	56	27
Property value (including slaves, $m)	11,000	5,500
Railroads (miles of track)	21,973	9,283
Farm value per acre ($)	25.67	10.40
Capital invested in manufacturing per capita ($)	43.73	13.25
Factories	110,000	18,000
Manufacturing workers	1,300,000	110,000
Per capita wealth of free population ($)	2,040	3,978
Per capita income of total population ($)	141	103
Percentage of labor force in agriculture	40%	81%
Percentage of total population literate	94%	58%
Percentage of free population literate	94%	83%
Percentage of free population ages 5–19 in school	72%	35%
Exports of U.S. products, value ($)	164,383,054	208,806,220
Imports of foreign products, value ($)	321,580,969	40,585,285

Sources: Adapted from Richard F. Selcer, *Civil War America, 1850 to 1875* (New York: Facts on File, 2006), 228–229; James M. McPherson, *Ordeal by Fire: The Civil War and Reconstruction,* 3rd ed. (Boston: McGraw-Hill, 2001), 28; and *Report of the Secretary of the Treasury Transmitting a Report from the Register of the Treasury of the Commerce and Navigation of the United States, for the Year Ending June 30, 1860* (Washington, DC: George W. Bowman, 1860), table 14, 552.

Note: For most rows, the label "North" indicates free states (and, in some cases, territories) in all regions, including the mid and far west; and the label "South" indicates slave states, irrespective of whether they tried to secede from the Union. In several rows, however, two or more border states (slave states that did not try to secede) are included as part of the "North," not the "South," depending on how the relevant source defined each region. The trade data, which omit re-exports, cover the period July 1, 1859 through June 30, 1860.

Scholars have long debated the effect of slavery on the Southern economy. Some historians have argued that slavery was inherently less productive than wage labor, in part because slaves lacked "the sheer need to go to work to survive, the promise of more pay for more work, and the added enticement of upward mobility in the long run."[71] However, quantitative analyses have challenged these arguments, demonstrating that slave labor was often highly productive and that planters often collected higher returns than Northern industrialists.[72] Planters' high profits, however, do not necessarily imply

TABLE 8.4

Regional Product per Capita (1840 dollars)

Region	1774	1800	1840	1860
New England	61.83	56.66	129.01	181.39
Middle Atlantic	73.81	68.73	119.68	186.65
South Atlantic	105.70	74.29	85.49	137.75
East North Central			71.50	135.78
West North Central			79.27	136.20
East South Central			85.49	132.83
West South Central			161.65	175.30
Mountain				209.07
Pacific				501.81
United States			101.03	160.16

Source: Adapted from Peter H. Lindert and Jeffrey G. Williamson, "American Incomes, 1774–1860," NBER Working Paper Series, National Bureau of Economic Research, September 2012, 33. Available at http://www.nber.org/papers/w18396.

broad economic benefits, even for the free population. Between a quarter and a third of white families in the South had slaves, but the majority of slaves worked on plantations owned by only 12 percent of slaveholders.[73] Although Southern per capita incomes were quite high, much of this income was funneled into relatively few households. Free Southerners outside of or at the margins of the cotton economy were typically far poorer than per capita figures suggest.[74] While scholars still debate the economics of slavery, the idea that the system was not only morally wrong, but economically damaging, was popular among Northerners in the 1850s. Comparing the North to the South in 1858, Senator Henry Wilson of Massachusetts argued that the North's "rugged soil yields abundance to the willing hands of free labor," whereas slavery had "left the traces of its ruinous power deeply furrowed on the face" of the South.[75]

"Bleeding Kansas"

The Kansas-Nebraska Act

Senator Douglas had once called the Missouri Compromise line "a sacred thing, which no ruthless hand would ever be reckless enough to disturb."

By January 1854 he had changed his mind. Douglas was an eager expansionist who believed that developing the West would "impart peace to the country & stability to the Union." However, Southerners fearful of new free states had recently blocked his proposals to incorporate a vast region above the Missouri Compromise line as a new territory.[76] To accommodate the opposition, Douglas proposed that Congress organize the land into two territories, Kansas and Nebraska, and repeal the Missouri Compromise so that the settlers could vote on slavery themselves.

As Douglas expected, the bill "raise[d] a hell of a storm" across the nation.[77] Self-described Independent Democrats such as Salmon Chase of Ohio and Charles Sumner of Massachusetts, who had migrated from the Free-Soil Party and sharply disagreed with Douglas, assailed the bill as "a gross violation of a sacred pledge . . . [and] a criminal betrayal of precious rights."[78] Even many Northerners who had traditionally taken no position on slavery joined the opposition, wary that slave plantations might take over lands historically available to the Northern population and the farmers who provided its food.[79] At the same time, Southerners and proponents of popular sovereignty applauded the bill, with one newspaper praising it as "the greatest advance movement in the direction of human freedom that has been made since the adoption of the Constitution."[80] Debates in Washington reflected these popular passions as congressmen brandished insults, threats, and even weapons against their opponents.[81] Despite fierce opposition, the Kansas-Nebraska Bill was enacted in May 1854.

Passage did not end the debate over the territories, however. Although the majority of Kansan settlers opposed the introduction of slavery, a large number of Missourians traveled across the eastern border of the territory, orchestrating massive voter fraud to install a pro-slavery government. The antislavery settlers set up a separate administration of their own, and by 1856 the rivalry collapsed into horrific violence that earned the territory the appellation "bleeding Kansas." Congress's debates over the issue also famously became bloody after Senator Charles Sumner's May 1856 speech against slavery, in which he mocked his South Carolinian colleague Andrew Pickens Butler. Representative Preston Brooks, a member of Butler's family, viciously beat Sumner with his cane in retaliation three days later. The incident provoked furious censure from the North but approval from many Southerners.[82]

Rise of the Republicans

The battle over Kansas effectively killed the Whig Party, which had been in decline ever since the late 1840s, when sectional debates divided its ranks. In 1852 the Whig presidential candidate Winfield Scott had won only 42 electoral votes to the 254 of pro-slavery New Hampshire Democrat Franklin Pierce, leading one Whig Party leader to declare, "There may be no political future for us."[83] Debates over the Kansas-Nebraska Act crippled the party, which saw its Southern wing break ranks to support the bill. "Whig, Democrat & free soil are now all 'obsolete ideas,' and all bygones are gone forever," announced one Whig, "and what shall we do next? What but unite on *principle* instead of *party*."[84]

The political crisis that erupted over Kansas provoked Northern Whigs, antislavery Democrats, and Free-Soilers to create a new Republican Party devoted to ending the admission of new slave states to the Union. Deriding slavery as "a great moral, social, and political evil," the Republican Party called for banning it in the territories, and some of its bolder members demanded its abolition in Washington, D.C., and repeal of the Fugitive Slave Act.[85] The Republicans quickly became the Democrats' principal rivals and secured the House speakership in 1855. Southerners were so alarmed that one Georgia senator warned that if the Republicans' presidential nominee, John Charles Frémont of California, won the 1856 election, it "would be the end of the Union, and ought to be."[86] Although Frémont lost to pro-slavery Pennsylvania Democrat James Buchanan (and secured only half a thousandth of a percent of the Southern vote), Republicans "rejoiced to see that [their] party, though beaten, [was] not conquered."[87] In a three-way race (the anti-immigrant Know-Nothing Party ran Millard Fillmore), the two-year-old Republican Party had attracted a plurality of Northern voters and had come in second overall. Many Republicans interpreted Buchanan's unimpressive performance—he had won only 45 percent of the popular vote—as a sign that they could succeed in 1860.[88]

Just two days after President Buchanan's inauguration in March 1857, the U.S. Supreme Court handed down a landmark decision that outraged Republicans. The case concerned the slave Dred Scott, who in the 1830s had traveled with his master out of Missouri and into the free state of Illinois and the free territory of Wisconsin before returning home. A suit on Scott's behalf argued that Scott was a free man because he had resided for years on free land.[89] The Supreme Court decided against Scott, concluding (1) that neither he nor any descendant of African slaves was a citizen of the United States and (2) that the defunct Missouri Compromise, "which prohibited a citizen from holding and owning [slave] property of this kind in the territory of the United States north of the line therein mentioned, is not warranted by the Constitution, and is therefore void."[90] By prohibiting Congress from abolishing slavery in the territories, the Court effectively declared that implementation of the Republicans' free-soil platform would be unconstitutional. Chief Justice Roger Taney, of Maryland, also wrote in the decision that territorial governments could not exercise any power denied to Congress, which after *Dred Scott* included abolishing slavery in the territories. This arguably banned the doctrine of popular sovereignty as well, though debate continued as to whether the decision was truly so sweeping.[91] In either case, Republicans lost little time in making the *Dred Scott* decision a rallying cry for their party. "Let the next President be Republican," the *Chicago Tribune* exclaimed, "and 1860 will mark an era kindred with that of 1776."[92]

Resolution in Kansas

By 1857 the violence in Kansas had largely dissipated, but the battle over slavery there continued. Soon after taking office, President Buchanan sent a new governor to combat the fraud that plagued Kansas's elections and had led to its competing administrations. Under this new regime, slavery opponents won a majority in the official, previously pro-slavery, territorial legislature. Pro-slavery activists, however, continued to intervene in Kansan affairs, and a convention at Lecompton, the territory's seat of government, soon passed a constitution for statehood that protected slavery. The free-soil legislature sought to undo the damage with a January 1858 referendum on the constitution. In a seemingly decisive victory, more than 10,000 voters rejected the constitution while fewer than 200 approved it.[93]

Southern Democrats refused to accept the referendum, insisting that Congress admit Kansas as a state under the Lecompton constitution. It was clear to all that the people there were likely, someday, to abolish slavery in Kansas either way, but if the settlers blocked statehood simply because their disputed constitution allowed slavery, it would deal a major blow to Southern principles and mark complete defeat in the protracted fight over Kansas.[94] Republicans naturally opposed the Lecompton constitution, but Northern

Democrats were no less critical. "If this constitution is to be forced down our throats, in violation of the fundamental principle of free government, under a mode of submission that is a mockery and insult," warned Stephen Douglas, "I will resist it to the last."[95]

Senate Democrats approved the constitution that Kansans themselves had opposed in the January referendum, but in the House twenty Democrats joined the Republicans in rejecting it. Congress finally finished wrangling over the issue in May 1858 with an ultimatum for Kansas: It would become a state and receive federal lands if its voters reapproved the Lecompton constitution, but would have to wait for statehood until its population had grown if they rejected it. Republicans and Douglas Democrats attacked the offer as a "bribe" to extend slavery. If so, the bribe was not enough, because in August Kansans again voted down the constitution.[96]

Abraham Lincoln and the Republican Party

One month later, in September 1858, Illinois Republicans nominated lawyer Abraham Lincoln to challenge Douglas for his Senate seat. In a historic acceptance speech, Lincoln spoke of the ominous sectional divide he had witnessed over the course of his political career. "A house divided against itself cannot stand," he famously said:

> I believe this government cannot endure permanently half slave and half free. I do not expect the Union to be dissolved; I do not expect the house to fall; but I do expect it will cease to be divided. It will become all one thing, or all the other. Either the opponents of slavery will arrest the further spread of it, and place it where the public mind shall rest in the belief that it is in the course of ultimate extinction, or its advocates will push it forward till it shall become alike lawful in all the States, old as well as new, North as well as South.[97]

Lincoln was born in a tiny log cabin in Kentucky in 1809 and had lived most of his life in Illinois. Through the 1830s and 1840s, he became a self-taught lawyer and was elected as a Whig to the state legislature and the U.S. House of Representatives, where he opposed the Mexican War and vigorously supported Zachary Taylor's presidential bid. Lincoln left the House after one term, but the Kansas-Nebraska Act aroused his political passions. Numerous times in 1854, Lincoln appeared uninvited at Senator Douglas's speeches to debate him, and later he helped organize the Illinois Republican Party.[98]

Lincoln again debated Douglas in 1858—this time as the Republican challenger for Douglas's seat in the U.S. Senate. The historic Lincoln-Douglas debates focused on slavery, and while Lincoln expressed his belief in the "superior position assigned to the white race," he insisted that slavery was an evil he hoped would someday disappear.[99] Lincoln particularly damaged Douglas's reputation within the Democratic Party when he questioned the senator about the effect of the *Dred Scott* decision on the popular sovereignty movement. Douglas maintained that settlers could still regulate slavery as they wished, and affirmed that he would "never violate or abandon that doctrine [of popular sovereignty], if I have to stand alone!"[100] This position rankled Southern Democrats, who believed that *Dred Scott* had rendered slavery in the territories immune from any possible intervention, including a popular vote.[101]

The Lincoln-Douglas debates boosted Lincoln's popularity and garnered him a national reputation, although he ultimately lost the Senate race to Douglas. Senators were chosen by state legislatures in that era, and although the Republicans running for the Illinois legislature won more total votes in 1858, Democrats won a majority of seats, and so selected Douglas. Undaunted, Lincoln assured his supporters that "we shall have fun again."[102] Throughout the following year, Lincoln gave speeches in several states and solidified his standing as a rising Republican star.

Southern Democrats, Northern Republicans

During the wider 1858 campaign season, New York Republican William Seward had asserted that the Democratic Party was "identical with the Slave Power." Although even many fellow Republicans found this rhetoric extreme, the developing alignment of Democrats with the South was evident in the election's results. The previous Congress had included 53 free-state and 75 slave-state Democrats, whereas in 1859 they would number 32 and 69, respectively. The increasingly Southern Democratic Party faced a strengthening—and almost entirely Northern—Republican Party. Republicans (and affiliated smaller parties) won a majority of House seats in nearly every Northern state in 1858, toppling the Democrats' House majority and further bolstering Republican hopes for the 1860 presidential race.[103]

Tensions grew in 1859 when, on October 16, the radical white abolitionist John Brown, originally from the Northeast, and a multiracial band of followers seized a federal arsenal at Harpers Ferry, Virginia, in order to incite a slave revolt. Local militia and a contingent of Marines, led by Lieutenant Colonel Robert E. Lee, thwarted the raid, and Brown was captured, tried, and hanged. Many Northern abolitionists hailed Brown as a martyr whose death would "make the gallows as glorious as the cross," while numerous Southerners attacked suspected Brown sympathizers and burned antislavery literature.[104] Although leading Republicans, including Lincoln, denounced Brown, Democrats asserted that Brown's actions were the "natural, logical, inevitable result of the doctrines and teachings of the Republican party."[105] Mounting sectional animosity virtually paralyzed Congress, meanwhile, as Southerners used parliamentary tricks and threats of secession to prevent the election of a Northern speaker of the House from any party.[106] "The only persons who do not have a revolver or a knife," commented one senator on the situation in Washington, "are those with two revolvers."[107]

The Democrats' Northern and Southern wings finally broke apart during the 1860 presidential election. Delegates at the party's nominating convention disagreed vehemently over slavery: Douglas and the Northern Democrats argued for popular sovereignty in the territories, while Southerners insisted on federal protections for slavery. When the convention indicated support for Douglas's position, Southern delegates walked out and organized a separate convention. The Northern Democrats nominated Douglas for president, while the Southerners chose Vice President John C. Breckinridge of Kentucky as their presidential candidate. Both would run against the Republican Abraham Lincoln as well as Tennessean John Bell, whose small Constitutional Union Party favored sectional reconciliation and recognized "no political principle other than THE CONSTITUTION OF THE COUNTRY, THE UNION OF THE STATES, AND THE ENFORCEMENT OF THE LAWS."[108]

Although Lincoln spoke relatively little during the campaign season, Southern Democrats were extremely vocal about their distaste—even abhorrence—for their opponent. Prior to Lincoln's nomination, one newspaper in Virginia mocked him as "an illiterate partisan . . . possessed only of his inveterate hatred of slavery and his openly avowed predilection of negro equality."[109] Numerous Southern governors and congressmen claimed they would favor secession from the Union if Lincoln won the election. "Your peace, your social system, your firesides are involved," warned Senator Robert Toombs of Georgia. "Never permit this Federal Government to pass into the traitorous hands of the Black Republican party."[110]

The results of the election on November 5, 1860, reflected the deep divisions that were fracturing the nation. Lincoln won the presidency with less than 40 percent of the popular vote by taking nearly all of the free states' electoral votes (New Jersey split its votes and gave some to Douglas). Douglas came in second in the national popular vote, but Breckinridge's sweep of the lower South and Bell's victories in Virginia, Kentucky, and Tennessee left the senator only Missouri. The sectional split of the electoral vote highlighted the fact that the North and South were essentially holding separate contests: the Republican Party did not exist south of the old Missouri Compromise line, so Lincoln received no votes there, while Breckinridge supporters mounted no campaign, and he received no votes, in New York, New Jersey, or Rhode Island.[111]

The Secession Crisis

South Carolina Secedes

When members of the South Carolina legislature learned that Lincoln had won, they immediately began discussing secession. Five days later, the chamber unanimously called for a convention to declare their state's independence. "The tea has been thrown overboard," announced one elated South Carolinian. "The revolution of 1860 has been initiated."[112] Despite their confidence, many lawmakers suspected that the people of South Carolina were not solidly behind secession. "I do not believe that the common people understand it," confessed one separatist, ". . . but whoever waited for the common people when a great move was to be made[?]"[113]

At first many Northerners doubted the secessionists' seriousness. The *New York Times* suggested that "disunion sentiment is rapidly losing ground in the South" and that Southerners had "done little else for the last ten years" but make empty secession threats.[114] Before long, however, skepticism gave way to alarm. In his address to Congress on December 3, several months prior to Lincoln's inauguration, President Buchanan denounced secession but blamed Northerners for forcing South Carolina's hand. He also claimed that he lacked the legal authority to compel a state to remain in the Union. "Congress possesses many means of preserving [the Union] by conciliation," he said, "but the sword was not placed in their hand to preserve it by force."[115]

Apparently convinced that reconciliation was the only way out, Buchanan sought to draw South Carolina back into the fold by requesting constitutional amendments that would definitively protect slavery. The most significant proposal came from Kentucky senator John Crittenden, who recommended multiple amendments to revive the Missouri Compromise line for the territories, ensure popular sovereignty over slavery for all new states, and guarantee compensation from the federal government for lost fugitive slaves. His plan also would require that these amendments could not themselves be amended in the future and that slavery would forever remain beyond Congress's power to abolish. Crittenden hoped that his program would see the slavery debate "permanently quieted and settled."[116]

As Congress deliberated over the Crittenden plan, the South Carolina convention announced the state's secession on December 20. Its official declaration listed numerous justifications for this action, including Northern violations of the Fugitive Slave Act, infringements of property rights, and the election of a president "whose opinions and purposes are hostile to Slavery." After airing these grievances, the document announced that "the Union heretofore existing between this State and the other States of North America is dissolved."[117]

Birth of the Confederacy

Panic in Washington grew as the government faced the reality of a state seceding for the first time in American history. In a message on January 8, President Buchanan reiterated that the states had no right to secede but that he in turn could not "make aggressive war upon any state," and again requested legislation that would save the Union.[118] Republican senators rejected the Crittenden plan just eight days later, however. Further proposals, as well as the loosening of antislavery laws by some free states, failed to satisfy the South Carolinians or others in the South who supported secession.[119]

Between January 9 and February 1, 1861, six states—Mississippi, Florida, Alabama, Louisiana, Georgia, and Texas—followed South Carolina in seceding from the Union. At a February convention, delegates from the seceded states formed the Confederate States of America and drafted a provisional

constitution modeled on the U.S. Constitution, but with some notable differences. The document asserted the sovereignty of each member state and prohibited any laws that would ban slavery or the transport of slaves into Confederate territories. The Confederate constitution also barred the Confederate
Congress from imposing tariffs and limited internal improvements to navigation projects. The Confederacy inaugurated its first president, Jefferson Davis
of Mississippi, a former U.S. senator and secretary of war, on February 18, and
established a temporary capital in Montgomery, Alabama.[120] At least from the
perspective of these Southern states, a new nation had been born.

Lincoln Confronts Secession

In the months leading up to his inauguration, President-elect Lincoln held
firmly to the position that the secession crisis would soon pass. Although he
mostly continued to avoid public statements, in November he had permitted
a friend to say on his behalf that he was "rather glad of this military preparation in the South. It will enable the people the more easily to suppress any
[secessionist] uprisings there, which their misrepresentations of purposes
may have encouraged."[121] Confident that the situation could be defused
without sacrificing Republican principles, Lincoln also advised congressional
Republicans to "entertain no proposition for a compromise in regard to the
extension of slavery."[122] Even after the seven Confederate states wrote and
ratified their new constitution, Lincoln insisted that *"there is no crisis . . . just
as other clouds have cleared away in due time, so will this."*[123]

    In his inaugural address on March 4, 1861, President Lincoln declared that
the seceded states had nothing to fear from his administration. He conceded
that he had "no lawful right . . . [and] no inclination" to "interfere with the
institution of slavery in the States where it exists," and he promised that his
government would enforce the Fugitive Slave Act. As he had made clear in
the past, he principally opposed the *spread,* not the existence, of slavery, and
he announced that he would not oppose a constitutional amendment, recently approved by Congress, "that the Federal Government shall never interfere with the domestic institutions of the States, including that of persons
held to service."[124]

    While showing some tolerance for slavery, the new president proved un-
wavering on the issue of secession and asserted that "no State upon its own

mere motion can lawfully get out of the Union" and that "resolves and ordinances to that effect are legally void." The Confederate states, he believed, remained part of the United States, and his government would continue to operate there as best it could. Although he promised that "there [would] be no invasion, no using of force against or among the people anywhere," he identified two exceptions where he would use force if necessary: "The power confided to me will be used to hold, occupy, and possess the property and places belonging to the government, and to collect the duties and imposts."[125]

Focus on Fort Sumter

News arrived the very next day that would test Lincoln's pledge to "hold, occupy, and possess" federal property. In December, South Carolina had requested that President Buchanan remove troops stationed at Fort Sumter in Charleston. Buchanan refused, but when he tried to resupply Sumter the next month, state artillery fired on the federal provision boat and forced it to withdraw. Buchanan had taken no further action, and now with supplies dwindling the Army general-in-chief Winfield Scott reported to Lincoln that he saw "no alternative but a surrender in some weeks."[126] Lincoln would either have to provision the fort, as Buchanan had attempted, or order its evacuation.

Rejecting Scott's early recommendation to evacuate, Lincoln consulted his Cabinet on March 15. He received much the same advice as he had from General Scott: evacuation was the best available option and attempting to provision the fort "would initiate a bloody and protracted conflict."[127] William Seward, the new secretary of state, particularly cautioned that a provocative move like provisioning could convince some of the slave states that had not seceded (including Virginia, Maryland, Kentucky, North Carolina, Tennessee, Missouri, and Arkansas) to join the Confederacy.* Only Postmaster-General Montgomery Blair fully supported the provisioning option.[128]

The near unanimity of the Cabinet in favor of evacuation led many political observers to believe that Lincoln was ready to go along. In fact, over the following days rumors abounded that Lincoln had already sent the order to evacuate. When Confederate commissioners approached Seward seeking

---

* Delaware was also a slave state, but Seward did not mention it.

U.S. recognition of the Confederacy, he softened his refusal by assuring them, without permission, that Lincoln would soon evacuate Sumter.[129]

President Lincoln was not yet convinced, however. He ordered a report on March 19 about the latest conditions at Fort Sumter and soon received word from the fort's commander, Major Robert Anderson, that while supplies would last until mid-April, the major believed reinforcement would be impossible. Lincoln also sent an investigatory team to determine the strength of pro-Union sentiment in Charleston.[130] After interviewing Charleston residents, the investigators reported "that separate nationality is a fixed fact . . . that there is no attachment to the Union."[131]

Outside of Lincoln's close circle of advisers, many Republicans strongly opposed evacuation. The Sumter crisis had come to be viewed as a test of the federal government's authority. As one Republican insisted, evacuation would represent "submission to a band of traitors." Another declared that if Lincoln continued to delay the decision, "the South will proclaim him a Damned fool, and the North a damned Rascal." On March 28, Senate Republicans introduced a resolution declaring that "it is the duty of the President to use all the means in his power to hold and protect the public property of the United States."[132]

That same day, a message from General Scott profoundly affected Lincoln's appraisal of the situation. Scott now pressed not only for evacuation of Sumter, but also of Fort Pickens, another facility the government still held in Confederate Florida. Floridians had allowed the government to continue provisioning Pickens as long as no reinforcements arrived, but Lincoln had recently prepared to reinforce the fort anyway, hoping to soften any blow to his credibility that a Sumter evacuation might bring.[133] Now Scott argued that abandoning both forts would relax tensions with the South, "give confidence to the eight remaining slave-holding states, and render their cordial adherence to the Union perpetual."[134] The message upset Lincoln. By advocating abandonment even of Fort Pickens, which Lincoln and others agreed would be a "humiliation and disgrace," Scott appeared to be acting on his own personal judgments rather than on the basis of his military expertise and the available intelligence. Even Scott's early dire assessment of the Sumter situation now seemed suspect.[135]

Lincoln consulted with members of his Cabinet again the next day, March 29, and found their opinions changed since March 15. After the revelation of how Scott's preferences may have colored his advice to evacuate, a majority of the Cabinet now favored provisioning.[136] "There is little probability that this will be permitted if the opposing forces can prevent it," wrote Navy Secretary Gideon Welles, ". . . but armed resistance to a peaceable attempt . . . will justify the government in using all the power at its command to reinforce the garrison and furnish the necessary supplies."[137] The most significant opposition came from Secretary of State Seward, who thought that attempting to supply Sumter would ultimately provoke war. With support from a Cabinet majority, however, Lincoln gave orders to prepare for provisioning Sumter.[138]

The president had now chosen to organize a mission to Sumter, but he would still have to decide whether or not to deploy the mission once it was ready. On April 1, Seward sent Lincoln a memorandum beseeching him to abandon Sumter and reinforce Pickens, an option the president continued to weigh. Meanwhile many Northerners were growing impatient with the government's inaction. "Wanted—A Policy!" declared the *New York Times* on April 3, announcing that the president "must adopt some clear and distinct policy in regard to secession, or the Union will not only be severed, but the country will be disgraced." Public pressure continued to build as the troops at Fort Sumter were rapidly running out of supplies. There was no question that the government would either have to evacuate or provision the fort in the coming weeks. Finally, on April 4, President Lincoln began writing a letter to Major Anderson at Fort Sumter describing his plan of action.[139]

NOTES

1. Quoted in Richard H. Sewell, *A House Divided* (Baltimore: Johns Hopkins University Press, 1988), 76.
2. "First Inaugural Address of Abraham Lincoln," available via Yale Law School's Avalon Project at http://avalon.law.yale.edu/19th_century/lincoln1.asp.
3. Donald L. Robinson, *Slavery in the Structure of American Politics, 1765–1820* (New York: Harcourt Brace Jovanovich, 1971), 19–21, 43.
4. *Historical Statistics of the United States,* Millennial Edition Online, http://hsus.cambridge.org/HSUSWeb/HSUSEntryServlet, series Eg 41–59. "The South" here refers to all the states and regions from Delaware down, including non-states Tennessee and Kentucky.
5. Silvia R. Frey, "Slavery and Anti-Slavery," in *A Companion to the American Revolution,* ed. Jack P. Greene and J. R. Pole (Malden, MA: Blackwell, 2004), 407–409. Because

these laws typically provided only for gradual emancipation, Northern slavery did not completely disappear for decades. Pennsylvania's law, for example, emancipated the children of slaves only after their twenty-eighth birthday. As a result, there were still slaves in Pennsylvania at least as late as 1840 (Robinson, *Slavery*, 30–31). Only Massachusetts and Vermont completely banned all slavery during this period (Frey, "Slavery and Anti-Slavery," 409–410; Robinson, *Slavery*, 28).

6. Elizabeth R. Varon, *Disunion!* (Chapel Hill: University of North Carolina Press, 2008), 40.

7. Robinson, *Slavery*, 269–271, 379–382, 402–405, 405; Varon, *Disunion!*, 39.

8. Massachusetts minister quoted in Robinson, *Slavery*, 277.

9. Rep. Philip Barbour (VA) quoted in John Ashworth, *Slavery, Capitalism, and Politics in the Antebellum Republic*, vol. 1 (New York: Cambridge University Press, 1995), 62.

10. Quoted in Ashworth, *Slavery, Capitalism, and Politics*, 20.

11. Robert Pierce Forbes, *The Missouri Compromise and Its Aftermath* (Chapel Hill: University of North Carolina Press, 2007), 34.

12. Arthur Livermore (NH) quoted in ibid., 42.

13. *Annals of Congress*, House of Representatives, 15th Congress, 2nd sess., 1213. Also quoted in Forbes, *Missouri Compromise*, 45.

14. Freeman Walker (GA) quoted in Ashworth, *Slavery, Capitalism, and Politics*, 65.

15. Jefferson expressed this argument in a letter to Marquis de Lafayette on 26 Dec. 1820. See "Quotations on Slavery and Emancipation," http://www.monticello.org/site/jefferson/quotations-slavery-and-emancipation, entry for 26 Dec. 1820. See also Forbes, *Missouri Compromise*, 48.

16. Forbes, *Missouri Compromise*, 51, 53, quotation from *New-York Daily Advertiser* at 51 (set in all-capitals in the original).

17. *Illinois Spectator* quoted in Forbes, *Missouri Compromise*, 54.

18. Quoted in Forbes, *Missouri Compromise*, at 99.

19. Thomas Jefferson, letter to John Holmes, 22 Apr. 1820, Library of Congress. http://www.loc.gov/exhibits/jefferson/159.html.

20. Thomas Jefferson, letter to Justice William Johnson, 27 Oct. 1822, http://www.let.rug.nl/usa/presidents/thomas-jefferson/letters of thomas jefferson/jefl269.php.

21. Michael F. Holt, *Political Parties and American Political Development from the Age of Jackson to the Age of Lincoln* (Baton Rouge: Louisiana State University Press, 1992), 33–35; Forbes, *Missouri Compromise*, 21.

22. Nathaniel Macon quoted in Forbes, *Missouri Compromise*, 7.

23. Thomas Cooper quoted in Irving H. Bartlett, *John C. Calhoun: A Biography* (New York: W. W. Norton, 1993), 143.

24. Varon, *Disunion!*, 57; William O. Lynch, *Fifty Years of Party Warfare, 1789–1837* (Gloucester, MA: Peter Smith, 1931), 338–339; Bartlett, *John C. Calhoun*, 142.

25. James Hamilton Jr. quoted in Lynch, *Fifty Years*, 342.

26. See Lynch, *Fifty Years*, 248, 284, on the protectionist intentions of tariff supporters.

27. Art. I, §8.

28. Bartlett, *John C. Calhoun,* 139–140.

29. Quoted in Richard Hofstadter, *The American Political Tradition and the Men Who Made It* (New York: Knopf, 1973), 70.

30. Lynch, *Fifty Years,* 427.

31. Quoted in Varon, *Disunion!,* 89.

32. "President Jackson's Proclamation Regarding Nullification, December 10, 1832," at the Avalon Project, Yale Law School, http://avalon.law.yale.edu/19th_century/jack01 .asp.

33. Quotations in Varon, *Disunion!,* at 89, 90.

34. See Sidney Ratner, *The Tariff in American History* (New York: Van Nostrand, 1972), chap. 2.

35. Lydia Maria Child quoted in Varon, *Disunion!,* 87, 91.

36. James M. McPherson, *Ordeal by Fire: The Civil War and Reconstruction,* 3rd ed. (Boston: McGraw-Hill, 2001), 45–46. Quotation in Varon, *Disunion!,* 71.

37. Varon, *Disunion!,* 96–97, 102.

38. Quotations in ibid. at 118, 121.

39. Quotation in ibid., at 107.

40. Ibid., 110; Joel H. Silbey, *The Shrine of Party: Congressional Voting Behavior, 1841–1852* (Westport, CT: Greenwood Press, 1981), chaps. 2 and 4.

41. Silbey, *The Shrine of Party,* 21, chaps. 2 and 4. See Ratner, *The Tariff,* 22, regarding sectional split over 1842 tariff. For regional alignments on 1840s tariff votes, see Douglas A. Irwin, "Antebellum Tariff Politics: Regional Coalitions and Shifting Economic Interests," *Journal of Law and Economics* 51, no. 4 (Nov. 2008): 721.

42. Varon, *Disunion!,* 172.

43. Northern Whigs quoted in ibid., 174.

44. Massachusetts legislature resolution quoted in James A. Rawley, *Secession: Disruption of the American Republic, 1844–1861* (Malabar, FL: Robert E. Krieger, 1990), 30.

45. Quotations in Rawley, *Secession,* at 24, 24–25.

46. James Dixon (CT) and Robert Barnwell Rhett (SC) quoted in Varon, *Disunion!,* 189–190, 192.

47. Rawley, *Secession,* 29.

48. Sewell, *A House Divided,* 25. Robert Toombs (GA) quoted in Rawley, *Secession,* 31.

49. Quotation in Rawley, *Secession,* 26.

50. Ibid., 34–37; David M. Potter, *The Impending Crisis* (New York: Harper and Row, 1976), 138–139. Quotation from Art. IV, §2, of the U.S. Constitution. The personal liberty laws were enabled by the Supreme Court decision *Prigg v. Pennsylvania* (1842), which suggested that the states had no obligation to actively assist in capturing fugitive slaves.

51. Quotation in Sewell, *A House Divided,* 31.

52. Potter, *The Impending Crisis,* 106; Rawley, *Secession,* 35. The lands considered New Mexico were at this time much larger than the modern state of New Mexico.

53. Quotation in Potter, *The Impending Crisis,* 99.

54. Henry Clay, *Speech of the Hon. Henry Clay of Kentucky on Presenting His Compromise Resolutions on the Subject of Slavery* (New York: Stringer and Townsend, 1850), 4.

55. Quotations in Sewell, *A House Divided,* 32; Thomas H. O'Connor, *The Disunited States* (New York: Harper and Row, 1978), 11. This speech was read by a surrogate. Calhoun was very ill and died shortly thereafter.

56. Sewell, *A House Divided,* 32–33.

57. Rawley, *Secession,* 40; Potter, *The Impending Crisis,* 113. The 1850 Fugitive Slave Act is available via the Yale Law School Avalon Project at http://avalon.law.yale.edu/19th _century/fugitive.asp. In the final agreement, New Mexico was divided into two territories, New Mexico and Utah.

58. Quotation in Sewell, *A House Divided,* 34.

59. Silbey, *The Shrine of Party,* 118–119, quotation at 119.

60. O'Connor, *The Disunited States,* 45–48; Potter, *The Impending Crisis,* 132–133.

61. Robert Barnwell Rhett quoted in Varon, *Disunion!,* 237.

62. Rawley, *Secession,* 48.

63. George F. Holmes excerpted in ibid., 182–184.

64. O'Connor, *The Disunited States,* 20.

65. Robert William Fogel and Stanley L. Engerman, *Time on the Cross: The Economics of American Negro Slavery* (New York: W. W. Norton, 1974), 53; Steven Deyle, *Carry Me Back: The Domestic Slave Trade in American Life* (New York: Oxford University Press, 2006), 291–296; O'Connor, *The Disunited States,* 22; McPherson, *Ordeal by Fire,* 38–41.

66. "Lecture on Slavery, No. 1" (1 Dec. 1850), in *Frederick Douglass: Selected Speeches and Writing,* ed. Philip S. Foner (Chicago: Lawrence Hill Books, 1999), 167.

67. Herbert Aptheker, *American Negro Slave Revolts,* 6th ed. (New York: International, 1993), 340.

68. John Hope Franklin and Loren Scheninger, *Runaway Slaves: Rebels on the Plantation* (New York: Oxford University Press, 1990); Aptheker, *American Negro Slave Revolts,* chap. 14.

69. Rawley, *Secession,* 52–57.

70. Ibid.; McPherson, *Ordeal by Fire,* 29–31. See Edward Pessen, "How Different from Each Other Were the Antebellum North and South?," *American Historical Review* 85, no. 5 (Dec. 1980): 1119–1149, which highlights some often-overlooked similarities between North and South prior to the Civil War. For a revisionist view of management techniques used on Southern plantations, see also Caitlin Rosenthal, "Plantations Practiced Modern Management" (interview), *Harvard Business Review* (Sept. 2013), 30–31.

71. James Oakes, *The Ruling Race: A History of American Slaveholders* (New York: Random House, 1982), cited in Charles Post, "Plantation Slavery and Economic Development in the Antebellum Southern United States," *Journal of Agrarian Change* 3, no. 3 (July 2003): 305. See also Mark M. Smith, *Debating Slavery: Economy and Society in the Antebellum American South* (New York: Cambridge University Press, 1998), 61, which highlights Eugene D. Genovese's argument about the profound inefficiency of slave labor.

72. Fogel and Engerman's *Time on the Cross* is a now-classic text suggesting the potential efficiency and profitability of slavery. See Smith, *Debating Slavery*, 65–67.

73. McPherson, *Ordeal by Fire*, 36. Whereas McPherson says one-third of white families in the South owned slaves in the 1850s, O'Connor (*The Disunited States*, 23) says one-quarter owned slaves at the end of the decade.

74. Smith, *Debating Slavery*, 83–85.

75. Speech of 20 Mar. 1858, quoted in Ashworth, *Slavery, Capitalism, and Politics*, 80.

76. Quotations in Sewell, *A House Divided*, at 44, 46.

77. Quoted in Rawley, *Secession*, 60.

78. "Appeal of the Independent Democrats," in Rawley, *Secession*, 191.

79. O'Connor, *The Disunited States*, 56–57.

80. Detroit *Free Press* quoted in O'Connor, *The Disunited States*, 54.

81. Sewell, *A House Divided*, 45.

82. O'Connor, *The Disunited States*, 62–63. On p. 63, O'Connor quotes an Alabama newspaper that wrote in reaction to the caning: "Let our Representative in Congress use the cowhide and hickory stick (and, if need be, the bowie knife and revolver) more frequently, and we'll bet our old hat that it will soon come to pass that our Southern institutions and Southern men will be respected." Brooks, who had broken his cane over Sumner's head, received many new canes from his admirers. One was inscribed "Hit him again." (Williamjames Hull Hoffer, *The Caning of Charles Sumner: Honor, Idealism, and the Origins of the Civil War* [Baltimore: Johns Hopkins University Press, 2010], 92.)

83. Thurlow Weed quoted in Rawley, *Secession*, 47.

84. Quoted in Sewell, *A House Divided*, 48. In the mid-1850s, before the Republican ascension, the Whigs were briefly replaced by an anti-immigrant American or "Know-Nothing" Party.

85. O'Connor, *The Disunited States*, 70; Sewell, *A House Divided*, 49, quotation at 49.

86. Robert Toombs quoted in David M. Potter, *Lincoln and His Party in the Secession Crisis* (New Haven, CT: Yale University Press, 1942), 2.

87. Rawley, *Secession*, 82. Benjamin Wade quoted in Sewell, *A House Divided*, 55.

88. O'Connor, *The Disunited States*, 81.

89. Sewell, *A House Divided*, 56–57.

90. *Dred Scott v. Sandford* is available online at http://caselaw.lp.findlaw.com/scripts /getcase.pl?court=US&vol=60&invol=393.

91. Don E. Fehrenbacher, *The Dred Scott Case* (New York: Oxford University Press, 1978), 379, 443.

92. Quoted in Sewell, *A House Divided*, 61.

93. Ibid., 62–64. Antislavery Kansans had boycotted elections for delegates to the Lecompton convention for fear of voter fraud. They later also sat out a first referendum on the Lecompton constitution, which only gave them the choice of whether or not the constitution would allow importation of slaves into Kansas. Recognizing that the constitution would be passed either way, they boycotted the

vote in protest. Fewer than 7,000 votes were cast in this referendum; Congress later determined that almost 3,000 of these were fraudulent.

94. Potter, *The Impending Crisis,* 317.

95. Quoted in Sewell, *A House Divided,* 65.

96. Ibid., 66.

97. "A House Divided," at InfoUSA, U.S. State Department, http://usinfo.org/enus /government/overview/22.html. Lincoln quoted the Bible in his opening: "Every kingdom divided against itself will be ruined, and every city or household divided against itself will not stand" (Matt. 12:25).

98. Matthew Pinsker, *Abraham Lincoln* (Washington, DC: CQ Press, 2002), 9–61.

99. Quoted in Rawley, *Secession,* 96.

100. Quoted in O'Connor, *The Disunited States,* 109. The *Dred Scott* decision had dealt a serious blow to Douglas's cherished principle of popular sovereignty. At this debate in the city of Freeport, Douglas communicated a belief in "residual" popular sovereignty, his contention that even if settlers who opposed slavery could not formally abolish it, they would successfully fight it in other ways. "If they do not want [slavery] they will drive it out, and you cannot force it upon them. Slavery cannot exist a day in the midst of an unfriendly people and unfriendly laws." Scholars refer to this school of thought as the Freeport doctrine. See Fehrenbacher, *The Dred Scott Case,* chap. 20, Douglas quoted at 490.

101. Pinsker, *Abraham Lincoln,* 63.

102. Quoted in ibid., 64.

103. Rawley, *Secession,* 98–99, quotation at 98.

104. Ralph Waldo Emerson quoted in Sewell, *A House Divided,* 70, see also 71.

105. Stephen Douglas quoted in Sewell, *A House Divided,* 70.

106. Sewell, *A House Divided,* 72.

107. James J. Hammond (SC) quoted in ibid., 72.

108. Rawley, *Secession,* 108–111; Constitutional Union Party Platform of May 1860, available at http://www.presidency.ucsb.edu/ws/index.php?pid=29571 (emphasis in the original).

109. Richmond *Enquirer* quoted in Rawley, *Secession,* 107.

110. Potter, *Lincoln,* 5–6, 4.

111. Ibid., 112; Sewell, *A House Divided,* 75–76.

112. Barnwell Rhett quoted in Potter, *Lincoln,* 45.

113. A. P. Aldrich quoted in ibid., 208.

114. Quoted in ibid., 63.

115. "President Buchanan's Fourth Annual Message to Congress," in Rawley, *Secession,* 234–235.

116. "Crittenden Peace Resolutions," in Rawley, *Secession,* 236–238.

117. "South Carolina Declaration on Causes of Secession," in Rawley, *Secession,* 231–233.

118. Quoted in O'Connor, *The Disunited States,* 142.

119. Rawley, *Secession,* 127–128.

120. O'Connor, *The Disunited States,* 140–141; Potter, *The Impending Crisis,* 499.

121. Lyman Trumbull quoted in Potter, *Lincoln,* 141.

122. Quoted in Rawley, *Secession,* 126.

123. Quoted in ibid., 126, emphasis in original.

124. "First Inaugural Address of Abraham Lincoln."

125. Ibid.

126. Quoted in Rawley, *Secession,* 134.

127. Secretary of War Simon Cameron quoted in Potter, *Lincoln,* 338.

128. *Complete Works of Abraham Lincoln,* ed. John G. Nicolay and John Hay (New York: Francis D. Tandy Co., 1905), 6:197, 214.

129. Potter, *Lincoln,* 339, 342–349.

130. Ibid., 339–340.

131. Stephen Hurlbut quoted in John G. Nicolay and John Hay, *Abraham Lincoln: A History* (New York: Century Co., 1890), 3:391.

132. Quotations in Potter, *Lincoln,* at 359–360, 360.

133. Potter, *Lincoln,* 359.

134. Quoted in ibid., 361.

135. Ibid., 358–361. Quote from J. H. Jordan on 358. See also Samuel Wylie Crawford, *The Genesis of the Civil War: The Story of Sumter, 1860–1861* (New York: Charles L. Webster and Co., 1887), 362–365.

136. Most historians accept this series of events regarding the Scott affair, which derives from the recollections of Postmaster Blair. See Potter, *The Impending Crisis,* 574n45, for a brief discussion of possible alternative timelines.

137. *Complete Works of Abraham Lincoln,* 6:228.

138. Potter, *The Impending Crisis,* 574.

139. Ibid., 576–578, quotation at 576–577.

·{ 9 }·

Race, Justice, and the Jury System in Postbellum Virginia (1880)

IN DECEMBER 1877 an all-white grand jury in Patrick County, Virginia, indicted two black teenagers, Lee and Burwell Reynolds, for killing a white man. After a series of trials, an all-white trial jury convicted Lee Reynolds of second-degree murder and sentenced him to prison. A separate all-white jury could not reach a verdict on Burwell Reynolds, and he was returned to jail to await another trial. During the proceedings, the defendants' attorneys had protested to the county judge that their clients could not get fair trials from all-white juries. They also complained that although black men were allowed on juries by Virginia law, no blacks were even in their clients' jury pools. The lawyers asked that special jury pools be created for their clients with blacks on them, but the judge denied their request. Finally, the lawyers petitioned a federal judge in the area, Alexander Rives, to move the trials to his court. In November 1878 Rives agreed to the petition and had the Reynolds brothers removed from state to federal custody.

Rives's act provoked strong protest from the State of Virginia. The legislature approved resolutions condemning his "usurpation of power," while the state attorney general appealed to the U.S. Supreme Court to order Rives to return the Reynolds brothers to state custody.

Rives responded to this challenge by charging two federal grand juries, both interracial, to investigate whether Virginia state courts had excluded blacks from jury pools just because they were black. This, he argued, would be a violation of both the Fourteenth Amendment to the U.S. Constitution (1868) and the federal Civil Rights Act of 1875. In February and March 1879,

Reprinted with permission from Harvard Business School Publishing. "Race, Justice, and the Jury System in Postbellum Virginia," HBS Case 716-047, February 2016. This case was prepared by Dean Grodzins and David A. Moss. Copyright ©2016 by the President and Fellows of Harvard College: all rights reserved.

the grand juries indicted fourteen Virginia county judges for keeping the jury pools they supervised all-white, among them the judge in the Reynolds trials. Another of the indicted judges, the first arrested, James Dodridge Coles of Pittsylvania County, refused to pay bail. Instead he petitioned the U.S. Supreme Court to release him, as did Virginia on his behalf, on the grounds that Rives had exceeded his authority.

These cases provoked intense national debate. Much of it concerned the problem of federal power over the states and the interpretation of the Constitution and recent civil rights laws. But beneath these concerns lay questions, debated for centuries, about what constituted a fair trial before a jury of "peers," and how both the right and the responsibility to serve on a jury intersected with citizenship, especially in a democracy. *Virginia v. Rives* and *Ex Parte Virginia* (the Coles case) were both argued before the U.S. Supreme Court in October 1879. It was now up to the nine justices to decide.

Ancient Juries

Jury trials have been linked to democratic forms of government since the ancient democracy of Athens. Athens was a version of what today would be called a "direct democracy." Laws were made by an assembly open to all citizens—which meant adult, free men of Athenian ancestry who had done military service, paid their taxes, and paid respect to the Greek deities. Charismatic figures, most famously the statesman and orator Pericles (ca. 495–429 BCE), often dominated the proceedings.

Athenian courts were similar. They consisted of assemblies of jurors, who were citizens over 30 years of age, chosen by lot, and paid for their service. Compared to juries in the Anglo-American tradition, these assemblies, called *dikasteria,* were very large, ranging in size from 201 citizens (for private disputes involving small amounts of money) to 2,500 (for important public cases). Athenians believed that the size of the juries and the randomness of their selection would protect against jury bias; no provisions were made to exclude anyone from a jury once chosen. The jury would hear the parties in the suit plead their own cases—the jurors were free to interrupt them, with shouts of approval or disapproval, for example—and then decide who was right, or guilty, by majority vote, using a secret ballot system. There were no judges.

The jurors themselves decided, based on their own knowledge of the law and precedent, how to interpret the former and whether to follow the latter.[1]

In 399 BCE, the philosopher Socrates was tried before such an assembly for the crimes of impiety and corrupting the young. A version of his speech defending himself is preserved in the *Apology*, a dialogue written years later by his student Plato. The jury was unpersuaded and condemned Socrates to death.

Anglo-American Juries until the U.S. Civil War

Most historians date the origins of English jury trials to shortly after the Norman Conquest of England in 1066. The Norman kings wanted to tax their new subjects and so had their officials summon groups of men from a given community to give sworn testimony as to who owned what. These officials began acting as judges in community disputes and would summon local men to assist them. Early jurors acted as witnesses for the judge, and in criminal cases offered him their opinion as to the guilt or innocence of the accused. Eventually British kings recognized two kinds of juries, which they called *grand* and *petit*. The grand jury, typically comprising up to twenty-four men (later, twenty-three), would collect evidence to see if a crime may have been committed, whereas the petit (or trial) jury, composed of twelve men, would determine the guilt or innocence of the accused. Trial jurors were often selected from among the grand jurors until concern arose that a trial juror might be biased by the evidence he had seen as a grand juror. Over time, the memberships of the two juries came to be distinct.[2] In each case, jurors were drawn from a pool of candidates, known as a "venire" (from the Latin term for a juror summons, *venire facias*, "to make to come"). By the fourteenth century, the practice was established, later followed in American courts, that trial jurors had to agree unanimously on a verdict for it to be valid.[3]

Trial by jury seems to have been claimed as a political right for the first time in 1215, when a group of rebellious barons forced King John to issue the "Great Charter of English Liberties," known by its Latin name, Magna Carta. One of its most important clauses declared that a "free man" could be exiled, or deprived of life, liberty, or property, only "by lawful judgement of his peers or by the law of the land."[4]

What was meant by the right to a jury of "peers"? The noblemen of 1215 seem to have been principally concerned that they themselves would only be tried before juries of fellow noblemen. Yet this right had been recognized in other contexts. In 1201 King John had granted English Jews a "Charter of Liberties," which declared that "if a Christian shall have a cause of action against a Jew, let him be tried by the Jew's peers." English courts came to interpret this provision, intended to protect against the anti-Semitism of Christian jurors, as guaranteeing a Jew, in a court process against a Christian, a half-Jewish jury. In 1354 King Edward III extended a similar privilege to all foreigners resident in England. They could now request a "mixed jury," composed partly of those who spoke their own language. English and, later, American defendants would continue to claim this right to a "jury *de medietate linguae*" into the early nineteenth century.[5]

In the seventeenth and eighteenth centuries, juries came to be seen as bulwarks against tyranny, owing to several celebrated trials in England and America in which juries refused to give the royal government the verdicts it demanded. In 1670, for example, a jury refused to convict William Penn of treason for preaching Quakerism, even though the judges locked the jurors up to force them to reconsider, threatened them with physical violence, and eventually levied heavy fines on them. One of the jurors subsequently filed a lawsuit regarding his mistreatment and won, and this "laid the groundwork for later legal developments allowing juries to nullify harsh laws or thwart unfair prosecutions." Another famous case, from colonial New York in 1735, involved the printer John Peter Zenger, whose newspaper had published slashing attacks on the corruption of the unpopular royal governor. The governor had Zenger arrested for seditious libel. According to legal precedent at the time, Zenger could not use the truth of his allegations as a defense. The judge, a political ally of the governor, tried to "stack the deck" against Zenger by disbarring the first two lawyers who offered to defend him. Yet a prominent lawyer from Pennsylvania, Andrew Hamilton, volunteered to represent Zenger, and in his argument before the jurors basically urged them to follow their conscience and the facts. When the jurors came back with a not-guilty verdict, Zenger and Hamilton became political heroes.[6]

By the time Americans wrote and ratified the U.S. Constitution and Bill of Rights (1787–1791), they had come to regard juries as so essential for the protection of liberty and the fair administration of justice that they included guarantees to the right to jury trials in three places. Article III of the Constitution, which creates the federal judiciary, mandates that the "Trial of all Crimes, except in Cases of Impeachment, shall be by Jury" (Art. III, §2); the Sixth Amendment mandates that in "all criminal prosecutions, the accused shall enjoy the right to a speedy and public trial, by an impartial jury of the State and district wherein the crime shall have been committed"; and the Seventh Amendment mandates that in "Suits at common law, where the value in controversy shall exceed twenty dollars, the right of trial by jury shall be preserved." These provisions applied only to federal courts, but the state constitutions all made similar guarantees. The U.S. Constitution did not explicitly guarantee a jury of "peers," although some state constitutions did so, nor did it explicitly establish a right to serve on a jury.

The American faith in jury trials was powerful enough before the Civil War that the right to them was extended to free blacks, who operated under severe political and civil disabilities in almost every state, North and South. In northern states, where blacks usually could not vote, they might still get a jury trial. In the South, where free blacks had still fewer rights—they were typically not allowed to testify against whites in court, for example—they might yet be tried before a jury. Virginia allowed free blacks jury trials until the panic following Nat Turner's bloody slave insurrection (1831), when the state rescinded this right. North Carolina allowed even slaves accused of crimes to be tried before a jury.[7]

Despite the consensus that jury trials should be made widely available, the right to serve on a jury was restricted to men and almost always to white men. Many early nineteenth-century jury reformers, who operated at the state level, wanted to restrict the jury pool still further, to white men who were "sober, propertied, responsible decisionmakers—the best people of the community."[8] These reformers demanded, and often got, state laws that excluded from the jury pool those white men who were thought unsuitable because they were poor, ill-educated, or possessed of what reformers deemed a bad character.[9] The various federal courts, meanwhile, generally followed the jury selection procedures of the states in which they were located.[10] The question of what constituted a jury of "peers" remained an issue, however, as indicated by courts occasionally allowing the creation of juries *de medietate linguae*.

Juries during and after the Civil War: The Problem of Confederates and Freedmen

The U.S. Civil War and its aftermath made the question of who could serve on juries a matter of national debate. Although a woman served on a jury for the first time in 1870, in Wyoming Territory, the claim of women to jury rights was not generally recognized.[11] The debate concerned men, and it fell along partisan lines. Republicans generally wanted to keep former supporters of the defeated Confederacy off juries, while putting blacks, most of them "freedmen" (former slaves), on juries. Democrats generally wanted the opposite.

During the war, Republicans controlled Congress and, with Abraham Lincoln, the presidency. They feared that in contested border state areas, Confederate sympathizers would get on federal juries and refuse to convict fellow rebels. In June 1862, therefore, Republicans enacted a law disqualifying anyone who had voluntarily aided or joined the rebellion from serving as a federal juror and requiring all federal jurors to swear an oath, declaring allegiance to the U.S. Constitution and denying they had ever assisted the rebellion.[12] Versions of these restrictions would stay in effect for the next seventeen years.

The year 1865 saw the end of the war, the assassination of President Lincoln, and the ratification of the Thirteenth Amendment to the Constitution, which abolished slavery. Almost immediately the rights of the newly freed slaves became a matter of national controversy between Democrats and Republicans. Andrew Johnson, the Unionist Democrat from Tennessee who succeeded Lincoln to the presidency, wanted the quick restoration of former Confederate states to the Union. Within months of the end of the war—and with President Johnson's encouragement—they elected new governments and congressional delegations under their old, prewar constitutions. Republicans, however, who still controlled Congress, were alarmed to see former Confederates elected both to Congress and to state government offices. The restored state governments, moreover, often approved laws that placed such severe restrictions on freed slaves as to re-create many of the features of slavery—for example, limiting the ability of freedmen to negotiate labor contracts and establishing severe punishments for criminal offenses that applied only to freedmen.[13]

The Republican Congress consequently refused to recognize the restored governments. Instead, in 1867 and 1868 it approved a series of Reconstruction Acts, over President Johnson's vetoes.[14] These laws established direct military rule in the former "rebel states," which were allowed to rejoin the Union only after they had called new constitutional conventions and rewritten their constitutions so as to guarantee black rights. The acts gave freed male slaves the right to vote for and serve as delegates to these conventions, but forbade former Confederates from doing either. Under these conditions, all of the former rebel states rewrote their constitutions and were readmitted to the Union by 1870. Federal troops continued to intervene in parts of the South until 1877, largely to prevent attacks against blacks and white Unionists by paramilitary groups dominated by former Confederates, such as the Ku Klux Klan.[15]

Meanwhile, in 1866, Congress sought to give protection to the rights of freed slaves by approving the Fourteenth Amendment to the Constitution. Ratified by the states two years later, the Fourteenth Amendment created the first national definition of American citizenship, comprising "all persons born or naturalized in the United States," and it committed the states to uphold core rights for all citizens. In particular, the amendment held that no state "shall make or enforce any law which shall abridge the privileges or immunities of citizens of the United States; nor shall any State deprive any person of life, liberty, or property, without due process of law; nor deny to any person within its jurisdiction the equal protection of the laws." It also abolished the three-fifths rule, requiring instead that representatives in Congress "shall be apportioned among the several States according to their respective numbers, counting the whole number of persons in each State"; prohibited any former Confederate, who had previously sworn an oath to the U.S. Constitution, from serving in federal or state office without a two-thirds vote of Congress; and granted Congress the "power to enforce, by appropriate legislation, the provisions of this article." Accelerating the adoption process, the Reconstruction Acts made ratification of the Fourteenth Amendment one of the prerequisites for a rebel state to be readmitted to the Union.

Simultaneously with the Fourteenth Amendment, Congress approved the Civil Rights Act of 1866, again over President Johnson's veto. The act declared that all U.S. citizens, "of every race and color, without regard to any previous condition of slavery or involuntary servitude," had the same rights "as . . . enjoyed by white citizens" to make and enforce contracts and buy and sell property, and were "subject to like punishments, pains, and penalties, and to none other."[16] The Civil Rights Act was unprecedented in scope and yet still was enacted with clear limits in mind. As the Republican congressman who introduced the legislation to the House explained, the act should not be understood to require "that all citizens shall sit on juries, or that their children shall attend the same schools. These are not civil rights and immunities."[17]

In the South, however, the new state constitutions that black delegates helped to write in the late 1860s removed racial requirements for jury service, and thus freedmen who were now voting and holding office began serving on juries as well. Some federal courts followed the jury selection practices of the states they were in and allowed blacks on juries. Finally, in 1875, Congress approved a new Civil Rights Act, which was signed into law by the Republican president who had succeeded Johnson, the former Union army commander Ulysses Grant.[18] The portion of the act dealing with jury service mandated, for the first time, that no citizen "possessing all other qualifications which are or may be prescribed by law shall be disqualified for service as a grand or petit juror in any court of the United States, or of any State, on account of race, color, or previous condition of servitude." The statute also specified that "any officer or other person charged with any duty in the selection or summoning of jurors who shall exclude or fail to summon any citizen for the cause aforesaid shall, on conviction thereof, be deemed guilty of a misdemeanor."[19]

Meanwhile, pressure mounted to repeal the loyalty restrictions for jurors. Federal prosecutors in some parts of the South complained that the restrictions ended up disqualifying so many potential jurors as to make the impaneling of grand and even trial juries difficult. Also, Democrats accused Republicans of using loyalty restrictions to purge juries of white southern Democrats. Republicans insisted that they were only trying to keep off juries those who were antagonistic to the enforcement of civil rights laws.[20]

Between 1869 and 1876, Democrats won control of one southern state after another, usually campaigning on a platform of restoring "white man's government" and often using violence to suppress black turnout.[21] In the 1876 presidential election, the Democratic candidate, Governor Samuel Tilden of

New York, appeared to have won a majority of the national popular vote, but Republicans alleged—and many historians agree—that numerous contests across the South were neither free nor fair, owing to the widespread suppression of black voters. The outcome in the electoral college was similarly contested because Tilden and his Republican rival, Ohio governor Rutherford Hayes, both claimed victory in three states: South Carolina, Louisiana, and Florida. These states had three of the last four remaining Republican governors in the South. Even apart from the presidential race, Democrats insisted that they had won all of these governorships in the 1876 elections. Republicans in Florida conceded defeat, but the Republican incumbents in South Carolina and Louisiana, rejecting the Democratic victories as fraudulent, refused to leave office. In both cases, Democratic-controlled militia would have forced them out, but federal troops guarded the statehouses.[22]

The electoral crisis was finally resolved with a political deal, known as the "Compromise of 1877." Congressional Democrats agreed that the electoral votes of the three contested states would go to Hayes, thereby giving him a one-vote majority in the electoral college, just enough to ensure that he would be the next president. In return, Hayes agreed to (among other things) order federal troops to stop protecting the governments of South Carolina and Louisiana, allowing Democrats to take power there. Historians generally date the end of Reconstruction to this point. Yet even with Democrats in charge in the South, as of 1877 many blacks there still voted, a few black Republicans still held office, and debates over jury rights continued.[23]

In the 1878 elections, Democrats won control of both houses of Congress for the first time since before the Civil War, and one of their top priorities, once in office, was to reform federal jury selection procedures. They approved legislation that repealed the loyalty oaths, arguing that Republican officials had exploited them for partisan purposes. Democrats also changed the procedure long used in most federal courts to summon jurors, which put the matter entirely in the hands of the federal marshal and court clerk. According to Democrats, these officials, nearly all at this time Republicans, had been carefully stacking juries with (in the words of one Democratic senator) "partisans and mere partisans alone; partisans of one political party; and but one."[24] The Democratic legislation therefore required all federal juries be selected from a box containing at least 300 names, which had been selected and placed there by a two-man, bipartisan commission. One of the men would be the court clerk, presumably a Republican; the other commissioner, appointed by the federal judge, had to be "a well-known member of the principal political party in the district in which the court is held opposing that to which the clerk may belong."[25]

When Republicans attacked this proposal as assuming federal juries would be filled with "rank partisans," Democrats added an amendment that the jurors would be chosen "without reference to party affiliations."[26] One Republican senator joked that this provision must mean "the republican is expected to select the democrats and the democrat is expected to select the republicans."[27] Of greater concern was the Republican charge that the Democratic commissioner would block the selection of black jurors. Fearing that President Hayes might veto the bill on this ground, Democrats added another amendment that "no citizen . . . shall be disqualified for service as grand or petit juror . . . on account of race, color, or previous condition of servitude."[28] Hayes was apparently satisfied with this formulation and did not veto the bill, which became law in June 1879.

Reconstructing Virginia

By many measures the Civil War inflicted greater damage on Virginia than on any other state. Not only did much of the fighting take place there, but the state split in two. In April 1861, when Virginia, politically dominated by tidewater planters who owned large numbers of slaves, decided to secede from the Union, the small farmers in the mountainous northwest, who had few or no slaves and had been battling the planters for decades over taxes and other issues, rebelled. A convention of western Unionists gathered in Wheeling, repudiated secession, established what they called the "Restored Government of Virginia," and elected as its governor the Republican Francis Pierpont. In December 1862 Congress passed legislation that would admit West Virginia to the Union as a separate state, with its own governor. Pierpont continued on as the "loyal" governor of Virginia in exile.[29]

After the Confederate surrender, Pierpont became the actual Virginia governor and oversaw the election of a new legislature under the prewar

Virginia constitution, by an all-white electorate. He encouraged the legislators to begin establishing public schools and to ratify the Fourteenth
Amendment. The legislature refused all his initiatives. Instead, it passed a
vagrancy law for blacks that re-created slavery in all but name, refused to
acknowledge the existence of West Virginia, and indicated that it wanted
Pierpont replaced as governor by the former Confederate commander,
Robert E. Lee.[30]

The legislature's fierce resistance to recognizing the results of the war
provoked the Republican Congress to refuse to readmit Virginia to the
Union. In 1867, the first Reconstruction Act abolished the legislature and reorganized the state as Military District Number One, under the administration of a Union general. Later that year federally supervised elections were
held for a new state constitutional convention, and blacks were allowed to
participate. Blacks made up a substantial portion of the state population—
43 percent in the 1860 census—and at this time probably a larger part of the
electorate, because the Reconstruction Acts barred many former Confederates from voting.[31] The result was that Radical Republicans elected three-
quarters of the convention delegates, and many of them were black. The
state constitution that they wrote allowed black men to vote, hold office, and
serve on juries. It also permanently barred nearly all former Confederate officeholders, meaning most of the white political class of Virginia, from
voting, holding office, or serving on juries.[32]

Moderate white Republicans joined with Democrats, however, in denouncing these disenfranchisement provisions as too severe. They protested to Republicans in Congress, who helped broker a compromise: in the
referendum to ratify the draft constitution, the controversial provisions were
to be voted on separately. As a result, Virginia voters approved the new constitution in July 1869 without Confederate disenfranchisement, and the
state was ultimately readmitted to the Union in January 1870.[33]

For much of the 1870s, Virginia was controlled by the Conservative Party,
a coalition of Democrats and moderate Republicans. Blacks continued to vote
in large numbers, however, and a few black Republicans served in the state
legislature. The dominant political issues in these years were the state debt
and the public schools.

Conservatives favored fully funding the prewar state debt, which with
interest stood in 1869 at about $45 million. It had been mostly accumulated

in the 1840s and 1850s to build roads and railroads. Yet the war had destroyed or severely damaged much of that infrastructure, while devastating the state tax base. A third of the state's prewar territory and population, including half of its prewar free taxpayers, were now part of West Virginia; the value of the remaining farmland had been halved; and the most valuable form of prewar taxable property, slaves, had been freed. Nonetheless, Conservatives insisted on paying the debt as a matter of state honor. Doing so meant, however, that the state would have difficulty funding its new public school system.[34]

The new state constitution had authorized the creation of the first public schools in Virginia. Although black leaders favored integrated schools, white resistance was so strong that they settled for a segregated system, which was established in 1870. Within a year it was educating 131,000 students. The new schools were very popular among blacks, who had been forbidden under slavery from learning to read and write. White opinion about public schools was divided. Some Conservative leaders feared that public education would have a dangerous "leveling" effect, leading laborers to despise honest work, while some poor whites resented seeing their black neighbors get educated. At the same time, many poor whites, particularly in areas with smaller black populations, favored the public schools, as did certain Conservative leaders, who came to see the improvement of public education as essential for the modernization of the state.[35]

By the late 1870s, the conflict over whether to finance the debt or the schools had created a split among Conservatives. On the one side were Funders, who wanted the debt paid in full, even if that meant closing the schools; on the other side were Readjusters, who wished to renegotiate the debt for the sake of the schools. The Readjusters made common cause with black Republicans, and in late 1879 this new coalition of blacks and whites won control of the legislature.[36]

Analysis of the vote shows that Readjusters garnered the most support among black voters in the tidewater region, and among white voters in the western part of the state, where there were relatively few blacks. The most contested area between Conservatives and Readjusters was the central, Piedmont region.[37] Perhaps not coincidentally, the dispute that launched the Virginia jury cases began with a racial incident involving one of the new black schools in the Piedmont county of Patrick.

The Killing of Aaron Shelton

According to court records, in mid-November 1877 a teenage member of the Shelton family—poor, white farmers in Patrick County, southern Virginia—marched up to the new "Negro school" in his neighborhood and shouted "School-butter!"[38] This taunt challenged schoolboys to risk a beating from their schoolmaster by rushing outside to fight. It had been used by white southern boys against each other since long before the Civil War, but here it had a political and racial charge. Many whites in Virginia opposed all public schools, especially those for emancipated slaves, while local blacks generally supported public schools. Also, before the Civil War, any slave child who fought back against a white one would have been severely beaten, or worse. Now a group of black students felt free to go after Shelton. He ran, but they caught him and "ducked" him in a creek—a standard punishment for anyone who risked yelling "school-butter" to a group of schoolboys in the nineteenth-century South. In this case, the duckers were led by Burwell Reynolds, then aged 19, whose father had a nearby farm.

Perhaps especially because Reynolds and his compatriots were black, the ducking infuriated Shelton's older brother, Aaron, aged 22. On November 27, he himself "hallooed school-butter" at the black school, on the way to help his uncle chop down trees in a nearby wood. None of the students chased him, possibly because Aaron was "of extraordinary physical development." Later that day, however, another of Aaron's younger brothers shouted "School-butter!" at the school and some schoolboys gave chase. The white boy ran for protection down a logging road to where his brother was working. There, one of the black boys told Aaron that Burwell Reynolds's younger sister, Puss, had called him a "rogue." Aaron, holding a rock and a stick, chased the black boys back to their school. He told them that his brother "might pass there when he damned pleased and halloo school-butter," and if they ducked his brother again, "he would shoot their heart-strings out, and if necessary would follow them into the school house to do so, and if the school-teacher interfered, he would shoot him." In the schoolyard, Aaron confronted Puss, threatening her with the stick. She denied that she had called him a rogue or that Burwell had ducked his brother—he had, she claimed, "only patted a little water on his head." Aaron responded with "abusive language" toward her. When Burwell and his younger brother Lee, aged 17 or 18, learned that Aaron had "abused" their sister, they seem to have decided to get even by rolling one of the logs Aaron and his uncle had cut and left on the logging road, ready to haul to the sawmill, off the road and down a hill.

They tried it that evening, but Aaron caught them, "cursed" them, and threatened to "thrash them." The Reynolds brothers left for home, stopping at the school, which was on their way. Soon Aaron and one of his brothers, also heading home, passed by them. Aaron's brother later testified that Lee was holding the school axe (probably used for firewood) and declared that he and Burwell were going to roll that log the next morning, and if Aaron "interfered they would shoot him, and if he ran they would make their dogs catch him." Burwell later denied that Lee made this threat. The following day, according to witnesses, Aaron received a message from Lee that Lee would shoot him if he tried to stop Lee from rolling the log, while Lee and Burwell heard from Aaron's uncle that Aaron would give them a beating if he saw them on the logging road. The next morning, November 29, as Burwell and Lee went to work on their father's farm, they again ran into Aaron's uncle, who reiterated the warning.

That afternoon, Burwell and Lee drove a sledge, laden with corn and pulled by a horse and oxen, down the logging road. Burwell, driving the team, carried an old butcher's knife, which his family used to cut tobacco, while Lee, who walked ahead, had a gun with him—one he or his brother often carried, possibly for hunting, now uncocked—and held a stick in his hands. The brothers found the road blocked by a newly cut log. When they started to push it out of the way, they saw Aaron himself, with one of his brothers, approaching on his wagon. Burwell quickly drove the sledge off the road. Aaron pulled up behind him, where Lee was now standing, and demanded to know what Lee was doing holding the stick.

Witnesses disagreed over what happened next. Either Lee said he had a right to carry the stick, or he said, "If you will get down, God damn you, I will show you." Aaron said, "Look here, boy, do you know who you are talking to?" and got down off the wagon. He told Lee to drop the stick. Either Lee dropped it and Aaron picked it up, or Aaron "jerked" it from him. Aaron pushed Lee backward until they reached the log. Lee may have tried to draw his gun on Aaron. Whether he did or not, witnesses agreed that he and Aaron wrestled over the gun, Aaron struck him with the stick, and knocked him over the log. Suddenly Burwell rushed up behind Aaron and stabbed him in the back. Aaron fell. Lee and Burwell fled in different directions. Aaron was carried, possibly by his brother and uncle, to a nearby house, where Aaron made a statement accusing Lee of threatening to murder him and Burwell of knifing him. Unable to write his name, Aaron signed the statement with a mark. He died on December 1.

Lee was found hiding in the woods near the killing, his gun cocked. Burwell was arrested in a neighboring county. The brothers were both locked in the Patrick County jail, and in January 1878 a Patrick County grand jury indicted them both for first-degree murder—killing "wilfully, and of their malice aforethought"—a crime punishable by death.[39] The grand jurors were all white.[40]

The Trials of Burwell and Lee Reynolds

The Reynolds family found two locally prominent white lawyers to represent the brothers. Andrew Murray Lybrook and William Martin had both served as officers in the Confederate army, and Lybrook, the lead counsel, would later be elected a state senator and appointed a county judge. Lybrook was a Readjuster Democrat (Readjusters tended to have some sympathy for black rights), and his wife's family, also named Reynolds, had before emancipation owned the black Reynolds family. An old story said that Burwell and Lee's mother, while a slave, had once saved Lybrook's father-in-law from being gored by a bull.[41] But regardless of why Lybrook took the case, he and Martin pursued the defense vigorously, and one of their main arguments had to do with jury rights.

The Reynolds brothers both pleaded not guilty and, at their request, were tried separately. The trials, first for Burwell, then for Lee, took place in April 1878 in the Patrick County Circuit Court. At the start of Burwell's trial, before the jury was selected, Lybrook and Martin protested to the judge, William Treadway, that the jury pool was "composed entirely of the white race." On behalf of their clients, they asked that the pool "be so modified as to allow one-third of . . . [it] to be composed of their race, they being colored." Judge Treadway denied the motion. He said that because the pool had been regularly drawn, he had no authority to change it. Lybrook and Martin then made the same request to the prosecuting attorneys, "waiving all objection to the illegality" of changing the pool. The prosecutors also refused them.[42]

Lybrook and Martin then petitioned that the trial be moved to federal court. Their petition pointed out that Virginia law allowed for "all male citizens twenty-one years of age and not over sixty, who are entitled to vote and hold office . . . [in] this State" to be jurors; that the law therefore allowed "the right as well as requires the duty of the race to which . . . [the accused] belong to serve as jurors"; but that the grand jury and the pool of the trial juries were all white. The lawyers alleged that "a strong prejudice" existed against the Reynolds brothers "independent of the merits of the case, and based solely upon the fact that . . . [they] are negroes, and that the man whom they are charged with having murdered was a white man," and that they therefore could not get an "impartial trial" before an all-white jury. Finally, the petition asserted that blacks "have never been allowed the right to serve as jurors, either in civil or criminal cases in the county of Patrick, in any case, civil or criminal, in which their race have ever been in any way interested up to the present time." Judge Treadway rejected the petition and ordered the trials to proceed.[43]

An all-white trial jury quickly convicted Burwell of first-degree murder. A few days later a different all-white jury convicted Lee of second-degree murder and recommended a sentence of fifteen years. In each case, Lybrook and Martin asked Judge Treadway to set aside the verdicts as "against the law and the evidence."[44] How could Burwell be guilty of premeditated murder when he seemed to have attacked Aaron Shelton spontaneously, in defense of his brother? And how could Lee be guilty of second-degree murder when he did not kill, or even apparently hurt, Shelton?

Judge Treadway set aside the verdict against Burwell and ordered a new trial, but decided not to set aside the verdict against Lee. Lybrook and Martin appealed Treadway's decision regarding Lee to the Virginia Supreme Court. It ruled, in July 1878, that "the facts certified as proved on the trial did not warrant the jury in finding the plaintiff in error, Lee Reynolds, guilty of the homicide charged in the indictment." The high court set aside Lee's verdict as "against the evidence" and granted him a new trial.[45]

Burwell and Lee each had their second trials, again in Judge Treadway's court, in October 1878. Again, the jury pool was all white. Before the trials started, Lybrook and Martin again petitioned to transfer the proceedings to federal court, on the grounds that their clients could not get a fair trial before all-white juries. Again, Treadway refused the petition. At Lee's second trial, the jury again convicted him of second-degree murder, but this time recommended a sentence of not fifteen but eighteen years. At Burwell's second trial, the jury deliberated for two days, then told the judge it could not reach a verdict. Lee and Burwell were sent back to the Patrick County jail, Lee to await his transfer to state prison, Burwell to await a third trial. On November 15, 1878, Lybrook and Martin petitioned directly to the federal district judge holding court in nearby Danville, Alexander Rives, and asked him to take over the case.[46]

Judge Rives came from a prominent Virginia slaveholding family, which had, however, opposed secession. One of his older brothers, William Cabell Rives, who had studied law under Thomas Jefferson and served as a U.S. senator from the state, had led state anti-secession forces during the crisis of 1860–1861. When Virginia left the Union anyway, William reluctantly accepted election to the Confederate Senate, but Alexander refused to serve in any capacity under the Confederate government. After the war, the younger Rives joined the Republican Party. In 1866 Governor Pierpont had appointed him to the Virginia Supreme Court, and five years later Republican president Ulysses Grant appointed him judge of the U.S. District Court for western Virginia. Rives remained active in the Virginia Republican Party even while on the bench, and in 1870 he ran unsuccessfully for Congress as a Republican.[47]

Rives responded favorably to the Reynoldses' petition. He was, he explained, "of [the] opinion that said petitioners had been denied such a trial as is secured to them by the laws of this State." He ordered a deputy U.S. marshal to take the Reynolds brothers into federal custody, so that they could be tried in his court by a jury selected "without distinction of race or color." The deputy marshal, with a writ in his pocket and accompanied by a posse of armed men, took the Reynolds brothers out of Patrick County jail and (as federal prisons did not yet exist) placed them in the custody of the senior deputy marshal, Jim Luck, which in this case meant transporting them eighty miles east to the jail in Pittsylvania County, where Luck lived.[48]

The high sheriff of Patrick County and Judge Treadway were absent when the Reynolds brothers were removed from their jail. Both later told reporters that had they been there, they would have protested. The sheriff said he would have objected in particular to the deputy taking Lee, who was a pris-

oner under sentence. Treadway, who was "indignant" over what he considered "a most flagrant violation of the rights of the State," said he would have
ordered the jailer "to refuse the keys of the jail" to the federal marshal.[49]

"Rives' Crusade"

No federal judge had ever assumed control over a state case on the grounds
of jury discrimination, and Rives's act received national attention. Within
weeks he found himself giving an interview to a major New York newspaper. He was aware, he explained to the reporter, that "the questions involved in his decision were grave, novel and delicate." He himself, in his
own court, had "always ordered mixed juries" and had "not discovered
that harm has resulted from it; on the contrary, the lawyers seem to
prefer them." Yet the civil rights law on which the Reynolds brothers had
based their petition to him was "not familiar to the Bar generally, and far
less to the public at large; hence any action under it is liable to be misun-
derstood and misrepresented."[50]

In fact, the press interpreted Rives's act in two different ways. One view,
expressed by a northern newspaper, was that Rives had "declared invalid the
conviction of a Negro by a white jury, on the ground that every man has a
right to be tried by his peers, wherefore a Negro should be tried by men of
his own color."[51] Another northern newspaper asserted, however, that Rives
had not taken this position, although if he had, it would have been no "novelty in jurisprudence," owing to the old precedent of courts allowing juries
de medietate linguae. But, this writer explained, the real question Rives had
raised was different: "Has the Nation yet enacted that white and colored men
shall be deemed equally competent for jury duty throughout the country,
forbidding a discrimination against jurors on the grounds of color, or is the
composition of juries a matter left to be freely regulated by State laws?"[52]
Both interpretations of Rives's actions would be debated in the coming
controversy.

It began almost immediately. On December 4, 1878, the Virginia legislature, dominated by the Funder faction, approved a resolution noting that
"certain persons held for trial under the laws of this commonwealth, by her
authority, charged with the murder of one of her citizens, on her soil, within
her jurisdiction, against her statutes, her peace and dignity, have been taken

from the custody of her proper officers." It called on the governor immediately to prepare an official report on what had happened. Governor Halliday turned to Judge Treadway and state Attorney General John G. Field, who swiftly prepared a report on what one newspaper described as "the 'capture' by Judge Rives of the Reynolds murderers from a State jail." Treadway argued the state should appeal to the U.S. Supreme Court for a writ ordering the prisoners returned to state custody. But first an appeal should be made for help from the U.S. attorney general on humanitarian grounds. Returning the "unfortunate prisoners" to state custody, Treadway explained, would only be fair to them, because whatever the result of their trial in federal court, "the State cannot surrender her jurisdiction." The punishments assigned them in his court would still apply, and the "harassment and imprisonment for trial in the Federal court will only be so much to protract their punishment in addition to necessary proceedings by the State."[53]

Attorney General Field argued not only that Judge Rives had committed a "serious and flagrant invasion of State rights," but also that his proceeding was "without law . . . without justification, or even excuse." First, the crime of which the Reynolds brothers were accused was against no U.S. law, but only against Virginia law, and so the federal courts had no jurisdiction. Second, the Reynoldses' civil rights had not been violated: "The rights of the white citizen constitute the standard erected by Congress for the ascertainment of the rights of all other citizens. In the trial of the Reynoldses was there any right denied to them which would have been accorded to the white citizen charged with the same or a similar offence . . . ? If there was, it is nowhere alleged or proved in the case." Field argued, moreover, that federal law nowhere guarantees the right to "a negro jury," any more than it does to a "negro judge." In fact, Field pointed out, neither federal law nor the U.S. Constitution provided for "a trial by jury of peers." The bill of rights of the state of Virginia did allow for such a right, but obviously it conferred no jurisdiction on a federal judge. Besides, continued Field, to say that blacks could not be tried fairly by a white jury was to make the obviously false claim that "the negro is not the peer of the white citizen before the law, or *vice versa*."[54]

Field further argued that if the right of a "negro" to demand a "negro jury" were upheld, the consequences would be absurd: "a Chinaman, in the city of Richmond . . . would have the right to demand for his trial a jury of

Chinamen, in whole, or in part, and as there are not Chinamen enough here to form a venire, the accused could not be tried at all." When summoning the jury pool for the Reynoldses' federal trial, Judge Rives had called for one "without distinction of race or color," yet the *"venire facias,* under which the jury was summoned in the circuit court of Patrick, made no distinction on account of race or color."[55] Continuing his argument, Field wrote: "If the Reynoldes [*sic*] were entitled to a jury of negroes, why did not Judge Rives put in his order that only negroes were to be summoned? If the negro jury is one of the civil rights conferred by Congress, then the serving of a single white person will vitiate the verdict. If a negro jury is a civil right, then Judge Rives has failed to discharge his duty in not ordering it, *in terms,* to be summoned. If it is not a civil right, then he has transcended the limits of his own jurisdiction and invaded that of the State court."[56]

After receiving the report from Halliday, Treadway, and Field, the Virginia legislature authorized the Joint Committee on Federal Relations to prepare its own report on the "usurpation of power by the federal judiciary in Virginia." This committee report advanced a broad constitutional argument that if "the government of the United States can . . . interfere in the rights of States to enforce their own laws . . . then it follows that the States exist only at the will and pleasure of the United States." If the federal government were required "to perform the functions of government for a State which refuses or neglects or fails to perform them according to the standard laid down by the majority who control the United States, then we shall see one State after another governed, not according to the will of its own people, but according to the opinions of people living in other States. . . . Then the government will not be by the people, of the people[,] for the people, but it will be power, maintaining itself by power, and relying on power alone."[57] From this perspective, the report argued that much of the Civil Rights Act of 1875 was unconstitutional.[58]

Specifically on the issue of juries, the legislative report objected that Rives had acted even though "there is no charge or insinuation" that Judge Treadway "is not pure, able, and impartial," or that the jurors "were not qualified, competent, intelligent, or just." Virginia law made no stipulation regarding the race of jurors, and nowhere in the court records of the Reynolds trials "is there anywhere found any suggestion that any of the parties, jurors, witnesses, or officers, were of any particular race or color, save and except only when placed on the record by the motion of the parties themselves, stating that they are negroes, and that the man they are charged with having murdered was a white man." The courts of Virginia, in other words, were color-blind by law. According to the committee report, the defendants' lawyers and Rives were the only ones injecting race into the case.[59]

The state Senate approved the committee report on January 18, 1879, along with a number of resolutions, including one instructing Attorney General Field to "institute proceedings in the name of this commonwealth, before the supreme court of the United States."[60] A few days later the lower house of the state legislature, the House of Delegates, also approved the report and resolutions. Here, however, they met opposition from Peter J. Carter, a black Republican from Northampton County, who proposed a substitute report. Carter's report called for the legislature not to interfere with Rives and declared that citizens of the state were denied equal protection of the law owing to "unequal administration of the laws," a problem that would be alleviated if blacks could serve on juries. According to the New York Times, Carter's report pointed out that "of persons indicted and tried for the same class of offenses, two colored men are convicted to one white man; that the terms of imprisonment imposed upon colored men thus convicted are nearly double those imposed upon whites similarly convicted; that in the face of innumerable killing of colored men by whites, it is of rare occurrence that whites are ever indicted for such homicides, and no white man has ever been hanged in this State for killing a colored man, while, on the other hand, hanging of colored men is of monthly occurrence."[61] The House passed over Carter's report "without action."[62]

Judge Rives, meanwhile, had chosen to challenge his critics by testing their claim that Virginia did not racially discriminate in the selection of jurors. Rives knew that Virginia law placed no color qualification on jurors, but also that Virginia county judges were responsible for making out and returning jury lists. As the Reynolds petition to him had alleged that no black jurors had ever served in Patrick County, Rives felt compelled to ask whether Judge Treadway and other county judges were deliberately excluding qualified men from juries simply because they were black. If so, Rives believed, these judges were not only violating the equal protection clause of the Fourteenth Amendment to the Constitution, but were committing a misdemeanor under the federal Civil Rights Act of 1875 and were subject to arrest and fine.[63]

In February 1879 Rives charged a racially mixed federal grand jury, sitting at Danville, to consider whether to indict state judges in the five counties from which the jurors were drawn: Patrick, Henry, Franklin, Charlotte, and Pittsylvania. Rives explained to the jurors how they should determine whether a judge from any of these counties should be charged: "If it should appear to you that by a long and systematic course [the judge] has never admitted to his list the names of colored men duly qualified, you would be compelled to infer his guilt and indict him for the offence, and let him repel by proof the fair presumptions of the law against him." He announced that he would travel to each seat in his district and summon new grand juries to consider further indictments and expressed the hope that his actions "will tend to remove one ground of interference with State courts, and assert the just supremacy of the Constitution and the laws of the United States."[64]

According to a news report, the Danville jurors heard testimony that the judge in Henry County had declared, "No nigger shall ever sit on a jury in my court!" They were told that in Franklin, Charlotte, and Patrick, where Judge Treadway presided, "a negro's name has never been upon the list of names from which juries are to be selected." They were told that in Pittsylvania County, "a negro has never been on a jury since the present judge [James Dodridge Coles] has been in office, and [that] on one occasion certainly, perhaps more, a mixed jury has been asked for by interested parties and denied." On February 27, 1879, the grand jurors indicted Treadway, Coles, and three other judges.[65]

The government of Virginia responded the next day. On February 28 the Virginia Senate passed resolutions denouncing the indictments as "arbitrary, outrageous, illegal and a usurpation." The resolutions directed Attorney General Field "to bring said proceedings to an adjudication by the supreme court of the United States, in order that such lawless measures may be checked." They also requested Virginian representatives in Congress to begin impeachment proceedings against Rives, on the grounds that he was "usurping judicial power for the purpose of bringing about an unnecessary conflict between state and federal authorities . . . [over] the criminal laws of Virginia, thereby endangering the harmony, peace and good order of this commonwealth." These resolutions passed the Senate of Virginia with only two dissenting votes (both Republicans) and within hours were also approved by the House of Delegates.[66]

Republican newspapers hailed Rives's "bold stand for the Negro's Rights," while Democratic papers called him "corrupt" and described his actions as "the antics of a fool on the bench," alleging that they had served only to re-awaken "prejudices between the races, which are gradually dying out."[67] Yet "Rives' Crusade," as one newspaper called it, proceeded.[68] In fact, Rives summoned a new grand jury on March 24 at Lynchburg.

This time he released his charge to the press in advance. Rives here noted that collision between state and federal courts could not be avoided if state courts disobeyed federal law, in this case the Civil Rights Act of 1875. He admitted that the intention of the judges to discriminate "may be difficult to prove," but again insisted that if a judge "has, by a long and unvarying course, refused to admit to his [jury] list the names of colored persons duly qualified," then the grand juror would have to accept this conduct as evidence of guilt. Rives referred obliquely to his critics when he declared himself "at a loss to conceive of any motive on the part of honorable and intelligent citizens to undertake in any way . . . to thwart the mission of the . . . [federal] Government in all its departments to give the equal protection of the laws to all its citizens without distinction."[69] On the basis of this charge, the Lynchburg grand jury soon indicted nine more county judges.

In the meantime, Rives had ordered Deputy Marshal Luck to arrest the first group of judges, but Luck declined to do so, announcing instead that he would only notify them when they were due to appear in court. Judge Coles of Pittsylvania County, an old friend of Luck's—among other connections, they had served together in Pickett's Charge at the Battle of Gettysburg—agreed to be arrested as a test case. On March 13, 1879, Luck served Coles with an arrest warrant, and Coles refused to pay bail. Luck took him under personal custody and gave him the liberty of the county, meaning he was confined to Pittsylvania. Coles immediately appealed to the U.S. Supreme Court to be released. Attorney General Field, acting for the State of Virginia, simultaneously filed an identical appeal on his behalf.[70]

By April, the U.S. Supreme Court had agreed to hear both of the "Virginia jury cases"—the one protesting Rives's decision to take over the Reynolds case *(Rives v. Virginia)* and the appeal of Judge Coles for release *(Ex Parte*

TABLE 9.1

Population as of 1880, by Race and Age, for Virginia Counties Where Judges Were Indicted in 1879 for Excluding Blacks from Juries

County	Total White Population	Total Black Population	All Males, 21 and Over
Amherst	10,001	8,702	4,000
Appomattox	5,153	4,927	2,064
Bedford	18,528	12,677	6,672
Botetourt	10,159	4,650	3,623
Buckingham	6,767	8,773	3,208
Campbell	17,297	18,953	8,286
Charlotte	5,704	10,949	3,453
Fluvanna	5,512	5,290	2,301
Franklin	17,069	8,015	5,155
Henry	8,614	7,395	3,247
Nelson	9,028	7,508	3,464
Patrick	10,099	2,734	2,458
Pittsylvania	25,389	27,200	11,823
Roanoke	8,273	4,828	2,809

Source: Adapted from *Statistics of the Population of the United States at the Tenth Census* (Washington, DC: GPO, 1883), 412–413, 665. For lists of the judges indicted, see Herman Melton, *Pittsylvania County's Historic Courthouse: The Story behind* Ex Parte Virginia *and the Making of a National Landmark* (Chatham, VA: Herman Melton and Pittsylvania Historical Society, 1999), 13, 16.

Virginia). The Court decided, however, "that such grave questions . . . should not be heard and decided in the hurry and confusion of the last days of the term, but should have the most deliberate consideration."[71] The justices therefore postponed hearings until the beginning of the next court term, in October.

At the Supreme Court

In the spring of 1879, collections were taken up in Virginia at black churches and at conventions of "colored men" to help "defray the expenses of counsel" to defend Judge Rives's acts before the Supreme Court. Black Virginians, reported the *New York Times,* "are evidently impressed with the idea that now is the time to strike for their rights if ever they are to have them."[72] The gesture turned out to be unnecessary. President Hayes's attorney general, the Massachusetts Republican and former Union Army general Charles Devens, agreed to represent Rives before the court. That Devens took on the cases indicated how politically important the jury question had become.

The Supreme Court heard arguments in the Virginia cases in the first days of its October term.[73] Representing Virginia was its attorney general, Field, and William Robertson, a prominent Virginia attorney who before the Civil War had sat on the Virginia Supreme Court. Opposing them were U.S. Attorney General Devens and two assistant attorneys general. Counsel argued over whether Rives had "invaded the sovereign rights" of Virginia. Field and Robertson maintained that only state courts could try questions of state law and that for a state to allow the federal government to determine how to select its jurors would be "an abdication of her sovereign right to administer her own laws." They noted that "no discrimination is made by the laws of Virginia between the races in the selection of jurors," and argued that Rives had no right to take over the Reynolds cases, because he did so on the grounds that civil rights were being violated, even though no right to all or partially black juries was guaranteed under federal law.[74] As for Coles, Field argued, according to a press report, the Civil Rights Act of 1875 could not constitutionally be used to punish the judicial acts of state judges:

> If Congress can fine a Judge for his judicial acts, it can imprison him during his whole term of service, or depose him from office. If it has the power claimed for it over the judicial officers of the State, it has like power over members of the Legislature who may vote for a law supposed by Congress to be in violation of any provision of the Constitution of the United States, and over the executive officers who may undertake to execute it. In short, he argued, "It converts this Government into a consolidated despotism, the despot being the Congressional majority of the day."[75]

U.S. Attorney General Devens and his assistants replied that such fears were exaggerated because the supervisory powers of the federal courts over state courts were very limited, but that the federal government could intervene in the administration of state law whenever "the equal protection of the laws is denied by a State to any class of its citizens." Such was the case here because "every person has the right to a trial by a jury constituted without discrimination against his own race or color."[76] It was, they argued, "idle . . . to say that there is no discrimination against colored men because the statute makes none, or because white men are tried by white jurors." If Judge Coles had excluded men from his jury lists "solely on account of race, color, or previous condition, this is a discrimination" and illegal.[77]

With the arguments over, the Supreme Court justices deliberated through the winter of 1879–1880. In *Ex Parte Virginia,* they had to decide whether Rives had gone too far in ordering the arrest of state judges. All of the justices seemed to agree that a federal court could not order the arrest of a state judge for having performed a judicial act, because this could result in the destruction of the state courts. But when Judge Coles had selected jurors, had he been performing a judicial act or merely an administrative one, which could be regulated by federal law? And what about Rives's presumption, in his charges to the Danville and Lynchburg grand juries, that if a county judge had never put blacks on jury lists, the judge should be presumed guilty of a criminal civil rights violation? In the face of such a presumption, one justice complained, an accused judge could make no defense, even if "he may have exercised at all times his best judgment in the selection of qualified persons, unless he could prove, what in most cases would be impossible, that in a county of many thousand inhabitants there was not a colored person qualified to serve as a juror."[78]

Then there was the *Rives* case. Although a majority of the court seemed to agree that the legal exclusion of blacks from juries would be a violation of the equal protection provisions of the Fourteenth Amendment and of the Civil Rights Act of 1875, the justices were not certain they faced this issue. Virginia law, after all, did not exclude blacks from juries. The lawyers for the Reynolds brothers had complained, instead, that no blacks appeared in the Patrick County jury pool. But did this omission ensure an unfair trial? If so, did the Fourteenth Amendment and the Civil Rights Act not only guarantee that blacks could not be excluded from juries, but that they must be included, at least in the jury pool, when the defendant was black? Also, in what sense could sitting on a jury be called a right, at least for men? These were among the questions with which the court would have to grapple before reaching a decision.

NOTES

1. John Keane, *The Life and Death of Democracy* (New York: W. W. Norton, 2009), 46–51.

2. Neil Vidmar and Valerie P. Hans, *American Juries: The Verdict* (Amherst, NY: Prometheus Books, 2007), 23–25.

3. Francis Leiber, "The Unanimity of Juries," *American Law Register* 15, no. 12 (Oct. 1867): 729.

4. Article 39. Translation from the Latin provided in J. C. Holt, *Magna Carta,* 2nd ed. (Cambridge: Cambridge University Press, 1992), 461.

5. Lewis H. LaRue, "A Jury of One's Peers," *Washington and Lee Law Review* 33 (1976): 849–855; Vidmar and Hans, *American Juries,* 69–70.

6. Vidmar and Hans, *American Juries,* 27–30, 41–47.

7. John Henderson Russell, *The Free Negro in Virginia, 1619–1865* (Baltimore: Johns Hopkins University Press, 1913), 103–104; Timothy S. Huebner, "The Roots of Fairness: *State v. Caesar* and Slave Justice in Antebellum North Carolina," in *Local Matters: Race, Crime, and Justice in the Nineteenth-Century South,* ed. Christopher Waldrep and Donald G. Nieman (Athens: University of Georgia Press, 2001), 29–52, esp. 30–32.

8. Benno C. Schmidt Jr., "Juries, Jurisdiction, and Race Discrimination: The Lost Promise of *Strauder v. West Virginia,*" *Texas Law Review* 61, no. 8 (May 1983): 1422.

9. LaRue, "Jury of One's Peers," 855–856.

10. This is the procedure outlined in the Federal Judiciary Act of 1789 (1 Stat. 73), §29.

11. Vidmar and Hans, *American Juries,* 73. Wyoming later rescinded the right of women to sit on juries. Women gradually won the permanent right to sit on state juries over the course of the twentieth century, starting in Washington in 1911 and continuing until South Carolina in 1967; Massachusetts women won the right to sit on juries in 1949. See Holly J. McCammon et al., "Movement Framing and Discursive Opportunity Structures: The Political Successes of the U.S. Women's Jury Movements," *American Sociological Review* 72, no. 5 (Oct. 2007): 727.

12. Drew L. Kershan, "The Jury Selection Act of 1879: Theory and Practice of Citizen Participation in the Judicial System," *University of Illinois Law Forum* (1980): 710.

13. On the history of the Reconstruction era, see, e.g., Eric Foner, *Reconstruction: America's Unfinished Revolution, 1863–1877* (New York: Harper Perennial, 2014); Mark Wahlgren Summers, *The Ordeal of the Reunion: A New History of Reconstruction* (Chapel Hill: University of North Carolina Press, 2014).

14. 14 Stat. 428 (1867); 15 Stat. 2 (1867); 15 Stat 14 (1867); 15 Stat. 41 (1868).

15. See esp. Foner, *Reconstruction,* chap. 9.

16. 14 Stat. 27 (1866), 27.

17. Quoted in Schmidt, "Juries," 1423.

18. 18 Stat. 335 (1875).

19. Ibid., §4.

20. One historian who has carefully examined the effect of the loyalty requirement on jury selection in Louisiana concludes that "the perceptions of both the Democrats and Republicans were based in reality." See Kershan, "Jury Selection Act," 722–726.

21. Foner, *Reconstruction,* 539, 549–553, 558–562.

22. Michael F. Holt, *By One Vote: The Disputed Presidential Election of 1876* (Lawrence: University Press of Kansas, 2008), 253–254 (table 5), 175, 181–183, 193; Foner, *Reconstruction,* 575–576; Summers, *Ordeal,* 383–384.

23. Foner, *Reconstruction,* 580–82, 595; Summers, *Ordeal,* 384–385, 389.

24. Kershan, "Jury Selection Act," 726.

25. 21 Stat. 43 (1879), 43.

26. Ibid.

27. Kershan, "Jury Selection Act," 745–746, n. 126.

28. 21 Stat. 43 (1879), 44.

29. Jane Dailey, *Before Jim Crow: The Politics of Race in Postemancipation Virginia* (Chapel Hill: University of North Carolina Press, 2000), 16–17; Stephen D. Engle, "Mountaineer Reconstruction: Blacks in the Political Reconstruction of West Virginia," *Journal of Negro History* 78, no. 3 (Summer 1993): 137. See also *Ordinances and Acts of the Restored Government of Virginia, Prior to the Formation of the State of West Virginia* (Wheeling, WV: John Frew, 1866).

30. Dailey, *Before Jim Crow,* 16–17.

31. See Michael R. Haines, "Virginia Population by Race, Sex, Age, Nativity, and Urban–Rural Residence: 1790–1990 [Present Boundaries]," in *Historical Statistics of the United States, Earliest Times to the Present: Millennial Edition,* ed. Susan B. Carter et al. (New York: Cambridge University Press, 2006), series Aa6101, Aa6103. The Reconstruction Acts required voters to swear a loyalty oath designed to exclude many of those who "engaged in insurrection or rebellion against the United States" (15 Stat. 2 [1867], 2).

32. Ibid., 19–20; *The Constitution of Virginia, Framed by the Convention which Met in Richmond . . . 1867* (Richmond, VA: New Nation, 1868), art. III, §1, clause 4, §§2–3.

33. Dailey, *Before Jim Crow,* 20–21.

34. Ibid., 17–18, 28–31.

35. Ibid., 22–25, 40.

36. Ibid., 30–32, 45–47.

37. Ibid., 32–35.

38. For this section ("The Killing of Aaron Shelton"), see Aaron Shelton's statement and the two "Bills of Exceptions and Facts," summarizing the testimony given at the two trials of Lee Reynolds, reprinted in *Senate Document No. 7: Communication from the Governor of Virginia, in Response to a Resolution of the Senate Calling for Information as the Exercise of Jurisdiction by Judge Rives* (Commonwealth of Virginia, 1878), 18, 20–22, 26–28, 30–32; hereafter cited as *Virginia Senate Document No. 7.* These accounts do not agree on certain key details, although we have tried to determine the most

plausible sequence of events. See also Herman Melton, *Pittsylvania County's Historic Courthouse: The Story Behind* Ex Parte Virginia *and the Making of a National Landmark* (Chatham, VA: Herman Melton and Pittsylvania Historical Society, 1999), 1–6.

39. *Virginia Senate Document No. 7,* 17–18.

40. Ibid., 21.

41. Melton, *Pittsylvania County's Historic Courthouse,* 8–9, 20. Melton says that Lybrook was a state senator in 1878, but the journal of the state senate that year does not list him.

42. *Virginia Senate Document No. 7,* 19, 20.

43. Ibid., 21.

44. Ibid., 22–23, 25–26.

45. Ibid., 23, 28–29.

46. Ibid., 29–30, 23–24; *Report of the Special Committee of the Senate and the Committee on Federal Relations of the House of Delegates of Virginia, as a Joint Committee of the General Assembly on Usurpation of Power by the Federal Judiciary in Virginia* (Richmond, VA: R. E. Fraser, 1879), 4–5. Although petitioning to transfer a case from state court to federal court was unusual, federal law permitted it under some circumstances. In March 1863 the Republican Congress enacted legislation that gave anyone involved in a case arising from the execution of a federal law the right to petition to remove the trial to federal circuit court (12 Stat. 755 [1863], 756–757 [§5]). During Reconstruction, Republicans feared that freedmen would not be treated fairly in southern state courts and so, in the Civil Rights Act of 1866, provided for civil rights cases to be removed to federal circuit court, using the procedures of the 1863 law (14 Stat. 27 [1866], 27). These procedures remained in place until 1875, when Congress approved a new, revised code of statutes. Although this code was generally understood, when approved, to be merely a compilation of existing law, the section that governed civil rights cases now seemed to allow petitions for removal only before trial (see Rev. Stat. §641 [1875]). Did the revised code bar defendants from petitioning a federal circuit court for removal *after* final judgment in state court, and could an appeal to federal circuit court be made if, as in the Reynolds case, a state court had refused a petition for removal before trial? In 1880, the answers remained unclear.

47. For a sketch of Rives's life until 1871, see Melton, *Pittsylvania County's Historic Courthouse,* 30–36. For examples of Rives's ongoing Republican political activities, see "Letter of Judge Rives Indorsing [sic] Grant and Colfax," *New York Times,* 20 Aug. 1868, 1; "Virginia Politics: The Republican State Convention," *New York Times,* 25 Apr. 1870, 2; "Political Notes," *New York Times,* 18 Oct. 1873, 9. On William Rives, the brother of Alexander, see Patrick Sowle, "The Trials of a Virginia Unionist: William Cabell Rives and the Secession Crisis," *Virginia Magazine of History and Biography* 80, no. 1 (Jan. 1972): 3–20.

48. *Report of the Special Committee,* 5; Melton, *Pittsylvania County's Historic Courthouse,* 1, 61–62.

49. "Courts Conflicting in Virginia," *Baltimore Sun*, 29 Nov. 1878, quoted in Melton, *Pittsylvania County's Historic Courthouse*, 12; "A Conflict between Courts," *New York Times*, 30 Nov. 1878, 2; *Virginia Senate Document No. 7*, 5.

50. "Virginia Juries" (Interview with Rives), *New York Herald*, 11 Dec. 1878, 3.

51. "Fact and Rumor," *Christian Union*, 4 Dec. 1878, 490.

52. "Mixed Juries," *New York Tribune*, 14 Apr. 1879, 4.

53. *Virginia Senate Document No. 7*, 1, 15; "Vexed Questions in Virginia," *New York Times*, 8 Dec. 1878, 1 ("the 'capture' by Judge Rives" quotation).

54. *Virginia Senate Document No. 7*, 4, 10, 6.

55. Ibid., 6.

56. Ibid., 6–7.

57. *Report of the Special Committee*, 8, 27.

58. Ibid., 29, 36.

59. Ibid., 6.

60. Ibid., 36.

61. "Virginia's Demand for Her Rights," *New York Times*, 1 Feb. 1879, 5.

62. Ibid.

63. "The Indicted Virginia Judges," *New York Tribune*, 15 Mar. 1879, 3.

64. Ibid.; Melton, *Pittsylvania County's Historic Courthouse*, 13.

65. "The Indicted Virginia Judges"; "Arresting the Judges," *Daily Constitution* (Atlanta, GA), 1 Mar. 1879, 1.

66. "The Indicted Virginia Judges"; "Arresting the Judges."

67. "The Indicted Virginia Judges"; "A Corrupt Judge," *Daily Constitution* (Atlanta, GA), 19 Mar. 1879, 1; "A Fine Federal Judge," *Daily Constitution*, 5 Mar. 1879, 2.

68. "Rives' Crusade," *Chicago Daily Tribune*, 21 Mar. 1879, 1.

69. "The Virginia Conflict," *Chicago Daily Tribune*, 20 Mar. 1879, 2.

70. "In General," *Daily Constitution* (Atlanta, GA), 5 Mar. 1879, 2; Melton, *Pittsylvania County's Historic Courthouse*, 61–63, 46 (reproduction of "The Conflict of Jurisdiction," *New York Herald*, 15 Mar. 1879, 4).

71. "Important Decisions," *Washington Post*, 15 Apr. 1879, 2.

72. "Counsel for Judge Rives," *New York Times*, 10 Apr. 1879, 7.

73. We do not discuss all aspects of the arguments. Coles, for example, had asked the court to issue a writ of habeas corpus to release him, and the attorneys debated whether the court had the authority to do so.

74. "Washington: Arguments in the Supreme Court on the Rives Case," *Chicago Daily Tribune*, 16 Oct. 1879, 4; "The Virginia Jury Cases," *Washington Post*, 15 Oct. 1879, 4.

75. "Virginia's State Rights Cases," *New York Times*, 17 Oct. 1879, 2.

76. See "State Rights in Question," *New York Tribune*, 16 Oct. 1879, 2; "Washington: Arguments in the Supreme Court on the Rives Case."

77. "Virginia's State Rights Cases."

78. Opinion of Justice Stephen J. Field, *Ex Parte Virginia*, 100 U.S. 339 (1880), 353.

An Australian Ballot for California? (1891)

ON MARCH 7, 1891, something was amiss at the California State Assembly in Sacramento. An important ballot reform bill was due to be voted on, but a number of Republican assemblymen who had pledged their support were absent from the floor and reportedly ill. As his colleagues debated the bill, Democratic assemblyman T. W. H. Shanahan requested a roll call, which found that twenty-three of the eighty members of the Republican-dominated Assembly were absent. Only nine had been granted leave, and most of the rest were San Francisco Republicans gone without permission. The missing assemblymen had presumably departed to avoid voting for the bill, which they had pledged to support during election season but apparently did not actually wish to pass. Shanahan moved that the Assembly's sergeant-at-arms should seek the missing assemblymen and return any he found to the legislature. Although this motion failed, the vote on the ballot measure was nevertheless postponed.[1]

The bill in question was a plan to reform California's elections with an "Australian" ballot. Under this new system, candidates from all qualifying parties would appear on uniform, official ballots, which would be printed by county and municipal governments and which voters would ultimately fill out in secret. This would mark a substantial departure from the existing way in which votes were cast in California, or for that matter in most of the United States. Traditionally, political groups prepared and distributed party-line ballots, called "tickets," for voters to submit at the polls. Because each party ticket was visually distinctive (in most cases, distinguished by a particular color), it was easy for observers to determine how individual citizens had voted as they handed in their ballots. Closely monitoring the ballot boxes, representatives of the party "political machines" frequently paid supporters who voted for the machine ticket and sought to punish those who did not. The system was also rife with opportunities for deception. The parties could hand out tickets that looked like those of another party to mislead illiterate voters, or sneak in extra votes by using tissue-thin tickets (called "pudding ballots") that allowed cooperative voters to cast multiple votes surreptitiously.[2] Supporters of the Australian ballot promised it would end these abuses, bring greater secrecy and honesty to California's elections, and loosen the grip of party machines on the state and municipal governments.

By March 9 most of the missing assemblymen had returned and, bound by their campaign pledges, helped approve the ballot bill. Only three Republican assemblymen voted against it, and just one Republican state senator opposed it when it reached the upper chamber two days later. The leading Republican opponent in the Assembly, Henry Dibble, had amended the bill to increase the number of supporters necessary for a candidate to appear on the ballot, and the final version allowed party-line voting with a single mark, but otherwise the bill was very similar to the one reformers had introduced. The bill now only needed the signature of Henry Markham, the recently elected Republican governor.[3] If Markham signed the bill into law, California would join a growing roster of U.S. states using the new, secret ballot, and reformers would claim another victory in their battle against political machines.

Party Politics and Political "Machines"

The political organizations (or "machines," as they were called by their critics) that controlled so much of American governance in the late nineteenth century arose out of the era's political parties. Contrary to the hopes of many of the Founding Fathers, who saw parties as distasteful and even dangerous, the nation's political culture had become highly partisan by 1840. In fact, from about that point forward, American politics were dominated at all levels by two major parties—first Democrats and Whigs, and later Democrats and Republicans.[4] The parties developed elaborate structures: local committees closely managed communications with voters and monitored their partisan allegiances, while county, state, and federal-level committees fashioned strategies, allocated party funds, and published partisan periodicals. Party leaders celebrated these structures as vital institutions of American democracy. "Arm a hundred thousand men with the most approved weapons of war, and put them in the field without drill or discipline, and what are they? A mere mob," argued one Democratic journal. "A political party is the same. Party organization is as necessary to the success of principles as truth is to their usefulness and vitality."[5]

In legal terms, parties were treated as private, voluntary associations in the nineteenth century. In general, American courts held that although states and the federal government had the authority to protect voting rights and prevent fraud on election day, neither had the authority to interfere with internal party affairs. Parties themselves determined their own membership, ran "primaries" (meaning local caucuses), held conventions, and nominated candidates, however they saw fit. As one political scientist has noted, "It was no more illegal to commit fraud in the party caucus or primary than it would be to do so in the election of officers of a drinking club."[6]

The Party Ticket

The rise of political parties in America coincided with the use of ticket ballots. Before tickets, and since ancient times, people voted in assemblies and by voice, although in some places they would put balls, stones, or beans in a pot—the original "ballots" (derived from the Italian word "ballotta," meaning "ball"). The use of written paper ballots first gained popularity in colonial New England in the early eighteenth century, possibly because literacy rates were relatively high there. Voters typically wrote out their ballots in front of election judges. This method spread to other parts of the country after the revolution, although voice voting persisted in some states for many years; Virginia did not require the use of written ballots until the 1860s. Meanwhile, the practice of casting votes by means of a printed ticket, prepared by a political party, and listing only the candidates of that party, seems to have first been introduced in Connecticut and Rhode Island in the late eighteenth century. By the mid-nineteenth century, ticket voting was common practice across much of the country.[7]

American political parties may have developed large and complex organizational structures at least in part to compete effectively with one another in printing and distributing tickets.[8] It was certainly a complicated undertaking. Each party had to print different tickets for each electoral district in each election—this in an era when many state and local elections were annual, and state, local, and national elections often took place on different days. Moreover, some states mandated that voters cast different ballots for each *office*, meaning parties had to print bundles of tickets for every voter in every election. Once printed, the tickets had to be handed out, often by the thousands, to party supporters, which became the job of a small army of operatives.

Any group that could print and distribute tickets could get votes on election day. As one historian points out, "the system punished party organizations if they were unresponsive to their members by making it easy to bolt the party's ticket."[9] But the system also allowed for the easy creation of phony political parties, such as the "piece clubs" of California, which used their tickets to extort money from legitimate office seekers, who were asked to pay to get their names listed. One San Francisco newspaper noted in 1877, "A candidate for a prominent office has received notices of assessments from [a] number of conventions, for amounts of $500, $300, $200, $375, $200." It was sometimes difficult for nominees to distinguish the piece clubs from genuine political groups, though occasionally their eclectic—and even racist—names may have given them away, as was the case with the "Independent Democratic Liberal Republican Anti-Coolie Labor Reform Party" of San Francisco.[10] A more general problem with the ticket system, however, concerned voter privacy.

Voting in the ticket era took place not in a booth but at a voting window (literally, a ticket window). The window was usually located in a private building, such as a home or saloon, and overlooked a street or public square. Inside would sit the election judges, usually a bipartisan panel of party operatives. Rival teams of ticket distributors would operate right outside the window. A voter (who, until after the Civil War, was almost always a white man) would approach the window through this boisterous, often drunken, and occasionally violent crowd, collecting the tickets he wanted as he went. Just in front of the window was usually a platform, on which the voter would have to step to reach the window. He would then hand his ticket or tickets to the judges, while calling out his name. The judges would call the voter's name to a clerk sitting behind them, who would write it down (often phonetically) in a ledger, then would deposit the ticket or tickets in the ballot box, which usually rested at their feet.[11]

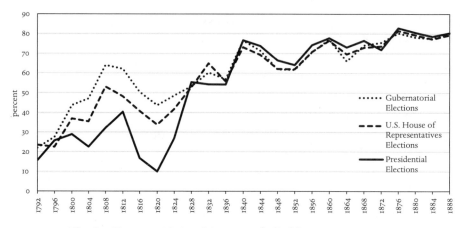

Election Turnout, National Average of Eligible Voters, 1792–1888

Source: Adapted from Curtis Gans and Matthew Mulling, *Voter Turnout in the United States, 1788–2009* (Washington, DC: CQ Press, 2011).

Note: After the election of 1860, eleven southern states declared their independence from the United States, but they ultimately lost the Civil War (1861–1865). Congress did not readmit congressional delegations from these states until 1868–1870. As a result, no congressional or presidential race took place in these states in 1864, and only one governor's race, in North Carolina, took place that year. In 1868 there were no gubernatorial, congressional, or presidential elections held in the three states not yet readmitted to the Union: Virginia, Mississippi, and Texas.

In this very public setting, the use of tickets allowed party operatives to observe how individuals voted. Although there were many ways to do this—noting, for example, which distributors a voter approached to collect his ticket—the easiest method was simply to look at what ticket the voter was holding. Each party made its tickets readily discernible from one another. Distinguishing features came in many varieties: Massachusetts Republicans, for example, used a ballot with a bright pink border in 1878, and an enterprising Tammany Democrat in New York once even perfumed his ballots to give them a distinct aroma.[12]

Many American voters apparently did not mind being watched. Voting had traditionally been public, and many commentators denounced secret voting as cowardly and dishonest.[13] Most voters also had strong partisan affiliations, and thus were often proud to show they were voting for their party. Besides, reformers found that making voting more private under the ticket system was difficult. In the 1850s, Massachusetts experimented with requiring voters to put their tickets in sealed envelopes, but critics denounced the system as unnecessary and cumbersome; after a couple of years the envelopes were made optional, which rendered them ineffective. Again, by 1881, fifteen states had passed laws trying to make tickets more uniform, and therefore less easily identifiable, mandating that tickets be printed in specific colors of paper and ink and regulating their size. California and Oregon even required that tickets be printed on a particular type of paper, provided by the secretary of state. But party officials usually found ways around these laws. In Ohio, for example, where tickets had to be white, the parties adopted distinctive shades of white—very bright for Republicans and darker for Democrats.[14] Yet reformers did not abandon their efforts to change the ticket system because they increasingly saw it as a bulwark for corrupt political "machines."

Political Machines and Corruption

By the 1830s some local and state party organizations had begun to develop elaborate and highly disciplined electoral operations. The most famous of these was the "Albany Regency," a New York Democratic Party organization led by Martin Van Buren, who would ultimately become president of the United States. By the late nineteenth century, such partisan organizations (now called "political machines") were commonplace, especially at the municipal level. Most operated in only a single urban ward or group of wards, although in some cases, and for certain periods of time, a machine might dominate the politics of an entire city.[15] Machines controlled the party nomination process and were adept a mobilizing party voters. Their leaders celebrated them as engines of democracy. A growing chorus of critics, however, charged them with having no agenda other than enriching themselves, and especially their "bosses."

Machines operated on the "spoils system" (from the expression "to the victor belong the spoils"), which involved awarding party nominations and government jobs to loyalists.[16] For example, after securing his grip on power in the early 1880s, "Blind Boss" Christopher Buckley, a saloon-keeper and leader of the San Francisco Democratic machine (who had lost his eyesight as a result of excessive drinking), made sure that public employees across the city, from hospital supervisors to janitors, were replaced with his friends, family members, and allies. To win a party nomination or get a government job, a candidate typically had to pay the machine money, sometimes in a bidding process. To keep their positions, appointees were generally required to make campaign contributions, known as "assessments," to the machine, commonly 2 to 7 percent of their salaries. When there were not enough patronage jobs to go around, machines would simply make more of them, using their control over government to establish new public boards and commissions. Machines also awarded their supporters lucrative, no-bid government contracts, notably to the printers who published the party newspaper and printed the party's election tickets. Printers favored by a machine were also frequently authorized to print government documents at prices several times the market rate, with the understanding that part of the resulting profits would be "donated" to the machine. One government printer in Albany, New York, boasted that between 1853 and 1859 his net profits totaled over $2 million (equivalent to nearly $58 million today, after adjusting for inflation).[17]

Public works contracts were commonly distributed in a similar fashion. The Tammany Hall machine, which dominated New York City under the leadership of William "Boss" Tweed, notoriously used construction of the New York County Courthouse as a pretext to dispense contracts to associates, who charged highly inflated prices for the work, with much of the proceeds ending up back in the pockets of Tweed and his friends. Tweed was eventually convicted of embezzlement and later died in prison, but the courthouse cost the city more than $13 million between 1869 and 1871 (approximately $240 million today, after adjusting for inflation) and remained unfinished until well after Tweed's departure. More generally, bosses were known to extort bribes from saloons and brothels in return for ensuring that temperance and antiprostitution laws were not enforced; to require companies to make payments (or grant stock) to the machine and its loyalists in return for a franchise (the exclusive right to operate a city service, such as a trolley line); and to exploit insider information for personal profit— buying land, for example, that was almost certain to increase in value because it was slotted for use in a city project.[18]

The control machines exercised over the levers of government also gave them substantial influence over the elections that kept them in power. Ticket distributors and other machine operatives maintained constant surveillance of voters at polling places, and election judges were themselves typically ma chine politicians. Even when organized as bipartisan panels on election day, these election judges frequently held a go-along, get-along attitude toward corruption that tolerated, in particular, the widespread practice of handing out cash in return for votes. Blind Boss Buckley was notorious for visiting polling places and paying loyal voters himself.[19] So long as a panel of election judges remained divided between both major parties, certain kinds of corruption that would give one party a notable advantage over the other remained off limits; but if one party was able to gain control of a panel, then nearly anything became possible.

Some of the tactics machines utilized required extensive organization. For example, a machine might "colonize" large numbers of paid voters, called "floaters," into a particular district on election day. In the hotly contested presidential election of 1888, the Republican national treasurer instructed local party leaders in Indiana to organize floaters into "blocks of five," each to be monitored and paid by a party representative. Democrats charged that the Republican presidential candidate, Benjamin Harrison, narrowly won Indiana and with it, the presidency, owing to these tactics, although historians dispute this allegation. Machines also hired "repeaters," who illegally cast multiple votes apiece. If these techniques failed to produce the desired results, machine operatives in some instances even falsified returns. One well-documented case that illustrated a whole host of shady activities occurred in the election of 1868, when New York City, then dominated by Boss Tweed, reported many more votes cast than eligible voters, for an apparent turnout rate of 143.8 percent.[20]

Reformers attacked the machines on a number of fronts. They tried to end the spoils system by instituting civil service reform: appointees would get their positions through merit examinations and could be dismissed only for cause, and assessments would be outlawed. Civil service reform made progress at the federal level, especially after Congress, in the face of public pressure, passed the Pendleton Act in 1883. The new law required federal appointees to take qualifying exams and barred them from paying party assessments. However, because the legislation applied only to certain federal jobs, patronage continued to flourish. Reformers also tried to end the use of floaters and repeaters by establishing voter registration systems, but these proved difficult to implement effectively, at least in part because election commissions usually remained under machine control and because a voter's qualifications had to be determined when he presented his ticket at the window—an often crowded and chaotic scene.[21] Increasingly, therefore, reformers began to see the ticket system itself as the root problem. Not only did it foster election-day disorder, in which corruption thrived, but all the various forms of voter bribery remained possible only when machine operatives could verify the votes they had paid for. The solution, reformers concluded, was to make voting secret, which meant replacing partisan tickets with an entirely new kind of ballot.

The Australian Ballot

Bribery, deception, and intimidation at election time were not uniquely American problems. In fact, the type of ballot reform that would soon prove popular in the United States was first implemented widely in Australia, which at that time was a collection of British colonies. "Before the [secret] ballot was in operation our elections were exceedingly riotous," one Australian politician recalled. "I have been in the balcony of an hotel during one of the city elections, when the raging mobs down in the street were so violent that I certainly would not have risked my life to have crossed the street."[22] In February and March 1856, three states—Tasmania, South Australia, and Victoria—passed election laws mandating a uniform ballot, printed at government expense and to be filled out by voters in secret. In the original Victorian system, voters crossed out the names of candidates they did not support, but similar laws that soon appeared throughout Australia had voters mark squares next to their desired candidates. The laws were widely regarded as successful.[23] According to one observer of the 1856 Victorian elections, "Subsequent experience has more than confirmed all the anticipations from this measure, both as to its nullifying effect upon bribery and intimidation, and, even more, its influence in restraining disorderly excesses and violence during the exciting times of political elections."[24]

Britain followed suit, adopting the "Australian ballot" in July 1872. Endorsement of the reform by such a prominent nation helped spark similar changes elsewhere over the next several years, including in Canada, Belgium, Luxembourg, and Italy. The new ballot finally reached the United States in February 1888 when the Kentucky state legislature mandated a secret ballot in the city of Louisville.[25] Greatly impressed with the reform, one Louisville

local reported later that year, "The election of last Tuesday was the first municipal election I have ever known which was not bought outright. As a
matter of fact no attempts at bribery were made."[26]

The first U.S. state to fully embrace the Australian ballot was Massachusetts. Members of the "Dutch Treat" club, a group of reformers from within
and outside the legislature, led the campaign, providing model legislation
from other jurisdictions and eventually drafting the bill signed into law in
May 1888.[27] Under the new statute, the secretary of the commonwealth was
responsible for the printing and delivery of ballots for statewide elections,
while city governments printed ballots for local elections and distributed
both the state-provided ballots and their own. Candidates could earn a spot
on the ballot by winning the nomination of a party that had received at least
3 percent of the vote in the previous election (in the relevant jurisdiction), or
via special conventions expressly organized for such nominations. Candidates could also qualify by submitting a petition with a sufficient number of
signatures: 1,000 for statewide elections, and 1 percent of the relevant electorate (but at least fifty) for subdivisions and municipal elections. The ballots listed candidates by office, with space for voters to write in their own
nominees, and "the party or political principle which he represent[ed]" was
recorded next to each candidate. The voter marked an X to the right of the
desired candidate. The law also abolished voting windows, requiring instead
private voting booths at all polling places, and mandated that only election
officials and voters filling out their ballots were allowed within six feet of
the booths or the ballot box. Any attempts by voters to communicate how
they were voting, or efforts by others to interfere with voting, were punishable with fines.[28]

After the Australian ballot was first used in Massachusetts in the 1889 election, supporters celebrated higher voter turnout and claimed numerous advantages, including greater efficiency and a fairer process.[29] Richard Henry
Dana III, the principal author of the law, boasted, "I have visited precincts
where, under the old system, coats were torn off the backs of voters, where
ballots of one kind have been snatched from voters' hands and others put in
their places, with threats against using any but the substituted ballots; and
under the new system all was orderly and peaceable."[30] Reactions from politicians outside reformist circles were mixed. Republicans in Massachusetts
were generally pleased, believing that the worst voter intimidation had

occurred in Democrat-controlled areas. Democrats, however, were divided: some welcomed the reform, but others worried that the secret ballot would weaken valuable party networks, depriving voters of a way to repay debts to party bosses or earn cash at election time. Some critics also charged that the new ballot was too complicated for illiterate voters, though the law did allow election officers to assist older voters who could not read and disabled voters who were unable to mark their ballots.[31]

After Massachusetts, the Australian ballot spread rapidly across numerous states. Later in 1889, Indiana, Minnesota, Missouri, Montana, Rhode Island, Wisconsin, and Tennessee (for some regions) passed similar laws. In 1890, Maryland, Mississippi, Vermont, Washington, and the territories of Oklahoma and Wyoming joined the movement. All of these laws followed the Australian model of a uniform ballot and secret voting, though their details varied. The Indiana ballot, for example, arranged candidates by party and allowed voters to vote party-line with a single mark. Some reformers, including Dana, worried that this would bias voters toward party-line voting and make it easy to discern how people had voted, since selecting individual candidates required more time in the voting booth.[32]

In New York State, meanwhile, despite having seen some of the earliest campaigning for ballot reform, legislative efforts to introduce the Australian ballot stalled. The state legislature passed bills in 1888 and 1889, but Governor David Hill, a Tammany Hall Democrat, vetoed both. In his 1889 veto message, Hill declared he was "unalterably opposed to any system of elections which will prevent the people from putting candidates in nomination at any time and voting for them by a printed ballot up to the very last moment before closing of the polls on election day. This is an inherent right under our free institutions, which the people will never knowingly surrender."[33] Reformers mounted another effort in 1890, this time presenting a petition with over 100,000 signatures to the state legislature. Although Hill continued to oppose the Australian ballot, he now invited the legislature to offer a less radical bill. The law that resulted included government printing of ballots and secret voting, but required separate ballots for each party. Voters were also permitted to bring completed "paster" tickets, provided by the parties, to attach to special blank ballots in order to facilitate party-line voting.[34]

The Ballot Debate in California

The success of ballot reforms in other states soon inspired activists in California. In the late 1880s an economic downturn, combined with a widespread perception that power was overly concentrated in the hands of bosses, provoked many Californians—especially in rural areas—to challenge the rule of Democratic and Republican machines. Thousands joined groups such as the antiplutocratic "Nationalist" clubs and the Farmers' Alliance, a reformist group founded in 1890 that opposed government subservience to "the narrow and selfish demands of a purse-proud oligarchy."[35] The emergence of these groups troubled the California political establishment. Wrote one worried Republican, "I don't think in my time I have seen so many evidences of disintegration in politics as now."[36] Recognizing that the parties continued to exercise outsized influence over elections through their control of the ballots, populist and labor activists began targeting this particular element of the machines' power as part of a wider campaign for political reform.[37]

The first major advocates for the Australian ballot in California were Franklin K. Lane and James G. Maguire. Lane had once been an organizer of the San Francisco Municipal Reform League, which had tried (and failed) to combat the influence of Blind Boss Buckley. By 1889, Lane led a group called the Young Men's Democratic League, which allied with the San Francisco Federated Trades Council (an association of labor unions) to lobby for ballot reform, and he organized a mass meeting in San Francisco that January in support of a bill. The next month, Maguire, a Democratic judge from San Francisco with close ties to the labor movement, addressed the state's joint legislative elections committee. "It is not a matter of Democracy and Republicanism, with the bosses, it is 'spoils,'" he declared. "Their motive is plunder and power."[38] Opponents claimed that the machinery associated with the Australian ballot was "ponderous and elaborate. It makes the whole act of approaching the polls, obtaining, marking and depositing the ballot, a weighty process, full of technical steps and bristling with penalties." Noting that the procedure "originated in an imperial colony," critics charged that it was "made for a people born and reared under the tutelage of the government, accustomed to bow to official authority."[39] Reformers, however, were undeterred.

Apparently influenced by Lane and Maguire (and their followers), the state Assembly in Sacramento passed an Australian ballot bill on March 1, 1889. Yet just three days later the Assembly reconsidered the bill and this time voted against it, with opposition coming from both major parties. Although the reasons for this reversal remain unclear, the defeat further convinced Lane that the Assembly was only after "boodle," referring to the income they allegedly reaped from bribery and corruption.[40]

Despite this initial setback, the California ballot reform movement gained strength in 1890. A number of San Francisco Democrats, who opposed the Blind Boss's control of their city, rallied for the Australian ballot at the state party convention that August. By the convention's end, the state Democratic platform included a promise that all party nominees would support the Australian ballot. At a rally with 2,000 supporters in San Francisco that October, Thomas V. Cator, a leader of the California Nationalist movement, exclaimed, "We have got a chance to down the bosses with the Australian ballot system: let us take advantage of it."[41]

The Democrats suffered heavy losses in the 1890 state elections, but by winter enough Republicans had voiced support for the Australian ballot that it seemed within reach. Four ballot reform bills appeared in the Assembly in early January 1891. The first, drafted by Maguire, called for the state to supply uniform ballot paper with a watermark kept secret until the election. Candidates would earn a spot on the ballot by obtaining the nomination of a party representing at least 3 percent of the voting population, or by turning in a petition with the signatures of 3 percent or 1,000 of the relevant jurisdiction's voters, whichever was lower. Each ballot would be numbered, and the number of each voter's ballot would be recorded and removed before the ballot was turned in. The second bill, proposed by the Democratic State Central Committee, was almost identical but included provisions that would allow party-line voting for presidential electors with a single mark, require matching time frames for nomination by party and petition, and guarantee workers two hours' paid leave to vote. The third bill, put forward by State Senator G. G. Goucher and Assemblyman F. H. Gould (both Democrats), was also similar but included no provisions for combating illegal voting and no paid leave. Finally, Republican Henry C. Dibble offered a reform bill without an Australian ballot. Under the system he proposed, parties would print their own tickets, but every voter would receive one of each from election officials. Inside the voting booth, the voter would choose a ticket and modify it as he wished before turning it in. The unused tickets would be destroyed, and the state would cover ticket-printing costs of any party that received at least 10 percent of the vote.[42]

The state Senate elections committee, meanwhile, offered a bill of its own on February 4, 1891. The committee had drafted it with input from Maguire and aimed to include "all the best features of the Australian law with such additions as the States using that law have found advisable." Not surprisingly, it closely resembled the bill Maguire had prepared for the Assembly.[43] In presenting the bill, the Senate committee promised that the "bribery and intimidation of voters would be effectually stopped," along with "the blackmailing practices of 'piece clubs' and other political parasites." The committee asserted that in other states, such as Massachusetts and Indiana, the Australian ballot had been "reported to be very effective . . . and to operate harmoniously and satisfactorily."[44]

Delays threatened the success of reform in the lower house. The bills introduced in January were formally read on February 12, after which they were placed in a long queue for a second reading. Assemblyman Gould, worried that the bills would not be taken up before the end of the legislative session, called for their immediate consideration on February 18. This special motion required two-thirds approval, however, and only forty-four assemblymen voted in favor, while thirty (all Republicans) opposed it. Numerous newspapers criticized lawmakers who had delayed the vote. The Sacramento *Record-Union* warned that they were "Digging a Republican Grave," because "no party can expect to bow to the will of the bosses in this matter and command the support of the people." Adoption of the measure, the paper added, would "[close] up the lucrative business of the vote hucksters."[45]

Acting more quickly than the Assembly, the Senate passed its bill with nearly unanimous support on February 26. The Assembly soon took up the Senate's substitute bill for consideration. Of its eighty members, thirty-eight were expected to vote for the Senate bill, only three short of a majority. With success hinging on such a small margin, both supporters and opponents waged vigorous campaigns to win over a few more votes. Reform groups lobbied members of the Assembly who had promised to support ballot reform in general but not yet the Senate bill in particular. Republican Assemblyman Henry Dibble, the leading opponent, threatened legal action against the lobbyist who led this effort. He also mocked the allegedly impractical size of the Australian ballot by circulating a three-foot-long "sample" ballot. Impassioned speeches on the Assembly floor complemented these efforts. In a March 6 speech, Dibble warned that the bill would "upset and overthrow our political system" and destroy the two major parties, and that "anarchy would follow." In response, Democratic Assemblyman T. W. H. Shanahan noted the widespread support for the Australian ballot and its potential to rein in the bosses. "The Legislature owe[s] more to the people than to any political organization," he declared, and "if either or both of the political parties had not the right to sustain them, both ought to go down."[46]

Dibble made a final effort to stop the bill the next day. Expecting a vote on March 7, he sent a number of San Francisco Republicans who had promised to support ballot reform away from Sacramento for the day. Dibble planned to bring his own ballot reform bill to a vote the next week, with the San Franciscans present to pass it. Before a vote was called on the Senate bill, however, Shanahan requested a roll call and noted the absences. Accusing the Republicans of trying to evade their ballot reform pledge, he insisted that the vote be postponed, and the Assembly agreed. Dibble then tried to bring his own bill up for consideration, but Shanahan succeeded in blocking the motion by a single vote.[47]

When most of the missing assemblymen returned on March 9, Dibble admitted defeat. Still, he proposed two amendments to the Senate bill, which Shanahan allowed so long as the Senate would be permitted to reject them. The first raised the threshold for nomination by parties or petitions from 3 percent to 5 percent; the second created an easy way to vote party-line for presidential electors. This amended bill easily passed the Assembly, 66 to 3, and the Senate approved it two days later.[48]

The final California bill had much in common with the Massachusetts law of 1888 and was most similar to the Assembly bill originally proposed by the Democratic State Central Committee. On the new government-printed ballots, candidates would be arranged by office, with their parties identified, and voters would mark each choice with an X. Ballots would be numbered for record-keeping purposes, and workers would receive two hours off, with pay, to vote. The bill provided for the same six-foot perimeter around the voters and the same prohibitions against outsider interference and voters announcing their choices as in the Massachusetts bill. County governments would provide ballots for state and county contests, while towns and cities would provide separate ballots for their own elections. All of the ballots—across all jurisdictions—would be printed on uniform, water-marked paper provided by California's secretary of state. Nominations and party-line presidential voting would operate as the Dibble amendments specified. Beyond those amendments, the only significant deviation from Maguire's original proposal was that the voter could also make a single mark to vote party-line across the entire ballot.[49]

The ballot reform bill ultimately arrived at the desk of Governor Henry Markham, a Republican elected the previous fall. In his inaugural address on January 8, 1891, he had refused to commit himself one way or the other on the Australian ballot:

> During the last campaign I received many communications, asking for an expression of my views on the Australian ballot system, which I answered by saying that I had no prejudices either for or against the system, and would approve any law that would materially improve the method now in use in this State. Nothing has transpired that has caused me to change my views, but I suggest that you make a thorough examination of the practical workings of the Australian system before determining to adopt it instead of our own. Every honest voter would hail with joy the adoption of this or any other method of conducting elections, whereby the sacredness of the ballot-box would be better preserved.[50]

Now, after two months of debate and politicking in the legislature, the future of the Australian ballot in California was in the governor's hands.

NOTES

1. "Our Solons in Sacramento," *Examiner* (San Francisco), 8 Mar. 1891; Erik Falk Petersen, "The Struggle for the Australian Ballot in California," *California Historical Quarterly* 51, no. 3 (Fall 1972): 238. See also *The Journal of the Assembly during the Twenty-Ninth Session of the Legislature of the State of California* (Sacramento, 1891), 681, available at http://books.google.com/books?id=JK03AAAAIAAJ.
2. Eldon Cobb Evans, *A History of the Australian Ballot System in the United States* (Chicago: University of Chicago Press, 1917), 7, 13.
3. *Journal of the Assembly*, 697; *The Journal of the Senate of the State of California during the Twenty-Ninth Session of the Legislature of the State of California* (Sacramento, 1891), 703,

available at http://books.google.com/books/reader?id=aSRNAAAAYAAJ; Petersen, "The Struggle," 239. The assemblymen's and senators' party affiliations can be found in Don A. Allen Sr., *Legislative Sourcebook: The California Legislature and Reapportionment, 1849–1965* (Assembly of the State of California, 1965).

4. Adam Winkler, "Voters' Rights and Parties' Wrongs: Early Political Party Regulation in the State Courts, 1886–1915," *Columbia Law Review* 100, no. 3 (Apr. 2000): 874. See also Richard Hofstadter, *The Idea of a Party System: The Rise of Legitimate Opposition in the United States, 1780–1840* (Berkeley: University of California Press, 1972).

5. Joel H. Silbey, *The American Political Nation, 1838–1893* (Stanford: Stanford University Press, 1991), 51–52; *Democratic Review* (Apr. 1856) quoted on 48.

6. Winkler, "Voters' Rights," 881, 876. Quotation from V. O. Key, *Politics, Parties, and Pressure Groups*, 4th ed. (New York: Thomas Y. Crowell, 1962), 411 (at 876 in Winkler).

7. Malcolm Crook and Tom Crook, "Reforming Voting Practices in a Global Age: The Making and Remaking of the Modern Secret Ballot in Britain, France and the United States, c. 1600 to c. 1950," *Past and Present* 212, no. 1 (2011): 203–207.

8. Richard Franklin Bensel, *The American Ballot Box in the Mid-Nineteenth Century* (Cambridge: Cambridge University Press, 2004), 16–17.

9. Ibid., 15.

10. Petersen, "The Struggle," 228. The article quoted appeared in the *San Francisco Bulletin*, 29 Sept. 1877. "Coolie" was a racial slur used against Chinese.

11. Bensel, *American Ballot Box*, 9–14, 40–42. When tallying returns, election judges would compare the number of names on the clerk's list to the number of votes cast. "Where there were too few votes, election officials simply assumed that some voters had not voted for that office or offices. . . . Where there were too many votes, . . . most officials . . . [would] put all the tickets back in the box and randomly draw out the requisite number of excess votes. These tickets were then destroyed and the count was appropriately adjusted" (50n56).

12. Evans, *Australian Ballot System*, 7. "Big Tim" Sullivan's perfumed ballots are mentioned in Morton Keller, *Affairs of State: Public Life in Nineteenth Century America* (Cambridge, MA: Belknap Press of Harvard University Press, 1977), 523.

13. This was not only the received wisdom but the view of leading European political philosophers, such as Rousseau, who considered secret balloting evidence of moral decline, and John Stewart Mill, who although he endorsed the secret ballot early in his career, in order to protect working-class voters from retribution by their employers, later renounced it, arguing that voters would be less likely to vote for purely self-interested reasons if they had to cast their vote publicly. On Rousseau, see Crook and Crook, "Reforming Voting Practices," 211; on Mill, see Bruce L. Kinzer, "J. S. Mill and the Secret Ballot," *Historical Reflections* 1 (Summer 1978): 19–39.

14. Michael Brunet, "The Secret Ballot Issue in Massachusetts Politics from 1851 to 1853," *New England Quarterly* 25, no. 3 (1952): 354–362; Evans, *Australian Ballot System*, 7–9.

15. M. Craig Brown and Charles M. Halaby, "Machine Politics in America, 1870–1945," *Journal of Interdisciplinary History* 17, no. 3 (1987): 587–612.

16. The term "spoils system" derives from an 1832 speech to the U.S. Senate by William Marcy, a leader of the Albany Regency: "The politicians of the United States are not so fastidious as some gentlemen are, as to disclosing the principles on which they act. They boldly preach what they practice. When they are contending for victory, they avow their intention of enjoying the fruits of it. If they are defeated, they expect to retire from office. If they are successful, they claim, as a matter of right, the advantages of success. They see nothing wrong in the rule, that to the victor belong the spoils of the enemy." Quoted in Hofstadter, *Idea of a Party System,* 250.

17. William A. Bullough, *The Blind Boss and His City* (Berkeley: University of California Press, 1979), 129–130; Alexander Callow Jr., "San Francisco's Blind Boss," *Pacific Historical Review* 25, no. 3 (Aug. 1956): 263–264; Mark W. Summers, *The Plundering Generation: Corruption and the Crisis of the Union, 1849–1861* (New York: Oxford University Press, 1987), 29, 26, 45; Ari Hoogenboom, "The Pendleton Act and the Civil Service," *American Historical Review* 64, no. 2 (1959): 302.

18. Keller, *Affairs of State,* 240; "Landmark Tweed Courthouse Has a Checkered History," Lower Manhattan Construction Command Center, 5 Mar. 2004, http://www .lowermanhattan.info/news/landmark_tweed_courthouse_has_65546.aspx; Terrence J. MacDonald, introduction to William Riorden, *Plunkitt of Tammany Hall: A Series of Very Plain Talks on Very Practical Politics* (Boston: Bedford Books, 1994), 7.

19. See Summers, *Plundering Generation,* 63, for details on prohibitions against bribing voters; Keller, *Affairs of State,* 523; Winkler, "Voters' Rights," 883.

20. Evans, *Australian Ballot System,* 11; L. E. Fredman, *The Australian Ballot: The Story of an American Reform* (Lansing: Michigan State University Press, 1968), 22; James L. Baumgardner, "The Election of 1888: How Corrupt?," *Presidential Studies Quarterly* 14, no. 3 (1984): 416–427; Bensel, *American Ballot Box,* 156–159; Walter Dean Burnham, "Those High Nineteenth-Century Turnout Rates: Fact or Fiction?," *Journal of Interdisciplinary History* 16, no. 4 (1986): 168. Burnham argues that such fraudulently high rates as reported in the New York City elections of 1868 were rare.

21. Hoogenboom, "Pendleton Act," 303, notes that the number of federal jobs covered by the Pendleton Act grew from 11 percent in 1883 to 46 percent in 1900. Bensel, *American Ballot Box,* 20–21. The first voter registration law was approved in Massachusetts in 1800, and an increasing number of such laws were passed after 1860, usually applied to large cities. Yet the ineffectiveness of these laws can be seen in the election of 1868 in New York City, mentioned in the text, which produced a turnout of 143.8 percent despite the fact that a voter registration law was supposedly in operation there. Joseph P. Harris, *The Registration of Voters in the United States* (Washington, DC: Brookings Institution, 1929), 65, 67, 71–74.

22. UK parliamentary testimony of Francis S. Dutton (1869), quoted in Evans, *Australian Ballot System,* 17.

23. Crook and Crook, "Reforming Voting Practices," 218; Fredman, *Australian Ballot,* 7–10.

24. William Westgarth, *The Colony of Victoria* (London: Sampson Low, Son, and Marston, 1864), 171.

25. Fredman, *Australian Ballot*, 11–17, 31–32; Evans, *Australian Ballot System*, 17–19; John H. Wigmore, *The Australian Ballot System as Embodied in the Legislation of Various Countries* (Boston: Charles C. Soule, 1889), 15–24.

26. *The Nation* (13 Dec. 1888), quoted in Wigmore, *Australian Ballot System*, 23–24.

27. Fredman, *Australian Ballot*, 38–40; Evans, *Australian Ballot System*, 19; Wigmore, *Australian Ballot System*, 25–26.

28. The Massachusetts law is reprinted in *Electoral Reform, with the Massachusetts Ballot Reform Act and New York (Saxton) Bill* (New York: Society for Political Education, 1889), 23–35. Quote from §5 on p. 25.

29. Fredman, *Australian Ballot*, 39.

30. *Annals of the American Academy of Political and Social Science,* quoted in Evans, *Australian Ballot System,* 23.

31. Geoffrey Blodgett, *The Gentle Reformers: Massachusetts Democrats in the Cleveland Era* (Cambridge, MA: Harvard University Press, 1966), 115–116. The provision for older illiterate voters and disabled voters was §25 of the law, which appears in *Electoral Reform,* 33–34.

32. Evans, *Australian Ballot System*, 27; Fredman, *Australian Ballot*, 48.

33. Quoted in Evans, *Australian Ballot System,* 24.

34. Ibid., 19–20; Richard L. McCormick, *From Realignment to Reform: Political Change in New York State, 1893–1910* (Ithaca, NY: Cornell University Press, 1981), 114–115; Fredman, *Australian Ballot,* 51–52.

35. R. Hal Williams, *The Democratic Party and California Politics, 1880–1896* (Stanford: Stanford University Press, 1973), 134–138, convention platform quoted on 138.

36. Letter from John F. Swift to Stephen M. White (29 Apr. 1890), quoted in ibid., 139.

37. Petersen, "The Struggle," 230.

38. Ibid., 230–231, quotation at 231.

39. "The Australian Ballot," *Daily Alta California* (San Francisco), 28. Jan. 1889, 4, available at http://cdnc.ucr.edu/cdnc.

40. Petersen, "The Struggle," 230–231.

41. Ibid., 232–233, quotation on 233.

42. Ibid., 234–235; "The Democratic Reform Bill," *Examiner* (San Francisco), 11 Jan. 1891.

43. Petersen, "The Struggle," 235, quoting "Proposed Laws," *Morning Call* (San Francisco), 29 Jan. 1891, 8; *Journal of the Senate,* 279, available at http://books.google.com/books/reader?id=aSRNAAAAYAAJ.

44. *Journal of the Senate,* 280.

45. Petersen, "The Struggle," 236; "Digging a Republican Grave," *Record-Union* (Sacramento), 26 Feb. 1891, 2, available at http://cdnc.ucr.edu/cdnc.

46. Petersen, "The Struggle," 236–238. Quotations are from "Among State Legislators: The Ballot Reform Bill the Cause of Several Long Arguments," *Examiner* (San Francisco), 7 Mar. 1891.

47. Petersen, "The Struggle," 238–239; "Our Solons in Sacramento."
48. Petersen, "The Struggle," 239.
49. *The Statutes of California and Amendments to the Codes Passed at the Twenty-Ninth Session of the Legislature* (Sacramento, 1891), 165–178, available at http://192.234.213.35/clerkarchive/archive/Statutes/1891/1891.PDF. See also Petersen, "The Struggle," 239.
50. The speech is available online at http://governors.library.ca.gov/addresses/18-Markham.html. Fredman, *Australian Ballot,* 66, gives the date of this speech as January 7.

·{ 11 }·

Labor, Capital, and Government:
The Anthracite Coal Strike of 1902

IN LATE OCTOBER 1902, President Theodore Roosevelt felt relieved after months of anxiety and uncertainty. Workers in Pennsylvania's anthracite coal industry had been on strike for five months, threatening to leave eastern cities in the cold without enough heating fuel for the winter. Anthracite workers and business owners had finally reached an agreement after months of stalemate, and anthracite production resumed on October 23. The threat of a severe fuel shortage had greatly disturbed the president, but with the crisis averted Roosevelt wrote that he felt "like throwing up my hands and going to the circus; but as that is not possible I think I shall try a turkey shoot or bear hunt or something of the kind instead."[1]

As the anthracite workers returned to the mines, they were joined by members of a federal commission, appointed by the president to research conditions in the industry. The compromise that the workers and employers had agreed to stipulated that this neutral body would ultimately decide terms of employment and various operational questions in the anthracite region. After a week-long investigation in the mines, the commission began in November to hear testimony from hundreds of representatives of the workers and their employers, the mine operators. The hearings closed in February 1903, after which the commission began formulating its final judgments.

At issue were numerous disagreements typical in labor disputes as well as a few that were unique to the anthracite industry. Nearly all of the workers who performed actual mining were paid by the amount of coal they extracted, while other workers at the mines were typically paid by the hour. Both groups often complained that their pay was too low for such a perilous industry and that their income failed to support a decent standard of living. The miners in particular charged that the mine operators often undercounted the amount mined, which cut further into compensation. Workers throughout the industry also argued that the length of the workday was too onerous, especially given the nature of the work. The mine operators denied all of this. Wages and hours, they insisted, were perfectly acceptable, and what the miners considered undercounting was simply appropriate accommodation for coal impurities.

Arguably the workers' most significant grievance was that their employers refused to recognize the national coal union, the United Mine Workers of America (UMW). At the commission hearings, UMW president John Mitchell had declared that anthracite workers had a right to collective action and that "experience shows that the trade agreement is the only effective method by which it is possible to regulate questions arising between employers and employed in large industries."[2] The mine operators countered that the UMW, which had originated outside of the anthracite fields, had no right to meddle in their industry and was indirectly responsible for violence and harassment against non-union men during the strike. This lack of discipline, they had long argued, demonstrated the UMW's inadequacy as a bargaining partner.

As the commission adjourned its hearings in mid-February 1903, its members knew that their work would set an important precedent for industrial governance going forward. The commission embodied a novel form of federal intervention into a labor dispute. Past U.S. presidents had helped put down strikes that threatened federal property or public safety, but the anthracite strike of 1902 marked the first time the government acted to resolve a strike both without force and without such a clear legal justification. The decisions of the commission would therefore have important ramifications, not only for the anthracite industry, but potentially for American business–labor relations more generally. With copious amounts of data, testimony, and research to inform them, the commission members began the process of deciding how an American industry should, and would, operate.

The American Labor Movement

The earliest American organized labor groups were skilled workers' "trade societies," first formed in the 1790s in response to the threat of mass manufacturing. As rising competition induced employers to lower prices and wages, urban "journeymen" craftsmen organized trade societies to resist what they viewed as "the cupidity of the employers, who not content with taking every advantage of the working men to reduce their wages, carried on a system of encroaching upon their time to such a degree, that they were literally reduced to a state of slavery."[3] These societies, essentially the first American labor unions, fought for increased wages, established product standards, and demanded less arduous working conditions. In pursuit of these goals, the societies orchestrated boycotts and strikes (which they called "turnouts"), demanded collective bargaining, and enforced closed shops (businesses essentially prohibited by their employees from hiring non-union workers) to pressure employers to meet their demands.[4] Although wage data from this period are scarce, evidence suggests that many skilled workers managed to maintain their status and their wages through the early 1800s.[5]

It was not until the late 1820s that American labor organized into what several historians consider a coherent "movement."[6] A recession beginning in 1819 wiped out many trade societies, but economic recovery in the 1820s brought about their return, along with the first labor unions among unskilled workers.[7] As before the recession, these groups initially focused on local issues without coordinating across organizations. The first sign of such coordination came in 1827 when Philadelphia unions partnered in forming the Mechanics' Union of Trade Associations, the first American labor organization to incorporate multiple trades. Leaving strikes and contract negotiations to its member unions, the Mechanics' Union focused on higher-level goals, such as economic equality and a common working-class identity. The latter, it was believed, would in turn facilitate "a just balance of power, both mental, moral, political, and scientific, between all the various classes and individuals which constitute society at large."[8]

This lofty conception of working-class interests turned labor leaders' attention to politics. The Philadelphia Mechanics' Union reflected this shift in 1828 when it called for workers to "unite under the banner of equal rights" and formed a Working Men's Party to compete in elections.[9] This party and others it inspired supported causes intended to empower the working class, such as public schooling, the end of debtors' prisons, direct election of government officers, and weakening of banks and industrial monopolies.[10] The workingmen's parties enjoyed widespread support in the northeastern states and even won some local contests, as a growing labor press presented their platforms and core principles to readers. Commenting on labor's rising political influence, one such paper boasted of "symptoms of a revolution, which will be second to none save that of '76."[11]

Despite their optimism and energy, the workingmen's parties were short-lived. Infighting among leaders and meddling by outside politicians led to their rapid decline in the early 1830s, and much of the labor vote shifted to the Democratic Party. The workingmen's parties left their mark, however, and in the ensuing years state governments considered and eventually acted upon a number of their proposals. In the 1830s and 1840s, for example, New York and Pennsylvania passed laws fostering public education, and numerous states banned debtors' prisons over the same period.[12]

A Revival of Union Activity in the 1830s

The dissolution of the workingmen's parties marked the end of the labor movement's first phase, but economic conditions in the mid-1830s set the stage for a new burst of union activity. A thriving economy, greater cohesiveness among laborers, and a rapidly increasing cost of living led to a proliferation of unions. Scholars estimate that union membership grew to more than 40,000 workers over the mid-1830s and that unions orchestrated at least 168 strikes between 1833 and 1837.[13] By 1836, this surge sparked thirteen multi-union "city central" organizations, similar to the defunct Philadelphia Mechanics' Union. These city centrals played a more active role in labor disputes than their predecessor by helping to organize member societies' strikes and boycotts.[14] Unions attempted national collaboration as well. Five trades formed nationwide organizations in the mid-1830s, and in 1834 several northeastern city centrals banded together to form the National Trades Union, America's first national labor association. These national bodies, however, exercised little tangible influence.[15]

One of the most significant victories for labor in the 1830s was the reduction of the traditional dawn-to-dusk workday to ten hours in many skilled crafts. Some unions had agitated for this beginning in the prior decade, but the movement took on new life during the economic boom of the mid-1830s. Reasoning that workers deserved "sufficient time each day for the cultivation of their mind and for self-improvement" (as one carpenters' union put it), unions across the country organized strikes for this purpose.[16] The most notable one came in 1835 when workers from seventeen different trades arranged the nation's first "general" strike in Philadelphia.[17] Although opponents argued that "to be idle several of the most useful hours of the morning and evening will surely lead to intemperance and ruin," skilled laborers in several cities and industries won ten-hour workdays as a standard.[18]

Employer Opposition

Employers fought back against the emergence of organized labor from the beginning. As early as 1806, for example, employers took journeymen's trade societies to court for violating the common law prohibition against malicious conspiracies. There were a number of successful suits against the societies, in which courts found laborers guilty of conspiring to inflate wages and to prevent employers from hiring whomever they wished.[19] "A combination of workmen to raise their wages," one judge declared, served only "to benefit themselves" and "to injure those who do not join their society. The rule of law condemns both."[20] Employers again turned to the courts for assistance in the 1830s. Although the employers often won these cases, unions proved effective in expressing their outrage. In one instance in 1836, 27,000 New Yorkers burned an effigy of a judge who had taken action against a tailors' union.[21] Labor historians have speculated that such reactions may have intimidated some judges into siding with unions in future cases, including one significant 1842 Massachusetts decision that held unions legal so long as they had "useful and honorable purposes."[22]

Economic Crisis and New Pressure for Reform

The 1842 Massachusetts decision arrived too late for many unions. A new economic downturn beginning in 1837 sent wages plummeting and triggered significant unemployment, nearly wiping out the journeymen's societies and factory unions and destroying all of the city and national bodies.[23] In addition, mounting competition and an influx of immigrant labor were said to have undercut both wages and working conditions.[24] Outside the workplace, poverty forced many urban laborers into crowded tenement houses, which one observer described as "perfect hive[s] of human beings without comforts and mostly without common necessaries; in many cases huddled together like brutes."[25]

As life in the cities and factories grew ever harder to bear, many laborers pondered societal reforms they hoped would offer an escape. Some dabbled in collectivist lifestyles, such as labor-based organized societies or worker-owned cooperative businesses, but most of these experiments failed.[26] Many workers also put their hopes in the "new agrarianism" movement, which demanded that workers receive tracts of public land to ensure a more equitable distribution of national wealth and end their dependence on employers. The National Reform Association, founded in 1845, championed a "Natural Right to Land" and gained many followers in its early years. However, the new agrarians did not achieve significant legislative success until much later, in 1862, when the Homestead Act opened western public lands to settlers.[27]

More relevant to the average laborer in the 1840s was the campaign to extend the ten-hour workday to factories. With backing from the National Reform Association and widespread public support—one Massachusetts petition for a ten-hour day was 130 feet long—several states enacted ten-hour laws in the late 1840s and 1850s.[28] These laws, however, almost always included caveats that allowed employees to agree to contracts with longer workdays. Employers argued that this freed workers to sell their labor as they wished, but reformers called the contract clauses "most egregious flummery," which effectively enabled employers to refuse a ten-hour day.[29] As the reformers expected, these watered-down laws did little to reduce working hours in practice.[30]

A New Direction

Labor unions, all but wiped out in the 1840s, reemerged in the next decade with a new focus on local and industry-specific problems. Not only were mid-century unions more independent, but many were more active than their predecessors, orchestrating approximately 400 strikes between 1853 and 1854, many of which proved successful. By 1854, for example, trade workers in New York City had seen an average raise of 20 to 25 percent over their 1850 wages.

This flurry of activity, however, was not to last. A recession in 1854–1855 and a steeper downturn in 1857 wiped out many unions, though some workers were able to retain their gains from earlier in the decade.[31]

A more durable resurgence began in the 1860s, as wartime activity lifted average wages but not always fast enough to keep pace with prices.[32] The number of American labor unions surged from 79 in 1863 to 270 by the end of 1864, with a record high of over 200,000 members. (This trend was almost entirely confined to the Northeast and Midwest. Only 3 of the 270 unions were located in the Confederacy.)[33] City and national organizations reappeared alongside a vocal labor press, which saw the creation of 120 new journals from 1863 to 1873. Despite the proliferation of labor groups, there were relatively few strikes during this period, as the unions were often able to secure better wages without such actions.[34] Frustrated employers complained that the rejuvenated unions made "business-like calculations and arrangements, especially such as involve prices for work, and time of completion and delivery . . . quite impracticable," and they formed associations of their own to resist labor's influence.[35]

The year 1866 saw the creation of the National Labor Union (NLU), which was supposed to coordinate the national labor movement. Under the charismatic leadership of iron molder William Sylvis, the NLU primarily pursued political reform. Its first major campaign was for an eight-hour workday. Although six states enacted eight-hour laws in response to NLU pressure, these laws contained the same loopholes that had weakened earlier ten-hour statutes. "For all practical purposes they might as well have never been placed on the statute books," complained one observer, "and can only be described as frauds on the laboring class." As workers voiced disappointment, the NLU shifted its attention to currency reform, aiming to replace the nation's gold-backed currency with a more flexible one linked, ultimately, to overall economic activity. Although NLU leaders believed such a shift would give "to laborers a fair compensation for their products, and to capital a just reward for its uses," they were unable to convince a large proportion of laborers.[36]

An Anthracite Union

In Pennsylvania the resurgent unionism of the 1860s saw the creation of the first industry-wide union of anthracite coal workers. Anthracite was a type of coal used for domestic heating, fueling steamboats and trains, and especially industrial iron smelting. The nation's supply of anthracite coal was concentrated almost exclusively in a 490-square-mile region of northeastern Pennsylvania.[37] Wage cuts in the late 1850s had caused "a degree of suffering and bitterness never before known in the region," and the mine operators had simultaneously ordered deeper excavation, heightening the risk of blasting accidents, mine collapses, and asphyxiation by toxic gas.[38] In response to these conditions, anthracite workers began forming local unions in 1860. These unions won raises from the operators as the Civil War boosted demand for coal and emptied the labor market. Wages fell back to antebellum lows, however, after the war and a number of failed strikes in 1865. By the late 1860s the scattered anthracite unions seemed largely powerless.[39]

Two developments spurred anthracite workers to organize on an industry-wide basis in 1869. First, mine operators had begun forming business associations, and their workers feared that they were colluding to depress wages and working conditions. Laborers from the different anthracite districts believed that only concerted opposition to these associations would prove effective. Second, in response to the NLU-led effort on working hours, the Pennsylvania legislature had passed an eight-hour law with the contract loophole in 1867. Workers from the southern and middle districts of the anthracite region had struck in July 1868 in an attempt to write airtight eight-hour-day provisions into their contracts. Their failure led many workers to seek greater coordination. Another ineffective strike in the southern district the following December only strengthened this conviction.[40]

In March 1869, unions throughout the region formed the General Council of the Workingmen's Associations of the Anthracite Coal Fields of Pennsylvania, commonly referred to as the Workingmen's Benefit Association (WBA).[41] The WBA made its first move on May 10 when members suspended mining to prevent a possible surplus of coal on the market and an expected wage cut. Some in the press attacked this effort to keep coal prices high, but the union insisted that it only sought a "steady, healthy market which will afford to the operators and dealers fair interest on their investments and at the same time receive for our share a fair day's wages for a fair day's work."[42] Although many workers in the northern district did not participate, the suspension exerted enough pressure on southern-district operators that they agreed to "sliding scale" wages, which would rise and fall with coal prices but could never decline below a set minimum. By autumn 1869, about 85 percent of the region's 35,000 anthracite workers had joined the WBA.[43]

The WBA's success in 1869 marked the height of its power. In November of that year southern-district mine operators created their own organization, the Anthracite Board of Trade, to defend their interests against the union. Over the next several years, the WBA and the Board were locked in battle, with further strikes in March–July 1870 and January–July 1871. Neither was as successful for the workers as the 1869 suspension, however, and each resulted in wage reductions rather than increases. The 1871 strike, which became violent at times and saw state militia sent in to maintain order, particularly weakened the WBA and nearly wiped it out altogether in the northern district.[44]

The Tumultuous 1870s

As anthracite workers struggled to maintain the WBA, the national labor movement coped with difficulties of its own in the early 1870s. Popular NLU leader William Sylvis had died in 1869, a loss that one labor paper called a "National Calamity."[45] Without Sylvis, the NLU quickly faded, largely disappearing by 1872. Meanwhile another major economic downturn struck in 1873, dramatically driving up joblessness. As desperate laborers abandoned efforts for better pay and working conditions, estimated union membership nationwide fell from 300,000 to just 50,000 by 1877.[46]

The depression fomented occasionally violent unrest among workers, which much of the public attributed to the influence of foreign socialists and anarchists. Many German Marxists immigrated to America in the 1870s, bringing with them revolutionary rhetoric and radical organizations. As these voices grew louder, an increasing number of Americans began to see all labor activism as radical.[47] At the same time, confrontations between unemployed protesters and law enforcement further damaged labor's reputation. Perhaps the most famous incident occurred on January 13, 1874, at New York City's Tompkins Square Park. A crowd of unemployed workers gathered hoping to make their needs known and expecting to hear Mayor William Havemeyer speak about relief, but police had withdrawn the group's permit after learning that radicals linked to the International Workingmen's Association, a European-based Marxist organization, planned to speak as well.

After an aggressive police intervention and ensuing panic injured numerous participants and bystanders, the *New York Times* reported that the "persons arrested yesterday seem all to have been foreigners—chiefly Germans or Irishmen. Communism is not a weed of native growth."[48]

The WBA Collapses

For a few years, the depression seemed to spare the anthracite industry, and coal prices remained steady at pre-1873 levels. A government investigation later attributed this stability to cartelization of the sector.[49] The railroads that served the anthracite fields had begun buying up coal lands and mines in the late 1860s, and a few powerful roads tightly controlled the industry. The Reading Railroad, for instance, held a third of the anthracite fields—over 95,000 acres—by the mid-1870s. This oligopoly began pooling coal distribution and managing prices in 1873, insulating the industry from the downturn and effectively protecting wages as well.[50]

Anthracite workers' relatively good fortune ended in 1875 when southern-district WBA members struck against an industry-wide wage cut. The loss of income during the "long strike," lasting from January to June, pushed strikers to their physical limits. According to one observer,

> Hundreds of families rose in the morning to breakfast on a crust of bread and a glass of water, who did not know where a bit of dinner was to come from. Day after day, men, women and children went to the adjoining woods to dig roots and pick herbs to keep body and soul together, and still the strike went on with no visible sign of surrender.[51]

The operators held firm, and the strike ultimately failed. In fact, the terms under which workers returned to the mines were worse than before the strike—for example, there would no longer be a guaranteed minimum rate for sliding-scale wages—and the crippled WBA soon dissolved.[52]

The infamous "Molly Maguire" trials of 1876 and 1877 further degraded the standing of anthracite workers in Pennsylvania. Throughout the 1860s and 1870s there had been a string of murders of mining and government officials in the region, including six in the months after the long strike, attributed to a rumored conspiracy of Irish laborers called the Molly Maguires.[53] National media had reported a "reign of lawlessness in the coal regions," which—in the minds of many readers—conflated all anthracite labor activity with the Mollies.[54] In 1873, Reading Railroad president Franklin Gowen hired the Pinkerton detective agency to sniff out Mollies in a local Irish fraternal organization, the Ancient Order of Hibernians. When the first suspects were tried in 1876, Gowen asserted that the Order and the Mollies were one and the same, and that their "purpose was to make the business of mining coal in this country a terror and a fear; to secure for the leading men in this society profitable positions and the control of . . . every colliery [coal mine]."[55] Prosecutors convicted about fifty workers of Molly-related crimes and sent twenty to the gallows. Although it is doubtful that a well-organized Molly Maguire conspiracy ever existed, the trials hardened negative public perceptions of anthracite workers and their possible connections to violent criminality.[56]

The Great Railroad Strike

The tensions of the 1870s climaxed in July 1877 when railroad workers across the country struck against wage cuts. The demonstrations interrupted rail operations nationwide, with such widespread effects that one paper deemed the event a "labor revolution."[57] The strike proved unusually destructive as striking workers in numerous cities engaged in violent confrontations with state troops. The worst occurred in Pittsburgh, which saw arson, vandalism, and looting as workers traded gunfire with Pennsylvania soldiers.[58] In the anthracite fields, mine workers struck as well in a demonstration that attracted 5,000 National Guardsmen to police the region.[59] Concerned about the chaotic and expanding strike, President Rutherford B. Hayes summoned an emergency Cabinet meeting on July 26 and soon commanded the military to use all force necessary to restore order. Troops intervened in several cities to protect railroad property, and within a few days the Great Railroad Strike was over.[60]

Although the public had at first been largely sympathetic to the strikers, the resulting chaos frightened many citizens and further blighted labor's reputation. Critics in the press raised questions about the influence of outside radicals, with one insisting that the revolt was "an attempt of communists and vagabonds to coerce society, [and] an endeavor to undermine American institutions."[61] In the strike's aftermath, businesses redoubled their opposition to organized labor by pressuring their employees not to join unions and pursuing conspiracy charges in the courts, and several states passed laws limiting unionization.[62]

Labor Resurgent

The Knights of Labor

Amid the disarray of the 1870s, the foundations were quietly laid for a labor organization of unprecedented influence. In December 1869, Philadelphia tailors had founded the Noble and Holy Order of the Knights of Labor, a secret society that aspired to collect "all branches of labor into a compact whole."[63] The Knights founded many assemblies over the 1870s, including a number among anthracite workers, and organized a national body in January 1878.[64] Three years later, the Knights dropped much of the secrecy from their operations and saw a rapid expansion to over 100,000 members by 1885. Although the reform-minded national leadership generally disapproved of strikes, walk-outs by local assemblies were often highly successful. One notable strike involving the Wabash Railroad in 1885, which crippled rail commerce in the Southwest, ended in a resounding victory that elevated the Knights' growing prestige. By 1886 the organization boasted over 700,000 members.[65]

The Knights of Labor peaked that year and soon declined. Southwestern railroad workers attempted another strike in 1886, but after strikebreakers and Pinkerton guards successfully foiled them, disappointed rail workers began leaving the Knights. The organization suffered another defeat in Chicago, where meatpackers had begun striking for an eight-hour day that spring. Terence Powderly, the strike-averse leader of the Knights, ordered them back to work in November. Furious meatpackers denounced national labor officials as "guilty of an act of heartless cruelty, as well as incompetency," and many left the Order altogether.[66]

Chicago had also been the scene of a notorious incident that same year, when four strikers seeking an eight-hour day were killed in a confrontation with police on May 3. At a protest the next day at Haymarket Square, an anarchist tossed a bomb at police, sparking a gunfight that killed eleven people and injured over a hundred others. Although no labor organization had anything to do with the bombing—the Knights insisted that they had "no affiliation, association, sympathy or respect for . . . anarchists"—the incident fed public suspicions that radicals controlled the labor movement.[67]

The Knights also faced setbacks in 1887, including among anthracite workers. A case in point was a strike jointly organized by the Knights and the Miners' and Laborers' Amalgamated Association, a coal union that had recently expanded into the anthracite fields. Beginning in September and continuing until March 1888, the strike eventually involved over 30,000 workers. As in 1875, however, mine operators demonstrated that they were better able to withstand the strike, and the "starved out" laborers mostly returned to work on their employers' terms.[68] A congressional investigation into the strike, which proved sympathetic to the workers, concluded that "most of the recent labor troubles in the anthracite regions of Pennsylvania arise from the railroads . . . being permitted to mine as well as transport coal." With railroads and mines under common ownership, the investigation suggested, employers had conspired to keep prices high and wages low. The report also determined that an influx of immigrants had created a "superabundance of labor" that depressed wages.[69]

In combination, the Haymarket episode, the failed strikes, and a botched eight-hour effort in 1886 ended up crippling the Knights of Labor. Its rolls fell to 75,000 by 1893, and the Order ultimately survived only as a small council for political reform—a shadow of its former self.[70]

The American Federation of Labor

As the Knights of Labor faded into obscurity, a new association, the American Federation of Labor (AFL), rose to take its place as the face of the American labor movement. Founded in December 1886, the AFL sought to "fight only for immediate objects—objects that can be realized in a few years," and focused on facilitating members' strikes and local campaigns for pro-labor legislation.[71] Under the leadership of cigar maker Samuel Gompers, the AFL grew to include 250,000 members by 1892. The new organization proved its staying power as it endured rising anti-union sentiment and a national recession beginning in 1893. As Gompers observed, "It is noteworthy that while in every previous industrial crisis the trade unions were literally mowed down and swept out of existence, the unions now in existence have manifested, not only the powers of resistance, but of stability and permanency."[72]

Two Historic Strikes

Two major strikes in the 1890s continued the pattern of violence of the two previous decades. The first began in Homestead, Pennsylvania, in July 1892, when a metalworkers' union struck in response to a company lockout and the threat of sharp wage cuts. On July 6 the strikers engaged in a horrific faceoff against a private army of Pinkerton men. In "a battle which for blood-thirstyness [*sic*] and boldness was not excelled in actual warfare," the strikers kept the Pinkerton soldiers at bay with gunfire, a cannon, and burning oil on the Monongahela River.[73] At least ten people were left dead. Six days later, state militia placed Homestead under martial law and replaced striking workers with non-union labor. When the strike finally ended in November, less than a quarter of the almost 4,000 strikers got their jobs back.[74]

Another major episode was the Pullman Strike of 1894. The Pullman Palace Car Company had cut wages and laid off many of its workers after the recession hit. Its remaining workers lived in the town of Pullman, Illinois, a company-organized community where the firm controlled the prices of rent, services, and utilities. Disgruntled Pullman workers struck in May 1894, and the next month the American Railway Union, led by Eugene V. Debs, ordered its approximately 150,000 members to stop working with any Pullman train cars. By July, the strike had expanded to such an extent that "nearly every railroad in the Middle West was affected, and the nation's entire transportation system was seriously threatened."[75]

Railroad managers, meanwhile, were working on a plan to draw in the federal government on their side of the strike. They paid outside workers to attach U.S. mail cars to Pullman cars, which in turn allowed them to accuse striking workers of interfering with mail delivery, a federal crime. U.S. Attorney General Richard Olney, who had previously worked as general counsel for a railway, dispatched 3,400 deputies to protect the rails, and the next month President Grover Cleveland summoned federal troops to assist. "If it takes every dollar in the Treasury and every soldier in the United States to deliver a postal card to Chicago, that postal card should be delivered," Cleveland reportedly declared. The troops' intervention angered strikers, who defied Debs's pleas for a peaceful response. Olney followed up with an injunction against any rail interference, which led to indictments against Debs and his associates. Debs was sentenced to six months in prison, and the strike soon ended in failure.[76]

The Fight for the Labor Vote

While major strikes figured prominently in the 1890s, the decade also saw a tug-of-war over the labor vote. The agrarian Populist (or People's) Party took the lead. Hoping to find common cause between farmers hit by falling agricultural prices and laborers facing declining wages, the Populists sought to appeal to workers by favoring immigration restriction, eight-hour laws, elimination of government injunctions in labor disputes, and an end to the Pinkertons. Although the Populists attracted the support of the weakened Knights of Labor and Eugene Debs, the AFL steered clear of party politics. Nevertheless, in the 1896 elections the Democratic Party adopted much of the Populist platform, and the Democrats' presidential candidate, William Jennings Bryan, declared that he would offer Samuel Gompers a Cabinet seat if elected. Bryan's Republican opponent, William McKinley, sought workers' votes as well, and his supporters circulated warnings that Bryan and "the socialistic and revolutionary forces" behind him would crash the economy and destroy jobs. McKinley, Republicans promised, would nourish a pro-business economy that delivered workers "a full dinner pail."[77] In November, McKinley won the presidency by capturing the industrial Northeast and Midwest.

The United Mine Workers of America

Although anthracite workers appeared less active in the 1890s, particularly after the failed strike of 1887–1888, the same was not true of bituminous coal workers, who formed the United Mine Workers of America (UMW) in January 1890. (Bituminous was another variety of coal that was mined more widely than anthracite throughout the United States.) About ninety UMW chapters appeared in the anthracite region over the decade and organized a few strikes, including a notorious 1897 confrontation with local militia that left nineteen strikers dead.[78] In general, however, the UMW found it difficult to organize effectively in the anthracite region during these years. As one observer complained, "As soon as one district is organized it is allowed to droop and die while another is being formed."[79]

The UMW finally established a foothold in anthracite, particularly in the northern fields, beginning in 1899. By January 1900, UMW membership among anthracite workers had reached close to 9,000—growth that UMW president John Mitchell called "almost phenomenal."[80] In August 1900, UMW anthracite workers convened in Hazleton, Pennsylvania, to draw up a list of grievances against employers. Besides complaints about wages, the list included a number of problems unique to the industry. As we have seen, many workers were paid by the hour, but the miners themselves were typically paid for the amount of coal they mined, either by the ton or by the carload. These miners claimed that supervisors often deducted, or "docked," too high a proportion of their output when accounting for impurities in the coal, thus reducing their pay. Miners paid by the carload also objected that the cars were not all of equal size, and those paid by the ton complained that the operators counted 3,360 pounds to the ton, instead of the more typical 2,240, again to compensate for impurities. Furthermore, the convention protested noncompliance with laws mandating semimonthly pay, inequality of wages within and between mines, pay reductions due to stopped machinery, high prices of blasting powder sold by the operators to the miners, and high prices at company stores and for doctors, among other issues. The petition also called for abolition of sliding-scale wages where they still existed (because, since the WBA's collapse, workers were no longer involved in setting them), and it requested a meeting with operators to discuss all of these issues.[81]

The Strike of 1900

When mine operators refused to hear the union's complaints, the workers struck on September 17, 1900. In fact, the number of workers who went out on strike—up to 100,000 on that first day—far exceeded the number of anthracite members of the UMW, and the total grew to an estimated 136,000 over the next eleven days.[82] Although the strike was not without occasional violence, it was more peaceful than many that had preceded it. There were indications, moreover, that public opinion leaned toward the workers, who were willing to bring in a neutral arbitrator, and against the mine operators, who resisted comprehensive solutions on the grounds that each mine's problems were distinctive. One popular journal found the operators' arguments "anything but convincing to the impartial mind."[83]

The strike presented a dilemma to President McKinley, who faced reelection in November. McKinley had won in 1896 promising a "full dinner pail," but the strike made it clear that anthracite workers were not satisfied with their dinner pails. As one Democratic paper argued, "The revolt of 140,000 miners against starvation wages and various forms of tyrannical impositions has fixed the gaze of the entire American people very sharply upon certain phases of McKinley prosperity. . . . No really permanent prosperity can rest upon the degradation of so many thousands of people."[84] Even before the strike had begun, Ohio senator and Republican National

Committee chairman Mark Hanna had attempted to persuade mine operators to settle with the UMW to prevent the strike.[85]

After some back-and-forth, Republicans finally convinced the mine operators to make concessions. On September 26 Hanna met with operators
to present UMW demands and "painted the . . . disastrous results that would
follow the placing in office of a Populist administration" if the strike spread
beyond Pennsylvania and McKinley lost to William Jennings Bryan.[86] Although the operators still refused to recognize the UMW, they announced
a 10 percent wage increase and a willingness to meet with workers on a firm-
by-firm basis. A UMW convention on October 12 accepted the offer, so long
as the operators promised to hold wages steady until April 1901, to abolish
the sliding scale, and to discuss grievances with committees of employees,
rather than only with individuals. The operators agreed, and the strike ended
on October 29, 1900. Eight days later President McKinley won reelection and
carried Pennsylvania by nearly 25 points.[87]

The Anthracite Strike of 1902

The period following the 1900 strike constituted what one historian has called
a "cold coal war" between workers and operators, where neither group was
satisfied with the strike's resolution.[88] Mine operators began building stock-
ades and coal storage depots in anticipation of future shutdowns. On the other
side, many workers remained frustrated that not all of their demands had been
met and, particularly, that the operators never recognized the union. In early
1901, with UMW membership among anthracite workers at over 53,000,
Mitchell repeatedly invited operators to negotiate what wage rates should be
after the existing arrangement expired in April. The operators rebuffed
Mitchell, however, announcing unilaterally that they were extending the current rates another year to April 1902.[89] "It seems to me," Mitchell wrote, "that
those laddie bucks . . . will have to be given another round before they will
realize the necessity of taking cognizance of our existence."[90]

Mounting Tension

As the UMW contemplated next steps, Mitchell sought help from the National Civic Federation, an organization recently established by representatives of big business and organized labor to foster mutually acceptable

reforms and mediate disputes. Leaders of the Civic Federation included the Republican reformer and former journalist Ralph Easley, Senator Hanna, AFL president Samuel Gompers, and Mitchell himself.[91] Easley and Hanna contacted the financier J. P. Morgan, who arranged a meeting between Mitchell and Erie Railroad president Eben B. Thomas on March 26, 1901. Thomas, whom Mitchell believed was speaking for several operators of the anthracite mines and railroads, promised to meet with workers' committees to settle grievances. Mitchell called this "a very important concession," despite the fact that it had already been part of the October agreement. Thomas further suggested that the operators might soon recognize the UMW if its members acted peacefully.[92]

Although the UMW urged members to display the "willingness and ability" to satisfy Thomas's request, many of its rank and file proved uncooperative.[93] In the months after the meeting with Thomas, mine workers launched a series of small strikes without UMW permission. The strikers charged that the mining companies discriminated against union members, cut wages, and interfered in the union's card-checking system used to ensure universal union membership. UMW members listed these grievances at an August 1901 convention and demanded a conference with the operators to produce binding rules. Mitchell requested a new meeting with Thomas, but Thomas refused.[94] "It was soon made clear," Easley wrote, "that [Thomas] was thoroughly disgusted with unions in general and the mineworkers in particular . . . [and] that it was simply a question that had to be fought out sooner or later as to who owned the mines, the miners or the operators."[95]

The UMW pressed its demands over the winter. At a convention in January 1902, Mitchell said that his principal goals for the anthracite workers were an eight-hour workday, union recognition by operators, and higher wages. The convention declared that it desired a conference with operators to set wage rates before existing rates expired in April, and that it was prepared to strike. After operators announced they would extend existing wages yet another year without UMW input, union members in the anthracite region convened on March 18 at Shamokin, Pennsylvania, to decide their next move. This convention refined the national statement, demanding recognition, the eight-hour day for hourly workers, and, for the miners paid by the amount of coal extracted, a 20 percent raise and payment by the 2,240-pound ton rather than the carload or heavier ton. At Mitchell's recommendation the convention agreed to appeal to the National Civic Federation for mediation, and it reiterated the threat of a strike to begin April 1.[96]

In the weeks following the Shamokin convention, UMW leaders, mine operators, and mediators repeatedly attempted to reach a compromise. On April 26 the operators finally met with UMW representatives at a session mediated by the Civic Federation. The only results, however, were promises by the UMW not to strike—and by the operators not to build up coal reserves—before a new meeting thirty days later. Follow-up meetings were no more productive. Although operators acknowledged they found Mitchell "a very fair and conservative man," they insisted that wage increases were financially untenable.[97] A final offer by the UMW on May 8 to have Catholic leaders in the Civic Federation arbitrate the dispute (since many mine workers were Catholic) was rejected by operators. President George F. Baer of the Reading Railroad reminded Mitchell that "anthracite mining is a business, and not a religious, sentimental, or academic proposition."[98]

Mediation having failed, the UMW ordered most anthracite workers to suspend work on May 12. Two days later, union delegates convened at Hazleton to discuss how to proceed. Mitchell opposed a full-blown strike. He noted that the workers were not sufficiently prepared to ensure victory, and he believed (most likely correctly) that the operators had greater respect for the UMW after meeting him in person. He asked the convention, "Is it better to go on improving your conditions, little by little, or to risk everything in one great fight?"[99] Although many delegates found Mitchell persuasive, their constituents had in most cases instructed them to vote for a strike. Ultimately, on May 15 the convention approved a strike by a vote of 461¼ to 349¾.[100] "Now that the strike is on," Mitchell wrote shortly after the vote, "I intend to do everything in my power to make it a success, at the same time using every possible effort to conciliate the coal operators and reach a settlement without a protracted contest." The *New York Times* reported that "it is freely predicted that the most serious labor struggle in the history of the country is about to begin."[101]

The Strike

On May 12, the first day of the UMW's work suspension, there were reports that none of the anthracite mines were functioning, and soon an estimated

145,000 workers were officially on strike. Many strikers left the region for other jobs, and by mid-June working-age men were almost completely absent from a number of local towns.[102] Many influential voices in the press initially supported the workers, believing they had been more willing to compromise than their employers. The Ann Arbor *Times* accused the latter of "greed, arrogance and contempt for men who work with their hands," and the Scranton *Times* expressed "no hesitation in placing the responsibility for this industrial war where it justly belongs, upon the coal carrying companies."[103]

Public support for the strike began to sour in June as reports emerged of strikers harassing non-union workers, whom they called "scabs." Local residents complained that strikers were hanging effigies of such men, boycotting businesses that served them, and even provoking strikes against unrelated businesses that hired their family members. In mid-June a Citizens' Alliance formed to combat the boycotts and prosecute strikers' crimes. Mitchell suggested that the Alliance was misguided and perhaps even in league with the mines. "Is it not rather strange that this organization was not formed at any time during the twenty-five years in which the anthracite coal companies were blacklisting, boycotting and driving from their homes and families all men who dared to assert their rights and join a labor organization?" he asked.[104] Declaring that he was "opposed to lawlessness of every character," Mitchell argued that only a small portion of his union was involved in any harassment and that the strike was in fact remarkably peaceful and orderly.[105]

In the meantime, bituminous UMW workers expressed interest in a "sympathetic strike" to demonstrate solidarity with anthracite strikers and to further pressure business leaders. Unlike the anthracite workers, however, bituminous workers *had* negotiated their contracts through the union, and a strike would violate these agreements. Easley and others insisted that such a strike would be "a suicidal act" that would destroy the credibility of the union, if not that of organized labor as a whole. Civic Federation representatives journeyed into the bituminous fields to argue against a strike, but the most important plea came from Mitchell himself at a July 17 convention in Indianapolis. Mitchell argued that "a disregard of the sacredness of contracts strikes at the very vitals of organized labor" and that the "effect of such action would be to destroy confidence, to array in open hostility to our cause all forces of society, and to crystallize public sentiment in opposition to our movement." He recommended that the bituminous members instead offer financial support, which they agreed to do. Voices in the press hailed Mitchell's leadership. The New York *World* praised his "temperative and conservative mood" and called for "corresponding willingness on the part of the anthracite operators to avoid pushing this industrial contest to extremities."[106]

Back in Pennsylvania, however, the strike grew more contentious. The "first serious violence" occurred on July 30, when a man was attacked and killed at Shenandoah as he headed to help his brother who was escorting non-union workers through the crowd. National Guardsmen soon arrived to police Shenandoah. UMW leaders condemned the death, but further violence over the ensuing months drew more troops into the region until the entire Pennsylvania National Guard was stationed there. Mitchell insisted this was an overreaction. "There is no reign of terror," he announced in late September, countering claims in the press, "and the miners are conducting themselves peaceably as when the strike started."[107]

Throughout the summer of 1902 there were several attempts to end the strike by bringing in a neutral party to investigate the industry and make recommendations. Despite numerous proposals from both business and government leaders, neither the UMW nor the operators proved willing to settle. Mitchell insisted that "the men will not return to work . . . until the strike is either won or lost or arbitrated."[108] For their part, the operators refused even to entertain outside arbitration for matters between employees and employers. Reported Senator Hanna, "It looks as if it was only to be settled when the miners are *starved* to it. And that may be weeks ahead as they are getting liberal supplies from their fellow workmen all over the country."[109]

President Roosevelt Intervenes

Early on, the strike captured the attention of Theodore Roosevelt, who had become president in September 1901 after McKinley was assassinated. In June 1902, Roosevelt ordered Labor Commissioner Carroll D. Wright to report on the conditions in Pennsylvania. Wright determined that the mine operators' core complaint was that they did not have a reliable negotiating partner—the 1901 strikes having convinced them that the workers could not be trusted. The operators attributed this to the arrival of the UMW and claimed they preferred a more disciplined, anthracite-only union to replace it. Regarding specific issues, Wright appeared to side with the workers, calling for coal weighing, a shorter workday, and the setting of wages by a joint conference between an anthracite-only union and owners. Overall, Wright concluded that the strike stemmed fundamentally from a lack of trust. "The way it appears to the average workman is that the operators do not want an agreement," he wrote, and "the operators contend that no such agreement would have any binding effect upon the miners. . . . Long-continued conditions on this basis of suspicion make the question one of great difficulty."[110] On June 28, President Roosevelt asked Attorney General Philander Knox for his opinion on the matter. Knox responded that the president had no business interfering in the strike and "that the Executive had no power whatever to take action in the matter."[111]

By autumn, however, Roosevelt was increasingly anxious about the strike. Anthracite typically cost a few dollars per ton, but by late September prices had reached as high as three times the normal rate. Because anthracite was the most important heating fuel in many eastern cities, a continued shortage threatened widespread suffering. As winter approached, numerous voices began demanding radical interventions to restore the coal supply.[112] Senator Henry Cabot Lodge, a leading Republican from Massachusetts, warned Roosevelt, "We are running straight on to what may become an overwhelming demand that the government take the mines—which would be an awful step, and we are being driven forward chiefly by the insensate folly as it seems to me of the operators."[113] Roosevelt replied, "There is literally nothing, so far as I have been able to find out, which the national government has any power to do in the matter . . . I am at my wits' end how to proceed."[114]

The Washington Conference

On September 29, Massachusetts governor W. Murray Crane recommended that the president meet with Mitchell and leading mine operators to discuss the situation. Roosevelt supported the idea, while acknowledging that it lacked precedent. Although much of the press and the public apparently also favored the proposed meeting, critics questioned the constitutional basis of such a move.[115] The attorney general himself had already said the president had no right or obligation to intervene in labor disputes, even if the industry in question was judged to be essential. Roosevelt, however, was confident of his course. As he later reasoned,

> There would be no warrant in interfering under similar conditions in a strike of iron workers. Iron is not a necessity. But I could no more see misery and death come to the great masses of the people in our large cities and sit by idly, because under ordinary conditions a strike is not a subject of interference by the President, than I could sit by idly and see one man kill another without interference because there is no statutory duty imposed upon the President to interfere in such cases.[116]

Mine operators and UMW leaders joined the president in Washington on October 3, 1902. Throughout the meeting, the operators made it clear that they would not compromise with the UMW. Baer complained of "intimidation, violence, and crime" by strikers and beseeched Roosevelt "not to waste time negotiating with the fomenters of this anarchy and insolent defiance of law."[117] He reiterated the operators' demand that grievances be settled separately at each firm and denied that Mitchell, as someone from outside the region, had any right to represent workers there. Mitchell countered with an offer to have the president appoint an arbitration tribunal, but the operators flatly refused. Instead, they insisted that Roosevelt take action against the UMW, either by sending in the military to end the strike or by indicting the union on charges of conspiracy. Exasperated, the president asked the operators if there was any plan of arbitration to which they would consent; they indicated there was not. The meeting adjourned soon thereafter. Roosevelt that night wrote to Senator Hanna: "Well, I have tried and failed."[118]

The operators' approach and demeanor at the conference did not sit well with either the president or the press. Roosevelt believed they had "showed extraordinary stupidity and bad temper" and admitted he was "insulted" by their insinuations that he had not fulfilled his duty to enforce order.[119] The only major fault he found with Mitchell was that he had perhaps not done enough to prevent violence.[120] Many in the media agreed with Roosevelt and pilloried the operators' "insolent defiance of public sentiment and disregard for public rights and interests."[121] The most vociferous critics called for drastic action against the mining companies—the Detroit *Tribune,* for instance, recommended making "the mines the legal property of the United States, to be operated by the government for the benefit of all the people."[122]

Roosevelt Seeks a Solution

The day after the conference, former president Cleveland recommended to Roosevelt that the workers and operators should agree to mine the coal needed for winter and resume the strike afterward, but Roosevelt responded that he was unwilling to propose any such plan to the recalcitrant operators. Additionally, he noted that he had researched Cleveland's intervention in the Pullman Strike, but that he could take no similar action because no federal property was affected and the state government had not requested federal assistance.[123] Unwilling to work with the operators, Roosevelt offered Mitchell a federal investigation if he would call off the strike, but Mitchell politely refused: "Having in mind our experience with the coal operators in the past we have no reason to feel any degree of confidence in their willingness to do us justice in the future."[124]

As the impasse continued, President Roosevelt received a bevy of recommendations on what to do. He complained to Senator Lodge, "A minor but very influential part desire that I send troops at once without a shadow of a warrant into the coal districts, or that I bring suit against the labor organization; the other demand that I bring suit against the operators, or that I . . . seize their property, or appoint a receiver, or do something else that is wholly impossible."[125] Once again Roosevelt asked Knox if there was anything he could do with regard to these recommendations, but Knox dismissed each proposed action as unconstitutional.[126]

Despite Knox's advice, in early October the president planned a secret maneuver to end the strike. As he had told Cleveland, one of the reasons he could not send troops was that Pennsylvania governor William Stone had not invited him to do so. Tired of failed offers and counteroffers, Roosevelt now sought simply to direct Stone to ask for federal military intervention. Once in the region, troops would seize the mines and directly oversee the resumption of mining operations. Roosevelt chose General

John M. Schofield, one of Cleveland's advisers during the Pullman Strike, to carry out the plan, instructing him "to pay no heed to any other authority, no heed to a writ from a judge or anything else excepting my commands" if the plan went forward.[127] "I do not know whether I would have had any precedents," Roosevelt explained in a private letter several weeks later, "but in my judgment it would have been imperative to act, precedent or no precedent—and I was in readiness."[128]

Finally, a Compromise

Such drastic measures proved unnecessary, however. On October 9, Secretary of War Elihu Root had suggested to J. P. Morgan a compromise that would establish a commission to investigate disputes between each firm and its employees, and whose decisions would be binding, industry-wide, for several years. Root believed his plan had promise because it offered the neutral arbitration the UMW desired without requiring mine operators to recognize the UMW. Roosevelt allowed Root to pursue his plan independently, and the secretary met with Morgan to work out the details. Ultimately it was decided that the commission's recommendations would be binding for three years. The commission, to be appointed by the president, would consist of a military engineer, a mining engineer unaffiliated with any coal firm, a federal judge from Pennsylvania, a sociologist, and an individual involved in mining and selling anthracite. Morgan, who had significant financial interests in the anthracite railroads, persuaded the operators to approve the plan, which Roosevelt published on October 13.[129]

Mitchell's only objection to the plan was that workers would have no representation on the commission. At Mitchell's urging, therefore, the president agreed to add a labor representative as well as a Catholic leader. When Roosevelt suggested this to Morgan's representatives, however, they made it clear that the operators would never allow a labor representative on the commission. Roosevelt argued with the Morgan men for two hours until he reached a surprising solution: he simply offered to name a labor representative under the label "sociologist." In what Roosevelt called "a most comic incident," the Morgan representatives immediately agreed, their true objection apparently having been to *acknowledging* labor's presence, rather than to labor's presence itself.[130]

With approval from both sides, Roosevelt soon assembled the commission, including Labor Commissioner Wright as recorder and Edgar E. Clark, leader of a railway conductors' union, as its sociologist. UMW anthracite workers accepted the proposed commission when they convened on October 20, 1902. Three days later they finally returned to work, after more than five months on strike.[131]

The Anthracite Commission

On October 27, Mitchell—now acting as a representative of the "workers" rather than of the UMW—presented a list of demands to the commission similar to the Shamokin declaration of the previous March. These demands included recognition of the UMW as well as a 20 percent pay raise for miners. While workers' representatives claimed "that the annual earnings of the mine workers are insufficient to maintain the American standard of living," the commission painted a different picture on the basis of its investigation. Housing and public life in anthracite communities, the commissioners observed, were generally acceptable, and wage rates were on par with other industries requiring similar skills. They particularly noted that because most miners were paid by weight, their individual incomes depended largely on their own productivity. The commission did, however, agree that anthracite mining was "perilous and extra hazardous," and that such risk deserved consideration when setting wages.[132]

In addition to higher wages, workers had also demanded an eight-hour workday for those paid on an hourly or daily basis, with no reduction in net pay. Workdays at the mines were a complex issue. While officially the mines operated under a ten-hour workday, actual hours varied greatly from day to day and across positions. Complicated processes and unreliable machinery often broke down or otherwise slowed work, and a majority of the firms studied by the commission were apparently already operating their mines fewer than eight hours a day on average. The commission noted that this unpredictability, as well as work stoppages brought about by market conditions, cut into miners' earnings. At the same time, certain positions (such as the firemen who fed the boilers) had to be manned around the clock to keep the mines running, and individual workers in these jobs often worked several consecutive shifts. Workers' representatives insisted that these jobs were extremely arduous, but operators contended that they required minimal effort and that workers often slept on the job.[133]

For determining miners' pay, Mitchell had demanded that the coal be weighed, rather than measured by the carload, and with workers paid a minimum of 60 cents per 2,240-pound ton. In its investigation of this matter, the commission also studied the practice of docking. It found that docking rates varied widely between mines, and reliably fell when a workers' representative was present to observe the process. The commission also noted that while weight and docking regulations similar to what the miners wanted already existed in Pennsylvania, these rules were typically avoided through provisions in the miners' contracts and would be difficult to fully implement.[134]

On February 12, 1903, in Philadelphia, the operators and workers offered their final statements to the commission, after months of testimony from 558 witnesses.[135] George Baer spoke on behalf of the operators. As at the October 3 conference, Baer focused on the violence and crime in the anthracite region. The operators, he explained, "concede to organized labor the same rights that we claim for organized capital," but insisted that organized workers had to behave within the law and, especially, respect the rights of non-union men to work without harassment. "We will not agree to turn over the management of our business to a labor organization because some of our employees belong to it," he declared. After reviewing the operators' objections to the workers' specific demands, he closed with a proposal for the commission: the operators would institute a 5 percent raise for wage workers for the months November 1902 to April 1903, followed by a revived sliding scale for three years with a guaranteed minimum wage at the existing rate.[136]

The closing speech on behalf of the mine workers was delivered by Clarence Darrow, the esteemed lawyer who had been their counsel throughout the hearings. Peppering his remarks with jokes at the operators' expense, Darrow dismissed complaints about violence as irrelevant to the proceedings. "So far as the demands of the Mine Workers are concerned, it makes no difference whatever crimes have been committed or not," he reasoned. "If John Smith earned $500 a year, it is no answer to say that Tom Jones murdered somebody in cold blood." As he reviewed the specific issues, Darrow repeatedly emphasized the dangers of mining. "Miners are not very good figurers," he quipped. "If they were going into a war and knew that when they went in that six out of a thousand would be killed in a year, they would hesitate . . . but they go down into the ground . . . where eighteen to twenty-four out of a thousand are killed, to say nothing of the hundreds of others who are maimed and crippled."[137]

The hearings closed and the commission returned to Washington to discuss its findings and decide what to do.[138] The commissioners knew that their role was without precedent in American history and that the public as well as the anthracite miners and operators were eagerly awaiting their recommendations. Their decisions not only would shape the anthracite industry, but could influence the broader path of American business–labor relations. With so much at stake, it was now up to the commissioners—and them alone—to fashion a settlement.

NOTES

1. Letter to Finley Peter Dunne (20 Oct. 1902), in *The Letters of Theodore Roosevelt,* ed. Elting E. Morison (Cambridge, MA: Harvard University Press, 1951) (hereafter cited as *Letters*), 3:357.

2. Miners' demands in Anthracite Coal Strike Commission, *Report to the President on the Anthracite Coal Strike of May–October, 1902* (Washington, DC: GPO, 1903), 94.

3. Melvyn Dubofsky and Foster Rhea Dulles, *Labor in America,* 8th ed. (Wheeling, IL: Harlan Davidson, 2010), 23–25. *Lancaster Journal* quoted in Philip Taft, *Organized Labor in American History* (New York: Harper and Row, 1964), 5.

4. Dubofsky and Dulles, *Labor in America,* 23, 26–27. The first trade societies evolved out of older organizations called "mutual aid societies," mostly organized in the late 1700s to foster camaraderie among both masters and journeymen and to provide financial assistance to members in need (ibid., 22–23).

5. Ibid., 25. Dubofsky and Dulles cite as evidence the plenitude of newspaper advertisements seeking skilled labor and promising high wages.

6. John R. Commons et al., *History of Labour in the United States,* 2 vols. (New York: Augustus M. Kelley, 1966), 1:25, says that the founding of the Philadelphia Mechanics' Union, when "wage-earners for the first time joined together as a class, regardless of trade lines," was "the beginning of American labour movements." Taft (*Organized Labor,* 12) and Dubofsky and Dulles (*Labor in America,* 53) come to a similar conclusion about the late 1820s.

7. Dubofsky and Dulles, *Labor in America*, 30–31; Commons et al., *History of Labour*, 1:134–136. Factory labor organizations of this era were the first to use the term "union" in their names (ibid., 1:156).

8. *Mechanics' Free Press*, 25 Oct. 1828, 1, also quoted in Commons et al., *History of Labour*, 1:190.

9. See Commons et al., *History of Labour*, 1:194–195. Quote in Dubofsky and Dulles, *Labor in America*, 32. Dubofsky and Dulles (34) point out that the end of property requirements for voting contributed to the influence of the workingmen's parties.

10. Dubofsky and Dulles, *Labor in America*, 33, 35, 43–46; Commons et al., *History of Labour*, 1:177–184.

11. *Newark Village Chronicle*, May 1830, quoted in Dubofsky and Dulles, *Labor in America*, 33.

12. Dubofsky and Dulles, *Labor in America*, 45–46; Commons et al., *History of Labour*, 1:326–332.

13. Dubofsky and Dulles, *Labor in America*, 54. At least 173 strikes are counted by Commons et al., *History of Labour*, 1:381, whose estimate of about 300,000 union members, derived from a labor publication (1:424), had long been cited by labor scholars. Maurice F. Neufeld, "The Size of the Jacksonian Labor Movement: A Cautionary Account," *Labor History* 23, no. 4 (Fall 1982): 599–607, has demonstrated that this high figure is unlikely to be accurate. Dubofsky and Dulles suggest that Neufeld's estimate of about 44,000 is more realistic.

14. Dubofsky and Dulles, *Labor in America*, 53; Priscilla Murolo and A. B. Chitty, *From the Folks Who Brought You the Weekend* (New York: New Press, 2001), 61; Commons et al., *History of Labour*, 1:364. Dulles and Dubofsky (53) note the potential confusion that may arise over what each sort of organization was called in the 1830s compared to today. The "city central" organizations discussed here were typically called "trades' unions," and their member organizations were usually "trade societies." However, the modern practice of calling the smaller organizations "trade unions" had begun to take hold.

15. Dubofsky and Dulles, *Labor in America*, 60–61; Commons et al., *History of Labour*, 1:441–453. The five trades were shoemaking, printing, comb making, carpentry, and hand loom weaving.

16. Quoted in Dulles and Dubofsky, *Labor in America*, 55.

17. Murolo and Chitty, *From the Folks*, 62.

18. Quoted in Dubofsky and Dulles, *Labor in America*, 56. See also Commons et al., *History of Labour*, 1:384–393.

19. Edward Pessen, "Builders of the Young Republic," in *A History of the American Worker*, ed. Richard B. Morris (Princeton, NJ: Princeton University Press, 1983), 50–51. See also Dubofsky and Dulles, *Labor in America*, 28–30.

20. Quoted in Dubofsky and Dulles, *Labor in America*, 28.

21. Dubofsky and Dulles, *Labor in America*, 58–59; Commons et al., *History of Labour*, 1:409–411.

22. Dubofsky and Dulles, *Labor in America*, 59; Commons et al., *History of Labour*, 1:411. Quotation in Murolo and Chitty, *From the Folks*, 63.

23. Murolo and Chitty, *From the Folks*, 63.

24. For example, the workweek of women weavers in Massachusetts grew to 75 hours by the late 1840s, and hatters' wages fell from $12 to $8 per week between 1835 and 1845. See Dubofsky and Dulles, *Labor in America*, 68–70.

25. Quotation at ibid., 71.

26. Ibid., 73–74; Commons et al., *History of Labour*, 1:496–510. As many as 8,000 people may have joined "phalanx" communities that followed the community-based socialist philosophy of Charles Fourier (Dubofsky and Dulles, *Labor in America*, 73).

27. Dubofsky and Dulles, *Labor in America*, 75–76, quotation from National Reform Association pledge at 75. See also Commons et al., *History of Labour*, 1:522–535.

28. Dubofsky and Dulles, *Labor in America*, 76–77.

29. Horace Greeley, quoted in ibid., 78.

30. Dubofsky and Dulles, *Labor in America*, 78.

31. Commons et al., *History of Labour*, 1:575, 610–611, 616; Pessen, "Builders of the Young Republic," 72. See also Dubofsky and Dulles, *Labor in America*, 79–81. One exception from the general labor downturn of the late 1850s was the February 1860 wage strike by New England shoemakers, which involved nearly 20,000 workers throughout the region. Although the strike was only partly successful, the press widely hailed it as a "Revolution in the North" (Dubofsky and Dulles, *Labor in America*, 80–81).

32. Commons et al., *History of Labour*, 2:15, which reports, for example, that by July 1863 prices had risen 43 percent since 1860, but wages only 12 percent.

33. Ibid., 2:18–19; Dubofsky and Dulles, *Labor in America*, 83. In the Confederacy, there was one union in Virginia and there were two in Tennessee.

34. Dubofsky and Dulles, *Labor in America*, 84; Commons et al., *History of Labour*, 2:23.

35. Employers' General Association of Michigan quoted in Commons et al., *History of Labour*, 2:27.

36. Dubofsky and Dulles, *Labor in America*, quotations at 97, 98–99. See also Commons et al., *History of Labour*, 2:119–124.

37. Robert J. Cornell, *The Anthracite Coal Strike of 1902* (Washington, DC: Catholic University of America Press, 1957), 7–8, 1.

38. C. K. Yearley Jr., *Enterprise and Anthracite: Economics and Democracy in Schuylkill County, 1820–1875* (Baltimore: Johns Hopkins Press, 1961), 172–173; Arthur E. Suffern, *Conciliation and Arbitration in the Coal Industry of America* (Boston: Riverside Press, 1915), quotation at 202 (from November 1897 *Bulletin of Bureau of Labor*). The first recorded strike among anthracite workers took place in July 1842, when workers in the southern Schuylkill region demonstrated against declining wages and the practice of paying those wages, in part, with goods from company-owned stores. The strike failed, and the record is quiet on further activity until 1848, when a small union formed in Schuylkill and struck the next year with similar grievances. This organization claimed to include 5,000 workers, but fell apart in 1850 when its founder

ran away with the union's funds. For a decade there may have been no new efforts to unionize, and small strikes in the 1850s were mostly unsuccessful. See Cornell, *Anthracite Coal Strike,* 12–13; Harold W. Aurand, "Early Mine Workers' Organizations in the Anthracite Region," *Pennsylvania History* 58, no. 4 (Oct. 1991): 300–301.

39. Cornell, *Anthracite Coal Strike,* 13–14; Aurand, "Early Mine Workers' Organizations," 301; Suffern, *Conciliation and Arbitration,* 202–203.

40. Cornell, *Anthracite Coal Strike,* 14–16; Suffern, *Conciliation and Arbitration,* 203–204. The December strike in the southern district was initially successful at preventing a 25 percent wage cut, but wages fell the next month to match northern rates.

41. Aurand, "Early Mine Workers' Organizations," 302.

42. Quoted in Cornell, *Anthracite Coal Strike,* 18.

43. Ibid., 17–19.

44. Ibid., 19–24; Aurand, "Early Mine Workers' Organizations," 302–304. The WBA also engaged in some political activism. Cornell (*Anthracite Coal Strike,* 26) mentions that the union contributed to the passage of the nation's first mine inspection act in 1869, an 1872 law protecting union members from conspiracy prosecution, and an 1875 act mandating payment by weight of coal mined, rather than by less precise means. Suffern (*Conciliation and Arbitration,* 214, 214n2) notes that loopholes rendered the 1875 act largely ineffective.

45. Quoted in Dubofsky and Dulles, *Labor in America,* 94.

46. Ibid., 99–100.

47. Ibid., 102–103.

48. Quoted in ibid., 104.

49. Cornell, *Anthracite Coal Strike,* 24; Suffern, *Conciliation and Arbitration,* 212. The government report was *Labor Troubles in the Anthracite Regions of Pennsylvania, 1887–1888* (Washington, DC: GPO, 1889), see xlviii–li.

50. Cornell, *Anthracite Coal Strike,* 8–12, 24; Suffern, *Conciliation and Arbitration,* 212.

51. Andrew Roy, *A History of the Coal Miners of the United States,* quoted in Cornell, *Anthracite Coal Strike,* 25.

52. Cornell, *Anthracite Coal Strike,* 25; Perry K. Blatz, *Democratic Miners: Work and Labor Relations in the Anthracite Coal Industry, 1875–1925* (Albany: SUNY Press, 1994), 91.

53. Kevin Kenny, *Making Sense of the Molly Maguires* (New York: Oxford University Press, 1998), 157–158.

54. *New York World* (1874) quoted in ibid., 166.

55. *Argument of Franklin B. Gowen in the Case of the Commonwealth v. Munley, 1877, for the Murder of Thomas Sanger,* quoted in Kenny, *Making Sense,* 235.

56. Cornell, *Anthracite Coal Strike,* 27–28. Much early writing on the Mollies took Gowen's accusation of a vast conspiracy at face value (ibid., 28). For example, Commons et al. (*History of Labour,* 2:181) write that the Mollies existed as a conspiracy and directly controlled the Hibernians. More recently, Kenny (*Making Sense,* 213–214) has written: "Some of the men convicted in the Molly Maguire trials were probably innocent. . . .

But even those who were wrongly convicted may well have been involved in other, similar activities. Many of the men who stood trial had engaged in violence, up to and including assassination. . . . But that they did so as evil terrorists in the type of conspiracy portrayed by the prosecution at the trials is beyond credibility."

57. *St. Louis Republic* quoted in Dubofsky and Dulles, *Labor in America,* 107.

58. Dubofsky and Dulles, *Labor in America,* 106–108.

59. Blatz, *Democratic Miners,* 39; Aurand, "Early Mine Workers' Organizations," 305.

60. Dubofsky and Dulles, *Labor in America,* 109; Michael A. Bellesiles, *1877: America's Year of Living Violently* (New York: New Press, 2010), 168–169.

61. Dubofsky and Dulles, *Labor in America,* 108–109, quotation at 108.

62. Dubofsky and Dulles, *Labor in America,* 109; Commons et al., *History of Labour,* 2:190–191.

63. Uriah Stephens quoted in Dubofsky and Dulles, *Labor in America,* 117.

64. Dubofsky and Dulles, *Labor in America,* 118–120. Information about the anthracite assemblies can be found in Commons et al., *History of Labour,* 2:199–200; Aurand, "Early Mine Workers' Organizations," 306; and Blatz, *Democratic Miners,* 39.

65. Dubofsky and Dulles, *Labor in America,* 120–121, 125–127.

66. Quoted in Taft, *Organized Labor,* 104.

67. Quoted in Dubofsky and Dulles, *Labor in America,* 112.

68. Aurand, "Early Mine Workers' Organizations," 306–307; Suffern, *Conciliation and Arbitration,* 235–237, quotation at 237.

69. *Labor Troubles in the Anthracite Regions,* ii, viii.

70. Dubofsky and Dulles, *Labor in America,* 132–133.

71. Ibid., 145–146, Adolph Strasser quoted on 135.

72. 1893 convention address quoted in ibid., 147.

73. *Chicago Tribune* (7 July 1892) quoted in Dubofsky and Dulles, *Labor in America,* 151.

74. Dubofsky and Dulles, *Labor in America,* 149–154.

75. Ibid., 154–156, quotation at 156.

76. Ibid., 158–161, quotation at 158.

77. Ibid., 162–165, quotations at 163, 164.

78. Cornell, *Anthracite Coal Strike,* 38; Blatz, *Democratic Miners,* 45–63.

79. Anonymous, "Mine Worker," *UMW Journal* (23 Mar. 1899), quoted in Blatz, *Democratic Miners,* 63.

80. Cornell, *Anthracite Coal Strike,* 38–39; Blatz, *Democratic Miners,* 79.

81. Blatz, *Democratic Miners,* 14, 88–92; See 148 for a clear explanation of docking.

82. Cornell, *Anthracite Coal Strike,* 46–47. Suffern (*Conciliation and Arbitration,* 243) reports that 112,000 struck on the first day, but Cornell (at 28n47) points out that John Mitchell later revised this estimate downward.

83. Cornell, *Anthracite Coal Strike,* 48–51, quotation from *Review of Reviews* (Nov. 1900) at 50.

84. Denver *News* quoted in *Literary Digest* (13 Oct. 1900) quoted in Cornell, *Anthracite Coal Strike,* 53–54.

85. Cornell, *Anthracite Coal Strike,* 44–45.

86. Ibid., 54–55, quotation of operator John Markle at 55n58.

87. Cornell, *Anthracite Coal Strike,* 56–59; Blatz, *Democratic Miners,* 94–96; David Leip, "Atlas of U.S. Presidential Elections," http://uselectionatlas.org/RESULTS/index .html.

88. Cornell, *Anthracite Coal Strike,* chap. 3.

89. Ibid., 60–63; Suffern, *Conciliation and Arbitration,* 244; Blatz, *Democratic Miners,* 102.

90. Letter to Harry N. Taylor (9 Mar. 1901) quoted in Cornell, *Anthracite Coal Strike,* 63.

91. For the formation and early history of the National Civic Federation, see Marguerite Green, *The National Civic Federation and the American Labor Movement, 1900–1925* (Washington, DC: Catholic University of America Press, 1956), chap. 1.

92. Cornell, *Anthracite Coal Strike,* 64–68; Blatz, *Democratic Miners,* 104. Letter to William B. Wilson (26 Mar. 1901) quoted in Cornell, *Anthracite Coal Strike,* 67, and Blatz, *Democratic Miners,* 104.

93. 29 Mar. 1901 committee circular quoted in Cornell, *Anthracite Coal Strike,* 68.

94. Cornell, *Anthracite Coal Strike,* 69–73. Blatz, *Democratic Miners,* 105–113, goes into significant detail about the individual 1901 strikes and the UMW leadership's struggle to enforce discipline.

95. Letter to Mitchell (11 Oct. 1901) quoted in Cornell, *Anthracite Coal Strike,* 72–73.

96. Cornell, *Anthracite Coal Strike,* 74–81.

97. Unspecified operator quoted in ibid., 85.

98. Letter to Mitchell (9 May 1902) quoted in Cornell, *Anthracite Coal Strike,* 90.

99. Quoted in Cornell, *Anthracite Coal Strike,* 92.

100. Ibid., 92–94; "Anthracite Miners Decide to Strike," *New York Times,* 16 May 1902, 1.

101. Letter from Mitchell to Bishop Michael Hoban, quoted in Cornell, *Anthracite Coal Strike,* 94; "Anthracite Miners Decide to Strike."

102. Cornell, *Anthracite Coal Strike,* 95; "Anthracite Miners Decide to Strike." Whereas the *New York Times* reported 145,000 on strike ("Anthracite Miners Decide to Strike"), the New York *Sun* (cited in Cornell, *Anthracite Coal Strike,* 95) reported 125,000. Engineers, firemen, and pumpmen initially did not join the strike because their services were needed to prevent flooding in the mines; these workers were finally ordered to strike on June 2 (Cornell, *Anthracite Coal Strike,* 98–99; "Goal Strike Crisis Will Come To-Day," *New York Times,* 2 June 1902, 1; "Strikers Fail to Flood Mines," *New York Times,* 3 June 1902, 3).

103. Quoted in Cornell, *Anthracite Coal Strike,* 96.

104. Ibid., 145–149, quotation at 147.

105. Open letter to the Citizens' Alliance (31 July 1902) quoted in ibid., 150. See also "President Mitchell's Reply," *New York Times,* 2 Aug. 1902, 1.

106. Cornell, *Anthracite Coal Strike,* quotations at 103, 117, 118–119.

107. Ibid., 151–155, quotations at 151, 155.

108. Quoted in ibid., 123–124.

109. Letter to President Roosevelt (29 Sept. 1902) quoted in ibid., 141.

110. C. D. Wright, *Report to the President on the Anthracite Coal Strike* (Washington: GPO, 1902), 1152–1153, 1166–1167, quotation at 1165.

111. Quoted in Cornell, *Anthracite Coal Strike*, 110.

112. Ibid., 173–175.

113. Letter to Roosevelt (25 Sept. 1902) quoted in ibid., 174.

114. Letter to Lodge (27 Sept. 1902) in *Letters*, 3:331–332. Also quoted in Cornell, *Anthracite Coal Strike*, 175.

115. Cornell, *Anthracite Coal Strike*, 176–181.

116. Letter to Mrs. W. S. Cowles (16 Oct. 1902), quoted in ibid., 181.

117. Quoted in Cornell, *Anthracite Coal Strike*, 184.

118. *Letters*, 3:337. Also quoted in Cornell, *Anthracite Coal Strike*, 187; the meeting is described on 181–187.

119. Letters to Crane (22 Oct. 1902) and Hanna (3 Oct. 1902), in *Letters*, 3:360, 338. Hanna letter also quoted in Cornell, *Anthracite Coal Strike*, 187.

120. Cornell, *Anthracite Coal Strike*, 189.

121. Charleston *Post* (4 Oct. 1902), quoted in ibid., 189.

122. Quoted in Cornell, *Anthracite Coal Strike*, 191.

123. Ibid., 195; letter to Cleveland in *Letters*, 3:338.

124. Quoted in Cornell, *Anthracite Coal Strike*, 198.

125. Letter (7 Oct. 1902) quoted in ibid., 207.

126. Cornell, *Anthracite Coal Strike*, 208.

127. Ibid., 210–212, quotation at 211. Though later in life Roosevelt denied revealing his plan to anyone else, he acknowledged later in October 1902 that he had told both Knox and Root that he was considering a military option. Apparently Roosevelt had warned both that he was prepared to move forward with the plan if necessary, that he would do so without consulting them, and that "they should both write letters of protest against it if they wished, so as to free themselves from responsibility." It is unclear if Root knew of Roosevelt's plan when he went to see Morgan (ibid., 213–214).

128. Letter to W. Murray Crane (22 Oct. 1902), *Letters*, 3:363. Also quoted in Cornell, *Anthracite Coal Strike*, 213.

129. Cornell, *Anthracite Coal Strike*, 215–217, 222–225.

130. Letter to W. Murray Crane (22 Oct. 1902), in *Letters*, 3:366. Also quoted in Cornell, *Anthracite Coal Strike*, 227, see also 224–227.

131. Cornell, *Anthracite Coal Strike*, 229–235.

132. Anthracite Coal Strike Commission, *Report*, 42–53, quotations at 42 and 51.

133. Blatz, *Democratic Miners*, 161–165; Anthracite Coal Strike Commission, *Report*, 50–51.

134. Blatz, *Democratic Miners*, 142–152; Anthracite Coal Strike Commission, *Report*, 70–71, 59–61.

135. Cornell, *Anthracite Coal Strike*, 252. The date of Feb. 12 comes from "Arguments during Proceedings of the Anthracite Coal Commission," online at the University

of Minnesota's Clarence Darrow Digital Collection, http://darrow.law.umn.edu
/documents/Anthracite_Arguments.pdf.

136. "Arguments during Proceedings," 9784, 9799, 9837.

137. Ibid., 9849, 9862.

138. Cornell, *Anthracite Coal Strike,* 252.

·{ 12 }·

The Jungle and the Debate over Federal
Meat Inspection (1906)

IN EARLY JUNE 1906, the House Committee on Agriculture grilled the president's investigators over which end of a dead hog had fallen into a Chicago slaughterhouse bathroom. President Theodore Roosevelt had sent the two investigators to verify allegations of unsanitary working conditions and diseased meat that had appeared in Upton Sinclair's recent novel, *The Jungle*. The investigators confirmed many of Sinclair's assertions, and noted that they had seen "a hog that had just been killed, cleaned, washed, and started on its way to the cooling room fall from the sliding rail to a dirty wooden floor and slide part way into a filthy men's privy" before being hung, uncleaned, with the other meat. The Agriculture Committee, which included many representatives friendly to the meatpacking industry, demanded details about the dropped hog and its subsequent processing.[1]

The hearing was part of a two-month congressional debate over possible meat inspection legislation, brought about by an unusual alliance between Roosevelt and Sinclair. The president, who sought to rein in industrial monopolies, had taken advantage of *The Jungle*'s popularity to campaign for a law to contain the "beef trust," a small group of meatpackers that dominated the industry. Not long before, however, Roosevelt had decried writers like Sinclair for "raking the muck" and engaging in dangerous sensationalism.[2] Attempting to explain his willingness to embrace Sinclair's work in this case, the president would later say: "In the beef packing business I found that Sinclair was of real use. I have an utter contempt for him. He is hysterical, unbalanced, and untruthful. Three-fourths of the things he said were absolute falsehoods. For some of the remainder there was only a basis of truth. Nevertheless, in this particular crisis he was of service to us, and yet I had to explain again and again to well-meaning people that I could not afford to disregard ugly things that had been found out simply because I did not like the man who had helped in finding them out."[3]

Although Sinclair, a committed socialist, had hoped *The Jungle* would awaken Americans to the plight of the working class and the abuses of big business, readers turned out to be more interested in his descriptions of repulsive slaughterhouse conditions and the implications for the meat they themselves consumed. "I aimed at the public's heart," he later wrote, "and by accident I hit it in the stomach."[4] As foreign and domestic demand for American meat declined, meatpacking firms vigorously denied Sinclair's charges, accusing him of outright fabrication.

On June 18, 1906, Speaker of the House Joseph Cannon presented a new draft of a meat inspection bill to the president. It was a compromise of sorts—a mixture of ideas from all sides that had grown out of a series of proposals and counterproposals through May and June. This latest version of the bill from the Agriculture Committee satisfied the president in some respects. In particular, it mandated inspection of meat products transported across state lines. Yet it also lacked provisions that Roosevelt favored, including dating of canned meats and fees on meatpackers to fund the inspections.[5]

Although the bill was hardly ideal from Roosevelt's perspective, he very much wanted to secure a statute before Congress adjourned only twelve days later. If he insisted on further negotiations, the momentum for a law spurred by *The Jungle* might dissipate, derailing the entire effort. On the other hand, if he endorsed the compromise bill, he would have to sell it to reformers in the Senate who were insisting on stricter legislation. With the congressional session rapidly winding down, Roosevelt had to decide whether to send the bill back to Capitol Hill with his blessing, or reject it and hope for something better.

The Rise of American Meatpacking

The explosive growth of the nation's railroad network in the mid-nineteenth century had stimulated domestic and foreign markets for western cattle and meats. By the 1850s, Chicago had become the principal gateway for eastbound shipments of these products, and further rail expansion ensured continual increases in the city's output. Cattle shipments from the Midwest to the East rose from 11,200 head in 1852 to 42,600 in 1858. To accommodate further growth, Chicago railroad and meatpacking interests constructed the Union Stockyards in 1865, with scale houses (for weighing cattle), an exchange building, and over 130 acres of stockyards all in convenient proximity.[6]

Unlike livestock, "dressed beef" was slaughtered and processed before transport. It was sold mainly on a seasonal basis until improved refrigerated railroad cars transformed it into a profitable year-round industry. Far cheaper to transport than livestock, dressed beef rapidly gained popularity in the 1880s and comprised 45 percent of Chicago's outbound beef by 1885.[7] Beef prices fell substantially as a consequence, and American per capita beef consumption rose 12 percent from the 1870s to the 1880s.[8]

The "Big Four" firms of Swift, Armour, Hammond, and Morris came to dominate the dressed-beef industry. Chicago newcomer Gustavus Swift had developed the refrigeration methods that enabled year-round shipment, and he used a vertical integration strategy—involving the ownership of nearly all stages of his beef's production and distribution, from slaughter to shipment to sale—in building his company. The other three, already in the meat business, successfully embraced Swift's novel strategy. The Big Four quickly surpassed competitors that failed to pursue vertical integration, and by 1887 they provided more than four-fifths of the dressed beef in the United States.[9]

The expansion of dressed beef also required significant changes in the industry's workforce and operations. When dressed beef was a seasonal product, small farmers seeking winter income often helped to prepare it in slaughterhouses and packing plants. As the industry shifted to year-round mass production, unskilled workers replaced farmers as the primary source of labor. Meatpacking firms streamlined their slaughterhouses with assembly-line-style division of labor and new machinery, boosting productivity but pushing their employees—some of whom were children—to work "inhumanly hard," in the words of one observer. Visitors to the slaughterhouses often reported appalling working conditions, including floors submerged in filthy water and dimly lit rooms, as well as pervasive disease.[10]

Because the livestock industry was a key source of business for the railroads, many railroad firms initially sought to protect it from the mounting competition of dressed beef. The railroads had invested in special cars and stockyards to assist livestock firms, but often refused to provide refrigerated cars or storage facilities to help the meatpackers.[11] Although the railroads did carry dressed beef, they frequently worked together to set prices in such a way that dressed beef would cost about the same in eastern markets as beef prepared locally from shipped livestock. One 1884 pricing policy, for example, charged 70 cents per 100 pounds to send dressed beef from Chicago to New York, as compared to only 40 cents for livestock, even though dressed beef was easier to transport than live cattle.[12]

These collusive pricing arrangements had a short life span, however. The temptation to attract the business of the Big Four meat producers was simply too large. Uncooperative railroad firms undercut the prearranged rates and sometimes gave secret rebates to the Big Four, provoking railroad price wars. In fact, once they realized how desperate the railroads were for their business, the Big Four colluded among themselves to exact ever lower rates for transporting their products.[13]

Regulating the Railroads

The railroads' scramble for dressed-beef traffic was symptomatic of the broader economics of the railroad industry. The sector consisted mainly of large firms with both high fixed costs (especially the large investments that went into laying the tracks and purchasing capital equipment) and relatively low variable costs (the expenses for fuel and personnel necessary to run the railroad on a day-to-day basis). To gain new customers, railroads frequently lowered their prices below what was necessary to recoup their fixed costs, and this forced competing railroads to do the same. In some cases, prices spiraled downward, putting nearly all of the railroads in financial jeopardy.[14] In fact, as a result of "destructive competition," as it was sometimes called, many railroads of the period fell into financial distress and entered receivership at some stage in their development.[15]

Major railroads attempted to address these challenges by organizing "pools" to set prices and allocate market shares among participating firms. These collusive arrangements proved difficult to maintain, however.[16] "The great defect in the present plan," pool organizer Albert Fink explained, "is that the co-operation of these railroad companies is entirely voluntary, and that they can withdraw from their agreements at pleasure."[17] By the 1880s Fink and other industry leaders favored government enforcement of these agreements, which they hoped would steady the market.[18]

Many other economic interests joined the call for rate regulation, but often for entirely different reasons. To attract business, the railroads had regularly offered lower rates and rebates to favored clients, such as those in the livestock industry and later the Big Four. These preferred customers were thus able to sell their goods at lower prices, which in the eyes of their competitors was akin to "letting one man steal another man's business."[19] The railroads also frequently charged higher prices per mile for short trips than for long ones, which handicapped certain clients in ways that felt "unjust."[20] Meanwhile others, such as water-based shipping companies and small merchants who sought to staunch the flow of cheap goods transported by rail, hoped that higher railroad rates would make their businesses more competitive.[21] For all of these reasons, a wide range of interests favored railroad rate regulation—at least of some kind.

There was much less support, however, for pooling arrangements that allocated market share. Many railroad executives believed that pooling agreements could effectively stabilize prices if backed by law. Yet most of their customers opposed government-sanctioned pooling. In testimony before a Senate committee, dressed-beef and livestock firms both asserted that such pools, if effective, would threaten their profitability.[22] As vulnerable as railroad owners and managers may have felt as a result of "destructive competition," their customers and numerous other interests claimed that the railroads had far too much influence over the markets already. One representative of New York merchants declared that stronger pooling arrangements would render Albert Fink "a greater power than the President of the United States by far."[23]

The debate over railroad regulation was thus largely over what form it should take, rather than whether any regulation should be enacted at all. Scholars disagree about which interests led the drive for railroad regulation in the 1880s,[24] but the only notable interests that opposed any sort of legislation were the relatively few firms—Swift, for example—that profited from rebates and the impotence of the existing pools.[25] With a widespread consensus for some sort of regulation, diverse interests drafted and debated a large range of legislative proposals throughout the 1870s and 1880s.[26]

By late 1886 the House and Senate had each passed a bill on the subject. With broad agreement that railroad rates should be stable and uniform, both bills included means for combating rebates and certain departures from published rates. The bills differed, however, in other important respects. The House bill favored railroad customers: it banned pooling, limited higher rates for shorter distances, and enforced its rules via the courts. The more railroad-friendly Senate bill, by contrast, allowed pooling (but did not include government enforcement, as the railroads wanted), was less strict about distance discrimination, and created a new commission to oversee the rules.[27]

Whether the courts or a commission would enforce the new law was an important point of contention as House and Senate conferees attempted to reconcile the two bills. Some railroad interests supported a commission on the belief that railroad-friendly commissioners would be appointed and interpret the law in their favor. "The older such a commission gets to be," one observer later mused, "the more inclined it will be found to take the business and railroad view of things. It thus becomes a sort of barrier between the railroad corporations and the people and a sort of protection against hasty and crude legislation hostile to railroad interests."[28] Opponents of a commission hoped that the courts would be more neutral arbiters of the law. Debate over enforcement dragged on until House leaders finally gave in and agreed to a commission.[29]

The long crusade for railroad regulation culminated in January 1887, when large majorities of both houses of Congress passed the Interstate Commerce Act. The act was a mixture of the House and Senate proposals. It banned pooling, rate discrimination, and rebates, required "reasonable" and "just" rates, and prohibited higher rates for shorter-distance shipments. It also created a new Interstate Commerce Commission (ICC) to administer these rules.[30]

Within the railroad industry there existed a wide range of views on the Interstate Commerce Act.[31] Some regarded it as a major defeat. Industry journal *Railway Review* declared that "the most merciless malice and the most careful deliberation could hardly have hit upon a measure more deadly and far-reaching in its effects."[32] Others, however, were prepared to withhold judgment until more was known about the approach and tilt of the commission.[33] "No matter what sort of bill you have," one railroad president had noted before the act passed, "everything depends upon the men who, so to speak, are inside of it, and who are to make it work."[34]

The early ICC proved friendly to the railroads. Its first chairman, Thomas Cooley, was a lawyer and ally of the industry.[35] Under Cooley, the ICC adopted a lenient interpretation of rate-setting rules, frequently gave legal advice to the railroad firms, and sometimes took years to settle complaints against the railways.[36] This apparently cozy relationship continued to frustrate critics of the ICC even after Cooley's departure in 1891. Merchant organizations that had hoped the Interstate Commerce Act would rein in the railroads were so disappointed with the ICC's performance that many petitioned for partial or total repeal of the legislation.[37]

Regulatory changes did not eliminate the industry's competitive pressures, however. Railroad income rose for a few months after passage of the Interstate Commerce Act, but before long the industry had returned to price-slashing competition. The leading firms—with ICC support—pleaded for Congress to legalize pooling, but to no avail. Railroad profits would not begin rising until the early years of the next century, after major roads entered into a series of mergers and a new law granted the ICC greater rate-setting powers.[38]

Collaboration by the Big Four

The dressed-beef industry managed to take advantage of the railroads' continued troubles, pressing for ever lower rates. Dressed-beef shipment rates from Chicago to the East Coast fell to under a dime per 100 pounds by July 1888, from as high as 65 cents the previous December. One key to the Big Four's influence in this period was that they were able to collaborate in ways that were now illegal for the railroads. The Interstate Commerce Act prohibited only the railroads from pooling, leaving their customers free to collude at their expense. The result, lamented one railroaders' magazine in 1890, was that the Big Four could collude to "precipitate such a [price] war as often as they choose."[39]

The Big Four collaborated not only to ensure lower railroad rates but also to protect themselves against the same economic pressures that had long plagued the railroads. The high fixed costs of the Big Four's vertically integrated operations, coupled with their saturation of the American market, heightened the competition between them. Dressed-beef profits and prices fell in the mid-1880s. Armour's profits, for example, declined from $1,618,000 in 1884 to about $1 million in 1887. Starting in 1886, however, the Big Four attempted a series of pooling schemes to divvy up available business, set prices, and counteract competitive pressures.[40]

Butchers and cattle raisers nationwide blamed the large meatpackers for their own losses during this period and accused them of forming a "beef trust"* that controlled the nation's meat industry. Cheap dressed beef had substantially reduced demand for traditional butchers. The butchers who remained lamented that the trust could "compel butchers in every town of any population, East or West, to purchase of them"; butchers who instead continued to dress their own beef would be priced out of the market.[41] Similarly, cattle firms blamed meatpacker collaboration for a sharp decline in livestock prices through the second half of the 1880s.[42] By the end of the decade, these interests were demanding national regulation to contain the packers, who they believed constituted "an unjust monopoly, and an unjust interference with legitimate trade."[43]

Their campaign against the big meatpackers broke into public view in 1888 when a Senate committee began investigating the Big Four's potential involvement in the collapse of livestock prices. Livestock and butcher interests were heavily represented at the resulting hearings. Although some of them agreed with the meatpackers that overproduction had caused the price collapse, many placed the blame squarely on the beef pools.[44] Testimony from the Armour company acknowledged that the large beef firms had pooled clients and collaborated in arranging price lists, but argued that such stabilizing measures were necessary and that the lists had been set "according to the state of the market as to supply and demand," with no intention of manipulating livestock prices.[45] The committee, however, rejected the meatpackers' arguments, concluding that their collaboration was "the principal cause of the depression in the prices paid to the cattle raiser."[46]

---

* At this point in time, the "beef trust" was not a formal trust, which was a specific form of business combination. Opponents used the term to insinuate that the meatpackers were colluding so extensively that they were effectively acting as one body.

The Larger Antitrust Movement

The crusade against the beef trust was just one facet of a larger movement against industrial monopolies and combinations. Prominent firms in the oil, sugar, and tobacco industries, among others, had colluded by various methods over the same period, and had begun merging into formal consolidated trusts in the 1880s. Small businesses—particularly agricultural interests—had since midcentury criticized big business collaborations as "detrimental to the public prosperity, corrupting in their management, and dangerous to republican institutions," and the rise of trusts had provoked further sharpening of such rhetoric.[47] By the late 1880s the antitrust movement had caught the attention of Congress. While the Senate investigated the beef trust, the House examined similar oligopolies in the sugar, oil, whiskey, and cotton-bagging industries.[48]

Certain that they were being targeted unjustly, representatives of big business complained that any sort of coordination between their companies, no matter how reasonable or appropriate, was now "denounced as a conspiracy."[49] In their eyes, cooperation between firms was still necessary to ease the dangerous competition that threatened the profitability of large-scale industries. One railroad leader claimed he could not name any trust that had ever damaged the public at large.[50]

In Congress, many lawmakers agreed that industrial coordination was a necessary response to the problem of excessive competition. Many also believed, however, that certain trusts had abused their positions, at the expense of consumers. According to Vermont representative John Wolcott Stewart, the "two great forces" of "competition and combination . . . are correctives of each other, and both ought to exist. Both ought to be under restraint. Either of them, if allowed to be unrestrained, is destructive of the material interests of this country."[51]

It was in this spirit that Congress passed the Sherman Antitrust Act in a nearly unanimous vote in 1890.[52] The act, according to sponsoring senator John Sherman, was meant to target only "the unlawful combination, tested by the rules of common law and human experience . . . and not the lawful and useful combination." It banned "every contract, combination in the form of a trust or otherwise, or conspiracy, in restraint of trade or commerce among the several States or with foreign nations."[53]

In spite of this language, the act had such a muted impact in its early years that some wondered if Congress had purposefully enacted a toothless law. The statute granted the Justice Department no new funds for enforcement, and the department soon found itself ill equipped to handle its growing caseload. Much of the law's language, meanwhile, was open to diverse interpretations, leaving the U.S. attorney general with considerable discretion. For example, Richard Olney, a former railroad attorney who became attorney general in 1892, openly insisted that trusts were a natural "economic evolution" unfairly victimized by "popular prejudice." Olney invoked the act only twice in his three-year tenure, writing in an official report that he believed many of the government's previous antitrust cases had reached outside of the law's authority.[54]

At least one scholar has suggested that the early weakness of the Sherman Act was evidenced by the continuation of the dressed-beef pools into the early years of the twentieth century. The Senate committee that investigated the beef trust in 1888 had endorsed antitrust legislation in its final report in the hope of combating collusion among the Big Four.[55] Yet the meatpacker pools survived through the 1890s and beyond. Even after the Supreme Court in 1899 ruled against their particular pooling methods, they apparently continued with no government action against them until the early 1900s.[56]

American Food and Drug Regulation
The Quality of American Meats

In addition to favoring antitrust action, the Senate committee of 1888 had also recommended a national meat inspection law. This was based in part on butchers' and small packers' accusations that the beef trust's indiscriminate processing of "diseased, tainted, or otherwise unwholesome meat" enabled unduly low prices.[57] These interests had supported earlier state-level inspection requirements to stymie the beef trust's interstate business, though few of these proposals became law. One prominent scholar has suggested that the small businessmen's accusations may have been primarily political in nature, because the most frequently cited cattle diseases, pleuropneumonia and Texas fever, were both rare and not threatening to humans.[58]

Although the federal government passed meat inspection laws soon after the hearings, it did so with the large packers' support and mainly for economic rather than health reasons. As early as 1879, several European nations had embargoed American meat over fears of trichinosis, a pork-borne illness.[59] Exports quickly plummeted.[60] Although many congressmen insisted that American pork was free of the disease, they favored inspection to remove any possible justification for the European embargoes. With the support of large meatpackers and livestock firms, Congress passed laws in 1890 and 1891 to guarantee the quality of American meats. The 1891 law mandated that the Agriculture Department inspect all cattle, hogs, and sheep (dead or alive) and meat products intended for export, as well as all livestock that would be slaughtered for interstate or international sales. The law also arranged for the inspection of meat products traded across state lines, though this was left voluntary and interstate trade in uninspected meat thus remained legal.[61] Although the interstate regulations were relatively weak and mostly optional, the 1891 law marked the first time the federal government had intervened in the quality of food intended for American households. The European nations, meanwhile, were apparently satisfied with the tougher regulations on meat for export: they lifted their embargoes in response to the new laws, and by 1895 U.S. meat sales had largely recovered.[62]

American meat again came under scrutiny during the 1898 Spanish-American War, when many soldiers complained about the beef that the Army provided. One officer attested that it "had an odor similar to that of a dead human after being injected with preservatives, and it tasted when cooked like decomposed boric acid . . . so bitter, nauseous, and unpalatable as to be quite impossible to use." Soldiers nicknamed the meat "embalmed beef," and many blamed the meat for widespread sickness among the men. Newspapers picked up on the scandal, conveying the soldiers' stomach-turning complaints to an astonished public.[63]

An official investigation contradicted the soldier's allegations, however. A military court found the beef to be sound, blamed the shipping and storage process as well as Cuba's heat for the poor taste, and attributed soldiers' sickness to environmental factors and lack of dietary variety. In fact, government investigators claimed that scientific analysis showed the beef was identical to that sold to American consumers. Still, the controversy persisted.[64]

The Pure Food and Drug Movement

The focus on meat safety complemented a larger effort during this period devoted to improving the quality of the nation's food and drugs. Since the mid-nineteenth century, activists had demanded state and federal laws against "adulteration." Reports claimed, for example, that producers diluted chocolate with peas, beans, and even soap, and that medicinal opium often contained significant quantities of crushed grapes.[65] Reformers insisted that such adulteration "poison[ed] and cheat[ed] the consumer,"[66] and one Harvard anatomy professor suggested "that if the whole materia medica, *as now used,* could be sunk to the bottom of the sea, it would be all the better for mankind,—and all the worse for the fishes."[67]

Some food producers accused their critics of being "sensational and unreliable" and of fomenting mistrust of the entire industry.[68] Others admitted that they adulterated in moderation, but not so much "as to be dangerous to health."[69] Still others acknowledged that adulteration was a grave problem. According to a biographer, H. J. Heinz believed that adulteration "creat[ed] suspicion of the quality and purity of all other products on the market," and he emerged as a leading supporter of pure-food legislation.[70]

Some businesses invoked the rhetoric of the pure-food movement to target rival firms. Dairy interests, for example, employed pure-food arguments in agitating for a tax on oleomargarine, a butter substitute. The major meatpackers had begun producing oleomargarine from beef fat in the 1880s, and butter interests saw it as a major threat.[71] In testimony before Congress, dairymen decried the product as an unhealthy "midnight assassin" that teemed with "spores, mold, hair, bristles, and portions of worms."[72] Oleomargarine defenders countered that the product was superior to butter in many ways and that the dairymen's health claims were unsubstantiated.[73] A federal oleomargarine tax eventually passed in 1886, though opponents criticized what they viewed as the "wrongful and fraudulent use of the taxing power" to serve an interest group.[74]

In the drug industry, tension arose between the pharmaceutical establishment and the "medicine men" who sold cheap "patent" or "proprietary" medicines to consumers and undiscerning doctors.[75] These patent medicines typically had little or no scientific merit, and many contained dangerous ingredients such as alcohol, morphine, or cocaine. Medical professionals had decried these "quack" medicines as early as the 1840s, but by the start of the 1900s they were still widely popular. Interests hostile to patent medicines demanded ingredient regulations and labeling requirements to protect consumers against potentially dangerous substances and to protect professional doctors from what appeared to be illegitimate competition.[76]

Speaking in support of his 1892 pure-food bill, Nebraska senator Algernon Paddock declared, "Take heed when the people demand bread that you continue not to give them a stone, lest the angry waves of popular discontent . . . engulf forever all that we most greatly value."[77] Yet despite such passionate exhortations and repeated efforts (at least one pure-food bill appeared in every Congress from 1879 until 1905), no comprehensive pure-food law was enacted during these years.[78]

The Muckrakers

In the early years of the twentieth century, a new cadre of investigative journalists called "muckrakers" would help to revitalize both the pure food and drug cause and the campaign for higher quality meats. In 1905, Edward Lowry's "The Senate Plot against Pure Food" asserted that industrialists controlling the Senate had foiled every attempt to regulate food and drugs. Starting later that year, Samuel Hopkins Adams's "The Great American Fraud" series in *Collier's Weekly* warned of fraudulent and adulterated drugs.[79] The meatpacking industry in particular faced the journalistic wrath of Charles Edward Russell, whose series "The Greatest Trust in the World" called the beef cartel "a great criminal organization" and "an active and pestilent public enemy."[80] These muckraking pieces, and others like them, reached readers across the nation, spreading alarm about what dangerous substances Americans might be consuming.

Muckraking itself had its roots in progressivism, a broad turn-of-the-century political movement that comprised reformers dedicated to everything from trust busting and fighting corruption to improving labor conditions and enfranchising women. Progressivism's first print champions were newspapers. The widely read *New York World* and *New York Morning Journal* investigated and editorialized against government corruption and questionable business practices, building support for political reforms. Faster printing machinery, cheaper newsprint, and novel picture-printing technologies developed in the late nineteenth century brought these crusades to wider audiences than ever before.[81]

Ultimately magazines, not newspapers, became most identified with progressive-era muckraking. In 1902, *McClure's* (a monthly magazine) published three sets of articles in an entirely new expository style: Ida Tarbell's exposé on Standard Oil, Lincoln Steffens's investigation of corruption in municipal and state governments, and Ray Baker's examination of American labor. This trio boosted *McClure's* circulation, and soon other magazines—including *Cosmopolitan, Everybody's,* and *Collier's*—were running investigative pieces of their own. By the decade's end, the circulation of these "muckraking" magazines exceeded 3 million, with more than 2,000 muckraking articles having appeared between 1903 and 1912.[82]

One popular 1906 series, David Graham Phillips's fiery "The Treason of the Senate," targeted the federal government itself. Since the ratification of the Constitution, states had enjoyed the authority to appoint U.S. senators with no direct input from the electorate. Phillips argued that this arrangement empowered elite political and business "interests" he considered "as hostile to the American people as any invading army . . . whose growth and power can only mean the degradation of the people." Phillips singled out specific senators' connections to these "interests" and, in his view, the corrupt legislation such relationships had produced. For example, he accused Illinois senator Shelby Cullom, a principal author of the Interstate Commerce Act, of being a railroad shill who had committed "treason to the people" by intentionally making the "so-called law" ineffective. Reasoning that "a servant obeys him who can punish and dismiss," Phillips maintained that such corruption would continue until the people could elect senators themselves.[83]

The initial reaction to "The Treason of the Senate" in both media and political circles was largely negative. One writer questioned whether Phillips was "sowing the seeds of anarchy," and even *Collier's,* a muckraking magazine that had carried Phillips's articles in the past, called the series "one shriek of accusations based on the distortion of such facts as were printed, and on the suppression of facts which were essential."[84] The most famous assault on this new brand of journalism came from President Theodore Roosevelt on April 14, 1906. Delivering a speech that popularized the term "muckraker" to describe Phillips and his colleagues, Roosevelt compared them to the "Man with the Muck-rake" character in John Bunyan's literary classic *The Pilgrim's Progress*. In Roosevelt's words, this character "typifies the man who in this life consistently refuses to see aught that is lofty, and fixes his eyes with solemn intentness only on that which is vile and debasing." Roosevelt continued:

> Now, it is very necessary that we should not flinch from seeing what is vile and debasing. There is filth on the floor, and it must be scraped up with the muck-rake; and there are times and places where this service is the most needed of all the services that can be performed. But the man who never does anything else, who never thinks or speaks or writes save of his feats with the muck-rake, speedily becomes, not a help to society, not an incitement to good, but one of the most potent forces of evil.[85]

Despite these attacks, much of the public proved receptive to Phillips and his fellow muckrakers. Their articles are said to have mobilized large armies of reformers, and the series "The Treason of the Senate," in particular, triggered a political movement for the direct election of senators. As one historian has written, "Perhaps no other single force was more responsible for the success of the progressive movement than the group of popular writers that emerged to write for the fast-flourishing muckrake magazines."[86] Even President Roosevelt could appreciate the muckrakers when their interests coincided with his. In fact, shortly before his April 1906 speech, he had already begun consulting with muckraker Upton Sinclair about the possibility of legislation to clean up the beef trust.[87]

Upton Sinclair and *The Jungle*

Sinclair was born in Baltimore in 1878. A lover of literature, he was a prolific writer from an early age.[88] Sinclair's novels from the start of the twentieth century communicated a deep dissatisfaction with American materialism and corruption—a melancholy presumably made worse by his unhappy marriage, precarious financial situation, and belief that society had as yet failed to recognize his genius. Sinclair encountered socialists for the first time in 1902 and found himself drawn to their political beliefs in a personal epiphany he later called "the falling down of prison walls about my mind." He incorporated socialist ideas into his next novel, *A Captain of Industry*. The book was not subtle. It told the story of a rich industrialist who quells labor strikes and exploits the stock market while living a vice-filled personal life. The industrialist ultimately dies on his yacht in a storm.[89]

A real-world conflict between organized labor and the beef trust inspired Sinclair's most famous work, *The Jungle*. In 1903 the Amalgamated Meat Cutters and Butcher Workmen of North America, the national meatpacking labor union, secured wage hikes and labor reforms from the big meatpackers. However, the firms cut pay the very next year, and Amalgamated responded with strikes in several cities. These turned violent as strikers attacked the workers brought in to replace them. In the end, the packers rehired the strikers at an even lower wage, and tens of thousands of disappointed members departed Amalgamated over subsequent years.[90]

Sinclair wrote several articles about the failed strike for the populist-socialist journal *Appeal to Reason*, and he ultimately decided to make the meatpacking industry the focus of a new socialist novel that he hoped would "blow the roof off the industrial tea-kettle."[91] Beginning in November 1904, Sinclair interviewed laborers and other members of the Chicago meatpacking industry, visiting workers' homes and investigating meatpacking plants both as an official visitor and, in disguise, as a worker. He began writing *The Jungle* that Christmas.[92]

The Novel

The Jungle's protagonist, Jurgis Rudkus, is a poor Lithuanian who emigrates to Chicago's Packingtown district with his family. Jurgis is proud when he quickly procures a meatpacking job. Despite his initial awe at the packing-house's efficiency, he soon witnesses horrific conditions, with workers tossing poisoned rats in with the meat and mixing sickly cows rejected by inspection with healthy ones. One notorious passage describes the packinghouse's dangers to its workers:

> There were those who worked in the chilling-rooms, and whose special disease was rheumatism; the time-limit that a man could work in the chilling-rooms was said to be five years. There were the wool-pluckers, whose hands went to pieces even sooner than the hands of the pickle-men; for the pelts of sheep had to be painted with acid to loosen the wool, and then the pluckers had to pull out this wool with their bare hands, till the acid had eaten their fingers off. There were those who made the tins for the canned-meat; and

their hands, too, were a maze of cuts, and each cut represented a chance for blood-poisoning. . . . [A]nd as for the other men, who worked in tank-rooms full of steam, and in some of which there were open vats near the level of the floor, their peculiar trouble was that they fell into the vats; and when they were fished out, there was never enough of them left to be worth exhibiting,—sometimes they would be overlooked for days, till all but the bones of them had gone out to the world as Durham's Pure Leaf Lard![93]

A worsening situation at Jurgis's home parallels the packinghouse horrors. His wife Ona's health suffers when she returns to work almost immediately after giving birth, and her boss soon rapes her. When Jurgis discovers this, he tries to kill the boss and is arrested. With Jurgis in jail for over a month, his family nearly starves. They also lose their home, unable to keep up with the payments. Ona dies not long after Jurgis is released, and in his grief Jurgis squanders the family's money on alcohol. He gets by on odd jobs until his son drowns, after which he escapes to the countryside and tries living "as a tramp."[94]

Upon returning to Chicago, Jurgis falls further into vice and criminality, and is enlisted by political bosses to help in their elections. At one point he hears a socialist orator and is intrigued by his ideas. Thrilled that there are others who disdain capitalism and the suffering of poor immigrants, Jurgis becomes a committed socialist and begins reading *Appeal to Reason*. The novel ends with the declaration "Chicago will be ours!"[95]

Publication and Reactions

The Jungle failed to catch the public eye when it first appeared serialized in *Appeal to Reason,* but it quickly became a sensation after Doubleday, Page & Co. published the full novel in February 1906. Doubleday had verified Sinclair's claims, with one editor reporting that he "was able to see with [his] own eyes much that Sinclair had never even heard about."[96] The publisher promoted the book heavily, providing early copies to newspapers nationwide and to influential individuals, including President Roosevelt. Although some early reviews dismissed it as sensationalist fiction and socialist propaganda, analysts estimated that over a million people had read *The Jungle* by year's end. Sinclair's descriptions of Chicago packinghouses astonished (and revolted) readers, and meat industry profits declined as many Americans avoided meat products and several nations barred American meat.[97]

J. Ogden Armour of the Armour Packing Company responded to *The Jungle* and other anti-meatpacking literature through pieces in the *Saturday Evening Post* that March.[98] Armour decried *"ignorantly or maliciously false statements"* and asserted that *"not one atom of any condemned animal or carcass finds its way, directly or indirectly, from any source, into any food-product or food-ingredient"* at his company.[99] He assured readers that the firm voluntarily had all of its meat inspected, because the government's stamp was good for business, and he argued that the packinghouses' transparency proved accusations of unsanitary conditions to be totally false. "Unfortunately," he wrote, "a good many people will always believe anything that is persistently told [to] them, particularly if it be about a corporation."[100]

Sinclair had hoped the book would help spark a socialist awakening. Descriptions of meatpacking filled only a fraction of the novel's pages, and the topic was largely incidental to his cause. Despite Sinclair's focus on the plight of industrial workers and his relative disinterest in the issue of food safety, *The Jungle* would ultimately play a prominent role in the development of American meat regulation.*

Meatpacking in the Early 1900s
Threats to the Major Meatpackers

New threats to the dressed-beef industry had emerged at the start of the 1900s. Many railroads had since merged into larger firms, with greater control over wider areas and better ability to bargain with packers. At roughly the same time, the original founders of the major meatpacking firms were aging and passing away, provoking uncertainty about both succession and

---

* Sinclair's book also played an important role in the broader drive for pure food and drug regulation. The Agriculture Department's chief chemist, Harvey Wiley, had made headlines in 1904 with a study concluding that preservatives in common food products were poisoning consumers, and in late 1905 the muckraking journalist Samuel Hopkins Adams had exposed dangers in the patent medicine industry in his "The Great American Fraud" series in *Collier's Weekly*. By early 1906 the combination of *The Jungle*, "The Great American Fraud," and Wiley's findings on food safety were pushing public demand for food and drug regulation to new heights, and proposals for a food and drug law were soon moving through both houses of Congress. See James Harvey Young, *Pure Food* (Princeton, NJ: Princeton University Press, 1989), esp. chaps. 8–11.

relationships within the industry. Beyond these pressures, there were questions about the structural and legal viability of their pooling arrangements. Twice over the course of the 1890s the emergence of a major new dressed-beef firm had broken the pooling agreements as members scrambled to compete with the newcomers. Although a new pool in 1898 incorporated the new companies, participants remained wary of future shocks.[101]

In 1902, meanwhile, the Justice Department finally began investigating the beef pools' legality under the Sherman Act. Despite meatpacker claims that their pooling and price setting served the "public good" by preventing market breakdowns, in 1903 an Illinois circuit court ruled against them and prohibited them from employing "any other method or device, the purpose and effect of which is to restrain commerce." However, the court still allowed the packers to limit their output "to prevent the over-accumulation of meats" on the market.[102]

Facing mounting legal and economic threats, and following a precedent set in the railroad and oil industries, Armour, Swift, and Morris (the "Big Three," after Armour bought out Hammond) merged with several other major meat firms into the National Packing Company in 1903, shortly after the Justice Department had launched its investigation. By combining through the formation of an immense holding company, the meatpackers could now coordinate their activities, communicate directly, and enact pooling-like policies all without violating the letter of the Sherman Act.[103]

Roosevelt versus the Beef Trust

Even before the National Packing Company took its place within the emerging pantheon of trusts, President Roosevelt was expressing deep concern about the degree of concentration in American business. "The great corporations which we have grown to speak of rather loosely as trusts are the creatures of the State," he declared in a 1902 address, "and the State not only has the right to control them, but it is duty bound to control them wherever the need of such control is shown."[104] Indeed, Roosevelt made it a goal of his young presidency to "strengthen the hand of the executive" in containing any trusts that proved detrimental to the country.[105] The merger of the meatpackers in 1903 quickly became a perfect illustration of what he hoped to combat. Roosevelt had experience with the meatpackers' products: as an officer in the Spanish-American War, he had sampled "embalmed beef" and found it inedible.[106] Perhaps in part as a result, he considered the beef trust "evil" and made it one of his very first targets.[107]

In 1904 the U.S. Bureau of Corporations began investigating the wide gap between low cattle prices and high beef prices. Roosevelt supported the investigation, hoping to find evidence of meatpacker misconduct, but the resulting 1905 report disappointed him and his antitrust allies.[108] Instead of revealing meatpacker wrongdoing, it concluded that their profits were entirely reasonable and that industry leaders had not restricted competition. The report found, for example, that while Swift's 1904 sales were about $200 million, its profits were only $3.85 million, or 1.93 percent of sales, far lower than popularly believed.[109] The report acknowledged that beef prices were high, but it concluded that this was because cattle prices were high as well, contrary to popular perceptions, and expressed skepticism that the packers were manipulating prices in any way.[110]

Antitrust activists and journalists assailed the report. The *New York Press* characterized the findings as "quite disgraceful" and "preposterous" and recommended that the Bureau's commissioner resign. The muckraker Charles Edward Russell derided "this airy skimming of dangerous facts, this agile turning of bad corners" and asked, "How does it happen that this defense is issued just at the time when it is most needed for the packing interests?"[111]

Roosevelt's efforts against the beef trust encountered further obstacles in 1905 and early 1906. In January 1905, the U.S. Supreme Court upheld the earlier Illinois decision against the packers, but found that the restrictions imposed had been too vague and onerous (even with the over-accumulation loophole), and loosened them accordingly. The next year, a district judge declared that immunity protections prevented any government case against the meatpackers from using information they had willfully supplied to the Bureau of Corporations during its investigation, dealing a large blow to the Justice Department's ongoing inquiry.[112]

Sinclair Shakes Up Washington

Despite these setbacks, the explosion of anti-meatpacker sentiment following release of *The Jungle* gave Roosevelt just the ammunition he needed to strike the packers. Almost immediately after the book was published, Secretary of Agriculture James Wilson tightened meatpacking sanitation rules and launched an investigation of the Chicago slaughterhouses and meat inspection system. However, both Wilson and Roosevelt feared that the Agriculture Department inquiry would not "get to the bottom of this matter," since a negative report would reflect badly on the department's existing inspections.[113] After consulting with Upton Sinclair, Roosevelt sent labor commissioner Charles Neill and social worker James Reynolds to conduct an investigation of their own.[114]

The two inquiries arrived at very different conclusions. While the Department of Agriculture team saw some room for improvement in the industry, it determined that *The Jungle* "greatly exaggerated" packinghouse sanitation issues and contained "willful and deliberate misrepresentations" of government inspectors as crooked and negligent.[115] The Neill-Reynolds findings, by contrast, were more in line with Sinclair's descriptions, telling of cold, unventilated rooms with wet floors where "drippings from the refrigerator rooms above trickled through the ceiling." Neill and Reynolds declared that these conditions were "a constant menace not only to [the laborers'] health, but to the health of those who use the food products prepared by them."[116]

The Neill-Reynolds findings alarmed major meatpackers, who already faced significant economic challenges. The growth of domestic meat consumption was slowing even as foreign competition was rising.[117] Worried that demand would decline further, the packers (along with livestock interests) urged the president not to release the report, promising that they would enact "reasonable, rational and just" reforms without government intervention.[118] Roosevelt kept the report quiet for the time being but rejected their offer to regulate themselves, asserting, "It is absolutely necessary that we shall have legislation which will prevent the recurrence of these wrongs."[119]

Two Proposals Face Off

The first lawmaker to answer Roosevelt's call for new legislation was Republican senator Albert Beveridge of Indiana, a fan of *The Jungle* (and an old friend of muckraker David Graham Phillips)[120] who had already been preparing a meat inspection amendment to the pending agricultural appropriations bill. After collaborating with Neill, Reynolds, and officials at the Agriculture Department, Beveridge introduced his amendment in May 1906. It called for stricter rules for the disposal of unfit meat, limitations on the use of dyes and chemicals, and date stamps on meat products. Firms, moreover, would only be allowed to sell meat products under "true name[s] which shall actually describe" their contents. Perhaps most significantly, Beveridge's amendment would require federal inspection of meat carcasses, products, and canned goods intended for interstate trade, as well as of meatpacking plants producing for interstate markets. All such inspections had been entirely optional under the 1890s laws.[121] Beveridge's proposal also mandated that packers would pay fees to fund the new inspections and that the Department of Agriculture would oversee packinghouse sanitation. Proud of his proposal, Beveridge touted it as "the most perfect meat inspection bill in the world" and "the most pronounced extension of federal power in every direction ever enacted."[122]

Although some meatpackers could see the commercial benefits of government inspections, as they had in the 1890s, they found the prospect of paying fees to fund them completely unacceptable.[123] As one meatpacking lobbyist later explained, the packers did not mind inspectors "provided [they did] not have to pay for them."[124] Under the existing system, inspection funding came from the government, which meant that meatpacking allies in the House could reduce the budget when inspections became too onerous.[125] Beveridge's plan would remove this option.

Beyond the funding provision, the meatpackers roundly opposed many of the Beveridge bill's other provisions as well. They feared that the new restrictions on naming products would destroy popular brands and that dating would lead consumers to reject sound, though aged, canned goods. One manager of the Morris company lamented that by empowering the Department of Agriculture with wide authority over sanitation, the amendment would place control of the industry "in the hands of theorists, chemists, [and] sociologists" without the oversight of the court system.[126]

Although the Beveridge amendment was approved in the Senate without opposition, in the House it competed with an alternate version prepared by Republicans James Wadsworth of New York and William Lorimer of Illinois. Both men were meatpacking allies: Wadsworth was a cattle breeder who considered *The Jungle* a "horrid, untruthful book," and Lorimer represented the Chicago meatpacking district.[127] Their far less onerous proposal had no dating requirements, protected brand names (even if they did not accurately

characterize the contents of the products), limited inspections to only carcasses and packinghouses, allowed greater use of preservatives, replaced the
packers' inspection fee with a budget appropriation, and allowed the meatpackers to appeal Agriculture Department rulings in court. It also left out the
critical Beveridge provision mandating inspection of meat and meat products
shipped across state lines. Although they had largely opposed any new regulation through early 1906, the meatpackers eventually expressed support for
legislation similar to the Wadsworth-Lorimer bill.[128]

The Wadsworth-Lorimer proposal infuriated Roosevelt. Dismissing it as
a "sham bill," he retaliated by releasing the official Neill-Reynolds report to
Congress on June 4.[129] Although he had hoped its publication would rally
support for the Beveridge bill, the report probably had minimal impact. An
impatient Sinclair had leaked the Neill-Reynolds findings to the *New York
Times* days earlier, and its contents, while unpleasant, were hardly shocking
to an American public already familiar with the even darker picture presented in *The Jungle*.[130]

The House Agriculture Committee soon began hearings on the Beveridge and Wadsworth-Lorimer proposals, though the committee was far
from impartial.[131] Not only were many members friendly to the meat industry, but Lorimer was a senior member of the committee and Wadsworth
its chair. The duo used the hearings to attack the Beveridge amendment and
initially summoned only industry-friendly witnesses to speak.[132] These witnesses assailed the Neill-Reynolds report as a "compendium of inaccuracies"
and argued that meatpacking was a dirty-looking business even when done
properly.[133] "I do not believe anybody ever expected to find a rose garden
in a slaughterhouse," one Illinois politician declared.[134]

When Neill and Reynolds testified, Wadsworth and his allies interrogated
them so aggressively that even some industry supporters thought they had
gone too far.[135] Wadsworth particularly harangued Neill over his claim that
workers had hung up with other clean carcasses a pig that had fallen into a
dirty bathroom, demanding precise details and explicitly challenging "the
credibility of the report."[136] Neill objected to this treatment, and one sympathetic congressman noted that Wadsworth was questioning Neill "as if he
were a culprit or as if he were being prosecuted."[137]

The committee passed a modified version of the Wadsworth-Lorimer
amendment on June 9.[138] Wadsworth and Lorimer had conceded some points

to Roosevelt after he indicated a willingness to compromise. They restored Beveridge's mandate on interstate inspections and expanded inspections to meat products and canned goods, but beyond these changes held firm to their original proposals. The amendment still had no dating requirements, protected brand names, would fund inspections through a budget appropriation rather than a fee assessed on the industry, and provided an easy path for meatpackers to appeal any of the agriculture secretary's rulings. Additionally, it instituted a year's delay between passage of the bill and formal appointment of inspectors, a policy that would likely give members of the Agriculture Committee considerable influence over the selection of inspectors in the interim.[139] Discouraged, President Roosevelt described the revised Wadsworth and Lorimer provisions as "so bad that . . . if they had been deliberately designed to prevent remedying of the evils complained of, they could not have been worse."[140]

Reaching a Compromise

Unfortunately for the president, he was now rapidly running out of time. The congressional session would end on June 30, only three weeks after the Agriculture Committee hearings ended. If Congress was unable to reach a better compromise by then, the cause might lose the energy that Sinclair's *Jungle* had provoked, scuttling hopes for a new law.

Although Roosevelt's Republican Party controlled both houses of Congress, the House and Senate were split over the issue. Reformers in the Senate wanted strong, Beveridge-style rules, while the House opposed such strict regulations. Fretting over the political implications of continued deadlock, Speaker of the House Joseph Cannon of Illinois approached Roosevelt about the possibility of a compromise that might placate both houses.[141]

At Cannon's suggestion, he and the president asked Wisconsin's Henry Adams, a moderate on the House Agriculture Committee and a pure-food advocate, to draft a new amendment that would incorporate elements of both the Beveridge and Wadsworth-Lorimer proposals. After consulting with James Reynolds and lawyers at the Agriculture Department, Adams produced an amendment that eliminated Wadsworth and Lorimer's yearlong delay in inspector appointments, restored the mandatory dating of canned meats, and removed the broad right of appeal on inspection decisions.

Inspections would still be funded by appropriation, as Wadsworth and Lorimer had demanded, but the agriculture secretary could impose fees if this funding proved inadequate. In Roosevelt's eyes, Adams's revision was "as good as the Beveridge amendment."[142]

Although members of the Agriculture Committee had informally approved the revision, Wadsworth and Lorimer had not been present for the meeting and quickly denounced the new proposal once they saw it. To accommodate these two stalwarts, Speaker Cannon permitted a few further changes to the bill. The committee eliminated dating of canned meats once again but met the reformers at least partway on most other issues. Brand names would still be acceptable, but only so long as they were "not false and deceptive." Although there would be no fees for inspection, the inspection appropriation would be raised high enough to accommodate future expansion of the meatpacking sector. The committee agreed to drop the right to appeal, so long as the bill no longer explicitly granted the secretary of agriculture "final and conclusive" authority over inspection decisions, and the committee consented to removing the one-year delay on inspector appointments.[143]

Cannon presented the new version to the president on June 18. Roosevelt was frustrated with the loss of dating requirements but feared that further negotiation would push the debate beyond Congress's adjournment twelve days later. At the same time, he worried about how the Senate would receive the new proposal. Beveridge had recently written to Roosevelt reasserting his commitment to imposing fees to fund inspections, and the senator strongly favored dating requirements.[144] If Roosevelt endorsed the latest House version, which contained neither provision, he would undoubtedly have a hard time selling it to Beveridge and his Senate allies. Yet he also wanted to avoid "an obstinate and wholly pointless fight about utterly trivial matters, or about matters as to which we may ultimately find ourselves forced to yield."[145] The question now was how to get the best possible law on the books. Should he endorse the newest House proposal, potentially alienating his Senate allies? Or should he demand a stricter bill from the House, risking a drawn-out fight that could sink the effort altogether? This was the choice the president faced as he considered the options before him.

NOTES

1. James Harvey Young, *Pure Food* (Princeton, NJ: Princeton University Press, 1989), 242–244, quotation at 242.

2. Address of President Roosevelt at the Laying of the Corner Stone of the Office Building of the House of Representatives, Saturday, Apr. 14, 1906 ("The Man with the Muck-Rake"), available at http://voicesofdemocracy.umd.edu/theodore-roosevelt-the-man-with-the-muck-rake-speech-text/.

3. Quoted in Young, *Pure Food,* 251.

4. Upton Sinclair, "What Life Means to Me," in *The Jungle,* ed. Clare Virginia Eby (New York: W. W. Norton, 2003), 351. He also wrote: "I do not eat much meat myself, and my general attitude toward the matter was one of indifference; I was of the opinion (and I am still of the opinion) that any man who takes into his stomach food which has been prepared under the direction of unscrupulous commercial pirates such as the Chicago packers, deserves all the poisoning he gets."

5. See, esp., Young, *Pure Food,* 248; John Braeman, "The Square Deal in Action," in *Change and Continuity in Twentieth-Century America,* ed. J. Braeman, R. H. Bremner, and E. Walters (Columbus: Ohio State University Press, 1964), 71–72.

6. Mary Yeager, *Competition and Regulation: The Development of Oligopoly in the Meat Packing Industry* (Greenwich, CT: JAI Press, 1981), 12–13, 14.

7. Ibid., 49–50, 69. In 1880, trains out of Chicago carried 416,204 tons of livestock and only 30,705 tons of dressed beef. By 1885, it was 281,022 tons of livestock and 231,634 tons of dressed beef. These numbers are from an 1886 U.S. Department of Agriculture report, cited in ibid., 69 (table III.3). The *Railroad Gazette* put dressed beef's proportion at 51.5 percent in 1885 (ibid., 98).

8. Gary D. Libecap, "The Rise of the Chicago Packers and the Origins of Meat Inspection and Antitrust," *Economic Inquiry* 30 (Apr. 1992): 247. The average price for a pound of beef tenderloin dropped from 27.5 cents to 16.75 cents between 1883 and 1889 (Yeager, *Competition and Regulation,* 70).

9. Yeager, *Competition and Regulation,* 58–64, 50, 112.

10. Jimmy M. Skaggs, *Prime Cut: Livestock Raising and Meatpacking in the United States, 1607–1983* (College Station: Texas A&M University Press, 1986), 108–110, quotation (from A. M. Simons's *Packingtown*) at 110.

11. Yeager, *Competition and Regulation,* 60, 88. In fact, the railroads' unwillingness to build refrigerator cars had spurred Swift to incorporate car construction into his firm and later pursue further vertical integration (ibid., 50).

12. Ibid., 88, 95.

13. Ibid., 88–90, 96–98.

14. Ibid., 27–28.

15. Gabriel Kolko, *Railroads and Regulation, 1877–1916* (New York: W. W. Norton, 1965), 7–8.

16. Yeager, *Competition and Regulation,* 31, 98–99; Kolko, *Railroads and Regulation,* 17–20.

17. Quoted in Kolko, *Railroads and Regulation,* 27.

18. Yeager, *Competition and Regulation,* 101; Kolko, *Railroads and Regulation,* 26–27.

19. Chicago businessman quoted in Edward A. Purcell Jr., "Ideas and Interests: Businessmen and the Interstate Commerce Act," *Journal of American History* 54, no. 3 (Dec. 1967): 567.

20. Herbert Hovenkamp, "Regulatory Conflict in the Gilded Age: Federalism and the Railroad Problem," *Yale Law Journal* 97, no. 6 (May 1988): 1046–1050, quotation at 1050. Hovenkamp offers several potential economic justifications for this practice.

21. Purcell, "Ideas and Interests," 562.

22. Yeager, *Competition and Regulation,* 100–101.

23. Simon Sterne, of the Board of Trade and Transportation of New York, in *Report of the Senate Select Committee on Interstate Commerce* (Washington, DC: GPO, 1886), 76.

24. Gabriel Kolko, in *Railroads and Regulation,* asserts that the railroads were the primary force behind the Interstate Commerce Act (see esp. chaps. 1–3). Lee Benson, in *Merchants, Farmers, and Railroads* (Cambridge, MA: Harvard University Press, 1955), posits that it was the New York merchant class. Edward Purcell, "Ideas and Interests," focuses on "businessmen" in general. Mary Yeager's brief account in *Competition and Regulation* (100–102) focuses on the role of shippers of livestock and dressed beef.

25. Kolko, *Railroads and Regulation,* 34.

26. See ibid., 20–36.

27. Thomas W. Gilligan, William J. Marshall, and Barry R. Weingast, "Regulation and the Theory of Legislative Choice: The Interstate Commerce Act of 1887," *Journal of Law and Economics* 32, no. 1 (Apr. 1989): 44–49.

28. Richard Olney, quoted in John P. Roche, "Entrepreneurial Liberty and the Commerce Power: Expansion, Contraction, and Casuistry in the Age of Enterprise," *University of Chicago Law Review* 30, no. 4 (Summer 1963): 686.

29. Kolko, *Railroads and Regulation,* 43–44.

30. Ibid., 44; Yeager, *Competition and Regulation,* 101.

31. Historians disagree about the position of the railroads on the Interstate Commerce Act. For example, Gabriel Kolko (*Railroads and Regulation,* 45) asserts that most railroads approved of the legislation, whereas Edward A. Purcell ("Ideas and Interests," 576) calls this conclusion "quite doubtful."

32. 22 Jan. 1887 issue quoted in Purcell, "Ideas and Interests," 577.

33. Kolko, *Railroads and Regulation,* 46–47.

34. Union Pacific railroad president Charles Francis Adams Jr., quoted in ibid., 37.

35. See Tim Innes, "Speech on the life of Thomas McIntyre Cooley," Thomas M. Cooley Law School, 2008 Biennial Reunion of the Cooley Family Association of America, Ann Arbor, Michigan, 2 Aug. 2008 (www.cooleyfamilyassociation.com/Cooley ThomasMcIntyre.pdf).

36. Kolko, *Railroads and Regulation,* 51–56. From 1890 to 1900, the ICC decided only 180 cases out of several thousand presented.

37. Ibid., 68, 53.

38. Ibid., 57, 62–64, 87–88, 117.

39. Yeager, *Competition and Regulation,* 102–104, quotation from *Railroad Gazette.*

40. Yeager, *Competition and Regulation,* 111–113.

41. Skaggs, *Prime Cut,* 108. Missouri representative Richard Bland quoted in Libecap, "The Rise," 258.

42. Libecap, "The Rise," 248 ($28.71 per head in 1885, to $20.67 per head in 1890, real prices).

43. Ibid., 253. Quote from George Beck in U.S. Congress, *Testimony Taken by the Select Committee of the United States Senate on the Transportation and Sale of Meat Products* (Washington, DC: GPO, 1889), 133.

44. Yeager, *Competition and Regulation,* 173–175.

45. U.S. Congress, *Testimony,* 426; Yeager, *Competition and Regulation,* 175.

46. Quoted in Yeager, *Competition and Regulation,* 173.

47. Quote from 1873 Illinois Farmers' Convention, quoted in William Letwin, *Law and Economic Policy in America* (Edinburgh: Edinburgh University Press, 1966), 67, see also 69–70; Libecap, "The Rise," 256.

48. Libecap, "The Rise," 256.

49. Railroader Charles Francis Adams, quoted in Letwin, *Law and Economic Policy,* 55.

50. Yeager, *Competition and Regulation,* 135–136; Letwin, *Law and Economic Policy,* 55.

51. Letwin, *Law and Economic Policy,* 96, 97, quotation at 97.

52. Ibid., 54.

53. Ibid., quotations at 96–97, 96.

54. Ibid., 100, 103, 119–123, quotations at 119.

55. Yeager, *Competition and Regulation,* 180, 177.

56. Ibid., 135, 180–181; on pools, see ibid., chap. 5. The case, *U.S. v. Addyston Pipe & Steel Co.* (175 U.S. 211), targeted an iron manufacturing pool, not the packers, but appeared to ban the packers' pooling methods (see ibid., 160n1).

57. U.S. Congress, *Testimony,* 150.

58. Libecap, "The Rise," 252–253, 250.

59. Young, *Pure Food,* 130–132. Trichinosis may not have been the Europeans' only concern: scholars suggest that worries on the part of German pork interests about American competition may have contributed to that nation's embargo policy (Libecap, "The Rise," 251).

60. Libecap, "The Rise," 251.

61. Young, *Pure Food,* 133; John Braeman, "Square Deal," 50. The 1890 and 1891 acts are reprinted in U.S. Bureau of Animal Husbandry, *Twenty-Third Annual Report of the Bureau of Animal Husbandry for the Year 1906* (Washington: GPO, 1906), 438–439.

62. Libecap, "The Rise," 255; Young, *Pure Food,* 132–133.

63. Young, *Pure Food,* 136–139, quotations at 136.

64. Ibid., 137–139.

65. Ibid., 9, 31–32.

66. Pure food activist George Angell, quoted in ibid., 47.

67. Oliver Wendell Holmes Sr., *Medical Essays, 1842–1882,* quoted in Young, *Pure Food,* 19.

68. *American Grocer* trade journal, quoted in Young, *Pure Food,* 49.

69. National Board of Trade, quoted in Young, *Pure Food,* 55.

70. Robert C. Alberts, *The Good Provider: H. J. Heinz and His 57 Varieties,* quoted in Donna J. Wood, "The Strategic Use of Public Policy: Business Support for the 1906 Food and Drug Act," *Business History Review* 59, no. 3 (Autumn 1985): 420.

71. Young, *Pure Food,* 73–74.

72. Ibid., 83–85, quotations from Albert Hopkins and MN congressman Milo White at 83 and 85.

73. Ibid., 86.

74. Ibid., 89–91, quotation from Texas senator Richard Coke at 89. In 1904 the Supreme Court decided in *McCray v. U.S.* (195 U.S. 27) that this tax and a 1902 expansion were constitutional. "The judiciary is without authority to avoid an act of Congress lawfully exerting the taxing power, even in a case where, to the judicial mind, it seems that Congress had, in putting such power in motion, abused its lawful authority by levying a tax which was unwise or oppressive . . . Congress may select the objects upon which the tax shall be levied, and, in exerting the power, no want of due process of law can possibly result, and the judiciary cannot usurp the functions of the legislature in order to control that branch of the Government in exercising its lawful functions." See http://supreme.justia.com/cases/federal/us/195/27 /case.html.

75. Wood, "Strategic Use," 409; Young, *Pure Food,* 119.

76. Wood, "Strategic Use," 410; Young, *Pure Food,* 26; Marc T. Law and Gary D. Libecap, "The Determinants of Progressive Era Reform: The Pure Food and Drugs Act of 1906," in *Corruption and Reform: Lessons from America's Economic History,* ed. Edward L Glaeser and Claudia Goldin (Chicago: University of Chicago Press, 2006), 330.

77. Quoted in Young, *Pure Food,* 99.

78. Ibid., 50.

79. Ibid., 195, 201. See also Samuel Hopkins Adams, *The Great American Fraud: A Series of Articles on the Patent Medicine Evil, Reprinted from Collier's Weekly* (Chicago: Press of the American Medical Association, 1906), available at https://books.google.com /books?id=fd_S2Van52EC.

80. Charles Edward Russell, *The Greatest Trust in the World* (New York: Ridgeway-Thayer Co., 1905), 251–252. Available at babel.hathitrust.org/cgi/pt?id=mdp.39015 030434685.

81. Arthur S. Link and Richard L. McCormick, *Progressivism* (Arlington Heights, IL: Harlan Davidson, 1983), 11–15, 29, 54–55; Edwin Emery and Henry Ladd Smith, *The Press and America* (New York: Prentice-Hall, 1954), 457, 459, 402–405.

82. Emery and Smith, *The Press and America,* 475–477; David M. Chalmers, "The Muckrakers and the Growth of Corporate Power: A Study in Productive Journalism," *American Journal of Economics and Sociology* 18, no. 3 (Apr. 1959): 297.

83. David Graham Phillips, *The Treason of the Senate,* ed. George E. Mowry (Chicago: Quadrangle Books, 1964), 59, 191, 59.

84. First quotation is F. Hopkinson Smith, cited in ibid., 38 (editor's introduction); second quotation is from *Collier's Weekly,* cited in Fred J. Cook, *The Muckrakers* (Garden City, NY: Doubleday, 1972), 171.

85. Quoted in Cook, *The Muckrakers,* 10.

86. George Mowry, quoted in Chalmers, "Muckrakers," 297.

87. See, e.g., Anthony Arthur, *Radical Innocent: Upton Sinclair* (New York: Random House, 2006), 72–75.

88. Sinclair claimed that beginning in 1896 he experienced visions in which he saw fictional characters and famous authors (such as Hamlet, Don Quixote, and Percy Shelley) celebrating at a campfire. He interpreted this as a sign of his potential to be a great writer. William A. Bloodworth Jr., *Upton Sinclair* (Boston: Twayne, 1977), 24.

89. Ibid., 15–31, 32–39, Sinclair's *Autobiography* quoted at 38.

90. Skaggs, *Prime Cut,* 115–116. Between 1904 and 1914, Amalgamated's membership declined from 56,000 to under 6,000.

91. Article in *Appeal to Reason,* 11 Feb. 1905, quoted in Bloodworth, *Upton Sinclair,* 48.

92. Bloodworth, *Upton Sinclair,* 44–48; Young, *Pure Food,* 224.

93. Sinclair, *The Jungle,* 97.

94. Ibid., 206.

95. Ibid., 328.

96. Isaac Marcosson, *Adventures in Interviewing,* quoted in Skaggs, *Prime Cut,* 119.

97. Young, *Pure Food,* 224, 229–230; James West Davidson and Mark Hamilton Lytle, *After the Fact: The Art of Historical Detection,* 3rd ed. (New York: McGraw-Hill, 1992), 213.

98. Yeager, *Competition and Regulation,* 199.

99. J. Ogden Armour, *The Packers, the Private Car Lines, and the People* (Philadelphia: Henry Altemus Co., 1906), 61, 62, emphasis in original.

100. Ibid., 364.

101. Yeager, *Competition and Regulation,* 136–138, 111–128.

102. Ibid., 181–184.

103. Ibid., 140–155.

104. Theodore Roosevelt, *Presidential Addresses and State Papers* (New York: Review of Reviews Co., 1910), 13:103.

105. Quoted in Yeager, *Competition and Regulation,* 185.

106. Young, *Pure Food,* 138.

107. Yeager, *Competition and Regulation,* 186.

108. Ibid., 186–188. Congress had, at Roosevelt's request, created the Bureau of Corporations within the Department of Labor and Commerce in 1903 to be an "agency of publicity" for his antitrust efforts (ibid., 186).

109. The report is cited in Francis Walker, "The 'Beef Trust' and the United States Government," *Economic Journal* 16, no. 64 (Dec. 1906): 501.

110. Yeager, *Competition and Regulation,* 187–188.

111. Quotations from ibid., 188.

112. Ibid., 184, 189.

113. Davidson and Lytle, *After the Fact,* 214.

114. Young, *Pure Food,* 232–233.

115. Quoted in Yeager, *Competition and Regulation,* 199, and Young, *Pure Food,* 232.

116. Quoted in Yeager, *Competition and Regulation,* 200.

117. Ibid., 202.

118. Louis Swift, quoted in ibid., at 201; livestock interests mentioned at ibid., 203.

119. Davidson and Lytle, *After the Fact,* 214.

120. Cook, *The Muckrakers,* 155.

121. Young, *Pure Food,* 236–237. Beveridge's proposal had to be presented as an amendment, instead of a bill, because inspection fees qualified as a form of revenue, and only the House can introduce revenue-related bills (Davidson and Lytle, *After the Fact,* 215). The amendment is reprinted in House of Representatives Committee on Agriculture, *Hearings before the Committee on Agriculture on the So-called "Beveridge Amendment" to the Agricultural Appropriation Bill (H.R. 18537) as Passed by the Senate May 25, 1906—to which are Added Various Documents Bearing upon the "Beveridge Amendment"* (Washington: GPO, 1906) (hereafter cited as *Hearings . . . Beveridge Amendment*), 351–356.

122. Quoted in Yeager, *Competition and Regulation,* 201, and Young, *Pure Food,* 237 (second quote originally in all capital letters).

123. Yeager, *Competition and Regulation,* 202.

124. Thomas Wilson, quoted in Young, *Pure Food,* 242–243.

125. Davidson and Lytle, *After the Fact,* 217.

126. Young, *Pure Food,* 238; Braeman, "Square Deal," 59. Quotation from Thomas Wilson, in Young, *Pure Food,* 238.

127. Quoted in Davidson and Lytle, *After the Fact,* 216.

128. Young, *Pure Food,* 240–243.

129. Davidson and Lytle, *After the Fact,* 218. Quotation in Young, *Pure Food,* 241.

130. Young, *Pure Food,* 240–241.

131. The hearing transcripts are contained in *Hearings . . . Beveridge Amendment.*

132. Davidson and Lytle, *After the Fact,* 219.

133. Thomas Wilson, quoted in ibid., 219.

134. Charles S. Charton, quoted in Yeager, *Competition and Regulation,* 207.

135. Davidson and Lytle, *After the Fact,* 219.

136. Quoted in Young, *Pure Food,* 245.

137. Sydney Johnston Bowie (AL), quoted in ibid., 245.

138. Davidson and Lytle, *After the Fact,* 219. This version of Wadsworth-Lorimer is reprinted in *Hearings . . . Beveridge Amendment,* 357–361.

139. Braeman, "Square Deal," 67–68.

140. Quoted in Davidson and Lytle, *After the Fact,* 219.

141. Davidson and Lytle, *After the Fact*, 221–222; Braeman, "Square Deal," 69–70.

142. Davidson and Lytle, *After the Fact*, 221; Braeman, "Square Deal," 70. The quotation appears in both sources.

143. Braeman, "Square Deal," 70–72, second quotation at 71. Provisions of this version are reprinted in William L. Snyder, *The Interstate Commerce Act and Anti-Trust Laws* (New York: Baker, Voorhis and Co., 1906), 144–152, first quotation at 147.

144. John Braeman, *Albert J. Beveridge* (Chicago: University of Chicago Press, 1971), 107–108.

145. Letter to Beveridge of 30 June 1906, quoted in Young, *Pure Food,* 247. The letter was written after the June 18 decision point featured in this case.

The Battle over the Initiative and Referendum in Massachusetts (1918)

IN THE FALL OF 1918, as state elections approached, Massachusetts voters had much on their minds, and not only about politics. Thousands of Bay State boys were "over there" in France, battling the imperial German army; the Spanish Flu pandemic was hitting the state hard, with tens of thousands of people sick and hundreds dying; and the Red Sox, led by star pitcher and slugger Babe Ruth, won an exciting World Series over the Chicago Cubs, leaving Boston fans confident of future victories. As for the elections, they included close races for governor and U.S. Senate. Voters would also have to choose whether or not to approve nineteen proposed amendments to the state constitution. Of these, the most controversial by far would establish a state process of initiative and referendum.

The initiative would empower private citizens to write both laws and constitutional amendments, and pass them, even over the opposition of a majority of the state legislature. The referendum would allow voters to rescind laws that the legislature had passed. Behind the proposal lay nearly three decades of agitation, both in the state and nationally, for "direct democracy" in America. The initiative and referendum—or "I&R" for short—had become a key demand of progressivism, the diverse movement for economic, social, and political reform that swept the nation for nearly two decades after 1900. By 1918, close to twenty states, mostly in the West, and hundreds of counties and municipalities, including a number of cities in Massachusetts, had adopted and implemented some form of I&R. Opposition to a statewide I&R provision in Massachusetts, however, remained fierce.

Opponents claimed the I&R would threaten the rights of minorities, give undue influence to small but well-organized interest groups, and place needless burdens on voters. Proponents urged the people to empower themselves and take back control of the state from the "invisible government" of party bosses and corporate lobbyists.[1] Now, with election day approaching, the voters would have to decide.

Progressive-Era Reforms

The progressive movement was said to have emerged in response to major political, economic, and cultural challenges arising out of rapid urbanization and industrialization, as well as a massive influx of "new stock" immigrants from eastern and southern Europe. Noting that key progressive leaders were usually "old stock" (descended from British or northern European immigrants) and from urban, middle-class backgrounds, some historians have argued that such people felt threatened by the rise of a new class of industrialist "plutocrats," on the one hand, and the emergence of a new, largely immigrant "proletariat" on the other. According to this view, middle-class reformers aimed to increase the influence of people like themselves. Other historians, meanwhile, have emphasized that many progressives came from the ranks of business, interested principally in "modernization," "order," and "efficiency." Still other historians have stressed that numerous immigrants, labor unionists, and small farmers also belonged to the progressive coalition and pushed their own agendas.[2]

In combination, Progressive-era reformers initiated a wide range of economic and political changes at the national, state, and local levels. These included new government efforts to rein in corporations—for example, through various attempts at "trust busting" (to break up monopolies), "Blue Sky" laws to protect investors, legislation to ensure the purity and safety of foods and drugs, and regulations to prevent railroads from engaging in price gouging or rate discrimination. The Progressive era saw the rise of government ownership of local utilities and transit systems, the establishment of the Federal Reserve System, and the introduction of campaign finance laws. Progressive reformers also helped to enact legislation that promoted workplace safety, compensated injured workers, set minimum wages and maximum hours (especially for women workers), and banned child factory labor.

Another major strain of progressivism was the attempt to "address . . . social and economic problems through changes in political structures." Virtually all progressives claimed to favor "democracy," but they broke with the vision of American democracy that sought to increase the number of elective offices and the frequency of elections, and which prized partisanship.[3] Progressives usually disliked partisanship, favored infrequent elections, and preferred to replace elected officials with "experts" who would act to advance the "public good."

Whereas democratic reforms of the nineteenth century extended the franchise to all white men and, during Reconstruction, to all men regardless of race, the late nineteenth and early twentieth centuries saw a very different set of developments related to the ballot box. States across the South and into the Southwest, starting with Mississippi in 1890 and continuing through Oklahoma in 1915, took the vote away from blacks (and some poor whites), usually in the name of electoral reform. In the North and West, state and local governments instituted policies that had the effect (often intentional) of discouraging illiterate immigrants from voting. In particular, the distinctive ballots that previously had been printed by each political party were replaced with uniform, state-printed "Australian ballots," which voters who could not read English often had difficulty using. As a consequence, many Americans who had the right to vote stopped voting, or voted less often. In presidential elections, voter participation fell from around 75–80 percent in the 1880s and 1890s to about 60 percent in 1916. There were similar declines in voter turnout in state and local elections.[4]

Yet even as voting was becoming more exclusive along some dimensions, it promised to become more expansive as a result of the women's suffrage movement. By 1910 only five states—Wyoming, Colorado, Idaho, Utah, and Washington—had granted women full suffrage rights (some women elsewhere were permitted to participate in certain elections, such as for school committees). By 1918, seven more states had joined the list, while others allowed women to vote in presidential elections. Congress, meanwhile, was debating an amendment to the U.S. Constitution that would guarantee that the right to vote could not "be denied or abridged by the United States or by any State on account of sex."[5]

Pure Democracy

While fights over the franchise were evident during this period, so too were debates over the nature of the democracy itself. "There is a radical difference between a democracy and a representative government," wrote J. W. Sullivan in 1892. "Democracy is direct rule by the majority, while representative government is rule by a succession of quasi-oligarchies, indirectly and remotely responsible to the majority." In the United States, Sullivan observed, the local, state, and federal governments were at best "quasi-oligarchies composed of representatives and executives" and all too often "complete oligarchies, composed in part of unending rings of politicians that directly control the law and the offices, and in part of the permanent plutocracy, who purchase legislation through the politicians." If, however, citizens could legislate for themselves, directly, then America could be transformed into a "pure democracy."[6]

Sullivan, a New York labor activist and self-described "radical," opened his book *Direct Legislation by the Citizenship* with these declarations. The tract would do more than any other book to excite public interest in the initiative and referendum by convincing readers that direct democracy was not just a "crazy" theory but a practicable plan.[7]

Sullivan pointed out that the I&R, although seemingly a novel concept, had many precedents in American history. One was the New England town meeting, where "any citizen may propose measures, and these the majority may accept or reject." Also, nearly every state used referenda to ratify constitutional amendments. Although at one time constitutional amendments were statements of general principle, and therefore distinct from ordinary laws, they were no longer always so. By 1892, amendments routinely dealt with questions once handled exclusively by legislation, such as "prohibiting or regulating the liquor traffic; prohibiting or chartering lotteries; determining tax rates; founding and locating state schools and other state institutions; establishing a legal rate of interest; fixing the salaries of public officials; drawing up railroad and other corporation regulations; and defining the relations of husbands and wives, and of debtors and creditors."[8]

Although Sullivan had to concede that no true system of direct legislation yet existed in the United States, he could point to one country that had such a system in operation: Switzerland. In some small Swiss cantons, governed by communal assemblies rather like New England town meetings, a kind of I&R had been practiced "from time immemorial." Specifically, any citizen could propose a law, and "the majority" could "actually enact the law." But what made the Swiss case so exciting for Sullivan was that in recent decades, large urban cantons such as Zurich had adopted the I&R, as had the confederation as a whole, with its three million citizens. The Swiss had shown the world, Sullivan argued, that "direct legislation is possible with large communities."[9]

According to Sullivan, the initiative and referendum in Switzerland had produced a revolution in politics comparable with the revolution in industry brought about by the steam engine. Partisanship had all but disappeared, along with "rancor, personalities, false reports, hatreds, and corruptions." Public debate had been transformed into an elevated discussion over policy. "Jobbery and extravagance are unknown," he announced, "and politics, as there is no money in it, has ceased to be a trade." Because the people directly controlled the public purse, they kept taxes low and fair, and made sure public moneys were spent efficiently. And because the people directly managed public resources, such as land, they made sure these resources were used to advance the public good, largely eliminating poverty. As a result of the initiative and referendum, Sullivan concluded, "the Swiss have advanced the line of justice to where it registers their political,—their mental and moral,—development. Above that, manifestly, it cannot be carried."[10]

Direct Legislation by the Citizenship reached a broad audience, selling 10,000 to 15,000 copies a year for three years running. Among its readers in the fall of 1892 was a young man living in a cabin in Milwaukee, Oregon. Largely self-educated, William Simon U'Ren had lived in several states and the Kingdom of Hawaii and had held jobs as (in this order) a blacksmith, miner, lawyer, small-town newspaper editor, and farmhand.[11] Sullivan's book so excited U'Ren that he stayed up an entire night to study it by the light of his kerosene lamp. Until this point, he had been active in various economic and political reforms. As he later recalled, however, Sullivan showed him that the "one important thing" was "to restore the law-making power where it belonged—into the hands of the people. Once give us that, we could get anything we wanted."[12] Reading Sullivan's book, U'Ren had found the cause that would become his life's work, and soon—with the backing of various farmer and labor groups—he organized a key reform organization, the Joint Committee on Direct Legislation.

"Fighting the Devil with Fire"

When U'Ren entered the Oregon political scene, public anger was palpable, particularly over the issue of political corruption. As one historian writes of Oregon in the 1890s, it was "common knowledge . . . that gangs of 'repeaters' cast multiple ballots for pay."[13] The big railroad companies, meanwhile, were generally understood to control the state legislature by doling out favors (such as free railway passes) and outright bribes.* Public discontent only worsened when a national financial panic struck in 1893, producing high unemployment across the state.[14]

Against this backdrop, U'Ren's Joint Committee went to work. It soon had lecturers traveling the state, selling the advantages of the initiative and referendum. It also distributed thousands of pro-I&R pamphlets. The committee promoted the initiative as a way to bypass the corrupt legislature and enact radical economic reforms. They also favored an "obligatory" form of referendum, under which no law passed by the legislature could take effect until voters approved it. Sullivan, in his book, had praised the obligatory referendum as much better than the optional form.[15]

During the 1894 elections, U'Ren's committee circulated a petition to add the initiative and obligatory referendum to the state constitution. Fourteen thousand voters, out of an electorate of 80,000, signed the petition. U'Ren also personally collected pledges of support from a majority of candidates for the state legislature. Yet when the legislature met in 1895, the amendment narrowly failed. U'Ren concluded that the only way to succeed would be by

---

* Public concerns about political corruption in Oregon would be validated in the next decade. Between 1903 and 1910, more than a hundred Oregon officials, including a majority of the state congressional delegation, were indicted for participating in the fraudulent sale of federal lands, and more than thirty of them, including the senior U.S. senator from Oregon, John Mitchell, were ultimately convicted. See John Messing, "Public Lands, Politics, and Progressives: The Oregon Land Fraud Trials, 1903–1910," *Pacific Historical Review* 35 (Feb. 1966): 35–66; Tom Marsh, *To the Promised Land: A History of Government and Politics in Oregon* (Corvallis: Oregon State University Press, 2012), 111–112.

beating the political operators at their own game—or, in his words, "by fighting the devil with fire."[16]

He got his opportunity in 1896. That year, U'Ren was elected to the state House of Representatives as a member of the Populist Party, just in time to participate in the selection of a U.S. senator. The federal Constitution required that senators be chosen by their state legislatures. In Oregon this process was notorious for lawmakers "auctioning" their votes in return for favors and bribes. Moreover, because the state constitution limited the legislature to one forty-day session every two years, two out of every three sessions involved a Senate election, which often crowded out other public business. In 1895, for example, lawmakers had taken fifty-two ballots, and all but eight days of the session, to select a Republican senator.[17] Two years later, in 1897, the Senate selection process would become even more tangled, thanks in large part to the efforts of U'Ren.

The principal campaign issue that year was silver.[18] As a result of persistent economic weakness in the mid-1890s, credit had contracted and prices were falling. While Populists and most Democrats proposed to expand the money supply by coining silver dollars alongside the traditional gold ones, most Republicans denounced this plan as an assault on the integrity of the dollar. Yet the incumbent Republican senator from Oregon, John Mitchell (later convicted in a land fraud scandal), knew that silver was popular in his state and therefore straddled the "bimetallism" issue. This strategy had the effect of alienating two important Republican factions in the legislature: the "gold bugs," led by the Republican boss of Portland, Joe Simon, and a pro-silver faction, led by Jonathan Bourne, who wanted to be speaker of the Oregon House. The Populists and Democrats controlled only a small number of seats but potentially held the balance of power between Mitchell and his critics. Mitchell thus met privately with U'Ren and offered to use his influence to get the legislature to pass an I&R amendment if the Populists would vote to reelect him. U'Ren agreed to the deal.

Soon, however, after Mitchell calculated that he had enough Republican votes without the Populists, he announced his opposition to the initiative-and-referendum amendment. U'Ren responded by joining with the Simon and Bourne factions, as well as the Democrats, in an obstructionist strategy. They refused to take their seats in the state House of Representatives, thereby preventing a quorum and ensuring that no legislative business, including the

Senate selection, could proceed. U'Ren and Bourne offered to support Mitchell once again if he endorsed both the I&R proposal and Bourne's candidacy for the House speakership, but Mitchell refused. As a result, the boycott continued until the legislative session expired, and no senator was chosen.* Good-government advocates decried this "hold-up" as a prime example of everything wrong with Oregon politics. U'Ren, however, secured an important ally, Bourne, who pledged (in this case sincerely) to support an I&R amendment in the next legislative session.[19]

U'Ren now aimed to win support for the initiative and referendum from the political mainstream. He broke with the Populists, whose influence was waning, and in 1898 founded a new organization, the Nonpartisan Direct Legislation League. Unlike the old Joint Committee, the League stopped talking about using the initiative to achieve radical economic reforms (which grew less popular as the economy recovered) and abandoned the idea of stripping the legislature of independent lawmaking authority by means of an obligatory referendum. Instead, the League favored an optional referendum, in which voters could petition to put a newly enacted law on the ballot. The League promoted the I&R as a tool to strengthen popular oversight and check corruption. The new, more moderate campaign cost the proposal some support among radicals, but it gained more than it lost, especially among "good government" Republicans. An influential Republican newspaper, the Portland *Oregonian,* as well as major industrialists and businessmen, now climbed aboard the I&R bandwagon.[20]

When the legislature met in 1899, U'Ren, although no longer a member of the House, worked the halls of power like the lobbyists he so often denounced. He cut deal after deal—pledging League support for the reelection of one lawmaker, and offering to back the pet project of another, so long as they voted for the I&R amendment. "We helped through measures we didn't believe in," he later explained, "to get help for our measures from members who didn't believe in them. That's corruption, yes; a kind of corruption, but our measures were to make corruption impossible in the end."[21]

The I&R amendment ended up passing the legislature with a large majority. According to the procedure in Oregon, however, a constitutional

---

* Mitchell was eventually returned to the U.S. Senate in 1901.

amendment had to be approved by two successive legislatures and then by the voters. As a result, U'Ren and the League kept up the public campaign and the private pressure, and they ultimately won a resounding victory. The 1901 legislature overwhelmingly reaffirmed the amendment, and most of the state's political leaders endorsed the proposal when it was put on the ballot in 1902. The electorate finally approved the amendment by a vote of 62,024 to 5,668, making Oregon the first state in the nation to put an I&R system into operation.[22]

The Oregon System

Under the "Oregon System," anyone could write a law or constitutional amendment and circulate a petition to put it on the ballot. To succeed, an initiative petition had to be signed by a number of voters equal to 8 percent of the total votes cast in the most recent election for a justice to the Oregon Supreme Court.* Voters could also call for referenda on laws passed by the legislature. Within ninety days of a law being enacted, a referendum petition had to be signed by a number of voters equal to 5 percent of the total votes cast in the most recent Supreme Court election. Legislators could also submit a law to voters for final enactment, a process called "legislative referral." Notably, the governor had no veto over voter-enacted laws.

By the time the I&R amendment was approved, U'Ren had emerged as a towering figure in Oregon politics. One Portland newspaper suggested that the state government now had four departments, "executive, legislative, judicial and Mr. U'Ren," and that U'Ren "outweighs any one, or perhaps all three" of the others.[23] His greatest triumphs came from using the initiative and referendum to further advance direct democracy. He scored his first major victory in 1904, when voters overwhelmingly endorsed his initiative measure for direct primaries.

In the nineteenth century the term "primary" referred to a local party caucus, run by party operatives according to party rules, which chose delegates to district and state party nominating conventions. Reformers had long

---

* At the time, Oregon had a Supreme Court composed of three justices, each elected for a six-year term in a statewide contest. Because the terms were staggered, a Supreme Court election took place every two years. See Constitution of Oregon (1857), Art. VII, §§3, 10.

TABLE 13.1

Selected Ballot Measures in Oregon, 1904–1916
(Initiatives unless otherwise noted)

Year	% Yes Vote	Description *Italics* = constitutional amendment **Boldface** = approved
1904	77.5%	**Direct primary**
	51.9%	**Local option liquor law**
1906	43.9%	*Equal suffrage for women*
1908	53.4%	**Effort to ban gillnet fishing on the Columbia River**
	65.0%	**Effort to ban fishwheel fishing on the Columbia River**
	38.6%	*Equal suffrage for women*
	65.3%	***Recall power on public officials***
	76.7%	***Instructing legislature to vote for people's choice for U.S. Senator***
1910	37.4%	*Permit female taxpayers to vote*
	41.6%	*Prohibit liquor traffic*
	51.0%	***Permit presidential primary***
	45.5%	*Extend I&R; six-year terms; proportional representation in legislature; etc.*
1912	51.8%	***Equal suffrage for women***
	57.3%	**Eight-hour day on public works**
	46.0%	Blue Sky law (investor protection)
	30.4%	*"U'Ren constitution"*
1913	43.9%	Sterilize habitual criminals [Referendum]
	69.0%	**Workmen's compensation act** [Referendum]
1914	57.7%	***Prohibition***
	80.5%	***Require voters to be U.S. citizens*** [Legislative Referral]
	50.0%	***Abolish death penalty***
	22.5%	*Proportional representation for the legislature*
	33.6%	*Abolish State Senate*
	22.7%	*Universal eight-hour workday*
	31.4%	*Establish a Department of Industry and Public Works to employ the unemployed and establish an inheritance tax for its maintenance*
1916	49.9%	End compulsory vaccination

Sources: Adapted from "Oregon Blue Book," http://bluebook.state.or.us, accessed July 1, 2013; Steven L. Piott, *Giving Voters a Voice: The Origins of the Initiative and Referendum in America* (Columbia: University of Missouri Press, 2003).

complained that only a small number of party activists ever participated in the primaries, and that party bosses used political chicanery to control the primaries and, in turn, the entire political system. Under the new law, primaries became publicly supervised elections. Although some party leaders objected that this unprecedented intrusion of the state into internal party matters violated the basic right of voluntary political associations to govern themselves, many Americans apparently disagreed.[24] The Oregon law, and a similar one approved in Wisconsin in 1903, were soon copied across much of the country.[25]

U'Ren also changed how Oregon chose its U.S. senators. Already in 1901 the legislature had approved an U'Ren-backed law to put the names of U.S. Senate candidates on the ballot, allowing voters to make their preferences known to the legislature. But in 1903, legislators bypassed the two top-vote-getting candidates and chose a third man, sparking a popular outcry. U'Ren's 1904 direct primary law required legislative candidates to sign one of two statements: Statement Number One declared that, if elected, the candidate would vote for whoever won the popular preference vote for senator; Statement Number Two declared that, if elected, the candidate would regard the popular vote as advisory. Whichever statement the candidate signed would be printed alongside his name on the ballot.[26]

In 1906 U'Ren ran the U.S. Senate campaign of his Republican ally from the 1897 contest, Jonathan Bourne. He and Bourne urged voters to elect only legislative candidates who subscribed to the first statement, and voters largely complied. As a result, when Bourne won the popular preference vote, the Oregon legislature sent him to Washington, where he became a champion of direct democracy.[27]

In 1908 U'Ren succeeded in putting an initiative on the ballot to make Statement Number One legally binding, and voters approved it overwhelmingly, 69,668 to 21,162. Owing to this law, in 1909 a majority-Republican legislature took just twenty-three minutes and a single ballot to select the Democrat who had won the 1908 preference poll as the next U.S. senator from Oregon.[28] Not only had U'Ren banished the ghost of the 1897 "hold-up," but his new way of electing senators was also copied in other states, building political momentum to change the U.S. Constitution so that senators would be elected directly by the voters.[29] This goal was finally achieved through the Seventeenth Amendment, ratified in 1913.

Besides direct primaries and the direct election of senators, U'Ren and his allies could point proudly to prominent pieces of reform legislation enacted in Oregon under the I&R process. These included a "corrupt practices act" (limiting lobbying and requiring all campaign contributions be publicly reported); an eight-hour workday for public employees; a workers' compensation system; new taxes on utilities, telegraph, and oil companies; constraints on the major railroads through regulation of freight rates and new railroad taxes; the creation and funding of Oregon State University; and abolition of the death penalty. Finally, there was women's suffrage. Although the male electorate rejected women's suffrage initiatives three times between 1906 and 1910, male voters finally agreed in 1912, by a margin of 61,265 to 57,104, to grant the right to vote to female citizens.[30]

Impressed by these achievements, progressive reformers outside of Oregon pushed their own states and communities to adopt the initiative and referendum, and U'Ren emerged as a leader of the national movement.[31] He also helped to convince two U.S. presidents—Theodore Roosevelt, a Republican, and Woodrow Wilson, a Democrat—to modify their positions on direct democracy.

Roosevelt, who had been skeptical about the initiative and referendum during his presidency (1901–1909), claimed to have warmed to the idea after a train ride with U'Ren through Oregon in 1911. They were discussing the Oregon System when they "heard some bird-song" through the compartment window. Roosevelt, an ardent naturalist, was "really pleased" that U'Ren could correctly identify it as the call of the western meadowlark. The former president remarked that he was glad to see that "those who most earnestly led and strove for the success of the radical democratic movement" continued to recognize the value and joy to be derived from "all that is beautiful . . . in the works of nature and of man." U'Ren replied that as social injustice was diminished, "the average man" would have more free time to devote to "things of the spirit." The remark, Roosevelt reported, "impressed" him.[32]

Wilson, who had been a political science professor and president of Princeton University before being elected governor of New Jersey in 1910, had denounced direct democracy in his books and class lectures. In 1909 he had become president of the national Short Ballot Association, an organization dedicated to reducing the number of elected officials in the name of governmental efficiency and accountability (the argument being that voters could monitor the acts of a few important, visible officials more easily than many minor, obscure ones). U'Ren served as the organization's secretary, and the two men wound up having many conversations. In the end, U'Ren helped convince Wilson, who had a reputation for rarely changing his mind, to do so in the case of I&R. In a 1911 interview, Wilson recalled he had "preached to the students of Princeton" that direct democracy was "bosh." But now, he said, "I want to apologize to those students. It is the safeguard of politics. It takes power from the boss and places it in the hands of the people. I want to say with all my power that I favor it."[33]

In the 1912 presidential race, Wilson became the Democratic nominee, while Roosevelt broke with the Republicans and became the standard bearer of a third party, the Progressives. They, along with a third I&R advocate, the Socialist Party candidate, Eugene V. Debs, together received 75 percent of the votes cast for president that year. Wilson won. Meanwhile, the only I&R opponent in the race, the Republican candidate and incumbent president, William Howard Taft, received just 23 percent of the vote.[34] Even as this apparent national consensus in favor of I&R took hold, however, U'Ren himself had come to believe that I&R did not go far enough.

Recall and Reorganization

In 1908 U'Ren promoted an Oregon initiative allowing voters to "recall" elected public officials—that is, remove them before their terms had expired. Under the plan, 25 percent of eligible voters had to sign a petition to trigger a recall election. U'Ren and many other progressives came to associate the recall so closely with the initiative and referendum that they began thinking of them as a single reform, the "I&R&R."[35] Yet public enthusiasm for the recall seemed lower than for the initiative and referendum. Particularly controversial were proposals to allow voters to recall judges. As one historian has explained, "even many Progressives . . . feared that recalling judges would dangerously undermine judicial independence."[36]

Oregon voters did ultimately approve U'Ren's recall plan, but only by 58,381 to 31,002, a far smaller margin than in the case of his earlier proposals. Over the coming years the issue of judicial recall would become a rallying point for critics of the I&R&R system across the country. In 1911, when

Congress approved a resolution admitting Arizona as a state, President Taft vetoed it because the proposed state constitution allowed for the recall of judges. Only after Arizonans abandoned this provision did Taft allow their state into the Union.[37]

Meanwhile U'Ren forged ahead, proposing a radical reorganization of state government. His reorganization plan became the platform of his new organization, the People's Power League. First published in 1909, the League plan went through various iterations over the next five years, but all aimed to reduce the number of elections and elective offices and to promote nonpartisanship.[38]

Instead of legislative elections every two years, a gubernatorial election every four, and elections for many other offices at two- or four-year intervals, the plan authorized a single statewide election every six years. In this single election, voters would choose a governor, an auditor, a board of three "People's Inspectors," and the entire legislature, which in later versions of the plan would be unicameral (a single house).[39] The governor would appoint almost all other officials, including many who previously had been elected independently, among them the attorney general, local sheriffs and district attorneys, and members of over forty commissions. The governor would also appoint a new state "business manager," whose job would be "to obtain the highest possible efficiency in the State's service and full value for the public money." The governor would, however, be limited to a single term; have no veto power; and be prohibited from appointing, transferring, promoting, or removing any official on the grounds of "personal preference or dislike or for political or party advantage." Legislators would be chosen by a system of proportional representation, where seats were allocated according to the percentage of the popular vote a party received. All members of the legislature would be required to pledge that they would not engage in "logrolling" (trading votes on one another's favored measures). If any ten "citizen freeholders" believed that a law had been passed by "bargaining, trading, logrolling, or other forms of undue influence," they could challenge it in court, and if they convinced a jury they were right, the measure would be put before the voters as a referendum.[40]

Promising fewer elections and elective offices, U'Ren's plan may have seemed as if it would take power away from the people. U'Ren insisted, however, that "the people" would be able to "protect their liberties" with "direct powers." His plan would authorize them to use the initiative and referendum at both the state and local levels, and allow them to recall not only any elected official, but even the entire legislature, as a body.[41] He also maintained that his plan would ensure that voters remained fully and accurately informed as to what their government was doing. This would be the job of the non-partisan "Board of People's Inspectors," elected by proportional representation. The inspectors would be responsible for investigating all state and local government activities, as well as "important experiments and developments in the science of government by other nations, States, counties, and cities," and would publish their findings in a bimonthly "gazette," mailed free to all voter households.[42]

Between 1910 and 1914, the People's Power League succeeded in putting components of this plan on the ballot, but Oregon voters rejected all of them. In 1910 they voted down an initiative creating the bimonthly gazette, 29,955 to 52,538, and another creating a legislature elected proportionately for six-year terms, 37,031 to 44,366. In 1912 they rejected a plan for a proportionately elected unicameral legislature (31,020 to 71,183), and in 1914 they overwhelmingly rejected an amendment to the state constitution that would have established proportional representation (39,740 to 137,116), and another abolishing the state senate (62,376 to 123,429).[43] Although U'Ren had little choice but to abandon the League plan in Oregon, similar plans were adopted around the country at the municipal level.

A City for the People

In the late nineteenth and early twentieth centuries, U.S. cities experienced explosive growth, fueled by migrants from rural areas and foreign lands. In 1880 about 13 million people, a quarter of all Americans, lived in urban areas. By 1920 the number had increased to more than 54 million, and the nation had an urban majority for the first time in its history. Municipal expenditures also exploded in this period, as cities rushed to meet the needs of their burgeoning populations for paved roads, dredged harbors, streetcar railways, police forces, schools, parks, libraries, and systems to supply fresh water, gas, and electricity and to dispose of sewage. By the first decade of the twentieth century, a majority of all public debt in the United States had been issued by local governments. Municipalities also managed most public services. One reformer declared in 1901, "Municipal government is the problem of the age. It touches us in our daily lives a dozen or a score of times while the State or National government touches us once."[44]

Progressives decried the corruption and inefficiency of most city administrations, which they blamed on the influence of political bosses and machines. Political organizations such as Tammany Hall in New York, run by Democrats, and the Gas Ring in Philadelphia, run by Republicans, used patronage and favors to win the support of many voters, and all too often fraud and intimidation to control many others. Certain bosses wielded enormous power—in some places no one could be elected to office, secure a government appointment, or win a government contract without their approval—and they often abused it. In New York City alone, the sums of public money lost to kickbacks, embezzlement, and inside deals under the leadership of the Tammany boss William Tweed, who eventually went to prison, reached at least $160 million, according to one estimate.[45]

Reformers proposed to create a new kind of "city for the People" by radically reorganizing how cities were governed. Their plans generally resembled U'Ren's plans for Oregon: fewer elections and elected officials (the "short ballot" reform) and less partisanship. U'Ren himself actively supported these efforts. In Oregon he successfully promoted an initiative to simplify the process by which cities could rewrite their charters (they would no longer need the approval of the legislature).[46] Also, as has been mentioned, he served as secretary of the national Short Ballot Association.

The urban government reform movement achieved sweeping victories. One indication of this was the rapid disappearance of the large, bicameral city council, its lower house elected by district. In 1890 such councils were the centerpiece of numerous American city governments; by 1920 reformers were well on their way to abolishing them.[47] In 1909, for example, Boston replaced its eight-member Board of Aldermen and seventy-five-member Common Council with a nine-member, nonpartisan unicameral council, elected at large.[48]

Reformers also transformed the office of the urban executive. In some cases the mayor was made more powerful, with his term extended (in Boston, from one to four years, for example), and his appointment powers increased. In other cases, executive power was invested in an unelected business manager, appointed by the city council. During the 1910s, more than a hundred cities adopted city manager charters.[49]

Perhaps the most popular new form of city government, however, was the commission. Under this arrangement, the mayor and city council were both replaced by a board of five to seven nonpartisan commissioners, elected at large and often by proportional representation. Each commissioner functioned as an executive in charge of a branch of municipal affairs (finance or public safety, for example), and collectively the commissioners served as the city council. In a common variant of the plan, commissioners hired a city business manager to supervise day-to-day administration. Business leaders in Galveston, Texas, established the first commission government in 1901, after a hurricane struck and the existing city government proved unable to deal with the resulting devastation. By 1913 more than 300 American cities had adopted some version of commission government.[50]

Most of the new city governments, and especially those of the commission type, included provisions in their charters for direct democracy.[51] In 1911 a political scientist offered the following explanation: "One of the most serious objections made to the commission government is that it concentrates too much power into the hands of a few individuals. . . . The initiative and referendum, coupled with the recall . . . have, therefore, been inserted in the later commission charters largely to overcome the objection that the new form of city government was undemocratic."[52]

The Representative Principle

Despite the growing popularity of the initiative and referendum, or perhaps because of it, criticism of direct democracy mounted steadily. A common objection to the Oregon System was that it needlessly burdened the electorate. Critics noted that in 1910, when thirty-two statewide initiatives appeared on Oregon ballots, the pamphlet sent to voters explaining them ran to 208 pages, while the ballot in Portland—listing candidates, statewide initiatives, and local initiatives—was more than three feet long.[53] A related objection was that the Oregon process set the threshold too low for putting questions on the ballot, resulting in small interest groups cluttering the ballot with initiatives of little interest to the average voter. Critics noted that as the

TABLE 13.2

Approval of State Ballot Measures in Oregon, 1904–1916

Year	Number of Ballot Measures	Number of Ballot Measures Approved by Voters	Average "Yes" Vote for All Ballot Measures
1904	3	3	67.2%
1906	11	8	68.3%
1908	19	12	52.5%
1910	32	9	39.5%
1912	37	11	44.0%
1913	5	4	57.4%
1914	29	4	36.4%
1916	11	6	50.9%

Sources: Adapted from "Oregon Blue Book," http://bluebook.state.or.us, accessed July 1, 2013; Steven L. Piott, *Giving Voters a Voice: The Origins of the Initiative and Referendum in America* (Columbia: University of Missouri Press, 2003). Ballot measures include legislative referrals.

number and variety of ballot measures increased in Oregon, voters there supported proportionately fewer of them. In 1904 and 1906, voters approved 11 out of 14 ballot measures; in 1913–1914, they approved only 8 out of 34.

Skeptics also questioned whether voters were capable of making fully informed decisions. An incident from the 1908 Oregon election became notorious. Two competing groups of salmon fishermen on the Columbia River, one that used gill-nets downstream and one that used fish wheels upstream, each put on the ballot, in the name of preserving fish stocks, an initiative that effectively banned the fishing method of the other. Voters approved both of them, thereby shutting down the state salmon fishing industry and creating a severe conflict with commercial fishermen from Washington State, who also caught salmon in the Columbia. A federal court ended up issuing an injunction to block enforcement of the two laws, and the legislature repealed both in 1909.[54]

Another objection to direct democracy was that it violated the U.S. Constitution. Advocates of direct democracy contrasted it with "representative government." Yet the founders of the country had made it clear they were establishing not a "democracy," but a "republic," based on representation. Opponents asked whether states that adopted direct democracy provisions had violated the constitutional guarantee that every state must have a "re-publican form of government." Indeed, this question lay at the heart of two major legal challenges to the Oregon System, both of which were turned back. The Oregon Supreme Court ruled in *Kadderly v. Portland* (1903) that a "republican form of government is a government administered by represen-tatives chosen or appointed by the people or their authority" and that Oregon, despite its I&R system, was by this standard still a republic: "The representative character of the government still remains. The people have simply reserved to themselves a larger share of legislative power."[55] The U.S. Supreme Court considered the same question in *Pacific States Telephone and Telegraph Company v. Oregon* (1912), but decided it had no authority over the issue. The high court ruled that the question of what constituted a repub-lican form of government was essentially political, not legal, and should be answered by Congress rather than the courts. Congress could show it no longer recognized Oregon as a republic simply by refusing to seat the Or-egon congressional delegation, but it had not done so.[56]

Neither of these decisions silenced the critics of direct democracy, who continued to insist it violated the "republican principle" and therefore threat-ened the foundations of American government. Among the most forceful advocates of this view was Senator Henry Cabot Lodge of Massachusetts. Lodge, a "Boston Brahmin" who had taught history at Harvard, had been elected as a Republican to the U.S. House of Representatives in 1886 and to the Senate six years later. In a series of speeches and lectures between 1907 and 1912, he argued that direct democracy and representative government were fundamentally incompatible, and that the latter was vastly superior.[57] The initiative and referendum, Lodge charged, typically produced worse laws than a legislature, or even than a New England town meeting. In a town meeting, as in a legislature, all measures were "open to debate, to amend-ment, to reference to a committee and to postponement." By contrast, the initiative and referendum processes rushed proposals before the voters, who could not modify them in any way, but had to vote them up or down in their entirety. This made no sense, Lodge argued, because there are many ques-tions that cannot be answered simply "yes" or "no." Besides, he charged, the initiative and referendum forced voters to act without adequate information, based merely on "what they happened to have read in the newspapers or to have heard from their neighbors." In pointing out these flaws of direct democracy, Lodge said he was no more questioning the ability of the people to govern themselves than he would be questioning their intelligence or education if he pointed out they could not read in the dark.[58]

Lodge also argued that the interests of the people as a whole could only be represented by legislatures and the courts. By contrast, initiatives and referenda merely registered the will of the voters—that "small portion of the people" qualified to vote—and, more specifically, the will of those who chose to cast ballots in a particular election. He noted that in nearly every election in which a law or constitutional amendment was on the ballot alongside candidates for office, many more people voted for the candidates than on the question. Lodge found cases in which questions were approved, even though a majority of those who went to the polls did not vote on them. The I&R system thus seemed to Lodge perfectly designed to allow small minorities, often "interested, fanatical, or corrupt factions," to use their "superior organization and intensity of purpose, to dictate the laws of the entire community."[59]

Lodge held, finally, that direct democracy would in the end undermine representative government, by taking from legislators all power and responsibility. As legislatures declined into insignificance, the power of the executive branch of government would have to grow. The end result, he concluded, would inevitably be despotism: "The advent of the strong man and the army is always coincident with the breaking down of representative government."[60]

Beyond Oregon

Despite such criticism, sixteen states beyond Oregon adopted I&R systems from 1904 to 1915. Yet perhaps in part because of the criticism, most of them attempted to limit the power of small "factions," typically by increasing the number of signatures required on a ballot petition. In many states, the percentage of voters who needed to sign a petition was increased to 10 percent, and in Oklahoma, Arizona, and Nebraska the trigger for a constitutional amendment was set at 15 percent. Nebraska, Maryland, and Ohio, meanwhile, required that signatures for ballot measures be geographically dispersed. A few states also mandated that for a referendum to be successful, a certain minimum percentage of the electorate had to participate, or that the votes had to be geographically dispersed.[61]

Perhaps the most significant departure from the Oregon System was the "indirect initiative." Some states, such as Michigan, adopted it in response to the criticism that initiative proposals could not be amended. The indirect process sent initiatives not straight to the voters, but first to the legislature, which then had the chance to enact it, reject it, or modify it. If it was rejected or modified, advocates of the original proposal could still petition to put it on the ballot. In some states the legislature was authorized to put the modified measure on the ballot alongside the original.[62]

One of the new states to adopt the initiative and referendum was California. There, as in neighboring Oregon, the direct democracy movement arose in response to public outrage over corruption—and especially over the immense political influence of the Southern Pacific Railroad. The grip the railroad appeared to have on nearly every aspect of state affairs gained it the nickname "The Octopus."[63] In 1910, a Progressive Republican, Hiram Johnson, swept into the governor's office pledging to restore control of the state to its people. One of Johnson's signature achievements, in 1911, was winning adoption of an I&R&R amendment to the state constitution.[64]

The California process resembled the Oregon System, with a simple 8 percent signature threshold for initiatives and a 5 percent threshold for referenda. Possibly as a consequence, statewide ballot measures proliferated as quickly in California as in Oregon. In 1912 and 1914, fifty-six laws and constitutional amendments were put before California voters, who approved twenty-nine of them. California progressives gave a nod to critics of direct democracy by creating an indirect initiative process, but made it optional. Sponsors of a measure could choose whether to take the direct or indirect route, and few bothered to go to the legislature.[65]

The Massachusetts Plan

In no state did the struggle to adopt the I&R take longer than in Massachusetts. Advocates appeared there early and were as fervent as in Oregon, but public opinion did not rally behind them as readily, in part because the state government was less obviously corrupt. The most prominent state politician was not, as in Oregon, the crooked John Mitchell, but rather the upright Henry Cabot Lodge.

Yet discontent simmered in Massachusetts, even if it never quite boiled. The women's suffrage movement had been agitating in the state since 1850, but women still lacked the right to vote. The labor movement felt stymied in its struggle to win worker protections, and recurring strikes, including a few that were large and violent, led many middle-class voters to worry that without reforms, "social unrest" would grow. Large numbers of immigrants, meanwhile, bridled under discrimination from the Yankee power structure. Also, Massachusetts was the second most urbanized state (after Rhode Island), with 76 percent of its population living in cities of over 8,000 by 1900. Local municipal reformers protested that although new, progressive-style city charters were urgently needed, the legislature had been slow to grant them.[66]

The first public call for the I&R in Massachusetts dates from 1891, when the journalist W. D. McCrackan, like J. W. Sullivan an ardent admirer of direct democracy in Switzerland, wrote an article for a Boston paper, *The Arena*. McCrackan declared that American democracy could not withstand the "corrupting influences, now at work in our midst" unless the "tyranny of Municipal, State, and Federal bosses, as unscrupulous as any feudal lordlings," were broken, and that this could be accomplished only by adopting the initiative and referendum.[67] In 1893, supporters organized a local Direct Legislation League and the following year succeeded in getting the Massachusetts legislature to consider an I&R amendment to the state constitution, but the amendment was defeated.[68]

Over the next decade, various I&R amendments were proposed but never passed the legislature. Supporters of the I&R therefore resorted to what one observer called the "flank movement" of a "public opinion" law.[69] It would allow petitioners to put nonbinding proposals on the state ballot; legislators were supposed to regard a majority "Yes" vote as an instruction from the people to take the proposal under consideration. Yet even this watered-down version failed to mollify conservatives—Lodge denounced it as auguring "a complete revolution in the fabric of our government"—while rousing little enthusiasm among direct democracy advocates, because it fell so far short of what they genuinely wanted. "Public opinion" bills failed to pass the legislature in 1906, 1907, and 1908.[70]

The political tide began to turn only when Democrats, who had the backing of labor and the growing immigrant population, allied with dissident, progressive-leaning Yankee Republicans. In 1910 this coalition elected Eugene Foss, a former Republican, as the first Democratic governor in fifteen years, and reelected him in 1911 and 1912. In his first inaugural address, he demanded an end to the "dictatorship by political bosses and by representatives of special interests" and advocated "direct legislation."[71] He was succeeded, in 1914, by another Democrat and I&R advocate, David Walsh (who was also the first Irish Catholic to be elected governor of Massachusetts).

By 1915 the legislature had approved a direct primary law, a constitutional amendment allowing the legislature to refer legislation to the people to be decided by referendum, a law allowing cities to adopt any of four standard progressive-style charters (each of which provided for a local initiative process), and a version of the public-opinion law, which allowed voters in particular legislative districts to hold nonbinding referenda. In 1914 and 1915, six such district referenda favored a state I&R.[72] Yet the legislature continued to reject the requisite constitutional amendment.

Direct democracy advocates, convinced they had to circumvent the legislature, began to push for a constitutional convention. This idea proved popular because even many opponents of direct democracy conceded that the Massachusetts constitution, written in 1780 principally by John Adams and "patched up by 44 amendments—several of them annulling previous changes," needed revision.[73] Many citizens wanted to remove the requirement that all state officials be elected annually—a practice they regarded as archaic and wasteful; others sought to add an "anti-aid" amendment, barring tax money from being appropriated to fund "religious" (meaning Catholic) charitable institutions; still others wanted to write female suffrage into the state constitution. In 1916 the legislature voted overwhelmingly to put a proposal for a convention before the voters, who approved it 217,293 to 120,979. That same year, thirty-seven districts held public-opinion referenda on whether to adopt the I&R. In all of them, the majority voted "Yes."[74]

Direct democracy advocates formed the Union for a Progressive Constitution to elect delegates to the convention who favored a "Massachusetts Plan" of I&R. According to one observer, "No sooner was a man's name broached as a possible candidate than he was promptly challenged to endorse the 'Massachusetts Plan.' Any demurring on his part made him an object of suspicion." Even those who planned to support "some form" of I&R, but not the Massachusetts Plan, "were heckled in public meetings and in the press as hide-bound reactionaries and servants of the 'interests.'"[75]

The Massachusetts Plan, versions of which had been in circulation since 1914, was generally understood to be the work of the Union chairman, Joseph Walker, a wealthy Progressive Republican from Brookline and former speaker of the state House of Representatives.[76] Its referendum provisions allowed a petition of 10,000 voters to put a law recently passed by the legislature on the ballot, so that voters had a chance to repeal it; 5,000 additional signatures could suspend the operation of the law before the vote took place. Initiatives would have to be submitted to the legislature—the petitions would need 25,000 signatures for a constitutional amendment and 15,000 for a law. After six months, if petitioners were dissatisfied with what the legislature had done or failed to do, they could put their initiative on the ballot by gathering 5,000 new signatures.[77]

Walker added a unique feature to the Massachusetts initiative plan, designed to remedy what he (like Henry Cabot Lodge) considered a serious defect of the Oregon System: "There is no opportunity to amend the proposed law after hearing and discussion." The plan designated the first ten signers of an initiative petition as a kind of committee—Walker at one point called them the "proposers"—and gave them amendment power.[78] If legislative debate over their initiative revealed to the proposers a flaw in it, they could decide, by majority vote, to add a "perfecting amendment." Doing so would not invalidate the signatures that the original version of the initiative had received. The initiative would then go on the ballot in its amended form. Walker provided, however, that if a hundred or more signers of the original initiative signed a protest against the amendment, only the original would appear on the ballot.[79]

Elections for 320 convention delegates took place in May 1917—just weeks after the United States declared war on Germany. Joseph Walker was chosen, while a number of prominent opponents of the I&R went down to defeat, among them A. Lawrence Lowell, a distinguished political scientist and the president of Harvard University. Walker himself estimated that 190 of the delegates were pledged, at least in "principle," to the I&R, but exactly how the convention would play out remained a mystery.[80]

The Con. Con. and the Campaign

The constitutional convention, known popularly as the "Con. Con.," assembled under the golden dome of the state House in Boston on June 6, 1917. Although the proceedings were overshadowed by the war (twenty delegates would eventually serve in the armed forces), everyone expected contentious debates over women's suffrage, an end to annual elections, the "anti-aid" amendment, and—above all—the I&R. Walker joined the committee to draft an I&R amendment, but critics of direct democracy sat on the committee as well. Over the following weeks it held hearings, and on July 23 it submitted a report proposing adoption of a version of Walker's Massachusetts Plan. The committee made only one major change from the original, dropping Walker's mechanism for "perfecting amendments."[81]

Seven of the fifteen committee members, however, issued a forceful dissent. They argued that majority rule without "permanent restrictions" was dangerous and threatened the rights of minorities, and that, besides, the I&R did not even allow true majority rule by the people, but only rule by small interest groups who had the "machinery" to collect the necessary signatures. The people, they declared, only form "real and certain opinions" on "great, simple, extraordinary, moral and political questions,—questions which have become thoroughly familiar through long public discussion." The people could not reasonably be expected to make informed decisions on ordinary ballot questions. Moreover, in every election in an I&R state in which both candidates and questions were on the ballot, the former always received more combined votes than the latter, suggesting that "people always take more interest in men than in measures." The dissenters even questioned whether there really was much public demand for the I&R in Massachusetts. They called the public-opinion referenda inconclusive (turnout in most of them had been light), and noted that during its hearings, the Walker committee had received no letters and the galleries had been empty, save for a "handful" of long-time I&R proponents.[82]

Walker replied to the committee's minority with a convention speech on August 7. He pointed out that public demand for the I&R had brought about the convention in the first place and reiterated that the I&R was needed to counter the influence of the "invisible government" of bosses and lobbyists. He conceded that a majority of those who vote did not represent the whole people, but declared it the only way that the will of the people had ever been legally expressed.[83]

With this speech began a debate that proceeded almost uninterrupted from August 7 to September 27, and continued in bursts until late November, for a total of forty-five days. Scores of amendments were proposed, and so many were adopted that the proposal went through six successive drafts, each longer than the last. Debates over some of the amendments proved so contentious that at one point a delegate had to be ejected. Finally, on November 27, 1917, the convention approved the I&R amendment, 163 to 125, and the following day voted to place it on the ballot for voters to approve or reject. The debate had been so protracted that the convention had missed the 1917 elections, and the popular decision had to wait until the following November.[84]

In its final form, the I&R amendment was over 3,700 words long—the most elaborate ever submitted to voters in any state (by contrast, the Oregon I&R amendment in 1902 was just 440 words). In general, the revised amendment still resembled Walker's Massachusetts Plan. The numbers of signatures needed on initiative and referendum petitions were the same as in the Massachusetts Plan, as was the distinction between two referendum processes—one that simply repealed a law with a majority vote and another that also suspended the law's operation until the vote took place at the next election. The proposed amendment also included Walker's idea to empower a majority of the first ten signers of an initiative petition to make perfecting amendments. Instead of allowing one hundred signers to challenge the proposed change, however, the state attorney general would now have to certify that the proposed modification did "not materially change the substance of the measure." The amended initiative then needed 5,000 additional signatures to get on the ballot.[85]

The proposed constitutional amendment also involved some major departures from the Massachusetts Plan. One was that an initiative amendment to the state constitution could not entirely bypass the legislature; it had to receive at least a quarter of the votes of both chambers in two successive legislatures before it could be placed before voters in a state election, and then at least 30 percent of the voters in the election had to participate in the referendum for approval to be valid. The signatures of all I&R petitions also had to be geographically distributed, with not more than a quarter coming from a single county. The most important difference, however, was the greatly expanded list of topics that were excluded from the I&R process. In the plan originally proposed to the convention, the only exclusions had been specific appropriations of money from the state treasury or laws involving a single town. Now added as exclusions were anything having to do with religion, anything inconsistent with the state bill of rights, or anything concerning the removal, recall, or pay of judges, the creation or abolition of courts, or the reversal of judicial decisions. Nor could these exclusions themselves be made the subjects of initiatives. The state attorney general was required to check all I&R proposals before they could go on the ballot to certify that they did not contain excluded subjects.[86]

Although some advocates of direct democracy complained that the Massachusetts I&R amendment placed too many shackles on the popular will, direct democracy critics still thought it went too far. One Boston newspaper even likened it to the Bolshevik Revolution, which had just taken place in Russia. Leading up to the 1918 vote, the anti-I&R campaign spent over $88,000, more than was "reported by any other [Massachusetts] political organization of that year," including the Democratic or Republican state committee, and dramatically more than was spent by I&R advocates.[87] Supporters of the amendment nonetheless waged a vigorous campaign, led by Walker. With the election looming in November, the fate of the amendment was now in the voters' hands.

NOTES

1. George H. Haynes, "How Massachusetts Adopted the Initiative and Referendum," *Political Science Quarterly* 34, no. 3 (Sept. 1919): 468–469, 473; Augustus Peabody Loring, "A Short Account of the Massachusetts Constitutional Convention, 1917–1919," *New England Quarterly* 5, no. 1, suppl. (Mar. 1933): 43–45, 75–76.

2. A good introductory summary of the historiographical debate can be found in Glenda Elizabeth Gilmore, ed., *Who Were the Progressives?* (Boston: Bedford / St. Martin's Press, 2002).

3. Sarah Henry, "Progressivism and Democracy: Electoral Reform in the United States, 1888–1919" (PhD diss., Columbia University, New York, 1995), 6, 20–22.

4. For statistics on turnout in presidential elections, see John P. McIver, "Voter Turnout in Presidential and Congressional Elections: National, South, and Non-South, 1824–1998," at *Historical Statistics of the United States, Millennial Edition Online,* series Eb114–122, http://hsus.cambridge.org.

5. Alex Keyssar, *The Right to Vote: The Contested History of Democracy in the United States* (New York: Basic Books, 2000), 186, 195, 206, 387–390 (tables A.17–19), 211–218.

6. J. W. Sullivan, *Direct Legislation by the Citizenship through the Initiative and Referendum* (New York: True Nationalist Pub. Co., 1893; 1st ed., 1892), 5–6.

7. Ibid., i, 90; Henry, "Progressivism and Democracy," 56–57.

8. Sullivan, *Direct Legislation,* 73, 82.

9. Ibid., 10, 7.

10. Ibid., 11, 26, 27, 60.

11. Steven L. Piott, *Giving Voters a Voice: The Origins of the Initiative and Referendum in America* (Columbia: University of Missouri Press, 2003), 4; Robert D. Johnston, *The Radical Middle Class: Populist Democracy and the Question of Capitalism in Progressive Era Portland* (Princeton, NJ: Princeton University Press, 2003), 129.

12. Piott, *Giving Voters a Voice,* 35; Henry, "Progressivism and Democracy," 139.

13. Piott, *Giving Voters a Voice,* 32.

14. Henry, "Progressivism and Democracy," 140.

15. Johnston, *Radical Middle Class,* 122; Sullivan, *Direct Legislation,* 17–21.

16. David Schuman, "The Origin of State Constitutional Direct Democracy: William Simon U'Ren and 'The Oregon System,'" *Temple Law Review* 67, no. 2 (Summer 1994): 953; Piott, *Giving Voters a Voice,* 37; Burton J. Hendrick, "The Initiative and Referendum and How Oregon Got Them," *McClure's Magazine* (July 1911): 246.

17. Henry, "Progressivism and Democracy," 152.

18. The following account of the 1897 election is based on Schuman, "Origin," 953–954; Piott, *Giving Voters a Voice,* 37–38; Henry, "Progressivism and Democracy," 151–153; Hendrick, "Initiative and Referendum," 244–248.

19. Hendrick, "Initiative and Referendum," 248. On the "hold-up," see, e.g., Tom Marsh, *To the Promised Land: A History of Government and Politics in Oregon* (Corvallis: Oregon State University Press, 2012), 94–97.

20. Henry, "Progressivism and Democracy," 159–162; Schuman, "Origin," 956; Piott, *Giving Voters a Voice,* 40.

21. Piott, *Giving Voters a Voice,* 39.

22. Ibid., 39–40; Schuman, "Origin," 956. South Dakota had authorized the creation of an I&R system in 1898, and Utah in 1900, but neither system was yet fully in operation. See Lloyd Sponholtz, "The Initiative and Referendum: Direct Democracy in Perspective, 1898–1920," *American Studies* 14, no. 2 (Fall 1973): 48, table I; Steven L. Piott, "The Origins of the Initiative and Referendum in South Dakota: The Political Context," *Great Plains Quarterly* 12 (Summer 1992): 190–191.

23. Schuman, "Origin," 951.

24. Moisey Ostrogorski, *Democracy and the Organization of Political Parties,* trans. Frederick Clarke (New York: Macmillan, 1902), 2:207–213, 223–224; H. G. Nicholas, "Political Parties in the Law in the United States," *Political Studies* 2, no. 3 (Oct. 1954): 258–270.

25. However, there did persist the idea that party-funded primaries were not public elections and thus that laws governing public elections did not apply to them. On this ground, the U.S. Supreme Court for many years declined to declare that "white primaries" in the South were a violation of the Fifteenth Amendment. The court did not rule white primaries unconstitutional until 1944 (*Smith v. Allwright,* 321 U.S. 649).

26. Henry, "Progressivism and Democracy," 179–180; Piott, *Giving Voters a Voice,* 42.

27. Marsh, *To the Promised Land,* 114–116; Henry, "Progressivism and Democracy," 192–195.

28. Henry, "Progressivism and Democracy," 181.

29. Marsh, *To the Promised Land,* 118–119.

30. Schumann, "Origin of State Constitutional Direct Democracy," 958; Piott, *Giving Voters a Voice,* 286–293; Henry, "Progressivism and Democracy," 196–206.

31. Henry, "Progressivism and Democracy," 154, 235; Johnston, *Radical Middle Class,* 132.

32. Theodore Roosevelt, "The People of the Pacific Coast," *The Outlook,* 23 Sept. 1911, 162; Johnston, *Radical Middle Class,* 127.

33. Quoted in Kenneth P. Miller, *Direct Democracy and the Courts* (New York: Cambridge University Press, 2009), 27; Johnston, *Radical Middle Class,* 127, 132; Henry, "Progressivism and Democracy," 80–81, 111, 223–224.

34. Miller, *Direct Democracy,* 25–29; Deborah Kalb, ed., *Guide to U.S. Elections,* 7th ed. (Washington, DC: CQ Press, 2016), 1:815.

35. See, for example, in Henry, "Progressivism and Democracy," 108.

36. Miller, *Direct Democracy,* 193.

37. Piott, *Giving Voters a Voice,* 145. After admission, Arizona reinstated judicial recall. By 1919, however, only three other states besides Oregon and Arizona allowed voters to dismiss judges: California, Colorado, and Nevada. See Miller, *Direct Democracy,* 192–193, 193n18.

38. Charles A. Beard and Birl E. Shultz, *Documents on the State-Wide Initiative, Referendum, and Recall* (New York: MacMillan Co., 1912), 349–383, see also 102–118; Henry, "Progressivism and Democracy," 219–221.

39. Beard and Shultz, *Documents,* 365, 374, 376, 380, 382; Henry, "Progressivism and Democracy," 220.

40. Beard and Shultz, *Documents,* 349–350, 376, 378, 366–368, 372–374, quotations at 376, 378, 373.

41. Ibid., 350, 362–363, 365, quotations at 350.

42. Ibid., 355, 359, 360–361, quotations at 359, 360.

43. Piott, *Giving Voters a Voice,* 289, 290, 293.

44. Michael R. Haines, "Population, by Race, Sex, and Urban–Rural Residence: 1880–1990," in *Historical Statistics of the United States,* series Aa716–775; James Weinstein, "Organized Business and the City Commission and Manager Movements," *Journal of Southern History* 28, no. 2 (May 1962): 167; John Joseph Wallace, "American

Government Finance in the Long Run, 1790–1990," *Journal of Economic Perspectives* 14, no. 1 (Winter 2000): 66 (table 2); C. F. Taylor, "Prefatory Note," in Frank Parsons, *The City for the People* (Philadelphia: C. F. Taylor, 1901), 4, quotation at 4.

45. Ostrogorski, *Democracy and the Organization of Political Parties,* 2:161–174 (estimates of the cost of the "Tweed Ring" to taxpayers at 165).

46. Piott, *Giving Voters a Voice,* 43–44.

47. According to the *Boston Globe,* the last American city with a bicameral council was Everett, Massachusetts, which voted to abolish it in 2011, effective 2014. See Steven A. Rosenberg, "Everett Finally Abandoning Its Bicameral Government: Last City in U.S. to Do So," *Boston Globe,* 8 Dec. 2011. On the rise and decline of bicameral city councils, see, e.g., Anirudh Virender Singh Ruhil, "Explorations in Twentieth Century Municipal Governance: The Case of Civil Service Commissions and Forms of Government" (PhD diss., SUNY at Stony Brook, 1999), 16, 64, 95, 129.

48. See *The City of Boston, Its Powers and Duties* (Boston: S. J. Parkhill, 1895); Boston City Charter (Prepared and Distributed by the Boston City Council, July 2007), append. A (39).

49. Henry, "Progressivism and Democracy," 74–76; Weinstein, "Organized Business," 170.

50. Weinstein, "Organized Business," 168–170. *A Model City Charter . . . of the National Municipal League* (Philadelphia, 1916) recommended a council-manager system of government, in which the council would be elected by one of two proportional representation systems (see esp. 54–59).

51. An indication of this development is *A Model City Charter,* which recommends an I&R&R system, at 18–28.

52. C. O. Gardner, "The Initiative and Referendum in Commission Cities," *Annals of the American Academy of Political and Social Science* 38, no. 3 (Nov. 1911): 154.

53. *A Pamphlet Containing a Copy of All Measures . . . to Be Submitted to the Legal Voters of the State of Oregon* (Salem, OR: William S. Duniway, 1910); Johnston, *Radical Middle Class,* 125.

54. See "Governor Chamberlain's Message Is Read to Legislature," *Morning Oregonian* (13 Jan. 1909), 6; *Debates in the Massachusetts Constitutional Convention, 1917–1918,* vol. 2, *The Initiative and Referendum* (Boston: Wright and Potter, 1918) (hereafter cited as *Initiative and Referendum Debates*), 55–56. See also Jim Lichatowich, *Salmon without Rivers: A History of the Pacific Salmon Crisis* (Washington, DC: Island Press, 1999), 107–108; John N. Cobb, *Pacific Salmon Fisheries,* 3rd ed. (Washington, DC: GPO, 1921), 101–103; "Protect the Salmon," Oregon History Project, http://www.oregonhistoryproject.org/articles /historical-records/protect-the-salmon-vote-332-x-yes.

55. *Kadderly v. Portland,* 44 Or 118 (1903), 145.

56. *Pacific States Telephone and Telegraph Company v. Oregon,* 223 U.S. 118 (1912). The Supreme Court here cites the precedent of *Luther v. Borden,* 48 U.S. 1 (1848), in which the court refused to adjudicate the claim made by a supporter of Dorr's Rebellion in Rhode Island that his state was not a republican form of government.

57. These are reprinted in Henry Cabot Lodge, *The Democracy of the Constitution and Other Addresses and Essays* (New York: Charles Scribner's Sons, 1915), 1–121.

58. Ibid., 12, 17, 16.

59. Ibid., 114–116, 81, 19–20, 110–112, 110n1, 115–116, 21, 89–90, quotations at 81 and 21.

60. Ibid., 29, see also 116.

61. Sponholtz, "Initiative and Referendum," 48, table I. In addition to the sixteen states that adopted I&R systems between 1904 and 1915, two other states—New Mexico (1911) and Maryland (1915)—adopted the referendum without the initiative (ibid.). One of the states that adopted the I&R in these years (Idaho, 1912) did not implement the system until 1933 (ibid.). In addition, Utah had adopted an I&R system in 1900 but did not implement it until 1917 (ibid.). South Dakota adopted the initiative and referendum as early as 1898, but implementation proved difficult and the first successful use of the initiative and referendum there came in 1908 (Piott, "Origins," 190).

62. National Council of State Legislatures, "The Indirect Initiative," http://www.ncsl .org/legislatures-elections/elections/the-indirect-initiative.aspx; Sponholtz, "Initiative and Referendum," 49.

63. Piott, *Giving Voters a Voice*, 148–165. On "The Octopus," see also John R. Robinson, *The Octopus: A History of the Construction, Conspiracies, Extortions, Robberies, and Villainous Acts of the Central Pacific, Southern Pacific of Kentucky, Union Pacific and Other Subsidized Railroads* (San Francisco, 1894); Frank Norris, *The Octopus: A Story of California* (New York: Bantam Books, 1971 [1901]), a novel in which the Southern Pacific appears, thinly disguised, as the "Pacific & Southwestern Railroad."

64. Piott, *Giving Voters a Voice*, 166–168.

65. Sponholtz, "Initiative and Referendum," 48 (table I); Piott, *Giving Voters a Voice*, 167, 263–265; National Council of State Legislatures, "The Indirect Initiative."

66. Henry, "Progressivism and Democracy," 405–416, 373–379; Piott, *Giving Voters a Voice*, 230–231, 234; Edward M. Hartwell, "The Cost of Municipal Government in Massachusetts," *Publications of the American Statistical Association* 11, no. 84 (Dec. 1908): 333–337; "Urban Population in 1900," *Census Bulletin*, no. 70 (Twelfth Census of the United States), 11 July 1901, 2 (table 1). In 1879, women did win a limited right to vote in school committee elections in Massachusetts. See Henry, "Progressivism and Democracy," 406.

67. W. D. McCrackan, "The Swiss Referendum," *The Arena*, 16 Mar. 1891, 458; Piott, *Giving Voters a Voice*, 231–232.

68. Piott, *Giving Voters a Voice*, 232–233.

69. Haynes, "How Massachusetts Adopted," 454.

70. Ibid., 454; Lodge, *Democracy of the Constitution*, 3; Piott, *Giving Voters a Voice*, 236.

71. Quoted in Piott, *Giving Voters a Voice*, 237.

72. Piott, *Giving Voters a Voice*, 237; "An Act to Simplify the Revision of City Charters," chap. 267, §§38–47, General Acts Passed by the General Court of Massachusetts, 1915; [Joseph Walker], *Initiative and Referendum: Massachusetts Plan, An Explanation of the Proposed Initiative and Referendum Amendment to the Constitution of Massachusetts and*

Some Reasons for Its Adoption, Prepared for the Use of the Public and the Members of the Massachusetts Constitutional Convention to Meet June 6, 1917 (Boston: Union for a Progressive Constitution, [1917]), 18.

73. Haynes, "How Massachusetts Adopted," 254–256, quotation at 255.

74. Loring, "Short Account," 10–11; Piott, *Giving Voters a Voice*, 238; George H. Haynes, "How Massachusetts Adopted," 254; [Walker], *Initiative and Referendum*, 18–22.

75. Haynes, "How Massachusetts Adopted," 456.

76. [Walker], *Initiative and Referendum*; see also [Joseph Walker], *The Massachusetts Plan for the Initiative and the Referendum* (Boston: Legislative Bureau of the Progressive Party, 1914). The 1917 version of the Massachusetts Plan, presented in [Walker], *Initiative and Referendum*, is the same in overall design as the 1914 version, presented in [Walker], *Massachusetts Plan*, but the two differ in details (for example, over the number of signatures required for an initiative, and exactly how a "perfecting amendment" would be proposed). Because the 1917 version was the one "prepared for the use of . . . the members of the Massachusetts Constitutional Convention," our references are to it, unless otherwise noted. On Walker, see Loring, "Short Account," 8; and Haynes, "How Massachusetts Adopted," 459 (where Walker is described without being named).

77. [Walker], *Initiative and Referendum*, 10–12.

78. [Walker], *Massachusetts Plan*, 5; [Walker], *Initiative and Referendum*, 11. The term "proposers" appears in [Walker], *Massachusetts Plan*, 3, 4, 5, 12. Note that in *Massachusetts Plan*, the committee of proposers has five members, who must unanimously agree to the perfecting amendment.

79. [Walker], *Initiative and Referendum*, 11.

80. Piott, *Giving Voters a Voice*, 238; Haynes, "How Massachusetts Adopted," 457; *Initiative and Referendum Debates*, 35.

81. *Journal of the Constitutional Convention of the Commonwealth of Massachusetts* (Boston: Wright and Potter, [1917, 1919]), 7, 385–388; *Initiative and Referendum Debates*, 3–6. The committee also increased the number of signatures required on initiative and referendum petitions. As an example of use of the nickname "Con. Con.," see "Kenny's Antidote for Con. Con. Wordiness," *Boston Herald* (12 Sep. 1917), 10.

82. *Initiative and Referendum Debates*, 7, 11, 13, 14.

83. Ibid., 15–38.

84. Loring, "Short Account," 43–44, 56; Haynes, "How Massachusetts Adopted," 549.

85. *Initiative and Referendum Debates*, 1050–1058.

86. Ibid.

87. Loring, "Short Account," 56, 75–76; Haynes, "How Massachusetts Adopted," 473–474, quotation at 473.

·{ 14 }·

Regulating Radio in the Age
of Broadcasting (1927)

On April 15, 1912, the *Titanic* met her tragic fate as she sank off the coast of Newfoundland in the North Atlantic. Of several nearby ships that might have heard her distress signals and staged a rescue, only one, the *Carpathia,* responded to the catastrophe. It took the *Carpathia* three and a half hours to reach the *Titanic.* Although 700 passengers and crew members were saved, it was by then too late for the 1,500 others who had not made it onto lifeboats. The *Lena,* a freight steamer, could have gotten there faster—perhaps in just ninety minutes—but it had no radio. The *Californian* may have been only an hour away but missed the distress signals because its radio operator was sleeping. In the aftermath of this unprecedented disaster, Congress moved swiftly to regulate radio, passing the Radio Act of 1912 four months later.[1]

At this stage, radio was still used principally for point-to-point, Morse code communications at sea, and the provisions of the Radio Act reflected this. The act contained important new rules for maritime radio and the handling of distress signals. It also implemented a new licensing scheme for radio stations, but did little to regulate radio transmissions beyond ensuring that the U.S. Navy, the arm of the federal government that most relied on radio, could transmit signals without interference.

The radio scene changed drastically in the early 1920s, however. Although point-to-point communication continued, this period saw the rise of broadcasting, with a growing number of broadcasters taking to the airwaves to deliver music and voice programs to the listening public. By 1927, more than 700 stations were fighting over the ninety-six available frequencies.[2] This crowding of the broadcast spectrum substantially diminished the quality of radio listening. Powerful stations were able to broadcast into markets thousands of miles away, and the airwaves were so full of interference that many citizens complained that it was often impossible to tune in to any station clearly. One federal official later claimed that the interference was "so bad at many points on the dial that the listener might suppose instead of a receiving set he had a peanut roaster with assorted whistles."[3]

In January 1926, both houses of Congress began considering sweeping bills to tackle the problem of interference and the question of how to allocate frequencies for broadcasting. They vigorously debated a broad set of issues, ranging from questions of ownership and regulatory authority to the protection of free speech and the prevention of monopoly. A bill endorsed by both the House and the Senate emerged a little over a year later, after the interference problem was said to have grown worse, and it finally arrived on the desk of President Calvin Coolidge on February 23, 1927.

The bill would create a Federal Radio Commission with the power to license radio stations for two years at a time. The Department of Commerce had assumed similar powers under the 1912 act, but recent court cases had virtually destroyed its ability to deny licenses or assign frequencies. The new bill expressly granted the commission the power to do both. Licensing authority, after one year, would revert to the Commerce Department, and the commission would survive as an advisory body. The bill stipulated that stations could appeal denials and revocations in court, but the licenses themselves would confer no property right to the frequencies in question. The entire spectrum, moreover, would effectively belong to the federal government and could be allocated by regulators, in accordance with the law.

President Coolidge had endorsed radio reform in his most recent annual message to Congress but had requested that all regulatory power be granted to the secretary of commerce, not to a commission. Now, with Congress having opted for a commission, he had to decide if the bill before him charted an acceptable path for American radio regulation.

Marconi's Invention

Radio had its roots in cutting-edge electromagnetic experiments of the late nineteenth century. Building on the work of scientific luminaries like Heinrich Hertz and Nikola Tesla, the Italian Guglielmo Marconi developed long-range wireless transmitters in the 1890s. His greatest demonstration of radio's promise came in 1901, when he transmitted a wireless signal across the Atlantic Ocean from England to Newfoundland, Canada. This early technology could only transmit unmodulated signals suitable for Morse code, and was thus called "wireless telegraphy." Despite this limitation, the technology proved very useful. Maritime navigators and their onshore associates were the earliest adopters, and by the early 1900s they were regularly communicating routes, schedules, and distress signals via wireless telegraphy.[4]

In 1897 Marconi had founded a company in England to make and distribute radio equipment, popularly known as "British Marconi." This company and its subsidiaries (such as "American Marconi") dominated the radio industry of the early twentieth century and were highly protective of their technology. The Marconi companies accused many competitors of violating their patents, regularly refused to communicate with non-Marconi stations, and often insisted on renting, not selling, their products to both private and public customers.[5]

Marconi's radio empire ran into trouble in 1902 when one of its stations refused to accept a transmission from Prince Henry of Prussia, brother of Germany's Kaiser Wilhelm, because he had sent it from a competitor's device. The German government condemned Marconi's domination of the airwaves and in August 1903 summoned a conference in Berlin to develop international protocols for radio transmissions. The meeting was attended by delegates representing Austria-Hungary, France, Germany, Great Britain, Italy, Spain, Russia, and the United States. Despite opposition from Britain and Italy (the two nations most closely tied to Marconi), the other countries agreed on the need for laws mandating that all wireless systems communicate with one another. At the conference, the American delegates observed the integral role that other governments and navies had played in developing their nations' radio networks. Worried that this might someday put the United States at a military disadvantage, they left the conference intent on increasing the American military's role in the development of radio at home.[6]

The Navy Takes Notice

The U.S. Navy had begun testing radio devices in 1899 and determined that "the system promises to be very useful in the future for the naval service."

That year, however, Navy officials rejected an offer from American Marconi to provide equipment, finding the price and terms of the contract too onerous.[7] In 1903 the Navy purchased a few radios manufactured by Slaby-Arco, the German firm whose product Prince Henry had used. The Navy also began constructing new shore stations and by 1904 had twenty operational stations transmitting signals, for both communications and navigational purposes.[8]

Concerns about the Private Sector

As early as 1902, leading figures in the Navy worried that proliferating signals from amateur radio operators might interfere with their own transmissions. That year, Admiral Royal B. Bradford, chief of the Navy's Bureau of Equipment, called for government regulation of radio. Bradford pointed out that other nations had already begun regulating radio, and he wanted the U.S. government to step in before commercial interests became powerful enough to block such a move at home. He recommended that the federal government not give private radio facilities access to any of its lighthouses or lightships, so that they could instead be used in a "national coast signal system." Writers for the *Army and Navy Journal* concurred in an editorial published that September, insisting, "In time of war such control would be almost indispensable to the safety of our squadrons at sea. It seems morally certain that wireless is destined to play a part of increasing importance in naval operations from this time forward."[9]

In early 1904 the Navy pressed the executive branch for guidance on wireless policy, citing various examples of troublesome interference. The new chief of the Navy's Bureau of Equipment, Rear Admiral George A. Converse, proposed that "the Government take control of the entire wireless-telegraph service along the coast as some foreign governments do with the land-telegraph service."[10] President Theodore Roosevelt's Cabinet discussed plans for radio regulation in April, and determined that the federal government should have regulatory oversight of the radio network during peacetime and total control during war. When Roosevelt asked the Navy General Board for comment, it offered an assessment similar to Converse's. Interference, the Board suggested, threatened the entire system, and a solution would require congressional action due to the interstate and international nature of wireless communication. The General Board, however, was hesitant to take control of private wireless stations, instead suggesting that they be put under the regulatory authority of the Department of Commerce and Labor and that construction of new stations be subjected to a government approval process.[11]

The Roosevelt Board

On June 24, 1904, President Roosevelt established the Interdepartmental Board of Wireless Telegraphy, commonly known as the "Roosevelt Board," to examine the potential for radio throughout the federal government. The board submitted its report on July 12. Its first recommendations concerned the government's own radio facilities. The board suggested that all coastal government radio stations be placed under Navy control (aside from a few under Army jurisdiction, which did not interfere with the Navy's system). Previously the Weather Bureau of the Agriculture Department had operated some stations, but the board wanted those transferred to the Navy. Beyond these existing stations, the board recommended that the Navy set up a wide-reaching radio network along the coasts to serve the whole government. The report added that this system should transmit and receive signals to and from ships for free, so long as it did not compete with commercial stations.[12] The board also concluded "that the Government must take the necessary steps to regulate the establishment of commercial wireless-telegraph stations among the States and between nations," and proposed legislation to that end. It argued that private stations should be prohibited "where they may interfere with the naval or military operations of the Government." The board further recommended that the Department of Commerce and Labor should oversee private stations in the nation's interior and that it should also be responsible for preventing "the control of wireless telegraphy by monopolies or trusts."[13]

President Roosevelt approved the report on July 29, 1904, and ordered that all pertinent departments of the executive branch adopt its recommendations.[14] Radio industry interests were quick to condemn the report. American Marconi complained that the Navy's free radio service would compete with its business operations and claimed that the Navy's equipment violated its patents. Another firm, the National Electric Signaling Company, asserted that if it was not permitted to establish stations that might conceivably interfere with government signals, it would effectively lose its maritime business.

It suggested that the government hold off on regulation because recent technological innovations were reducing the problem of interference. The company also noted that the government had no comparable regulations in place for telegraphs or telephones and had left such technologies to the private sector.[15] Several press outlets similarly criticized the government's plan. The *New York Times* echoed a common concern when it warned that the reform would "hamper enterprise by unduly restricting the application of wireless in time of peace."[16]

Although the Roosevelt Board's recommendations were controversial, the new policies that followed remained relatively narrow in scope. Roosevelt's 1904 order pertained only to the use and effectiveness of radio in the various departments of the federal government. Most measures to regulate radio in the private sector would require congressional legislation, which arose only haltingly in the early years of twentieth century.

Early Radio Regulation

In 1906 President Roosevelt experienced firsthand the problem of radio interference. One day when he was aboard a boat near Cape Cod, Massachusetts, interference made it impossible for him to receive radio transmissions. On September 29, after this frustrating incident, the president demanded a new report on the state of radio. The report, prepared by Rear Admiral Robley D. Evans, noted that many commercial radio signals were stronger than the Navy's, and that some stations (especially the Marconi stations) refused to assist in the delivery of government messages. Only stations transmitting at similar wavelengths, he observed, caused interference problems. Evans thus recommended that the Navy take control of all private coastal radio stations, and that no private inland stations with signals strong enough to reach the coast be permitted.[17]

That same year, another Berlin conference was held as a follow-up to the 1903 international meeting on radio. Twenty-seven nations sent delegates. The U.S. representatives reiterated support for a protocol requiring that different radio systems communicate with one another. Although the British, who had contracted with Marconi, resisted, the conference sided with the United States on this issue. The relevant clause was included in the treaty that emerged from the conference on November 3, 1906, to be ratified by the

participating governments. The conference also developed technical protocols for maritime radio, including the "SOS" distress signal.[18] Of particular
note, the conference agreed upon broad spectrum-allocation rules to regulate radio transmissions. The 500 kilohertz (kHz) and 1000 kHz frequencies,
for example, were "authorized for general public service," and all coastal
stations would have to tune signals to at least one of those frequencies.[19]

Despite the U.S. delegates' strong support for the provision requiring
communication across different radio platforms, the Senate refused to ratify
the new treaty when it first considered it in early 1908. John W. Griggs, president of American Marconi and a former U.S. attorney general, complained
to the Senate Committee on Foreign Relations that the treaty "represents
an enforced partnership to which the Marconi companies contribute everything and the German manufacturers of radio apparatus nothing" and that
"in effect, it is taking the property of the Marconi Company and subjecting
it to the use and service of others against the will of the owners, and to their
injury."[20] Navy officials and some smaller firms expressed their support for
the treaty at the hearings, but the Senate proved unsympathetic—at least in
1908. Further pieces of legislation that would have regulated American radio
failed both that year and the next. One naval historian has suggested that
Congress's close relationship to big business doomed these bills, as lawmakers
sought to appease industrial leaders after years of President Roosevelt's
trust-busting.[21]

Congress finally enacted radio regulation—for the first time—in June
1910. Partly inspired by a disaster at sea in January 1909, the legislation
required ocean-faring ships with fifty or more passengers to carry radio
equipment. The act also required companies installing such equipment "to
exchange . . . as far as may be physically practicable, to be determined by
the master of the vessel, messages with shore or ship stations using other
systems of radio-communication."[22] While not a universal application of the
intercommunication principle, the Wireless Ship Act of 1910 did meet several of the standards set forth at the Berlin Conference in 1906.[23]

With a third international conference on radio scheduled to meet in
London in June 1912, Americans were upset to discover that their invitation
was rescinded because the Senate had failed to approve the 1906 Convention.
Obviously displeased that the United States had become, in the words of *Electrical World* magazine, "an outcast among the nations," the Senate finally

ratified the treaty on April 3, 1912, fully committing the country to the agreement's provisions and earning the United States a seat at the negotiating table. The London Conference opened on June 4, 1912, with twenty-nine nations and several colonies represented. In the wake of the *Titanic* disaster of April 15, the conference decided on several new regulations relating to maritime radio equipment and distress signals, and reiterated and clarified rules agreed to in 1906 in Berlin.[24]

The *Titanic* tragedy may also have helped convince Congress to pass the era's most significant piece of radio legislation, the Radio Act of 1912, on August 13 of that year. In accordance with the London agreement, the new law mandated that every publicly accessible coastal radio station, and every ship radio, must accept signals from all others and grant priority to distress signals. Public service stations would operate on the two frequencies specified by the agreement. The law also created a licensing scheme, managed by the Department of Commerce and Labor, for all amateur and commercial radio stations. Each licensed station could only use frequencies within the bounds the Berlin and London conferences had set for nonpublic coastal stations (namely, below 187.5 kHz or above 500 kHz). Private stations near naval transmitters, and all amateurs, would be restricted to frequencies above 1500 kHz and limited to 1-kilowatt signal strength. The most desirable frequencies (187.5 to 500 kHz) were reserved mainly for government use (again in accordance with the Berlin and London agreements), and the Navy was empowered to collect fees on nongovernment signals handled by its stations.[25]

The Radio Act of 1912, along with the Wireless Ship Act of 1910, reportedly succeeded in improving maritime safety. In January 1913 a Marconi representative wrote in *Electrical World*, "While it is true that the laws enacted are not ideal and that more deliberate action would undoubtedly have produced a better result, it must be admitted that the lanes of the ocean have been rendered safer."[26]

There was one further attempt to regulate radio in the United States in the 1910s. A federal body, the Interdepartmental Radio Committee (IRC), recommended in November 1916 that the secretary of commerce be empowered to set the rates of private radio companies, that stations belonging to the federal government be permitted to compete with commercial stations, and that the Navy be authorized to "purchase at a reasonable valuation, any coastal radio station then in operation in the United States which the owner desired to sell." The IRC also suggested new spectrum-allocation rules. American Marconi strongly objected, claiming that "the proposed bill is evidence of a desire to limit private enterprise."[27] The debate was preempted, however, by America's entry into World War I in April 1917, particularly once the military invoked its wartime powers to seize the nation's commercial radio stations and prohibit amateur radio. Although amateur operators were allowed to return to the airwaves not long after the war ended in November 1918, and commercial stations reverted to their owners in March 1920, the push for new radio regulation had by this point largely disappeared.[28]

The Rise of Radio Broadcasting

The 1920s saw the flowering of broadcast radio—regularly scheduled transmissions intended for a wide public audience, made possible by advances in technology that enabled the transmission of voice and music over the air. Although many histories trace the first such broadcast to November 2, 1920, when Pittsburgh station KDKA announced Warren G. Harding's victory in that year's presidential election, several earlier stations paved the way, and scientists had been experimenting with broadcast technology at least since 1906. Nevertheless, KDKA's broadcast proved historic and set the stage for rapid expansion. By March 1923, there were 556 broadcast stations in operation across the country, delivering music, news, and other programming, and by the end of 1926 an estimated one in six American households had a radio capable of receiving broadcast programming.[29]

Four large companies dominated the American radio industry in the 1920s: American Telephone and Telegraph (AT&T), General Electric (GE), Westinghouse Broadcasting Corporation, and the Radio Corporation of America (RCA, which had been created in 1919 by General Electric after it bought American Marconi). These companies, along with a number of others, had pooled many of their radio patents between 1919 and 1922, bringing almost 2,000 patents under their common control. The rise of broadcasting caught them by surprise, however, and soon upset their alliance. AT&T, for example, insisted that under the existing agreements only it could produce and sell broadcast transmitters, sell advertising time ("toll broadcasting"), and provide wired connections across stations in different locations. Tensions between the firms generated legal battles and ultimately a new agreement in 1926 that granted AT&T a monopoly over wired connections between stations (an important technology allowing groups of stations, or networks, to broadcast the same content at the same time) but also required AT&T to sell its broadcasting network to RCA, which immediately used it to create the National Broadcasting Company (NBC).[30]

The Economics of Early Broadcasting

From the beginning, both commercial firms and independent experts grappled with the question of how to cover the costs of broadcasting. Two historians have written that "as late as the mid 1920s, even the most thoughtful scholars and journalists were unable to predict the dominant role that advertising would play in radio broadcasting by the start of the next decade. In fact, throughout much of the 1920s, there was no consensus that broadcasters would be able to sustain their operations without outside support."[31] Some stations initially solicited funds from listeners, offering to provide paying customers with written materials that complemented their programs, but this proved inadequate.[32] Hiram Jome, who undertook a detailed study of the economics of radio in 1925, identified the "who shall pay" problem as a central issue and ultimately suggested a tax on radios to help fund the stations.[33] The British government would soon impose an annual tax on radio sets to help finance its broadcasting company. The idea never gained traction in the United States, however.[34]

In these early years, many owners and operators of broadcasting stations probably never expected to make a profit. Perhaps as many as "one-quarter of stations . . . were nonprofits, ranging from religious stations to agricultural information stations to university stations."[35] Even among the other three-quarters, moreover, deriving profits directly from broadcasting was not always the main objective:

> Many for-profit owners . . . sought to make money only indirectly. According to [the journal] *Radio Broadcast,* these included "individual publicity stations operated by department stores, newspapers, radio companies, and other commercial institutions for the purpose of building good will for the owner, but not accepting outside pay for broadcasting." In fact, the first (and probably most prominent) station owners during the 1920s were radio manufacturers, who initially entered broadcasting to boost demand for their receivers.[36]

   The first documented commercial radio advertisement in the United States, carried by AT&T's station WEAF on August 28, 1922, promoted apartment housing in New York City. The housing company paid $100 for the ad and is said to have generated thousands of dollars in sales as a result.[37] Despite this early success, commercial radio advertising was slow to catch on, not least because interested parties of all sorts—listeners, regulators, and broadcasters—objected to funding radio by selling airtime to advertisers. In 1924 the American Radio Association, a listeners' group, reported rising complaints about radio advertising, and warned that the practice threatened the medium. Like-minded industry magazines compared commercial advertising to "an Old Man of the Sea—practically impossible to shake off once he got a good grasp" that would ruin radio "by creating an apathetic public, impairing listener interest and curtailing the sale of receiver sets."[38] Even some marketing firms feared that radio advertisements were so offensive to the listening public that they might endanger the entire advertising industry. By 1927 the question of whether radio broadcasters would be able to cover their costs remained very much alive.[39]

Allocating the Spectrum

The expansion of broadcast radio created a new demand for the radio spectrum and new questions about how best to allocate it. Accordingly, when Herbert Hoover became the secretary of commerce in March 1921, he made regulating broadcast radio one of his priorities. His Department of Commerce (formerly the Department of Commerce and Labor) initially dedicated only one frequency, 833.3 kHz, to broadcast radio in September 1921.* By that December, there was enough interest that the department opened 618.6 kHz to broadcasting as well, mainly for public service stations. Within just a few months, the rapid growth of radio demanded the opening of a third frequency, 750 kHz, which was reserved for a small number of the most powerful stations across the country.[40]

---

* At the time, the Department of Commerce typically referenced wavelengths (in meters) rather than frequencies (in kilocycles or, later, kilohertz). For example, contemporary documents referred to a wavelength of 360 meters rather than a frequency of 833 kilohertz (kHz), although the two approaches are equivalent and identify the same part of the radio spectrum. For consistency, this case will reference frequencies rather than wavelengths.

The crowding of the spectrum rapidly emerged as a problem within the radio community, despite the allocation of new frequencies, and federal capacity to address the issue remained limited. "One of the misfortunes of our present Government structure, and one which needs constructive thought," Hoover wrote early in his tenure at Commerce, "is that we have no bureau or central organized authority for dealing with the communications question."[41] On February 27, 1922, Hoover assembled a conference on radio that included fifteen government and private-sector leaders. The conference recommended further regulation of the spectrum, signal strength, and broadcasting schedules. The delegates expressed their belief "that radio communication is a public utility and as such should be regulated and controlled by the Federal Government in the public interest." They recommended further "that direct advertising in radio broadcasting service be absolutely prohibited and that indirect advertising be limited to a statement of the call letters of the station and of the name of the concern responsible for the matter broadcasted, subject to such regulations as the Secretary of Commerce may impose."[42]

Numerous bills to regulate the spectrum, including several encompassing the conference's proposals, failed to get through Congress in the early 1920s.[43] As a result, Secretary Hoover continued to regulate radio on the basis of the Radio Act of 1912. The 1912 Act had authorized licensing of radio stations, and Hoover interpreted the provision liberally. In one case, for example, he decided not to renew the license of New York's Intercity Radio Company, a radio telegraphy firm, after its license expired in August 1921. Hoover justified the decision saying that there were no available wavelengths "which would not interfere with government and private stations, and that under the provisions of the [1912] act of Congress the issuance or refusal of a license is a matter wholly within his discretion." The D.C. Court of Appeals disagreed, however, ruling in February 1923 that the department could not deny radio licenses to eligible stations: "The only discretionary act is in selecting a wave length, within the limitations prescribed in the statute, which, in his judgment, will result in the least possible interference."[44] Denying a license altogether was, in the opinion of the court, beyond the department's authority.

The following month, Hoover held a second radio conference, which proposed creating new spectrum-allocation rules and empowering the Commerce Department to exercise greater discretion in granting its broadcast licenses.[45] Soon thereafter, Hoover announced new spectrum rules. "Class A" stations, permitted to broadcast at no more than 500 watts, were assigned frequencies between 999.4 and 1365 kHz. "Class B" stations, broadcasting at 500 to 1000 watts, were assigned frequencies between 550 and 800 kHz as well as between 870 and 999.4 kHz. "Class C" low-power stations, meanwhile, were to broadcast only at 833.3 kHz.[46] Further conferences in October 1924 and November 1925 called for additional regulations and reflected mounting concern about the crowded airwaves.[47]

Congress Considers New Radio Regulation

After several failed attempts earlier in the decade, both houses of Congress again took up the issue of radio regulation at the start of 1926. On January 6 the House Committee on the Merchant Marine and Fisheries began discussing a bill introduced by Wallace H. White, a Maine Republican. The White bill "declared and reaffirmed that the ether within the limits of the United States, its Territories and possessions, is the inalienable possession of the people thereof."* The bill also would authorize the Commerce Department to issue licenses for all radio transmissions crossing state or national boundaries, and it empowered the department to set wavelengths, signal strength, and schedules for those stations. Under the bill, the department would be directed to issue a license to any station "if public convenience, interest, or necessity will be served thereby" and to refuse a license to any station "which has been found guilty by any Federal court of unlawfully monopolizing or attempting to unlawfully monopolize radio communications, directly or indirectly, through the control of the manufacture or sale of radio apparatus, through exclusive traffic arrangements, or by any other means." The licenses, the bill announced, represented "no vested property right" to the frequencies specified, could not be transferred to another person without the consent of the secretary of commerce, and could be revoked if the station violated the terms of the license or other laws. The licenses would

---

* Many early radio scientists believed that radio waves traveled via an invisible medium called the "ether." Later scientific discoveries disproved this theory, but the term survived in scientific papers until the late 1930s (Sterling and Kittross, *Stay Tuned*, 25–26).

last for a maximum of five years, but could be renewed. The Commerce Department would also issue permits to construct new radio stations, and no newly constructed station could receive a radio license without such a permit. All stations, moreover, would have to clearly state, at the time of broadcast, when their content was an advertisement and which firms sponsored their programs. Obscene or "superfluous" transmissions would be grounds for license suspension. Station operators would be entitled to appeal any revocation or refusal of a radio license or construction permit to the D.C. Court of Appeals. Finally, the bill would create a National Radio Commission, appointed by the U.S. president, to counsel the secretary of commerce on granting licenses and other issues related to the act. The secretary could choose when to consult the commission, but its decisions would be binding.[48]

Some representatives at the Merchant Marine and Fisheries hearings expressed concern that the White bill could threaten freedom of speech. Representative Frank R. Reid, an Illinois Republican, worried that the commerce secretary's authority over license renewal could be used for political ends. "Suppose some broadcasting station, during the Republican administration of the Government, is broadcasting a lot of Democratic documents which we thought were not for the good of the country," Reid said. "Would it be possible for him to refuse the license if, in his discretion, he thought that? Would it not be a limitation on the freedom of speech?" Reid's colleagues assured him that renewal rejections could be appealed in the courts, which appeared to alleviate his concerns.[49]

Several committee members also voiced concern about potential censorship by business, rather than government. At the hearings, W. E. Harkness, an assistant vice president at AT&T, claimed that on his company's radio stations, "We do not censor—we edit." AT&T, he explained, cut out potentially offensive content on its medical programs, and asked religious programs not to discuss controversial topics. He maintained that AT&T had given both major parties equal opportunities to broadcast at election time, and that its political debates were balanced, so as to attract audience members of all political leanings. Such assurances were not enough to satisfy Representative Ewin Davis of Tennessee, however, who later said, "We already have censorship . . . by the broadcasters themselves, who edit and pass upon whether this, that, or the other shall be broadcasted." Davis, who had helped draft the bill's advertising rules, explained that they would help to expose broadcasters' financial interests in particular types of programming.[50]

As the House debated White's bill, a similar discussion took place in the Senate. On January 8 the Committee on Interstate Commerce began examining two radio regulation bills. The first, sponsored by Nebraska Republican Robert B. Howell, was a short bill that merely declared the airwaves to be public property and authorized the secretary of commerce to issue two-year licenses to radio stations that sought to use them. The second bill, put forward by a Democrat from Washington State, Clarence C. Dill, closely resembled the White bill in the House. Unlike the White bill, however, Dill's proposal stated, "Nothing in this act shall be understood or construed to give the Secretary of Commerce the power of censorship . . . and no regulation or condition shall be promulgated or fixed by the Secretary of Commerce which shall interfere with the right of free speech and free entertainment by means of radio communications." Notably, Dill's bill did retain a prohibition on obscenity. It also excluded White's rules regarding advertising.[51]

At the Senate hearings, a number of senators expressed fears about the possibility that a few powerful firms could take control of the radio spectrum. Senator Howell explained that he had included in his bill a firm declaration that the airwaves were public property "to force to the surface now, and not 25 years from now, any claim of vested right [to frequencies] and put a period to such claim, or enable Congress to deal with them now in the infancy of this art." The Dill and White bills contained similar statements, but some senators wondered whether the bills' other provisions might provide means to skirt this principle. Senator James Couzens, a Michigan Republican, pointed out that the sale or transfer of radio licenses and licensed stations would still be allowed with the commerce secretary's consent. Because any growing radio company could, with the secretary's approval, buy up licensed stations, Couzens could "not see any way now, even in Senator Dill's bill, of preventing a monopoly of broadcasting." Ohio Republican Simeon D. Fess voiced similar concerns after Stephen B. Davis, Commerce Department solicitor, explained that any station "operated in accordance with the law and in accordance with its license" would have its license renewed. Because the spectrum was limited, Fess concluded, this would necessarily imply "favoritism" toward established stations, amounting to "perpetual franchise" and virtual ownership of the wavelengths.[52]

Others questioned whether Dill's framework for radio licenses was internally consistent. On the one hand, the bill explicitly stated that the licenses conferred no property rights. Yet on the other, the bill allowed anyone whose license was denied or revoked to appeal the Commerce Department's decision in court. "If there is no vested right, no property right," asked Albert B. Cummins, an Iowa Republican, at a second round of hearings in late February, "why is it not revocable at pleasure?" Putting an even finer point on the apparent contradiction, Cummins declared, "It says that the licensee has no vested right, when it is perfectly obvious that he has a vested right." By the end of the debate, Solicitor Davis conceded that the license *did* contain a vested right to the wavelength, but—he maintained—only for the term of the license.[53]

The House Passes a Bill

The House began considering an amended version of its bill on March 13. This version remained very similar to the original White bill, but now included language intended to ensure a more equitable distribution of licenses throughout the states.[54] In his opening statement, Representative White spoke of the importance of keeping the airwaves public rather than private. "Freedom to barter and sell licenses threatens the principle that only those who will render a public service may enjoy a license," he said. "It would make possible the acquisition of many stations by a few or by a single interest."[55]

One of the most outspoken critics at these debates was Thomas Blanton, a Democrat from Texas who repeatedly questioned whether White's bill adequately protected political candidates from slander or the political leanings of radio companies. "What greater monopoly could there be than for a radio corporation or a radio company engaged in the public business of broadcasting radio messages to grant one rate to one political party and charge an entirely discriminatory and different rate to another political party?" he asked. "What greater monopoly could exist than where a radio company would give the free use of its line to one candidate for office or one contender for some economic theory, and then deny such use to those who are on the other side of the question?"[56] Calling for an amendment that would have extended prohibitions on written slander and libel to speech broadcast over the radio, Blanton appealed directly to his fellow congressmen as politicians who would regularly need to run for office themselves:

I want to say this, gentlemen: This is one of the most important questions that can affect the whole people of this Government. It affects the seat in this House of every Congressman here. We are all to go home soon to our primaries. We are all to be elected in November in the general election. The night before the primary in your State some of your enemies could induce somebody in some other State, say 50 miles or 100 miles from where you live, to make derogatory statements about you in such a way that it might absolutely ruin you in the next day's primary or election, and they would be absolutely impervious to punishment, because now there is no law exactly covering the offense.

Do you want to take chances on that? Of course, they could not hurt you more than temporarily, but you would be defeated for office, and there would be no way to prevent the defeat. It would have already been done the night before your primary. When somebody the night before election puts a false statement out about you that injures your standing in the community, it is too late to remedy it when the primary is over, because your opponent has received the votes necessary to cut you out of the election. You could thus ruin a gubernatorial candidate; you thus could ruin a presidential candidate, or you could ruin a candidate for any elective office.[57]

The House rejected Blanton's amendment and passed the White bill on March 15, 1926, with only slight modifications.[58]

The Senate Rewrite

On May 8 the Senate's Interstate Commerce Committee presented the White bill to the whole Senate for consideration, recommending that it "pass with certain amendments."[59] These "certain amendments," however, were quite significant. In the version of the bill presented to senators, the committee struck out all of the language the House had passed and replaced it with new text. Instead of saying that the airwaves were public property, the new bill's introduction stated that "the Federal Government intends forever to preserve and maintain the channels of radio transmission as perpetual mediums under the control and for the people of the United States." It also specified that "such channels are not to be subject to acquisition by any individual, firm, or corporation, and only the use, but not the ownership thereof, may be allowed, for limited periods, under licenses in that behalf." The bill created a Federal Radio Commission, as the White bill did, but gave it all of the powers that White had granted the Department of Commerce, and transferred everyone in the department working on radio to the commission staff. This commission would oversee radio licensing in the United States under the new bill, with no comparable authority granted to the Commerce Department. The bill did not include any right to appeal the commission's decisions. It did provide explicit protection of free speech, and included White's rule for announcing advertising. Finally, it stipulated that licensees "shall make no discrimination" in presenting paid content "by a candidate or candidates for any public office, or for the discussion of any question affecting the public," and would have "no power to censor the material broadcast."[60]

The *Providence Journal* offered one hypothesis as to why the Senate committee had rewritten so much of the bill and disempowered the Commerce Department and, by extension, its secretary, Herbert Hoover:

> There is small room to doubt that the action of the Senate committee is tinged with politics. Senator [James] Watson, of Indiana, chairman of the Committee, is a prospective candidate for the Republican nomination for President, and must look upon Secretary Hoover as a possible rival. Senator [William] Borah, of Idaho, whose bill to create an independent radio commission is now before the Committee [and had inspired the rewrite], like Senator Watson, has no love for Secretary Hoover. Senator Couzens, of Michigan, who was active in securing the Committee vote, is regarded as an anti-administration and anti-Hoover senator. The same is to be said of Senator Howell, of Nebraska, another member of the Committee.[61]

The Senate began discussing the new bill on June 30. After Senator Dill reviewed it, Senators Sam G. Bratton and Joseph Taylor Robinson, Democrats from New Mexico and Arkansas, respectively, complained that the right of appeal had been dropped. Senator Cummins defended this change by reprising his arguments from February (that is, giving stations a right of appeal would imply a property right in the radio spectrum), but the majority ultimately sided with Bratton and Robinson and restored the provision allowing a right of appeal.[62]

Others worried about the power of the Federal Radio Commission. Senator William King, a Utah Democrat, declared his "inherent objection to the creation of more commissions," which he believed would "wind more and more the red tape of officialdom and bureaucracy around the people, to their discomfort if not their ultimate death." Hiram Bingham, a Republican from

Connecticut, offered a similar perspective. The bill stipulated that members of the five-person commission should represent diverse political parties and should have no financial interests in the radio industry, but Bingham doubted that these protections would be sufficient. "We object to giving one man a lot of power," he said, "and yet . . . we give one man of the majority party the power of settling all difficulties that may arise in this commission. Furthermore, no one will know which one of the five it is. . . . Why would it not be better to give it to one member of the Cabinet, who can be held responsible for the rules and regulations and for the decisions that are made?"[63]

Although Senator Dill did not compromise on the proposed commission, he did offer a significant amendment on July 1 that provoked notable debate in the chamber. Specifically, he suggested narrowing the political "no discrimination" rule to cover only "candidates for . . . public office," rather than both candidates and all questions "affecting the public," as in the prior draft. Senator Howell strongly objected. "To perpetuate in the hands of a comparatively few interests the opportunity of reaching the public by radio and allowing them alone to determine what the public shall and shall not hear is a tremendously dangerous course," he declared. "The discussion of public questions by radio is reaching the youth of this country, and will have a tremendous effect in the formation of their views. . . . Give me control of the character of the matter that goes out over our broadcasting stations and I will mold the views of the next generation. Again, as important as the rights of candidates are, do they compare in importance with some of the questions that are presented to the electorate of your municipalities at nearly every election?"[64]

The Senate approved Dill's amendment over Howell's objection, and passed the whole bill on July 2. Senate leaders had hoped that they could quickly reach an agreement with their House colleagues in conference, reconciling the House and Senate bills before the congressional session ended the next day, but they soon realized there would simply not be enough time to work out an acceptable compromise. Not wishing to have any long-term licenses issued or commitments made before Congress was able to finish work on the bill at the next opportunity, the conference committee hastily wrote up a brief resolution limiting the life of new broadcast licenses to ninety days and requiring that anyone receiving or renewing a broadcast license explicitly waive "any right or . . . any claim to any right" in the radio spectrum. The resolution never became official, however, because Vice President Charles Dawes, in his role as president of the Senate, failed to sign it before the session ended.[65]

Radio Goes to Court

United States v. Zenith Radio Corporation

As members of Congress worked unsuccessfully to pass radio legislation in 1926, their counterparts in the federal judiciary managed to transform the regulatory environment for radio, virtually with the stroke of a pen. In 1925 the Commerce Department had licensed Chicago's Zenith Radio Corporation for two hours per week at 930 kHz. As its business expanded, Zenith requested that it be allowed to broadcast on a preferable frequency (840, 910, or 960 kHz), but the department refused, having promised to leave those frequencies available for Canadian stations. When Zenith went ahead and began broadcasting at 910 kHz without permission, many other stations indicated that they might soon make similar moves, irrespective of their licenses. The Commerce Department sued Zenith, with many outside observers perhaps expecting an easy government victory. But in April 1926 the U.S. District Court for Northern Illinois ruled that the secretary of commerce lacked the authority to specify either frequencies or times of use in radio licenses.[66]

Hoover opted not to appeal the decision. Having turned to Acting Attorney General William J. Donovan for advice on the matter, Hoover was told he had a weak case. Donovan wrote in early July, "It is apparent from the answers contained in this opinion that the present legislation is inadequate to cover the art of broadcasting, which has been almost entirely developed since the passage of the 1912 Act. If the present situation requires control, I can only suggest that it be sought in new legislation, carefully adapted to meet the needs of both the present and future."[67]

The result was that Hoover's Commerce Department stopped trying to curb stations from broadcasting whenever and on whatever frequencies they wished, and it was said that chaos quickly overtook the airwaves. As one government official later recalled, "many stations jumped without restraint to new wave lengths which suited them better, regardless of the interference which they might thus be causing to other stations. Proper separation between established stations was destroyed by other stations coming in and camping in the middle of any open spaces they could find, each interloper thus impairing reception of three stations—his own and two others. . . . Indeed, every human ingenuity and selfish impulse seemed to have been exerted to complicate the tangle in the ether."[68] Attempts among stations to self-regulate by scheduling their broadcasts for different time slots were largely unsuccessful. Some scholars subsequently alleged that Hoover expected the period after *United States v. Zenith Radio Corporation* to be chaotic, and that he chose not to appeal the District Court's decision because he suspected that the resulting chaos would force Congress to enact comprehensive radio regulation. Several scholars have even noted that Secretary Hoover and Acting Attorney General Donovan were close friends, insinuating that Donovan may have given Hoover exactly the answer he wanted.[69]

Tribune Co. v. Oak Leaves Broadcasting Station

The *Zenith* decision helped trigger further litigation as chaos increasingly enveloped the airwaves. After *Zenith* freed it from the restrictions of its federal license, Chicago's Oak Leaves Broadcasting Co. had begun transmitting on a frequency near that of a station owned by the Tribune Company, causing interference on Tribune's station. Tribune sued Oak Leaves, and on November 17, 1926, Judge Francis Wilson ruled in Tribune's favor. Without either statutory guidance or a similar case to rely on in deciding who had the right to broadcast on a particular frequency, Wilson turned to common law principles, ruling "that a court of equity is compelled to recognize rights which have been acquired by reason of the outlay and expenditure of money and the investment of time." He determined that "the complainant has been using said wave length for a considerable length of time and has built up a large clientage, whereas the defendants are but newly in the field. . . . We are of the opinion further that, under the circumstances in this case, priority of time creates a superiority in right . . . it would be only just that the situation should be preserved in the status in which it was prior to the time that the defendant undertook to operate over or near the wave length of the complainant."[70] With this decision, Wilson declared that Tribune had a right to the frequency on which it had long broadcast, and which Oak Leaves had recently trespassed.[71]

Congress Resumes Its Efforts to Pass a Radio Bill

Congress reconvened in December 1926. Both houses quickly approved the joint resolution that had fizzled the previous July. This granted Commerce more flexibility in issuing ninety-day licenses but also waived private claims to individual wavelengths, provoking protest from many radio stations as a result. With complaints coming from numerous directions, a House-Senate conference committee immediately set to work on a compromise radio bill, searching for a more permanent solution.[72]

The committee finally produced a reconciled bill on January 28, 1927. The new draft declared that federal licenses would "provide for the use of [radio] channels, but not the ownership thereof." Senate negotiators had urged this language on the House conferees, claiming that the White bill's character-ization of the airwaves as "'the inalienable possession of the people' . . . was inadequate and indefinable."[73] Licensing power would initially be granted to the Federal Radio Commission, but after a year many of its duties would shift back to the Department of Commerce, with the commission reverting to the advisory role outlined in the original House proposals. The confer-ence bill also affirmed the right of free speech on the airwaves, mandated equal opportunity for competing political candidates (though not for com-peting opinions on questions of public importance), and required that spon-sored broadcasts and advertising be announced as such. Finally, station owners could appeal licensing decisions in the federal courts.[74]

Debate over the Conference Bill

The strongest opposition to the conference bill in the House came from Ewin Davis, who declared that it was "less protective of the public interests and more favorable to the monopoly and the profiteering interests than any radio bill that has passed either branch of Congress, or which has heretofore been reported to either branch of Congress." Davis noted that the new bill had dropped much of the White bill's original language designed to prevent pri-vate interests from owning the airwaves. The new bill, he argued, specified that the licenses conferred no right—but did *not* say that established stations had no vested right in the frequencies they had long occupied. "They are not going to claim vested rights under a license," Davis warned. "They are not making that claim now. They are going to claim vested rights upon the ground of prior use." Davis also worried that the licenses as defined in the new bill would be no stronger than under the existing system, and that the public interest would suffer no matter how courts interpreted the new language. If stations were deemed to have a vested right in their wavelengths, this would inevitably lead to monopoly, and if they were found to have no such rights, the result would be wave jumping and intolerable interference. To Davis, only a law that guaranteed fully public airwaves, which were tightly controlled by the government, would solve the dual threats of private monopoly, on the one hand, and debilitating interference, on the other.[75]

As Davis expected, however, the bill passed the House on January 29, and it was taken up in the Senate a few days later. Senator Dill, presenting its key features, explained that the new bill granted the Federal Radio Commission licensing power for one year in order to ensure that the first licenses under the new law were spread fairly throughout the country (a consequence, presumably, of the fact that commission members themselves would come from different regions). Furthermore, the initial year would allow commission members to accrue expertise that would inform their subsequent advisory role. When asked why the bill did not include a waiver of property rights as strong as the recent joint resolution, Dill contended that radio stations had complained that the waiver "was so broad that they did not know what they were giving away, and they feared it included even the right of due process of law to which they were entitled as against the United States seizing or using their apparatus. . . . The Senate conferees were fearful that such a waiver provision would be declared unconstitutional by the courts, and therefore we modified it."[76]

When the question was raised whether property rights in the "ether" would exist, Dill insisted that they would not—but also that the very idea of such a right was misleading. "What we are really trying to prevent is some one getting a vested right to operate apparatus at a certain rate of frequency, and the right to regulate that is the only right we have," he explained.

I am as anxious as any man can be—for I think I have given more attention to this one phase of the subject than any other phase of it—to prevent anybody, individual, firm, or corporation, from ever securing the right to use these frequencies on their apparatus as against the control of the United States; but we should not declare that we own all of the apparatus. We should not declare that we want to forbid anybody from possessing this apparatus. All we can do is to say that we shall regulate the use of it to the point even of preventing its use. This talk about air channels, this talk about owning the ether, has no real basis except as considered in terms of regulating the apparatus that sends its impulses out through the ether and the air and through everything on this earth. We never have been able to find anything that will stop the radio wave. You can own all the air and all the buildings and all the air channels you want to, but give me a piece of apparatus, and let me operate it at a certain frequency, and what good would it do anybody to own the air and the buildings and all that sort of thing?[77]

The Senate's leading opponent to the conference bill was Key Pittman, a Nevada Democrat. Pittman interrogated Dill throughout the debates about various features of the bill, with the hope of shelving it entirely so that a new bill could be drawn up and considered by the incoming Congress. In a long speech before the final vote on February 18, Pittman enumerated the legislation's flaws as he perceived them. Among other complaints, he pointed out that the prohibition against private possession of the airwaves had been softened, that the commission would be a better and more consistent judge of licensing questions after the first year than an ever-changing secretary of commerce, and that the bill set no limits on the total amount of advertising that would be allowed on the radio.[78] Pittman expressed particular concern that a radio monopoly would ultimately arise, forcing American listeners to pay for service, and that the powers granted to the commission and the Department of Commerce were far from sufficient:

What powers of regulation has this bill in it? It is the most astounding thing you ever read. It does not give to the officer that licenses and the commission that may revoke licenses the power to fix charges [i.e., prices]. It does not give either the Secretary or the commission the power to investigate charges. It does not give either the power to investigate discriminations. It does not give either the power to investigate lack of service.

Think of such a bill! Here you are seeking now to regulate a known monopoly, an inevitable monopoly, and yet you give to one man after a year the power to issue these licenses; you reserve the power to a commission to revoke them; and yet you do not give either one of those the authority to regulate the charges. There is no power in the bill to fix charges. You do not give them any power to regulate service. You do not give them any power to prevent discriminations.

That must appear to be a great mistake. You will have to have a firm control over this industry. If it is better to put it in the hand of one man, like the Secretary of Commerce, instead of in the hands of a commission, all right; but when you recognize the fact that this industry has to be controlled by a strong hand, why do you withhold from that strong hand the power to regulate? If there ever was a bill manufactured for the very purpose of preventing regulation, it is this bill.[79]

President Coolidge's Decision

Like Davis in the House, Pittman expected his colleagues to approve the bill over his objections, and they did. The Senate passed it on February 18, 1927, and it arrived at the desk of Republican president Calvin Coolidge several days later. In his message to Congress the previous December, Coolidge (using words written by Secretary Hoover) had voiced firm support for radio legislation and expressed a strong preference that regulatory authority be lodged in the Department of Commerce rather than in a commission.[80] The new radio bill, however, placed the Federal Radio Commission outside of the Commerce Department and granted the commission substantial powers in its first year. With this final bill now before him, President Coolidge had to decide whether to sign it or let it die.

NOTES

1. Eric Klinenberg, *Fighting for Air: The Battle to Control America's Media* (New York: Metropolitan Books, 2007), 17–18.
2. Susan J. Douglas, *Listening In: Radio and the American Imagination* (New York: Random House, 1999), 63. Of the ninety-six frequencies (or channels) allocated to broadcasting, six had been reserved for Canadian broadcasters by agreement.
3. *Annual Report of the Federal Radio Commission to the Congress of the United States for the Fiscal Year Ended June 30, 1927* (Washington, DC: GPO, 1927), 11.

4. Christopher H. Sterling and John Michael Kittross, *Stay Tuned: A History of American Broadcasting*, 3rd ed. (Mahwah, NJ: Erlbaum, 2002), 27–29, 33, 38–40.

5. Sterling and Kittross, *Stay Tuned*, 30–32; Linwood S. Howeth, *History of Communications-Electronics in the United States Navy* (Washington, DC: GPO, 1963), 19–22, 67–71.

6. Howeth, *History*, 71–72; Gleason L. Archer, *History of Radio to 1926* (New York: American Historical Society, 1938), 79; Sterling and Kittross, *Stay Tuned*, 41–42; Susan J. Douglas, *Inventing American Broadcasting, 1899–1922* (Baltimore: Johns Hopkins University Press, 1987), 122–123.

7. Sterling and Kittross, *Stay Tuned*, 40. See Howeth, *History*, chap. 3, for greater detail. The quote is from a letter from Bradford, the chief of the Bureau of Equipment, to the secretary of the Navy (1 Dec. 1899), quoted in Howeth, *History*, 34.

8. Sterling and Kittross, *Stay Tuned*, 40; Howeth, *History*, 71.

9. Howeth, *History*, 69–70, quotations at 70.

10. Letter to the secretary of the Navy (7 Mar. 1904), quoted in Howeth, *History*, 73.

11. Howeth, *History*, 74–76.

12. Ibid., 76–77; U.S. Inter-Departmental Board on Wireless Telegraphy, *Wireless Telegraphy* (Washington, DC: GPO, 1905), 9–11.

13. *Wireless Telegraphy*, 9, 11.

14. Howeth, *History*, 78. The exact language of the order is on 551 in the reprint of the report.

15. Ibid., 77–82.

16. Quoted from *New York Times* (10 Sep. 1906, 6) in Douglas, *Inventing American Broadcasting*, 126.

17. Howeth, *History*, 117.

18. Ibid., 118–124; Sterling and Kittross, *Stay Tuned*, 42.

19. *International Wireless Telegraph Convention* (Washington, DC: GPO, 1907), 31. The 1906 Berlin Convention is also available at http://earlyradiohistory.us/1906conv.htm. The Convention specified wavelengths, not frequencies. We reported frequencies to ensure consistency across the case.

20. Hearings on International Wireless Telegraph, quoted in Howeth, *History*, 124–125.

21. Howeth, *History*, 129–132, 153–155.

22. Quoted in Sterling and Kittross, *Stay Tuned*, 42.

23. Ibid., 43. Howeth, *History*, 158, insists that the law "did nothing . . . to compel intercommunication between commercial companies."

24. Howeth, *History*, 158–159 (quotation from the 9 Mar. 1912 issue), 160–161, 164–165. The London Convention is available at http://earlyradiohistory.us/1914reg.htm.

25. Howeth, *History*, 162–163. The text of the act is available at http://earlyradiohistory.us/1912act.htm.

26. John Bottomley, "Commercial Wireless Telegraph Development," *Electrical World*, 4 Jan. 1913, 25, quoted in Howeth, *History*, 164. Howeth mistakenly lists the date of the *Electrical World* issue as 3 Jan. 1914.

27. Howeth, *History*, 314–315, first quotation at 314; second quotation, from E. J. Nally, "The New Radio Legislation" (*The Wireless Age*, Jan. 1917, 236) at 315.

28. Sterling and Kittross, *Stay Tuned*, 56–57; Howeth, *History*, 315–317.

29. Sterling and Kittross, *Stay Tuned*, 63–67, 91.

30. Ibid., 57–63, 74–77, 116–117. Although RCA owned 50 percent of the newly created NBC, GE and Westinghouse owned the other 50 percent (ibid., 117).

31. David A. Moss and Jonathan B. L. Decker, "Capturing History: The Case of the Federal Radio Commission in 1927," in *Preventing Regulatory Capture: Special Interest Influence and How to Limit It*, ed. Daniel Carpenter and David A. Moss (Cambridge: Cambridge University Press, 2013), 201.

32. Susan Smulyan, *Selling Radio: The Commercialization of American Broadcasting, 1920–1934* (Washington, DC: Smithsonian Institution Press, 1994), 65–68.

33. Hiram Jome, *Economics of the Radio Industry* (New York: A. W. Shaw and Co., 1925), 177–178, 254.

34. Archer, *History of Radio*, 252.

35. Moss and Decker, "Capturing History," 201.

36. Ibid., 201–202.

37. Sterling and Kittross, *Stay Tuned*, 79.

38. Quotes from Joseph H. Jackson, "Should Radio Be Used for Advertising?," *Radio Broadcast*, Nov. 1922, and E. J. Van Brook, "How Bombastic Advertising Can Be Suppressed," *Broadcast Advertising*, July 1929, in Smulyan, *Selling Radio*, 68–69.

39. Smulyan, *Selling Radio*, 69; Sterling and Kittross, *Stay Tuned*, 80.

40. Sterling and Kittross, *Stay Tuned*, 93; Marvin R. Bensman, *The Beginning of Broadcast Regulation in the Twentieth Century* (Jefferson, NC: McFarland, 2000), 29, 74.

41. Letter to Ludwig Hesse (23 Mar. 1921) quoted in Bensman, *Broadcast Regulation*, 33.

42. The report from the first conference is available at http://earlyradiohistory.us /1922conf.htm. See also Sterling and Kittross, *Stay Tuned*, 94; Bensman, *Broadcast Regulation*, 47–55.

43. See Bensman, *Broadcast Regulation*, 33–36, 55–64, 95–101.

44. *Hoover v. Intercity Radio Co., Inc.*, 286 Fed. 1003 (1923), is available at https://apps.fcc .gov/edocs_public/attachmatch/DOC-328549A1.pdf. See also Laurence F. Schmeckebier, *The Federal Radio Commission: Its History, Activities and Organization* (Washington, DC: Brookings Institution, 1932), 5–6; Bensman, *Broadcast Regulation*, 44–47.

45. The report from the second conference is available at http://earlyradiohistory.us /1923conf.htm. See also Sterling and Kittross, *Stay Tuned*, 94; Bensman, *Broadcast Regulation*, 80–81.

46. Louise Benjamin, "Working It Out Together: Radio Policy from Hoover to the Radio Act of 1927," *Journal of Broadcasting & Electronic Media* 42, no. 2 (Spring 1998), 227–228; Bensman, *Broadcast Regulation*, 81; Schmeckebier, *The Federal Radio Commission*, 6–7; Sterling and Kittross, *Stay Tuned*, 94–96.

47. Sterling and Kittross, *Stay Tuned*, 96–97; Bensman, *Broadcast Regulation*, 101–114, 140–148. The reports for the third and fourth conferences are available at http://earlyradiohistory.us/1924conf.htm and . . . /1925conf.htm.

48. The bill (H.R. 5589) is reprinted in House Committee on the Merchant Marine and Fisheries, *To Regulate Radio Communication* (Washington, DC: GPO, 1926), 1–8. Available via HeinOnline. HeinOnline's Intellectual Property Law Collection has a collection called "Legislative History of the Radio Act of 1927" that contains many relevant documents.

49. *To Regulate Radio Communication*, 25–26.

50. Ibid., 56–58, 83–84.

51. The Howell (S. 1) and Dill (S. 1754) bills are reprinted in Senate Committee on Interstate Commerce, *Radio Control* (Washington, DC: GPO 1926), 1–8. Available via HeinOnline.

52. Senate, *Radio Control*, 34, 44, 87–88.

53. Ibid., 110–113.

54. This bill, H.R. 9971, is available via HeinOnline. There was another version in the interim, H.R. 9108.

55. *Congressional Record*, vol. 67 (hereafter cited as 67 CR), 5479. Available via HeinOnline, 67 Cong. Rec. 5479 (1926).

56. Ibid., 5561.

57. Ibid., 5573.

58. Ibid., 5645–5647. HeinOnline has the version of the bill passed by the House.

59. *Regulation of Radio Transmission*, Report no. 772 (submitted by Clarence Dill), 69th Congress, 1st sess. (8 May 1926), Senate, quotation at 1. Available via HeinOnline.

60. H.R. 9971 [Rept. No. 772], 69th Congress, 1st sess. (8 May 1926), quotations at 31, 50. This version of the bill is available on HeinOnline.

61. Quoted in Bensman, *Broadcast Regulation*, 193–194.

62. 67 CR, 12355.

63. Ibid., 12356–12357, 12498.

64. Ibid., 12502, 12503–12504.

65. Bensman, *Broadcast Regulation*, 193; 67 CR, 12959, quotation at 12959. The resolution (S.J. Res. 125) is available on HeinOnline.

66. Sterling and Kittross, *Stay Tuned*, 97; Bensman, *Broadcast Regulation*, 156–170. *United States v. Zenith Radio Corporation et al.*, 12 F. 2d 614 (1926), is available at https://apps.fcc.gov/edocs_public/attachmatch/DOC-328551A1.pdf.

67. Sterling and Kittross, *Stay Tuned*, 98; Bensman, *Broadcast Regulation*, 170–176; Schmeckebier, *The Federal Radio Commission*, 12–14; Charlotte Twight, "What Congressmen Knew and When They Knew It: Further Evidence on the Origins of U.S. Broadcasting Regulation," *Public Choice* 95, nos. 3–4 (June 1998): 250. Quotation from Donovan's opinion is from Schmeckebier, *The Federal Radio Commission*, 14.

68. FRC Commissioner Orestes H. Caldwell, in *Annual Report of the Federal Radio Commission* (1927), 11. Also quoted in Sterling and Kittross, *Stay Tuned*, 98.

69. Sterling and Kittross, *Stay Tuned,* 98; Twight, "What Congressmen Knew," 255–257; Thomas W. Hazlett, "The Rationality of U.S. Regulation of the Broadcast Spectrum," *Journal of Law and Economics* 33, no. 1 (Apr. 1990): 157–160.

70. *Tribune Co. v. Oak Leaves Broadcasting Station* (Cook County, IL Cir. Ct. 1926) as reproduced in *Congressional Record,* vol. 68 (hereafter cited as 68 CR), 216–219, quotations at 219. Available via HeinOnline, 68 Cong. Rec. 216 (1926). The Tribune Company also published the *Chicago Daily Tribune* newspaper.

71. See Twight, "What Congressmen Knew," 251.

72. Bensman, *Broadcast Regulation,* 197–199; 68 CR, 2574.

73. Frank Scott, in 68 CR, 2564.

74. Ibid., 2557–2568; Frank Scott, *Regulation of Radio Communication,* Report no. 1886, 69th Congress, 2nd sess. (27 Jan. 1927), House. Available on HeinOnline.

75. 68 CR, 2573, 2574, 2574–2575.

76. Ibid., 2869, 2871.

77. Ibid., 2873.

78. Ibid., 4109.

79. Ibid., 4110.

80. Bensman, *Broadcast Regulation,* 199, 196–197. See also President Coolidge's Dec. 1926 message, which is available via the American Presidency Project at http://www .presidency.ucsb.edu/ws/?pid=29567.

·{ 15 }·

The Pecora Hearings (1932–1934)

In late October 1929, Wall Street was badly shaken by what later came to be known as the "Great Crash." On Black Monday and Black Tuesday (October 28 and 29), the Dow Jones Industrial Average fell from 300 to 230, well down from its peak of 381 on September 3. It ultimately bottomed out at 41 during the summer of 1932. By this time hundreds of banks had failed, prices had dropped dramatically, U.S. real per capita GDP had fallen by nearly 30 percent, and the unemployment rate stood at over 20 percent.[1] Many blamed Wall Street for the onset of the Great Depression; and Franklin Delano Roosevelt, who ultimately won the 1932 presidential election by a wide margin, promised to enact strict regulations on the financial community and put "an end to speculation."[2]

In 1932 the Senate Banking Committee began a much-publicized investigation of the nation's financial sector. The hearings, which came to be known as the Pecora hearings after the Banking Committee's lead counsel, Ferdinand Pecora, revealed how the country's most respected financial institutions knowingly misled investors as to the desirability of certain securities, engaged in irresponsible investment behavior, and offered to insiders privileges that were not available to ordinary investors. During the famous "Hundred Day" congressional session that began his presidency, Roosevelt signed two bills meant to prevent some of these abuses. The first law required companies to register new securities with the Federal Trade Commission (FTC) and to publish prospectuses with detailed information on their business ventures before they could offer new securities to the public. The second law established insurance for bank deposits and forced financial institutions to choose between investment and commercial banking.[3]

Roosevelt also believed that the government should play a more active role in the financial system by regulating national securities exchanges. In February 1934 the president urged Congress to enact such legislation, prompting the introduction of a bill titled the National Securities Exchange Act. If enacted, this bill would force all securities exchanges to register with the Federal Trade Commission, would curtail the size of loans that could be advanced to securities investors, and would ban a number of practices (such as short-selling) that were thought to facilitate stock manipulation. Additionally, the legislation would require that all companies with exchange-listed securities publish detailed business reports as frequently as the FTC desired and would subject any company or exchange deemed to be in violation of the act's provisions to increased legal liability.[4]

Wall Street, represented in particular by New York Stock Exchange (NYSE) president Richard Whitney, took a strong position against the National Securities Exchange Act. Whitney quickly broadened the NYSE's internal anti-manipulation rules, in hopes of convincing Washington that stock exchanges could effectively police themselves without any government involvement. The NYSE president also warned of potentially disastrous effects of the bill, arguing that the publicity measures of the proposed legislation would enable the FTC to control companies' business practices and would prove so onerous that companies might choose to delist their securities from formal stock exchanges. He insisted, moreover, that the bill would reduce liquidity in securities markets and could even bring about a mass liquidation of shares as the result of its high margin requirements.[5]

While Whitney launched his assault on the bill, the Pecora Committee conducted a public inquiry into stock price manipulation at the New York Stock Exchange. Pecora detailed an instance just a few months earlier in which speculators, unbeknownst to the NYSE management, had artificially driven up the price of shares in alcohol (liquor) companies. Furthermore, the committee revealed that when the NYSE eventually conducted its own investigation into the matter, its final report concluded that nothing improper had occurred. Pecora claimed that this lax oversight by the NYSE confirmed that exchanges were incapable of adequately regulating themselves and therefore passage of the National Securities Exchange Act was vital.[6]

Spectacular financial abuses, like those involving the stocks of alcohol companies, had been routinely uncovered by the Pecora Committee for more

than a year, captivating the nation and helping to instill in citizens a strong
desire for financial reform. So when Richard Whitney was summoned to testify during the congressional hearings on the securities exchange bill in late
February 1934, he had the tough task of trying to prove to citizens and congressmen alike that the proposed legislation was too restrictive.[7] Would he
be able to convince lawmakers that the bill would impose overly burdensome regulations on exchanges and stifle American securities markets? Or
would his arguments fail to win over those who believed that strict regulations were exactly what financial markets required following the Great
Crash?

The Securities Market in the 1920s

During World War I, the U.S. government's massive Liberty Loan drives introduced large numbers of Americans to the idea of investing in bonds, a
prospect that would have seemed alien to many prior to the war. In 1917
and 1918, "the number of bond buyers in the United States increased from
350,000 to 25 million persons" as more and more citizens considered it their
patriotic duty to purchase Liberty Bonds.[8] According to historians, these far-
reaching wartime loan drives increased Americans' willingness to invest in
securities, priming them for the 1920s market surge.[9]

Indeed, stock indexes boomed in the 1920s as a suddenly investment-
hungry populace readily bought up a torrent of newly issued securities.
Over the decade as a whole, more than $28 billion in corporate debt secu-
rities were issued, far more than the roughly $12 billion issued during the
1910s. The growth in corporate equity issues was even more dramatic,
with the total value of common and preferred stock issues more than tri-
pling, from $5.8 billion in the 1910s to $18 billion in the 1920s. Likewise,
the total volume of stocks and the aggregate value of bonds traded on the
floor of the New York Stock Exchange nearly tripled from the 1910s to
the 1920s.[10]

Helping to fuel this massive surge in investment were margin loans,
which allowed investors to borrow heavily from their brokers (often as much
as 75 to 90 percent of the total cost) in order to buy securities. To fund their
customers' margin accounts, brokers in turn had to take out brokers' loans
from banks or other lenders. As a testament to the rapid increase in margin

financing during this time, aggregate brokers' loans surged from $7.6 billion in 1924 to more than $26.5 billion just five years later.[11]

Security Affiliates and Investment Trusts

Prior to the 1920s, commercial banks rarely participated in securities markets. Marked by a historic commitment to safe and conservative practices, and bound by state and federal legislation that barred them from partaking in any sort of "nonbanking" activities, commercial bankers tended to focus on their deposit and loan businesses. They generally kept their institutions' funds out of corporate securities and left the origination of stocks and bonds to J.P. Morgan and Company and other Wall Street investment firms.[12]

However, amid the stock market boom of the 1920s, many commercial banks abandoned their traditional outlooks and established subsidiary companies known as security affiliates. Numerous commercial banks had long maintained bond departments, through which they had sold Liberty Bonds during the war, but these new subsidiary organizations allowed bankers to circumvent the laws that forbid them to deal in the full spectrum of stocks and bonds. Additionally, by establishing such affiliates, many banks could bypass restrictions on interstate branching. Whereas only ten nationally chartered banks and eight state-chartered banks had security affiliates in 1922, 105 national banks and 75 state banks had securities-dealing subsidiaries by 1930.[13]

These security affiliates often acted as both investment houses and broker-dealers, not only helping to originate securities—by 1930, about half of all bonds were originated by banks' security affiliates—but also then facilitating customers' purchases of these securities. To attract walk-in clients, the affiliates often set up shop on the ground floor. Additionally, these companies would advertise in the era's most popular magazines, touting the virtues of an investment portfolio.[14]

Companies known as investment trusts, which were relatively new to the United States at the time, also found a niche selling securities during the 1920s, particularly to smaller investors. Like today's mutual funds, investment trusts sold shares in themselves to customers and invested the income in a securities portfolio. Their portfolios could be either fixed or actively managed and often included stocks, bonds, and sometimes even shares of other investment trusts. These investment companies experienced a tremendous rise in popularity during the decade, increasing in count from 40 to more than 750 from 1921 to 1929.[15]

Stock Market Manipulations

Schemes aimed at controlling security prices were common during the 1920s, and so-called stock pools or pool operations were among the most widespread stock market manipulations of the era.[16] The classic explanation of such practices was later given by John Kenneth Galbraith:

> The nature of these operations varied somewhat but, in a typical operation, a number of traders pooled their resources to boom a particular stock. They appointed a pool manager, promised not to double-cross each other by private operations, and the pool manager then took a position in the stock which might also include shares contributed by the participants. This buying would increase prices and attract the interest of people watching the tape across the country. The interest of the latter would then be further stimulated by active selling and buying, all of which gave the impression that something big was afloat. Tipsheets and market commentators would tell of exciting developments in the offing. If all went well, the public would come in to buy, and prices would rise on their own. The pool manager would then sell out [the pool's shares], pay himself a percentage of the profits, and divide the rest with his investors.[17]

In addition, some observers argued that certain stock pools also engaged in outright fraud, reporting "false statements or fictitious trades" to help inflate stock values.[18]

"Wash sales" were a specific form of manipulation that pool operators used to create the illusion of increased market activity in a given stock. In this practice, a stockholder would sell his shares on an exchange but would employ a broker working on his behalf to repurchase the shares, typically at a slightly higher value. Thus, by essentially selling his shares to himself, the market actor generated the appearance of active trading and exerted upward pressure on the stock's price, which in turn attracted other market participants to the stock. So-called matched sales were identical to wash sales, except that the market actor did not sell shares to himself, but instead sold them to another actor with whom he was colluding. By continually buying and selling the same shares back and forth between themselves, the actors could again entice outside investors to the stock by effecting the semblance of elevated market activity. Although these manipulative practices were recognized as fraudulent, they "were seldom detected or penalized by stock exchange officials" of the era.[19]

Unlike the preceding manipulations, "bear raids" sought the artificial depression of a stock's price. Through this practice, a group of market actors would engage in intense short-selling of a chosen stock, thereby applying downward pressure on its price. If the share price fell enough, many investors who held the stock on margin would receive margin calls. That is, those investors who had borrowed heavily to purchase the stock would receive calls from their brokers when the stock's price fell below a critical threshold. If the investors could not come up with enough money to cover their margin requirements, they would then be forced to sell off a portion or all of their shares, which, in turn, drove the stock's price down further.[20]

The Senate Banking Inquiry: A Shaky Start

In early 1932, with the depression deepening and stock indexes continuing to fall, President Herbert Hoover urged the leaders of the New York Stock Exchange to enact measures that would put an end to manipulative practices such as stock pools and bear raids. When the NYSE failed to take any substantive action, the president called on two members of the Senate Banking Committee, Republican senators Fredrick Walcott and Peter Norbeck, to lead an investigation of "vicious pools" and other manipulative stock practices. On March 4 the Senate officially authorized the inquiry and allotted $50,000 for the investigation.[21]

The Committee Falters

In early April, on rumors of an impending bear raid, Hoover urged the Banking Committee to begin formal hearings. The Banking Committee convened an emergency session on April 8 and called NYSE president Richard Whitney to testify on April 11. The committee chose the attorney Claude Branch to serve as its temporary lead counsel. Branch and the senators had little time to prepare for the inquiry, and Whitney captivated the audience during the inquiry's opening sessions.[22] Legal historian Joel Seligman later described the initial hearings:

For the first two days they were a near-total disaster. A smooth, haughty Richard Whitney was the lead-off witness. The self-confident stock exchange president dazzled the five hundred or so reporters and spectators jammed into the modestly proportioned committee room. Suavely he denied knowledge of a bear raid scheduled for the previous Saturday. Indeed, Whitney testified, "constant investigations have shown . . . bear raids [do] not exist." Nor did short-selling have much effect on market prices, accounting as it did for less than 5 percent of all stock exchange transactions. If they wanted culprits to blame for the exaggerated price movements of the great bull market and succeeding crash, Whitney suggested they look at "the high-powered political agents of prosperity," who misled the country into a "state of mind that . . . thought poverty was about to be abolished in our country forever."[23]

The early hearings went so poorly that Senator Norbeck, the Banking Committee's chairman, replaced Branch with the lead counsel's assistant, trial lawyer William Gray. By the end of the month, the investigation began to gather momentum when it was revealed that a publicist had received nearly $300,000 over a decade-long span to plant in respectable newspapers, such as the New York Times and the Wall Street Journal, articles that were aimed at increasing the share price of more than sixty different securities.[24]

In mid-May, after the committee had returned from a brief adjournment, Gray revealed that the brokerage firm M. J. Meehan and Company had earned $5 million over the course of a single week in March 1929 by organizing a pool operation in Radio Corporation of America stock. He also showed how various prominent investors had profited enormously through the exploitation of insider information and through securities-related tax evasion.[25]

While the Banking Committee's findings graced the front pages of the nation's leading newspapers, Gray's handling of the inquiry frustrated a number of the committee members. Gray could not substantiate his claims that some witnesses engaged in wash sales and other questionable stock transfers, and he failed to subpoena one particular witness who later escaped to Europe. In June, Senator Norbeck struggled to secure $50,000 to continue the investigation, and, to the public's surprise, the hearings officially adjourned on June 24. On the same day that the committee declared the suspension of the inquiry, it also determined that Gray's services would no longer be required.[26]

The Inquiry in Suspension

During the summer and fall of 1932, President Hoover gave little indication that he wished to resume the Banking Committee's hearings. In fact, Hoover seemed to shun any federal involvement in securities markets, believing instead that securities regulation should be left to the states. Additionally, his reelection platform made no mention of stock exchanges. Democratic presidential nominee Franklin Delano Roosevelt, on the other hand, devoted several planks of his campaign platform to the reform of securities trading, pledging to enact sweeping federal legislation to regulate the industry if elected. The Democrat's platform ultimately resonated much more strongly among the nation's voters, and only a little over a week after Roosevelt's landslide victory in November 1932, Senator Norbeck announced that the Banking Committee's hearings would resume when Congress convened its short lame-duck session in early December.[27]

Norbeck, however, encountered difficulties finding a replacement for William Gray. He was turned down by his first three choices before attorney Irving Ben Cooper agreed to take the post on January 10, 1933.[28] A week later Cooper resigned, claiming in a letter published in the *New York Times* that Norbeck had violated an agreement to grant him "a free hand in the conduct of the investigation."[29] On January 24, Norbeck announced that Cooper would be replaced by Ferdinand Pecora. The Sicilian-born lawyer had been recommended to Norbeck by former New York district attorney Joab H. Banton, who lauded Pecora as "the best qualified lawyer in the country" to pursue the inquiry.[30] Although Pecora was known to be quite theatrical, he was also regarded as an adept cross-examiner. After the Cooper debacle, Norbeck assured the public that his new hire would "have all the authority necessary to make a comprehensive investigation."[31] Indeed, the new general counsel would play such a major role in the proceedings over the following months that the Senate Banking Committee's investigative hearings became known as the Pecora hearings.

The Hearings under Pecora

With Pecora on board as general counsel, Banking Committee hearings recommenced in mid-February. The subjects on its agenda included two large financial empires whose machinations were of intense interest to the public—the Insull utilities empire, and the National City Bank and its security affiliate.

Insull Inquiry

The "Insull empire" was a once-massive group of utilities assembled by British-born Samuel Insull, who had worked for a time as Thomas Edison's business and financial manager before striking out on his own to Chicago. At its peak in the mid-1920s, the Insull empire was the nation's third-largest consortium of utility companies, providing an eighth of the country's electricity. In late 1931, however, shares in the Insull companies collapsed, with rumors of managerial ineptness and fraud hastening the empire's decline into insolvency. Hundreds of thousands of stockholders and bondholders were wiped out as a result, and the panic caused by the Insull crash led to runs that closed twenty-five Chicago-area banks. The Insull name, consequently, came to be widely reviled.[32] In the run-up to the 1932 election, Roosevelt had harshly criticized Samuel Insull and denounced the entire power industry as "evil."[33] At one particular campaign event, while condemning the selfish and monopolistic practices of industrial and financial barons, Roosevelt referred to "the lone wolf, the unethical competitor, the reckless promoter, the Ishmael or Insull whose hand is against every man's."[34]

Samuel Insull absconded to Greece in 1932 after learning of a pending federal indictment, prompting the Banking Committee to interview his son, Samuel Insull Jr., instead. With the empire's heir on the stand, the committee attempted to demonstrate that the Insull family had used its privileged position to take advantage of its companies' shareholders. Specifically, Pecora revealed that Insull family members had signed a contract giving them the option to purchase more than 1.2 million shares in the Insull Utility Investment Company for less than $12 million at a time when their value on the exchange was over $36 million. Insull Jr. defended his family's actions, claiming that the contract had been made at an earlier date and simply went unsigned for some time, and that nobody had expected the stock price to appreciate as it did.[35]

In addition to probing the family's questionable dealings in company stock, Pecora targeted the Insull consortium's notoriously convoluted organizational structure. The testimony of Owen D. Young, who served as chairman of General Electric and was one of the Insull companies' creditors, proved especially revealing:[36]

[The Insull group consisted of great] numbers of operating utilities, with holding companies superimposed on the utilities, and holding companies superimposed on those holding companies, investment companies and affiliates, which made it, as I thought then and think now, impossible for any man, however able, really to grasp the situation. . . . And if I may add: I should like to say here that I believe Mr. Samuel Insull was very largely the victim of that complicated structure, which got even beyond his power, competent as he was, to understand it. . . . [I]f I am right in thinking that Mr. Insull himself was not able ultimately to understand that structure, how can the ordinary investor . . . be expected to know, or even to inform themselves, conscientious and able as they might be, really as to the value of those securities?[37]

The highly fragmented structure of the utility empire allowed the Insull family to creatively bypass lending laws. By having their myriad companies borrow relatively small sums from a number of Illinois' biggest banks, the Insull group was able to evade a state law that prevented banks from lending more than 15 percent of their total capital and surplus to any one entity. That is, while no single Insull firm borrowed more than the 15 percent limit from any bank, certain individual banks' aggregate lending to all Insull-controlled companies far exceeded the statutory ceiling.[38]

The committee also revealed major accounting irregularities, including multiple occasions in which Insull firms recorded profits in their annual reports but reported losses on their official tax filings. Additionally, the committee drew attention to the actions of Halsey Stuart, an investment bank that owned large caches of Insull securities and shared many of its directors with Insull firms. Halsey Stuart, Pecora asserted, had used stock pools to maintain Insull company shares at inflated prices.[39]

National City Inquiry

After finishing its inquiry into the Insull empire, the Banking Committee commenced a headline-grabbing examination of National City Bank and National City Company, the latter having been established as a security affiliate of the former in 1911. During the booming 1920s, National City Bank had been the largest bank in the nation, while National City Company had been "reputed to be the world's largest distributor of securities," averaging $1.5 billion in annual securities sales at the height of its business.[40]

Pecora began the inquiry with a detailed questioning of Charles E. Mitchell, who, as chairman of National City's board, presided over both the bank and the company. The first few days of the hearings produced shocking revelations that *Time* magazine called the "Damnation of Mitchell." The banking committee revealed that Mitchell had received in compensation the then astounding sums of $1,081,230 in 1927, $1,341,634 in 1928, and $1,133,868 in 1929. Additionally, Mitchell came under heavy scrutiny for selling 18,000 shares in National City to his wife during the market crash. In so doing, Mitchell established a $2.8 million capital loss, which, in spite of his significant earnings, allowed him to avoid paying income taxes for the year 1929. The media feasted on these disclosures, and Mitchell quickly became the foremost scapegoat of the inquiry. Just five days into the National City hearings, Mitchell tendered his resignation, allegedly on the urging of then President-elect Roosevelt. Within a month the former Wall Street titan was indicted on charges of income tax evasion.[41]

Mitchell, however, was not Pecora's only target. The lawyer went on to attack all of the high-ranking officers of National City for their excesses, revealing that a "morale loan fund" had been established by National City in the weeks after the initial market crash. Through this fund, roughly a hundred of National City's officers borrowed $2.4 million of the firm's money to help them cover personal losses stemming from the market downturn. These officers did not need to pledge collateral to obtain such funds, and their loans bore no interest. By the time of the hearings, "only about five per cent of this money had been repaid" and National City had made no efforts to collect the remainder, simply writing much of it off as a loss.[42]

In addition to disgracing National City's officers, the Banking Committee attempted to demonstrate that National City Bank and National City Company were "inseparably interwoven" and thereby violated laws dividing commercial banking and investment banking functions.[43] Pecora revealed that the very same stockholders that owned the bank also owned the company; in fact, the bank's and the company's stock certificates were printed on the opposite sides of a single piece of paper. Additionally, Pecora disclosed that the company's initial capital had been quickly and easily obtained through the declaration of a onetime 40 percent dividend on the bank's stock, and that all voting power in the company was in the hands of three trustees, each of whom served as a director or officer at National City Bank.[44]

To highlight National City Company's high-pressure sales tactics, Pecora called witnesses, including ordinary investors, to testify. Questioning revealed that National City representatives had persuaded clients into taking on sizable loans to facilitate larger purchases, that many agents had actively dissuaded customers from cashing out, and that the company had vigorously pushed certain securities in which it had a particular interest. The company applied especially strong pressure on its customers to buy stock in National City itself, selling nearly 2 million shares in its parent company (totaling some $650 million) from mid-1927 to the end of 1930. Pecora also showed that National City Bank depositors were specifically targeted and solicited by company sales representatives, and that the management of National City aggressively encouraged agents to sell as many securities as possible—particularly those that were slumping, riskier, and harder to move—by making subtle threats on agents' job security and by holding frequent competitions that offered cash awards to top sellers.[45]

The inquiry also revealed numerous instances in which National City Company had willfully withheld pertinent information from its clients regarding certain securities it offered. The most dramatic example occurred in 1927 and 1928, when National City Company helped sponsor and market $90 million in Peruvian bonds in spite of repeated internal reports acknowledging that the country suffered from political instability, an unfavorable balance of trade, a poor credit history, and significant budget problems. The company's bond prospectuses, however, made no mention of Peru's adverse economic conditions. Within a few years the entire issue of Peruvian bonds had gone into default, costing bondholders some $75 million by early 1933.[46]

Pecora further demonstrated that National City Company had engaged in pool operations (though company officials used more euphemistic terms, such as "joint accounts") to prop up the price of particular securities in which it had a strong interest. Additionally, the company was shown to have traded heavily in National City Bank shares. Although banks were expressly forbidden from trading in their own stock, such dealing by National City Company effectively skirted the law because officially the company was only an affiliate of the bank.[47]

The Banking Committee also accused National City of offering special privileges to insiders that were not available to normal investors and shareholders. Pecora showed that National City Company had purchased a large quantity of shares in the newly organized Boeing Corporation in 1928, but instead of passing the stock on to the public as in normal investment banking procedure, National City distributed shares at favorable prices to an assortment of its "officers, directors, key men, and special friends."[48] When Boeing stock began trading on exchanges soon thereafter, prices immediately surpassed the rates paid by the firm's "special friends." Many, including National City Company itself, made handsome profits. Additionally, the Banking Committee highlighted an instance in 1931 in which National City Company, just weeks after underwriting a $66 million issue of bonds on behalf of the Port Authority of New York, extended an unsecured $10,000 loan to the Port Authority's general manager. By the time of the inquiry, Pecora noted, none of the loan had been repaid.[49]

Finally, Pecora showed how National City Bank used its security affiliate and its shareholders to bail itself out of bad loans. Amid a boom in sugar prices during World War I, the bank had lent significant sums to Cuban sugar firms. When sugar prices plummeted in the early 1920s, however, the Cuban firms proved unable to pay back their loans. In response, National City called on its shareholders to purchase $50 million in new stock. The shareholders complied, and the bank and the company evenly split the newly raised capital. Immediately the company used its share to acquire all of the stock in the newly created General Sugar Corporation. General Sugar in turn used the funds to take the worthless Cuban sugar loans off the books of National City Bank. Eventually the company valued its General Sugar holdings at just $1, effectively realizing a $25 million loss on the investment. Of course, the venture was never intended to make money for the company or its stockholders; instead it was a calculated plan by which the company was able to erase what would have been a serious point of concern—the imprudent loans to Cuban sugar companies—from its parent bank's balance sheet. At the time of the $50 million stock issue, investors were completely unaware of the chicanery that the bank and the company planned to employ, as National City opted not to inform shareholders of its true intent in raising the capital.[50]

Financial Reforms of 1933

On March 4, 1933, just two days after Pecora finished his examination of National City, Franklin Delano Roosevelt was sworn in as president. In his inaugural address, Roosevelt decried "unscrupulous money changers" and promised to bring about "strict supervision of all banking and credits and investments."[51] Indeed, with panicked depositors running on banks throughout the country, Roosevelt sprang into action, declaring a national bank holiday within two days of assuming the presidency. Roosevelt then publicly directed federal inspectors to scrutinize the finances of every single national bank in the United States, pledging to reopen all institutions that the inspectors deemed solvent.[52]

The Glass-Steagall Banking Act of 1933

With Roosevelt's bank holiday underscoring the dire straits of the American banking industry, Congress reconsidered and ultimately passed a banking reform bill that had been repeatedly revived and revised since its initial introduction in January 1932.[53] This legislation, which was popularly referred to as the Glass-Steagall Act* after its sponsors Senator Carter Glass and Representative Henry Steagall, reformed American banking in two major ways.[54]

The first of these reforms was the establishment of deposit insurance. A Temporary Deposit Insurance Fund, which was financed by contributions from member banks, was established on January 1, 1934, and provided $2,500 in insurance per depositor (this level was soon raised to $5,000 per depositor). Though slightly later than prescribed in the Glass-Steagall Act, this temporary entity was eventually replaced by the permanent Federal Deposit Insurance Corporation in 1935.[55] The banking legislation of 1933 and 1935 also provided for significant federal supervision of insured banks.[56]

The second major component of the Banking Act of 1933 separated the deposit banking and investment banking industries. In time, the term "Glass-Steagall" would come to be associated mainly with this part of the

---

* The Banking Act of 1933 should not be confused with the first Glass-Steagall Act passed in 1932. The first Glass-Steagall Act expanded the acceptable collateral that banks could post in order to receive Federal Reserve loans and also allowed the nation's money supply to be backed, in part, by Treasury securities. For more, see Milton Friedman and Anna Jacobson Schwartz, *A Monetary History of the United States, 1867–1960* (Princeton, NJ: Princeton University Press, 1963), 191, 321.

legislation. Specifically, the statute gave national banks, such as National City, one year to break with their security investment affiliates, and barred the officers and directors of a commercial bank from acting as officers or directors of an investment bank. The act also required private banks, like J.P. Morgan and Company, to choose between their deposit banking business and their securities underwriting business, as they could no longer engage in both.[57]

While Roosevelt praised the Glass-Steagall Act, which he signed into law on June 16, 1933, many in the banking community were highly critical of the new legislation. A number of detractors, including the president of the American Bankers' Association, attacked the act's deposit insurance provision, claiming that it would reward unstable banks at the expense of strong and solvent institutions. Other critics made broader arguments, claiming that the act was highly detrimental to the banking and investment industries and that it was "likely to slow up the recovery" from the ongoing depression.[58]

Securities Act of 1933

Back on March 29, when the American public was still fuming over the disclosures of Pecora's inquiry into National City, President Roosevelt presented Congress with his outline for new securities legislation, which he claimed would "give impetus to honest dealing in securities and thereby bring back public confidence."[59] Through such a bill, the president proposed to add to "the ancient rule of caveat emptor [let the buyer beware], the further doctrine 'let the seller also beware.'"[60] Over the next eight weeks, several versions of a securities bill were drawn up, debated, and revised.[61]

In its final form, the Securities Act of 1933, which was also known as the Truth in Securities Act, required issuers of new securities to file application papers with the Federal Trade Commission (FTC)* and to publish prospectuses providing extensive details about their companies, including:

---

* Many types of securities were exempt from FTC registration, including all extant securities, all securities issued by banks and savings and loan institutions, all railroad securities, and all federal, state, and local government securities. Other securities that had a repayment period of nine months or less, were not sold across state lines, represented "insurance an-

1.   The names and addresses of all directors, high-level officers, and large shareholders,* plus details about their overall holdings of the company's securities and their stakes in the impending securities issue.

2.   The amount of compensation received by each director, and the amount of compensation, if in excess of $25,000 annually, received by each officer or other employee.

3.   The names and addresses of those underwriting the issue of securities, and details about their stakes in the impending securities issue and their overall holdings of the company's securities.

4.   Detailed information about the company's operations and business dealings, and detailed information about all of its outstanding securities and options.

5.   Details on how the proceeds from the securities' sale were intended to be employed by the company, how the price was determined, and all compensation received by the issue's underwriters and promoters.

6.   A recent balance sheet noting all assets and liabilities, along with a profit and loss statement.[62]

According to the act, the FTC had twenty days to review the company's registration material before the firm would be allowed to offer its new securities for public sale, and the entire securities issue could be delayed if the FTC found any problems with the company's documentation. Also, the Securities Act contained stringent liability rules, allowing investors who discovered inaccuracies or material omissions in the FTC filing to sue all parties involved in the registration's preparation. In the event of such a suit, the act stated that the burden of proof would fall on the security issuer and all other parties involved in the security's issuance to demonstrate that they had not intentionally misled investors. Finally, the Truth in Securities Act gave the FTC the power to enact standardized accounting guidelines, as variability in such methods had been a cause of much confusion over the

---

nuity contracts," or totaled no more than $100,000 could also be exempted. For more see, Joel Seligman, *The Transformation of Wall Street* (Boston: Northeastern University Press, 1995), 71.
* Large shareholders were those owning or with the option to own greater than 10 percent of the company's overall stock, or those owning or with the option to own greater than 10 percent of any single class of the company's securities. For more, see "'Truth in Securities' Bill Repassed by House, Senate," *Wall Street Journal*, 25 May 1933, 10.

years and had thwarted investors from easily comparing one firm's books to another's.[63]

Exchange Control?

On the same day that he introduced the initial Truth in Securities bill in March 1933, Roosevelt made it clear that he wanted to extend government regulation to include securities exchanges. However, Roosevelt also stated that his administration was "not yet ready" to propose such legislation.[64] Fearing an eventual regulatory bill, New York Stock Exchange president Richard Whitney asked to meet with President Roosevelt. At their meeting Whitney attempted to convince Roosevelt that federal securities exchange regulations were unnecessary, stating that the NYSE was both willing and capable of policing itself. Whitney also tried to show that his organization's interests were in line with Roosevelt's, claiming that "the vast majority of the members of the Exchange are anxious to put the security business on a higher plane than it has ever been before."[65] Not long after the meeting, the NYSE enacted new internal regulations that required all trading pools and similar accounts to file weekly reports, imposed minimum balances on customers' margin accounts, and dissuaded securities distributors from engaging in aggressive sales policies. Nevertheless, it appeared that Roosevelt still favored federal regulation.[66]

Criticism and the Dickinson Committee

Criticism of the Securities Act began immediately and rose to a crescendo during the summer and fall of 1933. Detractors claimed that the law was too complex and that its liability rules were too harsh, making it virtually impossible for new companies to obtain start-up financing and for existing firms to increase capital. Because of these restrictive effects on business, opponents argued, the law could potentially exacerbate the ongoing depression. Some within the Roosevelt administration also came to believe that the legislation needed to be revised, and Roosevelt responded by having two separate committees study the bill's alleged detrimental effects on securities sales. One of the committees, the so-called Dickinson Committee, which was named after Assistant Commerce Secretary John Dickinson, was charged with the additional task of drafting an outline for a new bill to regulate securities exchanges.[67]

The Pecora Hearings Resume

On May 23, 1933, just four days before President Roosevelt signed the Securities Act into law, the Pecora Committee commence an investigation of J.P. Morgan and Company.

J.P. Morgan and Company

The publicity generated by the Pecora hearings peaked during the inquiry into the House of Morgan, which *Time* magazine had described as "the greatest and most legendary private business of modern times."[68] The company had traditionally kept a lower profile than other major Wall Street institutions, and its top partner, J.P. Morgan Jr., had long avoided the public spotlight. Thus, when the scion of the House of Morgan was called to testify, droves of reporters and spectators flocked to the Senate Office Building, forcing the Banking Committee to move the hearings to a larger venue.[69] During the first day of Morgan's testimony, Pecora's questioning revealed that neither the banker nor any of his partners had paid income taxes for the years 1931 and 1932. In fact, because of major investment losses, many of the nation's wealthiest citizens earned no net taxable income during these years, a revelation that proved to be one of the most sensational of the entire hearings and prompted the *Washington Post* to print an article titled "Rich Men Pay No Tax."[70]

Over the twelve-day inquiry, Pecora attempted to demonstrate that J.P. Morgan and Company's dealings had benefited insiders at the expense of ordinary investors and that the company had abandoned its exacting standards in order to capitalize on the market boom. Specifically, Pecora exposed how the company's use of "preferred lists" enabled well-connected investors to make enormous and immediate capital gains. On at least five occasions, J.P. Morgan offered stock to its firm members and other influential figures (including prominent national politicians and business leaders) at prices well below the prevailing market rates. For example, the company had given insiders a chance to purchase shares in the Alleghany Corporation for $20 while such securities were trading at $35 on the floor of the New York Stock Exchange. Those lucky enough to be on J.P. Morgan's preferred lists could make an immediate profit by quickly selling the stocks on the exchange. Such preferred lists violated no laws, but their existence strengthened the perception that Wall Street insiders were given opportunities not available to ordinary investors.[71]

Although Pecora admitted that "the investigation of the Morgan firm elicited no such disclosures of glaring abuses" as those exhibited by other Wall Street firms, the public was still outraged by the secretive and disreputable, albeit technically legal, practices that the Morgan hearings had uncovered.[72] An editorial in the *New York Times* announced:

> Here was a firm of bankers, perhaps the most famous and powerful in the whole world, which was certainly under no necessity of practicing the small arts of petty traders. Yet it failed under a test of its pride and prestige. By a mistake which had with the years swollen into a grievous fault, it sacrificed something intangible, imponderable, that has to do with the very highest repute. The members of such a partnership forgot that they must not only be beyond reproach in their financial dealings—as they doubtless are—but must always appear to be so.[73]

Some observers argued that the public's bitter reaction to the J.P. Morgan disclosures spurred support for the Glass-Steagall banking bill, which the Senate abruptly and resoundingly passed amid the Morgan hearings.[74]

Chase National Bank

After concluding its inquiry into the dealings of J.P. Morgan and Company, the Banking Committee investigated two more prominent investment banks, Kuhn, Loeb and Company and Dillon, Read and Company. In mid-October, however, Pecora turned his attention to Chase National Bank, which had overtaken National City in 1930 as the country's largest bank.[75]

Pecora revealed that Chase National Bank had established no fewer than five security affiliates, the most important of which was Chase Securities Company. Just like National City Company, Chase Securities Company was owned by the exact same stockholders as its parent bank, with the two companies' stock certificates again "printed on reverse sides of the same piece of paper."[76] The Banking Committee showed that Chase Securities Company had conducted pool operations in a wide range of corporate stocks and foreign bonds during the late 1920s and early 1930s. Additionally, it was shown that the security affiliate had participated in at least eight pool operations in its parent bank's stock, which, Pecora argued, had helped drive Chase's share price from $575 in the autumn of 1927 to $1,415 two years later.[77] When former Chase chairman Albert H. Wiggin was asked flatly why Chase Securities Company had decided to engage in such stock pools (Wiggin preferred the term "trading accounts"), he could only muster the response, "I think the times." Shortly thereafter, Wiggin suggested that he "certainly would not do anything today that, if it turned out unfortunately, was going to be criticized."[78]

Much as he had done with Charles E. Mitchell, Pecora went on the attack with Wiggin. Pecora focused on the former chairman's income, showing that in addition to his compensation from Chase, Wiggin held fifty-nine directorships in other firms, some of which paid him up to $40,000 annually for his services. Many of these firms were also clients of Chase National Bank. Pecora highlighted a particular instance in which Wiggin, who served on a committee of the Brooklyn-Manhattan Transit Company, used his inside knowledge of Brooklyn-Manhattan's financial dealings with Chase to sell off his personal holdings of the transit company's stock while its share price was still high. Had he waited to sell his shares until knowledge of the company's dealings became publicly known, as a lay investor would have, Wiggin's sale would likely have netted less than half of what it actually did.[79]

Additionally, the Banking Committee went on to show how Wiggin had established six companies, owned by either himself or his immediate family, which seemed to do little more than speculate and engage in stock pools with money borrowed from Chase National Bank. Through these companies Wiggin sold his own bank's stock short, resulting in a $4 million personal profit in just a three-month period in late 1929. Like Mitchell, Wiggin left the hearings in disgrace, having felt compelled by a "storm of popular disapproval" to refuse his $100,000 annual pension from Chase.[80]

The shocking disclosures regarding Chase National prompted the bank's current chairman, Winthrop T. Aldrich—who in May had already received stockholder consent to disaffiliate Chase Securities Company from Chase National Bank—to distance the firm further from Wiggin and the speculative practices of the 1920s. Said Aldrich, "As long as I have anything to do with the management, the market in Chase stock shall not be affected by the operation of trading accounts by the affiliates of the bank."[81] Aldrich backed his tough words by explicitly banning all of the bank's subsidiaries from engaging in pool operations in Chase stock.[82]

The Proposed Securities Exchange Act

In late January 1934, several weeks after Pecora finished up his examination of Chase National Bank, the Dickinson Committee released its official report on a new securities exchange bill.

The Dickinson Committee Report

Although the Dickinson group had previously announced that it was in favor of a bill that allowed exchanges to "discipline [their] own members and conduct their [own] affairs," the committee's formal report elaborated considerably on this initial sentiment.[83] Most notably, the report suggested the creation of a "Federal Stock Exchange Authority," either as an independent body or as a part of the Federal Trade Commission. The committee favored granting this new body the authority to study the securities industry further and make its own rules regarding pools, short selling, margin requirements (in conjunction with the Federal Reserve Banks), security listing requirements, reporting and accounting standards, and the role of exchange specialists.* Additionally, the Dickinson group maintained that the Federal Stock Exchange Authority should be given adequate power to punish violators.[84]

While the Dickinson Committee wanted to leave much of the regulatory decision making to the proposed Federal Stock Exchange Authority, the report did make a few specific recommendations. In particular, it suggested that all exchanges engaging in interstate commerce should be licensed by the federal government (licensure of over-the-counter exchanges and individual brokers, the committee stated, should not be required). Additionally, the Dickinson group advised that any new legislation should ban wash sales

---

* The Securities Exchange bill defined a specialist as "any person who specializes in the execution of orders in respect of any security or securities on an exchange and who commonly receives from other members of the exchange orders for execution in respect of such security or securities." See "Text of Bill for Regulating Stock Exchanges," *Wall Street Journal*, 10 Feb. 1934, 4.

and matched sales, and should compel all companies with listed securities to take steps to increase their transparency, including requiring them to release quarterly reports and to submit to annual examinations of their books by independent accountants.[85]

Introduction of the Bill

In private and at times in public, President Roosevelt showed signs of disagreement with the Dickinson Committee's recommended approach. Saying that he wanted legislation with "teeth in it," he appeared to support those members of his administration who favored more detailed and forceful legislation that would include specific rules and provide greater direction to officials charged with regulating the nation's exchanges. On February 9, 1934, the president wrote a message to Congress that briefly outlined his vision for a new securities exchange bill.[86] He stated:

> The exchanges in many parts of the country which deal in securities and commodities conduct, of course, a national business because their customers live in every part of the country. The managers of these exchanges have, it is true, often taken steps to correct certain obvious abuses. We must be certain that abuses are eliminated, and to this end a broad policy of national regulation is required.[87]

After the president's message was read on the Senate floor, Senator Duncan U. Fletcher, a Florida Democrat, introduced what he hoped would become the "National Securities Exchange Act of 1934." Members of the administration had played a key role in drafting the bill, and Representative Sam Rayburn, Democrat of Texas, was taking responsibility for introducing it in the House. As written, the bill would deny all exchanges the right to use the postal system or to engage in any form of interstate commerce unless they registered with the Federal Trade Commission. Additionally, the act would prohibit margin lending on any security not listed on a registered exchange. Margin lending would be permitted on exchange-listed securities, but would be capped at the higher of two values: either 40 percent of the security's current price, or 80 percent of the security's lowest selling price over the previous three years. In addition, the act would impose an outright ban on all wash sales, matched sales, any actions aimed at artificially raising or lowering a security's price (e.g., pool operations and bear raids), the dissemination of rumors or other deceptive information about a security, any actions aimed at holding a security's price steady (unless the FTC was first informed about such actions), cornering a security (i.e., taking a controlling stake in a security with the intent of manipulating its price), the exercising of options (such as puts and calls) on securities, and the short selling of exchange-listed securities "except in accordance with such rules and regulations as the Commission may prescribe." The bill would also impose strict civil liability rules on violators of its provisions, allowing injured parties to file suit.[88]

In addition, Fletcher's bill would ban exchange members and brokers from both underwriting securities and dealing in securities on their own accounts. The act would also require the registration of exchange specialists and would prohibit these specialists from disclosing information that was not publicly available. Furthermore, the bill would require all listed securities to be registered with both the exchange and the FTC. Securities issuers would also be compelled to publish reports detailing their business on an annual, quarterly, and even monthly basis. The act would require that exchanges, and all of those doing business on such exchanges, maintain detailed transaction records, which were to be made available for FTC inspection upon request. Additionally, the act contained a so-called anti-Wiggin rule, which would compel directors, officers, and major shareholders to disclose their dealings and holdings in their companies' securities and would forbid them from speculating in such securities. Also, the FTC would be empowered to revoke an exchange's or a security's registration if violations were discovered. Finally, the FTC would be given the authority to establish rules for over-the-counter (non-exchange-based) securities markets and be granted broad leeway to modify the abovementioned rules as it saw fit.[89]

Whitney Responds

On February 13, four days after Senator Fletcher introduced the National Securities Exchange bill (also known as Fletcher-Rayburn), Richard Whitney announced three additions to the New York Stock Exchange's governing regulations. The first new rule disallowed NYSE members, or their affiliated companies, from engaging in any trading pools or other actions aimed at "unfairly influencing the market price of any security." The second new regulation prohibited NYSE specialists, or their affiliated companies, from either granting or obtaining options relating to the securities in which they specialized. And the final new rule barred NYSE specialists from revealing any information about the orders with which they had been entrusted (certain NYSE committees were exempt from this final prohibition).[90]

In addition to announcing the new rules, Whitney gave his first interviews in over a year. He attacked a number of the "rigid and unworkable provisions" of the proposed bill, claiming that the New York Stock Exchange had already adopted sufficient rules "to prevent excessive speculation."[91] In particular, he argued that the bill's high margin requirements "might force the liquidation of many accounts," that the bill's prohibition on lending against unlisted securities would "deprive people owning unlisted securities of the right to use them as the basis of credit in brokerage accounts," and that the bill's ban on exchange members acting as securities dealers would unduly harm the nation's smaller regional securities markets and would "destroy the odd-lot business which now affords the only market to investors holding less than one hundred shares of stock."[92] But Whitney reserved his harshest criticism for the publishing requirements of the bill:

> Probably the worst features of the bill are those which purport to regulate corporations and corporate practices by imposing conditions upon the listing of securities upon exchanges. The bill requires every corporation listed on an exchange to register its securities with the Federal Trade Commission. The minimum requirements set forth in the bill are so burdensome that corporations may be unwilling to keep their securities listed on any exchange. Furthermore, the Federal Trade Commission is given unlimited power to require additional information in regard to corporate affairs which like all other reports or information furnished to the Commission, must be made available to the public. These powers are so extensive that the Federal Trade Commission might, in effect, control the management of every listed company.[93]

Additionally, Whitney stated that the potential dissemination of a company's "confidential statistics," which could result under the bill's publishing mandate, "would be destructive of American industry because it would furnish vital information to foreign competitors."[94]

Led by Whitney, the heads of the nation's stock exchanges and brokerages quickly began a wide-reaching campaign against the Fletcher-Rayburn bill, rallying their colleagues across the country via telegram and swamping congressmen with a flood of messages, phone calls, and letters aimed at crushing support for the bill. Brokers argued that the act was far too harsh and restrictive and that it would likely drive "speculation and investing in American stocks to foreign markets" if enacted.[95]

On February 15, Whitney sent a copy of the bill and a letter criticizing it to all companies listed on the NYSE, claiming that the proposed legislation could end up "destroying the market for their securities."[96] On the same day, he also sent a copy of the bill and a different letter to every member of the exchange. The letters, which were printed in the following day's *Wall Street Journal,* highlighted specific facets of the proposed legislation that exchange members and listed firms would likely find disagreeable. In his letter to listed companies, for example, Whitney drew attention to provisions in the bill that would impose high fines on firms for noncompliance, would increase companies' vulnerability to lawsuits brought by investors, and would place securities trading limitations on directors, officers, and other large shareholders. In his letter to NYSE members, Whitney highlighted a number of other provisions, including those that would ban short selling, limit how much members could borrow, and grant the FTC the right to suspend or expel exchange members for perceived violations.[97]

The *New York Times* wrote that Whitney's response to the bill "was regarded in Wall Street as the broadest program of education on a Federal measure which the Exchange has ever directed toward the financial and business communities."[98] Senator Fletcher chose different words to describe the response:

> The propaganda released by the Exchange officials is intended to persuade the people that regulation of that Exchange and the other Exchanges by the Federal Government will hurt business. Whose business? Only that of brokers who have lined their pockets by disregarding the interest of their customers.[99]

Pecora Attacks the NYSE

In mid-February, while Whitney and others were attempting to discredit the newly introduced securities exchange bill, Pecora was busy revealing several instances in which the New York Stock Exchange had failed to prevent the manipulation of security prices. Specifically, the Banking Committee detailed trading pools in the stock of alcohol corporations that had occurred over the previous summer. The committee presented an internal NYSE report which showed that the stock exchange had conducted its own examination of these suspect alcohol-stock transactions several months earlier. According to its report, the New York Stock Exchange had concluded that there had been "no material deliberate improprieties."[100] Pecora, however, showed that there had indeed been a concerted effort to artificially drive up the price of alcohol stocks and that those involved benefited considerably. Regarding the Banking Committee's findings, the chairman of the New York Stock Exchange's listing committee admitted to Pecora that "a cog slipped somewhere" and that his office was to blame for making a rare mistake.[101]

Whitney to Testify

On February 22, 1934, Whitney was called to testify at the first of two congressional hearings on the proposed National Securities Exchange Act (Fletcher-Rayburn).[102] He aimed to persuade lawmakers to reject the bill, but he faced significant resistance. The Pecora investigation had impressed upon the nation a desire for financial reform, and the recent inquiry into the 1933 alcohol pools had just shown that Whitney's New York Stock Exchange had failed in one key area of self-regulation. However, in the two weeks since the bill was introduced, Whitney had effectively mobilized much of the financial world to oppose the act and to publicly denounce it as a heavy-handed overreaction. With these two opposing forces at play, would Whitney be able to convince Congress that the proposed legislation granted the FTC too much regulatory power and that it was in the nation's best interest to let stock exchanges police themselves? Or would Whitney's comments fall on deaf ears, with the legacy of the Pecora hearings helping to carry another sweeping financial reform bill through to law?

NOTES

1. Dow Jones Averages, "Dow Jones Industrial Average Performance," http://www.djaverages.com/?go=industrial-index-data; Susan B. Carter, Richard Sutch, and Peter H. Lindert, "Labor Force, Employment, and Unemployment, 1890–1990," "Money and Banking: Money Supply, Monetary Base, and Banks Suspended, 1919–1939," "Gross Domestic Product, 1790–2002 [Continuous annual series]," and "Consumer Price Indexes, for All Items, 1774–2003," all in *Historical Statistics of the*

United States, Earliest Times to the Present: Millennial Edition, ed. Susan B. Carter et al. (New York: Cambridge University Press, 2006), series Ba475, Ca11, Ca16–17, Cb70, Cc1–2.

2. Franklin D. Roosevelt, "Inaugural Address," 4 Mar. 1933, American Presidency Project, http://www.presidency.ucsb.edu/ws/index.php?pid=14473.

3. Joel Seligman, The Transformation of Wall Street: A History of the Securities and Exchange Commission and Modern Corporate Finance (Boston: Northeastern University Press, 1995), 12–100; James Burk, Values in the Marketplace: The American Stock Market under Federal Securities Law (Berlin: Walter de Gruyter, 1988), 25–26.

4. Seligman, Transformation, 75–76, 85–86; Legislative History of the Securities Act of 1933 and Securities Exchange Act of 1934, compiled by J. S. Ellenberger and Ellen P. Mahar (South Hackensack, NJ: Rothman, 1973), 4:2264–2272, item no. 5.

5. "Three Tight Rules Added by Exchange," New York Times, 14 Feb. 1934, 29–30.

6. Seligman, Transformation, 87–88.

7. Susan Hoffmann, Politics and Banking: Ideas, Public Policy, and the Creation of Financial Institutions (Baltimore: Johns Hopkins University Press, 2001), 129; Seligman, Transformation, 21–90; "Whitney Testifies Today," New York Times, 22 Feb. 1934, 2.

8. Robert Alexander Halliburton, The Real Estate Bond House: A Study of Some of Its Financial Practices (Ann Arbor, MI: Edwards Bros., 1941), quotation at 6; John L. Snider, "Security Issues in the United States, 1909–20," Review of Economic Statistics 3, no. 5 (May 1921): 98–99.

9. Laylin K. James, "The Securities Act of 1933," Michigan Law Review 32, no. 5 (Mar. 1934): 625; Ernest M. Fisher, Urban Real Estate Markets: Characteristics and Financing (New York: National Bureau of Economic Research, 1951), 30–31.

10. Peter L. Rousseau, "Corporate Security Issues, 1910–1934," and "Sales of Stocks and Bonds on the New York Stock Exchange, 1879–1999," in Carter et al., Historical Statistics, series Cj834, Cj837, Cj857, Cj858.

11. Seth C. Anderson, Thomas Randolph Beard, and Jeffrey A. Born, Initial Public Offerings (Norwell, MA: Kluwer Academic, 1995), 8; Thomas E. Hall and J. David Ferguson, The Great Depression: An International Disaster of Perverse Economic Policies (Ann Arbor: University of Michigan Press, 1998), 24.

12. Seligman, Transformation, 23; Barry Eichengreen, "The U.S. Capital Market and Foreign Lending, 1920–1955," in Developing Country Debt and Economic Performance, vol. 1, The International Financial System, ed. Jeffrey D. Sachs (Chicago: University of Chicago Press, 1989), 121.

13. W. Nelson Peach, The Security Affiliates of National Banks (Baltimore: Johns Hopkins Press, 1941), 83; Eugene N. White, "The Stock Market Boom and Crash of 1929 Revisited," Journal of Economic Perspectives 4, no. 2 (Spring 1990): 69; Barry Eichengreen, "U.S. Foreign Financial Relations in the Twentieth Century," in The Cambridge Economic History of the United States, vol. 3, The Twentieth Century, ed. Stanley L. Engerman and Robert E. Gallman (New York: Cambridge University Press, 2000), 478; Eichengreen, "U.S. Capital Market," 121.

14. White, "Boom and Crash," 69; Peter Rappoport and Eugene N. White, "Was There a Bubble in the 1929 Stock Market?," NBER Working Paper no. 3612, Feb. 1991, 4–5; Eichengreen, "U.S. Capital Market," 121–122; Barry Eichengreen and Albert Fishlow, "Contending with Capital Flows: What Is Different about the 1990s?," in *Capital Flows and Financial Crises,* ed. Miles Kahler (Ithaca, NY: Cornell University Press, 1998), 29.

15. White, "Boom and Crash," 69; Eichengreen, "U.S. Capital Market," 122; Stephen J. Whitfield, *A Companion to 20th-Century America* (Malden, MA: Blackwell, 2004), 31.

16. Richard Jack Teweles and Edward S. Bradley, *The Stock Market* (New York: Wiley, 1998), 329–347; Robert Sobel, *Inside Wall Street* (Washington, DC: Beard Books, 1977), 117.

17. John Kenneth Galbraith, *The Great Crash, 1929* (Boston: Houghton Mifflin, 1979), 79.

18. Paul G. Mahoney, "The Stock Pools and the Securities Exchange Act," *Journal of Financial Economics* 51, no. 3 (Mar. 1999): 345.

19. Ferdinand Pecora, *Wall Street under Oath* (New York: Simon and Schuster, 1939), 264–265; Seligman, *Transformation,* 17–18n.

20. Markus K. Brunnermeier and Lasse Heje Pedersen, "Predatory Trading," NYU Working Paper, 7 Oct. 2004, 34–35; Zvi Bodie, Alex Kane, and Alan J. Marcus, *Investments,* 5th ed. (New York: McGraw-Hill / Irwin, 2002), 88.

21. Seligman, *Transformation,* 11–13, quotation at 12.

22. Ibid., 13, 15.

23. Ibid., 15.

24. Ibid., 15–17.

25. Ibid., 17; "Copper Profits of J.D. Ryan and Partners Bared," *Chicago Tribune,* 5 June 1932, 6.

26. Seligman, *Transformation,* 17–18; "Copper Profits," 6; "Raskob Challenges Short Sales Charge at Senate Inquiry," *New York Times,* 4 June 1932, 1, 16; "Wall St. Inquiry Suddenly Is Ended," *New York Times,* 25 June 1932, 19.

27. Seligman, *Transformation,* 18–20; "Senators to Sift Insull Collapse," *New York Times,* 18 Nov. 1932, 27; "Stock Trade Probe Will Be Resumed," *Wall Street Journal,* 18 Nov. 1932, 10; Arthur Krock, "Major Issues on Schedule," *New York Times,* 5 Dec. 1932, 1.

28. Seligman, *Transformation,* 20; "I. B. Cooper Heads Market Inquiry," *New York Times,* 11 Jan. 1933, 3.

29. Quoted in "Cooper, Hampered, Quits Stock Inquiry," *New York Times,* 18 Jan. 1933, 5.

30. Quoted in "Pecora Appointed for Stock Inquiry," *New York Times,* 25 Jan. 1933, 23.

31. Quoted in ibid., 23; Seligman, *Transformation,* 21.

32. Scott B. MacDonald and Jane E. Hughes, *Separating Fools from Their Money: A History of American Financial Scandals* (New Brunswick, NJ: Transaction, 2007), 103–108, 111–113; Seligman, *Transformation,* 21–22; Pecora, *Wall Street under Oath,* 226–227.

33. Christopher J. Castaneda and Clarance M. Smith, *Gas Pipelines and the Emergence of America's Regulatory State: A History of Panhandle Eastern Corporation, 1928–1993* (Cambridge: Cambridge University Press, 1996), 74.

34. Franklin D. Roosevelt, "Commonwealth Club Address," 23 Sept. 1932, at The New Deal: Franklin D. Roosevelt Speeches, Faculty Research, Pepperdine University School of Public Policy website, http://publicpolicy.pepperdine.edu/faculty-research /new-deal/roosevelt-speeches/fr092332.htm.

35. "Securities Given for Stock," New York Times, 16 Feb. 1933, 8; "Insull Stock Deal Netted $25,000,000," New York Times, 16 Feb. 1933, 8; Seligman, Transformation, 22.

36. "Dawes Concedes Bank Abused Law in Insull Loans," New York Times, 17 Feb. 1933, 1; "Insull Stock Deal," 8.

37. Quoted in Pecora, Wall Street under Oath, 225–228.

38. Seligman, Transformation, 23; "Dawes Concedes," 1, 12.

39. Seligman, Transformation, 23; "Dawes Concedes," 12.

40. Thomas F. Huertas and Joan L. Silverman, "Charles E. Mitchell: Scapegoat of the Crash?," Business History Review 60, no. 1 (Spring 1986): 82; "Mitchell Avoided Income Tax in 1929 by '2,800,000 Loss,'" New York Times, 22 Feb.1933, 1; Jerry W. Markham, A Financial History of the United States (Armonk, NY: M.E. Sharpe, 2002), 116; Seligman, Transformation, 23–24.

41. "Mitchell Avoided Income Tax," 1; "Damnation of Mitchell," Time, 6 Mar. 1933; Huertas and Silverman, "Charles E. Mitchell," 82, 88–91.

42. Pecora, Wall Street under Oath, 127, 127–128.

43. Quoted in ibid., 81.

44. Ibid., 78–79; Seligman, Transformation, 24.

45. "Damnation of Mitchell"; Pecora, Wall Street under Oath, 84–87, 111, 88–94; Seligman, Transformation, 24–25.

46. "National City Sold Peru Bond Issues in 'Honest Mistake,'" New York Times, 28 Feb. 1933, 1, 6; Seligman, Transformation, 27–28; Pecora, Wall Street under Oath, 96–104.

47. Pecora, Wall Street under Oath, 105–112; Markham, Financial History, 117.

48. Quoted in Pecora, Wall Street under Oath, 124.

49. Ibid., 125–126; "City Bank Officer Bares Ramsey Loan," New York Times, 2 Mar. 1933, 1, 9.

50. M. R. Werner, Privileged Characters (New York: R. M. McBride and Co., 1935), 467–469; Pecora, Wall Street under Oath, 121–123; Peach, Security Affiliates, 133.

51. Franklin D. Roosevelt, "Inaugural Address," 4 Mar. 1933; "Profit in Mergers Told to Senators," New York Times, 3 Mar. 1933, 25.

52. State banks were also inspected during the holiday, though these examinations were performed by state-level examiners. James S. Olson, Historical Dictionary of the Great Depression, 1929–1940 (Westport, CT: Greenwood Press, 2001), 22.

53. On January 21, 1932, the initial banking reform bill was presented to the Senate. This bill, which did not include a deposit insurance provision, resulted from more than a year's worth of investigation by a Senate Banking and Currency Committee subgroup. The bill was withdrawn, revised, and reintroduced on April 18, 1932. After passing the Senate, the bill died in the House, as the congressional session ended

before the bill was brought to a vote. On the very first day of the special congressional session that Roosevelt called following his inauguration, the bill was again introduced. The bill was disregarded, however, as Congress focused on the more pressing matter of the emergency bank holiday. Revised to include federal deposit insurance, the bill was again presented to the Senate on May 1, 1933. The revised Senate bill, proposed by Carter Glass, was eventually merged with a very similar bill proposed by Representative Henry Steagall. Congress passed the resulting Glass-Steagall bill on June 13, 1933. For more, see Edwin Walter Kemmerer, *The ABC of the Federal Reserve System,* 10th ed. (Princeton, NJ: Princeton University Press, 1936), 190–192; Marcus Nadler and Jules I. Bogen, *The Banking Crisis: The End of an Epoch* (New York: Dodd, Mead and Co., 1933), 52–53.

54. David A. Moss, *When All Else Fails: Government as the Ultimate Risk Manager* (Cambridge, MA: Harvard University Press, 2002), 117–118.

55. All member banks of the Federal Reserve System had to join the deposit insurance system. Banks that were not part of the Federal Reserve System could become insured as well, so long as federal officials approved and the banks themselves agreed to join the Federal Reserve System within a short period of time. All participant banks were required to contribute an amount equal to 0.25 percent of their deposits to the Temporary Deposit Insurance Fund, with another 0.25 percent being callable at the fund operators' discretion. This Temporary Deposit Insurance Fund backed each depositor up to $2,500 starting on January 1, 1934. On July 1 of that year, the Federal Deposit Insurance Corporation (FDIC), which was to be initially capitalized by contributions from the twelve regional Federal Reserve Banks and the Treasury, was supposed to permanently replace the temporary fund. This did not happen, however, and the temporary fund was extended by a year and expanded to insure up to $5,000 per depositor. In August of the following year, the Banking Act of 1935 replaced the temporary fund with the permanent FDIC and kept the insurance at the $5,000 level. At that time, member banks' payments to the now permanent insurance fund were reduced to 0.083 percent of their deposits. For more, see Charles W. Calomiris and Eugene N. White, "The Origins of Federal Deposit Insurance," in *The Regulated Economy: A Historical Approach to Political Economy,* ed. Claudia Goldin and Gary D. Libecap (Chicago: University of Chicago Press, 1994), 175–176.

56. Emmanuel N. Roussakis, *Commercial Banking in an Era of Deregulation,* 3rd ed. (Westport, CT: Praeger, 1997), 34.

57. "Drastic Changes in Bank Methods Expected Soon," *Chicago Daily Tribune,* 18 June 1933, A8; Pecora, *Wall Street under Oath,* 284–286. See also Stanley Irving Fosner, "New Epoch in Banking Opens under Glass-Steagall Act; the Law Provides Not Only for the Guarantee of Deposits but for Further Strengthening of the Federal Reserve System," *New York Times,* 25 June 1933. According to one student of the subject, writing in 1983, the sections of the Banking Act of 1933 that dealt "with the separation of commercial and investment banking . . . are usually the intended reference when the name Glass-Steagall is used" ("A Banker's Adventures in Brokerland: Looking

through Glass-Steagall at Discount Brokerage Services," *Michigan Law Review* 81, no. 6 [May 1983], 1501n12).

58. Quoted in "Bankers Assail Glass-Steagall 'Reform' Bill," *Chicago Daily Tribune,* 15 June 1933, 29–30; "Roosevelt Hails Goal," *New York Times,* 17 June 1933, 1.

59. Franklin D. Roosevelt, "Message to Congress on Federal Supervision of Investment Securities," 29 Mar. 1933, The American Presidency Project website, http://www .presidency.ucsb.edu/ws/index.php?pid=14602; "President Takes Lead," *New York Times,* 30 Mar. 1933, 1; Seligman, *Transformation,* 75.

60. Roosevelt, "Message to Congress."

61. Seligman, *Transformation,* 53–57, 63–70; Robert Sobel, *The Big Board: A History of the New York Stock Market* (Washington, DC: Beard Books, 2000), 294.

62. " 'Truth in Securities' Bill Repassed by House, Senate," *Wall Street Journal,* 25 May 1933, 10.

63. Seligman, *Transformation,* 48–49, 70–71.

64. Franklin D. Roosevelt, "Excerpts from the Press Conference," 29 Mar. 1933, The American Presidency Project website, http://www.presidency.ucsb.edu/ws/index .php?pid=14604.

65. Quoted in Seligman, *Transformation,* 75–76.

66. Ibid., 76; "Stock Exchange Curbs Gambling; High Margins Set, Pools Checked," *New York Times,* 3 Aug. 1933, 1.

67. Seligman, *Transformation,* 71–72, 76–81.

68. "J.P. Morgan Faces Questioning Today," *New York Times,* 23 May 1933, 27; "Now It Is Told," *Time,* 5 June 1933; Seligman, *Transformation,* 31; Pecora, *Wall Street under Oath,* 4; Sobel, *The Big Board,* 294.

69. Pecora, *Wall Street under Oath,* 4–5; Seligman, *Transformation,* 31–32.

70. "Rich Men Pay No Tax," *Washington Post,* 24 May 1933, 6; Seligman, *Transformation,* 33.

71. Seligman, *Transformation,* 34–35; Pecora, *Wall Street under Oath,* 20–34; Sobel, *The Big Board,* 238–239.

72. Pecora, *Wall Street under Oath,* 5; Seligman, *Transformation,* 37.

73. "Why It Hurts," *New York Times,* 27 May 1933, 12.

74. Seligman, *Transformation,* 38; "Glass Bank Bill Passed by Senate," *New York Times,* 26 May 1933, 1; "Roosevelt Hails Goal."

75. U.S. Senate, *Hearings before the Committee on Banking and Currency:* pt. 2 *J. P. Morgan & Co.; O. P. Van Sweringen, May 26, 31, June 1, 2, 5, 6, 7, 8 and 9, 1933* (Washington, DC: GPO, 1934), 307–956; pt. 3: *Kuhn Loeb; Pennroad Corporation, June 27, 28, 29, 30, and July 6, 1933* (Washington, DC: GPO, 1934), 957–1533; pt. 4: *Dillon, Read & Co., Oct. 3 to 13, 1933* (Washington, DC: GPO, 1934), 1535–2277; pt. 5: *Chase Securities Corporation, Oct. 17 to 25, 1933* (Washington, DC: GPO, 1934), 2279–2741; "Damnation of Mitchell."

76. Pecora, *Wall Street under Oath,* 137–138.

77. The price of Chase National stock just prior to the market crash of 1929 was actually $283 per share. However, because the stock had recently undergone a 5-for-1 split,

to accurately compare its value to 1927 prices, the 1929 share price had to be multiplied by five, thus resulting in the quoted value of $1,415. Pecora, *Wall Street under Oath*, 149–151, 184.

78. U.S. Senate, *Hearings before the Committee on Banking and Currency*, pt. 6: *Chase Securities Corporation (Continued), Oct. 26 to Nov. 10* (Washington, DC: GPO, 1934), 2435–2436, 2835.

79. Pecora, *Wall Street under Oath*, 142–146, 268–269.

80. Ibid., 147–158, 184, 200–201, quotation on 161; "'Tax-Saving' Deals Related by Wiggin: He Paid $4,624,905," *New York Times*, 2 Nov. 1933, 1; Arthur E. Wilmarth Jr., "Did Universal Banks Play a Significant Role in the U.S. Economy's Boom-and-Bust Cycle of 1921–33? A Preliminary Assessment," in *Current Developments in Monetary and Financial Law*, vol. 4 (Washington, DC: International Monetary Fund, 2005), 577.

81. Quoted in "Aldrich Bans Chase Pools; Wiggin Bares Huge Profits," *Washington Post*, 28 Oct. 1933, 1; "Chase Bank Drops Half of Its Board," *New York Times*, 17 May 1933, 23; Pecora, *Wall Street under Oath*, 140.

82. "Aldrich Bans Chase Pools," 1.

83. Quoted in Seligman, *Transformation*, 82–84.

84. Ellenberger and Mahar, *Legislative History*, 5:5–20, item no. 16.

85. Ibid., 5:4–20.

86. Seligman, *Transformation*, 84–85; Ellenberger and Mahar, *Legislative History*, 4:2264, item no. 5.

87. Quoted in Ellenberger and Mahar, *Legislative History*, 4:2264, item no. 5.

88. Ibid., 2264–2272, quotations at 2265, 2267; Seligman, *Transformation*, 85.

89. Ellenberger and Mahar, *Legislative History*, 4:2264–2272, item no. 5; Pecora, *Wall Street under Oath*, 269.

90. "Three Tight Rules," 29, quotation from Whitney at 29.

91. Whitney quoted in "Whitney Fears Rigidity of Regulatory Bill Might Freeze Organized Regulatory Markets," *Wall Street Journal*, 14 Feb. 1934, 1, 9; "Three Tight Rules," 29.

92. Whitney quoted in "Whitney Fears Rigidity," 9; "Three Tight Rules," 31.

93. Ibid.

94. Ibid.

95. "Stock Market Bill Viewed as Faulty," *New York Times*, 17 Feb. 1934, 21, quotation at 21; Seligman, *Transformation*, 89.

96. "Whitney's Views on Trading Bill," *Wall Street Journal*, 16 Feb. 1934, 7; "Whitney Extends Market Bill Fight," *New York Times*, 16 Feb. 1934, 27.

97. "Whitney's Views on Trading Bill," 7; Seligman, *Transformation*, 89.

98. "Whitney Extends Market Bill Fight," 27.

99. Senator Fletch quoted in "Fletcher's Statement on Stock 'Propaganda,'" *New York Times*, 22 Feb. 1934, 2.

100. Quoted in "Flexibility Urged in Exchange Bill," *New York Times*, 15 Feb. 1934, 20; "Exchange 'Slipped' on Alcohol Issue," *New York Times*, 17 Feb. 1934, 16; Pecora, *Wall Street under Oath*, 272–282.

101. "Exchange 'Slipped' on Alcohol Issue," 16; Pecora, *Wall Street under Oath*, 272–282.

102. "Whitney Testifies Today"; Seligman, *Transformation*, 90.

·{ 16 }·

Martin Luther King and the Struggle for Black Voting Rights (1965)

ON TUESDAY AFTERNOON, March 9, 1965, Martin Luther King Jr. led more than 2,000 protestors—blacks and whites, men in jackets and ties, women in dresses—on a march from Brown Chapel, an African Methodist Episcopal church in Selma, Alabama, to the Edmund Pettus Bridge, spanning the Alabama River, a short distance away. He faced an agonizing decision about whether to defy a federal court order by crossing the bridge.[1]

The 36-year-old Baptist minister and director of the Southern Christian Leadership Conference (SCLC) had recently won the Nobel Peace Prize for his leadership of the civil rights movement in the United States. The movement aimed to overturn state laws and customs requiring racial segregation in the South, as well as state laws and practices that disenfranchised black voters there. King had helped launch the movement in 1955 as the spokesman for a boycott against segregated buses in Montgomery, the state capital of Alabama, and had brought the segregation issue unprecedented attention with a campaign of mass nonviolent civil disobedience in Birmingham, Alabama, in 1963. In the summer of 1964 Congress had enacted a sweeping Civil Rights Act, largely banning legally enforced segregation. Yet suppression of black voters remained pervasive across the South, leading King to take the SCLC to Selma in January 1965 to start a campaign for voting rights.

Central to the campaign was a series of illegal but nonviolent protest marches. In February one of these marches had been broken up by white rioters, local lawmen (including Sheriff Jim Clark), and state troopers, one of whom had shot and killed a marcher, Jimmie Lee Jackson. In response,

491

the SCLC had announced a three-day protest march from Brown Chapel, their Selma headquarters, to the Alabama state capitol building in Montgomery, more than fifty miles away down Highway 80. The governor, George Wallace, who had risen to national fame as an opponent of the civil rights movement, banned the march. The leaders of the SCLC decided to defy his order, expecting that marchers would be arrested at the Pettus Bridge, which connected downtown Selma to the highway.

On March 7, 1965, a Sunday, 600 well-dressed marchers left the chapel in two orderly lines. King had followed events from Atlanta, Georgia, where he was preaching to his home church. When the marchers crossed the bridge, they found their way blocked by Sheriff Clark, his men, and state troopers. A trooper ordered the protesters to disperse. When they did not immediately do so, the troopers and lawmen advanced. Suddenly they charged, assaulting the marchers with clubs, cattle prods, and tear gas, and then chased those who retreated through the neighborhood around Brown Chapel, beating any black person they encountered. Many white onlookers cheered.

Television cameras had recorded everything. That evening all three national networks, ABC, NBC, and CBS, broadcast the footage. ABC's special report on the events in Alabama interrupted the television premier of an Oscar-nominated film, *Judgment at Nuremburg* (1961), an all-star drama about the Allied military trials of German judges who had enforced race-based laws against Jews during the Holocaust.

By midnight King had sent telegrams all over the country, announcing that he would personally lead another march from Selma on Tuesday and asking "clergy of all faiths" to join him.[2] The next day, Monday, an estimated 800 activists, many of them clergy and divinity students, both black and white, rushed to Selma by car, bus, and plane from as far away as Massachusetts and California. Sympathy marches were held across the country. In Washington, D.C., students occupied the corridor outside the offices of U.S. Attorney General Nicholas Katzenbach, demanding federal intervention; TV cameras filmed him in shirtsleeves, on one knee, pleading with them, unsuccessfully, to leave. Meanwhile, SCLC lawyers petitioned Alabama federal district judge Frank Johnson, who was seen as sympathetic to the civil rights movement, for an injunction to prevent state and local authorities from stopping the next march.

Judge Johnson refused to issue an injunction without a hearing, which he scheduled for Thursday, and instructed the SCLC to postpone the march. Also, President Lyndon Johnson let King know through intermediaries that he did not want him to march. The president, who had shepherded the Civil Rights Act through Congress and was now drafting a voting rights bill, feared that a new march might provoke more violence, which could threaten the prospects of voting rights legislation. King did not want to alienate the president, a critical ally, but King's advisers told him that feelings were now running so high among his supporters in Selma that they might defy him if he tried to cancel or postpone the march. King decided to proceed with the march as planned.

On Monday night he spoke to a rally at Brown Chapel, celebrating the clergy who had just arrived in town and urging everyone to be brave the next day. Later, at the home of a Selma supporter where he was staying, he received a midnight phone call from Attorney General Katzenbach, who urged him not to march. King argued with Katzenbach, finally telling him: "But Mr. Attorney General, you have not been a black man in America for three hundred years."[3] After the call, however, King and his advisers engaged in a long, inconclusive debate over what to do. King had slept only a few hours when he was awakened, at dawn, by news that two of President Johnson's men were at the front door. One was the assistant attorney general for civil rights, John Doar; the other, who had been flown in overnight on the president's orders by military plane from Washington, was former Florida governor Le Roy Collins, who had been appointed the first director of the new Community Relations Service, created to mediate racial conflicts. King, still in his pajamas, met with them at the dining room table.

They informed him that Judge Johnson had issued an injunction against the march. King had previously defied the injunctions of state and local judges, but never of a federal judge. The modern civil rights movement had always depended on the support of the federal courts. Collins suggested that King might not violate the terms of the injunction if he led marchers to the bridge but then, instead of crossing it, turned them around and led them back to the chapel. He said he would ask Clark, as well as the commander of the state troopers, Al Lingo, to agree to this plan. King gave him permission to try.

Hours later, King, at the chapel, had still not heard from Collins, and only his advisers as yet knew about the turnaround possibility. King told the crowd to "put on their walking shoes" and started them toward the bridge.[4] There, as before, the troopers and lawmen waited. According to at least one report, marchers began singing a freedom song, "Ain't Gonna Let Nobody Turn Me 'Round."[5] The TV cameras were again rolling. King now had to decide whether to try to turn the march around at the bridge, or to push forward as his fellow marchers were expecting.

The Rise and Fall of Black Voting in the South, 1867–1908

The year 1865 marked the victory of the Union in the Civil War and the ratification of the Thirteenth Amendment to the Constitution, abolishing slavery. By 1870 black freedmen were voting across the South. "Alone among the nations that abolished slavery in the nineteenth century," writes historian Eric Foner, "the United States, within a few years of emancipation, clothed its former slaves with citizenship rights equal to those of whites."[6] Before the war, 90 percent of U.S. blacks had been slaves, and only a few northern states allowed free blacks to vote; between 1799 and 1838, black voting was outlawed in eight states that had formerly allowed it.[7] From the late 1840s through 1865, activists, some eventually affiliated with the self-styled "Radical" wing of the antislavery Republican Party, made many attempts to amend northern state constitutions to allow black voting, but these efforts were always defeated. In 1867, one year after the Republican-controlled Congress had approved both the Fourteenth Amendment (which declared *all* persons born in the United States to be citizens) and the first-ever Civil Rights Act (which offered former slaves equal protection of the law), white voters in Kansas, Minnesota, and Ohio rejected equal-suffrage amendments to their state constitutions.[8]

Yet change was still palpable. During the war, sentiment among northern whites had grown to favor suffrage for black Union veterans; and after the war Radical Republicans, who had become the dominant force in their party, concluded that all freedmen must be given the vote to protect their new citizenship rights and to stop Democrats, especially former Confederates, from regaining power in the South. With the 1867 Reconstruction Act, Radicals forced the former rebel states to write new constitutions, and mandated that there be no color restriction on who could vote for or serve as delegates to the constitutional conventions. In huge numbers, ex-slaves participated in these special elections, and 265 were chosen as delegates to the various conventions—among the first black elected officials in American history. The new state constitutions that they helped to write eliminated race restrictions on voting. Black voters went on to form the backbone of the Republican Party in the South, and southern black Republican leaders were elected to state and local office and to Congress.[9]

The new black voters were mostly impoverished, unskilled, and illiterate; as slaves they had been taught never to challenge their masters' authority and had been subjected to cruel punishments if they dared to try. Yet now they seized the opportunity not only to vote, but to vote against their former masters, who were almost all Democrats. The freedmen felt empowered by their experiences in the Civil War, when tens of thousands had fled their masters, many joining the Union army, and its immediate aftermath, when they loosened many brutal restrictions that had constrained their lives as slaves. They "held mass meetings and religious services unrestrained by white surveillance, acquired dogs, guns, and liquor (all barred to them under slavery), and refused to yield the sidewalks to whites." No longer confined to their masters' plantations, they became mobile—"it seemed that half the South's black population took to the roads"—with many resettling permanently in new homes. They withdrew from the white churches they had been forced to attend and set up their own congregations; they founded their own voluntary associations; they crowded into the freedmen's schools set up first by northern missionaries and then by the federal government. Freedmen also sought to obtain their own farms. Most, being too poor to buy land outright, arranged to rent it, usually in return for part of the cotton they grew. This system of "sharecropping" took hold across the former plantation areas of the South. In this time of revolutionary achievements, large numbers of ex-slaves came to believe they could exercise independent political power and acted on that belief.[10]

Meanwhile, in 1870 the states ratified the Republican-sponsored Fifteenth Amendment to the U.S. Constitution, which declared that the "right of citizens of the United States to vote shall not be denied or abridged by the United States or by any State on account of race, color, or previous condition of servitude." Again, Republicans in Washington, D.C., responded forcefully when southern Democrats formed vigilante groups, such as the Ku Klux Klan (KKK), which in 1869–1870 began a campaign of terror against Republican officials and voters, white as well as black, across the South. The violence provoked Republicans in Congress to approve the Enforcement Acts (1870–1871), which not only banned Klan activity but declared that "all citizens of the United States who are or shall be otherwise qualified by law to vote at any election . . . shall be entitled and allowed to vote at all such elections, without distinction of race, color, or previous condition of servitude." The legislation also made illegal any attempt to use "force, intimidation, or threat to prevent any citizen of the United States lawfully entitled to vote from giving his support or advocacy in a lawful manner towards or in favor of the election of any lawfully qualified person as an elector of President or Vice-President of the United States, or as a member of the Congress of the United States."[11] At first the federal government vigorously enforced these laws, with more than a thousand prosecutions in 1873.[12]

Nonetheless, between 1869 and 1877, southern Democrats, promising to "redeem" the South from "Negro rule," solidified support from poor southern whites and took control of every former rebel state. They subsequently enacted laws transferring power to appoint election supervisors from county governments, where it had traditionally resided, to the governor, a state board, or the state legislature, which effectively put white Democrats in charge of supervising all elections, even in majority-black Republican districts. Electoral fraud in these districts became endemic. Democratic operatives stuffed ballot boxes with fake Democratic ballots, while destroying Republican ballots after they were cast or, in some cases, simply tallying them as Democratic. Collectively these methods were known as "counting out" black votes. Formerly solid Republican districts soon crumbled, all across the South. An example involved the "Black Belt" of southern Alabama, where Montgomery, Birmingham, and Selma were all located. The name of the region was inspired by the color of its soil, but during Reconstruction it came to refer to the color of its voters.[13] Soon after Alabama was "redeemed" in 1874, the Black Belt began producing majorities for the "white man's party," the Democrats.[14]

Meanwhile, between 1878 and 1890 the number of federal prosecutions for violations of the voting rights provisions of the Enforcement Acts fell to an average of fewer than one hundred per year. The decline resulted from many causes: the electoral recovery of the Democratic Party to national parity with the Republicans; the shift of public concern in many quarters away from civil rights and toward economic issues; and the growing sentiment among northern whites that conflict with the South had gone on long enough. Above all, a growing number of northern Republican elites, overwhelmingly white, Protestant, and middle class or affluent, grew skeptical about the value of universal suffrage. Writes historian Alex Keyssar, "The key precipitants of this ideological swing . . . resided . . . in the dramatic—even shocking—transformations in [northern] economic and social life that inescapably reverberated into politics."[15]

Northern cities were experiencing explosive growth, prompted by industrialization and the migration of millions of southern and eastern Europeans to the United States, "propertyless workers . . . who did not speak English, whose cultures were alien, and most of whom were Catholic or Jewish. . . . Poor, uneducated, ignorant of American traditions, the foreign-born men peopling the nation's industries . . . [lacked, their critics charged,] the judgment, knowledge, and commitment to American values necessary for salutary participation in elections."[16] Besides, most of these immigrants voted Democratic. Northern Republicans began enacting laws restricting immigrant suffrage in their home states by various means, including poll taxes and literacy tests. They therefore could not easily oppose southern Democrats using similar techniques to disenfranchise black Republicans. In 1892, Democrats won control of both houses of Congress and the presidency for the first time since the Civil War and seized the opportunity to wipe "every trace of the reconstruction measures . . . from the statute books" by repealing the Enforcement Acts. Northern Republicans mostly put up little resistance, believing that black voting was a lost cause.[17]

Some black Republicans did keep fighting. Among them were politicians, ministers, educators, businessmen, and editors of black newspapers that had been founded in towns across the South. The existence of this mostly urban middle class showed the strides some southern blacks had made in wealth and education since emancipation. Yet the majority of blacks remained rural, poor, and illiterate. They knew that if they voted Republican, Democrats would "count out" their votes. Their political despair was reinforced by the growing power of "the man"—the white landowner, the white sheriff, the white official—over rural black life. Sharecropping became a trap as tenants often found themselves owing far more to their landlords than they could ever repay, and many were forced into debt peonage. Reinforcing white power was the system of convict leasing, which became so pervasive in the South by 1890 that the region had "no prisons to speak of."[18] The system proved highly profitable for companies that rented convict workers from the state at rock-bottom prices and for sheriffs in black districts, who were paid for each convict they leased. A sheriff could arrest a black laborer on a vague charge—"vagrancy" was common—then have him subjected to a cursory hearing before a justice of the peace, often a crony or relative of the sheriff, with no lawyers present. The prisoner would be ordered to pay a fine and his court costs. Unable to do so, he would be required to work off the charge and shipped to a logging camp or a coal mine, where his white boss had little incentive to treat him decently, because his labor was so cheap, and could extend his sentence almost at will by fining him for alleged infractions, which meant more money to work off. Fear of being caught in this system, which one recent scholar has called "slavery by another name," cast a pall of fear over black rural districts. It was only thickened by the threat of lynching, which reached its peak in the South in the 1890s, with scores of black men murdered each year.[19] Perpetrators were rarely arrested, and, if arrested, were brought before "lily white" juries, who almost never voted to convict.[20]

It was within this context that southern Democrats launched a campaign to "eliminate" the black vote. The process began in 1889–1890, when Tennessee, Arkansas, and Florida approved new election laws, and continued through a series of state constitutional conventions called specifically to effect disenfranchisement: Mississippi (1890), Arkansas (1891), South Carolina (1895), Louisiana (1898), North Carolina (1900), Alabama (1901), Texas (1901), Virginia (1902), and Georgia (1908). The announced goals of this movement were, first, to end the threat of "Negro domination" and guarantee "white supremacy," and second, to end political corruption. As the Richmond [Virginia] Times urged in 1898, "If we disfranchise the great body of Negroes, let us do it openly and above board and let there be an end to all sorts of jugglery." Or as an Alabama Democratic congressman, representing a Black Belt district, confessed in a speech to the disenfranchisement convention in his state, he had always told his operatives "to go to it, boys, count [black votes] out. We had to do it. Unfortunately, I say it was a necessity. We could not help ourselves. We had to do it or do worse. But we have gone on from bad to worse until it has become a great evil. . . . White men have gotten to cheating each other until we don't have any honest elections. That is the trouble we have to grapple with."[21]

Because measures explicitly banning black voting would contradict the language of the Fifteenth Amendment and possibly compel federal courts to intervene, proponents of black disenfranchisement devised voting require-ments that were nominally color-blind but in effect discriminated on the basis of race.[22] For example, the requirement that registered voters pay a poll tax to stay on the voting rolls disproportionately affected blacks, because they were, on average, significantly poorer than whites. Also, as black illiteracy was higher than white, new literacy requirements on voting hit blacks hard. In some cases, actual tests were administered to separate the literate from the illiterate. A more indirect technique was to implement the "Australian" ballot. Through most of the nineteenth century, each political party printed its own ballots, listing only its own candidates. As a result, a party-line voter did not need to be able to read the ballot to cast it. By contrast, the "Austra-lian" ballot, which was printed by the state and listed all of the candidates for each office, had to be read to be used. Democrats in Tennessee, who en-acted the first southern Australian ballot law in 1889, initially implemented it only in predominantly black districts.[23]

No matter how cleverly these measures were weighted against black voters, however, they inevitably disenfranchised many whites as well. Demo-crats, worried about alienating their political base, devised schemes to pro-tect white voters. Among these were "grandfather clauses." Louisiana enacted the first in 1898, and it was imitated, with variants, in many other states. The Louisiana version exempted anyone descended from a man who could vote on January 1, 1867 (when the electorate was all white), from the new literacy and poll tax requirements. Yet some proponents of disenfranchisement warned that grandfather clauses would not survive a challenge in federal court, and the U.S. Supreme Court ruled in 1915 that they violated the Fif-teenth Amendment.[24]

Ultimately, the most effective method of protecting white voters and dis-couraging black ones was to give election registrars, all white Democrats, wide discretion over how to do their jobs. For instance, registrars were asked to ensure that voters were literate enough to "understand" the privileges and nature of citizenship, but they were allowed to improvise their tests and standards on a case-by-case basis. Such improvisation proved highly discriminatory. Alabama registrars turned away one black applicant because he declined to explain "the differences of Jeffersonian democracy and the Calhoun principles as compared to the Monroe Doctrine."[25]

Black Republicans repeatedly challenged the new registration procedures in federal court. The most important case was that of Jackson Giles, a U.S. postal clerk in Montgomery, Alabama, who had voted for decades until turned away by his County Board of Registrars in 1902. Giles petitioned a federal district court, alleging that his Fifteenth Amendment rights had been violated and asking it to order the board to register him and 5,000 other blacks. When the court ruled that it could not hear the petition, he appealed to the U.S. Supreme Court. In 1903 the high court ruled that if the registration requirements were, as Giles alleged, unconstitutional, then the solution was not for courts to force blacks to be registered under them; rather, Giles should seek "political" relief from the Alabama legislature or Congress. With no realistic possibility of obtaining such relief, black leaders denounced the ruling, comparing it to the proslavery *Dred Scott* decision of 1857.[26]

Although black southerners were not the only victims of the disenfranchisement movement—significant numbers of poor whites also lost the right to vote—the effect on the black electorate was grossly disproportionate. In Virginia, the number of black voters was reduced from 147,000 to 21,000; in Georgia, from 68,000 to 11,285; in Louisiana, from 130,344 to 5,320; in the fourteen "Black Belt" counties of Alabama, from 79,311 to 1,081. In 1893, a few years after disenfranchisement in Mississippi, where nearly 748,000 blacks lived, constituting more than 58 percent of the total state population, only 8,965 black voters remained. Without black votes to sustain them, the remaining black elected officials in the South quickly lost their positions. The last black congressman, George Henry White, Republican of North Carolina, left office in 1901, shortly after his state ratified its disenfranchising constitution. No African American would serve in Congress for another twenty-eight years.[27]

The capstone of disenfranchisement was the "white primary." Primary elections were an innovation of the direct democracy movement, which flourished during the Progressive Era, in the first two decades of the twentieth century. Progressive reformers championed direct primaries as a method to take party nominations out of the hands of "corrupt bosses," who controlled party nominating conventions, and give them to the citizenry. Between 1902 and 1908, Democrats in most southern states instituted direct primary systems, but with one distinctive feature: they did not allow blacks to vote in them. Democrats claimed that their white primaries were not inconsistent with the Fifteenth Amendment, because the amendment guaranteed to blacks only the right to vote in general elections, not the right to participate in the private, internal administration of a political party. In most states outside of the South, primaries were considered public elections and paid for by taxpayers. Southern Democrats, wishing to emphasize that their primaries were private, paid for them with party funds. Decades would pass before the Supreme Court decided that white primaries were unconstitutional.[28] Meanwhile, as the Republican Party was now moribund in the South, and Democratic nominees always won general elections there, white primaries ensured that even those few blacks who still voted would never affect an election outcome.

Jim Crow

In the same era as disenfranchisement, southern states legally enhanced racial segregation, a system that came to be known, after a black minstrel character, as "Jim Crow." During slavery, southern blacks and whites had lived and worked in intimate proximity. After emancipation the races in the South started to separate. Blacks withdrew from white churches to set up their own congregations, for example, while white leaders insisted that white and black children must not share schools; white businessmen, acting on their private initiative, segregated most hotels, theaters, and restaurants; and white homeowners increasingly blocked blacks from buying houses in their neighborhoods. "Over a period of about a half century," writes one historian, "the implications of segregation worked themselves into the interstices of southern society."[29]

In 1890, southern Democratic state legislatures began enacting "separate coach" laws, authorizing or requiring cities to segregate streetcars. These laws seemed directed at urban, middle-class blacks, who often protested, writing petitions, holding mass meetings, and, in at least twenty-seven southern cities, organizing streetcar boycotts. The protests never did more, however, than delay the implementation of the new rules.[30] Black leaders also launched a series of suits in federal court, arguing that Jim Crow streetcars violated the equal protection provisions of the Fourteenth Amendment. The U.S. Supreme Court rejected this claim in 1896. In the case of *Plessy v. Ferguson,* the court ruled that the "enforced separation of the two races" did not stamp "the colored race with a badge of inferiority" and that "separate but equal" facilities were therefore constitutional.[31]

In reality, "colored" facilities under Jim Crow were always inferior to "white" ones. Moreover, Jim Crow practices soon went beyond the law but were routinely enforced as if they were law. In 1955, for example, a black woman, Mrs. Rosa Parks, was arrested on a segregated bus in Montgomery, Alabama, for refusing to obey the order of the white driver to yield her seat to a white passenger and, as no other black seat was available, stand in the aisle. Yet the city ordinance governing bus segregation in Montgomery required that she yield her seat to whites only if she could move to a free black seat.[32] The police jailed Parks anyway. Whites in the South had grown accustomed to enforcing Jim Crow however they saw fit. Blacks had been powerless to stop them and the federal government had been unwilling to intervene. By 1955, however, this situation was changing.

The Changing Environment for Civil Rights, 1909–1960

Although Jim Crow remained solidly in place over the first half of the twentieth century, blacks themselves moved—to the cities and to the North. In 1910, 73 percent of U.S. blacks and 51 percent of whites lived in rural areas; by 1960, 73 percent of blacks were urban, as opposed to 70 percent of whites. Meanwhile, the share of blacks living in the South fell from 89 percent to 60 percent.[33]

Southern black urbanization resulted in part from a shift in regional agriculture away from small cotton farms, a process accelerated by the boll weevil. Between 1890 and 1930, this beetle, whose larvae fed on cotton, spread from Mexico across the southeastern United States, devastating cotton production in many areas. The weevil arrived in Dallas County, Alabama, where Selma was located, around 1910; production fell from 40,000 bales that year to 16,400 in 1920. Countless tenants, already deeply in debt, could not make their payments at all. Many landlords, meanwhile, found they could make higher profits by evicting their tenants and moving to larger-scale farming (involving mechanization and pesticides), or by shifting resources to raise cattle. At the same time, southern industry began to grow, especially during the Second World War, attracting black farmworkers to the cities. The resulting shifts can be seen in Dallas County: in 1930 more than half the land was still being cultivated by black tenants; by 1960, the figure had fallen to 9 percent. In southern cities, most blacks were limited to unskilled work and could not vote, but they still had the numbers and means to form large churches and support independent black business and cultural institutions. There were other positive developments as well, many linked to rising black economic independence and literacy. Convict leasing had largely disappeared by the 1930s, and debt peonage was suppressed by the federal government as it mobilized the economy for World War II (1941–1945). Lynchings of blacks fell from an average of ninety-five a year in the 1890–1910 era, to three a year between 1940 and 1949, to zero between 1952 and 1954.[34]

The black exodus from the South, meanwhile, began with middle-class leaders disgusted by disenfranchisement, Jim Crow, and lynching. Congressman White, for example, decided to leave his native state for the North, declaring, "I cannot live in North Carolina and be a man and be treated as a man."[35] What scholars call the "Great Migration," however, began a little later. The outbreak of the First World War, in 1914, largely stopped European immigration, and the U.S. entry into the war, in 1917, led to an economic boom. Yet millions of white northerners—as well as hundreds of thousands of blacks—were joining or being drafted into the military. Facing severe labor shortages, northern industrialists began recruiting southern black workers, offering higher wages and even in some cases promising to pay for or subsidize their trips north. Many blacks seized the opportunity and, once settled in their new homes, usually in large northern cities, were typically joined by family members. Between 1915 and 1920, more than half a million black Americans left the South, and some 900,000 more left by 1930. By 1940 the four largest black communities in the country were located in New York, Chicago, Philadelphia, and Detroit. The Second World War produced an industrial boom that drew still-larger numbers of black workers out of the South.[36]

Blacks who lived in northern cities were usually segregated in practice, if not by law, often in "ghettos" plagued by high rates of poverty and crime. Yet they had the numbers and money to form larger and more powerful black institutions and associations than in southern cities, and they could vote.

Indeed, they soon made their political influence felt. In 1928, the black neighborhoods of South Chicago elected the first black member of Congress since White—Oscar De Priest, a Republican and migrant from Alabama. In 1935, he would be replaced by a black Democrat, Arthur Mitchell, also an Alabama native; Mitchell would be succeeded in 1943 by another black Democrat, the Georgia migrant William Dawson, who would serve for twenty-seven years. In 1945, the Harlem neighborhood of New York City also elected a black Democrat, Adam Clayton Powell Jr. (born a northerner, but with southern parents), bringing the total number of blacks in Congress to two. Powell would become, in 1961, the first black to chair an important congressional committee (Education and Labor in the House).

The appearance of black Democratic congressmen evidenced a shift in black political allegiance. During the Great Depression, the New Deal programs and pro-labor policies of President Franklin Delano Roosevelt, a Democrat, drew poor and working-class voters to his party, blacks among them. FDR pursued a very cautious policy on civil rights, not wanting to alienate the powerful southern Democratic members of Congress whose support he needed to pass legislation.* Still, black support for the Democrats was strengthened by the pro-civil-rights stands of the First Lady, Eleanor Roosevelt. Most famously, in 1938, when the Daughters of the American Revolution (DAR) refused the use of their Washington, D.C., concert hall to a celebrated black opera singer, Marian Anderson, Mrs. Roosevelt resigned her DAR membership and helped Anderson organize an open-air concert at the Lincoln Memorial, which was broadcast live on national radio.[37]

Many blacks continued to vote Republican, however, and by the 1940s the two major parties recognized that in a close presidential race, black voters could swing key states. Partly as a result, both parties began to appeal to the black vote by announcing support for civil rights. This presented a problem

---

* In the congressional elections of 1932, Democrats won control of both House and Senate, and they maintained that control for forty-four of the next forty-eight years. Because southern Democrats after disenfranchisement never faced viable Republican challengers, they had the safest Democratic seats. They often constituted a majority or near majority of the Democratic caucus in both chambers, and most senior caucus members were southerners, who, owing to the seniority system, came to chair a majority of congressional committees, including many of the most powerful and prestigious ones. See Nicole C. Rea, *Southern Democrats* (New York: Oxford University Press, 1994), 66–67, 84, 96–97.

for the Democrats, however, dividing their northern and southern wings. In the 1948 presidential election, the incumbent, Harry Truman, trailing Republicans badly in the polls, pushed for a plank in the Democratic platform that called for all Americans to have "the right of full and equal political participation" and for "the right of equal treatment in the service and defense of our nation."[38] In response, southern delegates walked out of the national party convention. Their protest was among the first news events covered by the brand-new medium of network television.[39] Days later Truman issued executive orders beginning the desegregation of the U.S. armed forces. In the fall several southern states voted for a segregationist "Dixiecrat" third-party candidate, but Truman was returned to office, in part on the strength of black votes outside the South.[40]

By 1948, policies aimed at black disenfranchisement were losing ground in America. The depression had thrust so many voters into poverty that the poll tax grew increasingly unpopular, even in the South, and a movement arose to abolish it. American involvement in the Second World War, meanwhile, required mass mobilization of the population. At least a million blacks were drafted or volunteered, including many who could not vote. The idea that those who fought for their country were denied suffrage at home because of their race grew unpalatable to many American whites, especially because the United States was battling racist Nazi Germany. The United States declared as a war goal "the restoration of democracy to all European nations, as well as an end to racial and ethnic discrimination," writes Keyssar. "In the popular mind and in wartime propaganda, the ideology of racial superiority espoused by the Nazis loomed as an evil that had to be vanquished."[41] Owing to such developments, many white Americans increasingly viewed systematic discrimination in the South as a national problem in need of a solution.

Ready to take advantage of this shift in mood was an incipient civil rights movement. Its most conspicuous organization was the National Association for the Advancement of Colored People (NAACP). Founded in 1909 by a group of prominent intellectuals, both black and white and mostly from the North, it aimed, according to its charter, "to promote equality of rights and to eradicate caste or race prejudice among the citizens of the United States; to advance the interest of colored citizens; to secure for them impartial suffrage; and to increase their opportunities for securing justice in the courts, education for their children, employment according to their ability and complete equality before law."[42] By the 1920s the NAACP had branches in nearly every U.S. city. Appealing principally to the black middle class, it organized protests (for example, demonstrations outside showings of *Birth of a Nation,* an immensely popular but deeply racist motion picture), publicized examples of black achievement and racial injustice, and lobbied political leaders.[43] It became best known, however, for undertaking carefully publicized legal challenges to segregation and disenfranchisement in the federal courts. Year after year, the NAACP methodically established civil rights precedents and trained up a cadre of talented lawyers in what amounted to a new field of law.

One early NAACP triumph was the 1915 Supreme Court ruling that "grandfather clauses" were unconstitutional. Another major victory came in 1944, when the Supreme Court declared that the Fifteenth Amendment covered all primaries, even party-funded ones, and therefore that the "white primary" was unconstitutional. After this, the NAACP launched a campaign to register black voters in the South. Thousands responded, particularly members of the urban middle class, but progress was slow: white registrars still took full advantage of their power to block black applicants, and especially in rural areas, black applicants often faced violent intimidation and economic reprisals.[44]

The NAACP scored its most celebrated victory in May 1954. After chipping away for decades, case by case, at the doctrine of "separate but equal," it finally persuaded the Supreme Court to overturn the doctrine altogether. In *Brown v. Board of Education of Topeka, Kansas,* the justices decided unanimously that legally mandated racial segregation of public schools violated blacks' Fourteenth Amendment right to equal protection. "Separate educational facilities," the court declared, "are inherently unequal." The ruling sent shockwaves across the country and may have been the first piece of civil rights news to receive a banner headline on the front page of the *New York Times.*[45] After that, civil rights stories loomed larger in both the American and international press. In 1956, the civil rights story of the year—the one that most caught the attention of both press and public—was a black boycott of segregated buses in Montgomery, Alabama.

The Rise of the Civil Rights Movement, 1955–1960

Some observers were surprised to see the largest black protest in decades erupt in Montgomery, the self-proclaimed "cradle of the Confederacy" (during the Civil War, it had been the first capital of the South). Yet Montgomery blacks had a long tradition of civil rights activism, including their own branch of the NAACP since 1918. They had institutional resources to draw on, including a black college (Alabama State), their own newspaper and radio station, and many large churches. In August 1954 the community got its first activist black lawyer (and second black lawyer overall) when Fred Gray, a World War II veteran and part-time preacher, was admitted to the Alabama bar. The community also had voters. Following the abolition of the white primary in 1944, many local blacks had succeeded, through sheer perseverance, in clearing the remaining hurdles blocking black registration. Although all elected officials in the city were white, and blacks remained significantly underrepresented in the electorate—they comprised 37 percent of the city population in 1955, but only 7.5 percent of the voters—they nonetheless could swing a close municipal election when the white vote was narrowly divided, as happened a number of times in the years leading up to the boycott.[46]

Montgomery blacks had used their political leverage to get the city to establish its first black public high school in 1946, a second in 1949, its first black hospital in 1951, and a number of black public housing developments. In early 1954 they even persuaded the city to hire its first black police officers, assigned to patrol black neighborhoods. White city leaders who agreed to these changes appear to have done so, at least in part, to help buttress segregation. With NAACP court victories undercutting the "separate but equal" doctrine, it became increasingly clear that segregation would not stand unless "colored" facilities and services at least approximated "white" ones. In addition, a new generation of white businessmen wanted Montgomery to present a forward-looking image in order to attract investment from the North.[47] Local blacks, meanwhile, likely saw the improvements as steps on the road to integration.

Segregation on city buses proved to be a flashpoint. The front ten seats were reserved for whites. White bus drivers forbade blacks to sit in them even when there were no white passengers aboard and the black seats were full. The drivers required black passengers to pay in front and then exit the bus and reenter through the rear door, and they routinely ordered blacks to stand so that whites could sit. Although none of these practices were explicitly authorized by city segregation ordinances, they were nonetheless enforced by the police.[48]

Blacks in Montgomery ultimately boycotted the buses in response to the arrest of Rosa Parks, a black community leader and secretary of the local NAACP office, who on December 1, 1955, refused to yield her seat in the "colored section" of a city bus to a white passenger when the white section was full. After Fred Gray, who represented Mrs. Parks, pointed out that she had not violated any municipal ordinance, the city prosecutor charged her instead with violating a 1945 state bus segregation law that had never before been understood to apply to municipal lines.[49] The local trial court promptly convicted Parks on this charge, and Gray appealed.

The arrest of Parks struck local activists as the perfect occasion for a bus boycott. They had been considering one for some time, inspired by boycotts in Baton Rouge, Louisiana, in 1953, which had won better treatment for black riders, and New York City in 1941, which had led to the hiring of black drivers.[50] Montgomery blacks supported the boycott with such immediate and unanimous enthusiasm that even most black leaders were caught off guard. They quickly created the Montgomery Improvement Association (MIA) to run the boycott and chose as its president a 26-year-old Baptist minister and Atlanta native who had only recently settled in Montgomery, Martin Luther King Jr. He was selected because he was seen as articulate and respectable—he had just received a doctorate in theology from Boston University—and was not tied to any faction of the local black leadership. A new father and a first-time pastor, the busy King accepted the presidency of the MIA in part because he thought the boycott would be over in a few days.[51] In fact, it would last for over a year.

As the boycott wore on, King's stature grew. His insistence that the protesters "meet hate with love" helped transform the boycott, in the eyes of both participants and observers, from an expression of economic power into a near-religious pursuit. As one elderly black woman who now had to walk to work declared: "My feets is tired, but my soul is rested." Civil rights activists around the country began to see King's nonviolent, mass-movement approach to civil rights as an appealing alternative to the legal strategy so long pursued by the NAACP, and—most strikingly—as a way to turn even poor, nonvoting blacks into significant political actors.[52]

Although the boycott was not legally tied to the *Brown* decision, the political environment in which it took shape was deeply influenced by the 1954 ruling. The Supreme Court's decision had energized black Americans, especially in places like Montgomery where activism had been gathering momentum, with the hope that they could bring about integration soon. Yet the 1954 decision outraged many southern whites. One sign was the reemergence of the Ku Klux Klan, which now took the form of semisecret clubs pledged to stop the civil rights movement with violence.[53] More mainstream was the "White Citizens Councils" movement. Launched in Mississippi soon after the *Brown* ruling, these councils advocated "massive resistance" to integration. Believing that "without treacherous white assistance, blacks were powerless by themselves to achieve their integrationist goals," the councils concentrated their efforts on "eliminating all white dissent" and "silencing all public advocacy of racial moderation." Montgomery whites created their own council in October 1955, with 300 members. In response to the bus boycott, membership grew to 12,000 by February 1956.[54]

Initially, King and the MIA did not ask for an end to segregated buses, but merely that black drivers be hired for bus routes through black neighborhoods, that the segregated seating system be made more flexible, with whites taking seats from the front of the bus to the back, blacks back to front, and that no seats be reserved for whites only. The city government refused to agree to these proposals. It tried to disrupt the boycott by falsely announcing that black leaders had agreed to end it and subsequently ordered city police to tail black drivers, including King, who were carpooling black commuters to work. On January 26, 1956, while King was driving a carpool, police arrested him for going 30 miles per hour in a 25-mile-per-hour zone. He was jailed, although his friends quickly bailed him out. At this point, the MIA decided compromise was useless. On February 1, Fred Gray filed a suit in federal court on behalf of four black Montgomery women, demanding an injunction against segregated seating.[55]

Now that the fight had become about segregation itself, the NAACP got involved, offering legal and financial help to Gray and the MIA. The State of Alabama responded by demanding that the NAACP turn over its membership and financial records for inspection. When the NAACP refused, it was subjected to severe fines, forcing it to shut all its offices in the state; they would remain closed for years.[56] Also, the state draft board revoked Gray's ministerial exemption. Only direct intervention from the Selective Service Office in Washington prevented Gray from being called up for military service.[57] Meanwhile, on January 30, the KKK bombed King's home—his wife and daughter were there—and less than forty-eight hours later, also bombed the house of the former president of the local NAACP chapter. Fortunately no one was hurt in either attack. The city government denounced the bombings but the police made no arrests. On February 21, however, an all-white state grand jury indicted nearly a hundred MIA leaders under an old, half-forgotten state anti-boycott statute originally aimed at labor unions. The grand jury report declared, "We are committed to segregation by custom and by law [and] we intend to maintain it." King's case was the first to be tried. He was convicted on March 22 and appealed. These developments brought reporters from around the world to Montgomery to see what was happening. The boycott story moved from the back pages of the *New York Times* to page 1.[58]

The MIA decided to continue the boycott until its segregation case was resolved in federal court. In early June, a federal circuit court panel ruled 2–1 that segregated buses violated the Fourteenth Amendment. The state of Alabama appealed to the U.S. Supreme Court. In November an Alabama state judge issued an injunction against the MIA carpool system on the grounds that it violated the franchise rights of the company that ran the Montgomery bus service. This might have disrupted the boycott, had not the U.S. Supreme Court rejected the Alabama appeal that same day. Alabama asked for reconsideration. The Supreme Court again rejected the appeal on December 17. On December 20, 1956, federal injunctions arrived ordering bus integration. Only then did the MIA end the boycott.[59]

The Montgomery bus boycott made King a national figure. In February 1957, *Time* magazine put his picture on its cover, and in a long profile, titled "Attack on the Conscience," attempted to explain the significance of his accomplishment:

In Montgomery, Negroes are riding side by side with whites on integrated buses for the first time in history. They won this right by court order. But their presence is accepted, however reluctantly, by the majority of Montgomery's white citizens because of Martin King and the way he conducted a year-long boycott of the transit system. In terms of concrete victories, this makes King a poor second to the brigade of lawyers who won the big case before the Supreme Court in 1954, and who are now fighting their way from court to court, writ to writ, seeking to build the legal framework for desegregation. But King's leadership extends beyond any single battle: homes and churches were bombed and racial passions rose close to mass violence in Montgomery's year of the boycott, but King reached beyond lawbooks and writs, beyond violence and threats, to win his people—and challenge all people—with a spiritual force that aspired even to ending prejudice in man's mind.[60]

Time exaggerated the willingness of Montgomery's whites to comply; violent resistance to integration would persist there for years. Nonetheless, the boycott had created national political momentum for civil rights, and King worked to build on it. In February 1957 he helped to create what became the Southern Christian Leadership Conference (SCLC), with the idea of organizing black ministers for civil rights action. King began giving civil rights speeches all over the country, traveling hundreds of thousands of miles a year, and in 1958 published his first book, *Stride towards Freedom,* about the boycott. The book sold slowly, however, and although the SCLC attracted many ministers, its staff was tiny and it failed in its major push to register millions of new black voters.[61]

Meanwhile, in September 1957 a white mob blocked nine black students from entering Central High School in Little Rock, Arkansas, impeding a federal court order for integration. When the Arkansas governor mobilized the National Guard to stop the black students from enrolling, President Dwight Eisenhower sent in the 101st Airborne Division to restore order and enforce the court order. These events occasioned the "first on-site news extravaganza of the modern television era."[62] King, however, had little influence on these events.

Also in September 1957, Congress approved the first Civil Rights Act since Reconstruction. The NAACP hired its first congressional lobbyist to work on the bill, while King organized a prayer rally of 27,000 people in front of the Lincoln Memorial urging passage of a strong law.[63] The resulting statute, however, disappointed both King and the NAACP. It reflected the mainstream white view that civil rights reform should be "gradual."[64] It created a Civil Rights Commission to investigate and report on voting rights abuses and a small Civil Rights Division in the Justice Department, but it did not directly attack segregation, and the procedures it established to prosecute voting rights violations were aimed only at individuals, as if the problem was just a few "bad apples," not systematic state policy. The law was weak enough that southern Democratic senators chose not to organize a filibuster.[65] By

TABLE 16.1

U.S. Households with Radios and/or Televisions, 1946–1965

Year	Households with Radio Sets (thousands)	Households with TV Sets (thousands)
1946	33,998	8
1950	40,700	5,030
1955	45,900	30,700
1960	50,193	45,750
1965	55,200	52,700

Source: Adapted from Alexander J. Field, "Radio and television–stations, sets produced, and households with sets: 1921–2000," *Historical Statistics of the United States,* Millennial Edition Online, eds. Susan B. Carter, Scott Sigmund Gartner, Michael R. Haines, Alan L. Olmstead, Richard Sutch, and Gavin Wright (Cambridge University Press, 2006), Table Dg117–130.

1959, when a national Gallup poll asked respondents whether the Supreme Court ruling on segregation in the schools had "caused a lot more trouble than it was worth," 53 percent responded "yes."[66]

Civil Disobedience and Publicity, 1960–1963

On February 1, 1960, King resigned his pulpit in Montgomery; he was moving back to his hometown of Atlanta, Georgia, to become co-pastor with his father, a prominent minister, and because the SCLC was headquartered there. That same day four freshmen from the North Carolina Agricultural and Technical State University, a black school in Greensboro, walked to the local Woolworth's department store and asked to be served at the "whites only" lunch counter. The unplanned demonstration flustered the owners, and the students were not arrested. They came back the next day with friends. Soon hundreds of students were taking part. Within a week, the "sit-in" movement spread to four other North Carolina cities. An SCLC minister from Birmingham, Fred Shuttlesworth, was visiting the state to preach when he saw students marching to a sit-in. Impressed, he quickly telephoned SCLC administrator Ella Baker and urged her to "tell Martin that we must get with this."[67]

King had already been thinking about a civil disobedience campaign, as had his friend James Lawson, a student at the Divinity School at Vanderbilt

University in Nashville, Tennessee. Both men viewed civil disobedience as a form of religious witness and personal sacrifice, with the potential to bring about nonviolent political change by stirring the conscience of the oppressor. Lawson had been training students for civil disobedience and had sponsored a number of sit-in demonstrations, although "few of them had made the news, [and] all faded quickly from public notice." Now he rushed to support the new movement, and his trainees, led by Vanderbilt student Diane Nash, launched sit-ins at lunch counters in downtown Nashville. Hundreds were arrested, refused to pay their fines, and were jailed. Months of protests followed, producing front-page headlines across the country. The house of the lawyer representing the students was bombed, and the trustees of Vanderbilt summarily expelled Lawson. This led 400 faculty members to resign in protest, forcing his reinstatement. Eventually downtown Nashville businesses integrated their lunch counters. Similar victories were achieved in dozens of southern cities, including Greensboro, integrating restaurants, swimming pools, and libraries. In other cities, such as Montgomery, sit-ins provoked only harsh crackdowns.[68]

Meanwhile, in April 1960 the SCLC sponsored a national conference of student sit-in activists, led by the Nashville group. With the encouragement of Ella Baker, these activists established their own independent organization, the Student Nonviolent Coordinating Committee (SNCC). SNCC soon started a sit-in campaign in King's city, Atlanta, to integrate the snack bar at a prestigious downtown department store. They asked King to join them, and on October 19, 1960, he did so, deliberately seeking arrest for the first time. He and the students were convicted of trespassing and refused bail, and he spent his first night in jail. Public attention and protests mounted. Alarmed, the mayor of Atlanta brokered a deal to drop charges against the protesters and form a biracial commission to make recommendations on how to desegregate downtown businesses. This seemed like a victory for the activists until the state police unexpectedly removed King from the county jail in shackles.[69]

It turned out that in May, King had gotten a traffic ticket. State law required that he replace his Alabama driver's license with one from Georgia within ninety days of moving to the state, but he had not done so. In September he had challenged the ticket in court, lost, and paid a $25 fine. Unbeknownst to King, however, the judge had also put him on probation.

Apparently King's lawyer had agreed to the terms—that King not violate state or federal laws for a year—without actually telling King. Now this same judge, finding King had violated his probation, sentenced him to four months of hard labor. Denied bail, King was moved in shackles to a maximum security state prison, where he was locked alone in a cell. His lawyers and family could not contact him. The Georgia governor's press spokesman told reporters that prison might do King "good" and "make a law-abiding citizen out of him." King's family and many civil rights activists feared he would be murdered.[70]

This crisis unfolded in the final weeks of a close presidential election between Senator John F. Kennedy of Massachusetts, the Democratic candidate, and Vice President Richard Nixon of California, the Republican. King had endorsed neither candidate. Nixon hoped to win at least as much black support as Republicans had in the 1956 presidential election, when Eisenhower received nearly 40 percent of the black vote. Nixon had joined with black leaders in criticizing the 1957 Civil Rights Act as too weak and had friendly relations with King. In addition, the most famous black man in the country, Jackie Robinson, the first black player in major league baseball, was campaigning for Nixon. Kennedy, by contrast, did not have a strong civil rights record and had picked for his running mate Senator Lyndon Johnson of Texas, whom civil rights leaders distrusted. Some leading black ministers, including King's father, refused to back JFK because he was Catholic. Now, however, Nixon made no comment while JFK phoned King's pregnant wife, Coretta, expressing concern, and Robert F. Kennedy (RFK), the candidate's younger brother and campaign manager, called King's judge to convey his opinion as a lawyer that King had a constitutional right to post bail. The judge let King do so the next day, October 27.[71]

The white press at first hardly noticed the Kennedy intervention, but news of it swept through black communities. Although King himself still declined to make endorsements, many other black leaders, including King's father, announced they were now for JFK. On election day, November 8, JFK won a 0.02 percent plurality of the total vote, but 70 percent of the black vote, enough of a gain for the Democrats over 1956 to provide his margin of victory in five crucial states.[72] In the words of one leading historian of the civil rights movement, the Kennedy calls had "elevated King in national politics. He became the Negro whose name determined a president."[73]

Nevertheless, after taking office in January 1961, President Kennedy as well as Robert Kennedy, his new attorney general, proceeded cautiously on civil rights. They methodically launched voting rights lawsuits, but feared that doing anything dramatic on segregation would alienate southern whites, whose votes JFK had relied on to win the election and whose powerful representatives in Congress he needed to enact his domestic agenda. On the recommendation of southern Democrats, JFK even appointed a number of pro-segregation federal judges.[74] In May 1961, however, the civil rights movement provoked a crisis that forced the Kennedys to take a clearer stand.

The Supreme Court had ruled in 1946 and again in 1960 that segregated waiting rooms, restaurants, and bathrooms at interstate bus terminals violated black passengers' Fourteenth Amendment rights. The Interstate Commerce Commission (ICC) had banned segregated terminals in 1955, but southern states had refused to comply (some simply relabeled their interstate terminals "intrastate").[75] It was against this backdrop that the Congress of Racial Equality (CORE), a pacifist group founded in 1942 that had worked in obscurity, organized a "Freedom Ride" in 1961. On May 4, a group of activists (black and white, men and women, some students from SNCC but also a number of participants who were middle-aged) left Washington, D.C., on two regularly scheduled buses, one Greyhound and one Trailways, aiming to reach New Orleans on May 17, the seventh anniversary of the *Brown* decision. At each stop, the riders planned to "challenge . . . every form of segregation met by the bus passenger."[76]

On May 14, Mother's Day, mobs led by the KKK attacked the riders near Anniston, Alabama. One mob burned the Greyhound bus, nearly killing the passengers; an hour later another mob attacked the Trailways bus, brutally beating Freedom Riders aboard. The Anniston police did not intervene. The Trailways driver then drove the injured Riders to Birmingham, where another Klan mob attacked them in front of reporters, including Howard K. Smith, a CBS correspondent in town to investigate segregation. Again, no police were in sight. Smith filed live radio reports and drove bleeding Riders to his hotel to film interviews with them, but the local CBS TV affiliate, owned by a segregationist, refused to allow him to file a televised report that night, citing "technical difficulties." Nonetheless, and even though the mobs destroyed the cameras of anyone they noticed taking pictures, images of the burning bus and the bleeding Freedom Riders got out and appeared on front pages around the world. The Riders now decided to fly to New Orleans, but found themselves trapped at the Birmingham airport by bomb threats. RFK's personal representative rushed from Washington and arranged for them to take an unannounced flight.[77]

Newspapers declared the Freedom Rides over, but SNCC decided otherwise, sending a group of SNCC activists on a bus from Nashville to Birmingham. A mob met them at the terminal, and the Birmingham police commissioner, Eugene "Bull" Connor, had them arrested without charge (he claimed to be taking them into "protective custody"). After two nights in jail, during which the students fasted, the CBS network broadcast Smith's prime-time special *Who Speaks for Birmingham?* The program closed with his riot coverage. An hour and a half after the broadcast ended, in the middle of the night, Connor and his men ordered the Riders out of their cells and into unmarked cars, drove them to the Tennessee border, and dumped them on the side of the road. After reinforcements arrived from Nashville, the Riders snuck back into Birmingham. They again reached the bus terminal, where they were again trapped by a mob. Robert Kennedy threatened to send U.S. army troops to restore order unless the governor of Alabama provided the Riders with state police protection. The governor reluctantly did so on the next leg of the Riders' journey, to Montgomery, where city police were supposed to take over. Instead, Montgomery police allowed yet another mob to attack the Riders, as well as reporters and RFK's assistant, who was beaten unconscious. Once again, pictures of the bloody mayhem became big news, both on the front pages of newspapers and on television.[78]

A furious RFK ordered federal marshals to protect the Riders, while King rushed to Montgomery to hold a mass meeting on their behalf at a friend's church. That night, May 21, the church, with King and an audience of 1,500 inside, was surrounded by an angry white mob of many thousands, with only a couple of dozen federal marshals to keep them at bay. RFK, constantly on the phone with aides in Montgomery and with King, was about to ask his brother to mobilize the U.S. army when the governor, panicked by the unrest in his capital city, declared martial law and sent in the National Guard. RFK then negotiated with officials in Alabama and Mississippi to provide protection so the Rides could continue to Jackson, Mississippi, where by prearrangement all of the Riders were arrested (many spent over a month in a maximum security prison). At this point, RFK asked for a "cooling off period," but instead SNCC and CORE launched more rides, many of which were violently attacked. Finally, in September, owing to RFK's relentless lobbying, the ICC ordered immediate integration of interstate travel. Yet the Kennedys were reluctant to take further steps against segregation, having seen how politically explosive the issue was. Significantly, it seems that few, if any, of the Klan members who attacked the Riders spent more than a few days in jail.[79]

The crisis produced by the Rides influenced King's thinking about civil disobedience. He still viewed it primarily as a form of religious witness and personal sacrifice, but as he explained in a letter in October 1961, "Public relations is a very necessary part of any protest of civil disobedience. The main objective is to bring moral pressure to bear upon an unjust system or a particularly unjust law. . . . In effect, in the absence of justice in the established courts of the region, nonviolent protesters are asking for a hearing in the court of world opinion."[80]

King struggled, however, with how to apply this lesson. In 1961 and 1962, the SCLC concentrated its efforts on a desegregation campaign in the small city of Albany, Georgia. SNCC had instigated the Albany Movement, as the broad coalition of local black groups was called, in November 1961, aiming to get the new ICC desegregation order enforced in the airport, train station, and bus terminal, then to integrate buses, businesses, and public facilities, such as parks and the library. The Movement launched boycotts of buses and downtown stores and developed a new tactic: mass marches leading to mass arrests. The aim was to "fill the jails." With no place to put arrested demonstrators, local officials would have to negotiate. The Movement invited the SCLC to join them, and it did. King himself tried to excite national interest in Albany by getting himself arrested there three times. Yet Albany had no active KKK chapter to incite violence, and Albany officials took care to befriend northern reporters and deescalate tensions the Movement sought to create. The police chief had his men behave professionally and sent prisoners to surrounding towns, so the jails would not fill. In June 1962, when an Albany court convicted King of marching without a permit and King refused to pay bail, the mayor secretly arranged to have him bailed out within hours. Despite the efforts of SNCC and the SCLC, the Albany campaign never generated a sense of national crisis.[81]

Other civil rights matters did generate headlines. When the University of Mississippi, after years of resistance, admitted its first black student in June 1962, the Kennedy administration was forced to send in thousands of troops to stop a massive, armed white riot. But the failure in Albany was seen by King and others at the SCLC as a major setback. They decided they must, for the first time, instigate their own mass civil disobedience campaign in a place of their own choosing. In January 1963 they picked Birmingham, where SCLC minister Fred Shuttlesworth had already laid the groundwork through effective organizing.[82]

The leaders of the SCLC thought a victory in Birmingham would resonate nationally. Alabama had just elected George Wallace as governor, who in his inaugural address would declare, "I draw the line in the dust and toss the gauntlet before the feet of tyranny . . . and I say . . . segregation now . . . segregation tomorrow . . . segregation forever."[83] Birmingham, meanwhile, had received national press attention as a bastion of violent segregationism. Long and highly critical profiles of the city had appeared in the *New York Times* and *Time* magazine, even before the Freedom Ride riots had cemented its reputation. The local KKK subjected blacks to beatings, shootings, even (in one case) castration, and they resorted so often to dynamite that they won for the city the nickname "Bombingham." Shuttlesworth himself had barely escaped being blown up (he had been trapped in the ruins of his parsonage), and his church had been bombed three times.[84]

The intransigence of many Birmingham whites was embodied in its city police commissioner, "Bull" Connor. A former sportscaster who was first elected commissioner in 1937, he had made a name for himself shortly afterward by having his men challenge First Lady Eleanor Roosevelt for sitting in the black seats at a conference in his city.[85] Local business leaders tolerated his antics because he was an effective union buster, until revelations of personal and departmental "incompetence, moral turpitude, and corruption" forced him from office in 1952. Yet the *Brown* ruling, coupled with a municipal decision to consider hiring black patrolmen for black neighborhoods, produced a white backlash that Connor had been able to ride back to power. Reelected commissioner in 1957 (by a razor-thin margin) and again in 1961 (by a landslide), he had his officers harass civil rights activists, and he cooperated closely with the Klan. Everyone suspected, correctly, that he was responsible for the bloody Freedom Rides riot; in fact, he had passed word to his KKK friends beforehand that when the Riders' bus reached the terminal, the Klan would have fifteen minutes to do whatever it wanted before the police showed up. Leaders of the SCLC worried about the violence Connor might inflict on demonstrators, but decided he made a "perfect adversary" because "he wanted his name in the paper" and could be provoked into the kind of dramatic confrontation civil rights activists never got in Albany.[86]

King launched the Birmingham campaign in April 1963 with the goal of desegregating facilities and employment downtown. Yet local black enthusiasm for the campaign was low, because Connor appeared finally on the way out. White business leaders, anxious to persuade outside industries to relocate to their "Magic City," had grown embarrassed, especially after the Freedom Rides, that Connor was now the symbol of Birmingham to the world.[87] Because Connor had been reelected in 1961, businessmen launched a referendum campaign to replace the city commission with a mayor-council system, which would eliminate Connor's job. Their effort gained traction only weeks before the vote when a federal court ordered the integration of municipal parks. Businessmen proposed a plan of gradual compliance, but Connor and the commission denounced them as race traitors and closed the parks instead. This move satisfied the KKK but upset many of Connor's working-class constituents, whose children now had no playgrounds. They joined wealthier whites, who had been voting against Connor for a decade, and a small but united black electorate to make a majority, which approved the new charter in November 1962, and five months later defeated Connor's bid to be the first mayor. Connor remained in charge of the police—he insisted that the commissioners were legally entitled to serve out their terms, and the matter was being adjudicated in court—but many Birmingham blacks adopted a hopeful wait-and-see attitude. They regarded King's demonstrations, which started the day after Connor's mayoral defeat, as badly timed.[88]

The SCLC struggled for weeks without the Birmingham campaign catching fire. The press paid little attention; even the local newspapers kept the demonstrations off their front pages. The planned mass marches and civil disobedience sputtered, as few blacks volunteered to be arrested. When a state judge issued an injunction against the marches, King decided to defy it and seek jail, but his imprisonment generated little political reaction.* The tide turned only when the SCLC began recruiting black children. Thousands of children, mostly teens but some as young as six, responded to the SCLC call to leave school and go to jail for freedom. The first children's march took place on May 2. By nightfall 600 were in custody, packing the city jail. The following day Connor, unable to make further arrests and struggling to keep the marchers out of downtown, unleashed police dogs and water cannons on them. Appalled, local black leaders united behind King for the first time, while pictures of children being mauled and blasted appeared on television and on newspaper front pages around the world. President Kennedy told a group of White House visitors that the images made him "sick."[89]

The demonstrations did not let up. On May 6 young protesters snuck around Connor's men and made their way downtown, staging a mass sidewalk sit-in. White business leaders had to step over singing protestors to get to their offices. After round-the-clock negotiations with Robert Kennedy, local black leaders, and the SCLC, Birmingham business leaders announced a tentative desegregation agreement on May 7. President Kennedy immediately called a press conference and endorsed the plan. When a Birmingham judge tried to scuttle the deal by jailing King, again for parading without a permit, RFK rushed to get him bailed out. King refused to cooperate, however, until all of the children were bailed out as well, which would require $160,000. As the banks were closed for the weekend, RFK's men scrambled to collect the money in cash—mostly from organized labor—and then wire it to Birmingham. King emerged from jail in triumph, and he and Shuttlesworth (who had also been arrested) publicly agreed to the desegregation deal on Sunday, May 10. Ruling on the separate dispute over Birmingham's new city charter nearly two weeks later, the Alabama Supreme Court declared that the old city commissioners had to vacate their offices, which meant that Connor's reign as police commissioner was officially over.[90]

---

* While King was locked up, held in solitary, without a mattress or razor, anti-Connor white Birmingham clergy published a letter criticizing his protest as inopportune. In response King wrote his celebrated "Letter from Birmingham Jail," in which he passionately explained "why we can't wait." See King, *Why We Can't Wait* (New York: Harper and Row, 1964). Although King's letter did not immediately influence conditions on the ground in Birmingham, it would ultimately gain a large audience and prove highly influential.

In the meantime, however, on May 11, the Birmingham Klan bombed both the church of King's brother, Birmingham minister A. D. King, and the black motel that the SCLC had used as its headquarters. In response, local blacks rioted. Just as A. D. King and others were calming the situation, Alabama state troopers under the command of Al Lingo arrived and began beating any blacks they encountered. In August and September, the Klan bombed the homes of black community leaders; on September 15 it bombed a black church, killing four girls, a crime that shocked the nation. Amid this tumult, Birmingham desegregated only slowly. It would not hire a black police officer until 1966.[91]

Although Birmingham was not desegregated overnight, the protests there in April and May 1963—along with the violent reaction from law enforcement—deeply affected national public sentiment. From mid-May through July 1963, there were "758 racial demonstrations producing 14,733 arrests in 186 American cities."[92] Around this time a national survey of black Americans found that half said they were personally willing to sit in, march, or even go to jail in a civil rights protest, while nearly two-thirds said they were willing to boycott a segregated store.[93] King announced during this period that the SCLC was considering a march on Washington, and on June 11 President Kennedy pledged in a nationally televised address that he would propose a new civil rights law, targeting segregation:

> Are we to say to the world—and much more importantly, to each other— that this is the land of the free, except for Negroes, that we have no second-class citizens, except Negroes, that we have no class or caste system, no ghettoes, no master race, except with respect to Negroes? . . . The events in Birmingham and elsewhere have so increased the cries for equality that no city or state or legislative body can prudently choose to ignore them. . . . We face, therefore, a moral crisis as a country and as a people.[94]

The SCLC's planned march on Washington now became a march for the civil rights bill. On August 28, 1963, 250,000 gathered at the Lincoln Memorial and heard King's "I Have a Dream" speech, which was televised nationally. The following January, *Time* magazine named King its Man of the Year.[95]

Despite this newfound momentum for a civil rights law, opponents in the U.S. House of Representatives bottled up the bill in committee until tragedy rocked the nation on November 22, 1963: the assassination of President

Kennedy. Civil rights leaders, including King, did not know what to expect from Lyndon Johnson, the Texan who now occupied the Oval Office. As Senate majority leader, he had shepherded the Civil Rights Act of 1957 through Congress, but by 1963 that law seemed hopelessly weak. Upon becoming president, however, Johnson announced that Congress must enact the slain president's proposed civil rights bill as a tribute to his memory. He then used all his powers of personal persuasion and political maneuvering, which turned out to be formidable, to push the bill over one legislative hurdle after another, including a fifty-seven-day Senate filibuster by southern Democrats and some Republicans. King was invited to the White House to watch President Johnson sign the bill into law on July 2, 1964.[96]

King's leadership of the civil rights movement would result in his being awarded the Nobel Peace Prize that fall. But he had little chance to celebrate, because the movement was increasingly wracked by an issue the Civil Rights Act did little to address—voting rights.

The Campaign for Voting Rights

The civil rights movement had never ignored disenfranchisement. One of the SCLC's first initiatives, in 1957, had been a drive to register millions of voters, although it proved unsuccessful. The Civil Rights Commission, created that same year to investigate voting rights abuses, had held nationally televised hearings in Alabama in 1958 that showed a parade of black witnesses, all property owners and taxpayers, among them decorated veterans and college graduates, whose registration applications had been denied for unspecified reasons. Meanwhile, at the Justice Department, John Doar, a white Minnesotan whom the Eisenhower administration had made second in command at the new Civil Rights Division despite his lack of experience with the issue, had decided on his own initiative to travel through the South investigating voting rights abuses. His first trip, in the summer of 1960, had been to rural Tennessee to check out a complaint that a black tenant farmer had been evicted for trying to register. At a clapboard church he had introduced himself to the black congregation and asked if anyone there had received eviction notices. To his shock, nearly every hand went up. He soon indicted fifty white landlords for conspiring to violate black voting rights.[97]

TABLE 16.2

Percentage of Adult Population in the South Registered to Vote, by State

	Black Registered Voters as Percent of Black Voting Age Population, 1962	Black Registered Voters as Percent of Black Voting Age Population, March 1965	White Registered Voters as Percent of White Voting Age Population, March 1965
Alabama	13.4	19.3	69.2
Arkansas	34.0	40.4	n.a.
Florida	36.8	51.2	n.a.
Georgia	n.a.	27.4	62.6
Louisiana	27.8	31.6	80.5
Mississippi	5.3	6.7	69.9
North Carolina	35.8	46.8	96.8
South Carolina	22.9	37.3	75.7
Tennessee	49.8	69.4	n.a.
Texas	26.7	57.7	n.a.
Virginia	24.0	38.3	61.1

Source: Adapted from Steven F. Lawson, *Black Ballots: Voting Rights in the South, 1944–1969* (Lanham, MD: Lexington Books, 1999), Table 2 (p. 284); Bernard Grofman, Lisa Handley, and Richard G. Niemi, *Minority Representation and the Quest for Voting Equality* (New York: Cambridge University Press, 1992), Table 1 (p. 23).

Doar had been held over by the Kennedy administration, which gave him much more to do. When he arrived at the department, it had only three pending voting rights cases; under Robert Kennedy the department worked to launch at least one prosecution in every federal court district in the South.[98] The administration also sought to make a ban on poll taxes in federal elections part of the U.S. Constitution, which was not an especially controversial proposal, given that only four states still had these taxes. The ban was approved by Congress as the Twenty-Fourth Amendment in 1962 and ratified by the states in 1964. The administration worked as well to increase the number of black applicants for registration by launching the Voter Education Project (VEP). In the summer of 1961 the administration persuaded major private philanthropies to fund VEP and the leading civil rights groups, including SCLC, NAACP, CORE, and SNCC, to participate. The combination of Kennedy administration initiatives appears to have contributed to an increase of over 500,000 southern black voters between 1962 and 1964, although the numbers varied widely by state, and black registration still lagged notably behind white registration across the South.[99]

SNCC had joined the VEP only after internal debate. Many of the young activists believed the Kennedys were promoting it simply as a way to divert the movement from its highly visible fight against segregation. Sit-ins and Freedom Rides produced crises that attracted national attention, whereas the voting issue seemed to involve only tedious litigation and "laborious door-to-door canvassing and . . . [the establishment of] citizenship schools."[100] Nevertheless, Ella Baker, now a SNCC adviser, argued that fighting disenfranchisement would prove just as explosive as fighting Jim Crow. At her suggestion, SNCC split into two parts, one focused on segregation, the other on voting rights.[101]

One SNCC activist who took the voting rights cause to heart was Bob Moses, a soft-spoken, bespectacled black New Yorker with an MA in philosophy from Harvard. He believed that real social change was produced not by charismatic leaders like King, but by grassroots empowerment, of which voter registration could be a part. In 1961 he started a voting rights movement in rural Mississippi, which had the lowest rates of black voter registration in the country. Over the next two years, movement members were beaten, shot, and arrested, their meeting places were ransacked and burned, and one local black supporter was shot dead by a member of the Mississippi legislature, who was never prosecuted. Officials of two counties tried to quash local black interest in the movement by stopping distribution of federal food aid, on which the sharecroppers depended, for an entire winter. Each attack, however, seemed to gall a few more sharecroppers into trying to register, and Mississippi activists discovered that they could blend techniques of mass protest with voter drives by organizing marches of applicants to registration offices. Eventually the movement attracted press attention—in September 1962, CBS aired a special full-hour report, "Mississippi and the Fifteenth Amendment"—but it produced few new voters, because registrars continued to reject most applications from black citizens.[102]

In October 1963, Mississippi activists organized an alternative to the gubernatorial election then taking place. They nominated their own integrated ticket and printed provisional "Freedom Ballots" so that disenfranchised people could vote for it. They also recruited outside volunteers, mostly white college students from the North, to distribute the ballots door to door to black households. In November, more than 80,000 Freedom Ballots were cast; at the time there were only 24,000 registered black voters in the state. The students, meanwhile, returned to their campuses with reports of confronting violent harassment, which only seemed to excite the interest of more students in going south.[103]

They got their chance the following year, when Moses helped launch both the Mississippi Freedom Democratic Party (MFDP) and the Freedom Summer project. Northern college students, mostly white, joined local blacks to start voter-training schools and registration drives and to build support for the MFDP, which elected its own pro-Johnson delegation to the national Democratic convention, meeting in Atlantic City in August. Over the summer, a thousand voting rights activists were arrested, eighty were beaten, and nearly seventy black churches, homes, and businesses were burned or bombed. In early June three activists, two white northerners and a local black volunteer, vanished. Press flooded into the state, and President Johnson cajoled a reluctant FBI into investigating. Agents found the bodies in August, and eventually Klansmen confessed to the killings.[104]

Meanwhile, the integrated MFDP delegation arrived in Atlantic City, as did King, asking that they be seated instead of the all-white regular Mississippi delegation, whose members had not pledged support for Johnson owing to his stand on civil rights. Johnson, however, feared that seating the MFDP would exacerbate an emerging white backlash. In the spring George Wallace had launched a symbolic quest for the Democratic Party nomination and stunned observers by winning over a third of the vote in the primaries of Wisconsin, Indiana, and Maryland. At the same time, southern Democrats were defecting in large numbers and taking control of state Republican organizations. At the Republican national convention in July there had been no black delegates from the South for the first time since Reconstruction, and the presidential nominee was Senator Barry Goldwater of Arizona, one of a minority of congressional Republicans to vote against the Civil Rights Act of 1964.[105] In light of these developments, Johnson tried to impose a compromise on Mississippi, seating the regular delegates if they pledged to vote for him, choosing two MFDP members as at-large delegates, and promising that no segregated delegation would be seated in the future. The proposal infuriated southern Democrats; Mississippi delegates and most Alabama delegates walked out. But the MFDP rejected the compromise and walked out, too. "We're not here to bring politics to our morality," Moses declared, "but morality to our politics."[106] The convention nominated Johnson by acclamation. In November, Johnson lost five southern states that had not voted Republican since Reconstruction, among them Mississippi and Alabama, but won 61 percent of the national popular vote and 96 percent of the national black vote. Democrats also won lopsided majorities in Congress (68 to 32 in the Senate, 295 to 140 in the House).[107]

Although King had endorsed Johnson (and the SCLC had suspended protests during the fall campaign), the standoff in Atlantic City had proved painful for the civil rights leader. Torn between his alliance with the president and his loyalty to the activists, King had declined to back either Johnson's compromise proposal or the MFDP's rejection of it.[108] Nevertheless, the episode helped raise the profile of voting rights as an issue, and immediately after the election King announced a new campaign against disenfranchisement.

The SCLC decided to launch its battle for voting rights in Selma, which was the seat of Dallas County in Alabama. There were 15,000 blacks of voting age in Dallas County, a majority of the adult population, but fewer than 200 registered black voters. The local White Citizen's Council, closely affiliated to the city Democratic machine, effectively controlled city politics. There was an active KKK "klavern" in the area, and the county sheriff, Jim Clark, who liked to wear quasi-military uniforms and a lapel button stating his views on integration—"NEVER"—was known for his quick, violent temper. Yet white Selma seemed to be changing. The town had become economically dependent on Craig Air Force Base, which was integrated, and in early 1964 a young anti-machine candidate—an avowed segregationist but committed to modernization and economic development—had been elected mayor. One of his first acts had been to take city law enforcement out of Sheriff Clark's hands by creating a new office of Public Safety Director and giving the job to Wilson Baker, who considered Clark a disgrace to law enforcement.[109] Clark retained control, however, at the county level.

The black community in Selma had a long-established voting rights movement, with its own organization, the Dallas County Voters League (DCVL).[110] In late 1962 the DCVL had invited SNCC to begin a VEP-funded voting rights campaign in Selma, which increased the number of black applications for registration from three a month in January 1963 to 215 in

October, yet registrars rejected the overwhelming majority of them (all but 11 of the 215). SNCC also organized sit-ins (mostly by high school students), regular mass meetings at Brown Chapel, and marches to the registration office at the county courthouse, resulting in mass arrests. Then, in July 1964, a state judge named James Hare issued an injunction banning civil rights groups from holding marches and public meetings. With the SNCC campaign stalled, the DCVL asked King to bring the SCLC to Selma, which he did in January 1965.[111]

The movement in Selma soon took off, with mass meetings, mass marches to the county courthouse, protest marches in surrounding towns, and hundreds of arrests. King himself was jailed for three days. On February 4, while King was locked up, a federal judge, Daniel Thomas, ordered county registrars to let all applicants sign up for appointments in a book, to process at least a hundred applicants every day their office was open, and stop administering a citizenship test that in practice had been used to screen out black applicants. This order conceivably could have allowed all black residents of Selma who wanted to register to do so within a year, but the SCLC decided to boycott the appointment book and keep protesting. King thought the new registration process would be too slow and wanted to keep up political pressure for comprehensive federal voting rights reform.[112]

Although Baker, the public safety director in Selma, tried to ease tensions where possible, Sheriff Clark continually frustrated these efforts. Baker, for example, allowed protesters to march unmolested through the streets of Selma, refusing to enforce Judge Hare's injunction on the grounds that it was being appealed in federal court. When the marchers got to the county courthouse, however, which was Clark's domain, the sheriff and his men beat and arrested them. Clark also helped break up the February 18 march in which Jimmie Lee Jackson was shot, and he played a key role in orchestrating the assault on protesters at the Pettus Bridge on March 7.[113] Clark's brutality had outraged King's supporters, alarmed President Johnson, and brought national media attention to the voting rights issue. Now, on March 9, as King led marchers back to the Pettus Bridge, he had to decide whether to try to turn the march around before crossing, or to try to cross the bridge as his supporters fervently expected and wanted, but against President Johnson's wishes and in violation, for the first time in his career, of a federal court order. With much at stake, the time for a decision was upon him.

NOTES

1. This account—including the remainder of this introduction—is based on Charles E. Fager, *Selma: The March That Changed the South,* 2nd ed. (Boston: Beacon Press, 1985), 73–86, 92–105 (orig. pub. 1974); David J. Garrow, *Bearing the Cross: Martin Luther King, Jr., and the Southern Christian Leadership Conference* (New York: Vintage, 1988), 397–405; Taylor Branch, *Pillar of Fire: America in the King Years, 1963–65* (New York: Simon and Schuster, 1998), 592–594, 597–599; Taylor Branch, *At Canaan's Edge: America in the King Years, 1965–68* (New York: Simon and Schuster, 2006), 8–9, 24–25, 38–39, 44–78. For a map of Selma in 1965, see J. Mills Thornton III, *Dividing Lines: Municipal Politics and the Struggle for Civil Rights in Montgomery, Birmingham, and Selma* (Tuscaloosa: University of Alabama Press, 2002), 381.

2. Quoted in Fager, *Selma,* 98.

3. Quoted in Garrow, *Bearing the Cross,* 402.

4. Quoted in ibid., 403.

5. Fager, *Selma,* 103. The song started with the chorus, "Ain't gonna let nobody turn me 'round / Turn me 'round, turn me 'round / Ain't gonna let nobody turn me 'round / I'm gonna keep on a-walkin', keep on a-talkin' / marchin' down to freedom's land." As singers added choruses, they would improvise, substituting words for "nobody," such as "segregation," or "injustice," or "George Wallace." Branch, however, suggests that this song was sung at a later point in the march (*At Canaan's Edge,* 78).

6. Eric Foner, *Reconstruction: America's Unfinished Revolution, 1863–1877* (New York: Harper Perennial, 2014), 279.

7. Alexander Keyssar, *The Right to Vote: The Contested History of Democracy in the United States,* rev. ed. (New York: Basic Books, 2009), 44–47, 315–320. The eight states that outlawed black voting were Delaware, Kentucky, Maryland, Ohio, New Jersey, Connecticut, Tennessee, and Pennsylvania. New York, meanwhile, starting in 1821, established various special, discriminatory suffrage requirements to discourage black voting, among them high property qualifications. An exception to this pattern was Rhode Island, which gave black men the vote in 1842 as part of the sweeping expansion of suffrage associated with the popular uprising known as "Dorr's Rebellion." Before this, black men in Rhode Island had not been specifically excluded from voting, but had effectively been excluded, along with most white men, by high property requirements for suffrage. Blacks were allowed to vote in some school committee elections in Michigan starting in 1855; and in Ohio, two 1842 court rulings that legal restrictions on "Negroes" did not apply to "mulattoes" allowed mixed-race men to vote there until 1859, when the state legislature took away voting rights from anyone who showed "a distinct and visible admixture of African blood." See Paul Finkelman, "Prelude to the Fourteenth Amendment: Black Legal Rights in the Antebellum North," *Rutgers Law Journal* 7 (1985–1986): 424, 424–426n54, 425, table 2; Keyssar, *Right to Vote,* 317.

8. Eric Foner, *Free Soil, Free Labor, Free Men: The Ideology of the Republican Party before the Civil War* (New York: Oxford University Press, 1970), 281–288; Xi Wang, *The Trial of Democracy: Black Suffrage and Northern Republicans, 1860–1910* (Athens: University of Georgia Press, 2012), 5–6, 22; Foner, *Reconstruction*, 315.

9. Foner, *Reconstruction*, 318, 352–359.

10. Peter Kolchin, *First Freedom: The Responses of Alabama's Blacks to Emancipation and Reconstruction* (Westport, CT: Greenwood Press, 1972); Foner, *Reconstruction*, 7–10, 79, 80, 88–102.

11. 16 Stat 140 (1870), §1; 17 Stat 13 (1871), §2.

12. Keyssar, *Right to Vote*, 85.

13. Michael Perman, *Struggle for Mastery: Disfranchisement in the South, 1888–1908* (Chapel Hill: University of North Carolina Press, 2001), 18–19, 45–46, 11, 14. On the shifting meaning of "Black Belt," see Booker T. Washington, *Up from Slavery: An Autobiography* (Garden City, NY: Doubleday, 1901), 108.

14. On the shift in the Alabama Black Belt from Republican to Democrat, see Joseph H. Taylor, "Populism and Disfranchisement in Alabama," *Journal of Negro History* 34, no. 4 (1949): 413.

15. Keyssar, *Right to Vote*, 85, 96.

16. Ibid., 96–97, quotation at 97.

17. Perman, *Struggle for Mastery*, 46–47, quotation at 47. On voting restrictions outside the South, see also Keyssar, *Right to Vote*, 102–128.

18. Roger L. Ransom and Richard Sutch, "*One Kind of Freedom* Reconsidered (and Turbo Charged)," *Explorations in Economic History* 38 (2001): 6–39; Matthew J. Mancini, *One Dies, Get Another: Convict Leasing in the American South, 1866–1928* (Columbia: University of South Carolina Press, 1996), quotation at 1.

19. Douglas A. Blackmon, *Slavery by Another Name* (New York: Anchor Books, 2008); Jessie Carney Smith and Carrell Horton, eds., *Historical Statistics of Black America: Media to Vital Statistics* (Detroit: Gale Research, 1995), 1:493–494 (table 554).

20. On "lily-white" juries in the South resulting from the "virtually total" exclusion of blacks from juries, and how this exclusion was a key part of a "structure of lawful and lawless racism," see Benno C. Schmidt Jr., "Juries, Jurisdiction, and Race Discrimination: The Lost Promise of *Strauder v. West Virginia*," *Texas Law Review* 61, no. 8 (May 1983): 1406–1412. On the lack of prosecution for lynching of blacks, even in the mid-twentieth century, see Gunnar Myrdal's classic study, *An American Dilemma: The Negro Problem and Modern Democracy* (New Brunswick, NJ: Transaction, 1996 [1944]), esp. 2:562: "Lynchers are seldom indicted by a grand jury. Even more seldom are they sentenced, since the judge, the prosecutor, the jurors, and the witnesses are either in sympathy with the lynchers or do not want to press the case."

21. Perman, *Struggle for Mastery*, 15, 186. In sources from this period the older term "disfranchisement" was always used, but we use the more modern term "disenfranchisement" throughout the case, except in quotations.

22. The problem was succinctly stated in a *New York Times* headline regarding the Alabama convention: "Alabama's Negro Vote: Difficult Task Set Before the Constitutional Convention. Demand That White Supremacy Be Assured Is Attended by the Danger of Nullification." Quoted in R. Volney Riser, *Defying Disfranchisement: Black Voting Rights Activism in the Jim Crow South, 1890–1908* (Baton Rouge: LSU Press, 2010), 114.

23. Perman, *Struggle for Mastery,* 54.

24. Riser, *Defying Disfranchisement,* 78–79; *Guinn v. United States,* 238 U.S. 347 (1915). Grandfather clauses could have unintended effects. After Alabama instituted one, poor white voters turned out to be reluctant to take advantage of it, because they saw doing so as a humiliating admission of ignorance and poverty. See Riser, *Defying Disfranchisement,* 143, 149.

25. Riser, *Defying Disfranchisement,* 146.

26. *Giles v. Harris,* 189 US 475 (1903), 484–488; Riser, *Defying Disfranchisement,* 150, 1–2.

27. Perman, *Struggle for Mastery,* 298, 147, 193, 313, 33–35; Steven F. Lawson, *Black Ballots: Voting Rights in the South, 1944–1969* (Lanham, MD: Lexington Books, 1999), 14–15; Smith and Horton, *Historical Statistics of Black America,* 2:1293–1294 (table 1541).

28. Perman, *Struggle for Mastery,* 299–303, 307. The U.S. Supreme Court ruled in *Newberry v. United States,* 256 U.S. 232 (1921), that primaries were not part of the electoral process covered by the Fifteenth Amendment. Although *Newberry* did not directly concern the constitutionality of the white primary, civil rights activists came to recognize it as a ruling that had to be reversed before the white primary could be successfully challenged. See Lawson, *Black Ballots,* 40.

29. Perman, *Struggle for Mastery,* 245–246.

30. August Meier and Elliot Rudwick, "The Boycott Movement against Jim Crow Streetcars in the South, 1900–1906," in Meier and Rudwick, *Along the Color Line: Explorations in the Black Experience* (Urbana: University of Illinois Press, 1976), 267–289.

31. 163 U.S. 537 (1896), 551, 552.

32. Thornton, *Dividing Lines,* 44, 57–58.

33. See Smith and Horton, *Historical Statistics of Black America,* 2:1509, 1589–1590 (tables 1725, 1800).

34. Thornton, *Dividing Lines,* 384, 385; Blackmon, *Slavery by Another Name,* 377–382; Smith and Horton, *Historical Statistics of Black America,* 1:493–495 (table 554). The illiteracy rate among blacks in the South fell from 33.3 percent to 19.7 percent between 1910 and 1930 (Smith and Horton, *Historical Statistics of Black America,* 685 [table 811]). Martin Luther King Jr.'s father, the senior MLK, exemplified the educational opportunities afforded by urbanization. The son of sharecroppers, he moved from rural Georgia to Atlanta as a semiliterate teenager around 1915. Once there, he worked his way through high school, attended college, and in 1931 became pastor of one of the largest black churches in the city. See Taylor Branch, *Parting the Waters: America in the King Years, 1954–63* (New York: Simon and Schuster, 1988), 34–38.

35. White quoted in Eric Anderson, *Race and Politics in North Carolina, 1872–1901: The Black Second* (Baton Rouge: LSU Press, 1981), 308.

36. Isabel Wilkerson, *The Warmth of Other Suns: The Epic Story of America's Great Migration* (New York: Random House, 2010), 160–161, 217–218, 556n9; Smith and Horton, *Historical Statistics of Black America,* 2:1509–1510, table 1726.

37. On this episode, see Allida M. Black, "Championing a Champion: Eleanor Roosevelt and the Marian Anderson 'Freedom Concert,'" *Presidential Studies Quarterly* 20, no. 4 (1990): 719–736.

38. Democratic Platform, 1948. Available online at http://www.presidency.ucsb.edu/ws /?pid=29599.

39. Sasha Torres, "'In a Crisis, We Must Have a Sense of Drama': Civil Rights and Televisual Information," in *Channeling Blackness: Studies on Television and Race in America,* ed. Darnell M. Hunt (New York: Oxford University Press, 2005), 245.

40. Truman won a larger percentage of the black vote than Franklin Roosevelt ever had, and black votes seem to have provided his margin of victory in Ohio, Illinois, and California, which gave him his Electoral College majority. See Howard Sitkoff, "Harry Truman and the Election of 1948: The Coming of Age of Civil Rights in American Politics," *Journal of Southern History* 37, no. 4 (1971): 613.

41. Keyssar, *Right to Vote,* 182–183, quotation at 196.

42. Quoted in Langston Hughes, *Fight for Freedom and Other Writings on Civil Rights,* in *The Collected Works of Langston Hughes,* ed. Arnold Rampersad, vol. 10 (Columbia: University of Missouri Press, 2001), 41.

43. By the end of 1919 there were 310 NAACP branches with a total membership of 91,203 (42,588 in the South). Nine-tenths of the members were black. See Charles Flint Kellogg, *NAACP: A History of the National Association for the Advancement of Colored People,* vol. 1, *1909–1920* (Baltimore: Johns Hopkins University Press, 1967), 137. See also, Stephen Weinberger, "*The Birth of a Nation* and the Making of the NAACP," *Journal of American Studies* 45, no. 1 (2011), 77–93.

44. *Smith v. Allwright,* 321 U.S. 649 (1944); Lawson, *Black Ballots,* 124–139.

45. 347 U.S. 483 (1954), 495; "High Court Bans School Segregation; 9-to-0 Decision Grants Time to Comply," *New York Times,* 18 May 1954, 1.

46. Thornton, *Dividing Lines,* 29, 33, 53–54. On the founding of the NAACP branch, see http://naacp-al.org/.

47. Thornton, *Dividing Lines,* 37–39, 52. Business leaders were concerned that between 1953 and 1955, five large national corporations, including DuPont, had decided against building factories in Montgomery.

48. Ibid., 41–45.

49. Ibid., 57–62.

50. The unsuccessful black boycott against the introduction of Jim Crow streetcars in Montgomery itself in 1900–1902 seems to have been forgotten. See ibid., 57, 42–43; Branch, *Parting the Waters,* 145.

51. Thornton, *Dividing Lines,* 62–63; Garrow, *Bearing the Cross,* 17–18, 24–26; Branch, *Parting the Waters,* 137–138.

52. Branch, *Parting the Waters,* 166, 143, 189, 204–205, quotation at 149.

53. In 1915 a new Klan had been created in response to *Birth of a Nation,* the first Hollywood feature film and one of the most popular movies in history, which had portrayed the Reconstruction-era Klan as heroic. This new Klan flourished in the 1920s, mostly outside the South, with millions of members, its concerns more with immigrants and feminists than with blacks, before it declined in the wake of financial and ethical scandals involving its leaders. It had lingered on in the South, however, and revived during the civil rights era. See Wyn Craig Wade, *The Fiery Cross: The Ku Klux Klan in America* (New York: Simon and Schuster, 1987).

54. Thornton, *Dividing Lines,* 73, quotations at 97, 402, 403.

55. Ibid., 64–65, 72–77; Branch, *Parting the Waters,* 155–163. The boycotters initially also demanded that white drivers treat black passengers courteously, but the city government responded by denying that white drivers had ever been discourteous to blacks, "except in the rarest instances" (Thornton, *Dividing Lines,* 65).

56. The Supreme Court would rule in 1958 that Alabama had violated the constitutional rights of its citizens by its actions against the NAACP, but the state of Alabama refused to back down, and the issue would not be resolved until a second Supreme Court ruling in 1964. Branch, *Parting the Waters,* 186–187. See also *NAACP v. Alabama,* 357 U.S. 449 (1958) and *NAACP v. Alabama,* 377 U.S. 288 (1964).

57. Branch, *Parting the Waters,* 168. The two Democratic senators from Alabama denounced the Selective Service Office's "political" intervention in Gray's case and demanded a congressional investigation (ibid., 192n).

58. Ibid., 163–168, 173–174, 185; Thornton, 81–83, 88–89; Garrow, *Bearing the Cross,* quotation at 64. For the *New York Times* coverage, see, for example, the following: "Buses Boycotted over Race Issue," 5 Dec. 1955, 31; "Bus Boycott Continues," 10 Dec. 1955, 13; "Negro Bus Boycott Still On," 20 Dec. 1955, 33; "Alabama Indicts 115 in Negro Bus Boycott," 22 Feb. 1956, 1; "Negro Leaders Arrested in Alabama Bus Boycott," 23 Feb. 1956, 1; "Negroes Pledge to Keep Boycott," 24 Feb. 1956, 1.

59. Garrow, *Bearing the Cross,* 77–78, 80–82.

60. "The South: Attack on the Conscience," *Time,* 18 Feb. 1957, 19.

61. Branch, *Parting the Waters,* 225, 228–229, 231–232; Garrow, *Bearing the Cross,* 85–86, 90, 97, 102–104, 111; Martin Luther King Jr., *Stride towards Freedom: The Montgomery Story* (New York: Harper and Row, 1958).

62. Branch, *Parting the Waters,* 223.

63. Lawson, *Black Ballots,* 175–176.

64. A national Gallup poll, taken shortly after the 1957 Civil Rights Act was approved, found that 29 percent of adults surveyed thought segregation should be ended in the "near future," 45 percent thought it should be ended "gradually," and 19 percent said they opposed integration, with the balance expressing no opinion or not answering. See Gallup Poll #589, conducted 19–24 September 1957 (USAIPO1957-0589), question

29. The poll is available at https://ropercenter.cornell.edu/CFIDE/cf/action/catalog /abstract.cfm?archno=USAIPO1957-0589.

65. 71 Stat. 634. See Branch, *Parting the Waters*, 220–221; Lawson, *Black Ballots*, 140–202.

66. Thirty-seven percent responded "no," with the remainder expressing "no opinion" or not answering. See Gallup Poll #614, conducted 29 May to 3 June 1959 (USAIPO1959-0614), question 31A. The exact wording of the query was: "It's been five years now since the Supreme Court ruled on segregation in the schools. When you look at the record of what's happened since then, do you think this decision caused a lot more trouble than it was worth or not?" The poll is available at https:// ropercenter.cornell.edu/CFIDE/cf/action/catalog/abstract.cfm?archno=USAIPO 1959-0614.

67. Branch, *Parting the Waters*, 270–273.

68. Ibid., 272, 278–284; Thornton, *Dividing Lines*, 113–117.

69. Garrow, *Bearing the Cross*, 131–134, 143–145; Branch, *Parting the Waters*, 291–292, 350– 352, 356–358.

70. Garrow, *Bearing the Cross*, 142–143, 145–147; Branch, *Parting the Waters*, 359.

71. Lawson, *Black Ballots*, 141, 161–162, 251–257, 389n98; Garrow, *Bearing the Cross*, 118–119, 147–148; Branch, *Parting the Waters*, 343, 362–367.

72. Branch, *Parting the Waters*, 366–370, 373–378. See also Lawson, *Black Ballots*, 256: "An analysis of the returns demonstrated that Negro ballots were enough to give the Democratic contender a winning margin in New Jersey, Michigan, Illinois, Texas, and South Carolina, all states that had supported [Republican President Dwight] Eisenhower in 1956. Had the Republican–Democratic division in the black districts of these states broken down the same way as four years earlier, Richard Nixon would have become the thirty-fifth President."

73. Taylor Branch, *The King Years: Historic Moments in the Civil Rights Movement* (New York: Simon and Schuster, 2013), 24.

74. Branch, *Parting the Waters*, 408–411; Lawson, *Black Ballots*, 266–271, 273–274.

75. *Morgan v. Virginia*, 328 U.S. 373 (1946); *Boynton v. Virginia*, 364 U.S. 454 (1960); *Sarah Keys v. Carolina Coach Company*, 64 MCC 769 (1955); Branch, *Parting the Waters*, 417.

76. Branch, *Parting the Waters*, 412; Garrow, *Bearing the Cross*, quotation at 154–155.

77. Garrow, *Bearing the Cross*, 156; Branch, *Parting the Waters*, 417–424, 427–430; Raymond Arsenault, *Freedom Riders: 1961 and the Struggle for Racial Justice* (New York: Oxford University Press, 2006), 153, 159.

78. Branch, *Parting the Waters*, 430–432, 436–450; Arsenault, *Freedom Riders*, 137.

79. Branch, *Parting the Waters*, 451–478, 483–485; Arsenault, *Freedom Riders*, 164–173, 349– 358, 364, 422–423, 492.

80. Quoted in Garrow, *Bearing the Cross*, 172.

81. Ibid., 176, 180–188, 203–204; Branch, *Parting the Waters*, 524–558, 601–607.

82. Garrow, *Bearing the Cross*, 225–230; Branch, *Parting the Waters*, 647–671, 689–692. Shuttlesworth was still regarded as a leader in Birmingham even though in 1961 he had moved to become pastor of a church in Cincinnati, Ohio.

83. "Inaugural Address of Governor Wallace," http://digital.archives.alabama.gov/cdm /singleitem/collection/voices/id/2952/rec/5, p. 2. Ellipses in the original.

84. Thornton, *Dividing Lines,* 199–200, 221–222, 232–235; Branch, *Parting the Waters,* 198, 683.

85. Patricia Sullivan, ed., *Freedom Writer: Virginia Foster Durr, Letters from the Civil Rights Years* (Athens: University of Georgia Press, 2006), 11–12. Sullivan notes that when a "police officer informed the First Lady that she could not sit in the 'colored' section [because] it was against the law," Roosevelt "took her chair and placed it in the middle of the aisle separating the two groups" (11–12).

86. Thornton, *Dividing Lines,* 152–153, 179–184 (the charges against Connor, leading up to his initial departure in 1952, were serious even before investigators discovered, in 1954, that dozens of his officers had run a burglary ring), 201, 240–244, "incompetence" quotation at 181; Garrow, *Bearing the Cross,* quotation at 251.

87. In 1961 Sidney Smyer, the incoming president of the Birmingham Chamber of Commerce, was leading a business delegation to a Rotarian convention in Tokyo when photographs of the Freedom Ride riot in the Birmingham bus terminal appeared on front pages of Japanese newspapers. "Smyer found himself the object of cold stares and perplexed questions from his Japanese hosts and assembled international businessmen, who suddenly lost interest in Birmingham's climate of investment. Words failed Smyer and his Birmingham friends as they tried to explain that the incident was grossly unrepresentative of their city. . . . Smyer, though a stout segregationist and a Dixiecrat from 1948, told his Birmingham colleagues that something must be done about Bull Connor." Smyer became a leader of the effort to change the city charter to remove Connor from office. Branch, *Parting the Waters,* 425–426, 643–644.

88. Thornton, *Dividing Lines,* 251–259, 271–273, 285–286, 290, 297–299; Garrow, *Bearing the Cross,* 237–239.

89. Garrow, *Bearing the Cross,* 239–250; Branch, *Parting the Waters,* 756–764.

90. Branch, *Parting the Waters,* 774–791; Thornton, *Dividing Lines,* 332.

91. Branch, *Parting the Waters,* 793–796, 888–892; Thornton, *Dividing Lines,* 331–379.

92. Branch, *Parting the Waters,* 825.

93. Smith and Horton, *Historical Statistics of Black America,* 2:1260, table 1498.

94. Quoted in Branch, *Parting the Waters,* 824. Just minutes after Kennedy went off the air, an assassin shot and killed Medgar Evers, the director of the NAACP in Mississippi, outside his home.

95. Branch, *Parting the Waters,* 876–883; "America's Gandhi: Martin Luther King, Jr.," *Time,* 3 Jan. 1964.

96. 78 Stat. 241; Julian E. Zelizer, *The Fierce Urgency of Now: Lyndon Johnson, Congress, and the Battle for the Great Society* (New York: Penguin Press, 2015), 85–130; Taylor Branch, *Pillar of Fire: America in the King Years, 1963–1965* (New York: Simon and Schuster, 1998), 387–388.

97. Lawson, *Black Ballots*, 216–217, 415n4; Branch, *Parting the Waters*, 331–335.

98. Branch, *Parting the Waters*, 408–411; Lawson, *Black Ballots*, 266–271.

99. Keyssar, *Right to Vote*, 210; Lawson, *Black Ballots*, 261–265, 284 (table 2).

100. Lawson, *Black Ballots*, 261.

101. Barbara Ransby, *Ella Baker and the Black Freedom Movement: A Radical Democratic Vision* (Chapel Hill: University of North Carolina Press, 2003), 269–270.

102. Branch, *Parting the Waters*, 325–329, 486–487, 492–500, 503–504, 507–514, 518–523, 713–725; *Pillar of Fire*, 66–74, 351–352.

103. Lawson, *Black Ballots*, 285–286, 284 (table 2); Branch, *Pillar of Fire*, 156–159.

104. Doug McAdam, *Freedom Summer* (New York: Oxford University Press, 1988), 77, 96; Branch, *Pillar of Fire*, 361–374, 399–400, 508–509. The FBI had no office in Mississippi at this time, and the FBI director, J. Edgar Hoover, viewed King as a Communist-influenced threat to national security and so kept him under continual wiretap surveillance. He was also angered by King's occasional criticism of the way the FBI handled civil rights cases. In 1964, shortly before King went to Sweden to receive the Nobel Peace Prize, Hoover told reporters that he considered King "the most notorious liar in the United States" (Branch, *Pillar of Fire*, 526).

105. Branch, *Pillar of Fire*, 456–476, 291, 300, 310, 403, 405, 356–357. More than 80 percent of Republicans in the House and Senate had voted in favor of the Civil Rights Act.

106. Ibid., 466, 471–472, quotation at 474; Lawson, *Black Ballots*, 302–306. One of the Alabama delegates was Bull Connor.

107. Branch, *Pillar of Fire*, 522–523.

108. Garrow, *Bearing the Cross*, 349.

109. Branch, *Pillar of Fire*, 63; Thornton, *Dividing Lines*, 400, 406–407, 425–428, 420, 430–434, 467–468; Stephen Oakes, "Introduction," in Fager, *Selma*, xiii.

110. Representatives from the DCVL had been key witnesses before the televised hearings of the Civil Rights Commission in 1958, which had first dramatized disenfranchisement for many Americans. Thornton, *Dividing Lines*, 440.

111. Ibid., 448–452, 455, 458–459, 461, 463, 476–477.

112. Ibid., 481–485; Garrow, *Bearing the Cross*, 382–386. Fager (*Selma*, 58–59) portrays the injunction as a ruse, because the registrar's office did not have to stay open more than two days a month; yet Thornton notes that it could have stayed opened more days, and could and soon did process more than a hundred applications a day. The question was, would Judge Thomas have made the office stay open. Fager assumes, as did many civil rights activists, that he would not, because he regarded Thomas as at heart a segregationist, based on a series of conservative rulings Thomas had handed down in civil rights cases. Yet Thornton believes Thomas to have been, in fact, a moderate, who wanted segregation to end but thought (to quote Thomas himself) that racial issues "must be resolved, and should be resolved, by the people, and not by the courts." In the early 1960s Thomas had hoped that a go-slow approach of not forcing civil rights on the white South would achieve the peaceful, gradual

acquiescence of southern white officials to the new laws. By the time of his 1965 injunction, however, Thornton argues, Thomas had reluctantly concluded that not enough southern white officials were men of goodwill for this hands-off strategy to work. See Thornton, *Dividing Lines,* 442–446.

113. Thornton, *Dividing Lines,* 480, 486; Fager, *Selma,* 74.

·{ 17 }·

Democracy and Women's Rights in America: The Fight over the ERA (1982)

ON THE AFTERNOON OF JUNE 21, 1982, the Florida Senate prepared to vote on whether to ratify the proposed Equal Rights Amendment (ERA) to the U.S. Constitution. The amendment stated, "Equality of Rights under the law shall not be denied or abridged by the United States or by any State on account of sex." Supporters believed the ERA was essential to winning equal rights for women, who comprised a slim majority of the American population. Opponents claimed that the proposed amendment would dangerously expand federal power over the states, remove needed protections for women, and undermine the American family.

When Congress had sent the ERA to the states for ratification, in March 1972, it had done so through a joint resolution stipulating that for the amendment to be valid, state legislatures would have to ratify it within seven years. ERA supporters had expected the constitutionally requisite three-quarters of the states (38 of 50) to ratify well before March 1979. Opposition to the amendment mounted, however, and as the deadline neared only thirty-five states had ratified, four of which had later voted to rescind ratification, although ERA supporters denied that these rescissions were constitutional. In October 1978, Congress extended the ratification deadline to June 30, 1982. ERA opponents denounced the extension as unconstitutional. Over the next few years, one more state voted to rescind, and no new states ratified.

In 1982, ERA supporters made a final push for ratification. That June the governor of Florida, an ERA supporter, called the state legislature into special session to consider, among other issues, approval of the ERA. If Florida

ratified, supporters hoped that Illinois and either Oklahoma or North Carolina would immediately follow. On June 21, thousands of demonstrators, both
for and against the amendment, converged on the state capitol in Tallahassee.
That morning the Florida House voted in favor of the ERA, 60 to 58. Now it
was up to the Florida Senate to decide whether to ratify the amendment, or
to kill it.[1]

Women's Rights in the American Revolution and Early Republic

The ERA debate of the 1970s and 1980s was the latest episode in a long struggle
in America to define women's rights and to determine how best to secure
them, which began with the American Revolution.* In the colonial era, all
Americans had been royal subjects, bound by common allegiance to the
British king. In this hierarchical world, few colonists questioned that slaves
were subjects of their masters, or wives subjects of their husbands.[2] A
husband had the legal right both to "chastise" (beat) his wife and to force
her to have sex with him.[3] Moreover, under the British common law tradition of "coverture," as the British jurist William Blackstone explained
in his influential *Commentaries on the Laws of England* (1765–1769), "the
very being and existence of the woman [once married] is suspended . . .
or entirely merged and incorporated in that of the husband."[4] Ownership
of any property that a woman possessed before marriage or any income
she earned during marriage, as well as her ability to sign contracts or to
sue or be sued in court, passed to her husband. Nor was a wife even a
royal subject in and of herself, but only as a dependent of her husband,
who was in turn a subject of the king. For this reason, if a woman married a foreign man, she became a foreigner, and if a wife willfully killed
her husband, the crime was classified, not as murder, but as *"petit treason"*—
killing her "lord."[5] With the Revolution, however, Americans reenvisioned
themselves as independent citizens with natural rights, who joined together
freely to form a republic. They began to question many traditional forms

---

* "Women's rights," "women's suffrage," and the "women's movement" are modern terms.
Until the early twentieth century, people spoke of "woman's rights," "woman suffrage," and
the "woman movement." Outside of quotations, we will use the modern terms throughout.

of subjection, including that of slaves (with some states abolishing slavery at this time) and of women.

During the Revolution, American women had to decide whether or not to support the Patriot cause and so exposed as fiction the legal assumption that they could only choose a man, not a political allegiance. In fact, Patriot embargoes of imported British tea and cloth would have failed without active, public backing by women. Women hosted public teas at which only concoctions from local herbs were served and organized public spinning bees to make homespun cloth. As Americans championed the "rights of man," many began thinking about the "rights of woman."[6]

Abigail Adams was thinking about them when she wrote to her husband, future U.S. president John Adams, in March 1776. He was away in Philadelphia, trying to persuade his fellow delegates in the Continental Congress to break from Britain. She was at home in Quincy, Massachusetts, doing her best to maintain their farm, take care of their five young children (among them, future president John Quincy Adams), and even develop a plan to manufacture gunpowder for Patriot militia. She expressed her strong desire to hear that Congress had "declared an independancy" and added:

> In the new Code of Laws which I suppose it will be necessary for you to make I desire you would Remember the Ladies, and be more generous and favourable to them than your ancestors. Do not put such unlimited power into the hands of the Husbands. Remember all Men would be tyrants if they could. If perticuliar care and attention is not paid to the Laidies we are determined to foment a Rebelion, and will not hold ourselves bound by any Laws in which we have no voice, or Representation.[7]

John Adams, in his reply, dismissed his wife's concerns: "As to your extraordinary Code of Laws, I cannot but laugh. . . . We know better than to repeal our Masculine systems." He explained that "in Practice you know We are the subjects. We have only the Name of Masters," and giving up that symbolic remnant "would subject Us to the Despotism of the Peticoat."[8] Yet Abigail's remarks had alerted him to a new issue. A month later he wrote to a male correspondent that the case of men without property was like that of women. Neither, Adams believed, should be allowed to vote, because their private cares left them "too little acquainted with public Affairs to form a Right Judgment" on political matters, and their situations left them too dependent on others—men in one case, or their employers in the other—to "have a Will of their own." He urged that no attempt be made to lower traditional property restrictions on suffrage: "Depend upon it, sir, it is dangerous to open . . . [such] a Source of Controversy and Altercation, as would be opened by attempting to alter the Qualifications of Voters. There will be no End of it. New Claims will arise. Women will demand a Vote."[9]

In July 1776, the same month that the Continental Congress passed the Declaration of Independence, which proclaimed that "all men are created equal," New Jersey gave some women the vote. It approved a new state constitution granting suffrage to adult "inhabitants" who possessed a certain small amount of property, in effect enfranchising unmarried women and widows. As Adams had predicted it might, the move resulted from a debate over lowering the property qualification for suffrage. The authors of the New Jersey constitution, having decided to exclude from suffrage only men without any property at all, evidently could think of no logical reason to exclude women with property. Women would vote in New Jersey for the next thirty years. In the close presidential election of 1800, Alexander Hamilton himself was reported to have campaigned among female voters there on behalf of the Federalist Party.[10]

Yet no other state followed New Jersey in giving women the vote, and even there, women were not permitted to hold office or serve on juries. Nor could married women vote in New Jersey, because the new republic maintained the old laws regarding coverture, meaning that wives still could not possess property of their own. American laws at this time did begin to recognize the *citizenship* of women: "Passports were issued to them. They could be naturalized; they could claim the protection of the courts. They were subject to the laws and were obliged to pay taxes." In the new state legal codes, moreover, a wife who deliberately killed her husband was no longer classed as a traitor, but simply as a murderer. The recognition of female citizenship only went so far, however. When, in 1807, New Jersey legislators decided to expand suffrage to all taxpaying citizens, they simultaneously ended the only state experiment with women's suffrage.[11]

Over the next three decades, nearly all white men won the right to vote, and between 1820 and 1840 intense party rivalries would mobilize this all-male electorate, increasing voter turnout in state and national elections from around 40 percent to nearly 80 percent.[12] With these developments, most

Americans came to see partisan politics as a kind of male enclave: a site of boisterous, alcohol-fueled, sometimes violent, male rivalry and solidarity. Most commentators, including female ones, began to insist that women had no place in politics, and that their realm was the "domestic sphere," where they could quietly nurture morality and religion in their families.[13]

Despite these limits, women claimed a large, if nominally nonpolitical, role in American civic life. Between 1790 and 1830, for example, women founded hundreds of benevolent associations and institutions, such as orphanages and asylums. Legislatures often granted these organizations charters of incorporation, allowing the women who ran them to "exercise collective rights that they did not possess individually, especially if they were married," such as the right to own and manage large amounts of property, retain earnings, and sue and be sued. In fact, these organizations often operated as self-contained political communities: the "members were able to vote, run for office, hammer out platforms, and make decisions that affected others directly."[14]

It was also widely believed, among men as well as women, that the American republic would not survive if its female citizens lacked virtue, and that virtue required education. Between 1780 and 1830, Americans established nearly 200 private girls' academies (the equivalent of high schools) as well as several girls' "seminaries" (the equivalent of colleges).[15] Meanwhile, in the small, rural communities where most Americans of the era lived, girls began to be educated alongside boys in the common schools, as the nascent public schools were called. According to two historians of coeducation, this change happened with so little public comment that it "seems to have been one of those major transitions in practice in which citizens moved gradually from *why* to *why not.*" Women were increasingly hired to teach in the common schools as well, and by 1860 a majority of such teachers in New England were female. White female literacy rates, indicated by the ability to sign one's name, were only about half that of men in 1790, but drew equal to the male level by 1840, and by 1870 had surpassed it.[16]

The Petition Issue

The right of citizens to petition government officials for the redress of grievances was established in medieval England. By the seventeenth century,

British reformers had discovered that the process of circulating petitions could be an effective tool for rallying public opinion. In the Declaration of Independence, Americans justified breaking with England in part on the grounds that the king had refused to answer their petitions complaining of his abuses of power; and in the First Amendment to the U.S. Constitution (ratified in 1791), they guaranteed the right "to petition the Government for redress of grievances." In England and colonial America, where relatively few men could vote, petitions had been couched in the language of deference, as "prayers" to the powerful. In the United States, as suffrage among white men became universal, voters began addressing petitions to legislators as equals, making forthright demands.[17]

At the same time, Americans limited the petitioning rights of slaves and women. During the Revolution, slaves in Massachusetts had joined together to petition for a state emancipation law, and North Carolina women petitioned in favor of a Patriot boycott. But in 1797, and again in 1837, Congress voted not to accept petitions from slaves, on the grounds that slaves had no right to petition. Although most southern state legislatures continued to accept petitions from slaves until the Civil War, they seem to have done so only as an indulgence, granted only to individuals or small groups making personal requests, and nearly always only if a white person wrote the petition on the slave's behalf. Free women retained their right to petition, but it was circumscribed by strict conventions. Between 1790 and 1830, Congress accepted "petitions without number" from widows of soldiers asking for pensions, while state legislatures accepted hundreds of petitions from wealthy women requesting charters of incorporation for charitable institutions or girls' schools. Yet women were expected to petition using the old, deferential language; only to petition as individuals or in small groups; and never to petition on controversial political questions.[18]

By 1818, however, women had started signing petitions to local governments in favor of laws restricting liquor sales. Temperance was a controversial political question, but the female petitioners claimed to be acting nonpolitically—as wives and mothers trying to protect their families from the rum sellers. Again, in 1830–1831, more than 1,500 women from several northern states petitioned Congress, urging it not to expel the Cherokee Indians from their traditional lands in Georgia. Cherokee removal proved to be one of the most politically divisive issues of the era, but the female peti-

tioners insisted that they acted purely out of Christian charity. To emphasize the nonpolitical nature of their petitions, they made sure no men signed
them.[19]

Female petitioning for temperance and for protecting the Cherokee
aroused criticism, but female petitioning for the abolition of slavery provoked
outrage. Abolitionism, which grew in part from older antislavery activism,
particularly by Quakers and free blacks, emerged in the North as a distinct
movement around 1830. At the time, most northern whites admitted that
slavery was contrary to American ideals but thought that it was a problem
for the South to solve sometime in the future; also, many (perhaps most) considered America a "white man's country" and wanted free blacks "colonized"
to Africa. By contrast, abolitionists insisted that the North was complicit,
politically and economically, in the "sin" of slavery, and so was responsible for
doing something about it. They also insisted that the southern states should
begin to emancipate their slaves "immediately," that colonization was a
cruel hoax, and that free blacks deserved full civil equality with whites. Most
white Americans considered such views fanatical and incendiary. Abolitionism was in effect outlawed in the South, while in the North, abolitionists faced popular scorn, "social ostracism," and even mob violence. By 1837,
nonetheless, 100,000 northerners had joined either the principal national
abolitionist organization, the American Anti-Slavery Society (AASS), founded
in 1833, or one of its state, regional, or local affiliates. The original leaders of
the AASS were white men, the most famous being the Boston newspaper
editor William Lloyd Garrison. Northern free blacks, women as well as
men, although few in number, gave abolitionism critical support, but the
key to its initial spread is widely thought to have been its appeal to
northern white women, who were the core abolitionist constituency in
many communities.[20]

Women's reasons for embracing abolitionism were in part the same as
men's, but many women also recognized that slavery produced horrific
violations of the domestic ideals that they believed they had been tasked to
uphold. Accounts of masters forcing their slave women to act as concubines,
and of slave mothers and children weeping on the auction block as they were
separated forever by sale, became staples of abolitionist literature.[21]

In 1831–1832, Lucretia Mott, a Quaker preacher, persuaded 2,000 fellow
Pennsylvania women to sign petitions to Congress asking it to abolish slavery

and the slave trade in the District of Columbia.* Garrison criticized Mott's action on the grounds that only men should petition Congress. In 1834, however, he visited London and saw a petition presented to Parliament that had been signed by nearly 200,000 women, asking for abolition of slavery in the British colonies. In England, where only a minority of men could vote, few apparently questioned the right of nonvoting women to petition. Impressed, Garrison and others began calling on U.S. women to petition their lawmakers, and many responded. In 1835–1836 Congress received 174 antislavery petitions, 84 of them signed only by women; of the 34,000 total signatures, approximately 15,000 were from female signatories.[22]

The antislavery petitions outraged southern members of Congress. In February 1836, after months of debate, the House (followed later by the Senate) adopted a rule requiring that all petitions "relating in any way, or to any extent whatever, to the subject of slavery, or the abolition of slavery . . . be laid upon the table, and that no further action whatever shall be had thereon." Former president John Quincy Adams, now a congressman from Massachusetts, objected that the rule was "a direct violation of the constitution of the United States, of the rules of this House, and of the rights of my constituents." Abolitionists, meanwhile, denounced the rule as a "gag" on free speech. They recognized that Congress had unintentionally put "a 'firebrand' in our hands to light anew the flame of human sympathy and public indignation."[23]

Perhaps no group was more indignant about the gag rule in Congress than northern women, who saw petitioning as their principal tool to influence government decision making. In 1837 female abolitionists from across the North, black and white, met in Philadelphia—the first national women's convention—where they decided to launch an antislavery petitioning cam-

---

* The reigning constitutional consensus in the early nineteenth century held that Congress had no constitutional authority to abolish slavery in the southern states. (See, e.g., James Oakes, *Freedom National: The Destruction of Slavery in the United States, 1861–1865* [New York: W. W. Norton, 2013], 2–4.) Abolitionist petitions to Congress therefore focused on secondary issues, such as ending slavery and the slave trade in D.C. (where the Constitution explicitly granted Congress authority); opposing the admission of new slave states; banning slavery in the western territories; outlawing the interstate slave trade; and overturning the gag rule. Abolitionists also extensively petitioned northern state legislatures, asking them to pass resolutions or laws against slavery, or civil rights laws on behalf of northern free blacks.

paign in defiance of the gag rule. Among the delegates most active in organizing the campaign were Lucretia Mott and Angelina Grimké. The latter came from a prominent slaveholding family in South Carolina but had, along with her older sister Sarah, converted to Quakerism and abolitionism. Shortly afterward, the Grimké sisters launched a lecture tour around Massachusetts to promote antislavery petitioning and the formation of antislavery societies. Massachusetts clergy produced a circular letter condemning them, claiming that decent women did not give public speeches, but people flocked to hear them nonetheless. In 1838 Angelina spoke before the Massachusetts House of Representatives, the first woman to do so, to defend the right of women to petition.[24]

By late 1838, antislavery petitions flooded Congress, signed by 414,000 Americans, more than half of them women. John Quincy Adams made a grand spectacle of attempting to present the petitions over the shouts and objections of southern members. He would keep this political theater project going for years, as abolitionist petitions continued to pour in, until Congress finally rescinded the gag rule in 1844.[25]

Petition campaigns were often led by female canvassers, many in their teens or even younger. Although women and girls circulated only about a third of all antislavery petitions sent to Congress between 1833 and 1845, they collected 50 percent more signatures than "petitions on the same topics, passed through the same localities at the same time, but canvassed by men." Men could pass their petitions around their workplaces or post them in shops; they typically went door to door only when paid by a political party, and did not ask for women's signatures. Women, unpaid and seen as nonpartisan, had to carry their petitions door-to-door—especially to reach most other women, who often spent the day at home. The method proved effective for reaching men as well (and minors, whose signatures they also collected). As canvassers, women learned how to articulate political arguments and build political networks, experience that one recent study has found turned many of them into lifelong activists. A disproportionate number of women's rights leaders in 1870 turn out to have been former abolitionist canvassers.[26]

Over the course of the antebellum period—and particularly over the 1830s—the role of women in the petitioning process changed in a number of ways. Notably, men and women began signing petitions together (although for a time in separate columns), and the language that characterized female antislavery petitions moved closer to that of their male counterparts. Before 1836, women's petitions were written in the old deferential language. Whereas male antislavery petitioners used forms describing themselves as "citizens" who addressed "the Honorable Senate and House of Representatives," women used special forms, which described them as "ladies" addressing "the Fathers and Rulers of Our Country." By the late 1830s, women petitioners had abandoned the deferential pose and were using the same petition forms as men.[27]

At the same time, women's rights emerged as an issue within the abolition movement itself. Originally, female abolitionists had been members, not of the AASS or its state or regional affiliates, but of women's auxiliary organizations. In 1839, however, female abolitionists, with Garrison's support, demanded that they be admitted as full AASS members and be allowed to serve as AASS officers. The issue provoked bitter controversy, with many abolitionists arguing that the push for women's rights was a distraction from the antislavery cause. The issue contributed to a rupture within the abolitionist movement in 1840; Garrison and his female allies took complete control of the AASS, while their opponents bolted.[28]

During the 1840s the right of women to petition on the same terms as men had largely ceased to be contested, and agitation to end legal, economic, and social inequality between men and women was beginning to emerge in many places and forms. By 1850, when the first national women's rights convention was held in Worcester, Massachusetts, the agitation had finally coalesced into a movement.[29]

Women's Rights in the Nineteenth Century

The wide-ranging goals of the women's rights movement were well articulated at a small but historic gathering that took place in upstate New York, organized by Mott and Elizabeth Cady Stanton. The two women had met in 1840, shortly after the AASS split over women's rights, at an international antislavery convention in London. Mott had come with the AASS delegation, while Stanton was there on a honeymoon with her husband, a member of the group that had broken away. The convention, over Garrison's protests, had decided not to seat female delegates; as a result, Mott joined Stanton as an observer in the gallery, where the two became friends. In 1848 Mott visited Seneca Falls, New York, where Stanton was now living with her husband and children, and the two women decided to place a call for a women's rights convention in the local newspapers. The convention was held ten days later, on July 19–20, 1848, at the local Wesleyan Chapel.[30]

The local men and women who took part voted on resolutions and approved the Declaration of Sentiments that Stanton had written. In language mirroring the Declaration of Independence (and the Declaration of Sentiments that inaugurated the AASS), Stanton's declaration proclaimed:

> We hold these truths to be self-evident: that all men and women are created equal. . . . Now, in view of this entire disfranchisement of one-half the people of this country, their social and religious degradation . . . because women do feel themselves aggrieved, oppressed, and fraudulently deprived of their most sacred rights, we insist that they have immediate admission to all the rights and privileges which belong to them as citizens of the United States.[31]

The resolutions and Declaration asserted the right of women to be as well educated as men, to enter all the same "profitable employments," and to write and speak publicly on public issues. The documents denounced every aspect of coverture and demanded that American women "secure to themselves their sacred right to the elective franchise." Sixty-eight women and thirty-two men signed the Declaration, the most famous being Frederick Douglass— escaped slave, celebrated antislavery lecturer and author, and editor of the abolitionist newspaper in nearby Rochester, New York.[32]

Although Kentucky (in 1838) and Michigan (1855) granted women "school suffrage," allowing women to vote for local school boards (children's education was seen as a matter of special female concern), and although in the 1850s activists launched the first state campaigns for full female suffrage rights, the vote seemed a distant goal. Reformers achieved greater success chipping away at coverture. In 1848, shortly before Mott and Stanton called the Seneca Falls convention, New York State enacted a Married Women's Property Act, allowing wives to retain ownership of property they held at marriage; many other states followed. These laws had support beyond the women's rights movement: by protecting a wife's property from her husband's creditors, they helped keep families from poverty in an era of financial booms and busts, and they were seen as a matter of equity, extending to all women the privileges of brides with rich fathers, who had been protecting their daughters' property through family trusts. In 1860, New York enacted the first Earnings Act, also widely imitated, which allowed married women to own any money they made during marriage. It was seen as more radical than the Property Act, because it challenged the presumption that the husband ought to be the sole breadwinner. The New York Earnings Act came only after intense agitation led by, among others, Susan B. Anthony. Anthony, a temperance activist, had joined the women's rights movement in the early 1850s, becoming Stanton's close friend and collaborator. The effects of the property and earnings laws often were limited by state courts, however, which usually interpreted them narrowly.[33]

The multifaceted quality of the women's movement is well illustrated by the career of Lucy Stone. A former abolitionist canvasser, Stone was the first Massachusetts woman to graduate from Oberlin, which itself was the first coed college in America. Stone was a leading women's rights lecturer and a champion of suffrage and "dress reform"—urging women to wear comfortable trousers instead of restrictive corsets. In 1855 she married Henry Blackwell, the brother of one of her Oberlin classmates, Elizabeth Blackwell, who was the first woman in the United States to earn a medical degree. (Another Blackwell brother married another of Elizabeth's Oberlin friends, Antoinette Brown, the first woman in the United States to be ordained as a minister.) When Stone and Blackwell wed, Stone refused to take the traditional vow to "obey" him, and both bride and groom read statements, which they immediately published in the newspapers, rejecting the "whole system by which the legal existence of the wife is suspended during marriage" and the powers it gave the husband over the wife. They urged that "marriage should be an equal and permanent partnership, and so recognized by law." Stone refused to use her husband's last name, apparently the first American woman to take this step.[34]

Among the rights Stone and Blackwell rejected were his legal rights to beat and rape her. Over the course of the nineteenth century, courts slowly ceased to recognize these rights. Few men were prosecuted for beating their wives, however, and none for raping them.[35] Female activists supported laws that they thought would, if only indirectly, limit sexual violence against women, such as those restricting liquor sales. Female activists also led a successful crusade to raise the legal age of sexual consent, which in most states as late as 1885 was only 10, to 16 or higher by 1900. The activists' preferred means of limiting male violence against women, however, was moral suasion—exhorting men to control their anger and lust. This preference left most women's rights leaders uninterested in promoting contraception, and few of them objected when states, in the late nineteenth century, began outlawing abortions, allegedly because the procedure was medically unsafe. Women's rights leaders always insisted, however, that motherhood should be "voluntary," and some objected that the new anti-abortion laws were unfair in that they penalized the mothers but not the fathers.[36]

During the Civil War (1861–1865), antislavery women launched their largest petition campaign, successfully urging Congress to approve the Thirteenth Amendment to the U.S. Constitution, which officially abolished slavery once the amendment was ratified by the states in December 1865. Emancipation marked a turning point for the women's movement. During Reconstruction, Congress, and not just the states, became a focus of women's rights agitation, while suffrage became its principal (although never its only) issue. Just months after the war ended, Stanton, Anthony, Stone, Mott, Douglass, and others had established the American Equal Rights Association (AERA), the first national organization dedicated to winning universal suffrage. Over the next few years the organization splintered, however, over whether the rights of black freedmen or women, particularly white women, should be given priority. (Black women, among them Sojourner Truth, although active in the women's rights movement since its inception, struggled to be heard in this controversy.)[37]

In 1866 Congress passed the Fourteenth Amendment, which was ratified by the states in 1868. The first section of the amendment declared that "all persons born or naturalized in the United States, and subject to the jurisdiction thereof, are citizens of the United States and of the State wherein they reside," and that no state could deny their "privileges" as citizens without due process of law. Congress wrote this section with freedmen primarily in mind, but it seemed to strengthen the claim of women to full citizenship. The second section of the amendment, however, stipulated that if a state denied suffrage "to any of the male inhabitants of such State, being twenty-one years of age, and citizens of the United States," then its representation in Congress would be reduced "in the proportion which the number of such male citizens shall bear to the whole number of male citizens twenty-one years of age in such State." Leaders of the AERA lobbied and protested against this language for introducing the word "male" into the Constitution, objecting that it implied not only that women had no right to vote, but that they were not citizens in the same way as men. (In 1880, the U.S. Supreme

Court seemed to confirm this interpretation when it ruled that the Fourteenth Amendment only forbade the legal exclusion of black men, but not women, from jury service.)[38]

The AERA broke apart in 1869 when Congress passed the Fifteenth Amendment, which was ratified by the states the following year. Whereas the Fourteenth Amendment had offered states a political incentive not to deny votes to freedmen, the Fifteenth banned outright any voter restriction based on "race, color, or previous condition of servitude"—wording that also promised to expand the suffrage rights of male immigrants. Stanton and Anthony opposed the amendment, however, because it did not grant votes to women. They argued that educated white women deserved the vote more than freedmen or immigrants and proposed an alternate amendment that granted the vote to all literate citizens. As Stanton declared in a speech to the AERA, "Think of Patrick and Sambo and Hans and Yung Tung . . . who cannot read the Declaration of Independence or Webster's spelling book, making laws for Lucretia Mott . . . [or] Susan B. Anthony." Douglass, by contrast, insisted that black men in the South urgently needed political power to protect their newly won rights in the face of violent intimidation by whites. Stone, after trying and failing to get Congress to consider a universal suffrage amendment, sided with Douglass, arguing that freedmen must not be denied the vote just because women did not get it as well, and that the amendment was still a major step toward suffrage for all. When an AERA convention refused to back Stanton and Anthony, they withdrew to found the National Woman Suffrage Association. Stone responded by founding the American Woman Suffrage Association.[39]

The American Association, the larger of the two organizations, came to focus on suffrage campaigns at the state and local levels—an approach that looked promising to many reformers. In 1869 the newly organized Territory of Wyoming granted its few women the right to vote. Later, women won the vote in other western territories: Utah in 1870, although women's suffrage there was revoked by an act of Congress in 1887, and Washington in 1883, although it was there revoked by territorial Supreme Court decisions in 1887. While state suffrage campaigns all failed, some states granted "municipal suffrage," allowing female taxpayers to vote on local tax and bond questions, on the grounds that "municipal governance was a form of 'housekeeping,'" and more granted women school suffrage. Stone herself lived in Massachusetts, which granted school suffrage in 1879, but she was not allowed to cast a ballot because she refused to register under her husband's name.[40]

The National Association focused on trying to win women's suffrage at the national level, preferably through a constitutional amendment. Realizing the difficulty of getting one through Congress, however, the National Association in 1871 tried another strategy, known as the "New Departure," first conceived by Virginia and Francis Minor, a married couple from Missouri. They argued that because the Fourteenth Amendment made all native-born or naturalized "persons" citizens and prevented states from denying them the privileges of citizenship, and because voting was an essential privilege of citizenship, women already had the right to vote. Acting on this theory, many women, including Virginia Minor and Susan B. Anthony, attempted to vote in the 1872 presidential election. When Minor was turned away by her registrar, Reese Happersett, she sued him in state court, arguing that the Missouri constitution, which restricted suffrage to men, violated the Fourteenth Amendment. When Missouri courts ruled against her, she appealed to the U.S. Supreme Court. Anthony, meanwhile, succeeded in casting a ballot in New York, only to be arrested a few weeks later for having voted illegally. Her widely publicized trial, in 1873, made her a national celebrity, but she lost, was denied appeal, and was fined (she refused to pay). Two years later the U.S. Supreme Court ruled, in *Minor v. Happersett,* that suffrage was not an essential privilege of citizenship.[41]

With the failure of the New Departure strategy, the National Association again began agitating for a women's suffrage amendment to the U.S. Constitution, now in a version written by Stanton: "The right of citizens of the United States to vote shall not be denied or abridged by the United States or by any state on account of sex." This amendment was introduced to Congress repeatedly, starting in 1878. The National Association organized petition drives on its behalf, and Stanton herself testified to Congress in its favor. Congress did not vote on it, however, until 1887, when the Senate rejected it 34 to 16, with 25 abstentions.[42]

After this defeat the National Association decided to concentrate on state suffrage campaigns along with a national amendment. This shift of emphasis allowed the National and American Associations to end their two-decade feud and unite in 1890 as the National American Woman Suffrage Association

(NAWSA), under the leadership of Anthony and her protégées. Between 1890 and 1896, four western states gave women the vote. But no state did so for years after that. In the meantime, Stone died in 1893, Douglass in 1895, Stanton in 1902, and Anthony in 1906. Subsequently, between 1910 and 1919, twenty-three states granted women full or partial suffrage rights. In the 1916 presidential election, both the Republican Party and the Democratic Party endorsed women's suffrage in their platforms, the first time either had done so, although neither endorsed a federal suffrage amendment.[43] That November, Jeannette Rankin, Republican of Montana, became the first woman elected to Congress.

Votes for (White) Women

Women's suffrage gained momentum in America at about the same time that the male electorate was being narrowed in various ways. After 1890, in the North and West, laws were passed to discourage immigrants from voting. One technique involved the establishment of actual or de facto literacy requirements to vote. These requirements, among other potential factors, such as voter registration laws and the rise of the secret ballot, helped produce a general reduction in voter turnout between the 1880s and 1910s, from over 80 percent to below 60 percent (as a share of the voter-eligible population). Meanwhile, southern states instituted new voting requirements that had the effect of disenfranchising almost all black voters and enacted laws reinforcing the system of racial segregation that had emerged since Reconstruction, commonly known as "Jim Crow." Although black leaders protested that these laws violated the Fourteenth and Fifteenth Amendments, federal courts and Congress chose not to intervene.[44]

The NAWSA in 1909 repudiated the notion of educated suffrage and with great success began reaching out to white immigrant voters and the labor movement, allowing it to become a mass effort for the first time, with branches in every state and two million members.[45] Yet many Americans supported giving women the vote precisely to counterbalance the influence of immigrants. Immigrant voters, for example, were generally hostile to "prohibition" laws, banning the sale, manufacture, and importation of alcoholic beverages, whereas the women's rights movement had always been allied with the temperance cause.[46] Prohibition became national policy in

1919, with the ratification of the Eighteenth Amendment to the U.S. Constitution (the Twenty-First Amendment would repeal national Prohibition in 1933). NAWSA leaders, moreover, failed to oppose black disenfranchisement in the South, fearing that doing so would doom the suffrage cause there. They also feared offending national leaders of the Democratic Party, most of whom were southerners, including President Woodrow Wilson, a progressive New Jersey Democrat who was a native of Virginia and supported segregation. In 1919 the NAWSA president reassured southern audiences that "white supremacy will be strengthened, not weakened, by women's suffrage."[47] No southern state, however, gave women full suffrage rights at this time.

After 1910 a new generation of suffragists took the political stage, led by Alice Paul, who thought the NAWSA was not nearly militant enough. In 1913 Paul helped found the Congressional Union, which became the National Woman's Party (NWP) in 1916. Its members adopted confrontational tactics, such as picketing the White House—because President Wilson insisted suffrage was a state issue—and engaging in dramatic acts of civil disobedience. After 1917, when the United States entered the First World War, NWP activists kept up this controversial campaign; the NAWSA, by contrast, worked to mobilize women for the war effort—winning Wilson's gratitude in the process—and repudiated NWP tactics. Paul and her allies, meanwhile, were attacked in the streets, arrested, and imprisoned. They demanded recognition as political prisoners, and when denied, launched a hunger strike.[48]

The NWP campaign embarrassed Wilson, who had declared that the principal American war goal was to "make the world safe for democracy." In January 1918 he finally urged Congress to pass a women's suffrage amendment. The next day Jeannette Rankin introduced the amendment into the House, where it passed 274–136—the exact two-thirds majority it needed. In 1919, after continual agitation, and with Wilson's continued support, the Senate also approved the amendment by a two-thirds majority. On August 18, 1920, Tennessee, by a single vote in the legislature, became the required thirty-sixth state to ratify what was now the Nineteenth Amendment. It had the same wording as the amendment drafted by Stanton, first introduced in Congress in 1878.[49]

That November women across the country voted in the presidential election. To attract their support, both major parties pledged in their national platforms to repeal the nativist Expatriation Act of 1907, a federal law requiring American women who married foreigners to relinquish their citizenship (the U.S. Supreme Court had ruled in 1915 that the law did not violate women's Fourteenth Amendment rights). In 1922, however, Congress enacted only a partial repeal: a woman who married a foreigner could retain her citizenship only if the man she married was himself *eligible* to be a U.S. citizen (at the time, men from China and Japan, among others, were not eligible).[50]

Feminism and the Equal Rights Amendment

Around 1913, just as the final push for women's suffrage began, a new term entered the American lexicon: "feminism." Although all feminists were suffragists—Paul, for example, identified herself as feminist—not all suffragists were feminists. Unlike many suffragists, feminists generally opposed Prohibition, championed legalizing contraception for women, and considered winning the vote not an end but a beginning. They declared that they wanted "'a complete social revolution': freedom for all forms of women's active expression, elimination of all structural and psychological handicaps to women's economic independence, an end to the double standard of sexual morality, release from constraining sexual stereotypes, and opportunity to shine in every civic and professional capacity."[51]

After ratification of the Nineteenth Amendment, feminists fought for this wider agenda. The NWP documented that discrimination against women, both legal and customary, remained widespread. An obvious example was that as of 1923, only eighteen states allowed women to sit on juries, and those states that did usually made women's service optional.[52] Women were also excluded by law and custom from many occupations and most professional schools, and were generally paid less than men for the same work. State laws varied widely, moreover, regarding the degree of control women were granted over their economic and family lives.

Paul decided that to achieve her objectives an Equal Rights Amendment (ERA) had to be added to the U.S. Constitution. A few western states already had one, although even these states had a checkered record of actually applying the principle of equal rights in legislation and court rulings. Paul argued that a national amendment would be "more inclusive" than state laws, requiring "at one stroke" that "both federal and state governments . . . observe the principle of Equal Rights," and more permanent, as "Equal Rights measures passed by state legislatures . . . are subject to reversal by later legislatures." She also insisted that the amendment was a more "dignified" approach to equality than legislation: "The principle of Equal Rights for men and women is so important that it should be written into the framework of our National Government as one of the principles upon which our government is founded."[53]

In 1923 Paul and the NWP petitioned Congress to consider an ERA. The proposed text read: "Men and women shall have equal rights throughout the United States and every place subject to its jurisdiction. Congress shall have power to enforce this article by appropriate legislation."[54] A few months later it was introduced into Congress by two Kansas Republicans. In 1924 a subcommittee of the Senate Judiciary Committee held a widely publicized hearing on the amendment, but in the end made no recommendation, and the proposal died.[55] Owing to the relentless agitation of Paul and the NWP, however, an ERA was introduced into the next Congress, and each Congress thereafter, for several decades.[56]

Opponents of an ERA charged that if the provision were ratified, courts would face a flood of litigation over what the phrase "men and women shall have equal rights" actually meant. Apparently conceding that the language was too vague, ERA supporters in the 1940s changed the first sentence of the proposed amendment to read, "Equality of rights under the law shall not be denied or abridged by the United States or by any State on account of sex." Opponents also argued that an ERA, by giving Congress the authority to enforce equal rights, would produce a dangerous expansion of federal power because it would allow federal legislation on domestic relations, which had always been a state concern. ERA supporters insisted that no such thing would happen, but nonetheless for a time agreed to amend the second sentence of the proposed amendment so that it read, "Congress *and the several States* shall have power, *within their respective jurisdictions,* to enforce this article by appropriate legislation" (emphases added). Although these alterations were eventually dropped, supporters also added a third sentence to the proposed amendment, preventing it from taking effect for a number of years, in order to allow state legislatures time to "review and revise" their own laws in their own way.[57]

Many of the strongest objections made against the ERA in the mid-twentieth century, however, came from some of Paul's fellow feminists, who feared it would repeal "protective legislation" for working women. Until the early twentieth century, protective labor laws—limiting working hours, setting minimum wages, regulating workplace conditions—were routinely struck down by state and federal courts on the grounds that they violated "freedom of contract," which was said to be guaranteed to workers and employers by the "due process" clauses of the Fifth and Fourteenth Amendments. Several state courts, however, had upheld protective labor laws for women between 1876 and 1902; and in 1908, in the case of *Muller v. Oregon,* the U.S. Supreme Court adopted the same stance, upholding an Oregon law limiting the hours of female factory workers. In *Muller,* a team of reformers led by future Supreme Court Justice Louis Brandeis successfully argued that the state had a compelling interest to interfere with women's freedom of contract because women were physically frailer than men and thus required special protection.[58] After *Muller,* "states enacted a raft of women-only protective legislation: maximum hours and minimum wage laws, health and safety regulations, laws barring women from night work, mandating break time for them, limiting the loads they could carry, and excluding them from certain occupations altogether."[59]

Paul believed that such laws, however well intentioned, both demeaned women and limited their economic opportunities. She found allies both among women who believed that protective legislation limited their ability to compete directly with men and among political constituencies that opposed organized labor, including many Republicans and most southern Democrats. Among the staunchest early supporters of the ERA were professional and business women's clubs, whose members were mostly Republican. Partly owing to their influence, in 1940 the Republican Party became the first national party to endorse an ERA in its national platform.[60] The large majority of women workers in the early twentieth century, however, labored in largely gender-segregated trades. Not having to compete directly with men, they found protective legislation worked to their benefit. Perhaps as a result, the unions that represented them, as well as the broader labor movement, largely opposed the ERA, as did most liberal Democrats and feminists allied with the labor movement. Pro-labor feminists preferred to keep women's protective laws in place until they could be extended to men, and they proposed challenging sex discrimination on a case-by-case basis—for example, with state campaigns to grant women the right to sit on juries (which Paul's NWP also supported).[61]

The ERA made only slow progress during the presidency of Democrat Franklin Roosevelt (1933–1945). Roosevelt's political coalition, which included union workers as well as socially conservative Catholics and southerners, generally opposed the ERA; and both Secretary of Labor Frances Perkins, the highest-ranking female official in U.S. history to that point, and First Lady Eleanor Roosevelt opposed it as well (although Mrs. Roosevelt changed her mind in later life). President Roosevelt's New Deal programs, meanwhile, concentrated on lowering the staggering levels of unemployment during the Great Depression, and focused particularly on male breadwinners. The New Dealers seemed to assume, as one historian has dryly noted, that "no housewife [had] lost her job." In reality, however, about a quarter of all women over age 14 worked outside the home, and female unemployment similarly reached historic levels in the 1930s.[62]

By 1938 Congress approved the Fair Labor Standards Act (FLSA), establishing for the first time a federal minimum wage (25 cents an hour) and a forty-hour workweek for many workers, both male and female, and in 1941 the U.S. Supreme Court upheld the FLSA as constitutional. ERA supporters argued that because protective legislation could now be sustained without relying on the *Muller* doctrine of gender difference, the key labor objection to the ERA had been removed. Yet many labor groups continued to support state-level protective legislation for female workers, at least in part because the FLSA failed to cover occupations in which many women worked, such as agriculture, or that were dominated by women, such as domestic service. Two of the largest labor organizations, the American Federation of Labor (AFL) and the Congress of Industrial Organizations (CIO), continued to oppose an ERA.[63]

The role of labor and the nature of labor markets in the United States would change dramatically after the nation entered the Second World War in 1941. Sixteen million men eventually served in the American armed forces, 10 million of whom were drafted (as compared to approximately 350,000 women, all volunteer), resulting in a severe shortage of male workers needed to build everything from weapons to consumer products.[64] The U.S. government consequently called on women to work in heavy industry, and millions responded. Government propaganda celebrated the achievements of "Rosie the Riveter" during the war years, but as soon as the war was won, in 1945, women workers were quickly replaced by returning male veterans. Nonetheless, ERA supporters argued that this experience clearly disproved the notion that women should be treated differently from men and excluded from certain kinds of work because they were physically frail. This argument proved persuasive enough that in 1944 both Democrats and Republicans endorsed an ERA in their national party platforms.[65] In 1945 the United States signed the United Nations Charter, which in several places acknowledged the "equal rights of men and women," and in 1946 the American occupation force in Japan imposed a new constitution on that country that included an ERA provision, granting Japanese women equal political, economic, and social rights.[66] Also in 1946, an ERA for the first time was allowed before the full U.S. Senate for a vote. A majority of senators favored it—38 to 35—but not the required two-thirds majority.[67]

With the war over, U.S. marriage rates soared (from 84.5 per 1,000 women in 1945 to 120.7 in 1946) and the "baby boom" began. Notably, as historian Cynthia Harrison has observed, many married mothers soon returned to work: "Between 1950 and 1963, married women with husbands present and children between the ages of six and seventeen increased their labor force participation rate from 30.3 percent to 41.5 percent." Among all women in the United States, 37 percent had jobs by 1960, and nearly a third of them now worked alongside—and competed directly with—men. The number of women going to college steadily increased: approximately 103,000 received bachelor's degrees in 1950, as compared to about 127,000 nine years later.[68] Also, graduate and professional schools increasingly admitted female students. At Harvard, for example, the Medical School began admitting women regularly in 1946, the Law School in 1950, the Divinity School in 1955, and the Business School in 1963 (although for years women remained small minorities at each of these institutions).[69]

Amid these changes, the ERA push continued, now led in Congress by Senator Margaret Chase Smith, Republican of Maine. The Senate approved the ERA by greater than two-thirds majorities in 1950 and 1953, but in both cases only with the addition of an amendment, or "rider," proposed by Senator Carl Hayden, Democrat of Arizona. The rider, favored by labor unions and pro-labor feminists, read as follows: "The provisions of this article shall not be construed to impair any rights, benefits, or exemptions now or hereafter conferred by law upon persons of the female sex." The NWP refused to support this modified ERA, and opposition in the House of Representatives kept even this version from coming to a vote there.[70] Further progress on the ERA seemed stymied.

Indeed, by 1960 the main focus of American civil rights activists was not gender discrimination but racial segregation and racial disenfranchisement, especially in the South. Civil rights lawyers were persuading federal courts that segregation laws, known as "Jim Crow" laws, violated the equal protection clause of the Fourteenth Amendment, and public attention was increasingly riveted by boycotts, marches, and civil disobedience protests against Jim Crow, led most prominently by the Reverend Martin Luther King Jr. The civil rights movement ultimately inspired activism in other American groups facing discrimination, including a revived women's rights movement, which took shape in the early 1960s. In recognition of the achievements of the suffrage movement, this next phase came to be called "second-wave feminism."[71]

The "Second Wave"

John F. Kennedy, who became president in 1961, initially angered many feminists with his apparent lack of enthusiasm for the ERA and by making fewer female appointments than his supporters expected, including none at the cabinet level. Perhaps in part responding to feminist complaints, his administration backed the first federal Equal Pay law, enacted in 1963, which banned gender-based pay discrimination for covered wage workers doing "equal work on jobs the performance of which requires equal skill, effort and responsibility, and which are performed under similar working conditions."[72] Kennedy also appointed a Commission on the Status of Women, which issued a lengthy report in 1963. According to the journalist Gail Collins, the biggest impact of the commission was that "the state commissions . . . it spawned . . . brought together smart, achieving women who might otherwise have never met. And it required them to talk about women's rights, a subject that seldom came up in their normal work in government or academia." As a result the commission led many of these women to recognize more fully the degree of discrimination they had faced, and "to realize that inwardly," although they had always been polite about it, "they had been seething all along."[73]

The commission report did not endorse the ERA, but it did back a bold plan proposed by the African-American lawyer, civil rights activist, and feminist Pauli Murray. Murray noted that civil rights litigators were having great success in federal courts using the equal protection clause of the Fourteenth Amendment against Jim Crow, and she argued that equal protection litigation might be just as effective against state laws that discriminated against women, which she called "Jane Crow." For example, the U.S. Supreme Court, in a series of rulings beginning in the 1930s, had held that exclusion of black men from juries violated their equal protection rights, yet in 1963 three states (Alabama, Mississippi, and South Carolina) continued to exclude women from juries altogether, and most states, while making male jury service mandatory, still made female jury service optional and therefore rare. The Court itself had ruled in 1961 that women were not constitutionally required to sit on juries, at least in part because jury duty might interfere with their special role in "home and family life." Murray argued that if the exclusion of women from juries could be framed as an equal protection issue, federal courts would be compelled to rule against it. She also hoped that equal protection litigation, unlike an ERA, might spare women's protective legislation and so allow feminists who disagreed about such laws to work together. Such an approach, moreover, by allowing feminists and civil rights activists to pursue a common strategy, might help bridge the rift between these two movements.[74]

Meanwhile, also in 1963, the journalist and labor activist Betty Friedan published *The Feminine Mystique*. Friedan had graduated from Smith College, an all-women's school, in 1942. In 1957 she had conducted a detailed survey of her former classmates to gauge their satisfaction with their lives. Most were full-time "housewives," which was widely seen as an ideal female role, yet most declared themselves feeling dissatisfied, unhappy, and unfulfilled. From this survey Friedan developed a fierce and wide-ranging critique of the then-prevailing idea that women's place was in the home, arguing that it psychologically maimed women and weakened American society.[75] Her book became a national bestseller, and countless American women said they became feminists after reading it.

In 1964 Congress debated a sweeping Civil Rights Bill, which would largely ban racial segregation. The bill had the strong backing of the new Democratic president, Lyndon Johnson. Title VII of the bill would create an Equal Employment Opportunity Commission (EEOC) to enforce fair employment practices. Pro-segregationists in Congress did everything they could to block the legislation. Among them was the 80-year-old chair of the House Rules Committee, Howard Smith, Democrat of Virginia, who proposed an amendment to Title VII to give the EEOC authority to act on complaints of sexual as well as racial discrimination. Smith, a friend of Alice Paul and an ERA supporter, symbolized the long-held ties between segregationists and the NWP, which in a 1963 statement had cautioned that "the Civil Rights Bill would not . . . give protection against discrimination because of 'race, color, religion or national origins,' to a *White Woman, a Woman of the Christian Religion, or a Woman of United States Origin.*"[76] Smith later admitted that he had hoped his amendment would kill the bill, presumably by making it look unreasonable and spurring opposition from labor groups. Yet although many male members of Congress did oppose and mock the provision, others did not, and a few female members, including the influential Margaret Chase Smith, rallied Congress behind it. The bill became the Civil Rights Act of 1964 with Howard Smith's amendment included. After this the ERA increasingly came to be associated with support for the civil rights movement rather than opposition to it.[77]

The members of the EEOC began work expecting to focus on complaints about racial discrimination in the workplace, but they were shocked to find that in the first year alone they received more than 2,500 complaints concerning sex discrimination—over a quarter of the total. The large number of complaints also made it clear that many women no longer worked in sex-segregated industries but instead worked in direct competition with men. Moreover, hundreds of these sex discrimination complaints were filed against labor unions. These developments, which one union report described as "a new problem in a rather unexpected vein," prompted some labor leaders, female as well as male, to begin to question their long opposition to the ERA. For its part, the EEOC seemed to lack commitment to the sexual discrimination ban and was slow to act on sexual discrimination suits, infuriating feminists.[78]

In 1966, while attending a national meeting of state commissions on the status of women, Betty Friedan and others present shared their dissatisfaction with the EEOC and decided to form a new women's rights group. Friedan scribbled its name on the back of a napkin—the National Organization for Women (NOW). NOW soon held a national conference, organized protests at EEOC offices around the country, and came to be seen as the leading feminist organization. In 1967 it endorsed the ERA.[79]

Meanwhile, a "women's liberation" movement emerged that considered NOW too moderate. It was led by younger feminists already active in the protest movements for civil rights and against U.S. involvement in the Vietnam War, which was escalating in the late 1960s. These liberation feminists popularized a new word, "sexism," to describe a sexual "caste system" as well as prejudice against women, and they engaged in an ever-widening critique of gender norms, including in relationships and child rearing, politics, economics, religion, literature, art, and entertainment.[80] Many in the national media mocked "Women's Lib," which first gained prominence in 1968, when women picketed as sexist the Miss America beauty pageant in Atlantic City. The protesters had announced they would burn "implements of fashion-torture such as girdles and hair curlers," but the local fire department had not allowed them to do so. Although nothing was ultimately set on fire, the media sensationalized "bra-burning" as a symbol of "radical feminism."[81]

In 1969, in what is often seen as the symbolic start of the gay rights movement, gay men rioted against a police raid at the Stonewall Inn, a gay bar in New York City. Although there had been a "homophile" movement since the 1940s, it had concentrated on challenging the prevailing conception of "homosexuals," commonly defined at the time as people suffering from a dangerous sexual pathology. Activists had argued that psychologically healthy people could love others of the same sex, and that the differences between such people and others were so small that no rational basis existed for laws against them. Courts had rejected this view, however. In the 1960s, inspired by the civil rights movement, there emerged a new gay rights movement that saw gays and lesbians as a persecuted minority fighting for equal protection of the laws. In the 1970s, the relationship of gay rights to the ERA would become increasingly controversial.[82]

The Era of the ERA

Between 1966 and 1970 many feminist factions were able to coalesce around a common program. This program included pursuing Murray's idea of litigating sexual discrimination as an equal protection issue and working to enact women's rights legislation at the state and federal levels, but its centerpiece was the ERA.[83]

In 1970, members of Congress debated the ERA on the floor of the U.S. House of Representatives for the first time and passed it with more than a two-thirds majority. The ERA foundered in the Senate, however, when it became encumbered, as in the past, by amendments that feminists rejected, including one forbidding women from being drafted into the military.[84] Yet momentum for the ERA only increased in 1971, as three states, Illinois, Pennsylvania, and Virginia, added equal rights amendments to their own constitutions, the first states to do so in the twentieth century. On October 12, 1971, the U.S. House approved a joint resolution proposing the amendment, 354–23. The Senate then rejected all proposed changes and on March 22, 1972, approved the resolution, with its seven-year ratification deadline, by a vote of 84–8.[85]

By December 1972, twenty-two of the necessary thirty-eight states had ratified, and Helen Reddy's feminist anthem "I Am Woman, Hear Me Roar" was the number 1 song on the Billboard charts.[86] The next year, eight more states ratified, and the American Federation of Labor and the Congress of Industrial Organizations (which had merged in 1955, forming the largest coalition of labor unions in the country, the AFL-CIO) endorsed the ERA, ending five decades of opposition by organized labor.[87] The year 1974 saw three more state ratifications, while the Gallup public opinion poll found that nearly three-quarters of Americans backed the amendment. Also, between 1972 and 1974 eleven more states added equal rights provisions to their constitutions. In the 1976 presidential election, both the Republican incumbent, Gerald Ford, and his victorious Democratic challenger, Jimmy Carter, supported ERA ratification.[88]

TABLE 17.1

Equal Rights Amendments (ERAs), by State and Year, 1879–1980

State	ERA Added to State Constitution	Legislature Ratifies National ERA	ERA, State (S) or National (N), Rejected by Referendum	Legislature Rescinds Ratification of National ERA
Alabama				
Alaska	1972	1972		
Arizona				
Arkansas				
California	1879	1972		
Colorado	1973	1972		
Connecticut	1974	1973		
Delaware		1972		
Florida			1978 (S)	
Georgia				
Hawaii	1972, 1978	1972		
Idaho		1972		1977
Illinois	1971			
Indiana		1977		
Iowa		1972	1980 (S)	
Kansas		1972		
Kentucky		1972		1978
Louisiana	1974			
Maine		1974		
Maryland	1972	1972		
Massachusetts	1976	1972		
Michigan		1972		
Minnesota		1973		
Mississippi				
Missouri				
Montana	1973	1974		
Nebraska		1972		1973
Nevada			1978 (N)*	
New Hampshire	1974	1972		
New Jersey		1972	1975 (S)	
New Mexico	1973	1973		
New York		1972	1975 (S)	

State *	ERA Added to State Constitution	Legislature Ratifies National ERA	ERA, State (S) or National (N), Rejected by Referendum	Legislature Rescinds Ratification of National ERA
North Carolina				
North Dakota		1975		
Ohio		1974		
Oklahoma				
Oregon		1973	1978 (S)	
Pennsylvania	1971	1972		
Rhode Island		1972		
South Carolina				
South Dakota		1973		1979
Tennessee		1972		1974
Texas	1972	1972		
Utah	1896			
Vermont		1973		
Virginia	1971			
Washington	1972	1973		
West Virginia		1972		
Wisconsin		1972	1973 (S)	
Wyoming	1890	1973		

Sources: Adapted from Leslie Gladstone, "Equal Rights Amendments: State Provisions" (Congressional Research Service, 2004), 3–6; Sara A. Soule and Susan Olzak, "When Do Movements Matter? The Politics of Contingency and the Equal Rights Amendment," *American Sociological Review* 69, no. 4 (2004), 476; Nancy Elizabeth Baker, "Too Much to Lose, Too Little to Gain: The Role of Rescission Movements in the Equal Rights Amendment Battle" (PhD diss., Harvard University, 2003), esp. 97–153, 162, 256–289, 335, 353–354, 358–359, 373–376, 392; Laura E. Brock, "Religion, Sex & Politics: The Story of the Equal Rights Amendment in Florida" (PhD diss., Florida State University, 2013), 180–182; "Equal Rights Amendment" (Nevada Legislature, Background Paper 79-7, 1979), 3.

* The referendum was merely advisory, as only the state legislature had the constitutional authority to ratify the national ERA.

Meanwhile, the legal campaign to use the equal protection clause of the Fourteenth Amendment to expand women's rights had won its first of many victories before the U.S. Supreme Court in 1971. At issue in *Reed v. Reed* was an Idaho statute that required "males must be preferred to females" when two individuals in the same entitlement class (such as two parents) applied to become administrator of an estate.[89] Ruth Bader Ginsburg, later the second woman appointed to the U.S. Supreme Court, was principal author of the key brief. Ginsburg argued that sex-based classifications should be regarded by the courts in the same way that courts by this point regarded race-based classifications, as presumptively "suspect" under the equal protection clause, and so subject to the legal standard of "strict scrutiny."[90] Whereas equal protection litigation on race had concentrated on access to voting, juries, and public facilities, Ginsburg was extending it to a new area, one of central concern to the women's rights movement— family law. The Court ruled unanimously that sexual classifications did deserve special scrutiny, although not at the "strict" level, and that the Idaho law was unconstitutional.[91]

On the legislative front Congress passed the Equal Opportunity Employment Act in 1972, extending the antidiscrimination provisions of Title VII of the Civil Rights Act to cover schools, colleges, universities, state and local governments, and the federal government, and authorized the EEOC to go to court to enforce its rulings. Also in 1972, Congress approved the so-called Education Amendments, which included Title IX: "No person in the United States shall, on the basis of sex, be excluded from participation in, be denied the benefits of, or be subjected to discrimination under any educational program or activity receiving federal financial assistance."[92] Title IX became famous for its effects on collegiate sports, producing a large expansion of women's programs, yet it also has been credited with greatly expanding women's enrollment in graduate and professional schools. State legislatures, meanwhile, were beginning to reevaluate family law. In 1976, Nebraska became the first state to criminalize marital rape, although there was no prosecution of marital rape under the new statute until 1982.[93] By mid-1981, ten states recognized rape within marriage as a crime, and campaigns to criminalize it were under way in seven more.[94]

Despite these changes, momentum for the ERA slowed dramatically after 1974. By 1977, the year Alice Paul died at the age of 92, only two more states had ratified.[95] None did so over the remainder of the decade. In fact, between 1973 and 1978, the legislatures of four ratifying states—Nebraska, Tennessee, Idaho, and Kentucky—passed resolutions declaring that they had rescinded ratification (although the acting governor vetoed the Kentucky rescission). In addition, the legislature of nearly every ratifying state considered rescinding its own ratification. Whether a state could constitutionally rescind its prior approval of an amendment was a question that provoked consider-

TABLE 17.2

Public Opinion on the National ERA, in Polls by Gallup, Roper, and NBC (1974–1977)

	1974 (Gallup)	1975 (Gallup)	1975 (Roper)	1976 (Gallup)	1977 (NBC)	1977 (Roper)
Favor	74%	58%	60%	57%	53%	48%
Oppose	21%	24%	21%	24%	37%	20%
Not Sure / Don't Know	5%	18%	4%	19%	10%	4%
Have Mixed Feelings	n.a.	n.a.	15%	n.a.	n.a.	27%

Source: Adapted from Carol Finn Meyer, "Attitudes towards the Equal Rights Amendment" (PhD diss., CUNY, 1979), 14–15, tables 1 and 2. In the 1974 poll, Gallup gave respondents a ballot that included the ERA question as well as thirteen other questions, and asked respondents which ballot questions they would vote to approve. The 1975 and 1976 Gallup polls were of respondents who had heard of or read about the ERA. The 1977 NBC poll prefaced the question "Do you favor or oppose passage of the Equal Rights Amendment?" with a statement that the recent National Women's Conference had passed a resolution calling for approval of the ERA. The Roper polls prefaced the question about favoring or opposing the ERA with a statement saying "there is a lot of controversy for and against the amendment." The Roper polls also gave respondents the option of saying that they had "mixed feelings" about the ERA. In identifying respondents who were uncertain about the ERA, Gallup and NBC gave the option "Not Sure," and Roper gave the option "Don't Know."

able debate but had yet to be answered by the U.S. Supreme Court.* At roughly the same time, voters in several states, including New York and New Jersey, both of which had ratified the ERA, rejected equal rights amendments to their own state constitutions via referenda. Nonetheless, national and state polls indicated that the ERA retained relatively strong popular support, and several states had come close to ratification multiple times.[96]

---

* Supporters of the ERA in the 1970s and early 1980s denied that states had the constitutional authority to rescind ratification of a constitutional amendment. They noted that Article V of the U.S. Constitution mentions the power to "ratify" but not the power to rescind. Precedent for states rescinding ratification, however, dates to 1868, when the legislatures of Ohio and New Jersey voted to rescind their ratification of the Fourteenth Amendment. In that case, enough other states voted to ratify the amendment that adoption was assured, even without counting Ohio and New Jersey. In the end, Congress essentially ignored the rescissions, which is why Ohio and New Jersey still appear, without asterisks, on official lists of states that originally ratified the Fourteenth Amendment. In 1937 the Supreme Court ruled in a case involving a proposed (but never ratified) amendment banning child labor that a state could ratify an amendment after rejecting it, but whether it could do the opposite remained unclear. See esp. *State of Idaho v. Freeman,* 529 F. Supp 1107 (1981); William S. Sininger, "Can States Rescind ERA Ratification Votes?" *Human Rights* 8, no. 2 (July 1979), 46–47, 56; Nancy Elizabeth Baker, "Too Much to Lose, Too Little to Gain: The Role of Rescission Movements in the Equal Rights Amendment Battle" (PhD diss., Harvard University, 2003).

In October 1978, with the ERA ratification deadline of March 1979 fast approaching, but with at most 35 of the requisite 38 states having ratified (not counting rescissions), Congress took the unprecedented step of extending the deadline set by the original joint resolution in 1972. Congress approved the extension (as an amendment to the resolution) by a vote of 253 to 189 in the House and 60 to 36 in the Senate. Signed by President Carter, the provision reset the ERA ratification deadline to June 30, 1982.[97] The constitutionality of this extension, however, remained a matter of considerable controversy.[98]

Immediately after the extension vote, the president of NOW, Eleanor Smeal, told reporters that "the momentum is very, very strong right now" and that the remaining ratifications might occur even before the original 1979 deadline. None did, and in December 1979 South Dakota voted to rescind its ratification on the grounds that the extension violated states' rights. Nor had new ratifications occurred by December 1981, when a federal district judge in Idaho, Marion Callister, handed down a controversial decision in *Idaho v. Freeman,* a suit brought by anti-extension legislators from three states. Callister ruled both that states had the constitutional authority to rescind an amendment before it was ratified and that the deadline extension had been unconstitutional, because any congressional exercise of the amendment power, including amending a joint resolution, must be passed by a two-thirds vote. ERA supporters rejected the ruling and the authority of the court to make it, arguing that this was a political matter that courts should not adjudicate. NOW appealed the ruling to the U.S. Supreme Court, which took the unusual step of issuing a stay (normally issued only on judicial orders, not interpretations of law). The Court held off hearing the case, however, until after the June 30 deadline.[99]

Debate over the ERA, 1972–1982

The ratification process for the ERA ultimately stalled, at least in part, because opposition to it had coalesced into a well-organized movement. Opponents included both Democrats, especially from the South, and Republicans, particularly self-described conservatives. Although some Catholic groups, and many Jewish and mainline Protestant groups (as they were called), supported the ERA, major fundamentalist Protestant denominations and the National Council of Catholic Women campaigned against it. One of the most active opposition groups was the Church of Latter-Day Saints (LDS, or Mormons).

In 1976 the LDS First Presidency declared that the ERA, if ratified, would "stifle many God-given feminine instincts" and "strike at the family, human-kind's basic institution."[100] Thereafter church leaders urged members to reject the ERA and donated substantial funds to anti-ERA activists in battle-ground states such as Florida. In 1978 the church excommunicated an ERA supporter, Sonia Johnson, because she had urged Mormons to repudiate their leaders (and non-Mormons to turn away Mormon missionaries) on the issue. Shortly afterward, when *Idaho v. Freeman* first came before Judge Callister, NOW lawyers argued he should not hear the case because he was a promi-nent Mormon, and so "the Court's ability to consider the action before it in an impartial manner may be, or appear to be, impaired." NOW's efforts to get Callister to recuse himself or to convince another court to remove him proved unsuccessful.[101]

Although the ERA had many opponents through the 1970s and early 1980s, the most visible one—and arguably the most effective as well—was Phyllis Schlafly, a prominent conservative activist. After earning a master's degree in government from Radcliffe College in 1945, Schlafly became in-volved in Illinois Republican politics. In 1952 she ran as the Republican nom-inee for a seat in Congress, but lost. In 1964 she published her first book, *A Choice not an Echo,* a campaign biography of presidential hopeful Senator Barry Goldwater of Arizona, the leading Republican opponent of the 1964 Civil Rights Act. Her book sold 3.5 million copies in six months and may have helped Goldwater capture the Republican presidential nomination that year—celebrated by "grass-roots conservatives" as a victory over the "East Coast Establishment." Goldwater, however, suffered a landslide defeat to incumbent Lyndon Johnson in the presidential election that fall. In 1967 Schlafly started the *Phyllis Schlafly Report,* a conservative newsletter that soon gained a national readership, and in 1970 again ran unsuccessfully as a Republican for Congress (declaring, "a woman's place is in the House"). In 1972 she founded STOP-ERA, which emerged as the leading national organ-ization opposing the ERA. (Notably, she also earned a law degree at Wash-ington University in St. Louis in 1978.)[102]

Schlafly argued that the ERA would not expand women's rights, which were now fully protected by federal law, but would "transfer into the hands of the federal government the last remaining aspects of our life that the feds haven't yet got their meddling fingers into." She noted that federal courts were now interpreting the Fourteenth Amendment expansively to ban race discrimination, ruling for example that "you cannot discriminate on the basis of race even in private schools that get no public money whatsoever." Women's rights lawyers, she observed, were following "the same pattern of litigation and legal theories as civil rights lawyers," and so the ERA would lead federal courts to force "integration at every level." She added, "I do not dispute in the slightest what we are doing on the matter of race, but we do claim that sex should not be treated in the same way." For example, she charged that the ERA would "deprive you of your freedom of choice to attend an all-girls' or all-boys' school." Other ERA opponents argued it would mandate "unisex" bathrooms.[103]

Further, Schlafly maintained that the ERA would "take away a young girl's exemption from the draft" and require women to serve in combat, from which they had hitherto been excluded—a prospect that many Americans opposed. For their part, most leading feminists opposed the Vietnam War, which ended in 1975, and many supported men who resisted the military draft, which was suspended the same year. Many feminists nonetheless thought U.S. women would never win full recognition as citizens unless they could serve on equal terms with men in the military, and they noted that female soldiers had often risked their lives in "noncombat" roles, yet had been denied the promotion opportunities and veterans' benefits of male "combatants." Responding to feminist arguments, President Jimmy Carter proposed in 1980 that young women as well as young men should register equally for military service, although in the end Congress approved male-only registration.[104]

Beyond the focus on combat, Schlafly alleged that the ERA would change the "legal definition of marriage," threatening the prevailing understanding of marriage as between "a man and a woman."[105] NOW leaders insisted that the ERA "was not about gay liberation," and most Americans opposed gay marriage. Yet some gay rights activists, among them women's liberation feminists, had started to demand equal access to marriage for gay couples. In the 1970s, following the feminist lead, the gay rights movement began using civil rights precedents to sue for equal protection under the law. In 1967 the U.S. Supreme Court had used equal protection reasoning to overturn state bans on interracial marriage. Gay rights activists began using this precedent to launch equal protection lawsuits, and many thought the ERA would help their cause. Advocates of gay rights appeared in pro-ERA marches and rallies, and a gay rights lawsuit in Washington State in 1973 claimed that the state ERA, approved in 1970, had been intended to allow same-sex marriage (the state Supreme Court rejected this argument).[106]

Schlafly also objected that the ERA was "anti-children, and pro-abortion."[107] Many Americans, among them Catholics and a growing number of Protestant fundamentalists, viewed abortion as murder. Feminists, by contrast, saw the issue in light of their demand that women should have the right to decide whether to become mothers. They consequently pushed for states to liberalize their abortion laws and welcomed the U.S. Supreme Court decision in *Roe v. Wade* (1973), which held that women had a right to terminate pregnancy in its early stages. Some feminists filed suits in Hawaii and Massachusetts arguing that state ERAs gave women the right to tax-funded abortions.[108]

At the broadest level, Schlafly portrayed the ERA as part of an attack on traditional femininity, asserting that "women's libbers view the home as a prison, and the wife and mother as a slave. . . . [They] don't understand that most women want to be a wife, mother, and homemaker."[109] She insisted that she herself was first and foremost a mother of six and a homemaker and that she deferred to the decisions of her husband. Women who opposed the ERA often self-identified in a similar way. Some even emphasized their homemaking skills while lobbying male legislators, by wearing "little red aprons saying 'STOP ERA'" and presenting the lawmakers with gifts of homemade baked goods and jellies.[110]

In the 1980 presidential election, the Democratic Party platform endorsed registration of women for military service, abortion rights, and ratification of the ERA, while insisting that "past rescissions are invalid."[111] The party nominated for reelection President Carter, who had signed the ERA extension resolution in 1979 and whose administration had lobbied state legislatures to ratify the amendment. By contrast, the Republican platform took no position on women's selective service registration, and while conceding the party contained "differing views" on abortion, nonetheless endorsed "a constitutional amendment to restore protection of the right to life for unborn children." Having first endorsed the ERA in 1940, the Republican Party now declined to do so, saying: "We acknowledge the legitimate efforts of those who support or oppose ratification of the Equal Rights Amendment." The Republican platform also denounced the Carter administration's attempts to "pressure" states into ratifying the ERA and supported the right of states to rescind ratification. The Republican nominee, former California governor Ronald Reagan, had once supported the ERA but now opposed it.[112]

In the fall campaign, Reagan responded to Democratic charges that he was hostile to women's rights by promising that as president he would appoint the first woman to the U.S. Supreme Court. On election day he defeated Carter, carrying all but three states, and Republicans won control of the U.S. Senate for the first time since 1955. Exit polls indicated that Reagan had won support from 54 percent of male voters but only 47 percent of female voters—a difference NOW leaders labeled "the gender gap."[113]

Shortly after taking office President Reagan fulfilled his campaign pledge to appoint a woman to the Supreme Court, selecting Sandra Day O'Connor, a judge on the Arizona Court of Appeals, to be an Associate Justice. She had graduated third in her class at Stanford Law School in 1952 but had been "refused a job at every law firm to which she applied," presumably because she was a woman. Eventually she took a position as a prosecutor (an assistant county attorney) in Arizona. She worked for Goldwater in 1964 and served as a Republican in the Arizona State Senate, where she became the first female senate majority leader in any state legislature before entering the state judiciary. At her confirmation hearings before the U.S. Senate, she professed a personal "abhorrence" of abortion but refused to say whether she would vote to overturn *Roe v. Wade,* prompting anti-abortion groups to oppose her. The Senate nonetheless confirmed her nomination by a vote of 99 to 0. She was sworn in as an Associate Justice on September 25, 1981.[114]

If enough states ratified the ERA by the new deadline at the end of June 1982, Justice O'Connor would have the opportunity to help decide NOW's appeal of *Idaho v. Freeman.* But the clock was ticking, and by this point—with less than nine months to go—Florida was the key battleground state. If Florida ratified, Illinois and Oklahoma seemed primed to follow, bringing the total number of ratifications, not counting rescissions, to the required 38. If Florida did not ratify, then the ERA would most likely be dead, and the questions raised in the *Idaho* case would effectively disappear.

The ERA Fight in Florida

In March 1972, two days after Congress sent the amendment to the states, the Florida House of Representatives voted to ratify it—with no hearings, little debate, and by a margin of 84–3.[115] It might have passed the Florida Senate as well, but never came to a vote because the Senate president, an ERA opponent, blocked it with a procedural ruling.[116] Between January and March 1973 a joint Florida legislative committee held hearings on the ERA throughout the state. Although many witnesses supported the amendment, many also strongly opposed it. In April, when the Florida House debated the ratification resolution, the galleries were filled with women—supporters wearing green and opponents, red—a scene that would become a regular feature of legislative votes on the amendment in Florida. The ratification resolution failed, 54–64.* The following year the ERA resolution did not get out of committee in the Florida House and went down in the Senate, 19–21; the year after that, the resolution passed the House, 61–58, but again failed in the Senate, 17–21.[117]

In January 1977 commissioners in Dade County, Florida, approved an ordinance banning discrimination against gays and lesbians in hiring, housing, and access to public services. Anita Bryant, the TV spokeswoman for Florida orange juice, denounced the commissioners for polluting "the moral atmosphere" for her children. "Homosexuals cannot reproduce—so they must recruit," she asserted. "And to freshen their ranks, they must recruit the youth of America."[118] Her "Save Our Children" coalition waged a six-week campaign to repeal the ordinance by referendum, and county voters ultimately overturned it by a margin of 69 percent to 31 percent. The president of the Florida STOP-ERA chapter backed Bryant's campaign, later claiming the Dade County fight "went a long way in shaking church people out of lethargy" about opposing the ERA. Shortly thereafter the ERA again fell short in the Florida Senate, by a vote of 19–21. After the Senate defeat, supporters saw no point in holding a vote in the House, although 61 of 120 members had cosponsored an ERA resolution that session.[119]

In 1978 a state commission proposed adding the word "sex" to an existing constitutional declaration: "No person shall be deprived of any right because of race, religion, *sex,* or physical handicap." ERA opponents mobilized against

---

* In Florida, like every state except Illinois, a proposed federal constitutional amendment could be ratified by a simple majority vote in both chambers of the legislature; the Illinois state constitution required a three-fifths supermajority in both chambers. No state constitution explicitly required the governor to endorse a ratification resolution of a federal amendment, although governors typically did so, and the acting governor of Kentucky assumed the power to veto a resolution of the Kentucky legislature to rescind ratification of the ERA in 1978. See Nancy Elizabeth Baker, "Too Much to Lose, Too Little to Gain: The Role of Rescission Movements in the Equal Rights Amendment Battle" (PhD diss., Harvard University, 2003), 24–25n24, 358–359.

this "little ERA." In November, just weeks after Congress extended the national ERA deadline, Florida voters rejected the "little ERA" by a margin of 58 percent to 42 percent.[120] Nonetheless, public opinion polls continued to show that most Floridians favored the federal ERA.[121] In 1979 the ERA passed the Florida House 64–52, only to be defeated in the Senate, once again by a vote of 19–21.[122]

NOW pressured the state to ratify. In 1977 it began urging national organizations not to hold their conventions in Florida until it ratified. Many organizations complied, including the AFL-CIO, which "moved its biennial convention . . . from Miami Beach to Washington." In 1980 NOW called for a boycott of the entire $12 billion Florida tourism industry. Picketers began congregating along Interstate 4 near Disney World, urging tourists to forgo their Florida vacation plans.[123] Florida took no new legislative action on the ERA, however, until June 1982, when, with the new ratification deadline days away, the governor called a special session of the legislature.

In the weeks before the session, both sides mobilized, and on June 21, the day of the vote, thousands of demonstrators, mostly women, surrounded the state capitol and crowded its halls and galleries. ERA supporters were dressed in green and white, opponents in red. At about noon, the House voted for ratification. The Senate president ruled that a vote would be taken in his chamber by 2:00 p.m.[124] As the debate began, the nation watched.

NOTES

1. Laura E. Brock, "Religion, Sex & Politics: The Story of the Equal Rights Amendment in Florida" (PhD diss., Florida State University, 2013), 209–224.

2. Intellectuals had been discussing women's place or role in modern society since at least the seventeenth century. Rosemary Zagarri, *Revolutionary Backlash: Women and Politics in the Early American Republic* (Philadelphia: University of Pennsylvania Press, 2007), 12–19.

3. Jill Elaine Hasday, "Contest and Consent: A Legal History of Marital Rape," *California Law Review* 88 (2000): 1389–1392. Legal codes explicitly defined rape as something that a man did to a woman "other than his wife."

4. Quoted in Richard Geddes and Sharon Tennyson, "Passage of the Married Women's Property Acts and Earnings Acts in the United States: 1850 to 1920," *Research in Economic History* 29 (2013): 146.

5. Linda K. Kerber, *No Constitutional Right to be Ladies: Women and the Obligation of Citizenship* (New York: Hill and Wang, 1998), 11–14.

6. Mary Beth Norton, *Liberty's Daughters: The Revolutionary Experience of American Women, 1750–1800* (Boston: Little, Brown, 1980), 156–161, 166–169. A focus on the "rights of woman" was popularized by the English radical Mary Wollstonecraft when, inspired in part by Tom Paine's book *The Rights of Man* (1791), she published *A Vindication of the Rights of Woman* (1792). See Zagarri, *Revolutionary Backlash*, 40–41.

7. Abigail Adams to John Adams, 31 Mar. 1776, in *Adams Family Correspondence*, ed. L. H. Butterfield (Cambridge, MA: Harvard University Press, 1963–2015), 1:370. In the same letter (1:371), she mentions her intention to manufacture saltpeter, a key ingredient of gunpowder.

8. John Adams to Abigail Adams, 4 Apr. 1776, in *Adams Family Correspondence*, 1:382.

9. John Adams to James Sullivan, 26 May 1776, in Robert J. Taylor et al., *Papers of John Adams* (Cambridge, MA: Harvard University Press, 1977–2012), 4:208–212, quotations at 210–211.

10. Jan Ellen Lewis, "Rethinking Women's Suffrage in New Jersey, 1776–1807," *Rutgers Law Review* 63, no. 3 (Aug. 2011): 1022–1030.

11. Kerber, *No Constitutional Right*, xx (quotation), 13; Lewis, "Rethinking Women's Suffrage," 1032–1035.

12. Turnout figures come from Curtis Gans and Matthew Mullin, *Voter Turnout in the United States, 1788–2009* (Washington, DC: CQ Press, 2011).

13. For an account of the concept and workings of the female "domestic sphere"—how it limited women's opportunities yet how women were able to exploit it in certain ways to empower themselves—see Nancy Cott, *The Bonds of Womanhood: The Domestic Sphere in New England, 1780–1835* (New Haven, CT: Yale University Press, 1977; 2nd ed., 1997).

14. Anne M. Boylan, "Women and Politics in the Era before Seneca Falls," *Journal of the Early Republic* 10, no. 3 (1990): 363–382, quotations at 365.

15. Lucia McMahon, "'Of the Utmost Importance to Our Country': Women, Education, and Society, 1780–1820," *Journal of the Early Republic* 29, no. 3 (2009): 475–506; Mary Kelley, *Learning to Stand and Speak: Women, Education, and Public Life in America's Republic* (Chapel Hill: University of North Carolina Press, 2006).

16. David Tyak and Elizabeth Hansot, *Learning Together: A History of Coeducation in America* (New York: Russell Sage Foundation, 1992), 46–47; Susan Zaeske, *Signatures of Citizenship: Petitioning, Antislavery, and Women's Political Identity* (Chapel Hill: University of North Carolina Press, 2003), 106.

17. Zaeske, *Signatures of Citizenship*, 14–15, 13, 18–21.

18. Ibid., 16, 18–20, 78–81; "The petition of a Great Number of Blackes detained in a State of Slavery . . ." (January 13, 1777), *Collections of the Massachusetts Historical Society,* 5th ser., vol. 3 (Boston: Massachusetts Historical Society, 1877), 436–437, available at https://babel.hathitrust.org/cgi/pt?id=njp.32101076467586; Loren Schweninger, ed., *The Southern Debate over Slavery,* vol. 1: *Petitions to Southern Legislatures, 1778–1864*

(Urbana: University of Illinois Press, 2001); Kristin A. Collins, "'Petitions without Number': Widows' Petitions and the Early Nineteenth-Century Origins of Public Marriage-Based Entitlements," *Law and History Review* 31, no. 1 (2013): 1–60; Boylan, "Women and Politics," 370–372.

19. Zaeske, *Signatures of Citizenship,* 23–27; Alisse Theodore Portnoy, "'Female Petitioners Can Be Lawfully Heard': Negotiating Female Decorum, United States Politics, and Political Agency, 1829–1831," *Journal of the Early Republic* 23, no. 4 (2004): 573–610; Katheryn Kish Sklar, ed., *How Did the Removal of the Cherokee Nation from Georgia Shape Women's Activism in the North, 1817–1838?* (Binghamton: SUNY Press, 2004).

20. Julie Roy Jeffrey, *The Great Silent Army of Abolitionism: Ordinary Women in the Antislavery Movement* (Chapel Hill: University of North Carolina Press, 1998), 53, 1–3, "social ostracism" quotation at 3. See also Manisha Sinha, *The Slave's Cause: A History of Abolition* (New Haven, CT: Yale University Press, 2016), 266–278. The importance of female leadership to the creation and maintenance of organized abolitionism in Concord, Massachusetts, is stressed by Sandra Harbert Petrulionis, *To Set This World Right: The Antislavery Movement in Thoreau's Concord* (Ithaca, NY: Cornell University Press, 2006).

21. To cite just a few of countless examples, slave families being broken up by sale is a major theme of Harriet Beecher Stowe's *Uncle Tom's Cabin* (1852), whereas the sexual exploitation of slave women, repeatedly implied in that book and discussed more directly in Stowe's *Key to Uncle Tom's Cabin: Presenting the Original Documents and Facts on Which the Story Is Founded* (1853), is a major theme of Harriet Jacobs's now-famous memoir, originally published under the pseudonym "Linda Brent," *Incidents in the Life of a Slave Girl* (1861).

22. Zaeske, *Signatures of Citizenship,* 36–37, 42–44, 69.

23. Ibid., 69–73.

24. Ibid., 84–90, 112–114, 120–121. See also Sinha, *The Slave's Cause,* 282; Gerda Lerner, *The Grimké Sisters from South Carolina: Pioneers for Women's Rights and Abolition,* 2nd ed. (New York: Oxford University Press, 1998).

25. Zaeske, *Signatures of Citizenship,* 119, 78–81, 153. On the politics of the repeal, see ibid., 206n27.

26. Daniel Carpenter and Colin D. Moore, "When Canvassers Became Activists: Antislavery Petitioning and the Political Mobilization of American Women," *American Political Science Review* 108, no. 3 (2014): 480, 490–491, 493–494; Zaeske, *Signatures of Citizenship,* 110. Carpenter and Moore compare all petitions circulating in the same townships during the same sessions of Congress and find that those canvassed by females had a mean of eighty-five more signatures on them.

27. Zaeske, *Signatures of Citizenship,* 54–59, 97–99.

28. Ibid., 149–151.

29. See, e.g., *The Proceedings of the Woman's Rights Convention, Held at Worcester, October 23d & 24th, 1850* (Boston: Prentiss and Sawyer, 1851), available at https://babel .hathitrust.org/cgi/pt?id=hvd.rslfbk.

30. Sinha, *Signatures of Citizenship*, 288–292, 296–297; *Report of the Woman's Rights Convention, Held at Seneca Falls, New York, July 19th and 20th, 1848* (New York: Robert J. Johnson, 1870), 3. Stanton, and her collaborator Susan B. Anthony, later claimed (with some exaggeration) that the Seneca Falls convention was the founding event of the women's rights movement; in 1870, they even reissued this pamphlet with the title *The First Convention Ever Called to Discuss the Civil and Political Rights of Women*, presumably in order to enhance their authority during intramovement controversies after the Civil War. On the process by which they constructed the history of the women's rights movement, see Lisa Tetrault, *The Myth of Seneca Falls: Memory and the Women's Suffrage Movement, 1848–1898* (Chapel Hill, NC: University of North Carolina Press, 2014).

31. Elizabeth Cady Stanton, "Call to the Woman's Rights Convention and a Declaration of Sentiments," in *The First Convention Ever Called to Discuss the Civil and Political Rights of Women, Seneca Falls, N.Y., July 19, 20, 1848*, by Elizabeth Cady Stanton, Lucretia Mott, Martha C. Wright, Mary Ann McClintock and Jane C. Hunt (Seneca Falls, NY, 1848), 2–4.

32. *Report of the Woman's Rights Convention*, 4–5, 7–8. See also Stanton, *Elizabeth Cady Stanton as Revealed in Her Letters, Diary, and Reminiscences*, ed. Theodore Stanton and Harriet S. Blanche (New York: Harper and Row, 1922), 146–147.

33. See Alexander Keyssar, *The Right to Vote: The Contested History of Democracy in the United States* (New York: Basic Books, 2009), 141–143, 150, 365 (table A.17); Norma Basch, *In the Eyes of the Law: Married Women's Property Rights in Nineteenth-Century New York* (Ithaca, NY: Cornell University Press, 1982); Geddes and Tennyson, "Passage of the Married Women's Property Acts and Earnings Acts," 145–189.

34. Joelle Million, *Woman's Voice, Woman's Place: Lucy Stone and the Birth of the Women's Rights Movement* (Westport, CT: Praeger, 2003), 113–114, 194–196, quotations at 194.

35. Hasday, "Contest and Consent," 1424, 1464–1482. Hasday has found two cases in which a husband was prosecuted for helping another man to rape his wife, but none for a man raping his own wife. Hasday did find, however, a gradual recognition by American courts that under very special circumstances, such as when a wife had been ordered by a physician not to have sex, a husband's forcing her to have sex with him anyway might constitute marital cruelty and possibly serve as justifiable grounds for divorce.

36. Jane E. Larsen, "'Even a Worm Will Turn at Last': Rape Reform in Late Nineteenth Century America," *Yale Journal of Law & the Humanities* 9 (1997): 2–3; Hasday, "Contest and Consent," 1437–1438; Tracy A. Thomas, "Misappropriating Women's History in the Law and Politics of Abortion," *Seattle University Law Review* 36 (2012–2013): 20–30.

37. Zaeske, *Signatures of Citizenship*, 167–171; Tetrault, *Myth of Seneca Falls*, 19–22.

38. Nina Morais, "Sex Discrimination and the Fourteenth Amendment: Lost History," *Yale Law Journal* 97, no. 6 (May 1988): 1155–1163; *Strauder v. West Virginia*, 100 US 303 (1880), 310; Kerber, *No Constitutional Right*, 133–134.

39. Tetrault, *Myth of Seneca Falls*, 28–35, Stanton quotation at 28.

40. See Emmeline B. Wells, "Utah," in *History of Woman Suffrage,* vol. 4: *1883–1900,* ed. Elizabeth Cady Stanton, Susan B. Anthony, Ida Husted Harper, and Matilda Joslyn Gage et al. (Indianapolis: Hollenbeck Press, 1902), 936–940; and Martha Pike, "Washington," in Stanton et al., *History,* 4:967–968; Keyssar, *Right to Vote,* 151 ("municipal governance" quotation); Randolph Hollingsworth, "Introduction," in Alice Stone Blackwell, *Lucy Stone: Pioneer of Women's Rights* (Charlottesville: University Press of Virginia, 2001 [1930]), xviii.

41. Tetrault, *Myth of Seneca Falls,* 58–59, 66–68, 73–74; 88 U.S. 162 (1875).

42. Tetrault, *Myth of Seneca Falls,* 103 (quotation); Keyssar, *Right to Vote,* 149–150.

43. The party platforms can be found at http://www.presidency.ucsb.edu/platforms.php.

44. On these issues, see Cases 10 and 16. See also Dayna L. Cunningham, "Who Are to Be the Electors? A Reflection on the History of Voter Registration in the United States," *Yale Law & Policy Review* 9 (1991): 370–404; J. C. Heckelman, "The Effect of the Secret Ballot on Voter Turnout Rates," *Public Choice* 82 (1995): 107–124.

45. Keyssar, *The Right to Vote,* 163–171.

46. On the connections between suffrage, temperance, anti-immigrant and anti-black sentiment, see Brian Donovan, *White Slave Crusades: Race, Gender, and Anti-Vice Activism, 1887–1917* (Champaign: University of Illinois Press, 2005), 37–55.

47. "Suffragette's Remark Haunts College," *New York Times,* 5 May 1998; Stanton et al., *History of Woman Suffrage,* vols. 5–6: *1900–1920* (New York: NAWSA), 59–60, 82–83.

48. Keyssar, *Right to Vote,* 170–174; Karen Manners Smith, "New Paths to Power, 1890–1920," in *No Small Courage: A History of Women in the United States,* ed. Nancy F. Cott (New York: Oxford University Press, 2000), 409–410.

49. See Keyssar, *Right to Vote,* 174–175; Smith, "New Paths," 410–412.

50. The platforms can be found at http://www.presidency.ucsb.edu/platforms.php. Ann Marie Nicolosi, "'We Do Not Want Our Girls to Marry Foreigners': Gender, Race, and American Citizenship," *NWSA Journal* 13, no. 3 (2001): 1–21; Kerber, *No Constitutional Right,* 41–46.

51. Nancy F. Cott, *The Grounding of Modern Feminism* (New Haven, CT: Yale University Press, 1987), 13, 15.

52. Ruth Bader Ginsburg, "The Need for the Equal Rights Amendment," *American Bar Association Journal* 59, no. 9 (1973): 1013; Kerber, *No Constitutional Right,* 136–139.

53. Alice Paul, "PRO: Is Blanket Amendment Best Method in Equal Rights Campaign?," *Congressional Digest* 3, no. 6 (1924): 198. See also Alice Paul, "PRO: Should Congress Approve the Proposed Equal Rights Amendment to the Constitution?," *Congressional Digest* 22, no. 4 (1943): 107.

54. "The Pending Equal Rights Amendment to the U.S. Constitution," *Congressional Digest* 3, no. 6 (1924): 197.

55. "The Legislative Journey of the Equal-Rights Amendment, 1923–1943," *Congressional Digest* 22, no. 4 (1943): 105. The Republicans were Senator Charles Curtis, who would later become the Senate majority leader (1925–1929) and the U.S. vice president (1929–1933), and Representative Daniel R. Anthony, a nephew of Susan B. Anthony.

56. Ibid., 105–106; Gail Collins, *When Everything Changed: The Amazing Journey of American Women from 1960 to the Present* (New York: Back Bay Books, 2009), 67–68.

57. Marguerite M. Wells, "CON: Should Congress Approve the Proposed Equal Rights Amendment to the Constitution?," *Congressional Digest* 22, no. 4 (1943): 118; Birch Bayh, "PRO: The Question of Ratification of the Equal Rights Amendment," *Congressional Digest* 56, nos. 6/7 (1977): 172; Susan Louise Randall, "A Legislative History of the Equal Rights Amendment, 1923–1960" (PhD diss., University of Utah, 1979), 164, 173.

58. Suzanne B. Mettler, "Federalism, Gender, & the Fair Labor Standards Act of 1938," *Polity* 26, no. 4 (1994): 638–640; *Muller v. Oregon,* 208 U.S. 412 (1908). Brandeis's brief, famous as one of the first to make use of sociological data, may be found at http://www.law.louisville.edu/library/collections/brandeis/node/235.

59. Ruth Bader Ginsburg, "*Muller v. Oregon:* One Hundred Years Later," *Willamette Law Review* 45 (2008–2009): 366. Note, however, that in 1923 the Supreme Court ruled in the case of *Adkins v. Children's Hospital* that minimum wage laws for women (as opposed to maximum hour laws) were unconstitutional, although it reversed this ruling in 1937 in the case of *West Coast Hotel Co. v. Parrish.* Only after the latter ruling did Congress enact the first federal minimum wage. See Ginsburg, "*Muller v. Oregon,*" 367–368. See also David A. Moss, *Socializing Security: Progressive-Era Economists and the Origins of American Social Policy* (Cambridge, MA: Harvard University Press, 1996), esp. chap. 6 ("The Gendered Politics of Protection"), 97–116.

60. The platform called for "an amendment to the Constitution providing for equal rights for men and women." Quoted in Randall, "Legislative History." See also "Republican Party Platform of 1940," http://www.presidency.ucsb.edu/ws/index.php?pid=29640.

61. See Kathryn Kish Sklar, ed., *Who Won the Debate over the Equal Rights Amendment in the 1920s?* (Binghamton, NY: State University of New York at Binghamton, 2000). On the feminist jury rights movement, see Holly J. McCammon et al., "Becoming Full Citizens: The U.S. Women's Jury Rights Campaigns, the Pace of Reform, and Strategic Adaptation," *American Journal of Sociology* 13, no. 4 (2008): 1104–1147. McCammon et al. show that the League of Women Voters, which until 1954 opposed the ERA and did not endorse it until 1972, was central to the state jury campaign movement. On the League and the ERA, see The League of Women Voters, *Changed Forever: The League of Women Voters and the Equal Rights Amendment* (Washington, DC: League of Women Voters, 1988). On the conflict between the NWP and the League and other feminist groups in the 1920s and 1930s, see Susan D. Becker, *The Origins of the Equal Rights Amendment: American Feminism between the Wars* (Westport, CT: Greenwood Press, 1981), 197–234.

62. On the views of Perkins and Eleanor Roosevelt on the ERA, see Cynthia Harrison, *On Account of Sex: The Politics of Women's Issues, 1945–1968* (Berkeley: University of California Press, 1988), 21–22, 277–278n57; Susan Ware, "Women and the Great Depression," http://www.gilderlehrman.org/history-by-era/great-depression/essays/women-and-great-depression. On female unemployment during the Depression,

see Susan Ware, *Holding Their Own: American Women in the 1930s* (Boston: Twayne, 1984), 32.

63. Suzanne B. Mettler, "Federalism, Gender, & the Fair Labor Standards Act of 1938," *Polity* 26, no. 4 (1994): 635–654; Caroline Lexow Babcock, "PRO: Should Congress Approve the Proposed Equal Rights Amendment to the Constitution?," *Congressional Digest* 22, no. 44 (1943): 116–117; William Green, "CON: Should Congress Approve the Proposed Equal Rights Amendment to the Constitution?," *Congressional Digest* 22, no. 44 (1943): 120; Congress of Women's Auxiliaries, CIO, "CON: Should Congress Approve the Proposed Equal Rights Amendment to the Constitution?," *Congressional Digest* 22, no. 44 (1943): 125.

64. Scott Sigmund Gartner, "Military Personnel and Casualties, by War and Branch of Service: 1775–1991," and "Military Personnel on Active Duty, by Branch of Service and Sex: 1789–1995," both in *Historical Statistics of the United States, Earliest Times to the Present: Millennial Edition*, ed. Susan B. Carter et al. (New York: Cambridge University Press, 2006), series Ed1, Ed27; Beth Bailey, *America's Army: Making the All-Volunteer Force* (Cambridge, MA: Harvard University Press, 2009), 10; D'Ann Campbell, "Servicewomen of World War II," *Armed Forces & Society* 16, no. 2 (Winter 1990): 251, 253 (provides estimate of 350,000). See Kerber, *No Constitutional Right*, 248–249, on how the United States debated whether to follow the British example and draft women for nursing or war work.

65. Democratic Party Platform of 1944 (http://www.presidency.ucsb.edu/ws/?pid =29598): "We recommend to Congress the submission of a Constitutional amendment on equal rights for women." Republican Party Platform of 1944 (http://www.presidency.ucsb.edu/ws/index.php?pid=25835): "We favor submission by Congress to the States of an amendment to the Constitution providing for equal rights for men and women. We favor job opportunities in the postwar world open to men and women alike without discrimination in rate of pay because of sex." See also Randall, "Legislative History," 148–150.

66. On ERA advocates' use of the UN Charter, see Randall, "Legislative History," 202–205. The women's rights provisions in the Japanese constitution were largely the work of Beate Sirota Gordon, then a 22-year-old staffer in the American occupation government and a recently naturalized American citizen. For an account of this development from a postcolonial perspective, see Mire Koikari, "Exporting Democracy? American Women, 'Feminist Reforms,' and Politics of Imperialism in the U.S. Occupation of Japan, 1945–1952," *Frontiers: A Journal of Women Studies* 23, no. 1 (2002): 23–45.

67. Randall, "Legislative History," 170.

68. Harrison, *On Account of Sex*, 25; Miriam Schneir, ed., *Feminism in Our Time: The Essential Writings, World War II to the Present* (New York: Vintage, 1994), 38.

69. See "Harvard Medical School Opened to Women: School Ends Exclusion Policy of 136 Years—War Need Is Factor," *New York Times*, 26 Sept. 1944; Nora N. Nercessian, *Worthy of the Honor: A Brief History of Women at Harvard Medical School* (Boston: Presi-

dent and Fellows of Harvard College, ca.1995); "A Compilation in Commemoration of Celebration 50," *Harvard Women's Law Journal* 27 (2004): 299–410; Ann Braude, "A Short Half-Century: Fifty Years of Women at Harvard Divinity School," *Harvard Theological Review* 99, no. 4 (2006): 369–380; "50 Years of Women in the MBA Program," http://www.hbs.edu/women50/.

70. Harrison, *On Account of Sex*, 30–32, 35; Randall, "Legislative History," 299–306, 310–313 (the version of Hayden's amendment quoted, which passed the Senate in 1950 and 1953, appears at 302, 305, 312).

71. On the emergence of the civil rights movement, see Case 16. The "waves" model for understanding feminist movements continues to dominate scholarship on the topic. For an explanation and a critique of this model, see Hewitt's introduction to *No Permanent Waves: Recasting Histories of U.S. Feminism*, ed. Nancy A. Hewitt (New Brunswick, NJ: Rutgers University Press, 2010), 1–8.

72. Harrison, *On Account of Sex*, 73–81, 116–119; Equal Pay Act of 1963, Public Law 88-38,77 Stat. 56, quotation at §3(d)(1). See also "American Women: The Report of the President's Commission on the Status of Women," in Schneir, *Feminism in Our Time*, 38–47.

73. Collins, *When Everything Changed*, 72.

74. *Hoyt v. Florida*, 368 U.S. 57 (1961), 62; Kerber, *No Constitutional Right*, 188–194; Serena Mayeri, "Constitutional Choices: Legal Feminism and the Historical Dynamics of Change," *California Law Review* 92, no. 3 (2004): 762–769.

75. Betty Friedan, *The Feminine Mystique*, ed. Kirsten Fermaglich and Lisa M. Fine (New York: W. W. Norton, 2013).

76. Quoted in Mayeri, "Constitutional Choices," 771, emphasis in original.

77. Harrison, *On Account of Sex*, 176–181; Collins, *When Everything Changed*, 75–81; "Civil Rights Act of 1964, Title VII," in Schneir, *Feminism in Our Time*, 71–75; Mayeri, "Constitutional Choices," 770–773, 773–777.

78. Dennis A. Deslippe, "Organized Labor, National Politics, and Second-Wave Feminism in the United States, 1965–1975," *International Labor and Working Class History* 49 (1996): 147, quotation at 147.

79. Harrison, *On Account of Sex*, 192–195; Collins, *When Everything Changed*, 84–86; Mayeri, "Constitutional Choices," 785–792. For the NOW "Statement of Purpose," written by Friedan and adopted at the first NOW conference, see "National Organization for Women: Statement of Purpose," in Schneir, *Feminism in Our Time*, 95–102.

80. William H. Chafe, "The Road to Equality, 1962–Today," in Cott, *No Small Courage*, 548–554; Casey Hayden and Mary King, "A Kind of Memo . . . to a Number of Other Women in the Peace and Freedom Movements," and Beverly Jones, "Toward a Female Liberation Movement," in Schneir, *Feminism in Our Time*, 89–94, 108–124. On the origin of the term "sexism," see Andrea Rubinstein ("tekanji"), "The Origin of the Word 'Sexism,'" http://finallyfeminism101.wordpress.com/2007/10/19/feminism-friday-the-origins-of-the-word-sexism/.

81. Collins, *When Everything Changed*, 192–194.

82. See Craig J. Konnoth, "Created in Its Image: The Race Analogy, Gay Identity, and Gay Litigation in the 1950s–1970s," *Yale Law Journal* 119, no. 2 (2009): 329–352.

83. See Mayeri, "Constitutional Choices," 784–801; Ginsburg, "Need for an Equal Rights Amendment."

84. Eileen Shanahan, "Equal Rights Plan for Women Voted by House, 350–315; Amendment to Constitution, Introduced for 47 Years, Bars Discrimination; Foes are Led by [Rep. Emanuel] Celler [D-NY]; Senate Action This Year Is Uncertain, though Votes in Past Favored It," *New York Times*, 11 Aug. 1970, 1; Eileen Shanahan, "Senators Amend Equal Rights Bill; It May Die for '70; Provisions Allowing Prayers in Schools and Limiting Draft to Men; House Accord Unlikely; Measure May Be Shelved or Sent to a Conference Composed of Its Foes," *New York Times*, 14 Oct. 1970, 1. The prayer amendment added by the Senate to the ERA would have allowed public prayers in public schools, which had been ruled unconstitutional by the Supreme Court in 1963.

85. See Eileen Shanahan, "Equal Rights Amendment Passed by House, 354–23," *New York Times*, 13 Oct. 1971, 1; Eileen Shanahan, "Equal Rights Amendment Is Approved by Congress," *New York Times*, 23 Mar. 1972, 1.

86. Brock, "Religion, Sex & Politics," 1, n. 1.

87. Deslippe, "Organized Labor," 154–158; Donald T. Critchlow and Cynthia L. Stachecki, "The Equal Rights Amendment Reconsidered: Politics, Policy, and Social Mobilization in a Democracy," in *The Constitution and Public Policy in U.S. History*, ed. Bruce A. Schulman and Julian E. Zelizer (University Park: Penn State University Press, 2009), 159.

88. "Carter Reaffirms Equal Rights Stand," *New York Times*, 14 June 1976, 26; "Women's Equality Day Declared by President," *New York Times*, 27 Aug. 1976, 12. Note, however, that President Ford faced a strong challenge for the 1976 Republican nomination from former governor Ronald Reagan of California, whose supporters at the national party convention opposed including a pro-ERA plank in the party platform; the platform committee endorsed the ERA by a vote of only 51–47. See Richard L. Madden, "Platform Panel Votes to Endorse Equal Rights Plan; Opponents in G.O.P. Group May Fight the Proposal on Convention Floor," *New York Times*, 13 Aug. 1976, 1.

89. *Reed v. Reed*, 404 U.S. 71 (1971), 72–73.

90. Ginsburg, "Commentary on *Reed v. Reed*," *Women's Law Reporter* 1, no. 2 (1972): 7. Ginsburg acknowledged her debt to Murray by listing her, honorifically, as a coauthor of the brief. Kerber, *No Constitutional Right*, 199.

91. *Reed v. Reed*, 404 U.S. 71 (1971), 74–77. That civil rights litigation did not focus on family law has been attributed, by Pauli Murray and others, to male domination of the black civil rights movement. See Konnoth, "Created in Its Image," 359.

92. Quoted in Charlotte B. Hallam, "Legal Tools to Fight Sex Discrimination," *Labor Law Journal* 24, no. 12 (1973): 803.

93. Lalenya Weintraub Siegel, "The Marital Rape Exemption: Evolution to Extinction," *Cleveland State Law Review* 43 (1995): 364.

94. Joanne Schulman, "State-by-State Information on Marital Rape Exemption Laws [as of July 1, 1981]," in Diana E. H. Russell, *Rape in Marriage* (New York: MacMillan, 1982), 375–381 (append. 2); J. C. Barden, "Confronting the Moral and Legal Issue of Marital Rape: Among a Growing Number 'A Hostile and Brutal Act,'" *New York Times,* 1 June 1981), B5. Schulman indicates that eight states had entirely eliminated the "marital exemption" for rape, while two others had eliminated it for certain categories of aggravated rape (for example, when a weapon was involved).

95. On Paul in 1977, see Collins, *When Everything Changed,* 213, 399.

96. Nancy Elizabeth Baker, "Too Much to Lose, Too Little to Gain: The Role of Rescission Movements in the Equal Rights Amendment Battle" (PhD diss., Harvard University, 2003), 97–153, 162, 256–289, 353–354, 358–359. The New Jersey and New York referenda took place in 1975; New Jersey voters rejected the proposed state ERA by 60,000 votes, New York voters by a margin of 60 percent to 40 percent. On polls continuing to favor the ERA, and state debates over ERA ratification, see Collins, *When Everything Changed,* 239; Critchlow and Stachecki, "Equal Rights Amendment Reconsidered," 160, 162–163.

97. W. Dale Nelson, "ERA Backers Win Extension," *Washington Post,* 7 Oct. 1978, A1.

98. ERA advocates argued that Congress could extend the ratification deadline by a simple majority vote (instead of the two-thirds vote required of amendments, because the deadline in this case had not been written into the text of the amendment itself). Opponents vehemently disagreed, with many arguing that no extension was permissible at all under the Constitution. Notably, the constitutionality of ratification deadlines themselves had once been a point of contention. Congress set the first ratification deadline in 1917, in the text of the Eighteenth Amendment (Prohibition), which was ratified by the states in 1919. The validity of the Eighteenth Amendment was then challenged before the U.S. Supreme Court on the grounds that the deadline violated Article V of the Constitution, which indicates no limit on when states can ratify. In 1921 the Court ruled that the ratification deadline was constitutional. Whether the Court would rule that such a deadline could stand outside the text of an amendment or could be extended, including by a simple majority vote of Congress, remained uncertain. See, e.g., Mason Kalfus, "Why Time Limits on the Ratification of Constitutional Amendments Violate Article V," *University of Chicago Law Review* 66, no. 2 (Spring 1999): 437–467; "Ratification of Constitutional Amendments," http://www.usconstitution.net/constamrat.html.

99. Nelson, "ERA Backers Win Extension"; *State of Idaho v. Freeman,* 529 F. Supp. 1107 (1981); Baker, "Too Much to Lose," 380–390.

100. Brock, "Religion, Sex & Politics," 212–213, 196–199; National Council of Catholic Women, "CON: The Question of Ratification of the Equal Rights Amendment," *Congressional Digest* 56, nos. 6–7 (June–July 1977): 177, 179, 181; LDS Presidency quoted in

J. B. Hawes, *The Mormon Image in the American Mind: Fifty Years of Public Perception* (New York: Oxford University Press, 2013), 88–89.

101. Hawes, *The Mormon Image,* 92–94; *State of Idaho v. Freeman,* 478 F. Supp. 33 (D. Idaho 1979), quotation at 35.

102. Donald T. Critchlow, *Phyllis Schlafly and Grassroots Conservatism: A Woman's Crusade* (Princeton, NJ: Princeton University Press, 2005), 23–24, 47–61, 124–125, 128, 4, 194–202, 219, 239; Schlafly quoted in Carol Felsenthal, *The Sweetheart of the Silent Majority: The Biography of Phyllis Schlafly* (New York: Doubleday, 1981), 204.

103. Phyllis Schlafly, "The Question of Ratification of the Equal Rights Amendment: CON," *Congressional Digest* 56, nos. 6–7 (June–July 1977): 191 ("transfer into," "I do not dispute," and "deprive you" quotations); Schlafly quoted in Brock, "Religion, Sex & Politics," 162 ("you cannot discriminate" and "the same pattern" quotations). The accusation that the ERA would require unisex bathrooms is referred to in many contemporary sources. See, e.g., Brock, "Religion, Sex & Politics," 217; "ERA in Florida," *Washington Post,* 18 Apr. 1977, A18.

104. Schlafly, "CON,"189; Kerber, *No Constitutional Right,* 267, 284–288.

105. Schlafly, "CON," 189, 191.

106. Collins, *When Everything Changed,* 236; Brock, "Religion, Sex & Politics," 112; Konnoth, "Created in Its Image," 363–364, 364n219. The case was *Singer v. Hara,* 522 P. 2d 1187 (Washington Ct. App. 1974).

107. Quoted in Critchlow, *Phyllis Schlafly,* 218.

108. John T. McGreevy, *Catholicism and American Freedom: A History* (New York: W. W. Norton, 2003), 273–281; George M. Marsden, *Fundamentalism and American Culture* (New York: Oxford University Press, 2006), 243; Critchlow and Stachecki, "Equal Rights Amendment Reconsidered," 168–169. Feminists also argued that criminalizing abortion merely forced the practice underground, making it less safe.

109. Quoted in Critchlow, *Phyllis Schlafly,* 218.

110. See Brock, "Religion, Sex & Politics," 71. See also Phyllis Schlafly, *The Power of the Positive Woman* (New Rochelle, NY: Arlington House, 1977).

111. Democratic Party Platform of 1980, http://www.presidency.ucsb.edu/ws/?pid=29607. This transcription of the platform contains an obvious error: the text, as transcribed, declares that the party supports the "fabrication," rather than "ratification," of the ERA.

112. Republican Party Platform of 1980, http://www.presidency.ucsb.edu/ws/?pid=25844; Critchlow, *Phyllis Schlafly,* 280.

113. Lou Cannon, *President Reagan: The Role of a Lifetime* (New York: Simon and Schuster, 1991), 804; Collins, *When Everything Changed,* 326; "Gender Gap: Voting Choices in Presidential Elections," available from the Center for American Women and Politics, Eagleton Center for Politics, Rutgers University; Christina Wolbrecht, *The Politics of Women's Rights: Parties, Positions, and Change* (Princeton, NJ: Princeton University Press, 2010), 48. The year 1980 was by no means the first time men and women voted differently. See Richard Seltzer, Jody Newman, and Melissa Voorhees Leighton, *Sex*

as a Political Variable: Women as Candidates and Voters in U.S. Elections* (Boulder, CO: Lynn Reinner, 1997), 3–4.

114. Edward C. Burks, "Arizona Judge, a Woman, Is High Court Contender," *New York Times,* 2 July 1981, A17; Linda Greenhouse, "Justice O'Connor Seated on Nation's High Court," *New York Times,* 26 Sept. 1981, 1 ("refused a job" quotation); Nancy Maveety, *Justice Sandra Day O'Connor: Strategist on the Supreme Court* (New York: Rowman and Littlefield, 1996), 14–18, "abhorrence" quotation at 18; Ann Carey McFeatters, *Sandra Day O'Connor: Justice in the Balance* (Albuquerque: University of New Mexico Press, 2005), 43–50, 117–118.

115. Brock, "Religion, Sex & Politics," 238. Brock's article is the most complete account of the Florida ERA fight, but see also Joan S. Carver, "The Equal Rights Amendment and the Florida Legislature," *Florida Historical Quarterly* 60, no. 4 (Apr. 1982): 455–481, and Kimberly Wilmont Voss, "The Florida Fight for Equality: The Equal Rights Amendment, Senator Lori Wilson, and Mediated Catfights in the 1970s," *Florida Historical Quarterly* 88, no. 2 (2009): 173–208. In reporting legislative tallies, we follow Brock in not counting courtesy votes. In Florida, legislators absent for a roll-call were allowed to record a vote later, so long as their doing so did not affect the outcome (Brock, "Religion, Sex & Politics," 40n16). Owing to these courtesy votes, the final tally in the 1972 Florida House ERA vote, cited by both Carver and Voss, was 91–4.

116. The Florida Senate president claimed that no vote could take place because the state constitution forbade the legislature from voting on a federal constitutional amendment until after a general election. The Florida attorney general, however, held that this provision was void because it violated existing federal court rulings. After the failed 1972 Senate vote, ERA supporters in Florida challenged this provision of their state constitution in federal court, where it was overturned in 1973. See Brock, "Religion, Sex & Politics," 40–41.

117. Ibid., 46–47, 65, 238.

118. Anita Bryant, *The Anita Bryant Story,* quoted in Gillian Frank, " 'The Civil Rights of Parents': Race and Conservative Politics in Anita Bryant's Campaign against Gay Rights in 1970s Florida," *Journal of the History of Sexuality* 22, no. 1 (2013): 127.

119. Brock, "Religion, Sex & Politics," 140–143, 239.

120. Ibid., 180–182. Altogether, the commission proposed eight amendments; all eight were rejected in the same referendum as the "little ERA."

121. Brock, "Religion, Sex and Politics," 211n54, cites a news report from June 1982 regarding a Harris Poll, in which the pollsters asked respondents in Florida what they thought of specific arguments against the ERA, such as that it would expose women to military combat. Even when, in this way, the respondents were exposed to anti-ERA claims, they continued to favor the ERA by a margin of 57 percent to 37 percent.

122. The 1979 vote was unusual. The ERA was almost kept from a floor vote in Florida when the Senate Rules Committee voted against recommending a ratification resolution. A House supporter surprised opponents, however, by proposing ERA

ratification as an amendment to a human rights bill that the state Senate had already approved. The amended law passed the Florida House (64–52), and instead of being referred to the Rules Committee, as was customary, it was immediately brought before the full Senate for a vote. The law with the ERA rider attached was defeated (19–21) in the Florida Senate. See Brock, "Religion, Sex & Politics," 187–197, 239.

123. "AFL-CIO Moves Its Convention out of Florida; ERA Is Cited," *Chicago Tribune*, 6 Jan. 1979, W2 (quotation); Mark Albright, "ERA Supporters to Expand Boycott," *Evening Independent*, 5 May 1980; "Disney World Angers NOW," *Boca Raton News*, 20 Jan. 1981, 12A.

124. Brock, "Religion, Sex & Politics," 217–224. See also "Florida Senate," *News and Courier* (Charleston, SC), 22 June 1982.

18

Leadership and Independence at the Federal Reserve (2009)

"FROM THE GREAT DEPRESSION, to the stagflation of the seventies, to the current economic crisis caused by the housing bubble, every economic down-turn suffered by this country over the past century can be traced to Federal Reserve policy."[1] Ron Paul, a Republican from Texas, offered this damning diagnosis on the floor of the U.S. House of Representatives on February 3, 2009, as he introduced a bill to abolish the Federal Reserve (also known as the "Fed"). Paul had opposed the Fed for decades and had offered several bills to dismantle it, dating back to 1983. As with all of his previous attempts, the 2009 bill died in committee.[2]

Although few members of Congress shared Paul's desire to eliminate the Fed, the central bank's unprecedented interventions during the 2007–2009 financial crisis provoked new sources of resistance. At a minimum, many more Americans grew curious about the inner workings of the Fed, whose activities and decisions were frequently wrapped in secrecy. From its earliest days, the Fed's supporters had insisted that monetary policy had to be separated from electoral politics to prevent the manipulation of the money supply and interest rates for short-term political gain. Increasingly, however, critics questioned whether the costs of Federal Reserve independence and secrecy might outweigh the benefits.

By late 2009, mounting concerns in Congress had breathed new life into one of Representative Paul's milder proposals for containing the Fed. Though his ultimate goal was to "end the Fed," Paul had also repeatedly proposed a full audit of the institution. By November 19, 2009, his latest audit bill had

---

attracted 313 cosponsors, a record level of support, and the House Financial Services Committee was scheduled to vote that very day on whether to append a version of the proposal to a major financial reform bill that was then taking shape in Congress. If the audit provision became law, it would represent a notable change in policy, providing an unprecedented window on Fed activities and raising significant new questions about the nature of central bank independence in America.

Early American Banking

Distrust of central banking had a long history in the United States. In the country's earliest years, debates over establishing a national bank had helped give rise to the bitter rivalry between the Federalist Party and Democratic-Republicans. The Federalists won their bank (the Bank of the United States) in 1791, but Democratic-Republicans allowed its charter to expire in 1811. Only a few years later, however, facing financial challenges associated with the War of 1812, Democratic-Republicans reversed course and established the Second Bank of the United States in 1816. Some supporters desired it solely as a means of bolstering the national treasury, but most also aspired to create a national currency, via its banknotes, and to better utilize the nation's limited supply of specie (gold and silver coins). In late 1815, Treasury Secretary Alexander Dallas hoped that the bank would be "not an institution created for the purposes of commerce and profit alone, but more for the purposes of national policy, as an auxiliary in the exercise of some of the highest powers of the Government."[3]

The Second Bank of the United States drew the ire of state banks caught in the wake of its policies. When its first president, William Jones, undertook aggressive lending, smaller banks complained of the competition and encouraged state laws and taxes targeting the bank.* When Jones's successor, Langdon Cheves, moved in the opposite direction and contracted its lending, the resulting financial distress further fed the opposition. The bank's third and most famous president, Nicholas Biddle, resumed wider

---

* The landmark 1819 Supreme Court decision *McCulloch v. Maryland,* in addition to finding the Second Bank constitutional, struck down a Maryland tax on the Second Bank on the grounds that states could not tax legitimate federal operations.

lending and significantly strengthened the institution's financial position.[4] Biddle also adopted policies that aimed to stabilize the currency and ensure a healthy financial system, leading some historians to consider him a proto-typical central banker. "The Bank performed these functions deliberately and avowedly," according to historian Bray Hammond, "with a consciousness of quasi-governmental responsibility, and of the need to subordinate profit and private interest to that responsibility."[5]

The Bank War

Opposition to the Second Bank culminated during the presidency of Andrew Jackson, who rode to the White House in 1828 on a wave of populist opposition to political elites. After criticizing the Second Bank in his 1829 message to Congress, Jackson laid siege in July 1832 when he vetoed a bill to renew its charter (four years ahead of the charter's expiration).[6] In his veto message, Jackson claimed that the bank held powers "unauthorized by the Constitution, subversive of the rights of the States, and dangerous to the liberties of the people." He asserted that the bank was a monopoly that benefited a wealthy few who were unaccountable to the public, and he insisted that maintaining the bank reached beyond Congress's power to pass laws "necessary and proper" to fulfill its duties.[7]

Banking, after the Second Bank

After the Second Bank's federal charter expired in 1836, the United States was left once again without a national bank. State-chartered banks continued to issue their own unique banknotes, which fluctuated in value depending on a number of factors, including the riskiness of the issuing institution, but now there was no national bank to discipline the state banks by returning their notes for specie when they over-issued. Particularly after the Civil War began, many state-chartered banks stopped exchanging their notes for specie altogether, significantly diminishing the value of the notes on the market. When Congress issued its own "greenbacks" in 1862—in part to help pay for the war—the new currency, though officially legal tender, soon depreciated sharply. To shore up the currency system, Congress passed the National Banking Acts of 1863, 1864, and 1865, which authorized new federally chartered banks to issue national banknotes, backed by U.S. government debt. With their value tied exclusively to safe securities (and further backed by the

Treasury itself), these banknotes functioned as a more reliable national currency. The acts also effectively taxed state banknotes out of existence and created a new office, the Comptroller of the Currency, to regulate national banks and print their banknotes.[8] State-chartered banks continued to play a large role, but they now operated alongside the new national banks, chartered (and supervised) by the federal government.

Even after the National Banking Acts, crises and shocks continued to trouble the banking system. The Panics of 1873 and 1893 proved particularly severe.[9] It was only after another calamitous panic in 1907, however, that federal policymakers attempted a large-scale reform of the system.

The Panic of 1907

In October 1907, F. Augustus Heinze, E. R. Thomas, and Charles W. Morse "failed spectacularly" in their attempt to corner the market on United Copper Company stock. Although Heinze had helped to build United Copper, he was also active in the financial sector, as were Thomas and Morse. Almost as soon as the share price of United Copper collapsed, rumors began circulating that the financial firms these men were associated with must also be in trouble. The first to suffer a bank run, on October 16, was Mercantile National Bank, "which was under the control of Heinze, Morse and Thomas." Before long the panic spread to other banks, threatening the broader financial system.[10]

Clearly concerned, the financier J. P. Morgan assembled a prominent group from the financial sector to help bring the panic under control. On October 22 the group concluded that the Knickerbocker Trust Company—New York's third largest trust company, with $62 million in deposits, and whose president had known business dealings with Morse—was in too much trouble to rescue. This doomed the trust to close the next day, wreaking havoc on Wall Street and sparking widespread bankruptcies, well beyond New York. Morgan's group did intervene to save other institutions, however. It arranged $13 million to support the Trust Company of America and helped direct $35 million of U.S. Treasury funds into various New York banks. By October 28, Morgan had cobbled together nearly $40 million from numerous sources to support the New York Stock Exchange and $30 million for the City of New York itself.[11]

The worst of the Panic of 1907 was over by December, but its effects rippled through the economy for months. Bank vaults finally began refilling in February 1908, and economic growth returned starting in June.[12] In the wake of the panic, diverse voices in policy circles and the press faulted the banking system itself rather than external shocks. As the *New York Times* observed, "In 1907, we had neither war, pestilence, nor famine, earthquake nor conflagration."[13] At the same time, although many Americans appreciated the leadership J. P. Morgan had shown, many also worried about the power he had wielded. "Let us thank our lucky stars that in such an emergency we had that man," said one prominent banker in 1912. "But I believe that such enormous power, power great enough to stop a panic, power great enough to bring one on, should be in the hands of men who have no private interests to promote, but solely one duty to perform—that of service to the people."[14]

Creating the Federal Reserve

Federal lawmakers initially responded in May 1908 with the Aldrich-Vreeland Act. In addition to fashioning a mechanism for groups of banks to issue additional currency in an emergency, the act created the National Monetary Commission to study the nation's money and banking problems and to make recommendations for how best to solve them.[15]

The National Monetary Commission

The National Monetary Commission launched an extensive investigation that lasted several years and spanned multiple countries. Of particular inspiration was the thinking of Paul Warburg, a prominent German banker who had recently arrived in the United States as a partner at Kuhn, Loeb & Co., a prestigious New York investment bank. Like many banking experts of the time, Warburg believed that America suffered from an "inelastic" money supply that was largely unresponsive to ups and downs in the demand for money. These ups and downs were often associated with the agricultural calendar, with farmers typically short on cash at harvest time. Because the nation's money supply was largely inelastic even as the demand for money varied widely from month to month and season to season, interest rates often fluctuated dramatically over the course of a year.[16]

To address this problem, Warburg recommended an "elastic" currency backed by short-term commercial debt, which ideally would ensure that the money supply would expand and contract as needed, in line with expansions and contractions of real commercial activity. This idea was closely associated with the "real bills doctrine," which informed much of the era's banking theory. A "real bill" was a short-term commercial debt tied to physical goods, such as the debt of a distributor to a manufacturer for goods that the distributor expected to sell. The real bills doctrine held that these sorts of debts constituted the ideal backing for an elastic money supply: so long as banks only lent against real bills, tied to actual products circulating in the economy, the banks' creation of money through the lending process would presumably never be too large or too small, but always just right.[17]

Warburg also believed that, even beyond an elastic currency, the banking system required a centralized monetary authority that could concentrate reserves and make use of them as conditions required. In a 1907 pamphlet he had envisioned a central bank for the United States managed by banking leaders and unelected public officials. Their independence from the electorate, he argued, would prevent the encroachment of "politics in business," while explicit limitations on the central bank's power would erase "all danger of selfish or speculative use of its moneys." In Warburg's estimation, "We need some centralized power to protect us against others and to protect us from ourselves—some power, able to provide for the legitimate needs of the country and able at the same time to apply the brakes when the car is moving too fast." Such an institution, he observed, functioned well in Germany and other European countries, but was notably absent in America.[18]

Jekyll Island

In November 1910 the chairman of the National Monetary Commission, Senator Nelson Aldrich (R-RI), along with his assistant on the commission, Assistant Secretary of the Treasury A. Piatt Andrew, met secretly with a handful of the nation's most elite bankers, including Warburg, on Georgia's exclusive Jekyll Island. There they drafted a plan for a privately owned "bank of banks," called the Reserve Association of the United States (later, the National Reserve Association), to which commercial banks could subscribe. With only modest modifications, the Aldrich Plan first fashioned on Jekyll

Island became the basis of the National Monetary Commission's recommendations in January 1912.[19]

Under this plan, member banks would invest 20 percent of their capital in the National Reserve Association (though only half needed to be paid in). The association, in turn, would maintain fifteen regional branches, which would provide cash to member banks according to Warburg's model, facilitate banking processes, and always redeem association banknotes for gold upon demand. Local bankers would elect most of each branch's directors, and the association's board of directors would include thirty-nine members elected by branch directors, a governor appointed by the president of the United States, two deputy governors selected by the board, the secretaries of the Treasury, Agriculture, and Commerce and Labor, and the comptroller of the currency. The proposal also required the association to hold a gold reserve worth half the value of its circulating banknotes. Above all, the Aldrich Plan envisioned a centralized, quasi-public institution that had authority over monetary policy but was owned and largely controlled by private entities. As the report of the National Monetary Commission made clear, "While it may be contended that the issue of money of any kind is a distinctive function of sovereign power, the exercise of this authority directly by Governments has, as shown by the experience of the world, inevitably led to disastrous results."[20]

Congress Considers Reform

In January 1912, Congress considered a bill based on the Aldrich Plan. The bill never made it out of committee, however. It had little support from the beginning, but became even more unpopular after a House investigation drew additional attention to the issue of financial concentration on Wall Street. Even though there was support for banking reform across the political spectrum, the idea of creating a centralized National Reserve Association owned and run by banks themselves was a nonstarter.[21]

Although Democrats had already gained control of the U.S. House of Representatives in the 1910 elections, the elections of 1912 placed Democrats in charge of both houses of Congress and the White House. President-elect Woodrow Wilson wanted monetary reform, but was inclined toward a solution that would ensure both public control and a reasonable degree of centralization.[22] That December, Representative Carter Glass (D-VA) and economist Henry Parker Willis presented a plan to Wilson. Their proposal would create many local independent reserve banks, rather than one association, so as "to provide for local or home control . . . instead of granting centralized control."[23] Separately, however, Paul Warburg had helped to persuade Wilson (through an intermediary) that the banking system would benefit from a strong, centralized monetary authority. Because Congress would never vote for a single central bank, Wilson recommended creating a board to supervise the reserve banks. Glass opposed the board at first, fearing that "those who are seeking to mask the Aldrich plan and to give us dangerous centralization" had fooled Wilson, but he acquiesced after consulting with leading bankers.[24]

Glass and Willis included a central board in a bill they offered to Wilson in January 1913. Their version would have given bankers partial control over selection of the board as well as significant representation on it, but to satisfy populist Democrats the bill that Glass eventually introduced in Congress dramatically reduced the role of bankers on the board. The board would now consist of the secretaries of the Treasury and Agriculture, the comptroller of the currency, and four others selected by the president and approved by the Senate, only one of whom needed to have banking experience. Bankers objected, claiming that government control would push the board to pursue political ends at the expense of economic and financial stability. Warburg, in particular, worried that in the United States, "where the bid for votes and public favor is ever present in the politician's mind, where class prejudice and antagonism between East and West and North and South run high . . . a political management, apt to change every few years, would be a national disaster."[25]

Members of Congress naturally differed over what degree of centralization and government control should be sought. Republican representative Horace Towner of Iowa charged that the Glass bill absolutely "creates a 'central bank.' This plan is much more centralized, autocratic, and tyrannical than the Aldrich plan. It is true that we are to have . . . regional banks, but these are but the agents of the grand central board, which absolutely controls them. The power is not with them; they are not in any material matter given the right of independent action; they must obey orders from Washington."[26] In the Senate, where Robert Owen (D-OK) introduced a bill similar to Glass's, there was wider support for centralization. Senator Theodore Burton (R-OH) argued, "There can be no doubt but that eight or twelve regional banks cannot act as effectively to control our gold supply as a central bank."[27] After extensive discussion, the Glass and Owen bills were reconciled as the Glass-Owen bill, which both houses of Congress passed and President Wilson ultimately signed into law as the Federal Reserve Act on December 23, 1913.[28]

The Federal Reserve Act

The preamble to the Federal Reserve Act announced that it was intended "to provide for the establishment of Federal reserve banks, to furnish an elastic currency, to afford means of rediscounting commercial paper, to establish a more effective supervision of banking in the United States, and for other purposes." The act called for the establishment of at most twelve Federal Reserve Banks across the country. All federally chartered banks, known as national banks, were required to subscribe to their regional Reserve Bank, and state banks could join as well. The main advantage for member banks is that they could borrow from their Reserve Banks through a process known as discounting (described below). Each member bank was also required to maintain reserves against all of their deposits (the "reserve requirement") equal to approximately 12 to 18 percent for demand deposits and 5 percent for time deposits. Federal Reserve Banks, meanwhile, were authorized to distribute "Federal Reserve Notes," a new legal currency that could always be exchanged for gold at the U.S. Treasury or any Reserve Bank. Each Reserve Bank was required to hold full collateral for these Federal Reserve Notes (in the form of qualifying short-term assets) and maintain a gold reserve equal to at least 40 percent of the value of its notes.[29]

Overseeing the system would be the Federal Reserve Board, consisting of the secretary of the Treasury, the comptroller of the currency, and five others appointed by the president and confirmed by the Senate. Two of the five had to have banking or finance experience, but none could be an officer or stockholder of a bank. The Treasury secretary would serve as the chairman of the Board, and two of the appointees would serve as governor and vice governor, in charge of operations. Each Reserve Bank would have nine directors: three bankers elected by member banks, three from the fields of commerce, agriculture, or industry, also elected by member banks, and three selected by the national board. None but the three bankers could be officers or stockholders of a bank. Every Reserve Bank would send one representative to a Federal Advisory Council established to assist the Federal Reserve Board.[30]

The Early Years

The twelve Reserve Banks of the Federal Reserve system opened for business on November 16, 1914.* From the start, their most important monetary tool was the "discount window." Commercial banks in need of cash could come to the "window" and borrow funds, so long as they offered qualifying short-term assets ("notes, drafts, and bills of exchange arising out of actual commercial transactions") as collateral. In practice, the commercial banks would effectively sell these assets to their regional Reserve Bank at a discount—with the Reserve Bank paying slightly less than the face value of the asset, according to the Reserve Bank's discount rate. In this way commercial banks could convert noncash assets into cash for a small price. By raising or lowering the discount rate (effectively the interest rate it charged on loans to commercial banks), a Reserve Bank could discourage or encourage commercial bank borrowing at the discount window, and thus contract or expand the money supply. Although each Reserve Bank was allowed to set its own discount rate, the act required the Federal Reserve Board to approve each Bank's rate decisions.[31]

In the early years of the Federal Reserve, monetary policy was tied closely to the real bills doctrine and the gold standard. The real bills doctrine implied that the money supply should be responsive to commercial activity, because Reserve Banks would always be prepared to discount qualifying real bills, which represented commercial loans tied to real goods in the economy. The gold standard, meanwhile, required that Federal Reserve Banks hold a 40 percent gold reserve for their notes and always be prepared to exchange any Federal Reserve Note for gold, on demand. This represented an additional source of discipline, effectively requiring the Reserve Banks to raise

---

* The twelve Reserve Banks were located in Boston, New York City, Philadelphia, Cleveland, Richmond, Atlanta, Chicago, St. Louis, Minneapolis, Kansas City (Missouri), Dallas, and San Francisco.

their discount rates (to attract gold and contract the supply of Federal Reserve Notes) if their gold reserves started to run low.[32]

Importantly, each Federal Reserve Bank could also act as a "lender of last resort" in times of financial crisis or distress. In the event of an emerging panic, for example, a Reserve Bank was expected to quickly put out the fire by lending to commercial banks that were "temporarily illiquid but still fundamentally solvent," much as J. P. Morgan and his colleagues had attempted to do—on a private basis—during the Panic of 1907.[33] In fact, many observers believed that the creation of the Federal Reserve would eliminate panics altogether, with one Federal Reserve Board governor announcing, "Under the Federal Reserve system we shall see no more financial panics."[34]

At an organizational level, there were numerous debates in the early years about the authority and responsibility of the twelve Reserve Banks relative to the Federal Reserve Board in Washington, D.C. In December 1914, for example, the Reserve Bank governors created a Governors Conference to discuss policy independently of the Board. Under the leadership of Benjamin Strong, the governor of the New York Federal Reserve Bank, the conference coordinated policy, sent messages to Congress, and voiced disagreements with the Board. Strong, who had served as president of Banker's Trust Company and stood as one of the most prominent and respected officials at the Federal Reserve until his death in 1928, believed that the technical banking expertise of the Governors Conference complemented the Board's high-level view of the national economy.[35] However, the Board perceived the conference as a rival body that "assumed powers which [it did] not possess."[36] In January 1916 the Board stopped authorizing conference meetings until 1922, when it insisted that a Board member attend each meeting.[37]

Struggles with the Treasury

As Federal Reserve governors and Board members jockeyed for influence internally, the Federal Reserve and the U.S. Treasury engaged in a power struggle of their own. After the United States entered World War I in April 1917, the Federal Reserve Board "freely conceded that the great national emergency made it necessary to suspend the application of well-recognized principles of economics and finance which usually govern banking operations in times of peace."[38] In other words, the real bills doctrine and the gold standard would take a backseat to the demands of the war. The Federal

Reserve kept interest rates low (3 to 4.5 percent) so that the Treasury could easily sell low-interest bonds to finance rapidly mounting war expenditures. Fearing that lax monetary policy would stoke inflation, however, some members of the Federal Reserve Board argued that the war should be financed on the basis of higher taxes, rather than debt, which would free the Federal Reserve to exert more discipline over monetary affairs. Yet after Treasury Secretary William McAdoo threatened to take over the Federal Reserve, under the authority of a new wartime law, the Board quickly backed down.[39]

After the war ended in November 1918, with inflation rates exceeding 15 percent, officials at the Federal Reserve believed that interest rates needed to rise. The Treasury—headed by Carter Glass beginning that December— resisted. With no other options, the Federal Reserve Banks tried to persuade commercial banks to curtail lending, a tactic then called "direct pressure" but often referred to today as "moral suasion." Direct pressure proved ineffective, however, and in November 1919 the Federal Reserve finally began raising interest rates. Nevertheless, inflation remained high through the first half of 1920, even as a sharp recession began to take hold. By early 1921, inflation had given way to deflation.[40]

The Federal Reserve Banks kept discount rates high through much of the recession, angering credit-starved farmers, among many others. Such outrage provoked a congressional investigation in 1921, where the conflict between the Treasury and the Federal Reserve was on full display. At the hearings, Comptroller of the Currency John Skelton Williams attacked bankers on the Federal Reserve Board, claiming that "from the very outset Secretary McAdoo and the more liberal elements of the board had to combat and oppose the reactionary faction which fought for the centralization rather than the democratization of banking power." He suggested replacing sitting Board appointees and adding the secretary of agriculture to the Board. Governor Strong offered the most effective rebuttal, explaining that the rate hikes had been necessary after wartime excess. He promised that the economy was finally undergoing "readjustment and recovery—a period in which the suffering of the previous period is rewarded." In its final report the congressional investigation seemed to side mostly with the Federal Reserve, finding no evidence of ill will toward farmers, and criticizing the central bank for raising discount rates too late, rather than too early. The report proposed no major reorganization, though Congress did add an agricultural representative to the Federal Reserve Board in June 1922.[41]

Open Market Operations

The primary innovation at the Federal Reserve during the 1920s was the use of "open market operations," which involved the buying and selling of government bonds on the secondary market. Open market purchases of government bonds injected money into the economy, while open market sales of government bonds withdrew money. The Federal Reserve Banks had always been able to buy and sell government bonds—and had actively done so during World War I—but now Federal Reserve officials increasingly saw open market operations as a potentially effective means for managing the money supply, even apart from wartime conditions. In 1922 and 1923 the Federal Reserve set up committees to oversee open market operations, and it flexed its market muscle during a mild economic downturn in 1923 by buying $500 million in Treasury debt to expand the money supply. When the downturn quickly gave way to renewed growth, Governor Strong spoke of a "feeling of tranquility and contentment" after the apparently successful policy experiment.[42]

Despite the sharp recession in 1920–1921 and several later hiccups, the 1920s were generally seen as a prosperous decade—at least until the market crash in late 1929. Although historians disagree whether the Federal Reserve could have prevented the crash, some say the American central bank was too lax over much of the decade, allowing the rise of asset bubbles, while others suggest that things might have turned out differently if only Benjamin Strong had lived long enough to guide monetary policy through the rocky shoals of the late 1920s. Whatever the explanation, the economic downturn that became known as the Great Depression clearly put the Federal Reserve to the test.[43]

Depression and War

Officials at the Federal Reserve did not immediately adopt an activist (expansionary) stance in the early years of the Great Depression. In fact, many of the leading figures within the organization believed that a significant downturn and widespread liquidations of weak firms were necessary to cleanse the economy of its excesses from the Roaring Twenties. "The consequences of such an economic debauch are inevitable," said the governor of the Philadelphia Reserve Bank in 1930. "Can they be corrected or removed by cheap money? We do not believe that they can."[44] The real bills doctrine and the gold standard remained core guiding principles. As the crisis deepened and commercial banks ran out of qualifying assets to use as collateral for borrowing at the discount window, Federal Reserve officials largely refused to loosen their standards, even as bank failures were reaching record levels. Similarly, when Britain left the gold standard in September 1931, putting pressure on America's gold reserves, the Federal Reserve sharply raised interest rates to steady its gold supply, despite urgent cries for lower rates from across the country. President Herbert Hoover's administration was dumbfounded by the Federal Reserve's "policy of confirmed pessimism" and demanded in vain that it reverse course.[45]

With Federal Reserve officials apparently convinced that there was little they could do as the downturn intensified, Congress worked to expand their options. In 1932 it relaxed standards on acceptable collateral for Federal Reserve Notes and similarly broadened the types of securities eligible for discount at the Reserve Banks.

By the time Franklin Roosevelt assumed the presidency on March 4, 1933, the nation's banking system was in free fall and virtually nonfunctional. The new president immediately ordered the temporary closure of every bank in the nation, including the Federal Reserve Banks, in an unprecedented effort to staunch the hemorrhaging. On March 9 he signed the Emergency Banking Act, granting his administration greater regulatory authority over Federal Reserve member banks. He also radically overhauled the currency system with reforms in April and June that required Americans to cash in most of their gold, banned gold exports, and ended the use of gold as currency, although he kept the dollar on the gold standard. In May he signed legislation empowering the president to substantially devalue the dollar relative to gold and to instruct the Federal Reserve to buy government securities both on the open market and from the Treasury directly. The next month, the Banking Act of 1933 established federal deposit insurance, mandated the separation of commercial and investment banking (under its "Glass-Steagall" provisions), and created the Federal Open Market Committee (FOMC) within the Federal Reserve to help streamline open market operations.[46]

A Plan to Strengthen the Board

In November 1934, Treasury official Marriner Eccles drafted a memo for the president arguing that "the diffusion of power and responsibility" in the Federal Reserve led to internal stalemates over policy. Eccles believed that the best way out of the depression would be aggressive government spending "to bring about a rise in the national income," and that the Federal Reserve should support fiscal expansion by bringing down interest rates to facilitate the financing of emergency spending. The reason this was not happening, Eccles maintained, is that the Federal Reserve was dominated by the governors of the individual Reserve Banks, which put "banker interest . . . over the public interest." The solution, he suggested, was to empower the central Federal Reserve Board in Washington by giving it control over both open market operations (which were currently run by the governors) and the appointment of Reserve Bank governors themselves. "The adoption of these suggestions," Eccles concluded, "would introduce certain attributes of a real central bank capable of energetic and positive action without calling for a drastic revision of the whole Federal Reserve Act."[47]

Impressed with Eccles, President Roosevelt soon appointed him chairman of the Federal Reserve Board, and in early 1935 Eccles helped prepare a bill incorporating his earlier ideas for strengthening the Board. Carter Glass, now a U.S. senator, vigorously opposed the bill, fearing that it would lead the Federal Reserve to be "crushed by government" and hamper its ability "to serve the business interest of the country."[48] Glass, along with many in the banking sector, worried that strengthening the Board at the expense of the Reserve Bank governors would render the institution more sensitive to political pressure and thus less likely to tighten monetary policy during good economic times.[49] As one banker observed at the Senate hearings on the bill,

> We think it is no insult to either, to say that politics and banking do not mix. Their objectives and methods are widely divergent. Politics necessarily involves doing the popular thing; sound banking on the other hand frequently requires unpleasant and unpopular refusals.
>
> It has been said that the Federal Reserve System ought always to be unpopular, in that it ought always to be counteracting, or at least getting ready

to counteract, the economic tendencies of the moment. When the mood is confident, it is the duty of the System to be cautious; when the mood is fear, it ought to be more daring; it ought always to be courageous.

. . . there is a strong suspicion abroad that if the Federal Reserve authorities, back in 1927 and 1928, had been less afraid of political pressure from the vast public which was profiting from the boom, they would have taken the unpopular steps necessary to check the speculative madness which led to the collapse of 1929.[50]

Despite these protests, most of Eccles's plan passed into law in August as part of the Banking Act of 1935. The Board would now consist of seven presidential appointees, called "governors," without the Treasury secretary or comptroller of the currency. The Board's two leaders were retitled "chairman" and "vice chairman," and the former bank governors (of the individual Reserve Banks) were renamed "presidents." The Board governors would have fourteen-year terms, with chairmen serving four years at a time. The act also reorganized the FOMC to comprise the seven-member Board plus five Reserve Bank presidents.[51] President Roosevelt boasted that the Banking Act of 1935 concentrated monetary powers "to a greater degree than before in a single public body, so that they can be used promptly and effectively in accordance with the changing needs of the country."[52]

From the Peg to the Accord

Although the Treasury secretary had been removed from the Board, the Treasury continued to exercise considerable influence over Federal Reserve policy in the late 1930s and 1940s. Treasury Secretary Henry Morgenthau wanted low interest rates to help finance New Deal spending. Although Eccles himself had originally favored a similar policy, now as chairman of the Federal Reserve Board he feared that inflation might result, but still gave in after feeling pressure from President Roosevelt himself. American entry into World War II in December 1941 ensured further subordination to the Treasury, because massive borrowing was required to finance the war effort. Promising "an ample supply of funds," the Federal Reserve kept interest rates low to facilitate bond issues throughout the conflict.[53] In fact, in February 1942 it agreed to peg rates on government bonds at exceptionally low levels for as long as necessary and promised that no Treasury offering would fail.

This understanding, commonly referred to as the "peg," committed the Federal Reserve to following the Treasury's lead.[54]

Such cooperation masked what Eccles later called "a civil war within an international war."[55] Worried that the Treasury's spending was spurring inflation, Eccles pushed hard after the war to end the peg. This did not sit well with the Treasury or the new president, Harry Truman. Truman chose not to reappoint Eccles as chairman in January 1948 and installed Thomas McCabe, of the Philadelphia Reserve Bank, in his stead. Eccles remained a governor of the Federal Reserve Board, however, and stepped up his criticism only after losing his chairmanship, arguing that the peg "deprived [the Federal Reserve] of its only really effective instrument for curbing overexpansion of credit." The feud climaxed in January 1951, when the Federal Reserve allowed the price of one type of government bond to drop (thereby raising its effective interest rate) without consulting the Treasury. The change was small, but the move signaled the beginning of the end of the peg.[56]

The incident angered President Truman, who feared that a loss of faith in the federal government's credit would be disastrous for the ongoing war in Korea and the larger struggle against Communism. After a tumultuous back-and-forth between the Federal Reserve and the administration, the two sides in time began working to better define their respective roles. Finally, on March 4, 1951, they issued a joint statement announcing that they had "reached full accord with respect to debt management and monetary policies to be pursued in furthering their common purpose to assure the successful financing of the Government's requirements and, at the same time, to minimize monetization of the public debt."[57] Although the public announcement provided no further details, the "Accord"—as it came to be known—effectively ended the peg while specifying short-term measures to ease the transition away from Federal Reserve support for the federal bond market.[58] According to one of the leading historians of the Federal Reserve:

> The March 1951 Accord with the Treasury opened a new era in Federal Reserve history. Once again, the Federal Reserve could claim to be independent, as its founders intended. It could raise interest rates without prior approval or consultation with the Treasury [once the one-year transition came to a close].

The new arrangement reopened issues that had remained dormant. What did independence mean in practice? What goals should an independent central bank pursue? How could it reconcile independence with continued responsibility for the success of the Treasury debt management operations? . . . What guiding principles should govern practice?[59]

As officials at the Federal Reserve pondered these questions, lawmakers in Congress were struggling with similar questions of their own. The legislative branch had created the Federal Reserve, and yet the executive branch, via the Treasury, had the closest relationship with the Board. This upset many in Congress, and in March 1952 Representative Wright Patman (D-TX) led an investigation into the Federal Reserve's independence from the Treasury and from Congress.[60] In a letter to the investigating committee, New York Reserve Bank president Allan Sproul wrote that the Federal Reserve did not have "independence from the Government, but independence within the Government." He reiterated that "the Federal Reserve is an agency of the Congress set up in a special form to bear the responsibility for [monetary policy] which constitutionally belongs to the legislative branch of the government."[61]

Some experts at the hearings were highly critical of the Federal Reserve. The eminent monetary economist Milton Friedman alleged that it had "failed" to control inflation and instead offered monetary policy as a "sacrifice . . . on the altar of Government security prices." Perhaps most strikingly, he called for the elimination of the Federal Reserve itself:

> Despite the prevailing belief to the contrary, I am convinced that the Federal Reserve System has failed to promote the objectives for which it was established, and that this conclusion is abundantly supported by the historical evidence. The System facilitated inflation in two world wars, permitted or promoted unnecessary inflation immediately after both wars, had much to do with making the great depression of the 1930's as deep as it was, and even failed in the one function that its founders were most convinced it would perform: namely, the prevention of a banking panic. I do not believe that the failure of the System reflects ignorance or incompetence, or malice on the part of the group of men who have guided its destinies. On the contrary, they seem to me an unusually well-informed, able, and public-spirited group. I therefore believe that the solution, if there be one, lies in a fundamental reform of our monetary institutions. As a matter of long-run reform,

I would like to see the Federal Reserve System in its present form abolished and replaced by a 100-percent reserve-deposit banking system in which there was no monetary authority possessing discretionary powers over the quantity of money.[62]

Although it is unclear whether Friedman genuinely believed elimination of the Federal Reserve was likely—or even possible—there could hardly have been a more forceful critique of the institution than the one he offered to members of Congress in 1952.

Chairman Martin

President Truman appointed William McChesney Martin, a Treasury official who had worked on the Accord, to chair the Federal Reserve Board after McCabe resigned in March 1951. Martin believed that the Federal Reserve's primary mission was "to lean against the winds of deflation or inflation, whichever way they are blowing."[63] He inaugurated two new policies in the spirit of the Federal Reserve's newfound independence under the Accord. The first was that the FOMC would pursue only the "correction of disorderly conditions" in the Treasury bond market, rather than the more proactive "maintenance of orderly conditions," which implied keeping rates low.[64] The second was that the FOMC would adopt a "bills only" policy and deal solely in Treasury debt that matured in one year or less (i.e., short-term Treasury bills rather than long-term Treasury bonds). This would keep the Federal Reserve out of the Treasury's long-term borrowing and preclude any chance of returning to the peg.[65]

Martin maintained effective communications with the next two U.S. presidents through meetings of a group called the Quadriad. Created to ease communications with the Federal Reserve after a dispute with the Eisenhower administration over interest rates, the Quadriad consisted of the chairman of the Federal Reserve Board, the president of the United States, the Treasury secretary, and the chair of the president's Council of Economic Advisers. President John F. Kennedy continued the Quadriad meetings, and in 1961 his administration persuaded Martin to abandon "bills only" and buy long-term Treasury debt to help "nudge" down long-term interest rates. The goal of this unorthodox policy was to try to boost domestic investment through lower long-term rates while discouraging capital flows abroad by keeping short-term rates high. This plan, called "operation nudge," would later become known as "operation twist."[66]

Martin's close coordination with the executive branch ended after a confrontation with Kennedy's successor, Lyndon Johnson. In a June 1965 speech, delivered against the backdrop of a booming economy, Martin noted "disquieting similarities between our present prosperity and the fabulous twenties" and spoke of the need for tighter monetary policy.[67] When the Federal Reserve Board raised the discount rate in December, the move enraged Johnson, who had wanted to coordinate monetary policy with the demands of the Vietnam War and his "Great Society" programs. Johnson had expected to discuss such changes at the next Quadriad meeting, scheduled for just a few days after the rate increase was announced. When that meeting finally came, Martin and Johnson agreed that more direct communications would be helpful in the future.[68]

Combating Stagflation

Martin remained chairman of the Federal Reserve Board until President Richard Nixon appointed his own economic counselor, Arthur Burns, to the position in January 1970. Burns arrived as economists nationwide confronted a puzzle. Past experience suggested that unemployment and inflation tended to move in opposite directions, with unemployment falling and inflation rising when the economy was booming, and just the opposite (rising unemployment and falling inflation) when the economy slowed down. Between 1969 and 1970, however, unemployment had risen from 3.5 percent to 4.9 percent while inflation had jumped from 5 percent to 6 percent.[69] This unexpected combination of rising inflation and rising unemployment, called "stagflation," persisted through much of the 1970s.

Burns believed that inflation was the principal problem that deserved attention. In normal times the Fed* would have tightened credit to combat it, but Burns had doubts about this approach during a period of stagflation. He recommended instead that the government impose direct controls to stop

---

* The Federal Reserve came to be called the "Fed" in popular parlance over the course of the late 1960s (Shull, *The Fourth Branch*, 154).

wages and prices from rising. The suggestion at first shocked President Nixon, but he soon changed his mind and announced a bold package of economic policies in August 1971, including federal wage and price controls and the closing of the so-called gold window. The latter policy, which meant that foreign central banks could no longer exchange dollars for gold, effectively devalued the dollar and released American monetary policy from the constraints of the Bretton Woods gold exchange standard. The Fed, meanwhile, expanded the money supply over the following year, and by November 1972, when Nixon was up for reelection, the economy was surging ahead while inflation remained under 3.5 percent.[70] In fact, some journalists and scholars have accused Chairman Burns of loosening monetary policy specifically to boost the economy in time for the 1972 elections.[71]

Stagflation did not disappear for long, however. In 1973 inflation rose to 6.2 percent, and by the time Nixon resigned the next August, inflation had leaped into the double digits (in part as a result of an OPEC oil embargo) and the U.S. economy was facing its worst recession since the 1930s.[72] The new president, Gerald Ford, agreed with Burns that inflation was the paramount economic issue, and Burns himself began to tighten monetary policy. Despite frequent one-on-one meetings, Burns reported that Ford did not try to influence Fed decisions. "Every president I have known has made remarks about the independence of the Federal Reserve," Burns later recalled. "Gerry Ford believed it."[73]

Wright Patman had long been Congress's most vocal critic of the Fed, calling it "a self-appointed money trust" that "imperiled the welfare of our citizens."[74] Although Patman's stature in Congress had diminished by the 1970s (and he died in early 1976), the Fed's policies during the recession converted many members of Congress to his cause. Between 1975 and 1978, several new laws attempted to expand Congress's oversight of the Fed. In March 1975 Congress resolved that the Fed should provide targets for the coming year's money supply, four times each year. The Fed complied, but provided five different measures, and used a "rolling base" that projected the targets from a new start date at each consultation, confusing many lawmakers.[75] In 1977 Congress directed the Fed to offer public meetings, transcripts, and prompt policy announcements, but the Fed retained the right to restrict access to any meeting that might provoke financial speculation or instability. As it turned out, this exception covered just about every meeting

Fed officials held, which meant the new rules were virtually a dead letter.[76] The 1977 legislation also established the Federal Reserve's so-called dual mandate, requiring the Fed "to promote effectively the goals of maximum employment, stable prices and moderate long-term interest rates."[77] In 1978 Congress offered more precise specifications for Fed reporting on monetary targets, and it required the Fed to explain annually how its policies fit with the president's economic goals. Congress also attempted to audit the Fed's budget at this time, but the Fed "went to war" against this (in the words of one official), insisting that audits would compromise its independence from politics. A 1978 law ultimately did institute audits of some of the Fed's expenses, but not audits that covered any of its key financial or monetary activities.[78]

The Fed also weathered criticism from President Jimmy Carter, who took office in 1977. Carter hoped to stimulate a weak economy with increased public spending, tax cuts, and looser monetary policy, and during his campaign had said he wanted "a chairman of the Federal Reserve whose economic views are compatible with [the president's] own."[79] Burns, however, continued to focus on containing inflation with tight money. He publicly declared this was possible only due to the Fed's "considerable degree of independence it enjoys within the government."[80] When Burns's term ended in early 1978, Carter chose to replace him with G. William Miller, chairman of a large technology company. His tenure lasted only eighteen months. Miller supported expansionary monetary policy, but by 1979 rising inflation led many in the Fed as well as the Carter administration to support a return to tighter credit. That summer, Carter named Miller secretary of the Treasury and picked Paul Volcker, the New York Federal Reserve Bank president, as the new chairman of the Federal Reserve Board.[81]

Paul Volcker

In his thinking about monetary policy, Volcker was sympathetic to the "monetarist" school of thought. Monetarists held that stable, predictable growth of the money supply was best, and that adjusting it to address short-term needs only fostered instability. As chairman, Volcker sought to pursue "practical" monetarism. He believed that the Fed should announce money supply targets well in advance, strive to meet them, and revise them when necessary to respond to changes in the economy. In October 1979 the Fed announced a major policy change in line with monetarist principles. It raised the discount rate, the usual prescription when inflation was high, but also increased reserve requirements (the percentage of reserves banks were required to hold against deposited funds) and reformed its open market operations to target the money supply rather than interest rates.[82]

Although Volcker's methods proved highly controversial, they at least appeared to be effective in taming inflation. By 1983 inflation was down to about 3 percent (as compared to more than 10 percent just two years before).[83] The exceptionally tight monetary policy and high interest rates that Volcker's strategy had generated took a large toll, however, sparking numerous bank failures and producing a severe recession. Protests against the Fed, by both businesses and consumers, were widespread: construction firms mailed miniature wooden planks to the Board, "reminding [Fed officials] that high interest rates were destroying their businesses," while farmers surrounded the Fed's Washington offices with tractors.[84] In August 1982 Senator Robert Byrd announced that high interest rates were "public enemy no. 1" and authored a bill that would have forced the Fed to lower them.[85] Despite the outcry, Volcker earned the respect of many business leaders for slaying inflation. Even some members of Congress, in the words of one economist, "praise[d] him with faint damns" for finally beating stagflation.[86] President Reagan reappointed Volcker in 1983, and he remained chairman until he resigned in 1987.

The Greenspan Years

The new Fed chairman, Alan Greenspan, assumed office in August 1987 and almost immediately faced a trial by fire. On October 19 the American stock market crashed. The Dow Jones Industrial Average fell 22.6 percent, its largest-ever one-day decline. The next day the Fed declared "its readiness to serve as a source of liquidity to support the economic and financial system." It quickly expanded its open market purchases to provide extra liquidity and encouraged bankers to keep credit flowing. Over the next few weeks, several small financial institutions failed, but the broader financial system remained intact and the stock market gradually recovered.[87]

Once he was satisfied the immediate crisis had passed, Greenspan again tightened monetary policy, though he loosened it in response to small financial disturbances in 1989 and 1990. His decision to tighten again in mid-1990, just as a recession was beginning, provoked sharp criticism. President George H. W. Bush urged lower interest rates in his 1991 State of the Union address, and one senator complained to Greenspan that "people are going to starve out there and you're worried about inflation."[88] Although the official recession soon ended and Bush reappointed Greenspan, the economy continued to struggle through the early 1990s, despite lower interest rates. The Democrat Bill Clinton defeated Bush in November 1992, and Bush later blamed Greenspan, saying, "I think that if the interest rates had been lowered more dramatically that I would have been reelected. . . . I reappointed him, and he disappointed me."[89]

When Greenspan met with President-elect Bill Clinton in December 1992, the Fed chairman expressed concern about the almost $300 billion federal budget deficit. Such a high deficit, Greenspan believed, kept long-term interest rates high and diminished the Fed's ability to influence them. Greenspan thought that this helped explain why the economy had remained weak despite relatively loose monetary policy. Having seen the third-party candidate Ross Perot secure nearly 20 percent of the vote on an anti-deficit platform in the 1992 presidential election, Clinton quickly adopted a deficit reduction strategy as president, and in 1993 he signed an aggressive budget law (including significant tax increases) that he expected would cut the deficit by nearly $500 billion over five years.[90]

Given that the budget law had been designed at least in part to permit lower interest rates, Clinton was furious when the Fed still went ahead and raised rates in 1994. Various media outlets and members of Congress complained that Greenspan was battling an imaginary threat, since inflation was low, and Clinton's advisers reportedly "had to restrain" the president from publicly denouncing the policy. Criticisms notwithstanding, inflation dropped and remained below 3 percent through the end of the decade.[91] In the meantime, the economy shifted into high gear, with robust real GDP growth, low unemployment, and surging stock indexes, particularly in the technology sector. Even major financial crises in Mexico in 1994–1995 and in Asia in 1997–1998 failed to push the American economy off track. By the late 1990s, Greenspan was a national celebrity. Candidates from both parties praised him during the 2000 presidential election. Republican John McCain quipped, "If [Greenspan] would happen to die, God forbid . . . I would prop him up and put a pair of dark sunglasses on him."[92]

The good times of the 1990s appeared to come to a sudden stop at the dawn of the new decade. The surge in the technology sector that had helped fuel the boom of the late 1990s hit a wall in the year 2000. Technology stocks, especially Internet stocks, fell sharply in what was frequently characterized as the "collapse of the tech bubble." The economy soon fell into recession, and the Fed responded by lowering interest rates. It lowered them still further to shore up confidence after the devastating terrorist attacks on New York and Washington on September 11, 2001. Over the course of that year, the Fed cut the target federal funds rate—the rate banks charged each other on overnight loans—from 6.5 percent to 1.75 percent, and from there to an unusually low 1 percent. Supporters of Fed policy insisted that such low rates were appropriate because inflation remained tame, the job market appeared lackluster, and the economy continued to face significant risks on the downside, despite the fact that economic growth had returned. The Fed finally began to raise interest rates starting in 2004, as the economy seemed to strengthen. In fact, on January 31, 2006, Greenspan's last day as chairman, the Fed lifted the federal funds rate to 4.5 percent.[93]

Bernanke Confronts a Crisis

President George W. Bush selected Ben Bernanke, chairman of his Council of Economic Advisors, to replace Greenspan in 2006 as chairman of the Federal Reserve Board. Bernanke had served at the Fed from 2002 through 2005 (before joining the Council of Economic Advisors), and prior to that had been an economics professor at Princeton. His research included cutting-edge work on the Great Depression. Throughout 2006 Bernanke continued to follow Greenspan's lead and raised interest rates. Bernanke's major policy ambition in his first year was to begin announcing inflation targets. Greenspan had kept his targets secret, if he had them at all, but under Bernanke the Federal Reserve Banks began announcing long-term inflation "forecasts," which the financial community understood as targets.[94]

Although Bernanke had given a widely cited speech in February 2004 celebrating the "Great Moderation"—which he characterized as "a substantial decline in macroeconomic volatility" over the previous "20 years or so"— signs of trouble appeared about a year into Bernanke's tenure as chairman of the Federal Reserve.[95] The American housing market had risen substantially over the 2000s, fueled in part by the proliferation of subprime mortgages, which were high-interest loans for homebuyers who were generally considered too risky for regular (prime) mortgages. On the eve of the crisis, lenders and investors held over 7 million subprime mortgages, which were worth about $1.3 trillion and accounted for more than a tenth of all home mortgages. In early 2007 some lenders began filing for bankruptcy as defaults among subprime borrowers were on the rise. Housing prices had begun to fall, and by the spring 3.5 million mortgages were "under water," meaning that the amount owed was greater than the market value of the property.[96]

Problems in the housing sector in early 2007 attracted attention, but not alarm, from government officials. That July, Bernanke predicted "moderate" growth for the rest of the year and acceleration in 2008, noting a risk "that the ongoing housing correction might prove larger than anticipated."[97] Inflation remained his "predominant policy concern." The housing situation continued to deteriorate, however, worrying investors. Many large financial firms had packaged subprime mortgages into products called mortgage-backed securities (MBSs). With so many mortgages failing, the true value of these securities was difficult to discern. By August 2007 banks in both the United States and Europe were feeling the strain as housing troubles had "crossed into the banking system." In fact, as fears about American mortgages spread across the European banking sector in early August, the European Central Bank and the Fed injected vast amounts of liquidity to help stabilize financial markets.[98]

Over the autumn of 2007 the economic situation grew significantly worse than Bernanke had anticipated. In September the Fed cut the federal funds rate from 5.25 percent to 4.75 percent. Although a few indicators suggested the economy performed better into October, troubling signs soon reemerged. The Fed lowered the federal funds rate by 0.25 percent at the end of October and again in December. These cuts—particularly the one in December—were smaller than many financial analysts had expected, and stocks fell as investors worried that the Fed had "fallen way behind the curve."[99] On December 12 the Fed announced two unprecedented initiatives to stabilize the financial system. First, it created a mechanism called the Term Auction Facility (TAF), allowing it to auction funds to qualifying depository institutions.[100] Second, the Fed began authorizing large-scale currency swaps with foreign central banks to help meet a rising overseas demand for dollars.[101]

With the crisis showing no signs of abating, emergency measures continued in early 2008. At the end of January, in what the *Financial Times* called a "week that shook the world," the Fed cut the federal funds rate by a dramatic 0.75 percent, and soon another 0.50 percent, to 3.00 percent.[102] On February 7 Congress passed $168 billion in tax cuts and rebates to stimulate the economy. The Fed expanded TAF in March and created a new program, the Term Securities Lending Facility (TSLF), to temporarily exchange Treasury debt for MBSs and other collateralized obligations, an intervention one economist at the European Central Bank described as being "as close as [the Fed] can get to going really nuclear."[103]

Rescue Operations

Bear Stearns

In early March there were rumors that a large investment bank, Bear Stearns, was in trouble. A leaked email from Goldman Sachs expressing such fears helped trigger a run. On March 13 Bear Stearns notified the Fed that collapse was imminent. By that night the bank held less than $2 billion in cash, a steep fall from $18 billion just two days earlier. Because Bear Stearns played a pivotal role in many complex financial transactions involving (both directly and indirectly) countless financial actors, some experts worried its failure could threaten the broader financial system.[104]

On Friday, March 14, Fed and Treasury officials decided that the Fed would loan Bear Stearns $12.9 billion to see it through the weekend.* Bear Stearns repaid the loan on March 17, with interest, but the intervention troubled many at the Fed. As an investment bank, not a commercial bank, Bear Stearns technically fell under the jurisdiction of the Securities and Exchange Commission (SEC), not the Federal Reserve. Fed officials had cited an obscure clause from a 1932 law, allowing the Fed to lend "to any individual, partnership or corporation" in "unusual and exigent circumstances," as legal justification for the loan. The Fed had rarely used this power, and never for a loan as big as this. New York Federal Reserve Bank president Timothy

---

* Over this weekend, the Fed also created a new program called the Primary Dealer Credit Facility (PDCF), through which other investment banks could borrow overnight from the Fed (Wessel, *In Fed We Trust,* 170–171; Thomas, *The Financial Crisis,* 169).

Geithner called the loan "an extraordinary step," but said "it seemed irresponsible for us not to use that authority in this unique situation."[105]

Over the weekend of the loan, the Fed and the Treasury helped Bear Stearns' top leadership sell the company to avoid bankruptcy. JPMorgan Chase, one of the nation's largest financial firms, was interested in buying, but feared Bear Stearns' potentially toxic portfolio of mortgage-related assets. To seal the deal, the Fed assumed risk for $29 billion of those securities, employing some rather intricate financial maneuvers to do so. By the end of 2008, the bundle of securities had fallen in value by more than $4 billion. Chairman Bernanke later testified, "This cost . . . must be weighed against the effects on the American economy and American financial system of allowing [Bear Stearns] to collapse."[106]

The Bear Stearns rescue briefly lifted spirits, but weak economic forecasts, growing concerns about inflation, and low consumer confidence soon soured expectations. On April 2, Chairman Bernanke acknowledged that a recession might be imminent. His timing was off: though it was not widely recognized at the time, economists would later date the start of the recession to December 2007.[107]

Fannie Mae and Freddie Mac

In July 2008 the Fed confronted an emergency that, in the words of one retired Fed official, "dwarf[ed] the Bear Stearns issue."[108] In 1938 Congress had created the Federal National Mortgage Association, or "Fannie Mae," to buy certain types of mortgages on the secondary market. Congress sold Fannie Mae to private investors in 1968, though the company continued to be seen as a quasi-public entity that had the implicit financial backing of the federal government. Congress later created another similar organization, the Federal Home Loan Mortgage Corporation, or "Freddie Mac." Fannie Mae and Freddie Mac began issuing (and effectively insuring) mortgage-backed securities in the 1970s and 1980s, typically bundling very safe mortgages. In the 2000s, however, as the subprime market was becoming ever more popular with private investors, Fannie and Freddie increasingly moved into riskier assets. This, combined with the collapse of housing prices in 2007 and 2008, left both Fannie and Freddie facing large losses.[109] In the first half of 2008, shares in both companies had declined more than 60 percent. Foreign investors in Fannie and Freddie wondered if the U.S. government would meet its unofficial responsibility to support the firms. Many observers worried that if Fannie and Freddie were ever allowed to fail, the results could prove catastrophic because together they held or backed more than 30 million mortgages, valued at about $5.5 trillion.[110]

On July 13, Treasury Secretary Henry Paulson announced his and Chairman Bernanke's plan for Fannie and Freddie. He requested that Congress empower him to use Treasury funds to assist the companies. Until such a law passed, the Fed would again declare "unusual and exigent circumstances" and lend funds to Fannie and Freddie as needed. Congress passed the requested legislation by the end of the month, and Paulson soon used his new power in an unexpected way. On September 7, federal regulators seized control of both companies. The Treasury committed up to $100 billion to support each firm—four times what it estimated was necessary, but an unambiguous signal that it would not abandon Fannie and Freddie.[111] Bernanke called it "a brilliant operation, absolutely necessary," which "stabilized an important part of the financial system at a critical time."[112]

Lehman Brothers

The next emergency arrived within a week. The investment bank Lehman Brothers had seen its commercial real estate holdings lose $6.7 billion in six months, and its shares were down 90 percent since January. On September 12, with bankruptcy imminent, Secretary Paulson, New York Federal Reserve Bank President Timothy Geithner, and SEC Chairman Christopher Cox met with the leaders of major financial firms to persuade them to rescue Lehman. The government apparently had no interest in a federal rescue in this case. Paulson had complained of his unwanted reputation as "Mr. Bailout," and Geithner insisted that there was "no political will" for a Bear Stearns–style intervention. By the next evening the British bank Barclays appeared interested in purchasing Lehman, but the deal soon fell apart. The only remaining way to save Lehman would have been an intervention by the Fed, estimated to cost over $60 billion, but this was never put on the table. Instead the company was left to fail, and on September 15, 2008, Lehman Brothers commenced the biggest bankruptcy in American history.[113]

Stock markets fell sharply, and critics demanded to know why federal officials—including those at the Fed—had allowed Lehman to go down. In congressional testimony on September 24, Bernanke claimed that "the troubles at Lehman had been well known for some time, and investors clearly recognized . . . that the failure of the firm was a significant possibility. Thus, we judged that investors and counterparties had had time to take precautionary measures."[114] In later interviews, however, those involved in the decision not to intervene argued that the Fed, like the Treasury, had been powerless to step in. The "unusual and exigent circumstances" rule required that any loans be sufficiently secured, Geithner and Bernanke explained, but Lehman lacked the necessary collateral. More generally, federal officials insisted that they did not yet have the legal authority to execute a government bailout. In January 2009 Paulson reported that they had avoided this explanation at first—that is, that officials at both the Fed and the Treasury had been powerless to save Lehman—because it would have diminished public faith in the government's ability to respond to the crisis.[115]

AIG

After letting Lehman fail, Bernanke immediately turned his attention to the American International Group (AIG), the world's largest insurance company. In addition to insurance, AIG had a sizable Financial Products Division, which had lost $18.5 billion between September 2007 and June 2008. AIG's CEO warned Geithner on September 11 that the firm was struggling, and on September 16 the company alerted the government that it might not survive the day. As an insurance company, AIG was ineligible for many government programs aimed at supporting banks. However, the Fed judged that AIG's businesses were vital enough to secure "unusual and exigent" loans. That afternoon the Fed offered to lend AIG up to $85 billion at a high interest rate, with caveats that the government would take a controlling stake in the company and replace the CEO. AIG accepted, and the Fed kept its wire system open late that night to transfer the funds.[116]

Tensions ran high after the one-two punch of Lehman Brothers and AIG. Bernanke later testified that the AIG ordeal upset him more than any other incident during the crisis. As an insurer that was also involved in other areas of finance, "AIG exploited a huge gap in the regulatory system," Bernanke noted. The Fed, in his view, "really had no choice" other than a bailout because AIG's collapse would have been "disastrous for the economy."[117]

The AIG rescue also troubled many members of Congress. In a meeting with congressional leaders to explain the AIG operation, Bernanke let them know that the Fed had $800 billion to use for emergency loans.[118] This disturbed Barney Frank, Democrat from Massachusetts and chair of the House Financial Services Committee. "I think [Bernanke and Paulson] are doing well," he said, "although I think it's been inappropriate in a democracy to have them in this position where they were doing this stuff unilaterally. . . . No one in a democracy, unelected, should have $800 billion to spend as he sees fit."[119]

TARP

On September 17, 2008, the day after the AIG rescue, the Dow Jones Industrial Average fell 4.1 percent and interbank lending slowed dramatically. In an interview later that month, Secretary Paulson named September 17 as the most frightening point of the crisis thus far. According to the *Wall Street Journal,* that was the day Chairman Bernanke placed an urgent call to Secretary Paulson:

> The Fed chairman, a Princeton academic with an occasional quaver in his voice, leaned toward the speakerphone on his office coffee table and spoke unusually bluntly to Mr. Paulson, a strong-willed former college football player and Wall Street executive.
> The Fed had been stretched to its limits and couldn't do it any more, Mr. Bernanke said. Although Mr. Paulson had been resisting such a move for months, Mr. Bernanke said it was time for the Treasury secretary to go to Congress to seek funds and authority for a broader rescue. Mr. Paulson didn't commit, but by the next morning, he had.[120]

Bernanke had studied past financial crises and knew that governments facing a financial storm often had resorted to such measures to shore up their banking systems. The next day, Thursday, September 18, Bernanke and Paulson warned President Bush that without quick action, the country could fall into a deep depression, possibly even worse than in the 1930s. Convinced that the Fed had exhausted its own options, Bush approved their plan.[121]

Bernanke and Paulson scheduled an emergency meeting with congressional leaders that evening to make their case. Citing a participant at the meeting, the *Washington Post* reported that "Paulson and Bernanke presented a 'chilling' picture of the state of the financial system."[122] As Senator Christopher Dodd later recalled, "I had no idea I was going to hear what I heard, sitting in that room with Hank Paulson saying to us in very measured tones that, 'Unless you act, the financial system of this country and the world will melt down in a matter of days.' There was literally a pause in that room where the oxygen left."[123] Warning of a potential depression, Paulson said the Treasury needed $700 billion by Monday to stabilize the situation, and leaders from both parties indicated that they were prepared to do whatever was necessary. There were a few practical objections, however. Harry Reid (D-NV), the Senate majority leader, worried about political fallout and about the timing. "You are coming here to ask taxpayers to spend hundreds of billions of dollars," he reminded them. "We're elected. You're not. This needs hearings." Richard Shelby (R-AL), of the Senate Banking Committee, feared that Congress would be writing "a blank check."[124]

The plan failed its first vote in the House on September 29. Americans across the political spectrum, it turned out, opposed bailing out huge financial institutions with taxpayer money. "I've read the Constitution," one North Carolinian had written in a letter. "Nowhere does it say that taxpayers are the default dumping ground for mortgages made to people who cannot afford them." Many members of the House were similarly incensed and rejected the bill. Once it was voted down, however, stocks fell sharply and lawmakers quickly reversed course. After the Senate passed the bill on October 1, the House did the same on October 3, and President Bush immediately signed it into law. The new statute created the Troubled Asset Relief Program (TARP) and allocated $700 billion to it to stabilize the financial system.[125]

On October 13, Bernanke, Paulson, and Geithner met with leading bankers to ensure their participation in TARP. Although the program's architects had originally aimed to buy "toxic" assets from the banks (and had justified the plan to Congress on this basis), they now believed that a better approach would be to buy billions of dollars of nonvoting equity in the banks instead. The purpose of the meeting was to make sure that all of the relevant banks were on board, healthy and sick alike, because all of the banks could use a cushion and because buying equity only in the weakest ones would send an ominous signal to the public, possibly provoking mass withdrawals from those institutions. By the end of the day, all of the banks represented at the meeting had agreed to the deal, which consumed $125 billion of the $700 billion TARP appropriation.[126]

As Congress and the nation were debating TARP, the Fed had been working to sort out additional problems among some of the nation's largest financial firms. On September 21 it facilitated the conversion of investment banks Morgan Stanley and Goldman Sachs into bank holding companies, which gave the Fed greater oversight of their activities and ensured that both institutions would have access to the Fed discount window and other programs in an emergency. Over the following week the Fed assisted in the sale of Washington Mutual to JPMorgan Chase. The Fed also created two new programs during this period to help address the scarcity of private credit in the marketplace: the Commercial Paper Funding Facility (CPFF) and the Asset-Backed Commercial Paper Money Market Mutual Fund Liquidity Facility (AMLF).[127]

Coping with Recession

After Barack Obama won the presidency in November 2008, Chairman Bernanke encouraged further fiscal stimulation of the economy. The Fed planned to do its part by driving the federal funds rate, already at just 1 percent, even lower. At its December 2008 meeting, the FOMC cut the rate to near zero—an unprecedented move. With the federal funds rate essentially as low as it could go, the FOMC also resolved to begin "quantitative easing" (QE), a novel strategy for increasing the money supply through the purchase of diverse assets, including commercial and long-term assets, not just short-term Treasury debt. Some observers, including certain members of the FOMC itself, worried about the implications of QE. Noted economist John Taylor wondered, in a January 2009 article, "Will [QE] interventions only take place in recessions, or will the Fed officials use them in the future to try to make economic expansions stronger or to assist certain sectors and industries for other reasons?"[128]

New efforts to revive the battered economy were initiated in 2009. In February President Obama approved $787 billion in tax cuts and new spending.[129] QE accelerated the next month, with the Fed's announcement of $1.75 trillion in purchases of government agency and Treasury securities over the coming year, including $1.25 trillion of MBSs from agencies like Fannie Mae and Freddie Mac.[130] A joint Treasury–Federal Reserve program called the Term Asset-Backed Securities Loan Facility (TALF), announced the previous November, also began in March. Its purpose was to encourage investment in asset-backed securities tied to consumer and small-business loans, a market that had largely dried up and thus diminished the availability of such loans. By year's end TALF had lent $47 billion of its $200 billion allocation.[131] The FOMC, meanwhile, had declared that it anticipated "that economic conditions are likely to warrant exceptionally low levels of the federal funds rate for some time."[132]

Congress and the Fed

Throughout 2009, Congress held numerous hearings to investigate the financial sector, the crisis, and the government agencies that had intervened.[133] Many lawmakers were particularly interested in the Federal Reserve.

Power and Accountability

On February 10, 2009, the House Financial Services Committee held a hearing on the Fed's "extraordinary" efforts to support the financial system. As the hearing opened, several committee members expressed discomfort with the Fed's interventions. Barney Frank, the chairman, declared, "It does not seem to me healthy in our democracy for the amount of power that is lodged in the Federal Reserve with very few restrictions to continue." Spencer Bachus (R-AL) worried that while the public had devoted its attention to TARP and the stimulus package, such expenditures paled in comparison to the trillions of dollars quietly loaned by the Fed. Chairman Bernanke testified on behalf of the Fed, claiming that its policies had stabilized the financial system. Acknowledging the committee's concerns, he stated that "central banks should be as transparent as possible, both for reasons of democratic accountability and because many of our policies are likely to be more effective if they are well understood by markets and the public." Bernanke also noted that the Fed had rescued Bear Stearns and AIG "with great reluctance," and that if Congress created a program to handle such emergencies in the future, "the Federal Reserve would be more than delighted to step aside from such operations."[134]

The House Subcommittee on Domestic Monetary Policy and Technology, part of the Financial Services Committee, called a hearing for July 9, 2009, to discuss the Fed and its multiple roles. In June the Obama administration had recommended that the Fed take responsibility for regulating large financial firms. The subcommittee explored the proposal, particularly in light of the Fed's monetary responsibilities and its desired political independence.[135] Republicans at the hearing criticized the proposal. Representative Bachus insisted that the Fed should have less regulatory authority, not more, so that it could focus on monetary policy. The administration proposal, he argued, "would statutorily bless what [Republicans] consider an unwise cycle of bailouts, picking winners and losers, and obligating the taxpayers." Congressmen Ron Paul (R-TX) and Michael Castle (R-DE) also criticized the Fed's independence from political oversight and proposed an audit of its operations.[136]

The Federal Reserve's vice chairman, Donald Kohn, attempted to rebut Paul and Castle, arguing that central bank independence "tends to yield a monetary policy that best promotes economic growth and price stability." Independence, he suggested, "prevents governments from succumbing to the temptation to use the central bank to fund budget deficits" and "enables policymakers to look beyond the short term as they weigh the effects of their monetary policy actions on price stability and employment." Thorough audits would be "contrary to the public interest," Kohn maintained, because "financial markets likely would see the grant of such authority as tending to undermine monetary independence, and this would have adverse consequences for interest rates and economic stability."[137]

On July 16 the same subcommittee considered the Fed once more—this time against the backdrop of the administration's proposal to create a Consumer Financial Protection Agency to oversee the regulation of retail financial products. Such an agency, proponents suggested, might have detected the subprime mortgage problem before the crisis started.[138] The hearing investigated the Fed's role in consumer protection and how it would relate to the proposed agency. After an introduction by Chairman Melvin Watt (D-NC), Congressman Paul accused the Fed of abandoning consumers throughout its history, by allowing inflation at numerous points in the twentieth century and bailing out banks at taxpayers' expense during the crisis.[139] Representative Brad Sherman (D-CA) similarly charged that the Fed was too cozy with banks, pointing out that bankers held significant power in selecting Federal Reserve Bank presidents and, in turn, members of the FOMC. He called this an "incredible and offensive exception" to the American democratic tradition and "an affront to the Constitution."[140] Elizabeth Duke, of the Federal Reserve Board, delivered the Fed's view that a new consumer protection agency was unnecessary. She said Congress should formally grant such responsibilities to the Fed itself, which already had numerous consumer protection initiatives under way.[141]

An Audit?

On September 25, 2009, the House Financial Services Committee gathered to discuss the "Federal Reserve Transparency Act of 2009," sponsored by Representative Paul and cosponsored by 295 other members of the House. The bill would direct the Government Accountability Office (GAO) to perform a complete audit of the Federal Reserve Board and the twelve Federal Reserve Banks. Paul had submitted an audit bill as early as 1981, but this was the first time his proposal had received a hearing.[142]

Scott Alvarez, general counsel to the Federal Reserve Board, offered the Fed's opinion. He began by highlighting ways in which the Fed was already transparent. The FOMC announced policy decisions after each meeting and provided minutes three weeks afterward. Chairman Bernanke testified regularly before Congress. Moreover, an independent firm and the GAO regularly audited certain Fed activities each year, and their findings were public. Alvarez conceded that these audits excluded activities related to monetary policy, but repeated Vice Chairman Kohn's words from July that "considerable experience shows that monetary policy independence, within a framework of legislatively established objectives and public accountability, tends to yield a monetary policy that best promotes price stability and economic growth." An audit, he insisted, would provoke "concerns that monetary policy judgments would become subject to political considerations," "chill the unfettered and wide-ranging internal debates that are essential for identifying and implementing the best policy options," and "reduce the effectiveness of our discount window and liquidity programs by increasing potential borrowers' fear of stigma or adverse reactions from participating in these programs."[143]

The House Committee on Financial Services considered a version of the Federal Reserve Transparency Act on November 19, 2009, as an amendment to a major financial reform bill. By then Paul's bill had 313 cosponsors.[144] Lawmakers working on the financial reform legislation had already included in their drafts various transparency provisions regarding the Fed's "unusual and exigent" powers.[145] This new amendment, by Paul and Alan Grayson (D-FL), would expand that transparency by requiring a complete audit of the Fed. The only limitations were that the GAO could not look into unreleased transcripts of FOMC meetings, and that it could not release findings on the Fed's market actions until 180 days had passed. The amendment stated that none of its provisions "shall be construed . . . as interference in or dictation of monetary policy to the Federal Reserve System by the Congress or the Government Accountability Office."[146] In a letter to the committee, Paul and Grayson wrote, "We also reject the false dichotomy between transparency and independence. The Paul-Grayson amendment would achieve the necessary transparency of the trillions of dollars of Fed interventions while keeping Congress from directly intervening in the decision-making process. Independence should not be synonymous with secrecy."[147]

At the November 19 meeting, Chairman Frank—who still supported an audit of the special crisis-related programs—worried that the Paul-Grayson amendment would compromise the Fed's ability to resist political pressure.[148] Melvin Watt, another concerned Democrat, suggested a milder alternative. Watt's amendment allowed for an audit of the Fed's "unusual and exigent" loans as well as its regulatory functions, financial statements, and some structural details of its emergency liquidity programs. Watt's amendment, however, would adhere to existing limitations on Fed audits and would bar any audits of monetary policy actions or the financial details of liquidity programs.[149] In a letter to the committee Watt insisted, "My amendment strikes the appropriate balance of increasing Federal Reserve transparency while preventing political interference with monetary policy," though he noted it would "certainly fall short of demands by those intent on destroying the independence (if not the existence) of the Fed." Representative Grayson announced in response that Watt's plan would not allow auditors to do much more than "count the pencils on the desks."[150]

Once the debate ended, the committee prepared to vote on the two amendments. If the broader Paul-Grayson amendment prevailed, Representative

Ron Paul's long-hoped-for investigation of the Fed's inner workings would be one step closer to reality.

NOTES

1. *Congressional Record,* 111th Congress, 3 Feb. 2009, E192. Available at thomas.loc .gov.

2. See H.R. 875 of the 98th Congress, "A bill to repeal the Federal Reserve Act." Available at thomas.loc.gov.

3. George Rogers Taylor, "A Brief History of the Second Bank of the United States," in George Rogers Taylor (ed.), *Jackson vs. Biddle's Bank* (Lexington, MA: Heath, 1972), 1–3 (quotation from a letter to John Calhoun, 24 Dec. 1815, at 3); Bernard Shull, *The Fourth Branch* (Westport, CT: Praeger, 2005), 19.

4. Taylor, "Brief History," 4–7.

5. Hammond's *Banks and Politics in America* (1957) quoted in Shull, *The Fourth Branch,* 20. Taylor ("A Brief History," 8) disputes Hammond's argument and claims that the Treasury, not the Bank, was the chief executor of federal monetary policy during this period.

6. Shull, *The Fourth Branch,* 20–21.

7. Jackson's veto message is available at Yale Law School's Avalon Project, http: //avalon .law.yale.edu/19th_century/ajveto01.asp.

8. Shull, *The Fourth Branch,* 22–23; Elgin Groseclose, *Fifty Years of Managed Money* (London: Macmillan, 1965), 6.

9. Shull, *The Fourth Branch,* 23–25.

10. Ibid., 29–31; Groseclose, *Fifty Years,* 29–30; Lloyd B. Thomas, *The Financial Crisis and Federal Reserve Policy* (New York: Palgrave Macmillan, 2011), 38–39; Carola Frydman, Eric Hilt, and Lily Y. Zhou, "The Panic of 1907: JP Morgan, Trust Companies, and the Impact of the Financial Crisis," unpublished working paper (www.vanderbilt.edu /econ/sempapers/Frydman.pdf), 8–11 (quotations at 9).

11. Shull, *The Fourth Branch,* 30–35; Groseclose, *Fifty Years,* 29–33.

12. Shull, *The Fourth Branch,* 33.

13. Quoted in Groseclose, *Fifty Years,* 37.

14. John Harsen Rhoades, "Who Shall Control Our Financial Destiny?," speech to the Finance Forum of New York City (18 Dec. 1912), quoted in Shull, *The Fourth Branch,* 35–36.

15. Shull, *The Fourth Branch,* 41; Groseclose, *Fifty Years,* 49–50.

16. Donald F. Kettl, *Leadership at the Fed* (New Haven: Yale University Press, 1986), 18.

17. Groseclose, *Fifty Years,* 55–56; Kettl, *Leadership at the Fed,* 23; David Moss and Cole Bolton, "The Federal Reserve and the Banking Crisis of 1931," HBS Case No. 9-709-040 (Boston: Harvard Business School Publishing, 2009), 8.

18. Paul Moritz Warburg, *A Plan for a Modified Central Bank* (1907), 3–6, available at http://books.google.com/books?id=tYEuAAAAYAAJ, quotations at 5 and 6; final quote also in Groseclose, *Fifty Years,* 57.

19. See Roger Lowenstein, *America's Bank: The Epic Struggle to Create the Federal Reserve* (New York: Penguin Press, 2015), esp. chap. 7; David Kinley, "The Specie Reserve in a Banking System," *Journal of Political Economy* 20, no. 1 (Jan. 1912): 21 ("bank of banks" quotation); Murray N. Rothbard, "The Origins of the Federal Reserve," *Quarterly Journal of Austrian Economics* 2, no. 3 (Fall 1999): 46–47.

20. United States National Monetary Commission, *Report of the National Monetary Commission,* vol. 1 (Washington: GPO, 1912), 10–18 (quotation at 18). For a clear summary of the proposal, see Robert Craig West, *Banking Reform and the Federal Reserve, 1863–1923* (Ithaca, NY: Cornell University Press, 1977), 71–79.

21. J. Lawrence Broz, *The International Origins of the Federal Reserve System* (Ithaca, NY: Cornell University Press, 1997), 184, 190–193. To drum up support for the Aldrich plan, proponents created a "National Citizens' League" in 1911 to educate the public about central banking issues. See ibid., 185–190; West, *Banking Reform,* 79–82; Paul M. Warburg, *The Federal Reserve System: Its Origin and Growth* (New York: Macmillan, 1930), 1:68–76.

22. Broz, *International Origins,* 190; Kettl, *Leadership at the Fed,* 20.

23. Broz, *International Origins,* 195. Quote from Henry Parker Willis, *The Federal Reserve System: Legislation, Organization and Operation* (New York: Ronald Press Co., 1923), 145, also quoted on Broz 195.

24. Broz, *International Origins,* 195–196, quotation from a letter to Willis, 29 Dec. 1912, at 196.

25. Ibid., 196–199, quotation from Paul M. Warburg at 199. See also Groseclose, *Fifty Years,* 77.

26. Quoted in West, *Banking Reform,* 119.

27. Quoted in Willis, *The Federal Reserve System,* 499.

28. West, *Banking Reform,* 113, 126–127. For a thorough account of the debates in both houses of Congress, see Willis, *The Federal Reserve System,* chaps. 16 and 20.

29. Federal Reserve Act of 1913, 12 U.S.C. §221 (1913).

30. Federal Reserve Act of 1913.

31. Ibid. (quote from §13). For brief summaries of the Federal Reserve Act, see Shull, *The Fourth Branch,* 48–57; Carl H. Moore, *The Federal Reserve System* (Jefferson, NC: McFarland, 1990), 7–9; Moss and Bolton, "Federal Reserve," 6–7. A version of the act with comparisons to the House and Senate bills is available at http://fraser.stlouisfed.org/docs/historical/congressional/19131218sen_bankcurrbill.pdf.

32. Kettl, *Leadership at the Fed,* 23; Wyatt Wells and David Moss, "Crisis at the Federal Reserve: Arthur Burns at the Stagflation of 1973–75," HBS Case No. 9-797-079 (Boston: Harvard Business School Publishing, 1997), 2.

33. Quoted in Moss and Bolton, "Federal Reserve," 7.

34. Quoted in ibid., 8.

35. A. Jerome Clifford, *The Independence of the Federal Reserve System* (Philadelphia: University of Pennsylvania Press, 1965), 93–96; Allan H. Meltzer, *A History of the Federal Reserve* (Chicago: University of Chicago Press, 2003), 1:77–78.

36. Quoted in Meltzer, *A History*, 1:80.

37. Clifford, *Independence*, 95.

38. Federal Reserve Board, *Annual Report for 1920*, quoted in Shull, *The Fourth Branch*, 65.

39. Wells and Moss, "Crisis at the Federal Reserve," 2; Meltzer, *A History*, 1:87; Clifford, *Independence*, 100.

40. Shull, *The Fourth Branch*, 65–72.

41. Ibid., 72–73, 75, 75–78, 78, 80, 80–81, quotations at 75, 80.

42. Kettl, *Leadership at the Fed*, 31–32; Moore, *The Federal Reserve System*, 65–66. Quotation in Kettl at 32 and in Moore at 66.

43. Moss and Bolton, "Federal Reserve," 10–11; Wells and Moss, "Crisis at the Federal Reserve," 3; Kettl, *Leadership at the Fed*, 33.

44. Kettl, *Leadership at the Fed*, 37.

45. Ibid., 36–41; quotation from a letter from P. J. Croghan to Commerce Secretary Robert LaMont, 26 Apr. 1930, at 38.

46. Shull, *The Fourth Branch*, 98–107.

47. [Marriner Eccles], "Desirable Changes in the Administration of the Federal Reserve System," Memo given to the President, Nov, 3, 1934, http: //fraser.stlouisfed.org/docs /historical/eccles/004_01_0002.pdf. See also Shull, *The Fourth Branch*, 111–113; Kettl, *Leadership at the Fed*, 47–48.

48. Quoted in Shull, *The Fourth Branch*, 114.

49. Kettl, *Leadership at the Fed*, 51.

50. *Banking Act of 1935: Hearings before a Subcommittee of the Committee on Banking and Currency, United States Senate, Seventy-Fourth Congress, First Session, on S. 1715 a Bill to Provide for the Sound, Effective, and Uninterrupted Operation of the Banking System, and for Other Purposes, April 19 to May 13, 14 to May 22, 1935* (Washington, DC: GPO, 1935), 262–263 (testimony of Elwyn Evans, representing the Clearing House Banks, Wilmington, Delaware).

51. Shull, *The Fourth Branch*, 115–116. The law is available online at http: //fraser.stlouisfed .org/docs/historical/congressional/1935_bankingact_publiclaw305.pdf.

52. *Federal Reserve Bulletin* (Nov. 1937), quoted in Kettl, *Leadership at the Fed*, 54.

53. Moore, *The Federal Reserve System*, 95; Kettl, *Leadership at the Fed*, 55–59, quotation from Board of Governors of the Federal Reserve System, *Twenty-Eighth Annual Report* (1941), at 59.

54. Kettl, *Leadership at the Fed*, 59.

55. Quoted in Clifford, *Independence*, 190.

56. Kettl, *Leadership at the Fed*, 60–66, 70, quotation from Senate subcommittee testimony at 66.

57. *Joint Announcement by the Secretary of the Treasury and the Chairman of the Board of Governors, and of the Federal Open Market Committee, of the Federal Reserve System,* press

release, 4 Mar. 1951, http: //www.richmondfed.org/publications/research/special_ reports/treasury_fed_accord/historical_documents/pdf/accord_announce- ment_03_04_1951.pdf.

58. Kettl, *Leadership at the Fed,* 70–71, 74–75.

59. Meltzer, *A History,* 2:41–42.

60. Kettl, *Leadership at the Fed,* 75–77. The hearings are reprinted in U.S. Congress, Joint Committee on the Economic Report, Subcommittee on General Credit Control and Debt Management, *Monetary Policy and the Management of the Public Debt* (1952), http: // fraser.stlouisfed.org/docs/publications/mpmpd/1952jc_mpmpd_hearings.pdf.

61. Joint Committee, *Monetary Policy,* 983–985. Also quoted in Kettl, *Leadership at the Fed,* 76, 77.

62. Joint Committee, *Monetary Policy,* 689–691.

63. Kettl, *Leadership at the Fed,* 74–75, 83, Senate testimony quoted on 83.

64. Quotes from U.S. Congress, Joint Economic Committee, Subcommittee on Economic Stabilization, *United States Monetary Policy: Recent Thinking and Experience* (1954), in Kettl, *Leadership at the Fed,* 86.

65. Kettl, *Leadership at the Fed,* 86.

66. Ibid., 92, 96–102.

67. *New York Times* (2 June 1965) quoted in ibid., 103.

68. Kettl, *Leadership at the Fed,* 103–107.

69. Ibid., 116.

70. Ibid., 122–123, 127; Wells and Moss, "Crisis at the Federal Reserve," 5.

71. See Kettl, *Leadership at the Fed,* 113–116. Kettl disputes the theory.

72. Shull, *The Fourth Branch,* 130; Kettl, *Leadership at the Fed,* 131.

73. Kettl, *Leadership at the Fed,* 131–135, quotation from an interview by Kettl at 132.

74. U.S. Congress, Joint Economic Committee, *Standards for Guiding Monetary Action* (1968), quoted in Kettl, *Leadership at the Fed,* 141.

75. Kettl, *Leadership at the Fed,* 145–147; Moore, *The Federal Reserve System,* 141. These requirements, originally included in a resolution, were formally made law in 1975.

76. Kettl, *Leadership at the Fed,* 151–153; Moore, *The Federal Reserve System,* 142–144.

77. Laurence H. Meyer, "Inflation Targets and Inflation Targeting," *North American Journal of Economics and Finance* 13 (2002): 149.

78. Kettl, *Leadership at the Fed,* 149, 154–159, "went to war" quote from a Fed official, in an interview with Kettl, at 154; Moore, *The Federal Reserve System,* 141–142, 144–145.

79. Quoted in Kettl, *Leadership at the Fed,* 167.

80. 1977 speech at Jacksonville University quoted in ibid., 168.

81. Kettl, *Leadership at the Fed,* 167–172; Moore, *The Federal Reserve System,* 145.

82. Kettl, *Leadership at the Fed,* 118, 172–173, 175–177; Moore, *The Federal Reserve System,* 154; Shull, *The Fourth Branch,* 136–137.

83. Shull, *The Fourth Branch,* 140.

84. Moore, *The Federal Reserve System,* 154–155; Shull, *The Fourth Branch,* 142, quotation at 142.

85. Quoted in Kettl, *Leadership at the Fed,* 182.

86. Andrew H. Bartels, "Volcker's Revolution at the Fed" (1985), quoted in Kettl, *Leadership at the Fed,* 188.

87. Justin Martin, *Greenspan: The Man Behind Money* (Cambridge, MA: Perseus, 2001), 174, 176, 177–179, quotation at 176.

88. Ibid., 187–196, quotation from NY senator Alphonse D'Amato, House Budget Committee testimony (22 Jan. 1991), at 196.

89. Martin, *Greenspan,* 197–198, quotation from an A&E interview with David Frost (25 Aug. 1998) at 198.

90. Ibid., 200–203.

91. Ibid., 204–205, 208–209, 212, quotation (from Alice Rivlin) at 205.

92. Ibid., 218–226, quotation from a 2000 Republican primary debate at 226.

93. David Wessel, *In Fed We Trust: Ben Bernanke's War on the Great Panic* (New York: Crown Business, 2009), 55; Stephen H. Axilrod, *Inside the Fed: Monetary Policy and Its Management, Martin through Greenspan to Bernanke,* rev. ed. (Cambridge: MIT Press, 2011), 145–147.

94. Wessel, *In Fed We Trust,* 74–75, 80, 84, 86–87.

95. Ben Bernanke, "The Great Moderation," remarks at the meetings of the Eastern Economic Association, Washington, DC, 20 Feb. 2004, http://www.federalreserve .gov/Boarddocs/Speeches/2004/20040220/.

96. Thomas, *The Financial Crisis,* 56, 58, 70–71.

97. Bernanke's report to Congress, 18 July 2007, quoted in Wessel, *In Fed We Trust,* 93. The report is available at http://federalreserve.gov/newsevents/testimony/ber nanke20070718a.htm.

98. Wessel, *In Fed We Trust,* 93 ("predominant policy concern" quotation), 100–102, "crossed" quotation from Fed vice chairman Donald Kohn at 102; Thomas, *The Financial Crisis,* 152.

99. Wessel, *In Fed We Trust,* 127, 129, 135–136; Johan Van Overtveldt, *Bernanke's Test: Ben Bernanke, Alan Greenspan, and the Drama of the Central Banker* (Chicago: Agate, 2009), 166–168. Quotation from Morgan Stanley economist David Greenlaw in Greg Ip, "Rate Cut Fails to Cheer Market; Fed Sifts Options," *Wall Street Journal,* 12 Dec. 2007, in Wessel, *In Fed We Trust,* 135–136.

100. Wessel, *In Fed We Trust,* 137–138; Thomas, *The Financial Crisis,* 165–167.

101. Wessel, *In Fed We Trust,* 139–142; Thomas, *The Financial Crisis,* 167–168; Van Overtveldt, *Bernanke's Test,* 168–169.

102. Wessel, *In Fed We Trust,* 144–145; Van Overtveldt, *Bernanke's Test,* 172–173, quotation from the *Financial Times,* 26 Jan. 2008, at 172.

103. Van Overtveldt, *Bernanke's Test,* 173, 175–176, quotation from an anonymous ECB economist at 175; Wessel, *In Fed We Trust,* 151–152.

104. Van Overtveldt, *Bernanke's Test,* 177–179; Wessel, *In Fed We Trust,* 153–154; Thomas, *The Financial Crisis,* 84.

105. Wessel, *In Fed We Trust,* 148, 158–163, quotations at 148, 160, 162.

106. Wessel, *In Fed We Trust,* 165–173, Bernanke's testimony to Senate Banking Committee (3 Apr. 2008) quoted at 173.

107. Van Overtveldt, *Bernanke's Test,* 183–185; Wessel, *In Fed We Trust,* 142.

108. Quotation from retired Richmond Reserve Bank president Alfred Broaddus from Bloomberg.com (10 July 2008) in Van Overtveldt, *Bernanke's Test,* 189.

109. Van Overtveldt, *Bernanke's Test,* 190; Wessel, *In Fed We Trust,* 180; Thomas, *The Financial Crisis,* 84–86.

110. Wessel, *In Fed We Trust,* 182; Thomas, *The Financial Crisis,* 86.

111. Wessel, *In Fed We Trust,* 182–186; Thomas, *The Financial Crisis,* 86. Months later this was lifted to $200 billion each.

112. Quoted in Wessel, *In Fed We Trust,* 187.

113. Ibid., 10, 14–16, 18–20, quotations at 14 and 16; Van Overtveldt, *Bernanke's Test,* 198–199.

114. Wessel, *In Fed We Trust,* 22–23, quotation at 23, also in Van Overtveldt, *Bernanke's Test,* 199.

115. Wessel, *In Fed We Trust,* 24–25; Phillip Swagel, "Why Lehman Wasn't Rescued," *New York Times,* 13 Sept. 2013.

116. Van Overtveldt, *Bernanke's Test,* 199; Wessel, *In Fed We Trust,* 192, 189–191, 193–197.

117. March 2009 congressional testimony quoted in Wessel, *In Fed We Trust,* 194.

118. Wessel, *In Fed We Trust,* 197–198.

119. Quotation from Brian Blackstone and Patrick Yoest, "Bailouts Turn Up Heat on Fed Chief," *Wall Street Journal,* 19 Sept. 2008, in Wessel, *In Fed We Trust,* 7.

120. Jon Hilsenrath, Deborah Solomon, and Damian Paletta, "Paulson, Bernanke Strained for Consensus in Bailout," *Wall Street Journal,* 10 Nov. 2008.

121. Wessel, *In Fed We Trust,* 199–203.

122. Binyamin Appelbaum and Lori Montgomery, "Citing Grave Financial Threats, Officials Ready Massive Rescue," *Washington Post,* 19 Sept. 2008.

123. Michael Kirk, "Inside the Meltdown," transcript for *Frontline,* PBS, 17 Feb. 2009.

124. Wessel, *In Fed We Trust,* 203–205, quotations at 204–205.

125. Ibid., 214, 226–227, quotation at 214.

126. Ibid., 227, 236–240.

127. Ibid., 217–229; Thomas, *The Financial Crisis,* 168–170.

128. Wessel, *In Fed We Trust,* 241–254, quotation from John B. Taylor at 254.

129. Sheryl Gay Stolberg, "Signing Stimulus, Obama Doesn't Rule Out More, *New York Times,* 17 Feb. 2009.

130. Marc Labonte, "Federal Reserve: Unconventional Monetary Policy Options," Congressional Research Service, 19 Feb. 2013, 7, available at http: //www.fas.org/sgp /crs/misc/R42962.pdf. See also FOMC press release, 18 Mar. 2009, http: //www .federalreserve.gov/newsevents/press/monetary/20090318a.htm.

131. Wessel, *In Fed We Trust,* 254–255; Thomas, *The Financial Crisis,* 169–170.

132. Quotation from Federal Reserve press release, 28 Jan. 2009, http: //www.fed eralreserve.gov/newsevents/press/monetary/20090128a.htm. See also Labonte,

"Unconventional Monetary Policy Options," 20; Ben Bernanke, "Monetary Policy since the Onset of the Crisis," speech to Federal Reserve Bank of Kansas City Economic Symposium, 31 Aug. 2012, http: //www.federalreserve.gov/newsevents /speech/bernanke20120831a.htm.

133. See "Dodd-Frank Wall Street Reform and Consumer Financial Protection Act: A Brief Legislative History with Links, Reports, and Summaries," Law Librarians' Society of Washington, DC, at http: //www.llsdc.org/.

134. House Committee on Financial Services, "An Examination of the Extraordinary Efforts by the Federal Reserve Bank to Provide Liquidity in the Current Financial Crisis," 10 Feb. 2009 (Washington, DC: GPO, 2009), 2, 3, 5–8, 9, 12, quotations at 2, 9, and 12.

135. House Subcommittee on Domestic Monetary Policy and Technology, "Regulatory Restructuring: Balancing the Independence of the Federal Reserve in Monetary Policy with Systemic Risk Regulation," 9 July 2009 (Washington, DC: GPO, 2009), 1–2. The administration policy proposal, "Financial Regulatory Reform—A New Foundation: Rebuilding Financial Supervision," is available at http: //www.treasury .gov/initiatives/Documents/FinalReport_web.pdf.

136. House Subcommittee, "Regulatory Restructuring: Balancing," 3, 4–6, quotation at 3.

137. Ibid., 7, 8.

138. "Financial Regulatory Reform," 57.

139. House Subcommittee on Domestic Monetary Policy and Technology, "Regulatory Restructuring: Safeguarding Consumer Protection and the Role of the Federal Reserve," 16 July 2009 (Washington, DC: GPO, 2009), 3.

140. Ibid., 4.

141. Ibid., 7–8. Governor Duke's full prepared statement and appendices, on 72–160, describes these initiatives in detail.

142. House Committee on Financial Services, "H.R. 1207, the Federal Reserve Transparency Act of 2009," 25 Sept. 2009 (Washington, DC: GPO, 2009), 1–3. Paul's earliest audit bill was H.R. 2322 of the 97th Congress, though the earliest bill mentioned in this testimony dates from 1983. The 2009 bill is available at http: //thomas.loc.gov /cgi-bin/query/z?c111:H.R.1207.

143. House Committee, "H.R. 1207," 12–13.

144. See http: //www.govtrack.us/congress/bills/111/hr1207.

145. See H.R. 3996, §1701, at http: //www.gpo.gov/fdsys/pkg/BILLS-111hr3996ih/html /BILLS-111hr3996ih.htm; and the Nov. 10 Senate discussion draft at http: //www.llsdc .org/assets/DoddFrankdocs/bill-111th-s3217-discussion-draft.pdf, 1126–1127.

146. The amendment is available at http: //democrats.financialservices.house.gov/media /file/markups/111/paul_grayson.pdf. Procedurally, this amendment was presented as a substitute amendment to Watt's amendment. For details, see http: //democrats .financialservices.house.gov/Hearings/hearingDetails.aspx?NewsID=799.

147. Letter reprinted at http: //archive.lewrockwell.com/paul/paul608.html.

148. Edmund L. Andrews, "Panel Votes to Broaden Oversight of the Fed," *New York Times,* 19 Nov. 2009.

149. The amendment is available at http: //democrats.financialservices.house.gov/media /file/markups/111/watt_001_xml.pdf.

150. Watt's letter and Grayson quotes from Ryan Grim, "Audit the Fed Effort under Threat in House," *Huffington Post,* 25 May 2011.

19

Citizens United and Corporate
Speech (2010)

THE STORY OF *Citizens United* began in late 2007, as leading members of the Republican and Democratic parties were preparing for the 2008 presidential primaries. Democrats expected a three-way contest in their party between Senator Barack Obama of Illinois, Senator (and former first lady) Hillary Clinton of New York, and former senator John Edwards of North Carolina.[1] In anticipation of the primary election season, a nonprofit corporation named Citizens United made a film, *Hillary: The Movie,* which attacked Senator Clinton's character, activities in Washington, and fitness for the presidency. People interviewed in the film described Clinton as "steeped in controversy [and] steeped in sleaze," "deceitful," "ruthless," "vindictive," "venal," "sneaky," and "intolerant."[2]

Citizens United released *Hillary: The Movie* in cinemas and on DVD, but also wished to show the film via on-demand video. Although the group sought to promote the on-demand release with television commercials, it worried that both the on-demand release and the associated advertisements could be deemed illegal. The Federal Election Campaign Act of 1971 (United States Code, Title 2, §441b), building on earlier campaign finance legislation dating back to 1907 (see the timeline at the end of this case), banned corporations and labor unions from using internal treasury funds to assist with the election or defeat of candidates for certain federal offices. Prohibited assistance included both direct monetary and in-kind donations, as well as independent expenditures on relevant materials or events. The 2002 Bipartisan Campaign Reform Act (BCRA) had expanded this ban to include any "electioneering communication" within thirty days of a primary election or sixty days of a general election that could reach 50,000 or more people in the relevant jurisdiction. In spite of these constraints, corporations and unions were allowed to organize political action committees (PACs) to contribute to campaigns. The money a PAC spent on electoral campaigns could not come from the general treasury of its sponsoring corporation or union. However, the PAC could raise money by soliciting donations from people affiliated with the corporation or union. Both contributions to PACs and expenditures by PACs were subject to numerous limits and restrictions.[3]

Citizens United pled in District Court that the laws restricting corporate speech were unconstitutional. It also targeted other clauses in the BCRA that mandated disclosure of major spenders on electioneering communications and the use of identifying disclaimers in the communications themselves. The District Court ruled against Citizens United on all of these issues, but the U.S. Supreme Court soon took up the case. Lawyers representing Citizens United and the Federal Election Commission (FEC) twice argued before the Court, once in May 2009 and again that September. On January 21, 2010, the Supreme Court announced its ruling.[4]

In a 5–4 decision, the Court declared that limiting corporations' independent expenditures on election speech was unconstitutional. In reaching this verdict, the Court overturned two of its own precedents: *Austin v. Michigan Chamber of Commerce* (1990), which had upheld a law that banned corporate independent expenditures on state elections, and part of *McConnell v. Federal Election Commission* (2003), which had permitted limitations on electioneering communications. The majority opinion in *Citizens United,* penned by Justice Anthony Kennedy, announced that corporations had First Amendment rights and that existing federal law improperly infringed on these rights. The four justices in the minority joined in a spirited dissent, written by Justice John Paul Stevens, which expressed deep concern over the influence of corporate spending on elections.*

---

* The justices in the majority on the major issues were Kennedy, Chief Justice John Roberts, Antonin Scalia, Samuel Alito, and Clarence Thomas. The dissenters were Stevens, Ruth Bader Ginsburg, Stephen Breyer, and Sonia Sotomayor. All of the justices except Thomas concurred that the disclosure and disclaimer rules that Citizens United also challenged were constitutional.

The remainder of this case is based mainly on extended excerpts from the opinions that make up *Citizens United,* with only very limited explanatory scaffolding. The reason for this is twofold. First, the *Citizens United* decision is recent history, and historians are often cautious when it comes to interpreting recent events. Second and more importantly, readers have now grappled with eighteen vital moments in American democracy and have had the chance in each one to step into a decision-maker's shoes. This case, by contrast, allows readers to scrutinize the decision-making process itself, giving them a front-row seat on one of the most controversial legal verdicts in recent years, and one that had considerable implications for the conduct of American democracy. The justices' opinions not only reveal their final decision but also provide a precious window on how they reached it and where they perceive the most important fault lines to lie.

Although the full text of *Citizens United* is not reprinted here, the excerpts that follow convey many of the justices' core arguments. Headings—and a few brief explanations—have been added as signposts. In addition, a time-line and several data exhibits have been included at the end for context. The heart of the case, however, is the immensely consequential judicial handiwork that appears in the indented excerpts themselves.

The Majority Opinion
Confronting Constitutional Issues

The first question taken up by the majority was whether an extensive review of existing campaign finance law was in fact required. The nonprofit corporation Citizens United had offered—in addition to broad arguments about corporate speech—narrow arguments as to why §441b might not apply to *Hillary: The Movie.* If accepted by the Court, such arguments would have obviated the need for a more extensive examination of the law. Citizens United claimed that the film was not an "electioneering communication" or "express advocacy," that on-demand video differed from traditional television enough to merit different rules, and that nonprofit corporations funded mostly by individuals deserved exemption from §441b.[5] The majority quickly dispensed with these arguments, however. On the difference between on-demand video and regular television, Justice Kennedy wrote:

Citizens United contends . . . that [video on-demand] has a lower risk of distorting the political process than do television ads. . . . On what we might call conventional television, advertising spots reach viewers who have chosen a channel or a program for reasons unrelated to the advertising. . . . [A]ny effort by the Judiciary to decide which means of communication are to be preferred for the particular type of message and speaker would raise questions as to the court's own lawful authority. . . . The interpretive process itself would create an inevitable, pervasive, and serious risk of chilling protected speech pending the drawing of fine distinctions that, in the end, would themselves be questionable.[6]

Regarding the creation of an exception for corporations mostly funded by individuals, he wrote:

There is no principled basis for doing this without rewriting *Austin's* holding that the Government can restrict corporate independent expenditures for political speech. Though it is true that the Court should construe statutes as necessary to avoid constitutional questions, the series of steps suggested would be difficult to take in view of the language of the statute. . . . We decline to adopt an interpretation that requires intricate case-by-case determinations to verify whether political speech is banned, especially if we are convinced that, in the end, this corporation has a constitutional right to speak on this subject.[7]

Having rejected narrower arguments, Kennedy explained why it was appropriate—and, in fact, necessary—for the Court to examine the constitutionality of §441b. Although Citizens United had initially issued a "facial" challenge to the law, demanding such a broad review, it later dropped that challenge. The majority, however, insisted it was still able and obligated to rule on the constitutionality of the law:

[T]he Court cannot resolve this case on a narrower ground without chilling political speech . . . It is not judicial restraint to accept an unsound, narrow argument just so the Court can avoid another argument with broader implications. Indeed, a court would be remiss in performing its duties were it to accept an unsound principle merely to avoid the necessity of making a broader ruling. . . . [T]hroughout the litigation, Citizens United has asserted a claim that the FEC has violated its First Amendment right to free speech. All concede that this claim is properly before us. And " '[o]nce a federal claim is properly presented, a party can make any argument in support of that claim; parties are not limited to the precise arguments they made below.'" . . . [T]he distinction between facial and as-applied challenges is not so well defined that it has some automatic effect or that it must always control the pleadings and disposition in every case involving a constitutional challenge . . . The parties cannot enter into a stipulation that prevents the Court from considering certain remedies if those remedies are necessary to resolve a claim that has been preserved. Citizens United has preserved its First Amendment challenge to §441b as applied to the facts of its case; and given all the circumstances, we cannot easily address that issue without assuming a premise—the permissibility of restricting corporate political speech—that is itself in doubt.[8] . . .

Consideration of the facial validity of §441b is further supported by the following reasons. First is the uncertainty caused by the litigating position of the Government . . . [T]he Government suggests, as an alternative argument, that an as-applied challenge might have merit . . . When the Government holds out the possibility of ruling for Citizens United on a narrow ground yet refrains from adopting that position, the added uncertainty demonstrates the necessity to address the question of statutory validity. Second, substantial time would be required to bring clarity to the application of the statutory provision on these points in order to avoid any chilling effect . . . A speaker's ability to engage in political speech that could have a chance of persuading voters is stifled if the speaker must first commence a protracted lawsuit . . . Third is the primary importance of speech itself to the integrity of the election process. As additional rules are created for regulating political speech, any speech arguably within their reach is chilled . . . The ongoing chill upon speech that is beyond all doubt protected makes it necessary in this case to invoke the earlier precedents that a statute which chills speech can and must be invalidated where its facial invalidity has been demonstrated.[9]

Corporate Speech

Justice Kennedy next took up the issue of corporate speech, arguing forcefully that §441b violated the First Amendment:

[T]he following acts would all be felonies under §441b: The Sierra Club runs an ad, within the crucial phase of 60 days before the general election, that exhorts the public to disapprove of a Congressman who favors logging in national forests; the National Rifle Association publishes a book urging the public to vote for the challenger because the incumbent U.S. Senator supports a handgun ban; and the American Civil Liberties Union creates a Web site telling the public to vote for a Presidential candidate in light of that candidate's defense of free speech. These prohibitions are classic examples of censorship. Section 441b is a ban on corporate speech notwithstanding the fact that a PAC created by a corporation can still speak. . . . PACs are burdensome alternatives; they are expensive to administer and subject to extensive regulations. . . . This might explain why fewer than 2,000 of the millions of corporations in this country have PACs.[10] . . .

Section 441b's prohibition on corporate independent expenditures is thus a ban on speech. As a "restriction on the amount of money a person or group can spend on political communication during a campaign," that statute "necessarily reduces the quantity of expression by restricting the number of issues discussed, the depth of their exploration, and the size of the audience reached." . . . Were the Court to uphold these restrictions, the Government could repress speech by silencing certain voices at any of the various points in the speech process. . . . If §441b applied to individuals, no one would believe that it is merely a time, place, or manner restriction on speech. Its purpose and effect are to silence entities whose voices the Government deems to be suspect.[11] . . .

Speech is an essential mechanism of democracy, for it is the means to hold officials accountable to the people . . . The right of citizens to inquire, to hear, to speak, and to use information to reach consensus is a precondition to enlightened self-government and a necessary means to protect it. The First Amendment "'has its fullest and most urgent application' to speech uttered during a campaign for political office" . . . Speech restrictions based on the identity of the speaker are all too often simply a means to control content. Quite apart from the purpose or effect of regulating content, moreover, the Government may commit a constitutional wrong when by law it identifies certain preferred speakers. By taking the right to speak from some and giving it to others, the Government deprives the disadvantaged person or class of the right to use speech to strive to establish worth, standing, and respect for the speaker's voice. The Government may not by these means deprive the public of the right and privilege to determine for itself what speech and speakers are worthy of consideration. The First Amendment protects speech and speaker, and the ideas that flow from each.[12]

Kennedy proceeded to review the legal and judicial history of corporate speech:

> The Court has recognized that First Amendment protection extends to corporations . . . This protection has been extended by explicit holdings to the context of political speech . . . The Court has thus rejected the argument that political speech of corporations or other associations should be treated differently under the First Amendment simply because such associations are not "natural persons."[13] . . .
>
> At least since the latter part of the 19th century, the laws of some States and of the United States imposed a ban on corporate direct contributions to candidates. . . . For almost three decades thereafter, the Court did not reach the question whether restrictions on corporate and union expenditures are constitutional. . . . The question was in the background of *United States v. CIO* [1948] . . . There, a labor union endorsed a congressional candidate in its weekly periodical. The Court stated that "the gravest doubt would arise in our minds as to [the federal expenditure prohibition's] constitutionality" if it were construed to suppress that writing . . . The Court engaged in statutory interpretation and found the statute did not cover the publication . . . Four Justices, however, said they would reach the constitutional question and invalidate the Labor Management Relations Act's expenditure ban . . . The concurrence explained that any "'undue influence'" generated by a speaker's "large expenditures" was outweighed "by the loss for democratic processes resulting from the restrictions upon free and full public discussion" . . . In *United States v. Automobile Workers* [1957] . . . [t]hree Justices dissented, arguing that the Court should have reached the constitutional question and that the ban on independent expenditures was unconstitutional.[14] . . .
>
> In [*Buckley v. Valeo* (1976)] the Court addressed various challenges to . . . an independent expenditure ban . . . that applied to individuals as well as corporations and labor unions . . . *Buckley* first upheld . . . limits on direct contributions to candidates. The *Buckley* Court recognized a "sufficiently important" governmental interest in "the prevention of corruption and the appearance of corruption" . . . The *Buckley* Court explained that the potential for *quid pro quo* corruption distinguished direct contributions to candidates from independent expenditures. The Court emphasized that "the independent expenditure ceiling . . . fails to serve any substantial governmental interest in stemming the reality or appearance of corruption in the

electoral process," . . . because "[t]he absence of prearrangement and coordination . . . alleviates the danger that expenditures will be given as a *quid pro quo* for improper commitments from the candidate" . . . *Buckley* did not consider [an existing] separate ban on corporate and union independent expenditures . . . Had [the separate ban] been challenged in the wake of *Buckley,* however, it could not have been squared with the reasoning and analysis of that precedent.[15] . . .

[*First Nat. Bank of Boston v. Bellotti* (1978)] reaffirmed the First Amendment principle that the Government cannot restrict political speech based on the speaker's corporate identity . . . when it struck down a state-law prohibition on corporate independent expenditures related to referenda issues: . . . "In the realm of protected speech, the legislature is constitutionally disqualified from dictating the subjects about which persons may speak and the speakers who may address a public issue" . . . *Bellotti* did not address the constitutionality of the State's ban on corporate independent expenditures to support candidates. In our view, however, that restriction would have been unconstitutional under *Bellotti*'s central principle: that the First Amendment does not allow political speech restrictions based on a speaker's corporate identity.[16] . . .

Thus the law stood until Austin . . . To bypass Buckley and Bellotti, the Austin Court identified a new governmental interest in limiting political speech: an antidistortion interest. Austin found a compelling governmental interest in preventing "the corrosive and distorting effects of immense aggregations of wealth that are accumulated with the help of the corporate form and that have little or no correlation to the public's support for the corporation's political ideas" . . . The Court is thus confronted with conflicting lines of precedent: a pre-Austin line that forbids restrictions on political speech based on the speaker's corporate identity and a post-Austin line that permits them.[17]

Antidistortion

As for *Austin*'s antidistortion rationale, the Government does little to defend it . . . And with good reason, for the rationale cannot support §441b . . . If the First Amendment has any force, it prohibits Congress from fining or jailing citizens, or associations of citizens, for simply engaging in political speech. If the antidistortion rationale were to be accepted, however, it would permit Government to ban political speech simply because the speaker is an association that has taken on the corporate form. The Government contends that *Austin* permits it to ban corporate expenditures for almost all forms of communication stemming from a corporation. . . . If *Austin* were correct, the Government could prohibit a corporation from expressing political views in media beyond those presented here, such as by printing books. . . . Political speech is "indispensable to decisionmaking in a democracy, and this is no less true because the speech comes from a corporation rather than an individual." . . . The rule that political speech cannot be limited based on a speaker's wealth is a necessary consequence of the premise that the First Amendment generally prohibits the suppression of political speech based on the speaker's identity . . . It is irrelevant for purposes of the First Amendment that corporate funds may "have little or no correlation to the public's support for the corporation's political ideas." . . . All speakers, including individuals and the media, use money amassed from the economic marketplace to fund their speech. The First Amendment protects the resulting speech, even if it was enabled by economic transactions with persons or entities who disagree with the speaker's ideas.[18] . . .

Austin's antidistortion rationale would produce the dangerous, and unacceptable, consequence that Congress could ban political speech of media corporations . . . Media corporations are now exempt from §441b's ban on corporate expenditures . . . Yet media corporations accumulate wealth with the help of the corporate form . . . and the views expressed by media corporations often "have little or no correlation to the public's support" for those views . . . Thus, under the Government's reasoning, wealthy media corporations could have their voices diminished . . . There is no precedent supporting laws that attempt to distinguish between corporations which are deemed to be exempt as media corporations and those which are not. . . . The great debates between the Federalists and Anti-Federalists over our founding document were published and expressed in the most important means of mass communication of that era—newspapers owned by individuals.[19] . . .

Austin interferes with the "open marketplace" of ideas protected by the First Amendment . . . It permits the Government to ban the political speech of millions of associations of citizens . . . Most of these are small corporations without large amounts of wealth . . . (more than 75% of corporations whose income is taxed under federal law . . . have less than $1 million in receipts per year). This fact belies the Government's argument that the statute is justified on the ground that it prevents the "distorting effects of immense aggregations of wealth."[20] . . .

By suppressing the speech of manifold corporations, both for-profit and non-profit, the Government prevents their voices and viewpoints from reaching the public and advising voters on which persons or entities are hostile to their interests. Factions will necessarily form in our Republic, but the remedy of "destroying the liberty" of some factions is "worse than the disease." Factions should be checked by permitting them all to speak . . . and by entrusting the people to judge what is true and what is false.[21] . . .

Even if §441b's expenditure ban were constitutional, wealthy corporations could still lobby elected officials, although smaller corporations may not have the resources to do so. And wealthy individuals and unincorporated associations can spend unlimited amounts on independent expenditures . . . Yet certain disfavored associations of citizens—those that have taken on the corporate form—are penalized for engaging in the same political speech.[22]

Corruption

For the most part relinquishing the antidistortion rationale, the Government falls back on the argument that corporate political speech can be banned in order to prevent corruption or its appearance . . . [W]e now conclude that independent expenditures, including those made by corporations, do not give rise to corruption or the appearance of corruption . . . The fact that speakers may have influence over or access to elected officials does not mean that those officials are corrupt: . . . "It is in the nature of an elected representative to favor certain policies, and, by necessary corollary, to favor the voters and contributors who support those policies. It is well understood that a substantial and legitimate reason, if not the only reason, to cast a vote for, or to make a contribution to, one candidate over another is that the candidate will respond by producing those political outcomes the supporter favors. Democracy is premised on responsiveness" . . . The appearance of influence or access, furthermore, will not cause the electorate to lose faith in our democracy . . . The fact that a corporation, or any other speaker, is willing to spend money to try to persuade voters presupposes that the people have the ultimate influence over elected officials.[23] . . .

The *McConnell* record was over "100,000 pages" long . . . yet it "does not have any direct examples of votes being exchanged for . . . expenditures" . . . This confirms *Buckley*'s reasoning that independent expenditures do not lead to, or create the appearance of, *quid pro quo* corruption. In fact, there is only scant evidence that independent expenditures even ingratiate . . . The BCRA record establishes that certain donations to political parties, called "soft money," were made to gain access to elected officials . . . This case, however, is about independent expenditures, not soft money. When Congress finds that a problem exists, we must give that finding due deference; but Congress may not choose an unconstitutional remedy. If elected officials succumb to improper influences from independent expenditures; if they surrender their best judgment; and if they put expediency before principle, then surely there is cause for concern. We must give weight to attempts by Congress to seek to dispel either the appearance or the reality of these influences. The remedies enacted by law, however, must comply with the First Amendment; and, it is our law and our tradition that more speech, not less, is the governing rule. An outright ban on corporate political speech during the critical pre-election period is not a permissible remedy.[24]

Shareholder Protection

The Government contends further that corporate independent expenditures can be limited because of its interest in protecting dissenting shareholders from being compelled to fund corporate political speech. This asserted interest, like *Austin*'s antidistortion rationale, would allow the Government to ban the political speech even of media corporations . . . There is, furthermore, little evidence of abuse that cannot be corrected by shareholders "through the procedures of corporate democracy" . . . [M]oreover, the statute is both underinclusive and overinclusive. As to the first, if Congress had been seeking to protect dissenting shareholders, it would not have banned corporate speech in only certain media within 30 or 60 days before an election. A dissenting shareholder's interests would be implicated by speech in any media at any time. As to the second, the statute is overinclusive because it covers all corporations, including nonprofit corporations and for-profit corporations with only single shareholders.[25]

"Civic Discourse Belongs to the People"

Modern day movies, television comedies, or skits on Youtube.com might portray public officials or public policies in unflattering ways. Yet if a covered transmission during the blackout period creates the background for candidate endorsement or opposition, a felony occurs solely because a corporation, other than an exempt media corporation, has made the "purchase, payment, distribution, loan, advance, deposit, or gift of money or anything of value" in order to engage in political speech . . . Speech would be suppressed in the realm where its necessity is most evident: in the public dialogue preceding a real election. Governments are often hostile to speech, but under our law and our tradition it seems stranger than fiction for our Government to make this political speech a crime. Yet this is the statute's purpose and design.[26]

Some members of the public might consider *Hillary* to be insightful and instructive; some might find it to be neither high art nor a fair discussion on how to set the Nation's course; still others simply might suspend judgment on these points but decide to think more about issues and candidates. Those choices and assessments, however, are not for the Government to make. "The First Amendment underwrites the freedom to experiment and to create in the realm of thought and speech. Citizens must be free to use new forms, and new forums, for the expression of ideas. The civic discourse belongs to the people, and the Government may not prescribe the means used to conduct it."[27]

The Concurring Opinions of Roberts and Scalia

Chief Justice John Roberts and Justice Antonin Scalia each wrote concurring opinions. Roberts's concurrence primarily addressed *stare decisis,* the principle that courts should adhere to precedent. Defending the majority's decision to overturn *Austin* and *McConnell,* Roberts wrote:

> When considering whether to reexamine a prior erroneous holding, we must balance the importance of having constitutional questions decided against the importance of having them decided right . . . In conducting this balancing, we must keep in mind that stare decisis is not an end in itself. It is instead "the means by which we ensure that the law will not merely change erratically, but will develop in principled and intelligible fashion" . . . Its greatest purpose is to serve a constitutional ideal—the rule of law. It follows that in the unusual circumstance when fidelity to any particular precedent does more damage to this constitutional ideal than to advance it, we must be more willing to depart from that precedent . . . Abrogating the errant precedent, rather than reaffirming or extending it, might better preserve the law's coherence and curtail the precedent's disruptive effects.[28]

Justice Scalia's concurrence pertained to how the Framers of the Constitution viewed corporations and freedom of speech.

> Of course the Framers' personal affection or disaffection for corporations is relevant only insofar as it can be thought to be reflected in the understood

meaning of the text they enacted—not, as the dissent suggests, as a free-standing substitute for that text . . . Despite the corporation-hating quotations the dissent has dredged up, it is far from clear that by the end of the 18th century corporations were despised. . . . Most of the Founders' resentment towards corporations was directed at the state-granted monopoly privileges that individually chartered corporations enjoyed. Modern corporations do not have such privileges, and would probably have been favored by most of our enterprising founders—excluding, perhaps, Thomas Jefferson and others favoring perpetuation of an agrarian society.[29] . . .

All the provisions of the Bill of Rights set forth the rights of individual men and women—not, for example, of trees or polar bears. But the individual person's right to speak includes the right to speak in association with other individual persons. Surely the dissent does not believe that speech by the Republican Party or the Democratic Party can be censored because it is not the speech of "an individual American."[30] . . .

The [First] Amendment is written in terms of "speech," not speakers. Its text offers no foothold for excluding any category of speaker, from single individuals to partnerships of individuals, to unincorporated associations of individuals, to incorporated associations of individuals—and the dissent offers no evidence about the original meaning of the text to support any such exclusion. We are therefore simply left with the question whether the speech at issue in this case is "speech" covered by the First Amendment. No one says otherwise.[31]

The Dissent

In the dissent, Justice Stevens not only disagreed strongly with the majority's opinion regarding the constitutionality of §441b, but also objected that the majority had raised the question at all.

Our colleagues' suggestion that "we are asked to reconsider *Austin* and, in effect, *McConnell*" . . . would be more accurate if rephrased to state that "we have asked ourselves" to reconsider those cases . . . Essentially, the five Justices were unhappy with the limited nature of the case before us, so they changed the case to give themselves an opportunity to change the law.[32] . . .

The majority suggests that a facial ruling is necessary because anything less would chill too much protected speech . . . The majority suggests that, even though it expressly dismissed its facial challenge, Citizens United nevertheless preserved it—not as a freestanding "claim," but as a potential argument in support of "a claim that the FEC has violated its First Amendment right to free speech." . . . By this novel logic, virtually any submission could be reconceptualized as "a claim that the Government has violated my rights," and it would then be available to the Court to entertain any conceivable issue that might be relevant to that claim's disposition.[33] . . .

It is all the more distressing that our colleagues have manufactured a facial challenge, because the parties have advanced numerous ways to resolve the case that would facilitate electioneering by nonprofit advocacy corporations such as Citizens United, without toppling statutes and precedents. Which is to say, the majority has transgressed yet another "cardinal" principle of the judicial process: "[I]f it is not necessary to decide more, it is necessary not to decide more."[34] . . .

The Court's central argument for why *stare decisis* ought to be trumped is that it does not like *Austin*. The opinion "was not well reasoned," our colleagues assert, and it conflicts with First Amendment principles . . . I am perfectly willing to concede that if one of our precedents were dead wrong in its reasoning or irreconcilable with the rest of our doctrine, there would be a compelling basis for revisiting it. But neither is true of *Austin,* as I explain at length. . . . The majority also contends that the Government's hesitation to rely on *Austin's* antidistortion rationale "diminishe[s]" "the principle of adhering to that precedent" . . . Why it diminishes the value of *stare decisis* is left unexplained. We have never thought fit to overrule a precedent because a litigant has taken any particular tack.[35]

Corporate Speech

Pervading the Court's analysis is the ominous image of a "categorical ba[n]" on corporate speech . . . This characterization is highly misleading, and needs to be corrected . . . "The ability to form and administer separate segregated funds," we observed in *McConnell,* "has provided corporations and unions with a constitutionally sufficient opportunity to engage in express advocacy. That has been this Court's unanimous view" . . . Administering a PAC entails some administrative burden, but so does complying with the disclaimer, disclosure, and reporting requirements that the Court today upholds . . . To the extent the majority is worried about this issue, it is important to keep in mind that we have no record to show how substantial the burden really is, just the majority's own unsupported factfinding . . . Like all other natural persons, every shareholder of every corporation remains entirely free under *Austin* and *McConnell* to do however much electioneering she pleases outside of the corporate form. The owners of a "mom & pop" store can simply place ads in their own names, rather than the store's. If ideologically aligned individuals wish to make unlimited expenditures through the corporate form, they may utilize an *MCFL* organization* that has policies in place to avoid becoming a conduit for business or union interests.[36] . . .

So let us be clear: Neither *Austin* nor *McConnell* held or implied that corporations may be silenced; the FEC is not a "censor"; and in the years since these cases were decided, corporations have continued to play a major role in the national dialogue. Laws such as §203[†] target a class of communications that is especially likely to corrupt the political process, that is at least one degree removed from the views of individual citizens, and that may not even reflect the views of those who pay for it. Such laws burden political speech, and that is always a serious matter, demanding careful scrutiny. But the majority's incessant talk of a "ban" aims at a straw man.[37] . . .

The second pillar of the Court's opinion is its assertion that "the Government cannot restrict political speech based on the speaker's . . . identity." . . . [T]he authority of legislatures to enact viewpoint-neutral regulations based on content and identity is well settled. We have upheld statutes that prohibit the distribution or display of campaign materials near a polling place . . . Although we have not reviewed them directly, we have never cast doubt on laws that place special restrictions on campaign spending by foreign nationals. . . . And we have consistently approved laws that bar Government employees, but not others, from contributing to or participating in political activities.[38] . . .

The same logic applies to this case with additional force because it is the identity of corporations, rather than individuals, that the Legislature has taken into account . . . Not only has the distinctive potential of corporations to corrupt the electoral process long been recognized, but within the area of campaign finance, corporate spending is also "furthest from the core of political expression, since corporations' First Amendment speech and association interests are derived largely from those of their members and of the

---

* *Federal Election Commission* v. *Massachusetts Citizens for Life* (1986) (a.k.a. *MCFL*) allowed independent expenditures by corporations created solely for political ends that did not accept money from for-profit sources.

[†] 203 was §441b's section number in the original BCRA. Stevens uses §203 to signify the rule Kennedy referred to as §441b.

public in receiving information" . . . Campaign finance distinctions based on corporate identity tend to be less worrisome, in other words, because the "speakers" are not natural persons, much less members of our political community, and the governmental interests are of the highest order.[39] . . .

If taken seriously, our colleagues' assumption that the identity of a speaker has *no* relevance to the Government's ability to regulate political speech would lead to some remarkable conclusions. Such an assumption would have accorded the propaganda broadcasts to our troops by "Tokyo Rose" during World War II the same protection as speech by Allied commanders. More pertinently, it would appear to afford the same protection to multinational corporations controlled by foreigners as to individual Americans: To do otherwise, after all, could "'enhance the relative voice'" of some (*i.e.,* humans) over others (*i.e.,* nonhumans) . . . Under the majority's view, I suppose it may be a First Amendment problem that corporations are not permitted to vote, given that voting is, among other things, a form of speech.[40]

History and Precedent

The individualized charter mode of incorporation reflected the "cloud of disfavor under which corporations labored" in the early years of this Nation . . . Thomas Jefferson famously fretted that corporations would subvert the Republic . . . The Framers thus took it as a given that corporations could be comprehensively regulated in the service of the public welfare. Unlike our colleagues, they had little trouble distinguishing corporations from human beings, and when they constitutionalized the right to free speech in the First Amendment, it was the free speech of individual Americans that they had in mind. While individuals might join together to exercise their speech rights, business corporations, at least, were plainly not seen as facilitating such associational or expressive ends. Even "the notion that business corporations could invoke the First Amendment would probably have been quite a novelty," given that "at the time, the legitimacy of every corporate activity was thought to rest entirely in a concession of the sovereign" . . . If no prominent Framer bothered to articulate that corporate speech would have lesser status than individual speech, that may well be because the contrary proposition—if not also the very notion of "corporate speech"—was inconceivable.[41] . . .

[T]he Free Press Clause might be turned against Justice Scalia, for two reasons. First, we learn from it that the drafters of the First Amendment did draw distinctions—explicit distinctions—between types of "speakers," or speech outlets or forms. Second, the Court's strongest historical evidence all relates to the Framers' views on the press . . . yet while the Court tries to sweep this evidence into the Free Speech Clause, the Free Press Clause provides a more natural textual home. The text and history highlighted by our colleagues suggests why one type of corporation, those that are part of the press, might be able to claim special First Amendment status, and therefore why some kinds of "identity"-based distinctions might be permissible after all. Once one accepts that much, the intellectual edifice of the majority opinion crumbles.[42] . . .

A century of more recent history puts to rest any notion that today's ruling is faithful to our First Amendment tradition. At the federal level, the express distinction between corporate and individual political spending on elections stretches back to 1907, when Congress passed the Tillman Act . . . banning all corporate contributions to candidates. The Senate Report on the legislation observed that "[t]he evils of the use of [corporate] money in connection with political elections are so generally recognized that the committee deems it unnecessary to make any argument in favor of the general purpose of this measure. It is in the interest of good government and calculated to promote purity in the selection of public officials" . . . Our colleagues emphasize that in two cases from the middle of the 20th century, several Justices wrote separately to criticize the expenditure restriction as applied to unions . . . [T]heir position failed to command a majority. Prior to today, this was a fact we found significant in evaluating precedents.[43] . . .

It is worth remembering for present purposes that the four *MCFL* dissenters, led by Chief Justice Rehnquist, thought the Court was carrying the First Amendment *too far*. They would have recognized congressional authority to bar general treasury electioneering expenditures even by this class of nonprofits; they acknowledged that "the threat from corporate political activity will vary depending on the particular characteristics of a given corporation," but believed these "distinctions among corporations" were "distinctions in degree," not "in kind," and thus "more properly drawn by the Legislature than by the Judiciary."[44] . . .

In the Court's view, *Buckley* and *Bellotti* decisively rejected the possibility of distinguishing corporations from natural persons in the 1970's; it just so happens that in every single case in which the Court has reviewed campaign finance legislation in the decades since, the majority failed to grasp this truth . . . The majority emphasizes *Buckley*'s statement that " '[t]he concept that government may restrict the speech of some elements of our society in order to enhance the relative voice of others is wholly foreign to the First Amendment.'" . . . But this elegant phrase cannot bear the weight that our colleagues have placed on it. For one thing, the Constitution does, in fact, permit numerous "restrictions on the speech of some in order to prevent a few from drowning out the many" . . . For another, the *Buckley* Court used this line in evaluating "the ancillary governmental interest in equalizing the relative ability of individuals and groups to influence the outcome of elections." . . . It is not apparent why this is relevant to the case before us . . . Indeed, we *expressly* ruled [in *Austin*] that the compelling interest was not one of "'equaliz[ing] the relative influence of speakers on elections'" . . . but rather the need to confront the distinctive corrupting potential of corporate electoral advocacy financed by general treasury dollars.[45] . . .

Bellotti ruled, in an explicit limitation on the scope of its holding, that "our consideration of a corporation's right to speak on issues of general public interest implies no comparable right in the quite different context of participation in a political campaign for election to public office." . . . *Bellotti*, in other words, did not touch the question presented in *Austin* and *McConnell*, and the opinion squarely disavowed the proposition for which the majority cites it . . . The majority attempts to explain away the distinction *Bellotti* drew—between general corporate speech and campaign speech intended to promote or prevent the election of specific candidates for office—as inconsistent with the rest of the opinion and with *Buckley* . . . Yet the basis for this distinction is perfectly coherent: The anticorruption interests that animate regulations of corporate participation in candidate elections, the "importance" of which "has never been doubted," . . . do not apply equally to regulations of corporate participation in referenda. A referendum cannot owe a political debt to a corporation, seek to curry favor with a corporation, or fear the corporation's retaliation.[46] . . .

The *Bellotti* Court confronted a dramatically different factual situation from the one that confronts us in this case: a state statute that barred business corporations' expenditures on some referenda but not others. Specifically, the statute barred a business corporation "from making contributions or expenditures 'for the purpose of . . . influencing or affecting the vote on any question submitted to the voters, other than one materially affecting any of the property, business or assets of the corporation'" . . . and it went so far as to provide that referenda related to income taxation would not "'be deemed materially to affect the property, business or assets of the corporation. . . .'" As might be guessed, the legislature had enacted this statute in order to limit corporate speech on a proposed state constitutional amendment to authorize a graduated income tax. The statute was a transparent attempt to prevent corporations from spending money to defeat this amendment, which was favored by a majority of legislators but had been repeatedly rejected by the voters. . . . We said that "where, as here, the legislature's suppression of speech suggests an attempt to give one side of a debatable public question an advantage in expressing its views to the people, the First Amendment is plainly offended."[47] . . .

Bellotti thus involved a *viewpoint-discriminatory* statute, created to effect a particular policy outcome. Even Justice Rehnquist, in dissent, had to acknowledge that "a very persuasive argument could be made that the [Massachusetts Legislature], desiring to impose a personal income tax but more than once defeated in that desire by the combination of the Commonwealth's referendum provision and corporate expenditures in opposition to such a tax, simply decided to muzzle corporations on this sort of issue so that it could succeed in its desire." . . . To make matters worse, the law at issue did not make any allowance for corporations to spend money through PACs. . . . We acknowledged in *Bellotti* that numerous "interests of the highest importance" can justify campaign finance regulation. . . . But we found no evidence that these interests were served by the Massachusetts law. . . . We left open the possibility that our decision might have been different if there had been "record or legislative findings that corporate advocacy threatened imminently to undermine democratic processes, thereby denigrating rather than serving First Amendment interests."[48] . . .

Austin and *McConnell,* then, sit perfectly well with *Bellotti.* Indeed, all six Members of the *Austin* majority had been on the Court at the time of *Bellotti,* and none so much as hinted in *Austin* that they saw any tension between the decisions. The difference between the cases is not that *Austin* and *McConnell* rejected First Amendment protection for corporations whereas *Bellotti* accepted it. The difference is that the statute at issue in *Bellotti* smacked of viewpoint discrimination, targeted one class of corporations, and provided no PAC option; and the State has a greater interest in regulating independent corporate expenditures on candidate elections than on referenda, because in a functioning democracy the public must have faith that its representatives owe their positions to the people, not to the corporations with the deepest pockets.[49] . . .

In sum, over the course of the past century Congress has demonstrated a recurrent need to regulate corporate participation in candidate elections to " '[p]reserv[e] the integrity of the electoral process, preven[t] corruption, . . . sustai[n] the active, alert responsibility of the individual citizen,' " protect the expressive interests of shareholders, and " '[p]reserv[e] . . . the individual citizen's confidence in government.' " . . . These understandings provided the combined impetus behind the Tillman Act in 1907 . . . the Taft-Hartley Act in 1947 . . . FECA in 1971 . . . and BCRA in 2002. . . . Continuously for over 100 years, this line of "[c]ampaign finance reform has been a series of reactions to documented threats to electoral integrity obvious to any voter, posed by large sums of money from corporate or union treasuries." . . . Time and again, we have recognized these realities in approving measures that Congress and the States have taken. None of the cases the majority cites is to the contrary. The only thing new about *Austin* was the dissent, with its stunning failure to appreciate the legitimacy of interests recognized in the name of democratic integrity since the days of the Progressives.[50]

Corruption

On numerous occasions we have recognized Congress' legitimate interest in preventing the money that is spent on elections from exerting an " 'undue influence on an officeholder's judgment' " and from creating " 'the appearance of such influence,' " beyond the sphere of *quid pro quo* relationships . . . Corruption can take many forms. Bribery may be the paradigm case. But the difference between selling a vote and selling access is a matter of degree, not kind. And selling access is not qualitatively different from giving special preference to those who spent money on one's behalf. Corruption operates along a spectrum, and the majority's apparent belief that *quid pro quo* arrangements can be neatly demarcated from other improper influences does not accord with the theory or reality of politics. It certainly does not accord with the record Congress developed in passing BCRA, a record that stands as a remarkable testament to the energy and ingenuity with which corporations, unions, lobbyists, and politicians may go about scratching each other's backs—and which amply supported Congress' determination to target a limited set of especially destructive practices.[51]

The District Court that adjudicated the initial challenge to BCRA pored over this record . . . "The factual findings of the Court illustrate that corporations and labor unions routinely notify Members of Congress as soon as they air electioneering communications relevant to the Members' elections. The record also indicates that Members express appreciation to organizations for the airing of these election-related advertisements . . . Political consultants testify that campaigns are quite aware of who is running advertisements on the candidate's behalf, when they are being run, and where they are being run. Likewise, a prominent lobbyist testifies that these organizations use issue advocacy as a means to influence various Members of Congress. . . . After the election, these organizations often seek credit for their support. . . . Finally, a large majority of Americans (80%) are of the view that corporations and other organizations that engage in electioneering communications, which benefit specific elected officials, receive special consideration from those officials when matters arise that affect these corporations and organizations."[52] . . .

[T]his broader understanding of corruption has deep roots in the Nation's history. "During debates on the earliest [campaign finance] reform acts, the terms 'corruption' and 'undue influence' were used nearly interchangeably" . . . [W]e have ample evidence to suggest that [the Framers] would have been appalled by the evidence of corruption that Congress unearthed in developing BCRA and that the Court today discounts to irrelevance. It is fair to say that "[t]he Framers were obsessed with corruption," which they understood to encompass the dependency of public officeholders on private interests . . . They discussed corruption "more often in the Constitutional Convention than factions, violence, or instability." When they brought our constitutional order into being, the Framers had their minds trained on a threat to republican self-government that this Court has lost sight of.[53]

Antidistortion

The fact that corporations are different from human beings might seem to need no elaboration, except that the majority opinion almost completely elides it . . . Unlike other interest groups, business corporations have been "effectively delegated responsibility for ensuring society's economic welfare"; they inescapably structure the life of every citizen. " '[T]he resources in the treasury of a business corporation,' " furthermore, " 'are not an indication of popular support for the corporation's political ideas.' " . . . " 'They reflect instead the economically motivated decisions of investors and customers. The availability of these resources may make a corporation a formidable political presence, even though the power of the corporation may be no reflection of the power of its ideas.' " . . . It might also be added that corporations have no consciences, no beliefs, no feelings, no thoughts, no desires. Corporations help structure and facilitate the activities of human beings, to be sure, and their "personhood" often serves as a useful legal fiction. But they are not themselves members of "We the People" by whom and for whom our Constitution was established.[54] . . .

It is an interesting question "who" is even speaking when a business corporation places an advertisement that endorses or attacks a particular candidate. Presumably it is not the customers or employees, who typically have no say in such matters. It cannot realistically be said to be the shareholders, who tend to be far removed from the day-to-day decisions of the firm and whose political preferences may be opaque to management. Perhaps the officers or directors of the corporation have the best claim to be the ones speaking, except their fiduciary duties generally prohibit them from using corporate funds for personal ends. Some individuals associated with the corporation must make the decision to place the ad, but the idea that these individuals are thereby fostering their self-expression or cultivating their critical faculties is fanciful. It is entirely possible that the corporation's electoral message will *conflict* with their personal convictions. Take away the ability to use general treasury funds for some of those ads, and no one's autonomy, dignity, or political equality has been impinged upon in the least.[55] . . .

Austin recognized that there are substantial reasons why a legislature might conclude that unregulated general treasury expenditures will give corporations "unfai[r] influence" in the electoral process . . . and distort public debate in ways that undermine rather than advance the interests of listeners. The legal structure of corporations allows them to amass and deploy financial resources on a scale few natural persons can match. The structure of a business corporation, furthermore, draws a line between the corporation's economic interests and the political preferences of the individuals associated with the corporation; the corporation must engage the electoral process with the aim "to enhance the profitability of the company, no matter how persuasive the arguments for a broader or conflicting set of priorities" . . . [W]hen corporations grab up the prime broadcasting slots on the eve of an election, they can flood the market with advocacy that bears "little or no correlation" to the ideas of natural persons or to any broader notion of the public good . . . The opinions of real people may be marginalized.[56] . . .

In addition to this immediate drowning out of noncorporate voices, there may be deleterious effects that follow soon thereafter. Corporate "domination" of electioneering . . . can generate the impression that corporations dominate our democracy. When citizens turn on their televisions and radios before an election and hear only corporate electioneering, they may lose faith in their capacity, as citizens, to influence public policy . . . To the extent that corporations are allowed to exert undue influence in electoral races, the speech of the eventual winners of those races may also be chilled. Politicians who fear that a certain corporation can make or break their reelection chances may be cowed into silence about that corporation.[57] . . .

Our colleagues ridicule the idea of regulating expenditures based on "nothing more" than a fear that corporations have a special "ability to persuade," . . . as if corporations were our society's ablest debaters and viewpoint-neutral laws such as §203 were created to suppress their best arguments . . . All of the majority's theoretical arguments turn on a proposition with undeniable surface appeal but little grounding in evidence or experience, "that there is no such thing as too much speech" . . . If individuals in our society had infinite free time to listen to and contemplate every last bit of speech uttered by anyone, anywhere; and if broadcast advertisements had no special ability to influence elections apart from the merits of their arguments (to the extent they make any); and if legislators always operated with nothing less than perfect virtue; then I suppose the majority's premise would be sound. In the real world, we have seen, corporate domination of the airwaves prior to an election may decrease the average listener's exposure to relevant viewpoints, and it may diminish citizens' willingness and capacity to participate in the democratic process.[58] . . .

In critiquing *Austin*'s antidistortion rationale and campaign finance regulation more generally, our colleagues place tremendous weight on the example of media corporations . . . There would be absolutely no reason to consider the issue of media corporations if the majority did not, first, transform Citizens United's as-applied challenge into a facial challenge and, second, invent the theory that legislatures must eschew all "identity"-based distinctions and treat a local nonprofit news outlet exactly the same as General Motors.[59]

Shareholder Interest

Interwoven with *Austin*'s concern to protect the integrity of the electoral process is a concern to protect the rights of shareholders from a kind of coerced speech: electioneering expenditures that do not "reflec[t] [their] support" . . .

When corporations use general treasury funds to praise or attack a particular candidate for office, it is the shareholders, as the residual claimants, who are effectively footing the bill. Those shareholders who disagree with the corporation's electoral message may find their financial investments being used to undermine their political convictions . . . The Court dismisses this interest on the ground that abuses of shareholder money can be corrected "through the procedures of corporate democracy," . . . and, it seems, through Internet-based disclosures . . . By "corporate democracy," presumably the Court means the rights of shareholders to vote and to bring derivative suits for breach of fiduciary duty. In practice, however, many corporate lawyers will tell you that "these rights are so limited as to be almost nonexistent," given the internal authority wielded by boards and managers and the expansive protections afforded by the business judgment rule . . . Modern technology may help make it easier to track corporate activity, including electoral advocacy, but it is utopian to believe that it solves the problem. Most American households that own stock do so through intermediaries such as mutual funds and pension plans . . . which makes it more difficult both to monitor and to alter particular holdings. Studies show that a majority of individual investors make no trades at all during a given year.[60] . . .

If and when shareholders learn that a corporation has been spending general treasury money on objectionable electioneering, they can divest. Even assuming that they reliably learn as much, however, this solution is only partial. The injury to the shareholders' expressive rights has already occurred; they might have preferred to keep that corporation's stock in their portfolio for any number of economic reasons; and they may incur a capital gains tax or other penalty from selling their shares, changing their pension plan, or the like. The shareholder protection rationale has been criticized as underinclusive, in that corporations also spend money on lobbying and charitable contributions in ways that any particular shareholder might disapprove. But those expenditures do not implicate the selection of public officials, an area in which "the interests of unwilling . . . corporate shareholders [in not being] forced to subsidize that speech" "are at their zenith."[61]

"Distinctive Corrupting Potential of Corporate Electioneering"

In a democratic society, the longstanding consensus on the need to limit corporate campaign spending should outweigh the wooden application of judge-made rules . . . At bottom, the Court's opinion is thus a rejection of the common sense of the American people, who have recognized a need to prevent corporations from undermining self-government since the founding, and who have fought against the distinctive corrupting potential of corporate electioneering since the days of Theodore Roosevelt. It is a strange time to repudiate that common sense. While American democracy is imperfect, few outside the majority of this Court would have thought its flaws included a dearth of corporate money in politics.[62]

Timeline of Campaign Finance Legislation and Court Decisions prior to *Citizens United*[63]

1867—The first federal campaign finance law bans federal employees from soliciting campaign donations from Navy yard workers.

1883—The Pendleton Act expands the 1867 rules to protect all federal employees.

1907—The Tillman Act bans all corporations from donating money to election campaigns for federal office, and it bans federally chartered corporations and national banks from donating money to any election campaign; but the legislation is widely viewed as ineffective.

1910—The Federal Corrupt Practices Act, or Publicity Act, mandates that House campaign committees disclose their receipts and expenditures after elections are over.

1911—Congress expands the Publicity Act to cover Senate elections, individual candidates, and primary elections, and limits spending for all congressional campaigns. Receipts and expenditures must now be disclosed ten days before an election.

1921—In *Newberry v. United States,* the Supreme Court strikes down the 1911 restrictions as applied to primary elections: "We cannot conclude that authority to control party primaries or conventions for designating candidates was bestowed on Congress by the grant of power to regulate the manner of holding elections."

1925—A revised Federal Corrupt Practices Act tightens disclosure requirements and expands coverage, but also lacks enforcement provisions.

1939—The Hatch Act, including its amendments in 1940, bans federal workers and some contractors and state workers from contributing to campaigns, limits individual contributions in federal elections, and applies campaign finance regulations to primary elections.

1941—In *United States v. Classic,* the Supreme Court decides that Congress can regulate primary elections: "Where the state law has made the primary an integral part of the procedure of choice, or where, in fact, the primary effectively controls the choice, the right of the elector to have his ballot counted at the primary, is likewise included in the right protected by Article I, §2. And this right of participation is protected just as is the right to vote at the election, where the primary is by law made an integral part of the election machinery, whether the voter exercises his right in a party primary which invariably, sometimes, or never determines the ultimate choice of the representative."

1943—The Smith-Connally Act bans unions from using their dues to donate to campaigns until the end of World War II.

1944—In order to circumvent Smith-Connally, the Congress of Industrial Organizations (CIO) creates the first PAC to provide campaign donations from sources other than union funds.

1947—The Taft-Hartley Act extends the ban on labor unions (and corporations) donating to federal elections and bars both unions and corporations from making "independent expenditures" to support or oppose federal candidates.

1971—The Federal Election Campaign Act (FECA) consolidates existing campaign finance law. It also mandates comprehensive reports of federal campaign contributions and spending, widens the definition of "contributions" and "expenditures," limits spending on advertisements, and restricts campaign donations from candidates themselves or their family members. FECA defines the legal structure for PACs, through which corporations and labor unions can solicit donations for political causes. A separate law, the Revenue Act, creates a fund of federal tax dollars for presidential campaigns.

1974—Amendments to FECA create the Federal Election Commission to enforce the law, impose new limits on donations to and spending by federal election campaigns, expand public funding for presidential campaigns, and remove some Hatch Act restrictions on state government employees.

1976—In *Buckley v. Valeo,* the Supreme Court strikes down limitations on spending by privately funded campaigns, and on "issue ads" that aren't "express advocacy" for a campaign, declaring "A restriction on the amount of money a person or group can spend on political communication during a campaign necessarily reduces the quantity of expression by restricting the number of issues discussed, the depth of their exploration, and the size of the audience reached." The Court upholds limits on contributions, however, arguing that "a limitation upon the amount that any one person or group may contribute to a candidate or political committee entails only a marginal restriction upon the contributor's ability to engage in free communication. A contribution serves as a general expression of support for the candidate and his views, but does not communicate the underlying basis for the support. The quantity of communication by the contributor does not increase perceptibly with the size of his contribution, since the expression rests solely on the undifferentiated, symbolic act of contributing."

1978—In *First National Bank of Boston v. Bellotti,* the Supreme Court rejects a Massachusetts law that limits corporate spending on state referenda. "We thus find no support in the First or Fourteenth Amendment, or in the decisions of this Court, for the proposition that speech that otherwise would be within the protection of the First Amendment loses that protection simply because its source is a corporation that cannot prove, to the satisfaction of a court, a material effect on its business or property."

1979—An amendment to FECA allows corporations, unions, and individuals to donate without limit to national party committees, so long as the money is intended for "party-building" efforts instead of a particular campaign. This "soft money loophole" leads to heavy corporate and labor donations to political parties.

1986—In *FEC v. Massachusetts Citizens for Life,* the Supreme Court decides that FECA limitations on corporate independent expenditures are unconstitutional when applied to nonprofits created expressly for political purposes and unaffiliated with any campaign, business, or labor union.

1990—In *Austin v. Michigan Chamber of Commerce,* the Supreme Court upholds a Michigan law prohibiting nonmedia corporations from making independent expenditures in support of campaigns.

2002—The Bipartisan Campaign Reform Act (BCRA), or "McCain-Feingold," ends soft-money contributions to political parties and imposes new rules on "electioneering communications" before an election.

2003—In *McConnell v. FEC,* the Supreme Court upholds McCain-Feingold's ban on soft money.

2006—In *Wisconsin Right to Life v. FEC,* the Supreme Court exempts electioneering communications from McCain-Feingold's regulations if they are

TABLE 19.1A

Presidential Campaign Expenses, Republicans and Democrats, 1860–1988 (dollars)

	Republican		Democrat	
Election	Candidate	Expenses	Candidate	Expenses
1860	Abraham Lincoln*	100,000	Stephen Douglas	50,000
1864	Abraham Lincoln*	125,000	George B. McClellan	50,000
1868	Ulysses S. Grant*	150,000	Horatio Seymour	75,000
1872	Ulysses S. Grant*	250,000	Horace Greeley	50,000
1876	Rutherford B. Hayes*	950,000	Samuel J. Tilden	900,000
1880	James Garfield*	1,100,000	Winfield Scott Hancock	335,000
1884	James G. Blaine	1,300,000	Grover Cleveland*	1,400,000
1888	Benjamin Harrison*	1,350,000	Grover Cleveland	855,000
1892	Benjamin Harrison	1,700,000	Grover Cleveland*	2,350,000
1896	William McKinley*	3,350,000	William Jennings Bryan	675,000
1900	William McKinley*	3,000,000	William Jennings Bryan	425,000
1904	Theodore Roosevelt*	2,096,000	Alton B. Parker	700,000
1908	William Howard Taft*	1,655,518	William Jennings Bryan	629,341
1912	William Howard Taft	1,071,549	Woodrow Wilson*	1,134,848
1916	Charles Evans Hughes	2,441,565	Woodrow Wilson*	2,284,590
1920	Warren G. Harding*	5,417,501	James M. Cox	1,470,371
1924	Calvin Coolidge*	4,020,478	John W. Davis	1,108,836
1928	Herbert Hoover*	6,256,111	Al Smith	5,342,350
1932	Herbert Hoover	2,900,052	Franklin D. Roosevelt*	2,245,975
1936	Alf Landon	8,892,972	Franklin D. Roosevelt*	5,194,741
1940	Wendell Willkie	3,451,310	Franklin D. Roosevelt*	2,783,654
1944	Thomas E. Dewey	2,828,652	Franklin D. Roosevelt*	2,169,077
1948	Thomas E. Dewey	2,127,296	Harry S. Truman*	2,736,334
1952	Dwight D. Eisenhower*	6,608,623	Adlai Stevenson	5,032,926
1956	Dwight D. Eisenhower*	7,778,702	Adlai Stevenson	5,106,651
1960	Richard Nixon	10,128,000	John F. Kennedy*	9,797,000
1964	Barry Goldwater	16,026,000	Lyndon Johnson*	8,757,000
1968	Richard Nixon*	25,402,000	Hubert Humphrey	11,594,000
1972	Richard Nixon*	61,400,000	George McGovern	30,000,000
1976	Gerald Ford	21,786,641	Jimmy Carter*	21,800,000
1980	Ronald Reagan*	29,188,188	Jimmy Carter	29,352,767
1984	Ronald Reagan*	40,400,000	Walter Mondale	40,400,000
1988	George H. W. Bush*	46,100,000	Michael Dukakis	46,100,000

Source: Herbert E. Alexander, *Financing Elections: Money, Elections, and Political Reform*, 4th ed. (Washington, DC: CQ Press, 1992), 80.

*Winner of election

TABLE 19.1B

Sources of Presidential Campaign Funds, 1992–2008 (dollars)

Election	Candidate	Federal Matching Funds	Individual Donors	Party Committees and PACs	Other	Total Receipts
1992	Bill Clinton (D)	67,776,130	31,072,409	14,651	16,427,263	115,261,535
	George H. W. Bush (R)	65,358,246	31,496,588	61,225	3,594,026	100,510,119
1996	Bill Clinton (D)	75,232,194	35,282,097	1,861	8,555,712	119,604,182
	Bob Dole (R)*	75,365,768	30,431,191	1,315,837	31,381,495	138,549,762
2000	George W. Bush (R)	67,560,000	99,508,269	2,164,263	2,929,667	172,162,199
	Al Gore (D)	83,016,081	44,922,272	0	423,175	128,361,528
2004	George W. Bush (R)	74,620,000	269,777,919	2,699,895	15,313,777	362,411,591
	John Kerry (D)	74,620,000	224,580,021	322,705	21,635,279	321,158,005
2008	Barack Obama (D)	0	659,128,072	1,580	88,625,373	747,755,026
	John McCain (R)	0	190,411,677	1,301,134	27,878,240	219,591,051

Source: Adapted from Federal Election Commission, Presidential Data Summary Tables, http://www.fec.gov/press/campaign_finance_statistics.shtml.
The winner of each election is listed first. Figures are for the two calendar years up to the end of the election year. All columns exclude refunds and repayments. "Other" column includes transfers from other campaign committees, loans and contributions from the candidate, other loans, and other unspecified sources of funds.

* All figures, including totals, are drawn from the Federal Election Commission data. In some rows, the components do not sum exactly to the totals.

TABLE 19.2

**Large Individual Contributions to Candidates, Parties, PACs,
by Contribution Size, 1990–2008**

Election	Number of Donors	Total Donations ($millions)	Number of Donors	Total Donations ($millions)
	$10,000+		$100,000+	
1990	3,329	62	3	<1
1992	6,341	137	98	14
1994	4,783	105	81	12
1996	7,215	192	307	48
1998	7,001	174	206	39
2000	14,919	447	726	152
2002	10,708	340	387	133
	$10,000+		$95,000+	
2004	25,819	724	464	123
2006	22,551	577	515	64
2008	37,061	1,015	1,093	128

Source: Adapted from the Center for Responsive Politics, "Donor Demographics," http://www
.opensecrets.org/bigpicture/donordemographics.php. Donation size categories are inclusive of categories above them.

TABLE 19.3

**Individual Contributions to Congressional Campaigns,
by Contribution Size, 2002–2008**

Election	<$200	$200–$499	$500–$749	$750+	Total
2002	$136,147,367	$55,526,051	$86,946,952	$259,222,356	$537,842,726
2004	$158,849,255	$61,263,839	$95,215,696	$405,487,176	$720,815,966
2006	$192,830,849	$70,707,499	$106,018,666	$491,652,376	$861,209,390
2008	$159,664,485	$74,637,179	$99,727,505	$464,844,760	$798,873,929

Source: Federal Election Commission, "Individual Contributions to Congressional Campaigns by
Size 2007–2008," http://fec.gov/press/press2009/2009Dec29Cong/3Indiv2008.pdf.

TABLE 19.4

Outside Spending on Federal Elections, 1990–2008, Excluding Party Committees (dollars)

Election	Independent Expenditures	Electioneering Communications	Communication Costs
1990	5,650,524		1,562,695
1992	10,947,342		8,687,781
1994	5,219,215		4,319,629
1996	10,167,742		7,716,301
1998	10,266,937		4,924,170
2000	33,034,631		17,761,961
2002	16,588,844		10,700,441
2004	67,170,150	98,898,197	30,345,480
2006	37,401,996	15,152,326	16,305,587
2008	143,618,022	194,781,901	NA

Source: Adapted from the Center for Responsive Politics, "Total Outside Spending by Election Cycle, Excluding Party Committees," http://www.opensecrets.org/outsidespending/cycle_tots.php.

Note: Communication costs "are internal political messages generally aimed only at the members of a union or organization, or company executives. These may be coordinated with the candidates and can be paid for directly from the organization's treasury."

TABLE 19.5

PAC Spending, 1990–2008 (dollars)

Election	Number of PACs	Contributions to Candidates	Independent Expenditures	Contributions to Parties
1990	4,677	159,121,496	5,152,987	14,815,921
1992	4,727	188,927,768	10,640,476	18,334,359
1994	4,621	189,631,119	5,082,487	17,667,613
1996	4,528	217,830,619	10,552,367	23,916,931
1998	4,599	219,943,566	9,335,701	22,239,161
2000	4,499	259,829,774	21,041,789	26,988,229
2002	4,594	282,041,446	14,008,019	24,495,911
2004	4,867	310,489,001	57,374,392	42,632,290
2006	5,091	372,102,747	37,822,259	47,463,538
2008	5,210	412,847,552	135,181,501	52,743,398

Source: Adapted from Federal Election Commission, "Summary of PAC Activity 1990–2008," http://www.fec.gov/press/press2009/20090415PAC/documents/4sumhistory2008_000.pdf.

Note: Figures are for the two calendar years up to the end of the election year.

about legislative issues and not "express advocacy" regarding candidates or elections.

NOTES

1. Patrick Healy and Julie Bosman, "With New Poll Results, Candidates Scramble for Edge in Caucuses," *New York Times,* 31 Dec. 2007, A13.

2. Quotations are from the film trailer posted by Citizens United on YouTube, http://www.youtube.com/watch?v=BOYcM1z5fTs.

3. *Citizens United v. Federal Election Commission,* 558 U.S. 310 (2010), majority opinion, 2–4. The decision and all concurring and dissenting opinions are available at http://www.supremecourt.gov/opinions/09pdf/08-205.pdf. See also Federal Election Commission, "Federal Election Commission Campaign Guide: Corporations and Labor Organizations," January 2007, http://www.fec.gov/pdf/colagui.pdf.

4. *Citizens United,* majority opinion, 1, 4–5.

5. Ibid., 5–12.

6. Ibid., 9–10.

7. Ibid., 11–12.

8. Ibid., 12–14. The internal quotation is from *Lebron v. National Railroad Passenger Corporation,* 513 U. S. 374, 379 (1995), quoting *Yee v. Escondido* 503 U. S. 519, 534 (1992).

9. Ibid., 16–17, 19.

10. Ibid., 20–22.

11. Ibid., 22–23. The internal quotation is from *Buckley v. Valeo,* 424 U. S. 1, 19 (1976).

12. Ibid., 23–24. The internal quotation is from *Eu v. San Francisco County Democratic Central Comm.,* 489 U. S. 214, 223 (1989), quoting *Monitor Patriot Co. v. Roy,* 401 U. S. 265, 272 (1971).

13. Ibid., 25–26. The internal quotation is from *First Nat. Bank of Boston v. Bellotti,* 435 U. S. 765, 776 (1978).

14. Ibid., 26–28. The brackets around "the federal expenditure prohibition's" are from the decision. The internal quotations are from *United States v. CIO,* 335 U. S. 106, 121, 143 (1948).

15. Ibid., 28–29. The quotations are from *Buckley v. Valeo,* 424 U. S. 1, 25, 47–48, 47 (1976).

16. Ibid., 30–31. The internal quotations are from *Bellotti,* at 784–785.

17. Ibid., 31–32. The internal quotation is from *Austin v. Michigan Chamber of Commerce,* 494 U. S. 652, 660 (1990).

18. Ibid., 32–35. The internal quotations are from *Bellotti,* at 777, and *Austin,* at 660.

19. Ibid., 35–37.

20. Ibid., 38. The first internal quotation is from *New York State Bd. of Elections v. Lopez Torres,* 552 U. S. 196, 208 (2008). The second one is from *Austin,* at 660.

21. Ibid., 38–39. The internal quotation is from James Madison, "Federalist 10," in *The Federalist,* ed. Benjamin Fletcher Wright (Cambridge: Harvard University Press, 1961), 130.

22. Ibid., 40.

23. Ibid., 40, 42–44. The internal quotation is from *McConnell v. Federal Election Comm'n,* 540 U. S. 93, 297 (2003).

24. Ibid., 45. The first two internal quotations are from *McConnell v. Federal Election Comm'n,* 251 F. Supp. 2d 176, 209, 560 (DC 2003).

25. Ibid., 46. The internal quotation is from *Bellotti,* at 794.

26. Ibid., 56–57. The internal quotation is from the U.S. Code, 2 U. S. C. §431(9)(A)(i).

27. Ibid., 57. The final quotation is from *McConnell,* 540 U. S., at 341.

28. *Citizens United,* Roberts's concurrence, 7. The internal quotation is from *Vasquez v. Hillery,* 474 U. S. 254, 265 (1986).

29. *Citizens United,* Scalia's concurrence, 2–3.

30. Ibid., 7–8.

31. Ibid., 8–9.

32. *Citizens United,* dissent, 4, 6.

33. Ibid., 10–11.

34. Ibid., 14. The internal quotation is from *PDK Labs., Inc. v. Drug Enforcement Admin.,* 362 F. 3d 786, 799 (CADC 2004).

35. Ibid., 17–19.

36. Ibid., 23–25. The internal quotation starting with "The ability" is from *McConnell,* 540 U. S., at 203.

37. Ibid., 28.

38. Ibid., 28, 31–32.

39. Ibid., 32–33. The internal quotation is from *FEC v. Beaumont,* 539 U. S. 146, at 161n8 (2003).

40. Ibid., 33–34. The internal quotation is from the majority opinion, at 33 (quoting *Buckley,* at 49).

41. Ibid., 35–37, 39–40. The first quotation is from William Meade Fletcher, *Cyclopedia of the Law of Corporations,* vol. 1 (Eagan, MN: Thomson / West, 2006), 8. The second quotation is from David Shelledy, "Autonomy, Debate, and Corporate Speech," *Hastings Constitutional Law Quarterly* 18 (Spring 1991): 578.

42. *Citizens United,* dissent, 40n57.

43. Ibid., 42–44. The internal quotation is from S. Rep. No. 3056, 59th Cong., 1st sess., 2 (1906).

44. Ibid., 47. The internal quotations are from *FEC v. Massachusetts Citizens for Life, Inc.,* 479 U. S. 238, 268 (1986) (hereafter *MCFL*).

45. Ibid., 49–52. The first internal quotation is from the majority opinion, at 33 (quoting *Bellotti,* at 48–49). The second quotation is from *Nixon v. Shrink Missouri Government PAC,* 528 U. S. 377, 402 (2000). The third quotation is from *Buckley,* at 48. The fourth quotation is from *Austin,* at 660.

46. Ibid., 52–53. The internal quotations are from *Bellotti,* at 788n26.

47. Ibid., 53–54. The internal quotation is from *Bellotti,* at 785–786.

48. Ibid., 54–55. The internal quotations are from *Bellotti,* at 788–789.

49. Ibid., 55.

50. Ibid., 55–56. The quotations are from, respectively, *McConnell,* 540 U. S., at 206–207 (quoting *Bellotti,* at 788–789), and *FEC v. Wisconsin Right to Life, Inc.,* 551 U. S. 449, 522 (2007).

51. *Citizens United,* dissent, 57. The internal quotations are from *McConnell,* 540 U. S, at 152.

52. Ibid., 57–59. The internal quotation is from *McConnell,* 251 F. Supp. 2d, at 623–624.

53. Ibid., 61–62. The first quotation is from Frank Pasquale, "Reclaiming Egalitarianism in the Political Theory of Campaign Finance Reform," *University of Illinois Law Review* 2008, no. 2 (2008): 601. The latter quotations are from Zephyr Teachout, "The Anti-Corruption Principle," *Cornell Law Review* 94 (2009): 348, 352.

54. *Citizens United,* dissent, 75–76. The first quotation is from Milton C. Regan Jr., "Corporate Speech and Civic Virtue," in *Debating Democracy's Discontent: Essays on American Politics, Law, and Public Philosophy,* ed. Anita L. Allen and Milton C. Regan Jr. (New York: Oxford University Press, 1998), 302. The subsequent quotations are from *Austin,* at 659 (quoting *MCFL,* at 258).

55. Ibid., 77.

56. Ibid., 80. The first and third quotations are from *Austin,* at 660. The second quotation is from an *Amicus* brief by American Independent Business Alliance, 11.

57. Ibid., 81.

58. Ibid., 83. The "nothing more" and "ability to persuade" quotations are from the opinion of Roberts, at 11. The "that there is no such thing" quotation is from Scalia's dissent in *Austin,* at 695.

59. Ibid., 84–85.

60. Ibid., 86–88. The first quotation is from *Austin,* at 660–661. The second quotation is from the majority opinion, at 46. The third quotation is from Margaret M. Blair and Lynn A. Stout, "A Team Production Theory of Corporate Law," *Virginia Law Review* 85, no. 2 (Mar. 1999): 320.

61. Ibid., 88. The quotations are from Brennan's concurrence in *Austin,* at 677.

62. Ibid., 90.

63. See Victor W. Geraci, "Campaign Finance Reform Historical Timeline," via the Connecticut Network, http://ct-n.com/civics/campaign_finance/Support%20Materials/CTN%20CFR%20Timeline.pdf; "A Century of U.S. Campaign Finance Law," National Public Radio, http://www.npr.org/templates/story/story.php?storyId=121293380; Marc A. Triebwasser, Campaign Finance Timeline, via Central Connecticut State University, http://www.polisci.ccsu.edu/trieb/timeline.htm; FEC, "The Federal Election Campaign Laws: A Short History," http://www.fec.gov/info/appfour.htm; and Melvin I. Urofsky, *Money and Free Speech: Campaign Finance Reform and the Courts* (Lawrence: University Press of Kansas, 2005). The FEC keeps a

thorough record of campaign finance court cases at http://www.fec.gov/law /litigation.shtml; History Commons, Center for Grassroots Oversight, http://www .historycommons.org; Center for Public Integrity, "Important Dates: Federal Campaign Finance Legislation," 19 May 2014, https://www.publicintegrity.org/2004/03 /25/5852/important-dates-federal-campaign-finance-legislation.

Conclusion

As READERS TAKE A MOMENT to catch their breath, having worked through one case study after another, we now have a chance to draw a few conclusions from the exercise and consider what they might tell us about the state of the nation's democracy today.

There has certainly been tremendous change in the American republic since its founding in the late eighteenth century. In some ways, especially given the existence of slavery and the narrowness of the electorate in those early years, the new nation had more in common with the democracy of ancient Athens, over 2,000 years prior, than with our own democracy today, less than 250 years later.[1] Slavery, in particular, reflects a historical disjunction so extreme that it is difficult to think of the early period as being fully continuous with our own times.

Still, the essential structures of republican government and the foundational principles of representative democracy and individual liberty were evident from a very early stage in America, even if some of those principles initially remained largely aspirational. Already by the beginning of the nineteenth century, the country exhibited a vibrant culture of democracy, as Alexis de Tocqueville astutely observed, as well as an increasingly complex web of institutions, both formal and informal, that shaped political decision making in the most intricate of ways. Who, for example, would have imagined that an extralegal state constitutional convention led by a Harvard-educated lawyer named Thomas Dorr would have helped to eliminate property restrictions on voting—and led to his own imprisonment for treason—in antebellum Rhode Island (Case 5)? Or that the creation of a novel partisan organization under the direction of Martin Van Buren in antebellum New York would have helped lay the foundation for the modern political party, which has remained a defining feature of American politics ever since (Case 4)?

Although the federal Constitution provided a vital framework for governance, the full workings of democratic decision making always extended far beyond the formal institutions of government. This can be seen not only in Dorr's Rebellion and Van Buren's Albany Regency, but in everything from the critical role of the press in informing the public to the immense power of social reform movements in reshaping the political landscape. Corporations, labor unions, social and civic organizations, religious bodies, educational institutions, special interest groups of every imaginable variety—these too have proved integral to the workings of American democracy in a multitude of ways.

Such institutional complexity is surely part of the reason why accurately identifying and diagnosing democratic maladies has always proved challenging. Even among the most sophisticated of observers, there is often a tendency to focus mainly on formal institutions, such as the filibuster in the U.S. Senate or the process of redrawing congressional districts in the states or the rules surrounding money in political campaigns. If only this or that rule or process could be corrected, we're often told, democratic dysfunction could be resolved, or at least dramatically reduced. Yet in a system as complex as ours, problems (and solutions) can easily take root in less visible places, including far away from the official organs of power.

Over recent years numerous commentators have told us that American democracy is broken, or nearly so, and that the culprits include everything from rising income inequality and excessive money in politics to the decline of traditional news media. Perhaps more than anything else, pundits have blamed extreme partisan and ideological divisions for impairing the political process, and for inciting varying degrees of discontent, frustration, and anger in the nation's electorate. Political scientists, meanwhile, have shown that partisan polarization in Congress has reached record levels—that Democrats and Republicans effectively occupy separate spheres on Capitol Hill and that individual members are extremely unlikely to break ranks with their party caucuses when it comes to voting.[2]

By itself, partisan conflict should not be a cause for alarm because it has always been one of the hallmarks of American political life. Yet as we have seen, partisan conflict, while generally constructive, can also prove destructive at times, with the balance depending at least in part on the degree of shared commitment to the democracy itself. Although Americans continue to demonstrate a deep faith in democratic governance, it is nonetheless possible that something important has changed in this regard—that our culture of democracy has atrophied in some way.

For years now, there have been subtle indications that the nation's policy debates have become more focused on specific policy goals and less infused with discussions of democracy—democratic processes, solutions, and objectives—than they once were. Numerous budget hawks in Congress, for example, have called for a balanced budget amendment to the Constitution but without anything like the democratic escape hatch that was so central to the Barnburners' efforts to limit public borrowing in 1840s New York (Case 6). Similarly, education reformers, in urging improvements in the nation's schools, have focused on the promise of enhanced skill sets and a more competitive workforce, but not nearly as often on the promise of more capable citizens and a stronger democracy, which figured so prominently in the common school movement of the mid-nineteenth century (Case 7).

There are also numerous signs that partisan divisions in America are extending well beyond standard political settings, reaching ever further into everyday life. Over recent decades, residential neighborhoods in the United States have become significantly more homogeneous in terms of partisan identification, and a substantially larger number of parents in the United States say they would be upset if their child married someone from a different political party.[3] Since 1960, moreover, Americans have become far less likely to view someone from the other party as "intelligent" and far more likely to view someone from the other party as "selfish."[4]

At the same time, trust in government has fallen to record lows. When asked "How much of the time do you think you can trust government in Washington to do what is right?," the proportion saying "just about always" or "most of the time" declined from 73 percent in 1958 to 36 percent in 1974 to 24 percent in 2014.[5] Perhaps even more striking, when asked "How much trust and confidence do you have in the American people as a whole when it comes to making judgments under our democratic system about the issues facing our country?," the number saying "not very much" or "none at all" increased from 15 percent in 1974 to a high of 43 percent in 2015.[6]

This last shift merits particular attention. If shared faith in the democracy is ultimately the glue that holds Americans together—making one out of many and, in turn, rendering partisan conflict constructive rather than destructive—then any diminution in Americans' faith in each other and in their capacity for self-government is cause for concern. What might account for these changes? Much of the rest of this chapter explores three broad historical developments that, over time, may have eroded citizens' faith and engagement in the democracy, in ways both large and small.

An Unwelcome Consequence of More Orderly Elections

We start with the simple act of voting and how it has changed over time. As we saw in the Australian ballot case (Case 10), American elections looked dramatically different in the nineteenth century from what would become standard practice in the twentieth and still remains the norm today. Although the shift toward the secret ballot is regularly celebrated in civics classes for having cleaned up elections, it might also have wrung some of the life out of our democracy, leaving us with a political system that is a good deal more dignified but perhaps a little less exciting as well.

For much of the nineteenth century, election days were typically lively community events: citizens converged on polling places, which took on an almost carnival atmosphere. There was no shortage of raucous behavior—plenty of drinking, gambling, and even some fighting and "physical intimidation" of opponents.[7] Yet the festivities also engendered a profusion of animated discussion and debate among friends and neighbors. This was democracy in action, with voter turnout during the second half of the nineteenth century regularly reaching as high as 75 to 80 percent in presidential election years.

The system was far from perfect, of course. More than half of the adult population lacked the franchise. And because voting was conducted in public, based on preprinted ballots that were color-coded by party (and produced by the parties themselves), partisan operatives found it easy to buy votes. After paying a voter to cast this or that ballot, an operative could confirm with his own eyes that he had gotten what he paid for, simply by keeping a close watch on the voting window and what color ballot the voter turned in.

Against this backdrop, the introduction of the Australian ballot in the late nineteenth century profoundly changed both the conduct and the tenor of American elections. As reformers had promised, secret voting likely made it more difficult for party machines to buy votes. The shift from party-printed ballots (one per party) to uniform government-printed ballots probably weakened the parties' hold over election days. It may also have strengthened the position of the two major parties relative to third parties, because the latter now found it difficult to get their candidates listed on the official ballot, which had limited space.[8]

Perhaps most important of all, the new focus on secrecy in casting ballots—combined with the new prohibitions on politicking in the immediate vicinity of polling places—very likely dampened the social character of elections all across the country. There was still great excitement and anxiety on election days about who would win and who would lose, but the festive atmosphere that had long been part of the voting process largely disappeared after Australian ballot laws were enacted between the late 1880s and the early 1900s. Elections became "silent and single purpose events" in which citizens came "just to vote and depart for work or home."[9] This was a far cry from the "engaging social experience" that characterized nineteenth-century elections, where voters "talked with friends, threw down shots of free whiskey, listened to lively entertainment, and generally had a good time."[10]

Perhaps not surprisingly, voter turnout declined precipitously at the start of the new century, quickly falling below 65 percent by 1912 and reaching as low as 49 percent by 1920. In fact, turnout has remained between about 50 and 65 percent in presidential elections ever since.

Historians have identified many causes for this sharp drop in turnout. At about the same time that states were adopting Australian ballot laws, most were also introducing voter registration laws that required that each citizen formally register to vote if he wanted to cast a ballot on election day. In some cases these new rules (along with now-notorious devices of disenfranchisement, such as literacy tests) were used intentionally to suppress voting by African Americans and immigrants. Turnout fell especially far in the southern states, where black disenfranchisement was aggressively pursued. But even where the motives for adopting Australian ballot laws and voter registration laws were mainly to attack partisan corruption, the effect was almost always to make voting more difficult, especially for those who had trouble reading and writing English.

Other factors likely played a role as well. The dawn of women's suffrage, in particular, almost certainly contributed to declining turnout in the early twentieth century. Apparently women were initially less likely to vote than men, pulling down overall voter turnout rates once women became part of the electorate. Although the effect was at first quite significant, it was also

Voter Turnout in Presidential Elections, 1840–2000 (percent)

Source: Adapted from John P. McIver, "Voter Turnout in Presidential Elections, by State: 1824–2000," table Eb62-113, in *Historical Statistics of the United States, Earliest Times to the Present: Millennial Edition*, ed. Susan B. Carter et al. (New York: Cambridge University Press, 2006), series Eb62.

relatively short-lived, disappearing entirely among cohorts of women born after ratification of the Nineteenth Amendment in 1920.[11]

Of all the various factors that have been singled out, the passage of Australian ballot laws probably had the largest impact over the long term.[12] The shift to Australian-style ballots made voting both more burdensome and, frankly, less lucrative for individual voters. Instead of simply handing in party-printed ballots as in the past, voters now had to fill out government-printed ballots, which included candidates from all major parties. This made the act of voting more challenging, especially for those who had little or no schooling, and it complicated the operations of party machines by making split-ticket voting far more likely.[13] At the same time, as we have seen, the fact that voting was now secret ensured that party operatives would find it less attractive to pay for votes, because they could no longer confirm how individual citizens had voted after illicitly agreeing to trade their votes for money.[14]

Harder to measure, but probably also more fundamental in their effects on turnout, were profound changes in the very character of voting in

America. Vote buying receded, to be sure, but so too did the festive atmosphere of polling places on election day. With the introduction of secret ballots, voting was transformed from a highly social activity into an intensely individualized one. Elections became cleaner and more orderly, but also dramatically less exciting and a lot less fun.[15] Although turnout declined, the change was ultimately about more than just turnout. It was, in an important sense, about the nation's *culture of democracy*.

Over the second half of the nineteenth century, what historian Michael McGerr has called "spectacular displays of exuberant partisanship" were the heart and soul of a very public style of mass politics, tightly tied to—and largely orchestrated by—the major political parties. In presidential election years, once the party nominating conventions had chosen their candidates, typically by late summer, "local party members 'ratified' the ticket with speeches, parades, bell-ringing, and cannon fire." From that point until election day, public displays of party loyalty—including mass rallies, torchlight parades, marching companies, and open meetings—were pervasive, particularly in the North. It was, as McGerr explains, part of an "extroverted concept of partisanship" in which men "voted twice . . . once at the polls by casting a ballot, and once in the streets by participating in campaign pageantry."[16]

For most of these men, partisanship was a vital element of personal identity, helping to shape how they saw themselves and others, with whom they associated, what publications they read, and how they interpreted local and national events. Partisan identification was, in turn, one of the central cleavages of American life, closely aligned with ethnic and religious divisions as well as a sharply partitioned press, with most newspapers solidly in one partisan camp or the other.[17] In fact, the extreme partisanship of the late nineteenth century bears more than a passing resemblance to today's intense partisan polarization, in which citizens of opposing parties hold drastically different worldviews, concentrate in different geographic areas, and increasingly rely on different sources for news.

Yet the resemblance goes only so far. The highly social, public, and engaged partisanship of the nineteenth century, marked by exuberance more than cynicism, has little analogue today. Although we obviously cannot compare public opinion surveys across the two periods, today's deteriorating trust in the "American people as a whole" might have felt strangely out of place—even vaguely unpatriotic—in the late nineteenth century. As James Bryce observed, writing in 1894, Americans of the time held a "reverence for 'the People,'" which "makes them believe that the majority are right."[18]

By the start of the twentieth century, the style of mass politics that had become such a visible and distinguishing feature of American life was notably in retreat. Not only had polling places gone quiet and turnout declined, but the mass rallies, torchlight parades, and other pageantry of nineteenth-century presidential campaigns were rapidly disappearing as well.[19] Historians will continue to argue about whether the Australian ballot was one of the key triggers for this shift or whether, alternatively, the rise of the Australian ballot was simply one piece of a broader transition at the turn of the century toward a less brash, less communal, and far less partisan style of politics.

Either way, the consequences were profound. The corruption and even violence that had accompanied the rough-and-tumble of nineteenth-century electoral politics mercifully abated, but so too, it seems, did the energy and engagement of a significant slice of the American electorate. One result was that American voters were left with less of a common democratic experience, as their campaign marches and meetings and their raucous festivities on election day rapidly became relics of a bygone era.

Reaching the Limit of Universal Suffrage

A second unexpected challenge to America's culture of democracy emerged later in the twentieth century, with the achievement of near-universal suffrage among adult citizens. It may seem strange to characterize the attainment of universal suffrage this way—as a concern—when it clearly represents a great triumph of democratic values. Yet this triumph, paradoxically, also presents a problem, because the battles to expand suffrage over roughly the first two centuries after independence had often helped to stimulate democratic commitments and engagement. Now that the long struggle for universal suffrage is largely complete—with no group of adult Americans apart from recent immigrants and felons legally barred from voting—the restorative power of broad-based suffrage movements has apparently reached its limit as well.

This power was already visible in the push for universal white male suffrage, especially in the early nineteenth century (Case 5); in the fight for women's suffrage, which culminated in 1920 with ratification of the Nineteenth Amendment (Case 17); and in the campaign for black voting rights after the Civil War and again in the 1960s, following nearly a century of vicious race-based disenfranchisement (Case 16). In each case, reformers successfully forced an extended public discussion of the most basic of democratic values, the franchise, and effectively pressed countless Americans to confront the reality of incomplete democratic representation. Whether it was Thomas Dorr or Alice Paul or Martin Luther King Jr., leading suffrage reformers across the nation's history found novel ways to shock the conscience of the electorate, bringing into full view severe contradictions in American democracy that had previously been hiding in plain sight.[20]

King's strategy in Selma in 1965 is especially revealing in this regard. Since the late 1950s, he and his compatriots in the civil rights movement had discovered that even a poor and largely disenfranchised group could grab hold of the national agenda by harnessing the press in service to their cause. As we saw in the meat inspection case (Case 12), voters often remain uninformed about major public policy problems because they have little incentive to investigate them on their own, which has the effect of empowering special interests.[21] The press, however, can fundamentally change the equation, informing and even mobilizing the public on important policy issues through stories that dramatically seize the people's attention.[22]

What King and other leaders of the civil rights movement discovered in the years leading up to Selma—perhaps particularly from the so-called children's crusade in Birmingham in 1963—is that they could essentially *create* a scandal that the press would cover (or, more precisely, bring a long-running scandal into dramatically sharper focus) by peacefully provoking a violent response from white officials. They learned in particular that if they picked their locations and their officials carefully (such as Birmingham with Police Commissioner Eugene "Bull" Connor, or Selma with Sheriff Jim Clark), they could virtually guarantee a violent episode that would attract the press and capture national attention. By harnessing the press—and especially television—in this way, King and his colleagues were able to bring the horrors of black disenfranchisement into American living rooms nationwide, creating a political groundswell for change that led directly to the Voting Rights Act of 1965.[23]

Although the use of television was new, mass suffrage movements had long highlighted tensions between prejudice and principle in American democracy. From a modern vantage point, historical discussions of democratic principle can set off countless alarm bells. College students regularly complain that ostensibly principled declarations from the past—for example, that "all men are created equal" or that governments derive "their just powers from the consent of the governed"—were profoundly hypocritical across much of the nation's history, particularly over the long period when African Americans were enslaved and the still longer period when the majority of adults lacked the right to vote. Sadly, even in a democracy with a deep faith in the rule of law, fierce prejudice can and does prevail—including on a legal basis—over long periods of time, and rank hypocrisy is an inevitable by-product.

One lesson from the suffrage movements, however, is that political hypocrisy can have an upside—or, to put it another way, aspirational principles can prove to be of great value, even when they are egregiously violated in practice. After all, it is precisely when hypocrisy of this sort is dramatically exposed (as it was in Birmingham and Selma), and when Americans are thus forced to choose between their prejudices, on the one hand, and the principles they hold dear, on the other, that profound democratic values are most likely to be honored in practice. This is not always the outcome, of course. Too often, prejudice prevails—sometimes in naked form, but more frequently dressed up as virtue. Nevertheless, democratic principle has fortunately triumphed often enough (after Selma and many other battles) to create a positive trajectory—a long, hard path of progress—and to remind us, ultimately, that democratic ideals matter.

In manifold ways, therefore, the great suffrage movements of the nineteenth and twentieth centuries revived and bolstered democratic culture, periodically putting democracy itself at the center of public discourse and turning the whole nation into a grand civics classroom. Now, however, with the right to vote having become nearly universal since the 1970s, the days of mass suffrage movements are almost certainly behind us. If so, this means that another vital source of democratic energy and uplift may be gone—gone for the best of reasons, but gone nonetheless.

Expanding a More Distant Level of Government

A third long-term challenge to the nation's culture of democracy stems from
the dramatic expansion of the federal government, relative to both state and
local governments, since the early 1930s. There is obviously intense debate
in the United States about whether the enlargement of federal authority
has been good or bad for the country. Whichever way one comes out on
this question, some increase in the size and scope of the federal government
was likely inevitable, given both the growth of economic activity across state
lines and the intensity of the Great Depression in the early 1930s. The point
here, however, is not to litigate the proper role of the federal government,
economic or otherwise, but instead to suggest that the federal government
is inherently more distant from the people—not only because of geography

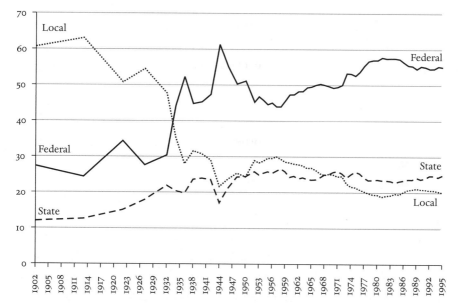

**Shares of Nonmilitary Government Expenditure, by Level of Government,
1902–1995 (percent)**

Sources: Concept for this chart drawn from John Joseph Wallis, "The Birth of the
Old Federalism: Financing the New Deal, 1932–1940," *Journal of Economic History* 44,
no. 1 (Mar. 1984): 141. Data from *Historical Statistics of the United States* (2006), series
Ea15-17, Ea134, Ea177, Ea350-352, Ea490-493. Intergovernmental transfers are attributed to
the level of government making the transfer, rather than to the level receiving it.

(physical distance), but also because it has long been more insulated from popular influence as compared to state and local governments.

Today, along numerous dimensions, the federal government is arguably less democratic—or, at least, less open to popular influence—than its state and local counterparts. Although all members of the U.S. Congress, in both the House and the Senate, are chosen by popular election, only the House is apportioned according to population. No member of the federal judiciary, nor any member of the federal executive branch other than the president and vice president, is elected by the people. In fact, even the presidential ticket itself is officially decided indirectly through the electoral college, allowing a presidential candidate who secured fewer popular votes than his opponent to win the presidency as recently as 2000. There is no such thing, moreover, as a federal initiative, referendum, or recall, meaning that direct democracy plays no role in federal decision making at all.

These limits on popular electoral input at the federal level naturally stem from the federal Constitution, which was drafted in 1787 when the idea of implementing representative democracy on a large scale was still quite new. Indeed, many of the nation's political leaders at the time actively worried about an "excess of democracy," as Elbridge Gerry of Massachusetts put it at the Constitutional Convention in 1787.[24] The thirteen original states, most of which had adopted their own constitutions early in the Revolutionary War, imposed similar restrictions, sharply limiting the number of elective offices and permitting no direct democracy at all.

Before long, however, state-level democracy had dramatically opened up, as new constitutions were adopted and old ones thoroughly amended. At roughly the same time that states were dismantling property requirements on voting, they were also significantly expanding the number of elective offices. Lower houses of the legislative branch had already been popularly elected in colonial times, but after independence the election of upper houses also became common, though in some cases with more restrictive voting requirements. Elective offices multiplied in the executive branch as well. By 1820, out of the 23 states that then made up the union, 13 provided for popular election of the governor, 8 for the lieutenant governor, and 2 for the state treasurer. By 1860, out of 33 states, 31 allowed for the popular election of the governor, 21 for the lieutenant governor, 17 for the secretary of state, 17 for the state treasurer, 12 for the auditor or comptroller, and 11 for the attorney general.[25]

Currently, beyond providing for the popular election of the governor and members of the upper and lower houses of the legislature, the vast majority of states elect at least five other government officials, and some elect as many as nine or more.[26] There are also typically many elective offices populating local governments. In her book *Becoming a Candidate,* Jennifer Lawless writes, "At the local level, literally hundreds of thousands of women and men serve as mayors, city and town council members, school board members, parks commissioners, dog catchers, sheriffs, soil and water conservation directors, coroners, auditors, sewage disposal authorities, tax collectors, and recorders of deeds, to name just a handful of elective positions."[27]

Direct democracy, meanwhile, was occasionally tried at the state level during the nineteenth century, as we saw in antebellum New York (Cases 6 and 7), but the initiative, referendum, and recall were adopted—and used—on a much broader basis at both the state and local levels beginning in the early twentieth century (Case 13). Already by the end of 1918, twenty states and a great many cities had adopted the initiative, mostly but not exclusively in the West; and by 2003, twenty-four states and about half of all American cities had the initiative. John Matsusaka estimated in 2004 that upward of 200 million Americans (approximately 70 percent of the total population) "live in either a city or state with the initiative, and by most indications the numbers are growing."[28]

Similarly, with respect to the judiciary, the popular election of judges at the state level began to take off starting in 1846, when New York State adopted a new constitution providing for the election of judges (Case 6). Although there had been a few scattered experiments with judicial elections before that, including in Georgia in 1812 and Mississippi in 1832, the year 1846 was a turning point. From that point forward, all new states adopted some form of judicial elections, and many of the existing ones also joined the trend. Most states modified these arrangements over time, with some adopting nonpartisan elections or retention elections for judges, and others abandoning certain judicial elections altogether, yet the overall direction remained clear.[29] Today the American Bar Association reports that 38 states hold some form of election for their highest courts, 31 hold elections for their appellate courts (of the 39 states that have intermediate appellate courts), and 39 states hold elections of some type for their trial courts.[30]

In sharp contrast to these dramatic changes at the state and local levels since the late eighteenth century, there has been far less expansion of formal popular influence at the federal level. At least part of the reason for this difference, it appears, is that the federal Constitution is exceedingly difficult to amend, particularly as compared to the state constitutions, as we saw in the case of the Equal Rights Amendment (Case 17). Whereas the federal Constitution has been amended only twenty-seven times since it was first ratified in 1788 (and only seventeen times since the first ten amendments—the Bill of Rights—were ratified at the end of 1791), the total number of successful amendments to state constitutions has been 7,481, or about 150 per state, on average.[31] Notably, of the twenty-seven federal amendments, three expanded the franchise (to African American men in 1870, to women in 1920, and to those 18 to 20 years old in 1971), and one (the Seventeenth Amendment, ratified in 1913) required the popular election of U.S. senators. Apart from these changes, however, the opportunities for citizens to vote on federal officials, let alone federal policies, remain today largely as they were when George Washington was elected president—by way of the electoral college—in 1788–1789.

By design, therefore, the U.S. Constitution offers only a limited number of formal avenues for popular influence over federal decision making. Those avenues have widened since the late eighteenth century as a result of expanded suffrage, but the *number* of avenues has increased by only one, with adoption of the Seventeenth Amendment. Limited popular influence presumably seemed perfectly reasonable in the early years of the republic when the federal government was relatively small and citizens intersected with it only infrequently in their daily lives. Yet even when the federal government greatly expanded its reach in the twentieth century—regulating our foods and drugs, insuring our bank accounts, providing for our retirement, and so forth—there was little corresponding effort to expand the formal structures of democratic accountability at the federal level.

The result, to steal a phrase, was a mounting democratic deficit, in which the fastest-growing level of government continued to offer the fewest opportunities for voter input at election time. If Americans' common faith in democratic governance and their trust in government itself have both declined over the past forty to fifty years, as public opinion polls strongly suggest, then perhaps this federal democratic deficit is at least part of the reason why. Indeed, it may be more than a coincidence that state and local governments, both of which offer a profusion of voting opportunities for citizens, have seen their measures of public trust hold up quite well over the past half century, whereas analogous measures of trust in the federal government have fallen sharply.[32]

Of course, constitutional constraints are not the only reason federal decision making can feel distant for the average citizen. As we saw in Case 18, twentieth-century lawmakers took pains to insulate the Federal Reserve from popular influence, presumably on the theory that monetary policy is best left to disinterested experts. A standard critique of the federal government more generally, particularly since the 1930s, has been that too much authority is placed in the hands of experts, without adequate oversight and input from elected representatives or the people themselves. There is no need to get into the substance of those debates here. Rather, it is simply worth noting that the federal government has faced—and will likely continue to face—significant questions about democratic accountability, with implications not only for the way public policy is made, but also, as I have tried to suggest, for the nation's culture of democracy, which goes to the heart of the political system itself.

Revitalizing the Nation's Culture of Democracy

Perhaps no other student of American politics recognized the central importance of political culture as early or as clearly as Alexis de Tocqueville. In *Democracy in America,* he wrote about the vital of role of "manners" and "customs" in maintaining the "democratic republic in the United States."[33] Nearly twenty years later, in 1853, he penned a letter to a friend emphasizing the limited role of formal institutions in shaping a political system and the much larger role of culture:

> I accord institutions only a secondary influence over the destiny of men. . . . I am thoroughly convinced that political societies are not what their laws make them but what they are prepared in advance to be by the feelings, the beliefs, the ideas, the habits of heart and mind of the men who compose them, and what native disposition and education made these men to be.[34]

For Tocqueville, the essence of a political system ultimately rested on these cultural attributes—"the habits of heart and mind" that shape individuals' modes of understanding, their behavior, and their social interactions more profoundly than any law. As we now turn to consider the health of America's democracy in the twenty-first century, amid myriad claims about its deficiencies and dysfunction, we need to focus especially on the nation's democratic culture and how it is faring.

In the introduction to this volume, we explored the remarkable power of political conflict for both good and ill, and what factors may have distinguished productive from destructive conflict over the course of American history. We saw that political culture—and particularly citizens' commitment to the democracy and the democratic process—may have been of distinct importance in this respect. Over much of the nation's history, a common and deeply felt commitment to the democracy appears to have served as a sort of societal glue, binding people together even in the face of intense political disagreement. This common commitment arguably helped to render even some of the most bitter partisan battles constructive rather than destructive; and its breakdown in the late 1850s—especially in the southern states, where faith in the national democracy had withered—may have opened the way to the most destructive of all conflicts in American history, the Civil War.

In the opening pages of this conclusion, we saw scattered pieces of evidence, mostly from public opinion surveys, suggesting that Americans' common commitment to the democracy has weakened in recent decades, and we explored three long-term historical shifts that may have contributed to this change: the decline of a boisterous, outdoor style of politics so typical of the late nineteenth century; the end of mass suffrage movements and the democratic energy they unleashed; and the rise of a federal democratic deficit, which accompanied the dramatic growth of the federal government during and after the Great Depression. So long as there was a sufficient degree of consensus across the major political parties, as has frequently been suggested by historians of mid-twentieth-century America, the effects of a weakened culture of democracy may not have been especially large or troublesome.[35] Once partisan polarization started to rise, however, as it did beginning especially in the late 1970s and early 1980s, the situation became considerably more fraught.[36]

If our culture of democracy has in fact become less robust over recent decades, leaving the nation less able to capitalize on the benefits of partisan conflict and more exposed to the dangers, is there anything that can be done about this? What follows are a few tentative suggestions for revitalizing democratic engagement and commitment, based largely on the historical analysis outlined above.

Fourth of July in November?

One idea for refreshing the nation's political culture starts with the act of voting and potentially reinjecting some life into the process. Although it would be a mistake to repeal Australian ballot laws and risk return to the days of voter intimidation, vote buying, and corrupt party machines, there may be ways to restore some of the energy and community spirit that characterized elections in the late nineteenth century without abandoning the secret ballot. One option would be to make Election Day a day of celebration, much like the Fourth of July. There have been many proposals over the years to turn the "first Tuesday after the first Monday in November" into a national holiday. The main goal, however, should not simply be to give citizens time off from work in order to vote, but also to create an exciting, social environment around voting, which—as we have seen—was correlated with high levels of turnout in the nineteenth century.

Remarkably, three political scientists from Yale and Tufts set out to test this very proposition about a decade ago. Noting that "Americans have lost touch with the festive milieu surrounding nineteenth century elections," the researchers ran a series of randomized experiments to determine the effect of a "more celebratory and community-focused atmosphere" on voter turnout. To do this, they organized festivals at a series of polling places (offering "food, fun, and music," but not alcohol), and they found a moderately large and statistically significant impact on voting.[37]

There has also long been what amounts to a large natural experiment in Puerto Rico, where Election Day is in fact a holiday, the atmosphere around elections has been described as "carnavalesque" (involving "countless rallies, caravans, and festivities"), and voter turnout is dramatically higher than on the mainland. In fact, a doctoral dissertation on the subject, finished in 1999, notes that the "environment surrounding elections in Puerto Rico is very similar to that seen last century in the United States."[38]

According to the economist Richard Freeman, voter turnout in Puerto Rico in the years 1992–2000 was 77 percent in general elections, sharply higher than turnout for U.S. presidential elections in the states and "nearly double the voting rate for Puerto Ricans residing in the US." Not surprisingly, Freeman suggests that one reason for the high turnout is that "Puerto Rico makes its general elections a holiday and treats the day as a special political event, with political parties mobilizing their supporters throughout the day."[39]

Voter turnout is only one aspect of citizen engagement in a democracy, and high levels of voter participation do not necessarily signal the sort of deep democratic commitment needed to bring citizens together and help ensure that political conflict remains productive. But buoyant elections with high turnout nevertheless seem like a good start and may be something that can be re-created from an earlier time, even without giving up the obvious benefits of the secret ballot.

Echoes of Thomas Dorr?

Closely connected with the question of how we vote is who votes and who is allowed to vote. Over time, mass suffrage movements have played a powerful role in American life—not only by vastly expanding the electorate in line with core democratic principles (and often elevating the principles themselves), but also by fostering outpourings of civic energy and self-reflection along the way. With universal adult suffrage now largely in place and new mass suffrage movements—we hope—no longer needed, are there constructive ways to reignite national discussions about the integrity of our democracy and the meaning of "We the People"?

To an extent this is already happening, through debates over such things as voter identification laws, the disenfranchisement of felons, and paths to citizenship for immigrants, legal and illegal alike. Even if large-scale changes in the franchise, comparable to the Nineteenth Amendment or the Voting Rights Act, are unlikely to come again, there will always be significant issues related to suffrage on the public agenda. What is far less certain is whether these issues can capture public attention on anything like the scale of a mass suffrage movement.

A campaign for a constitutional amendment focused on election law could conceivably provide such a catalyst, and reformers of various stripes have already suggested many such amendments. Given partisan polarization in Congress, however, the likelihood that both the House and the Senate would muster the necessary two-thirds majorities to send a proposed amendment to the states—on virtually any issue—seems exceedingly low. In fact, the last time Congress sent a proposed amendment to the states (the District of Columbia Voting Rights Amendment, which was never ratified) was in 1978, making the current dry spell the third longest on record at the time of this writing, just two years short of the forty-year stretch from 1869 to 1909 and thirteen years behind the fifty-one-year stretch starting in 1810.[40]

One intriguing alternative to working through the official amendment process would involve taking a page from Thomas Dorr, the suffrage reformer in antebellum Rhode Island who helped organize an extralegal state constitutional convention, an extralegal ratification process of the "People's Constitution," and an extralegal election of a rebel government (Case 5). Although Dorr was ultimately convicted of treason for agreeing to serve as governor of the rebel government, the original process of drafting and ratifying an alternative constitution was simply an exercise in free speech, which ended up captivating the state. The fact that a majority of men across Rhode Island, both legal voters and nonvoters alike, approved a mock constitution eliminating property requirements on voting was an immense moral victory. So large, in fact, that the official state government soon felt compelled to move toward universal white male suffrage, even after Dorr himself had been imprisoned.

The question today is whether something similar could be done at the national level that would have anything like the moral force of the People's Constitution in Rhode Island. Imagine, for example, a reform-minded group proposing one or more election-related amendments to the U.S. Constitution, and then organizing an extralegal ratification process that involved unofficial popular voting—possibly online—in every state of the nation. Imagine further that the group announced at the start that "ratification" would require popular majority votes in at least three-fourths of the states. If the number of adults voting by state turned out to be sizable and the three-fourths requirement were achieved, would lawmakers feel compelled to take up the amendments on an official basis, even though the exercise itself had no legal force? Equally important, might the gambit provoke a vigorous national discussion, of both the amendments themselves and why it had been necessary to circumvent Congress in the first place?

Much would depend not only on the organizational capacity and integrity of the reformers involved, but also on the proposed amendments and whether and how deeply they resonated with the American people. Possible amendments could range from the symbolic (introducing a national right to vote, which, remarkably, has not yet been guaranteed in the Constitution) to the practical (establishing Election Day as a national holiday) to the dramatic (overturning a controversial Supreme Court decision, such as *Citizens United,* or dismantling the electoral college). As with Dorr's alternative constitution, the goal would be to find a proposal or set of proposals that could not conceivably be passed in the existing political climate but that nonetheless reflects core democratic principles, exposing a contradiction that would demand civic engagement, debate, and ultimately action—much as the mass suffrage movements did in the past.

Of, by, and for the People?

Turning now to the federal government and its rather limited opportunities for formal input from the citizenry, there are naturally more than a few ways to address this challenge. The most extreme approach would involve the creation of additional federal elective offices. Imagine, for instance, a constitutional amendment mandating the direct election of the U.S. attorney general and the U.S. Treasury secretary. Although there is ample precedent at the state level for such a move, this would mark a radical change in the federal executive branch, where the process for selecting cabinet officers has remained largely fixed in place since 1789. As a result, even if an effective argument could be made that the benefits of such a shift would outweigh the costs (which remains an open question, to say the least), the odds of securing the necessary constitutional changes are exceedingly low.

A more promising approach might focus on the creation of new channels of popular influence over federal policy, even if they did not involve formal lawmaking power. Congress, for example, could authorize a federal initiative-and-referendum system that would be strictly advisory in nature. To get on the ballot, proposed initiative and referendum items would have to meet certain minimum signature requirements and potentially other tests of strength as well, such as preliminary approval by voters in more than a minimum number of states. Once on the federal ballot, these items would require a simple majority (or, if Congress preferred, a supermajority) in a national election. Although the results of these votes could not—without a constitutional amendment—be anything more than advisory to Congress, they would presumably carry significant political weight, clearly signaling lawmakers about voters' concerns and intentions. At the same time, such an experiment in direct democracy at the federal level could help to engage and educate the national electorate, providing citizens with new opportunities both to get involved in an otherwise distant political process and to express their interests and views on the national stage.

Another way to increase citizen involvement in federal policymaking would look toward small groups of citizens rather than the electorate as a whole. In particular, it might be possible to expand the use of juries well beyond their traditional role in the nation's courtrooms. The jury is certainly a remarkable institution. By virtually all accounts, the vast majority of citizens who are called to jury duty take their responsibility extremely seriously.[41] And although no institution is perfect, juries have apparently functioned well enough that Americans have continued to entrust them with the most consequential of decisions in both criminal and civil trials. In a survey conducted for the American Bar Association in 2004, 75 percent of those polled agreed with the statement "If I were a participant in a trial I would want a jury to decide my case, rather than a judge."[42] Given the success of juries in a judicial context, perhaps we should try to utilize the same basic institution in other contexts as well.

In fact, there have already been a number experiments in a variety of countries bringing citizen juries—and numerically larger citizen assemblies— into the policymaking process.[43] The political scientist Archon Fung, for example, has reported on an effort in British Columbia in which 160 people were selected at random from voting lists and asked to serve thirty days over a year-long period and ultimately recommend a new electoral system for the Canadian province. Based in part on this example, Fung has suggested that citizen assemblies be used in the United States for redistricting decisions to help solve the age-old problem of partisan gerrymandering.[44] Juries (or assemblies) of this sort might also be useful for a range of other policy purposes, from weighing difficult budget decisions to recommending which military bases or post offices ought to be closed in the face of budget pressures.

Utilizing randomly selected groups of citizens in this way promises two related benefits. First, it could inject a valuable citizens' perspective into policy debates. In evaluating a policy question—such as which of several budget proposals would best serve public needs—a citizen jury, like a trial jury, would not only deliberate on its own but also listen to witnesses, including expert witnesses, and sift through available evidence over an extended period of time. Whereas elected representatives often finish a legislative hearing or debate with precisely the same view they went in with, the members of citizen juries—according to researchers who have studied them—often change their minds in response to evidence or arguments.[45] The report of a citizen jury would always be strictly advisory, absent a constitutional amendment that conferred specific lawmaking authority. Still, such a report might bring a less partisan, less ideological orientation to a policy problem and confer significant legitimacy on the recommended solution.

Second, and equally important, the use of juries in a policymaking context could help reduce the sense of distance between the citizenry and the federal government. Those who are selected to sit on these juries would have a chance to influence federal policy directly, and there is evidence suggesting that many jurors increase their civic engagement, including their likelihood of voting, after serving.[46] Even the much larger number of citizens not selected to serve, moreover, could well feel a greater sense of confidence in the policy process, so long as lawmakers appear to take the work of the citizen juries seriously. Just as the trial jury is a highly respected institution in the United States that increases confidence in the judicial system, the citizen jury could potentially serve a similar role with respect to the two other branches of government.

Remarkably, the special role of the trial jury in helping to influence American political culture was already evident to Tocqueville when he published the first volume of *Democracy in America* in 1835. The "system of the jury," in his view, was as important to "the sovereignty of the people as universal suffrage. These institutions are two instruments of equal power, which contribute to the supremacy of the majority."[47] Tocqueville argued further that the jury system not only empowered the people, but also fundamentally shaped them:

In whatever manner the jury be applied, it cannot fail to exercise a powerful influence upon the national character. . . . It invests each citizen with a kind of magistracy, it makes them all feel the duties which they are bound to discharge toward society, and the part which they take in the Government. By obliging men to turn their attention to affairs which are not exclusively their own, it rubs off that individual egotism which is the rust of society.[48]

Although Tocqueville never suggested that the jury be used outside of the judicial system, he certainly understood its enormous power as an institution. "Thus the jury," he wrote, "which is the most energetic means of making the people rule, is also the most efficacious means of teaching it to rule well." It was, he thought, a vital source of civic education, "a gratuitous public school ever open."[49] Nearly 200 years after Tocqueville penned these words, it may be time to expand the province of the jury so that the legislative and executive branches can benefit from it as well.

Reprising Horace Mann?

One last proposal for helping to sustain and strengthen the nation's culture of democracy—very much in line with Tocqueville's metaphor—relates to education and the role of civics in our schools.[50] As we saw in Case 7, the Massachusetts reformer Horace Mann believed that a broad system of public education was essential for nurturing strong citizens and sustaining a healthy democracy. Toward this end, he suggested it was necessary not only to teach students to read and write and to train them in moral behavior and thought, but also to provide instruction on the history and workings of American government. "Citizens of a Republic," he wrote in 1848, must "understand something of the true nature and functions of the government under which they live."[51]

Mann was by no means the first American to make these arguments. Thomas Jefferson had raised similar ideas in calling for free schools in Virginia in 1779, and Benjamin Rush of Philadelphia, who like Jefferson had signed the Declaration of Independence, sketched a curriculum in republican citizenship in 1798. Yet Mann, as the first secretary of the State Board of Education in Massachusetts, was able to carry these ideas further than his predecessors.[52]

Still, the teaching of civics in the nation's schools appears to have been rather limited over much of the nineteenth century, only beginning to take off in the early 1900s, particularly in the North. "Throughout the Progressive era," writes Jeffrey Mirel, a historian of American education, "the teaching of Bible-based morality in urban public schools faded away and nonsectarian civic education rapidly filled the void." With immigrants arriving in large numbers, educational leaders renewed the push for "Americanization," but in an increasingly secular context. As Mirel put it, "Teaching the 'old time religion' was supplanted by teaching students the American civil religion."[53] In 1916 two blue-ribbon panels recommended an increased focus on civics, government, and democracy in the nation's schools, helping to "set the pattern that persisted for more than four decades, a pattern that included civics courses, usually at the eighth or ninth grade, and government courses, usually at the twelfth grade." U.S. history classes also became standard practice across virtually all districts, reaching 97 percent of high school students by the early 1960s.[54]

Many proponents believe that civics education subsequently suffered a sharp decline in the United States, especially following the social and political turmoil of the late 1960s and early 1970s.[55] Although some analysts suggest that the percentage of high school students taking American government courses began rising again in the 1990s, concerns about the state of civics education remain widespread.[56] In fact, a growing chorus of voices characterizes the current state of civics education as woefully inadequate. "The evidence that we have failed to transmit basic civic knowledge to young adults," writes policy analyst William Galston, "is now incontrovertible."[57] Critics note that over two-thirds of students failed to reach proficiency on a national civics assessment in 2006, that there were large disparities in performance by race and income, and that students "continue to be bored by civics and social studies and to rate them among their least favorite subjects," in the words of Sandra Day O'Connor, a former U.S. Supreme Court Justice.[58]

Recent years have seen the rise of numerous organizations dedicated to improving and expanding civics instruction in the nation's schools. Many reformers insist that effective civics education promises highly tangible results, including increased rates of voting and other forms of political participation.[59] Research in this area is thin, however, and the studies that have been conducted, especially regarding the effects of civics education on voting, have shown mixed results.[60]

The deeper question is not whether there are discernible changes in rates of participation, however attractive that would be, but rather whether educating students in the dynamics of democracy contributes to a more capable and effective citizenry, better able to govern even amid sharp disagreements over public policy. Although this question may never be definitively answered, there are good reasons to believe the answer is closer to yes than to no.

In particular, civics education may be of crucial importance precisely because it is so easy for young citizens—indeed, for all of us—to take democracy for granted. Given how much can go wrong in a political system and how many political catastrophes litter the world's historical landscape, it is nothing short of miraculous when a political system works at all, let alone year after year and generation after generation. Fostering an appreciation of all that is necessary to make our democracy work—and how much is at stake—may be at least one way to inspire citizens and heighten their interest in the hard work of governing.

If so, the next question is how exactly to foster that appreciation—that is, what to teach and how best to teach it. Many who favor a revival of civics in the nation's schools stress the importance of factual knowledge, including key events and personalities in American history and the core structures and mechanics of government under the Constitution. Others highlight the value of active or experiential learning, such as simulations of key governmental processes and decisions or in-class debates about current events. One of the great advantages of teaching history by the case method is that it brings together both objectives in a highly dynamic way. In fact, the hope of developing a new and more engaging way to teach about these issues was one of the main reasons for creating a case-based course on the history of American democracy in the first place, and thus a core motivation for this book as well.

Whatever educators decide are the best ways to teach their students about governance and citizenship, the point here is simply that the potential benefits, including to the nation's culture of democracy, are hard to overstate. Indeed, the benefits could begin to accrue even before any new classroom sessions begin, since a lively public debate about the future of civics curricula—about what to cover and how best to cover it—could prove enormously salutary in and of itself.

As Horace Mann declared in the middle of the nineteenth century, with perhaps just a touch of hyperbole, "It may be an easy thing to make a republic; but it is a very laborious thing to make republicans; and woe to the republic that rests upon no better foundations than ignorance, selfishness, and passion!"[61] Clearly, we have our work cut out for us.

Finally, as we think about these and other proposals for strengthening American democracy, it is worth remembering that the nation's political system has proved surprisingly resilient in the past. In almost every generation, pundits have warned that the republic was faltering and that political calamity was just around the corner, yet in the vast majority of cases the calamity never came.

In 1810, for example, the fiercely pro-Federalist *Connecticut Courant* warned that "the great American republic has of late been travelling fast in the broad road to despotism and ruin."[62] Eighty-two years later, the journalist William D. McCracken, who strongly favored adoption of the initiative and referendum, announced that it "has become somewhat of a commonplace assertion that politics in the United States have reached the lowest stage to which they may safely go. . . . [N]o democracy can hope to withstand the corrupting influences now at work in our midst, unless certain radical reforms are carried to a successful conclusion."[63] Fast-forward roughly another eighty years and John Kenneth Galbraith is said to have mused "that every publisher wants his author's book to be entitled 'The Crisis in American Democracy'—because he knows that that title will sell."[64] Like the biblical burning bush, the American political system regularly appears to be aflame, but so far—apart from the devastation of the Civil War—it has never actually been consumed.

Given this pattern, we need to ask ourselves whether oft-repeated concerns about the health of the democracy are perhaps overstated. Professional commentators, of course, have an interest in making dire predictions to help build their audience, and tough talk about impending crises can make us all feel a little more important, which may help to explain why politicians tell us every election cycle, without exception, that this is the most consequential election of our lifetime. It is also possible, of course, that the democracy's weaknesses are simply more visible than its strengths, leading even the most objective observers to underestimate its staying power. At the same time, there is always the chance that the pessimists are right—this time around—because something fundamental has changed. There is no way to know for sure.

Fortunately, if we are going to err on one side or the other, it is probably better to worry too much about the health of the democracy than to worry too little. There may even be some benefit from this sort of political hypochondria, if it ends up driving greater interest in potential reforms of the democratic system. Given the constant push of special interests to influence policymaking, often at the expense of the general public, there could well be an advantage to changing the rules from time to time, even if the new rules are not intrinsically better than the old. Special interests, after all, are constantly searching for cracks in the policy process that they can exploit to exert disproportionate influence over policy outcomes. By changing the process periodically—for example, by shifting the locus of policymaking in a given area from a legislature to an independent commission, or back again—we force special interests to look anew for cracks to exploit, potentially keeping them off balance. Some degree of political hypochondria, therefore, may help to ensure ongoing renewal of the democracy, and may even be one of the sources of its remarkable resilience over time.

So what are we to make of the countless warnings over recent years that American democracy is in trouble? While we can take comfort in the fact that the most ominous forecasts have almost always proved inaccurate in the past, it would be a mistake to ignore them altogether. With careful observers expressing fears about everything from relentless partisan warfare and excessive money in politics to rising economic inequality and mounting anger within the electorate, a historical perspective offers not only some welcome rays of hope but also guidance on what might be most needed to steady the ship of state in a stormy sea.

In the introduction to this volume and again here in the conclusion, I have emphasized one challenge above all others, relating to the nation's culture of democracy. Healthy democratic governance, I have argued, rests principally on productive tension in the nation's politics. What is required is not a broad consensus on policy issues, as pundits sometimes suggest, but rather a vigorous contest of ideas and interests that is mediated—and ultimately rendered constructive—by a common faith in the democracy itself. The question I have raised is whether political conflict in the United States has become somehow less constructive over recent decades as that common faith has waned, even perhaps just a little bit.

Beyond this tentative diagnosis and the various prescriptions that flow from it, my abiding hope for this book is that it stimulates vigorous debate about the nature of American democracy—how it has functioned and changed over time, why it has lasted so long, and what we can do to sustain and strengthen it going forward. Indeed, I can think of no better way to honor our democracy than to engage in this debate, whether in a high school classroom or the halls of Congress.

In a 1788 letter to his friend Thomas Jefferson, James Madison suggested that rights written into the Constitution are just "parchment barriers," profoundly vulnerable to "overbearing majorities," unless those rights "become incorporated with the national sentiment."[65] The essence of democratic governance, in other words, always comes back to the people, their conception of how collective decisions ought to be made, and to what end. This is why ongoing debate about the democracy itself—both past and present—has historically been such a vital part of American life and why, I believe, it remains as important as ever today.

NOTES

1. Of course, unlike Athens, a city-state, the young United States adopted representative rather than direct democracy.

2. See Nolan McCarty, Keith T. Poole, and Howard Rosenthal, *Polarized America: The Dance of Ideology and Unequal Riches* (Cambridge, MA: MIT Press, 2006). Updated data, through 2014, available at http://voteview.com/political_polarization_2014.html.

3. Shanto Iyengar and Sean J. Westwood, "Fear and Loathing across Party Lines: New Evidence on Group Polarization," Working Paper, June 2014, 6, https://pcl.stanford.edu/research/2014/iyengar-ajps-group-polarization.pdf. Experimental studies suggest, moreover, that citizens are far more likely to award a scholarship based on partisan identification than on merit—and that partisan bias is now larger than racial bias in this regard (14–19).

4. Shanto Iyengar, Gaurav Sood, and Yphtach Lelkes, "Affect, Not Ideology: A Social Identity Perspective on Polarization," *Public Opinion Quarterly* 76, no. 3 (Fall 2012): 418–420. By 2013, according to one survey, 64 percent of Republicans perceived other

Republicans as "intelligent," but only 11 percent of Republicans perceived Democrats as "intelligent." The gap was smaller for Democrats but still significant (at 15 percent and 48 percent for Republicans and Democrats, respectively). The survey showed similar partisan gaps for honesty, patriotism, and generosity. See The Economist / YouGov Poll, 19–21 Jan. 2013, 59–60, https://d25d2506sfb94s.cloudfront.net /cumulus_uploads/document/d3ms2sphnu/20130119econTabReport.pdf.

5. See Gallup, "Trust in Government," http://www.gallup.com/poll/5392/trust -government.aspx; and Pew Research Center, "Public Trust in Government: 1958–2014," 13 Nov. 2014, http://www.people-press.org/2014/11/13/public-trust-in -government. See also "CNN Poll: Trust in Government at All-Time Low," CNN, 8 Aug. 2014, http://politicalticker.blogs.cnn.com/2014/08/08/cnn-poll-trust -in-government-at-all-time-low-2.

6. Gallup, "Trust in Government."

7. Richard Franklin Bensel, *The American Ballot Box in the Mid-Nineteenth Century* (New York: Cambridge University Press, 2004), 8, 11–13, quotation at 13.

8. See, e.g., Adam Winkler, "Voters' Rights and Parties' Wrongs: Early Political Party Regulation in the State Courts, 1886–1915," *Columbia Law Review* 100, no. 3 (Apr. 2000): 873–900.

9. Glenn C. Altschuler and Stuart M. Blumin, *Rude Republic: Americans and Their Politics in the Nineteenth Century* (Princeton, NJ: Princeton University Press, 2000), 75.

10. Elizabeth M. Addonizio, Donald P. Green, and James M. Glaser, "Putting the Party Back into Politics: An Experiment Testing whether Election Day Festivals Increase Voter Turnout," *PS: Political Science and Politics* 40, no. 4 (Oct. 2007): 721.

11. See Erik J. Engstrom, "The Rise and Decline of Turnout in Congressional Elections: Electoral Institutions, Competition, and Strategic Mobilization," *American Journal of Political Science* 56, no. 2 (Apr. 2012): 376, 379, 382. Glenn Firebaugh and Kevin Chen, in their "Vote Turnout of Nineteenth Amendment Women: The Enduring Effect of Disenfranchisement," *American Journal of Sociology* 100, no. 4 (Jan. 1995): 972–996, note that "post-amendment men and women vote at the same rate" (984). See also Charles Edward Merriam and Harold Foote Gosnell, *Non-Voting: Causes and Methods of Control* (Chicago: University of Chicago Press, 1924).

12. For an empirical analysis of which factors most contributed to the drop in voter turnout in the early twentieth century, see Engstrom, "Rise and Decline of Turnout," esp. 382.

13. Social scientists have found that of the two types of secret ballots that came into common use in the late nineteenth century—one that made party-line voting relatively easy (the party-column format) and another that did not (the office-bloc format)—both were associated with lower turnout than before the advent of secret ballots, but the office-bloc format (which made party-line voting more difficult) was associated with the lowest turnout rates of all. See esp. ibid., 381–382. On the Australian ballot and split-ticket voting, see also Jerrold G. Rusk, "The Effect of the

Australian Ballot Reform on Split Ticket Voting: 1876–1908," *American Political Science Review* 64, no. 4 (Dec. 1970): 1220–1238.

14. See, e.g., J. C. Heckelman, "The Effect of the Secret Ballot on Voter Turnout Rates," *Public Choice* 82, nos. 1–2 (1995): 107–124, which stresses that the Australian ballot system made voting less attractive by reducing payments to voters from the major political parties. By contrast, Daniel C. Reed, "Reevaluating the Vote-Market Hypothesis: Effects of Australian Ballot Reform on Voter Turnout," *Social Science History* 38, nos. 3–4 (Fall–Winter 2014): 277–290, argues that the more decisive factor with respect to turnout was the added burden that the Australian ballot system (and particularly the office-bloc format) placed on voters.

15. See, e.g., Michael Schudson, "Politics as Cultural Practice," *Political Communication* 18, no. 4 (2001): 426–427; Bensel, *American Ballot Box,* xii.

16. Michael E. McGerr, *The Decline of Popular Politics: The American North, 1865–1928* (New York: Oxford University Press, 1986), esp. 22, 26–27, 39, and 37.

17. For example, McGerr writes, "Party membership was a part of men's identity; as such, their partisanship had to be paraded and asserted in public" (*Decline of Popular Politics,* 14).

18. James Bryce, *The American Commonwealth,* 3rd ed. (New York: Macmillan, 1907), 2:210, orig. pub. 1894. Also quoted in McGerr, *Decline of Popular Politics,* 39.

19. McGerr, *Decline of Popular Politics,* esp. chap. 3 ("Partisanship Redefined").

20. Although the expansion of suffrage in the early nineteenth century is widely characterized by historians as a significant development that sparked controversy at the time, Donald Ratcliffe offers a competing view, suggesting that already by the start of the nineteenth century the vast majority of adult white men were able to vote in most states, despite official property requirements. Ratcliffe maintains that apart from Rhode Island, where property requirements on voting had been more strictly enforced, the formal shift toward universal suffrage among adult white males in early nineteenth-century America was not nearly as contentious or significant as commonly portrayed. See Donald Ratcliffe, "The Right to Vote and the Rise of Democracy, 1787–1828," *Journal of the Early Republic* 33 (Summer 2013): 219–253. For the more widely accepted view, see esp. Alexander Keyssar, *The Right to Vote: The Contested History of Democracy in the United States* (New York: Basic Books, 2000).

21. The political economist Anthony Downs famously called this decision to remain uninformed "rational ignorance" on the part of voters. See Downs, "An Economic Theory of Political Action in a Democracy," *Journal of Political Economy* 65, no. 2 (Apr. 1957): 149.

22. The classic example is Upton Sinclair's lurid exposé on the meatpacking industry in his 1906 novel *The Jungle,* which scandalized and activated the public and, in turn, laid the political foundation for both the Meat Inspection Act and the Pure Food and Drugs Act later that same year. See esp. Marc T. Law and Gary D. Libecap, "The Determinants of Progressive Era Reform: The Pure Food and Drugs Act of 1906,"

in *Corruption and Reform: Lessons from America's Economic History,* ed. Edward L. Glaeser and Claudia Goldin (Chicago: University of Chicago Press, 2006), 319–342; Alexander Dyck, David Moss, and Luigi Zingales, "Media versus Special Interests," *Journal of Law and Economics* 56, no. 3 (Aug. 2013): 521–553.

23. See David Moss and Mary Oey, "The Paranoid Style in the Study of American Politics," in *Government and Markets: Toward a New Theory of Regulation,* ed. Edward J. Balleisen and David Moss (Cambridge: Cambridge University Press, 2010), esp. 262–267.

24. Quoted in James Madison, *Notes of Debates in the Federal Convention of 1787* (Athens: Ohio University Press, 1984), 39 (31 May 1787).

25. Ratcliffe, "The Right to Vote," 228–229; Mary Barbara McCarthy, *The Widening Scope of American Constitutions* (PhD diss., Catholic University of America, 1928), 52–54.

26. Stephen Ansolabehere and James M. Snyder Jr., "The Incumbency Advantage in U.S. Elections: An Analysis of State and Federal Offices, 1942–2000," *Election Law Journal* 1, no. 3 (2002): table A.1 (p. 330).

27. Jennifer L. Lawless, *Becoming a Candidate: Political Ambition and the Decision to Run for Office* (Cambridge: Cambridge University Press, 2012), 32. Although dogcatcher (animal control) was once an elected office in many local communities, the position has mostly disappeared. See Philip Bump, "A Brief History of People Who Have Actually Been Elected Dog Catcher," *Washington Post* (online), 2 June 2014, https://www.washingtonpost.com/news/the-fix/wp/2014/06/02/a-brief-history-of -people-who-have-actually-been-elected-dog-catcher/. For a recent exception to the rule, see Miranda Orso, "Duxbury Voters Share Laughs, Concerns," StoweToday .com, 6 Mar. 2014, http://www.stowetoday.com/waterbury_record/article_46ba5b98 -a49a-11e3-b853-0019bb2963f4.html. In Duxbury, Vermont, Zeb Towne was elected dogcatcher "despite a 'no' vote from his wife that [caused] laughter to erupt in the room."

28. Daniel A. Smith and Dustin Fridkin, "Delegating Direct Democracy: Interparty Legislative Competition and the Adoption of the Initiative in the American States," *American Political Science Review* 102, no. 3 (Aug. 2008): 333; John G. Matsusaka, "Direct Democracy Works," *Journal of Economic Perspectives* 19, no. 2 (Spring 2005): 188–189; Matsusaka, *For the Many or the Few: The Initiative, Public Policy, and American Democracy* (Chicago: University of Chicago Press, 2004), 1.

29. Glenn R. Winters, "Selection of Judges: An Historical Introduction," *Texas Law Review* 44 (1966): 1081–1087. See also Evan Haynes, *The Selection and Tenure of Judges* (1944; Clarke, NJ: Lawbook Exchange, 2005).

30. American Bar Association, "Fact Sheet on Judicial Selection Methods in the States," http://www.americanbar.org/content/dam/aba/migrated/leadership/fact_sheet .authcheckdam.pdf. Regarding high courts in particular, seven states hold partisan elections for high-court judges, fourteen hold nonpartisan elections, and seventeen hold uncontested elections regarding the retention of high-court judges after their initial appointment (ibid.).

31. John Dinan, "State Constitutional Developments in 2014," in *The Book of the States,* vol. 47 (Lexington, KY: Council of State Governments, 2015), table 1.1 (pp. 11–12). See also Dinan, "State Constitutional Amendments and Individual Rights in the Twenty-First Century," *Albany Law Review* 76, no. 4 (2012–2013): esp. 2106. It is worth noting that in addition to frequently amending their constitutions, most states have replaced their constitutions altogether one or more times through state constitutional conventions.

32. See esp. Gallup, "Trust in Government"; Pew Research Center, "Public Trust in Government: 1958–2014"; "Gallup Poll Social Series: Governance," *Gallup News Service,* 4–7 Sept. 2014, questions 12 and 13, http://www.gallup.com/file/poll/177188/Confidence _in_St_and_Local_Govt_140922%20.pdf; Pew Research Center, *Beyond Distrust: How Americans View Their Government,* Nov. 2015, http://www.people-press.org/files /2015/11/11-23-2015-Governance-release.pdf, esp. 59.

33. Alexis de Tocqueville, *Democracy in America,* vol. 1, trans. Henry Reeve (New York: D. Appleton and Co., 1899), 322.

34. Quoted in Richard Herr, *Tocqueville and the Old Regime* (Princeton, NJ: Princeton University Press, 1962), 35–36.

35. For a critique of the traditional "consensus" view, see, e.g., Meg Jacobs, "The Uncertain Future of American Politics, 1940–1973," in *American History Now,* ed. Eric Foner and Lisa McGirr (Philadelphia: Temple University Press, 2011), 151–174.

36. On the rise of polarization and its timing, see McCarty, Poole, and Rosenthal, *Polarized America,* updated data online at http://voteview.com/political_polarization _2014.html.

37. Addonizio, Green, and Glaser, "Putting the Party Back into Politics," esp. 721–723.

38. Luis Raúl Cámara, "The Madness of Every Four Years: A Comparative Study of Voting, Candidate Selection and Turnout in Puerto Rico and the United States" (PhD diss., University of Michigan, 1999), 152.

39. Richard B. Freeman, "What, Me Vote?," NBER Working Paper 9896, Aug. 2003, http://www.nber.org/papers/w9896, 20.

40. See David C. Huckabee, "Ratification of Amendments to the U.S. Constitution," CRS Report to Congress, 97-922 GOV, 30 Sept. 1997, http://www.au.af.mil/au/awc /awcgate/crs/97-922.pdf. On May 1, 1810, Congress sent to the states an amendment regarding "Titles of Nobility," which was not ultimately ratified, and next sent an amendment to the states on March 2, 1861. The latter, which also was not ratified by the states, would have barred constitutional amendments authorizing Congress to ban slavery. The next amendment actually approved by Congress (31 Jan. 1865) and ratified by the states (6 Dec. 1865) was the Thirteenth Amendment, which banned slavery directly. The Fifteenth Amendment, which held that the right to vote could not be "denied or abridged . . . on account of race," was passed by Congress on February 26, 1869, and ratified by the states on February 3, 1870. The next proposed amendment passed by Congress was the Sixteenth, authorizing a federal income tax.

Approved by Congress on July 12, 1909, it was ultimately ratified by the requisite number of states on February 3, 1913.

41. When polled on the question of jury duty in 2004, 84 percent of respondents (including 87 percent of those who had been called for jury duty and 80 percent of those who had not) agreed with the statement "Jury duty is an important civic duty I should meet even if it is inconvenient." See HarrisInteractive, "Jury Service: Is Fulfilling Your Civic Duty a Trial," prepared for the American Bar Association, July 2004, p. 9, available at http://www.americanbar.org/content/dam/aba/migrated /2011_build/american_jury/harris_poll_report.authcheckdam.pdf.

42. HarrisInteractive, "Jury Service," 11. See also Julian V. Roberts and Mike Hough, "Public Attitudes to the Criminal Jury: A Review of Recent Findings," *Howard Journal of Criminal Justice* 50, no. 3 (July 2011): esp. table 6 (p. 254). It is possible that the preference for juries over judges has declined in recent years. When the Rasmussen polling service asked in April 2012, "Who do you trust more to determine the guilt or innocence of someone accused of criminal behavior—a judge or a jury?," 65 percent of respondents chose "jury," 21 percent chose "judge," and 15 percent were undecided. When the same question was asked in February 2014, 58 percent chose "jury," 22 percent "judge," and 20 percent undecided. See "65% Trust Jury More Than a Judge," Rasmussen Reports, 19 Apr. 2012, http://www.rasmussenreports.com/public _content/lifestyle/general_lifestyle/april_2012/65_trust_jury_more_than_a _judge; "58% Still Trust a Jury's Verdict More Than a Judge's," Rasmussen Reports, 19 Feb. 2014, http://www.rasmussenreports.com/public_content/lifestyle/general _lifestyle/february_2014/58_still_trust_a_jury_s_verdict_more_than_a_judge_s. Questions for the Rasmussen polls are available at http://www.rasmussenreports .com/public_content/business/econ_survey_questions/april_2012/questions _trayvon_martin_april_11_12_2012.

43. See, e.g., Graham Smith and Corinne Wales, "Citizens' Juries and Deliberative Democracy," *Political Studies* 48 (2000): 51–65.

44. Archon Fung, "Let Citizen Assemblies Draw Districts" (part of a group of pieces under the heading "Six Ways to Reform Democracy"), *Boston Review,* 6 Sept. 2006.

45. Smith and Wales, "Citizens' Juries and Deliberative Democracy," 60.

46. On citizen juries and civic engagement, see esp. ibid., 60–61. On trial juries and civic engagement, see John Gastil, E. Pierre Deess, Phil Weiser, and Jordan Meade, "Jury Service and Electoral Participation: A Test of the Participation Hypothesis," *Journal of Politics* 70, no. 2 (Apr. 2008): 351–367; Valerie P. Hans, John Gastil, and Traci Feller, "Deliberative Democracy and the American Civil Jury," *Journal of Empirical Legal Studies* 11, no. 4 (Dec. 2014): 697–717. See also John Gastil, E. Pierre Deess, Phil Weiser, and Cindy Simmons, *The Jury and Democracy: How Jury Deliberation Promotes Civic Engagement and Political Participation* (New York: Oxford University Press, 2010).

47. Tocqueville, *Democracy in America,* vol. 1, chap. 16, p. 303.

48. Ibid., 305.

49. Ibid., 307, 305.

50. Unlike the other proposals offered here, this one is not targeted at any of the historical shifts highlighted over the first half of this chapter. It will not make voting more exciting or re-create the energy of a mass suffrage movement or help to close the federal democratic deficit—at least not directly. It merits attention simply because education has always been intimately tied to political culture and thus may be a vital part of any solution.

51. Horace Mann, "Twelfth Annual Report of the Secretary of the Board of Education for Massachusetts, 1848," reprinted as "Report for 1848," in *Life and Works of Horace Mann*, vol. 4, ed. Mary Mann (Boston: Lee and Shepard, 1891), 277, 283.

52. Sandra Day O'Connor, "The Democratic Purpose of Education: From the Founders to Horace Mann to Today," in *Teaching America: The Case for Civic Education*, ed. David J. Feith (Lanham, MD: Rowman and Littlefield Education, 2011), 3–5. See also Benjamin Rush, "On the Mode of Education Proper in a Republic," in Rush, *Essays, Literary, Moral and Philosophical* (Philadelphia: Thomas and William Bradford, 1806), 6–20.

53. Jeffrey Mirel, "The Decline of Civic Education," *Daedalus* 131, no. 3 (Summer 2002): 51.

54. Richard G. Niemi and Julia Smith, "Enrollments in High School Government Classes: Are We Short-Changing Both Citizenship and Political Science Training?," *PS: Political Science & Politics* 34, no. 2 (June 2001): 281, table 1 (p. 282).

55. O'Connor, "The Democratic Purpose of Education," 6.

56. On the expansion of civics education in the 1990s, see Niemi and Smith, "Enrollments in High School," 282. For a critique of civics education in the United States today, see, e.g., Jonathan Gould, ed., *Guardian of Democracy: The Civic Mission of Schools* (Philadelphia: Leonore Annenberg Institute for Civics of the Annenberg Public Policy Center at the University of Pennsylvania, and the Campaign for the Civic Mission of Schools, 2011), http://civicmission.s3.amazonaws.com/118/f0/5/171/1/Guardian-of-Democracy-report.pdf.

57. William A. Galston, "Civic Education and Political Participation," *Phi Kappa Phi Forum* 84, no. 1 (Winter 2004): 38.

58. O'Connor, "The Democratic Purpose of Education," 7, 9. See also Anthony D. Lutkus and Andrew R. Weiss, *The Nation's Report Card: Civics 2006* (Washington, DC: National Center for Education Statistics, U.S. Department of Education, 2007); Meira Levinson, "The Civic Achievement Gap," Circle Working Paper 51, Jan. 2007, https://dash.harvard.edu/bitstream/handle/1/10861134/WP51Levinson.pdf.

59. See, e.g., Gould, *Guardian of Democracy*, 17.

60. See esp. Nathan Manning and Kathy Edwards, "Does Civic Education for Young People Increase Political Participation? A Systematic Review," *Educational Review* 66, no. 1 (2014): 22–45.

61. Mann, "Twelfth Annual Report," in *Life and Works*, 4:271.

62. "The Worm at the Root," *Connecticut Courant*, 14 Mar. 1810, 3.

63. William Denison McCracken, *The Rise of the Swiss Republic: A History* (1892; repr., London: Forgotten Books, 2013), 342.

64. Arthur Herman, *The Idea of Decline in Western History* (New York: Free Press, 1997), 2.

65. James Madison to Thomas Jefferson (17 Oct. 1788), in *The Papers of James Madison Digital Edition,* ed. J. C. A. Stagg, http://rotunda.upress.virginia.edu/founders/JSMN .html.

APPENDIX: FOLLOW-UPS TO CASES

Case 1: James Madison, the "Federal Negative," and the Making of the U.S. Constitution (1787)—The Follow-Up

The delegates to the Constitutional Convention rejected James Madison's proposal for an absolute federal negative by a convincing margin on June 8, 1787. This was not quite the end of the story, however. A narrower version of the negative, which would apply only to state laws that Congress believed violated the Constitution, lived on in the working draft of the document. Yet this clause, too, soon came under attack. On June 20, John Lansing of New York declared that if the federal government were granted a veto, even a narrow one, "the States must be entirely abolished." Delegates debated the clause again on July 17 and ultimately voted it down, despite Madison's pleas that it was "essential to the efficacy & security of the General Government." Charles Pinckney of South Carolina tried one last time to revive a modified version of the provision (this one would have required a two-thirds vote of each house of Congress to overturn a state law) but it failed as well, ensuring that there would be no "negative"—no congressional authority to invalidate state laws—in the U.S. Constitution.[1]

Thomas Jefferson, who opposed the federal negative, had suggested to Madison that state laws that violated the Constitution would be better handled in the courts. Although Madison disagreed, strongly favoring a legislative rather than a judicial solution, responsibility for overturning laws that violated the Constitution was ultimately vested in the courts—through judicial review—just as Jefferson had hoped.[2]

In fact, in an ironic twist, both Jefferson and Madison were personally involved in the landmark case that ended up establishing the federal courts' authority to review (and strike down) legislative acts. In the extremely bitter presidential election of 1800, Thomas Jefferson defeated the incumbent John Adams after only one term. Adams, however, subsequently appointed several new judicial officers in his final days as president. Shortly after Jefferson took over as president, he blocked the appointees from assuming office by refusing to deliver the necessary commissions. William Marbury, one of the appointees who did not receive his commission, took his case directly to the Supreme Court. Remarkably, the member of the administration who was responsible for delivering the commissions to Marbury and the other appointees was the new secretary of state—none other than James Madison. Ultimately, U.S. Supreme Court Chief Justice John Marshall ruled in the case of *Marbury v. Madison* in 1803 that although the Jefferson administration's decision to withhold the commissions was not legal, the Court had no jurisdiction over the matter because the federal legislation allowing Marbury take his case directly to the Supreme Court (the Judiciary Act of 1789) was itself unconstitutional.[3]

In *Marbury v. Madison,* therefore, Marshall asserted the power of judicial review over legislative acts. It was certainly not the sort of federal negative that Madison had wanted, being judicial rather than legislative, but it nevertheless provided—and continues to provide—a check on legislation, both federal and state, that violates the Constitution.

Case 2: Battle over a Bank: Defining the Limits of Federal Power under a New Constitution (1791)—The Follow-Up

Facing intense pressure from both supporters and opponents of a national bank, President George Washington signed the bill authorizing incorporation of what would become the Bank of the United States on February 25, 1791. Just ten months later, Americans witnessed another major development in the evolving definition of federal power when ten of the twelve constitutional amendments that Congress had proposed as the Bill of Rights were finally adopted by the states, once Virginia became the eleventh state to ratify on December 15.[4]

In the meantime, the Bank of the United States had opened its doors in Philadelphia on December 12, marking a triumph for Secretary of the Treasury Alexander Hamilton. Not long afterward, however, in early 1792, the new nation suffered its first major financial panic, centered, appropriately enough, on Wall Street in New York City. Thomas Jefferson, among many others, blamed the crisis on Hamilton's Bank of the United States and vowed to destroy it, ensuring that the bank would remain a fiercely debated issue in American politics.[5]

Notably, the year 1792 saw not only a financial panic but also the birth of what has come to be known as the First Party System in the United States. The Federalist Party took shape under Hamilton's leadership, mainly in the North and with a clear preference for a more energetic federal government and policies favoring economic and business development. The Democratic-Republican Party, which was more southern and agrarian in orientation and generally favored smaller government, formed under the leadership of Jefferson and Madison. Although the Federalists dominated the federal government until 1800, the Democratic-Republicans took over after that, controlling both Congress and the presidency for the next quarter century.[6]

Continuing to oppose the Bank of the United States, the Democratic-Republicans allowed its charter to expire in 1811. Just five years later, however, in the wake of the War of 1812 and the financial tumult that followed, even Democratic-Republicans felt the need to create another national bank, leading Congress to pass—and President Madison to sign—legislation establishing the Second Bank of the United States in 1816.[7]

The U.S. Supreme Court ultimately upheld the constitutionality of the Second Bank of the United States in 1819 in the landmark case of *McCulloch v. Maryland*. The court noted that both Congress and President Washington had approved a national bank in 1791, and that even many of the staunchest opponents of the idea had since accepted its constitutionality. Indeed, the court largely embraced Hamilton's reading of the issue, including his interpretation of the "necessary and proper" clause: "Congress is authorized to pass all laws 'necessary and proper' to carry into execution the powers conferred on it. . . . A bank is a proper and suitable instrument to assist the operations of the government."[8] Thus, in what would become an enduring debate over implied powers and the proper role of the federal government, Hamilton's more expansive view carried the first round.

Case 3: Democracy, Sovereignty, and the Struggle over Cherokee Removal (1836)—The Follow-Up

The U.S. Senate ratified the Treaty of New Echota by the required two-thirds margin—but without a single vote to spare—on May 18, 1836. President Andrew Jackson signed the treaty on May 23, and forced removal of the

Cherokee began roughly two years later. In the meantime some Cherokee left preemptively, but most stayed and followed Chief Ross's lead of what was essentially passive resistance.[9] General John E. Wool of the U.S. Army, who commanded troops in Cherokee territory, wrote in a letter on February 18, 1837:

> I called them [the Cherokee] together and made a short speech. It is, however, vain to talk to a people almost universally opposed to the treaty and who maintain that they never made such a treaty. So determined are they in their opposition that not one of all those who were present and voted at the council . . . however poor or destitute, would receive either rations or clothing from the United States lest they might compromise themselves in regard to the treaty.[10]

When the brutal process of removal finally commenced in June 1838, it proved catastrophic. More than 4,000 Cherokee are said to have perished, out of roughly 16,000, in what came to be known as the Trail of Tears. Even Chief Ross lost his wife during the migration.[11] One U.S. Army private, John G. Burnett, offered his own account many decades later, on December 11, 1890, his eightieth birthday:

> Being acquainted with many of the Indians and able to fluently speak their language, I was sent as interpreter into the Smoky Mountain Country in May, 1838, and witnessed the execution [of] the most brutal order in the history of American warfare. I saw helpless Cherokees arrested and dragged from their homes, and driven at the bayonet point into the stockades. And in the chill of a drizzling rain on an October morning, I saw them loaded like cattle or sheep into six hundred and forty-five wagons and started toward the west. . . .
>
> On the morning of November the 17th we encountered a terrific sleet and snow storm with freezing temperatures and from that day until we reached the end of the fateful journey on March the 26th, 1839, the sufferings of the Cherokees were awful. The trail of the exiles was a trail of death.[12]

Nor did the catastrophe end with the migration itself. Just a few months after the last set of migrants arrived in 1839, the former leaders of the Treaty Party—Major Ridge, John Ridge, and Elias Boudinot—were all assassinated by Cherokee enraged over removal. Major Ridge had said when he signed the Treaty of New Echota that he was signing his own death warrant, and that prediction proved tragically accurate.[13]

Case 4: Banking and Politics in Antebellum New York (1838)—The Follow-Up

Looking beyond the concerns of some fellow Democrats, Governor William L. Marcy signed the free banking bill into law on April 18, 1838. As expected, the number of banks in New York State increased significantly over subsequent years, rising from 98 in 1837 to 165 in 1840 to 274 in 1855.[14] Banknotes, meanwhile, proved remarkably safe under the new regime, presumably because the legislation's note-security requirement meant that all free-bank notes were fully backed with high-grade securities.[15] At the same time, the Free Banking Act of 1838 exerted a dramatic effect on the state's political system, largely eliminating the bank chartering system that had long served as a political weapon in Albany. In the words of one historian of the subject, "Free banking depoliticized the business corporation."[16]

Although most of these consequences were anticipated by proponents of the legislation, not everything worked out as expected. In particular, New York's free banking law did not eliminate banking panics as some supporters had predicted. Although banknotes became extremely safe under the new system, circulating with minuscule or zero discounts, both bankers and their customers increasingly relied on a new and more flexible form of money, checking accounts (demand deposits), which came into widespread use across New York State. Checking accounts were attractive to bankers precisely because they did not have to be backed one-for-one with high-grade assets under the free banking law and thus could be used to expand bank lending. In this way, checking accounts (and other types of deposits) supported the enlargement of credit, as banknotes had before the adoption of free banking, but also emerged as a new locus of instability in the financial system. When the next banking panic struck in 1857, New York's governor announced a novel development—that it was the depositors, not the noteholders, who "made the run upon the banks which forced them into suspension."[17] Although the state's Free Banking Act had succeeded in many respects, political as well as economic, it had failed to eliminate banking panics, which continued to wreak havoc on a periodic basis, even if now in a new guise.

Case 5: Property, Suffrage, and the "Right of Revolution" in Rhode Island (1842)—The Follow-Up

Poorly equipped and with no military training, Thomas Dorr led 250 men in the early hours of May 18, 1842, in an effort to take control of the Providence Arsenal. From there he intended to install the People's Government by force. The attack did not come as a surprise to the charter government, however, which had posted placards on May 17 calling for volunteers to protect the arsenal. Several of Dorr's own family members, including his father and brother, are said to have volunteered to guard the arsenal against him. In the end, Dorr's attempted use of force was a spectacular—almost comical— failure, as his forces were unable to fire their cannon and many of his troops rapidly deserted in the darkness.[18]

Although Dorr himself avoided arrest for the time being, the People's Government quickly collapsed after his ill-fated raid, and the broader suffrage movement was severely weakened as well. Wrote one compatriot in a letter to Dorr, "I can hardly find a suffrage man in the city with whom to advise or consult, so completely have we been defeated."[19] After fleeing to Connecticut, Dorr attempted to organize—but did not carry out—another military operation in June, and then escaped to New Hampshire, where he was given sanctuary by the governor. He finally returned to Rhode Island on October 31, 1843, intending to surrender and stand trial, and was immediately arrested on the charge of high treason. He was subsequently tried, convicted, and sentenced to life in prison "at hard labor in separate confinement."[20]

In the meantime, the charter government had both imposed martial law, ostensibly to restore order, and called for yet another constitutional convention to help reestablish governmental legitimacy.[21] The new constitution, which was ratified by a huge margin and went into effect in 1843, dramatically expanded suffrage among native-born males, both white and black, while also imposing tough restrictions on voting among foreign-born males, many of whom were Irish-Catholic.[22] By one estimate, the "new constitution increased the electorate by about 60 per cent."[23] Ironically, despite the humiliating defeat they faced after resorting to arms, Dorr and his supporters ended up getting much of what they wanted in terms of expanded suffrage, apart from the severe restrictions on foreign-born males.

As for Dorr himself, he enjoyed considerable support from Democrats, who saw his prison sentence as an outrage. The charter government offered to let him go free if he swore allegiance to the government, but he refused. The state legislature subsequently passed resolutions in June 1845 approving both his release from prison and the annulment of his conviction. He was released the same day, but by this point he was in poor health. He died nine years later, in December 1854, at 49 years of age.[24]

The U.S. Supreme Court was ultimately asked to weigh in on the legitimacy of Dorr's rebellion and, implicitly, on whether Americans had a "right of revolution" in their states. The case grew out of the tumultuous events of 1842. Once Dorr had fled the state following his failed attack on the Providence Arsenal and the charter government had declared martial law, several charter loyalists ransacked the home of a Dorr supporter, Martin Luther, in an attempt to arrest him. Incensed, Luther later sued on the grounds of criminal trespass. The defendants in the case claimed they had acted properly under martial law, but Luther countered that the government that had imposed martial law, the charter government, was by that point no longer the legitimate government of Rhode Island. Although the case gave the Supreme Court the opportunity to render an opinion on the legitimacy of the People's Constitution and the People's Government, it ultimately decided not to render any opinion at all on these questions—ruling simply that the question of which government was legitimate in Rhode Island was a political one that properly belonged with Congress rather than the Court.[25]

Case 6: Debt and Democracy: The New York Constitutional Convention of 1846—The Follow-Up

Delegates to the New York State Constitutional Convention approved Michael Hoffman's anti-debt provision on September 23, 1846, by a vote of 72 to 36, and the state's electorate overwhelmingly approved the new constitution itself by a vote of 221,528 to 92,436 on November 3.[26] Although Hoffman's provision proved highly restrictive, Whigs looked feverishly for ways to finance large projects, including especially expansion of the Erie Canal, which had been on their agenda since the 1830s.

Most notably, in 1851 Whigs attempted to circumvent the restriction on public debt, proposing to raise $9 million for enlargement of the canal through the issuance of "certificates" that would be tied to canal revenues. Confident that enlargement would pay for itself over time and that the bill would ensure this result "without an increase of the State Debt and without a resort to taxation," Whigs insisted that the measure was entirely constitutional—that the "certificates" were not "bonds"—and they even enlisted the esteemed jurist Daniel Webster to attest to the bill's constitutionality. Opponents would have none of it, however, with one opposition newspaper calling the bill "a trick . . . a paltry and dirty evasion of the prohibition of the constitution." In a desperate effort to block the legislation, a dozen Democrats abruptly resigned from the state senate in April to deny Whigs a quorum. Although the "Nine Million Bill" was ultimately passed in July in an extra session of the legislature called specially for this purpose by the governor, the measure was struck down as unconstitutional the following year by the Court of Appeals, though not before $1.5 million had already been raised through the sale of "certificates."[27]

Still determined to enlarge the canal, Whigs (along with Democratic allies from western New York, who supported enlargement) now decided they needed a constitutional amendment that would permit the necessary financing. Although Democrats had largely taken control of the state government in the elections of 1852, they nonetheless felt considerable pressure for action on the canal issue. Accordingly, two Democratic factions proposed two different plans, and Governor Horatio Seymour, also a Democrat, brokered a compromise that would authorize borrowing of $2.25 million per year over four years to finance enlargement of the Erie Canal and related work on several lateral canals, as well as $1.5 million to redeem the canal certificates that had already been issued. The compromise amendment was eventually approved by the legislature, which had since returned to Whig control, and then by the voters (185,771 to 60,526) in a referendum on February 15, 1854.[28] The Whig publisher and politician Thurlow Weed declared, "For the third, and we trust the last time, the People have literally 'crushed out' the opposition to the Canals. . . . The Enlargement of the Erie Canal is now a part of the Constitution of the State."[29]

In part as a result of these special measures, public debt continued to grow in New York. One scholar estimates that New York State debt increased from $21.8 million in 1841 to $24.3 in 1853 to $33.6 million in 1860. By 1870, however, eight years after enlargement of the Erie Canal was complete and five years after the end of the Civil War, the state's public debt had fallen slightly to $32.4 million, and it subsequently fell sharply to just $7.7 million in 1880 and $2.3 million in 1890.[30] By 1894, when New York held another constitutional convention, state debt had fallen to essentially zero and convention delegates decided to leave Hoffman's anti-debt provision largely untouched, apparently attributing the dramatic drop in debt "to the workings of the constitutional restrictions adopted in 1846."[31] Hoffman's influence also extended far beyond New York's borders, as numerous other states ended up adopting either constitutional or legislative measures to contain public borrowing, very much along the lines Hoffman had first sketched in New York.[32]

Although Michael Hoffman cast a long shadow in New York and across the country, his fiscal framework was nonetheless challenged in numerous ways over subsequent years. Not only was the framework officially circumvented in New York in the 1850s to allow enlargement of the Erie Canal, as we have seen, but it was effectively circumvented again as *municipal* governments, in New York and beyond, began borrowing on an unprecedented scale, starting especially in the second half of the nineteenth century.[33] By 1902 the sum of local debt nationwide had grown larger than state debt and federal debt combined.[34] Back in New York, moreover, there were growing concerns among state lawmakers in the early twentieth century that greater fiscal flexibility was sometimes needed, particularly in the face of economic recessions. Facing a large unexpected deficit as a result of an economic downturn in 1914, for example, state officials concluded they had no time to call a referendum and simply "borrowed the money anyway," basing their "right to do so on the theory of implied powers." The state constitution was again amended in 1920 to allow short-term borrowing in anticipation of expected revenues.[35]

Nevertheless, despite numerous changes and workarounds over the years, the essence of Hoffman's fiscal framework—involving strict limits on state borrowing along with a democratic escape hatch—remains a key part of the New York State constitution to this day. Article VII, §11, reads as follows:

Except the debts or refunding debts specified in sections 9, 10 and 13 of this article, no debt shall be hereafter contracted by or in behalf of the state, unless such debt shall be authorized by law, for some single work or purpose, to be distinctly specified therein. No such law shall take effect until it shall, at a general election, have been submitted to the people, and have received a majority of all the votes cast for and against it.[36]

In these words and many others spread across New York's constitution, the weighty decisions of 1846 remain very much alive.

Case 7: The Struggle over Public Education in Early America (1851)—The Follow-Up

Although New York State's voters had approved the Free School Law of 1849 in a statewide referendum and rejected the legislature's call for repeal the following year, state legislators nonetheless passed the Burroughs-Ferris bill by large margins (72–21 in the House and 22–4 in the Senate) just about six months later, and the governor signed the bill into law on April 12, 1851. Curiously titled "An Act to Establish Free Schools throughout the State," the 1851 law effectively repealed and replaced the Free School Law of 1849, allocating $800,000 annually for the support of common schools but requiring the reintroduction of rate-bills (tuition payments) for any remaining costs that were not covered locally.[37]

Lawmakers had faced intense pressure to act. Despite an apparent mandate by the voters, the 1849 law had proved extraordinarily divisive. As the superintendent of common schools explained in his report of January 1, 1853:

Though the majority of the people twice expressed their approbation of free schools . . . the [1849] law met with an opposition which neutralized the benefits which its friends anticipated for it. The strifes which it gave rise to, in the language of the Executive, in 1851, "disturbed the harmony of society." Districts were rent with contention; litigation in school matters rapidly increased; the inhabitants in many instances refused to carry out the provisions of the law, and in others, directly resisted it, as unconstitutional and oppressive.[38]

Against this backdrop the superintendent appropriately characterized the 1851 law as "a compromise between the views of the advocates and opponents of the law of 1849."[39]

Adding yet another nail to the coffin, the New York Court of Appeals subsequently struck down the already defunct 1849 law as unconstitutional, ruling in 1853 that the legislature had improperly delegated its exclusive lawmaking authority to the people when it conditioned enactment of the law on a statewide referendum. "All legislative power is derived from the people," Chief Judge Charles H. Ruggles announced, "but when the people adopted the constitution, they surrendered the power of making laws to the legislature." The sole exception, in his view, was the anti-debt provision Michael Hoffman had inserted into the Constitution of 1846, requiring that voters approve increases in public debt over $1 million. "In this special and single case, the people by the constitution reserved legislative power to themselves." One of his colleagues, Judge John Willard, added in a concurring opinion, "There is no other part of the constitution that recognizes, even by implication, the right of the legislature thus to delegate their trust." In fact, Willard was so concerned about the dangers of direct democracy that he concluded his opinion with the following warning: "If this mode of legislation is permitted and becomes general, it will soon bring to a close the whole system of representative government which has been so justly our pride. . . . All the checks against improvident legislation will be swept away; and the character of the constitution will be radically changed."[40]

Although the Free School Law of 1849 had now been killed twice—once by legislative act in 1851 and once by judicial act in 1853—the notion of tuition-free schools was hardly a dead letter. Even before 1849, many cities, from New York to Buffalo, had secured special legislation allowing the elimination of rate-bills, and the trend continued after the collapse of the 1849 law.[41] One early historian of American education, Andrew Draper, explained simply that "the cities would not tolerate the rate bill." Tuition-free education spread still further in New York after 1853, when the legislature passed "An Act to Provide for the Establishment of Union Free Schools." Although the legislation did not ensure tuition-free schools statewide, it did allow districts to eliminate rate-bills on their own. According to Draper, the new system "authorized districts to combine and establish a graded school, and meet the expenses by a general tax, thus obviating the necessity for the rate bill in communities adopting it."[42]

Finally, in the Free School Act of 1867, state lawmakers dispensed with rate-bills altogether. "Hereafter," the statute read, "all moneys authorized by any special acts to be collected by rate bill for the payment of teachers' wages, shall be collected by tax, and not by rate bill." The legislation also directed districts to raise taxes as needed "to pay whatever deficiency there may be in teachers' wages after the public money apportioned to the district shall have been applied thereto."[43]

Characterizing the new law as "abolishing rate bills, and establishing free schools," the state superintendent of public instruction, Victor M. Rice, noted shortly after its passage that from 1828 to 1866, the amount collected through rate-bills had averaged over $400,000 per year and was likely to reach approximately $700,000 in the year ending September 30, 1867, before the new law took effect. The Free School Act, he said, would do "away with that feature in the system . . . which has been burdensome and odious to the poor . . . and which has been the great cause of irregular attendance and absenteeism."[44] Nearly two decades after the enactment of the Free School Law of 1849, the core objective of that legislation had, it seemed, finally been achieved.

Case 8: A Nation Divided: The United States and the Challenge of Secession (1861)—The Follow-Up

In a letter drafted on April 4, 1861, to Major Robert Anderson at Fort Sumter, President Abraham Lincoln conveyed his decision to send provisions to the fort in unarmed boats. He would send military reinforcements only if the secessionists attacked and fired on the supply boats. Learning on April 6 that Fort Pickens in Florida was at risk, he finally sent to Major Anderson the letter he had penned two days before. He also informed the government of South Carolina of his plans to reprovision the fort, and the supply boats departed on their mission on April 9. Confederate leaders decided on the same day, however, that they would take the fort by force if necessary. After several requests for an immediate but peaceful surrender, Confederate forces began firing on Fort Sumter at about 4:30 A.M. on April 12. The first shot—a "10-inch mortar shell sent as a signal round to activate the other batteries"—was fired by Captain George S. James, who had resigned from the U.S. Army on February 1 and was now commanding Confederate forces at nearby Fort Johnson.[45]

Enduring heavy bombardment and dramatically outgunned, Major Anderson agreed to surrender Fort Sumter on April 14. Permitted to withdraw with their arms and belongings, but not to salute their flag, Anderson and his troops "marched out of the fort 'with colors flying and drums beating.'"[46] With that, the spiral into near total war had begun.

Over roughly the next seven weeks, four more states—Virginia, Arkansas, North Carolina, and Tennessee—joined the Confederacy. Four other slave states—the border states of Maryland, Delaware, Kentucky, and Missouri—remained with the Union.

Although Lincoln initially called up troops for ninety days, the Civil War ultimately lasted until 1865. Traditional estimates suggest the war claimed 620,000 dead, though the actual number was likely closer to 750,000, or even higher. The war is also said to have left nearly half a million wounded. Ultimately becoming one of the casualties himself, Lincoln was assassinated by John Wilkes Booth on April 14, 1865, just five days after General Robert E. Lee surrendered his Confederate forces to Ulysses S. Grant, the commanding general of the U.S. Army.[47]

Upon assuming the presidency, Lincoln had fiercely opposed the *spread* of slavery but had accepted the so-called federal consensus, which held that the federal government had no authority under the Constitution to eliminate slavery in states where it already existed. The intensity and brutality of the war ultimately changed that. Lincoln issued the Emancipation Proclamation on January 1, 1863, officially freeing all slaves in states that had seceded from the Union and that were not yet under Union control. Although the president's order did not instantly free all slaves in rebel territory, because it was not recognized by the Confederacy, the Emancipation Proclamation nevertheless ensured that as Union armies took control of territory in the South, slaves living there would gain their freedom. Yet even as Union victory neared in 1865, at least 85 percent of those who had been enslaved in the South as of 1860 still had not been freed. Many Republicans feared that the Emancipation Proclamation—which had been issued as an emergency military measure—might not be valid once the war ended, and they set their sights on changing the Constitution itself. Accordingly, Congress sent the Thirteenth Amendment to the states in January 1865. Ratified in December, eight months after the Confederate surrender, the amendment outlawed slavery in the United States.[48]

Case 9: Race, Justice, and the Jury System in Postbellum Virginia (1880)—The Follow-Up

On March 1, 1880, the U.S. Supreme Court announced its decisions regarding both *Virginia v. Rives* and *Ex Parte Virginia.* The first case concerned Judge Alexander Rives's decision to take Lee and Burwell Reynolds from state custody with the intention of trying them in his federal courtroom. Rives believed that because black citizens had effectively been kept off the grand and petit juries, the Reynolds brothers had been deprived of equal protection under the law. Justice William Strong, writing for the Court, disagreed, insisting that an all-white jury was not itself a violation of the defendants' rights, so long as Virginia law did not explicitly exclude blacks from juries. "A mixed [race] jury in a particular case is not essential to the equal protection of the laws," Strong declared, "and the right to it is not given by any law of Virginia or by any Federal statute. It is not, therefore, guaranteed by the Fourteenth Amendment, or within the purview of sect. 641 [of the 1875 Civil Rights Act]."[49]

The very same day, Justice Strong penned another majority decision in the case of *Strauder v. West Virginia,* in which the court struck down the murder conviction of a black defendant in West Virginia on the grounds that West Virginia law wrongly excluded black citizens from juries.[50] The key difference in this case is that West Virginia law explicitly discriminated against blacks in the formation of juries. Because Virginia law, by contrast, was not itself discriminatory against black jurors, the court concluded that there was no violation of equal protection, even if juries in Virginia regularly ended up all white.

The Supreme Court thus ruled against Judge Rives and ordered the Reynolds brothers remanded to state custody. After a number of twists and turns, state prosecutors dropped the case against Lee Reynolds. Burwell Reynolds, however, was tried yet again in state court in June 1880. This time a special jury was formed with eight white members and four black members who were, according to one contemporary account, "leading white and colored citizens of Danville." Burwell Reynolds was convicted of manslaughter and sentenced to five years in prison.[51]

Finally, in the case of *Ex Parte Virginia,* also decided on March 1, 1880, the Supreme Court concluded that Judge Rives had not violated the law or the Constitution in securing federal indictments against the county judges. The Fourteenth Amendment was clear, requiring "equal protection of the law" and, importantly, authorizing Congress "to enforce, by appropriate legislation, the provisions of this article." Congress in turn had mandated in the Civil Rights Act of 1875 that equal protection of the law applied to juries and that no citizen "shall be disqualified for service [as a juror] on account of race, color, or previous condition of servitude." With this legal infrastructure in place, the Supreme Court rejected the argument that the Commonwealth of Virginia was not subject to congressional authority, because in this case the federal Constitution had specifically empowered Congress to act: "In exercising her rights, a State cannot disregard the limitations which the Federal Constitution has applied to her power. . . . Nor can she deny to the general government the right to exercise all its granted powers."[52]

The Court determined further that when county judges participated in the process of selecting jurors, they were acting in an administrative rather than a judicial capacity. As a consequence these judges were subject to the provision of the Civil Rights Act of 1875 holding that "any officer or other person charged with any duty in the selection or summoning of jurors who shall exclude or fail to summon any citizen for the cause aforesaid shall, on conviction thereof, be deemed guilty of a misdemeanor."[53] The Court determined, in other words, that the federal prosecutions of thirteen county judges in Virginia, which Judge Rives had initiated, could proceed.

In the end, none of the indicted county judges was convicted. At least one was acquitted and another faced a hung jury. When Judge Coles came up for trial, in November 1880, the court announced that the Coles case and all of the remaining cases would be dropped. According to one report, "The courtroom was crowded, and the announcement of the Court's order was received with surprise and applause."[54]

The effective exclusion of blacks from juries would become commonplace in the South until well into the twentieth century, and the prosecutions that Judge Rives initiated were the last cases anywhere in the United States in which a state official was prosecuted in federal court for excluding citizens from jury pools on the basis of race.[55] Judge Rives himself retired from the bench in 1882 and died three years later.[56]

Case 10: An Australian Ballot for California? (1891)—
The Follow-Up

Governor Henry H. Markham signed California's ballot reform bill into law on March 20, 1891. Remarkably, California was one of seventeen states to adopt the Australian ballot that year, bringing the total number of states that had passed similar laws (starting with Massachusetts in 1888) to about thirty. By the end of 1909, the number of states with full-fledged Australian ballot laws had reached forty; four other states and one territory had partial measures in place; and only two states, Georgia and South Carolina, had resisted the movement entirely. In 1950, South Carolina became the last state to adopt an Australian ballot law.[57]

Just a little over two weeks after the California measure was enacted in 1891, the *Sunday Union* of Sacramento called the Australian ballot the "greatest political reform of the age."[58] Historians have generally offered more qualified assessments. "The Australian ballot did not fulfill all the high expectations of its advocates," writes Erik Falk Peterson, a historian of electoral reform in California. "By eliminating piece clubs and the traffic in votes on election day, it delivered only a glancing blow to the armor of the political boss. . . . Nevertheless, the movement for the Australian ballot in California was the opening round of a twenty year campaign for election reform which had impressive results."[59] A historian of American political parties, meanwhile, suggests that the "Australian ballot did not immediately produce major changes in behavior. . . . But over time the effects of this new voting procedure were immense."[60] Some of the long-term effects that are most commonly attributed to the Australian ballot include sharp reductions in the selling of votes on election day, dramatic increases in split-ticket voting, more orderly polling places, and reduced voter turnout, which never again reached the highs of 75 to 80 percent achieved in the nineteenth century (see the Conclusion).

Case 11: Labor, Capital, and Government: The Anthracite Coal
Strike of 1902—The Follow-Up

President Theodore Roosevelt released the report of the Anthracite Coal Strike Commission on March 18, 1903. The commission commented in great detail about the conditions that workers faced in the mines, and it rendered a set of decisions that mostly split the difference between workers' and employers' demands.[61]

Whereas the workers had asked for a 20 percent increase in pay, the commission awarded raises of about 10 percent to most workers, though in some cases this took the form of a reduction in hours without a corresponding decrease in pay. Similarly, where the workers had asked for a 20 percent reduction in hours, the commission awarded a 10 percent reduction, which meant a change from a 10-hour day to a 9-hour day for many classes of workers, with extra pay for overtime. Notably, the commission was unwilling to render a verdict on the proper weight of a ton of coal (e.g., 2,240 pounds versus 3,360 pounds) for purposes of compensating workers who were paid by the ton. Finally, although the commission did not require employers to recognize the union, it did prohibit discrimination based on membership or non-membership in a union, and it established an ongoing board of conciliation for labor disputes, with three members appointed by labor representatives and three by the operators. The decisions of the board would be "final and binding on all parties." Where the board was unable to reach a decision, the dispute would be referred to an "umpire," whose decisions would similarly be "final and binding." All of the commission's mandatory policies (including those covering wages, hours, and dispute resolution) were to remain in force until end of March 1906.[62]

According to a historian of the subject, "the press generally viewed the settlement as a victory for the mine workers and their union." John Mitchell, the president of the United Mine Workers, stated publicly that he saw it that way as well. Nevertheless, at least some mine operators believed that they—rather than the workers—had won. Characterizing the report as "a great and sweeping victory," one mine operator relished the fact that the commission had not required recognition of the union and that the commission's decisions regarding wages and hours were "no more than we all expected."[63]

Still, years later, labor leader Samuel Gompers continued to regard the anthracite coal strike of 1902 as a seminal event in the history of American labor, writing the following in his autobiography: "Several times I have been asked what in my opinion was the most important single incident in the labor movement in the United States and I have invariably replied: the strike of the anthracite miners in Pennsylvania . . . from then on the miners became not merely human machines to produce coal but men and citizens. . . . The strike was evidence of the effectiveness of trade unions."[64]

Case 12: *The Jungle* and the Debate over Federal Meat Inspection (1906)—The Follow-Up

According to newspaper reports about the House meat inspection bill, President Theodore Roosevelt agreed to the compromise that Speaker of the House Joseph Cannon suggested during their meeting at the White House on June 18, 1906. While prevailing on several issues, the president apparently yielded on the questions of whether meatpackers would be required to stamp a date on each can of meat they produced (they would not) and whether they would have to pay for the federally mandated inspections (again, they would not). Once the compromise was reached, the House Agriculture Committee quickly sent the redrafted bill to the full House, which approved it the following day.[65]

The Beveridge bill that the Senate passed a few days later included neither of these concessions, thus ensuring a fight when House and Senate conferees met to reconcile the two versions of the legislation. Although President Roosevelt was said to have accepted the concessions on June 18, he now publicly threw his weight behind the stronger Beveridge bill. With the House-Senate conference already under way, the *San Francisco Chronicle* reported on June 26 that President Roosevelt "has said that he will not be satisfied with the bill unless the amendment is accepted providing for the date of packing to be placed on the cans." The *Chronicle* story also noted, however, that the "general expectation is that the Senate conferees will agree to the House provisions."[66]

In fact, the House conferees issued an ultimatum on June 27 that if the Senate did not agree to the key provisions in the House bill, there would be no final legislation on meat inspection at all.[67] The wrangling continued for two more days, and President Roosevelt continued to tell Senate conferees that "he preferred . . . an agreement . . . whereby the packers would be compelled to pay the cost of inspection and that the dates of inspection should be placed on cans of meat," but the Senate negotiators ultimately had little choice but to capitulate to the demands of their counterparts in the House. On June 29, Senator Knute Nelson of Minnesota acknowledged, "We have been whipped," and a *New York Times* headline announced, "Upper House Surrenders and Government Foots the Bill."[68]

Senator Albert Beveridge, however, "took a cheerful view" of the outcome. According to the *New York Times,* he believed "it was better to gain the main object of the legislation [mandatory federal meat inspection] than to imperil the bill by insisting on what was a minor detail." The *Times* reported, moreover, that Beveridge "closed by saying this inspection bill was the greatest legislative act of this end of the century."[69]

The final legislation, which was nearly identical to the House bill, was passed by both the House and the Senate on the morning of June 30, and President Roosevelt signed it into law that same day, the final day of the congressional session.[70] The president subsequently sent the pen he used to sign the bill to the 44-year-old Senator Beveridge, writing "You were the man who first called my attention to the abuses in the packing houses."[71] Meat inspection has been a responsibility of the U.S. Department of Agriculture ever since.

Case 13: The Battle over the Initiative and Referendum in Massachusetts (1918)—The Follow-Up

Massachusetts voters approved the Initiative and Referendum Amendment by a narrow margin, 170,646 to 162,103, on November 5, 1918. In filling out their ballots, 96,698 voters left the I&R question blank. As a result, although 51.3 percent of those who addressed the question voted "yes," only 39.7 percent of voters who went to the polls that day approved the amendment, and in only two counties—Suffolk (which includes Boston) and Plymouth (which includes Brockton)—did more citizens vote "yes" than "no" on the amendment.[72]

The very first law that Massachusetts enacted by initiative, in November 1920, redefined beer, cider, and light wines with less than 2.75 percent alcohol as nonalcoholic, presumably in an effort to exempt these beverages from Prohibition, which had taken effect nationally less than a year before. The Massachusetts state legislature had approved a similar law earlier in the year, but Governor Calvin Coolidge vetoed it on May 6, saying that it violated the Eighteenth Amendment and was little more than an attempt to "deceive ourselves." Not willing to give up, supporters of the measure submitted it as an initiative, which was approved by the electorate by a vote of 442,215 to 432,951 on November 2. Although officially enacted into law by the people of Massachusetts under the new I&R process, it remained "inoperative by reason of its conflict with the Volstead Act," which Congress had passed to enforce Prohibition.[73] Overall, through 2012, Massachusetts voters used the I&R system to adopt three constitutional amendments by initiative, enact seventy-two laws by initiative, and rescind nineteen statutes by referendum.[74]

When Massachusetts adopted the initiative in 1918, it was the twentieth state to do so—a trend that had started tentatively with South Dakota in 1898 and produced the famous "Oregon System" in 1902. Notably, however, no other states followed Massachusetts until Alaska in 1956, Wyoming and Florida in 1968, and Illinois in 1970. Mississippi, which had seen its 1914 initiative provision struck down by the state's high court in 1922, readopted the initiative in 1992, bringing the total number with statewide initiative processes to twenty-four. It is estimated that about half of all U.S. cities also have initiative processes, many of which were first adopted in the early years of the twentieth century.[75]

Case 14: Regulating Radio in the Age of Broadcasting (1927)—The Follow-Up

President Calvin Coolidge signed the Radio Act on February 23, 1927, officially creating the Federal Radio Commission (FRC), which began operations in March. Although the FRC's licensing authority was supposed to last only a year (and then revert back to the Commerce Department), Congress extended the FRC's authority several times and ultimately made it permanent in 1929. As a result the Commerce Department never again exercised authority over radio broadcasting. Five years later, in 1934, the FRC was replaced by the Federal Communications Commission (FCC), which is still with us today.[76]

Case 15: The Pecora Hearings (1932–1934)—The Follow-Up

When Richard Whitney, the president of the New York Stock Exchange, testified before the House Committee on Interstate and Foreign Commerce on February 22, 1934, he offered a scathing critique of the bill that Senator

Duncan Fletcher and Representative Sam Rayburn had put forward to regulate the nation's securities exchanges. Whitney insisted that the powers granted under the bill to the Federal Trade Commission (FTC) were "so great that many of the functions of management [of listed corporations] are, in effect, transferred to an administrative department of the Government." He also charged that "this bill seeks to regulate exchanges to the point where it will destroy the free and open market for securities."[77]

As an alternative, Whitney suggested the creation of a seven-member "stock exchange coordinating authority," which would include two cabinet officials, two members specially appointed by the president, one selected by the Federal Reserve Open Market Committee, and two representing the nation's securities exchanges. The fact that Whitney was recommending an independent authority of any sort was a significant departure from his position just a year before, when he insisted in his meeting with President Franklin Roosevelt that self-regulation by the New York Stock Exchange would be sufficient. Although he now rejected many aspects of the Fletcher-Rayburn bill—including the placement of regulatory authority in the FTC and bans on certain financial instruments—he nonetheless recommended granting the new stock exchange authority extensive power to regulate securities exchanges. This included "plenary power" both to control margin requirements and to "require stock exchanges to adopt rules and regulations preventing not only dishonest practices but also all practices which unfairly influence the price of securities or unduly stimulate speculation."[78]

When on June 1, 1934, the House and Senate finally approved a revised and reconciled version of the Fletcher-Rayburn bill, it included elements of both the original bill, which Fletcher had introduced in the Senate in early February on behalf of the president, and the counterproposal that Whitney had outlined in his House testimony later that same month. Specifically, the Securities Exchange Act of 1934, which President Roosevelt signed into law on June 6, created a new body, the Securities and Exchange Commission (SEC), whose five members were to be appointed by the president on a bipartisan basis. Registration requirements were mainly retained from the original bill. Although the law did not include some of the outright bans that had been present in the original bill, it did impose explicit restrictions on wash sales, bear raids, and other forms of manipulation highlighted during the Pecora hearings. In general, most decisions regarding the proper regulation of securities exchanges and listed securities—on topics ranging from short-selling to margin requirements—were left largely to the discretion of regulators at the SEC and the Federal Reserve.[79]

On June 30 President Roosevelt named the five inaugural members of the Securities and Exchange Commission: Joseph P. Kennedy, a well-known businessman and financier who was widely thought to have engaged in numerous forms of stock manipulation himself during the 1920s; George C. Mathews, a member of the FTC; James M. Landis, a Harvard Law School professor and member of the FTC who had helped draft the Fletcher-Rayburn bill; Robert E. Healy, a former judge and chief counsel at the FTC; and Ferdinand Pecora, who had led the nation's most famous investigation of Wall Street in 1933–1934 as chief counsel for the Senate Banking and Currency Committee.[80]

One final postscript to the story deserves mention. On March 8, 1938, in a stunning announcement, Richard Whitney's securities firm was officially suspended from the New York Stock Exchange for insolvency. Whitney, it turns out, had for several years been engaged in an increasingly desperate—and illegal—effort to cover massive losses that he had suffered during the mid-1930s. This included "posting securities belonging to other people . . . as collateral for his loans."[81] Ironically, new SEC disclosure rules—not unlike ones Whitney had vehemently opposed during his fight against the original Fletcher-Rayburn bill—"quite unexpectedly, turned up irregularities in the affairs of Richard Whitney and Company."[82] Whitney was officially charged with grand larceny on March 10 and, after pleading guilty, "was handcuffed between two other freshly minted convicts (for rape and extortion) and hauled off to Sing Sing," where he remained for three years until released on parole. When President Roosevelt, who had attended the same schools as Whitney, heard about the indictment, he is reported to have said, "Poor Groton. Poor Harvard. Poor Dick."[83]

Case 16: Martin Luther King and the Struggle for Black Voting Rights (1965)—The Follow-Up

On March 9, 1965, as Martin Luther King Jr. led marchers to the Edmund Pettus Bridge, they stopped briefly at the foot of the bridge where a deputy U.S. marshal read them Judge Frank Johnson's federal court order barring them from crossing. The marshal stepped aside once King indicated he was "aware of the order" and intended to continue, but King and the marchers stopped again as they reached the end of the bridge and the sea of state law enforcement officers on the other side. Nearly all the marchers expected the procession to continue beyond the bridge, despite the troopers and the court order, hopeful that an unusually large media presence would dissuade law enforcement from a violent response. King, however, had other plans. While still on the bridge, he asked everyone to kneel down and pray together, and the marchers broke into song, including "We Shall Overcome." The head of the state troopers, meanwhile, positioned just beyond the bridge, called Governor George Wallace for instructions and was told that his men should step aside, as if to invite the marchers to continue on to Montgomery, in violation of the federal court order. With just a moment to decide what to do, King refused to take the bait and instead turned the marchers around, leading them back to Brown Chapel in Selma. Some protesters felt upset and even betrayed, believing that King had backed down at a crucial moment. Whereas March 7 had been "Bloody Sunday," March 9 quickly became known as "Turnaround Tuesday." King called it "the greatest demonstration for freedom, the greatest confrontation so far in the South."[84]

Although the Tuesday march ended peacefully, violence erupted again that night when four white men in Selma severely beat a white minister, James Reeb, who had traveled from Boston to participate in the march. Reeb died two days later. With national outrage over the events in Selma mounting, President Lyndon Johnson "pushed for specific actions the administration could take to meet another crescendo of unrest."[85] The president and the first lady also spoke with James Reeb's widow, soon after Reeb was pronounced dead, in what Lady Bird Johnson described as a "helpless, painful talk with Mrs. Reeb."[86] Although grief and anger over the minister's death were widely shared across the country, some Americans—especially in the civil rights movement—questioned why a white death captured so much more attention than a black one, mindful of the "official silence that accompanied the death of Jimmie Lee Jackson" just two weeks before.[87]

Protests in Washington continued, including a sit-in inside the White House on March 11, and President Johnson addressed Congress on March 15. Speaking about the marchers in Selma, he said: "Their cause must be our cause too. Because it is not just Negroes, but really it is all of us, who must overcome the crippling legacy of bigotry and injustice. And we shall overcome."[88] Two days later, on March 17, the president's Voting Rights Act arrived on Capitol Hill, and Judge Johnson issued an order that same day finally permitting King to lead a march from Selma to Montgomery.[89]

The Selma-to-Montgomery march, which began with about 3,000 people, ultimately covered more than fifty miles in five days and attracted intense media coverage. At one point, President Johnson sent federal agents to protect the marchers, when Governor Wallace refused to do so. The march neared its conclusion with a huge rally and a concert that featured Harry Belafonte, Sammy Davis Jr., Tony Bennett, Leonard Bernstein, Joan Baez, and Pete Seeger, among many others. When the procession finally arrived in Montgomery, on March 25, there were an estimated 25,000 marchers, including a large cast of celebrities. Protesters held a mass rally on the steps of the capitol in Montgomery, and King delivered one of his most moving addresses. Asking "How long will it take?" he answered: "How long? Not long, because the arc of the moral universe is long, but it bends toward justice." As if to confirm the length of that arc, Governor George Wallace refused to meet with the marchers, who had sought to deliver a petition on voting rights; and yet another civil rights volunteer, Viola Liuzzo from Michigan, was killed by Klansmen soon after the Montgomery rally ended.[90]

Back in Washington, debate in the Senate over the Voting Rights Act started on April 22. In time the threat of a southern-led filibuster was put down, and the Voting Rights Act was ultimately passed by large majorities in both the House (328–74) and the Senate (79–18) and was signed into law by President Johnson on August 6.[91]

Upon signing the bill, which attempted to end most of the abuses that had kept blacks from registering and voting, President Johnson called the legislation "one of the most monumental laws in the entire history of American freedom."[92] In just two years, from 1965 to 1967, black registration rates in the South increased from 29 percent to 52 percent (in Alabama from 19 percent to 52 percent, and in Mississippi from 7 percent to 60 percent). This was still lower than white registration rates, which averaged about 80 percent, but it was a dramatic improvement nonetheless.[93]

The civil rights leader John Lewis, who was the president of SNCC in 1965 and had helped lead the "Bloody Sunday" march, later called the Voting Rights Act "a high point in modern America, probably the finest hour in terms of civil rights."[94] Still, violence did not abate, and King himself, just 39 years old, was shot and killed by an assassin in Memphis on April 4, 1968.

Case 17: Democracy and Women's Rights in America: The Fight over the ERA (1982)—The Follow-Up

After a vigorous debate, the Florida State Senate rejected the Equal Rights Amendment on June 21, 1982, by a vote of 16 to 21. This effectively marked the end of the line for the ERA. No other states approved the amendment before the June 30 deadline, leaving the total number of states that had ratified at thirty-five, three short of the thirty-eight required to meet the constitutional threshold of three-quarters of the states.[95]

Supporters continued to reintroduce the ERA in subsequent congressional sessions, with the hope of beginning the ratification process anew.[96] Although the U.S. House and Senate never mustered the necessary two-thirds votes to send the amendment back to the states, some ERA proponents concluded in the 1990s that they did not need to start all over again— that three more states were all that was required for ratification.[97]

The reason for this change is that in 1992, Michigan officially became the thirty-eighth state to ratify a constitutional amendment regarding pay raises for Congress that had first been sent to the states in 1789. Of twelve amendments that Congress sent to the states that year, ten were ratified in 1791 and became the Bill of Rights. Although the pay-raise amendment (also known as the "Madison Amendment," after its author) was not approved by a sufficient number of states to be ratified along with the others, it gradually picked up support over the next two centuries. Angry about a congressional pay raise, Ohio lawmakers approved the amendment in 1873, and Wyoming did the same a little over a hundred years later, in 1978. Thirty more states followed suit from 1983 to 1992, with Michigan making ratification complete when it became the thirty-eighth state to endorse what is now the Twenty-Seventh Amendment to the Constitution. The U.S. Supreme Court had ruled in 1939 that it was up to Congress whether or not to set a time limit on a ratification process, and no time limit had been set by Congress with respect to the Madison Amendment in 1789.[98]

Seeing a 203-year-old amendment becoming part of the Constitution in 1992, ERA supporters began calling on Congress to eliminate the deadline it had originally imposed on the ERA, believing that if Congress took this step and several more states approved, the amendment would be officially ratified. Some argued, moreover, that Congress's time limit had been illegitimate from the start, and thus that no congressional action was needed. Many supporters of the ERA also claimed, based on prior precedents (especially related to the Fourteenth Amendment), that a state could not rescind its approval of an amendment, once granted. If so, then the thirty-five states that initially approved the ERA would still be on the list, and just three more states would be needed to get to thirty-eight.[99]

A few states have come close to approving the ERA in more recent years— including Illinois, where the House (but not the Senate) approved the amendment in 2003.[100] At the time of this writing, however, no additional states beyond the initial thirty-five have approved the Equal Rights Amendment, and the legal status of continuing a ratification process beyond the original deadline set by Congress remains uncertain.

Case 18: Leadership and Independence at the Federal Reserve (2009)—The Follow-Up

On Thursday, November 19, 2009, the House Financial Services Committee rejected the Watt amendment and proceeded to pass Paul-Grayson by a vote of 43 to 26. The Paul-Grayson amendment would subject the Federal Reserve to a far more expansive "audit" than under existing law. It prevailed despite opposition from the Democratic chairman of the committee, Barney Frank, and notable resistance coming from the Federal Reserve itself. In the end, fifteen Democrats joined twenty-eight Republicans on the committee to pass the measure, which was incorporated into the broader financial reform bill that the House passed by a vote of 223–202 on December 11, 2009.[101]

Five months later the Senate unanimously passed a narrower audit provision proposed by Independent Senator Bernie Sanders of Vermont. Like the failed Watt amendment in the House, the Sanders provision would require a General Accountability Office (GAO) examination of the Federal Reserve's emergency loans during the recent financial crisis, but not a broader examination of monetary policy itself. Sanders had originally proposed a more expansive audit, but he "agreed to scale it back in the face of opposition from the White House, the Fed, the Treasury and some Senate colleagues." In addition, Republican Senator David Vitter of Louisiana pro-

posed an amendment—with the support of thirty Republicans, six Democrats, and the Independent Sanders—that would have nearly replicated the
House's audit provision, but it was voted down, 62 to 37.[102]

When the House and Senate bills arrived in conference for reconciliation
in June, negotiators agreed on audit provisions that were much closer to the
Senate version than the House version, in part because Barney Frank and
other top Democratic representatives themselves opposed the stricter version that had come out of the House. According to the *Washington Post*,
"House Democrats blocked an attempt by GOP colleagues to revive a more
aggressive approach by Rep. Ron Paul (R-Tex.), which won wide support in
the House last fall and would have opened the Fed to extensive audits, including on its decision-making regarding monetary policy."[103] In the end, the
Wall Street Reform and Consumer Protection Act (Dodd-Frank), signed into
law by President Barack Obama on July 21, 2010, directed the GAO to audit
the Federal Reserve's special credit facilities, "all loans and other financial
assistance" extended by the Fed during the financial crisis, as well as the Fed's
system of governance.[104]

Disappointed that the audit requirements ultimately included in Dodd-
Frank were relatively narrow in scope, Representative Ron Paul continued
to press for increased auditing of the Federal Reserve. In July 2012 the House
overwhelmingly passed his bill for a "full audit," but the proposal subsequently died in the Senate. The House passed a similar measure in 2015. Early
in the following year, the Senate came close to passing an expansive "Audit
the Fed" bill—this one put forward by Ron Paul's son, Senator Rand Paul.
Despite nearly unanimous support from Senate Republicans, along with
Democratic presidential candidate Bernie Sanders, the bill failed to secure the
sixty votes needed for cloture in the Senate. Although the proposal for a "full
audit" had failed repeatedly, support for the measure remained widespread,
and there could be little doubt that political battles would continue over the
dueling goals of "independence and accountability" at the Federal Reserve.[105]

Case 19: *Citizens United* and Corporate Speech (2010)
—The Follow-Up

In the aftermath of the *Citizens United* decision, handed down on January 21,
2010, independent election expenditures rose sharply in the United States. Not
everyone agreed that the Court's decision had been the trigger for all, or even

most, of the increase, but the dramatic growth in spending was undeniable. Between 2008 and 2012, independent expenditures on federal elections increased from $143.6 million to just over $1 billion. Similarly, in nonpresidential years, independent expenditures on federal elections increased from $37.8 million in 2006 to $205.5 million in 2010 to $549.0 million in 2014. (Recall that independent expenditures are used to specifically support or oppose a candidate, but may not be coordinated with a candidate or his or her campaign.)[106]

A large part of the increase in independent expenditures was funded by so-called Super PACs, which emerged for the first time in 2010 following a federal appeals court decision *(Speechnow.org v. FEC)* that itself grew out of *Citizens United*. Until 2010 and still today, individuals wishing to contribute money to federal candidates face strict limits under federal election law, but they face no limit on independent expenditures. SpeechNow.org had formed as a nonprofit association in 2007 for the purpose of pooling resources solely from individuals to fund independent expenditures beginning in the 2008 election cycle. In a draft opinion, the Federal Election Commission advised SpeechNow that if it wished to collect contributions from individuals, it would need to register as a political committee, which in turn would limit the amounts it could collect to $5,000 per person per year. Convinced that this restriction violated First Amendment protections, SpeechNow took its case to court. Although a federal district judge decided against SpeechNow in 2008, a federal appeals court unanimously ruled in its favor in March 2010, just two months after the Supreme Court handed down *Citizens United*. "Given [the] analysis from *Citizens United*," the appeals court explained, "we must conclude that the government has no anti-corruption interest in limiting contributions to an independent expenditure group such as SpeechNow."[107]

Together, *Citizens United* and *Speechnow.org* cleared the way for "independent expenditure committees," more commonly known as Super PACs. So long as these entities undertook only independent expenditures, and never gave directly to federal candidates, they could accept unlimited contributions from individuals, corporations, and unions.[108] Appearing for the first time in the 2010 election cycle, 83 Super PACs reported independent expenditures totaling $62.6 million. Two years later, in the 2012 election cycle, 1,310 Super PACs reported a total of $609.4 million in independent expenditures. The Center for Responsive Politics finds that individuals—especially very wealthy ones—accounted for two-thirds of contributions to Super PACs in the 2012 cycle, with 30 percent of these individual contributions going to liberal Super PACs and 69 percent going to conservative Super PACs. Of the remaining one-third of contributions coming from organizations (particularly unions, corporations, and trade associations), 56 percent went to liberal Super PACs and 42 percent to conservative ones. An early study conducted by several political scientists suggests that major business corporations played a relatively small role in funding Super PACs in the 2012 cycle and that they likely gave significantly less to Super PACs in both that cycle and the 2014 cycle than did labor unions.[109]

Perhaps not surprisingly, the *Citizens United* decision sparked controversy from the day it was issued. Opinion polls taken over the next five years suggest that the public's reaction was overwhelmingly negative, among Democrats and Republicans alike. In a Washington Post–ABC News poll conducted February 4–8, 2010, just two weeks after the *Citizens United* ruling was handed down, 80 percent of respondents said they opposed the decision, including 85 percent of Democrats, 81 percent of Independents, and 76 percent of Republicans. Five and a half years later, a Bloomberg poll found nearly identical results: 78 percent of respondents thought that *Citizens United* should be overturned and only 17 percent thought it was a "good decision." Notably, the preference to overturn was shared by 83 percent of Democrats, 80 percent of Republicans, and 71 percent of Independents.[110]

Ironically, in a country sharply divided across partisan lines on issue after issue, the Supreme Court had managed to provoke a rare degree of unity against its decision. Whether the public would gradually warm to the Court's reading of the First Amendment, or whether the Court itself would reverse course, or perhaps be overruled by a constitutional amendment, was anyone's guess. There could be little question, however, that the role of money and business in electoral politics remained a live issue on the American stage. The Court had ruled decisively in the latest act, but the larger drama appeared far from over.

NOTES

1. James Madison, *Notes of Debates in the Federal Convention of 1787* (Athens: Ohio University Press, 1984), 92, 156, 304–305, 518–519.

2. See esp. Jefferson to Madison, 20 June 1787, and Madison to Jefferson, 24 Oct. 1787, in *The Papers of James Madison Digital Edition*, ed. J. C. A. Stagg, rotunda.upress .virginia.edu.

3. See, e.g., Kevin R. C. Gutzman, *James Madison and the Making of America* (New York: St. Martin's Press, 2012), 285–286.

4. See David Jack Cowen, *The Origins and Economic Impact of the First Bank of the United States, 1791–1797* (New York: Garland, 2000), 22; Robert Allen Rutland, *The Birth of the Bill of Rights, 1776–1791* (Boston: Northeastern University Press, 1991), 217. Of the two amendments that Congress proposed but that were not ratified by a sufficient number of states, one (which would have reapportioned the U.S. House of Representatives) was never ratified, while the other (which would impose new rules on salary changes for Congress) was ultimately ratified 200 years later, in 1992, as the Twenty-Seventh Amendment to the Constitution.

5. See Cowen, *Origins and Economic Impact,* 38–39, 58, 89–136.

6. See John C. Miller, *The Federalist Era, 1789–1801* (New York: Harper, 1960), chap. 7.

7. Ralph C. H. Catterall, *The Second Bank of the United States* (Chicago: University of Chicago Press, 1960 [1902]), chap. 1.

8. *McCulloch v. Maryland,* 4 Wheat. 316, 324 (1819).

9. See esp. A. J. Langguth, *Driven West: Andrew Jackson and the Trail of Tears to the Civil War* (New York: Simon and Schuster, 2010); Brian Hicks, *Toward the Setting Sun: John Ross, the Cherokees, and the Trail of Tears* (New York: Atlantic Monthly Press, 2011).

10. Quoted in J. W. Powell, *Fifth Annual Report of the Bureau of Ethnology to the Secretary of the Smithsonian Institution, 1883–'84* (Washington, DC: GPO, 1887), 286.

11. See Russell Thornton, *The Cherokees: A Population History* (Lincoln: University of Nebraska Press, 1990), 73–76; Langguth, *Driven West,* 311.

12. Quoted in "Two Accounts of the Trail of Tears: Wahnenauhi and Private John G. Burnett," Digital History (ID 1147), available at http://www.digitalhistory.uh.edu /disp_textbook.cfm?smtID=3&psid=1147. For a skeptical view of Burnett's report, see John Ehle, *Trail of Tears: The Rise and Fall of the Cherokee Nation* (New York: Anchor Books, 1988), 393–394. Noting that Burnett was writing long after the events in question, Ehle suggests that the account suffers from "exaggeration and factual errors" (394) and that it was motivated by Burnett's effort to "assure his grandchildren of his own purity of past actions" (393).

13. Hicks, *Toward the Setting Sun,* 282, 322–330; Langguth, *Driven West,* 313–317, 235, 423.

14. Warren E. Weber, "Early State Banks in the United States: How Many Were There and When Did They Exist?," *Federal Reserve Bank of Minneapolis Quarterly Review* 30, no. 1 (Sept. 2006): table 1 (p. 35). See also David A. Moss and Sarah Brennan, "Managing Money Risk in Antebellum New York," *Studies in American Political Development* 15, no. 2 (Fall 2001): 138–162.

15. On the safety of banknotes under New York's free banking law, see esp. Arthur J. Rolnick and Warren E. Weber, "New Evidence on the Free Banking Era," *American Economic Review* 73, no. 5 (Dec. 1983): 1087–1088.

16. Howard Bodenhorn, "Bank Chartering and Political Corruption in Antebellum New York: Free Banking as Reform," in *Corruption and Reform: Lessons from America's Eco-*

nomic History, ed. Edward L. Glaeser and Claudia Goldin (Chicago: University of Chicago Press, 2006), 252.

17. See esp. Moss and Brennan, "Managing Money Risk," 155–160 (quote on 160). See also David A. Moss and Sarah Brennan, "Regulation and Reaction: The Other Side of Free Banking in Antebellum New York," Harvard Business School Working Paper 04-038, 31 Mar. 2004.

18. Arthur May Mowry, *The Dorr War* (Providence: Preston and Rounds, 1901), 182–188; Edward Field, ed., *State of Rhode Island and Providence Plantations at the End of the Century: A History* (Boston: Mason, 1902), 344; Rory Raven, *The Dorr War: Treason, Rebellion and the Fight for Reform in Rhode Island* (Charleston: History Press, 2010), 60–64.

19. Quoted in Raven, *The Dorr War,* 67.

20. Field, *State of Rhode Island,* 344–349. The final quote from the judgment against Dorr can be found in Marvin E. Gettleman, *The Dorr Rebellion: A Study in American Radicalism, 1833–1849* (New York: Random House, 1973), 165.

21. Field, *State of Rhode Island,* 345–346.

22. Specifically, all native-born males who either owned $134 of "real and personal" property or paid a $1 poll tax would be permitted to vote, whereas naturalized citizens could qualify to vote only by meeting the $134 freehold property requirement. See Chilton Williamson, "Rhode Island Suffrage since the Dorr War," *New England Quarterly* 28, no. 1 (Mar. 1955): 36. By 1850 (the first year for which relevant data are available), foreign-born residents of Rhode Island comprised just over 16 percent of the state's total population. See Michael R. Haines, "Rhode Island Population by Race, Sex, Age, Nativity, and Urban-Rural Residence: 1790–1990," in *Historical Statistics of the United States, Earliest Times to the Present: Millennial Edition,* ed. Susan B. Carter, Scott Sigmund Gartner, Michael R. Haines, Alan L. Olmstead, Richard Sutch, and Gavin Wright (New York: Cambridge University Press, 2006), series Aa5508 and Aa5516.

23. Williamson, "Rhode Island Suffrage," 37.

24. Field, *State of Rhode Island,* 348–352; Mowry, *The Dorr War,* 255–259; Gettleman, *The Dorr Rebellion,* 171–173.

25. *Luther v. Borden,* 48 U.S. 1 (1849). See also Alexander Keyssar, *The Right to Vote: The Contested History of Democracy in the United States* (New York: Basic Books, 2000), 75.

26. William G. Bishop and William H. Attree, *Report of the Debates and Proceedings of the Convention for the Revision of the Constitution of the State of New York* (Albany, NY: Evening Atlas, 1846), 950; S. Croswell and R. Sutton, *Debates and Proceedings in the New-York State Convention for the Revision of the Constitution* (Albany, NY: Albany Argus, 1846), 726; De Alva Stanwood Alexander, *A Political History of the State of New York, 1833–1861* (New York: Henry Holt and Co., 1906), 2:113.

27. Ronald E. Shaw, *Erie Water West: A History of the Erie Canal, 1792–1854* (Lexington: University Press of Kentucky, 1990), 365–374, quoted passages at 368, 366; J. Hampden Dougherty, *Constitutional History of the State of New York,* 2nd ed. (Clark, NJ: Lawbook Exchange, 2004 [1915]), 174–175.

28. Shaw, *Erie Water West,* 379–395; Dougherty, *Constitutional History,* 175; "Communication from the Secretary of State, Transmitting a Copy of the Certificate of the Board of State Canvassers," doc. no. 65, 4 Mar. 1854, in *Documents of the Senate of the State of New-York, Seventy-Seventh Session,* vol. 2 (Albany, NY: C. Van Benthuysen, 1854).

29. Quoted in Shaw, *Erie Water West,* 395. The original can be found in "The Enlargement Triumphant," Albany *Evening Journal,* 16 Mar. 1854, 2, col. 3, http://fultonhistory .com/newspapers%20Disk3/Albany%20NY%20Evening%20Journal/Albany%20 NY%20Evening%20Journal%201854.pdf/Albany%20NY%20Evening%20 Journal%201854%20-%200152.pdf.

30. B. U. Ratchford, *American State Debts* (Durham, NC: Duke University Press, 1941), table 9 (p. 127) and table 20 (p. 254); Shaw, *Erie Water West,* 396.

31. *Problems Relating to Taxation and Finance: Reports of the New York Constitutional Convention of 1938,* vol. 10 (Albany, NY: J. B. Lyon Co., 1938), 67.

32. James A. Henretta, "The Strange Birth of Liberal America: Michael Hoffman and the New York Constitution of 1846," *New York History* 77, no. 2 (Apr. 1996): 151–152.

33. On the experience in New York, see, e.g., Henretta, "Strange Birth of Liberal America," 173–176.

34. John Joseph Wallis, "American Government Finance in the Long Run: 1790 to 1990," *Journal of Economic Perspectives* 14, no. 1 (Winter 2000): table 1 (p. 65).

35. *Problems Relating to Taxation and Finance,* 68–70, quotations at 68.

36. *New York State Constitution, as Revised, Including Amendments Effective January 1, 2015* (available online at https://www.dos.ny.gov/info/pdfs/Constitution.pdf), Art. VII, §11 (p. 26).

37. S. S. Randall, *History of the Common School System of the State of New York, from Its Origin in 1795 to the Present Time* (New York: Ivison, Blakeman, Taylor, and Co., 1871), 284–285.

38. "The State Schools: Report of the Superintendent of Common Schools," *New-York Daily Times,* 7 Jan. 1853, 3.

39. Ibid., 3.

40. *Barto v. Himrod,* 4 Seld. 483 (1853). Quoted passages from 491, 488, 493, 496–497.

41. Ellwood P. Cubberly, *Public Education in the United States: A Study and Interpretation of American Educational History* (Boston: Houghton Mifflin Co., 1919), 148; Randall, *History of the Common School System,* 312–322.

42. Andrew S. Draper, *Origin and Development of the Common School System of the State of New York* (Syracuse, NY: C. W. Bardeen, 1903), 51, 52. See also *117th Annual Report of the Regents of the University of the State of New York,* transmitted to the Legislature on 6 Jan. 1904 (Albany, 1904), 16, available online at https://books.google.com/ books?id=nB4tAAAAYAAJ.

43. "An Act to Amend an Act Entitled 'An Act to Revise and Consolidate the General Acts Relating to Public Instruction,' Passed May 2, 1864, and to Abolish Rate Bills Authorized by Special Act," enacted 16 Apr. 1867, New York State, reprinted in

Thomas E. Finegan, *Free Schools: A Documentary History of the Free School Movement in New York State* (Albany: University of the State of New York, 1921), 555, 550.

44. Quoted in Finegan, *Free Schools,* 556.

45. David M. Potter, *The Impending Crisis, 1848–1861* (New York: Harper and Row, 1976), 578–583; David J. Eicher, *The Longest Night: A Military History of the Civil War* (New York: Simon and Schuster, 2001), 38, quotation at 38; Robert Lebby, "The First Shot on Fort Sumter," *South Carolina Historical and Genealogical Magazine* 12, no. 3 (July 1911): 141–145; "Officers of the United States Army, 1861, Who Resigned to Enter the Confederate Army," *Post Almanac,* Jan. 1901, 262.

46. Eicher, *The Longest Night,* 38–41, quotation at 41.

47. Armin Rappaport, "The Replacement System during the Civil War," *Military Affairs* 15, no. 2 (Summer 1951): 95; Lisa Tendrich Frank, ed., *The World of the Civil War: A Daily Life Encyclopedia* (Santa Barbara, CA: Greenwood, 2015), 425–428; J. David Hacker, A Census Based Count of the Civil War Dead," *Civil War History* 57, no. 4 (Dec. 2011): 307–348; James M. McPherson, *Ordeal by Fire: The Civil War and Reconstruction* (Boston: McGraw-Hill, 2001), 163–173, 519.

48. McPherson, *Ordeal by Fire,* 316–317, 321, 502–503; Michael Vorenberg, *Final Freedom: The Civil War, the Abolition of Slavery, and the Thirteenth Amendment* (Cambridge: Cambridge University Press, 2004); James Oakes, *Freedom National: The Destruction of Slavery in the United States, 1861–1865* (New York: W. W. Norton, 2013), xiv, 227–230, 422–427, 430–445.

49. *Virginia v. Rives,* 100 U.S. 313 (1880), 323.

50. *Strauder v. West Virginia,* 100 U.S. 303 (1880).

51. "The Lee Reynolds Case," *Daily Dispatch* (Richmond, VA), 22 Apr. 1880, 2, col. 2 (http://chroniclingamerica.loc.gov/lccn/sn84024738/1880-04-22/ed-1/seq-2/); "The Reynolds Case Ended," *Staunton Spectator* (Staunton, VA), 29 June 1880, 2, col. 2 (http://chroniclingamerica.loc.gov/lccn/sn84024718/1880-06-29/ed-1/seq-2/); "Distinguished Arrivals," *Daily Dispatch* (Richmond, VA), 30 June 1880, 1, col. 3 (http://chroniclingamerica.loc.gov/lccn/sn84024738/1880-06-30/ed-1/seq-1/). Quote from "Reynolds Case Ended."

52. *Ex Parte Virginia,* 100 U.S. 339 (1879), 346.

53. Quoted in ibid., 344.

54. "Trial of the Judges," *Daily Dispatch* (Richmond, VA), 23 Mar. 1880, 2, col. 3, http://chroniclingamerica.loc.gov/lccn/sn84024738/1880-03-23/ed-1/seq-2/); "Lynchburg: Judge Griffin's Case," *Daily Dispatch* (Richmond, VA), 1 Apr. 1880, 2, col. 2 (http://chroniclingamerica.loc.gov/lccn/sn84024738/1880-04-01/ed-1/seq-2/); "A Nolle Prosequi Entered in the Cases of the Virginia Judges Indicted," *Daily Dispatch* (Richmond, VA), 18 Nov. 1880, 3, col. 3 (http://chroniclingamerica.loc.gov/lccn/sn84024738/1880-11-18/ed-1/seq-3/). Quote from "A Nolle Prosequi Entered."

55. Benno C. Schmidt Jr., "Juries, Jurisdiction, and Race Discrimination: The Lost Promise of *Strauder v. West Virginia,*" *Texas Law Review* 61, no. 8 (May 1983): 1475.

56. "U.S. District Courts for the Districts of Virginia—Judges of the Western District of Virginia—Rives, Alexander," History of the Federal Judiciary, Federal Judiciary Center (http://www.fjc.gov/servlet/nGetInfo?jid=2018&cid=166&ctype=dc&instate=va).

57. *The Statutes of California and Amendments to the Codes, Passed at the Twenty-Ninth Session of the Legislature, 1891* (Sacramento, CA: A. J. Johnston, Supt. State Printing, 1891), 165, http://clerk.assembly.ca.gov/sites/clerk.assembly.ca.gov/files/archive/Statutes /1891/1891.PDF. See also Erik Falk Peterson, "The Struggle for the Australian Ballot in California," *California Historical Quarterly* 51, no. 3 (Fall 1972): 239; Charles A. Beard, *American Government and Politics* (New York: Macmillan, 1917), 677–679; A. James Reichley, *The Life of the Parties: A History of American Political Parties* (Lanham, MD: Rowman and Littlefield, 1992), 167.

58. "More History of the Ballot," *Sunday Union* (Sacramento, CA), 5 Apr. 1891, 2, col. 1, http://cdnc.ucr.edu/cgi-bin/cdnc?a=d&d=SDU18910405.2.27&srpos=5&e=01-03 -1891-01-05-1891.

59. Peterson, "Struggle for the Australian Ballot," 239–240.

60. Reichley, *Life of the Parties*, 168.

61. Anthracite Coal Strike Commission, *Report to the President on the Anthracite Coal Strike of May–October, 1902* (Washington: GPO, 1903).

62. Ibid., 39–68, 79–83, quotations at 67.

63. Perry K. Blatz, *Democratic Miners: Work and Labor Relations in the Anthracite Coal Industry, 1875–1925* (Albany: SUNY Press, 1994), 171.

64. Quoted in Jonathan Grossman, "The Coal Strike of 1902: Turning Point in U.S. Policy," *Monthly Labor Review* 98 (Oct. 1975): 26.

65. "Meat Fight Ends: Both Sides Win," *Chicago Daily Tribune,* 19 June 1906, 1; "Meat Bill Is Amended," *Boston Daily Globe,* 19 June 1906, 10; and "The Week: Leading Events—Congress," *Ohio Farmer,* 30 June 1906, 635.

66. "Conferences on the Agriculture Bill," *San Francisco Chronicle,* 26 June 1906, 3.

67. "Two Bills—Await the Last Touch," *Cincinnati Enquirer,* 28 June 1906, 7.

68. "Leaves Issue to Conferees: President's Wishes on Meat Inspection," *Boston Daily Globe,* 29 June 1906, 11; "House Defeats Senate on Meat Inspection," *New York Times,* 30 June 1906, 4.

69. "House Defeats Senate," 4.

70. "The News This Morning," *New-York Tribune,* 30 June 1906, 6; "Off for Oyster Bay: President Starts for His Summer Home at Midnight," *The Sun* (Baltimore), 1 July 1906, 2.

71. "Credit to Whom Credit Is Due," *The Sun* (Baltimore), 6 July 1906, 5.

72. George H. Haynes, "How Massachusetts Adopted the Initiative and Referendum," *Political Science Quarterly* 34, no. 3 (Sept. 1919): 469; "Coolidge Beats Long," *Boston Daily Globe,* 6 Nov. 1918, 1.

73. Wendell D. Howie, "Three Hundred Years of the Liquor Problem in Massachusetts," *Massachusetts Law Quarterly* 18, no. 4 (May 1933): 251–253, 281.

74. "Ballot Measures by Type of Question," website of the Secretary of the Commonwealth of Massachusetts, http://www.sec.state.ma.us/ele/elebalm/balmtype ofquestion.html.

75. John G. Matsusaka, "Direct Democracy Works," *Journal of Economic Perspectives* 19, no. 2 (Spring 2005): 188–189; Sarah M. Henry, "Progressivism and Democracy: Electoral Reform in the United States, 1898–1919" (PhD diss., Columbia University, 1995), 337–351.

76. See David Moss and Michael R. Fein, "Radio Regulation Revisited: Coase, the FCC, and the Public Interest," *Journal of Policy History* 15, no. 4 (2003): 389–416; David Moss and Jonathan Lackow, "Capturing History: The Case of the Federal Radio Commission in 1927," in *Preventing Regulatory Capture: Special Interest Influence, and How to Limit It,* ed. Daniel Carpenter and David Moss (New York: Cambridge University Press, 2014), chap. 8.

77. Statement of Richard Whitney, president of the New York Stock Exchange, in regard to HB 7852—the short title of which is "National Securities Exchange Act of 1934," Committee on Interstate and Foreign Commerce, United States House of Representatives, 22–23 Feb. 1934, reprinted in "Stock Exchange Practices" (Hearing), Committee on Banking and Currency, United States Senate, 28 Feb. 1934, 6624–6625, https://fraser.stlouisfed.org/docs/publications/sensep/sensep_19340228.pdf. See also Joel Seligman, *The Transformation of Wall Street: A History of the Securities and Exchange Commission and Modern Corporate Finance,* rev. ed. (Boston: Northeastern University Press, 1995), 90.

78. Statement of Richard Whitney, 6641; Seligman, *Transformation of Wall Street,* 90–91.

79. "Stock Control Bill Voted by Congress," *New York Times,* 2 June 1934, 1; Ernest K. Lindley, "Exchange Becomes Bill Law, Ending 20-Yr. U. S. Crusade," *New York Herald Tribune,* 7 June 1934, 1; John E. Tracy and Alfred Brunson MacChesney, "The Securities Exchange Act of 1934," *Michigan Law Review* 32, no. 8 (June 1934): esp. 1037–1058; Seligman, *Transformation of Wall Street,* 92–100.

80. "Exchange, Labor Boards Named," *New York Times,* 1 July 1934, 1; Stephen A. Zeff, "The SEC Rules Historical Cost Accounting: 1934 to the 1970s," *Accounting and Business Research* 37, suppl. 1 (2007): 1–2.

81. John Kenneth Galbraith, *The Great Crash 1929* (Boston: Houghton Mifflin Harcourt, 2009), 159–163 (quotation at 162).

82. Thomas K. McCraw, "With Consent of the Governed: SEC's Formative Years," *Journal of Policy Analysis and Management* 1, no. 3 (Spring 1982): 356.

83. Michael Beschloss, "From White Knight to Thief," The Upshot, *New York Times* online, 13 Sept. 2014 (http://www.nytimes.com/2014/09/14/upshot/from-white-knight-to-thief.html). On the downfall of Richard Whitney and especially its impact on the NYSE and the SEC, see Seligman, *Transformation of Wall Street,* 167–174.

84. Taylor Branch, *At Canaan's Edge: America in the King Years, 1965–68* (New York: Simon and Schuster, 2006), 75–79 (quotes from King at 76, 78).

85. Ibid., 80–85, quotation at 85.

86. Ibid., 89.

87. Sara Bullard, *Free At Last: A History of the Civil Rights Movement and Those Who Died in the Struggle* (New York: Oxford University Press, 1993), 79.

88. Quoted in Branch, *At Canaan's Edge,* 114. See also Laurie Collier Hillstrom, *The Voting Rights Act of 1965* (Detroit: Omnigraphics, 2009), 89, 201.

89. Charles Mohr, "Bill to Reinforce the Right to Vote Goes to Congress," *New York Times,* 18 Mar. 1965, 1; "Text of Bill to Guarantee Voting Rights," *New York Times,* 18 Mar. 1965, 20; Ben A. Franklin, "U.S. Court Allows Alabama March, Enjoins Wallace," *New York Times,* 18 Mar. 1965, 1; "Ala. Is Ordered to Allow March," *Newsday* (New York), 18 Mar. 1965, 3.

90. Hillstrom, *Voting Rights Act,* 89–91; Branch, *At Canaan's Edge,* 157–163; "Mirth in the Mud: World's Highest Paid Stars Give Free Show for Alabama Marchers," *Philadelphia Inquirer,* 30 Mar. 1965, 14; Renata Adler, "Letter from Selma," *New Yorker,* 10 Apr. 1965; Martin Luther King, "Our God Is Marching On," 25 Mar. 1965, https://kinginstitute.stanford.edu/our-god-marching.

91. Hillstrom, *Voting Rights Act,* 94; "Decline and Fall of Dixie Veto," *Call and Post* (Cleveland), 5 June 1965, 2C.

92. Quoted in Hillstrom, *Voting Rights Act of 1965,* 94. See also Lyndon B. Johnson, "Remarks in the Capitol Rotunda at the Signing of the Voting Rights Act, August 6, 1965," in *Public Papers of the Presidents of the United States: Lyndon B. Johnson, 1965,* bk. 2 (Washington, DC: GPO, 1966), 841.

93. Bernard Grofman, Lisa Handley, and Richard G. Niemi, *Minority Representation and the Quest for Voting Equality* (Cambridge: Cambridge University Press, 1992), table 1 (p. 23).

94. Quoted in Hillstrom, *Voting Rights Act of 1965,* 94.

95. "Senate in Florida Votes against ERA," *Boston Globe,* 22 June 1982, 4; Joanne Omang, "Rejection by Fla. May Dash ERA's Chances," *Washington Post,* 22 June 1982, A5; Laura E. Brock, "Religion, Sex, and Politics: The Story of the Equal Rights Amendment in Florida" (PhD diss., Florida State University, 2013), 229–230.

96. Ellen Creager, "ERA Is Back: Congress to Try Again in Bush Administration," *Chicago Tribune,* 5 Mar. 1989, §6 (p. 8).

97. See Dana Candey, "Advocates of Equal Rights Amendment Resume Their Fight," *New York Times,* 4 May 2003, N41; George F. Will, "ERA: Still Ticking," *Washington Post,* 12 Sept. 1999, B7; Jonathan Turley, "Revival of the Equal Rights Amendment," *Roll Call,* 16 Apr. 2007, 1; Allison L. Held, Sheryl L. Herndon, and Danielle M. Stager, "The Equal Rights Amendment: Why the Era Remains Legally Viable and Properly Before the States," *William & Mary Journal of Women and the Law* 3, no. 1 (1997): 113–136.

98. Richard B. Bernstein, "The Sleeper Wakes: The History and Legacy of the Twenty-Seventh Amendment," *Fordham Law Review* 61, no. 3 (1992): 497–557, esp. 534, 537–539, 544–547. See also William J. Eaton, "Pay Raise Amendment Wins Ratification," *Los Angeles Times,* 8 May 1992, A30.

99. See esp. Will, "ERA: Still Ticking"; Turley, "Revival of the Equal Rights Amendment"; and Held, Herndon, and Stager, "Equal Rights Amendment." See also Roberta W. Francis, "The Equal Rights Amendment: Frequently Asked Questions," ERA Task Force, National Council of Women's Organizations, July 2015, http://www.equalrightsamendment.org/misc/faq.pdf.

100. Francis, "Equal Rights Amendment," 3–4.

101. Ryan Grim, "Fed Beaten: Bill to Audit Federal Reserve Passes Key Hurdle," *Huffington Post,* 19 Nov. 2009 (http://www.huffingtonpost.com/2009/11/19/fed-beaten-bill-toaudit_n_364546.html); Damian Paletta and Robin Sidel, "House Strikes at Wall Street: Bill Would Usher in Biggest Change to Finance Regulation since '30s," *Wall Street Journal,* 12 Dec. 2009, A1.

102. David M. Herszhenhorn, "Senate Votes Unanimously for an Audit of Fed's Actions in Financial Crisis," *New York Times,* 12 May 2010, B3.

103. Brady Dennis, "Lawmakers Agree to Expand Audit of Federal Reserve," *Washington Post,* 17 June 2010, A15.

104. Public Law 111-203, 21 July 2010 (available at https://www.gpo.gov/fdsys/pkg/PLAW-111publ203/pdf/PLAW-111publ203.pdf), §1102 (2115–2117), §1109 (2127–2129).

105. David Grant, "Ron Paul's Last Hurrah: A Big, Bipartisan Vote to 'Audit the Fed,'" *Christian Science Monitor,* 25 July 2012, 17; Steven Nelson, "Democrats Kill Rand Paul's Audit the Fed Bill, Though Sanders Votes Yes," *U.S. News & World Report,* 12 Jan. 2016 (http://www.usnews.com/news/articles/2016-01-12/democrats-kill-rand-pauls-audit-the-fed-bill-though-sanders-votes-yes); Sarah Binder and Mark Spindel, "Independence and Accountability: Congress and the Fed in a Polarized Era," Center for Effective Public Management, Brookings Institution, April 2016 (http://www.brookings.edu/~/media/research/files/papers/2016/04/01-congress-and-the-fed-binder/monetary-politics.pdf). See also Sarah Binder, "A Brief History of Attempts to Audit the Fed (Rand Paul Is a Latecomer)," WashingtonPost.com, 11 Jan. 2016, https://www.washingtonpost.com/news/monkey-cage/wp/2016/01/11/a-brief-history-of-attempts-to-audit-the-fed-rand-paul-is-a-latecomer/.

106. "Total Outside Spending by Election Cycle, Excluding Party Committees," Opensecrets.org (https://www.opensecrets.org/outsidespending/cycle_tots.php). See also Wendy L. Hansen, Michael S. Rocca, and Brittany Leigh Ortiz, "The Effects of Citizens United on Corporate Spending in the 2012 Presidential Election," *Journal of Politics* 77, no. 2 (2015): 535–545.

107. *SpeechNow.org v. FEC,* 599 F.3d 686 (D.C. Cir. 2010), 14.

108. See, e.g., Bradley A. Smith, "Super PACs and the Role of 'Coordination' in Campaign Finance Law," *Willamette Law Review* 49 (2013): 604.

109. "Super PACs," OpenSecrets.org, https://www.opensecrets.org/pacs/superpacs.php?cycle=2010 and https://www.opensecrets.org/pacs/superpacs.php?cycle=2012; "2012 Super PACs: How Many Donors Give," OpenSecrets.org, http://www.opensecrets.org/outsidespending/donor_stats.php?cycle=2012; Hansen, Rocca, and Ortiz, "Effects of Citizens United on Corporate Spending," 535–545, esp. 535, 543–544.

110. Dan Eggen, "Poll: Large Majority Opposes Supreme Court's Decision on Campaign Financing," Washingtonpost.com, 17 Feb. 2010, http://www.washingtonpost.com /wp-dyn/content/article/2010/02/17/AR2010021701151.html; Greg Stohr, "Bloomberg Poll: Americans Want Supreme Court to Turn Off Political Spending Spigot," Bloom-bergPolitics, 28 Sept. 2015, http://www.bloomberg.com/politics/articles/2015-09-28 /bloomberg-poll-americans-want-supreme-court-to-turn-off-political-spending -spigot.

ACKNOWLEDGMENTS

In developing the cases that make up this book, I worked closely with nine outstanding co-authors and research associates: Marc Campasano, Dean Grodzins, Tim Lambert, Cole Bolton, Amy Smekar, Colin Donovan, Eugene Kintgen, Gregory DiBella, and Rachel Wilf. Without their tireless and painstaking efforts, this project would never have reached fruition. I am profoundly grateful for the phenomenal work that they did and for their support and friendship throughout.

Along the way, many other colleagues and friends helped make the book better by suggesting new paths to explore, reading and critiquing portions of the manuscript, pointing out problems, highlighting parallels, and providing advice and encouragement at critical moments. I am especially indebted to Lisa Adams, Ed Balleisen, Joanna Beinhorn, John Bell, Alex Berlin, Dan Carpenter, John Cisternino, Steve Cohen, Jon Decker, Susan Donnelly, Alex Dyck, Walter Friedman, Archon Fung, Doris Kearns Goodwin, Rebecca Henderson, Anna Hopper, David Kaufman, Alex Keyssar, Stephanie Khurana, Julia Kirby, Greg Kornbluh, Naomi Lamoreaux, Charlie Ledley, Dutch Leonard, Roger Lowenstein, Jamie Mai, Wendy Nelson, Beth Neustadt, Bill Novak, Zach Nowak, Mary Oey, Danny Orbach, Mel Parker, David Paydarfar, Amanda Peery, Jamie Piltch, Tobi Resch, Karthik Ramanna, Forest Reinhardt, Meg Rithmire, Jan Rivkin, Julio Rotemberg, Arthur Segel, Liat Spiro, Melanie Wachtell Stinnett, Jim Stone, Gunnar Trumbull, Dick Vietor, John Wallis, Mitch Weiss, Lou Wells, and Luigi Zingales for their insights, inspiration, support, and counsel.

I owe particular thanks to my editor at Harvard University Press, Thomas LeBien, who helped to envision the book at the outset, consistently provided superb advice, and gently pushed as needed to ensure that the project reached completion.

I am also grateful to the Harvard undergraduates and MBA students who participated in the History of American Democracy course, from which the book took shape. In ways both large and small, these students tested and challenged my ideas, offered new perspectives and insights, and vetted draft cases. It was truly a privilege getting to work with them.

Without the remarkable support and encouragement of Nitin Nohria, dean of Harvard Business School, there would have been no course at all and, in turn, no book. I am enormously appreciative for all he did and for his willingness to take a bet on this project. Nor would the course have been possible without Stephanie Kenen and Ned Hall, who made it part of the Program in General Education at Harvard College. I am grateful for their efforts. I am also thankful for the very generous financial support provided by the Division of Research and Faculty Development at Harvard Business School.

Finally, and above all, I am forever indebted to my family—to my wife, Abby, and my daughters, Julia and Emily, whose love, patience, and reassurance make everything possible; my sisters, Kathy and Debbie, who have led the way and guided me more often than they know; and my parents, to whom this book is dedicated, who have, through their love and example, laid a strong foundation for growth and instilled within me the values I hold most dear.

INDEX